INTERNATIONAL ACCOUNTING/FINANCIAL REPORTING STANDARDS GUIDE

David Alexander

and

Simon Archer

This publication is designed to provide accurate and authoritative information in regard to the subject matter covered. It is sold with the understanding that the publisher is not engaged in rendering legal, accounting, or other professional services. If legal advice or other professional assistance is required, the services of a competent professional person should be sought

—From a *Declaration of Principles* jointly adopted by a Committee of the American Bar Association and a Committee of Publishers and Associations

ISBN: 978-0-8080-2656-3

No claim is made to original government works; however, within this Product or Publication, the following are subject to CCH's copyright: (1) the gathering, compilation, and arrangement of such government materials; (2) the magnetic translation and digital conversion of data, if applicable; (3) the historical, statutory and other notes and references; and (4) the commentary and other materials.

Portions of this work were published in previous editions.

Portions of this publication have their origins in copyrighted materials from the International Accounting Standards Committee Foundation (IASCF). The IASB logo "Hexagon Device," "IAS," "IASB," "IASCF," "IASC," and "International Accounting Standards" are trademarks of the International Accounting Standards Committee Foundation. Copyright ©2008 International Accounting Standards Committee Foundation.

Full texts of the original standards can be ordered directly from the IASB Publications, 166 Fleet Street, London EC4A 2DY, United Kingdom. Internet: http://www.iasb.org.uk.

Printed in the United States of America.

International Accounting/Financial Reporting Standards Guide

by David Alexander and Simon Archer

Highlights

CCH's *International Accounting/Financial Reporting Standards Guide* features comprehensive coverage of all current International Accounting Standards (IASs) and International Financial Reporting Standards (IFRSs) promulgated by the International Accounting Standards Board (IASB), plus related Interpretations issued by the International Financial Reporting Interpretations Committee (IFRIC). General and industry-specific standards are organized by topic, with the main difference between IASB and GAAP identified as well.

2012 Edition

The 2012 Edition of the *International Accounting/Financial Reporting Standards Guide* keeps you up-to-date on the latest International Financial Reporting Standards and the proposed changes on the immediate horizon that will most likely alter the way in which you must account for and disclose information.

An understanding of this material is also essential for those who need to understand or interpret financial statements prepared under IASB GAAP, which includes thousands of large enterprises in Europe and Australia. Further, the implications of the promised increasing "convergence" between U.S. and IASB GAAP can only be appreciated with a knowledge of IASB pronouncements.

As detailed in the Preface, this edition is fully up to date as of requirements issued by early August 2011.

CCH Learning Center

CCH's goal is to provide you with the clearest, most concise, and up-to-date accounting and auditing information to help further your professional development, as well as a convenient method to help you satisfy your continuing professional education requirements. The CCH Learning Center* offers a complete line of self-study courses covering complex and constantly evolving accounting and auditing issues. We are continually adding new courses to the library to help you stay current on all the latest developments. The CCH

---

* CCH is registered with the National Association of State Boards of Accountancy (NASBA) as a sponsor of continuing professional education on the National Registry of CPE Sponsors. State boards of accountancy have final authority on the acceptance of individual courses for CPE credit. Complaints regarding registered sponsors may be addressed to the National Registry of CPE Sponsors, 150 Fourth Avenue North, Nashville, TN 37219-2417. Telephone: 615-880-4200.

*CCH is registered with the National Association of State Boards of Accountancy as a Quality Assurance Service (QAS) sponsor of continuing professional education. Participating state boards of accountancy have final authority on the acceptance of individual courses for CPE credit. Complaints regarding QAS program sponsors may be addressed to NASBA, 150 Fourth Avenue North, Suite 700, Nashville, TN 37219-2417. Telephone: 615-880-4200.

Learning Center courses are available 24 hours a day, seven days a week. You'll get immediate exam results and certification. To view our complete accounting and auditing course catalog, go to: **http:/cch.learningcenter.com**.

Accounting Research Manager™

Accounting Research Manager is the most comprehensive, up-to-date, and objective online database of financial reporting literature. It includes all authoritative and proposed accounting, auditing, and SEC literature, plus independent, expert-written interpretive guidance.

Our Weekly Summary e-mail newsletter highlights the key developments of the week, giving you the assurance that you have the most current information. It provides links to new FASB, AICPA, SEC, PCAOB, EITF, and IASB authoritative and proposal-stage literature, plus insightful guidance from financial reporting experts.

Our outstanding team of content experts take pride in updating the system on a daily basis, so you stay as current as possible. You'll learn of newly released literature and deliberations of current financial reporting projects as soon they occur! Plus, you benefit from their easy-to-understand technical translations.

With **Accounting Research Manager**, you maximize the efficiency of your research time while enhancing your results. Learn more about our content, our experts, and how you can request a FREE trial by visiting us at **http:/www.accountingresearchmanager.com**.

11/11

Preface

The new 2012 *International Accounting/Financial Reporting Standards Guide* explains and analyzes International Accounting Standards (IASs) and International Financial Reporting Standards (IFRSs) promulgated by the International Accounting Standards Board (IASB). IASs are the standards issued by the IASB's predecessor body, the International Accounting Standards Committee (IASC), while IFRSs are those issued by the IASB. However, some of the IASs have been subject to major revisions by the IASB.

International accounting and financial reporting standards are playing an increasing role in the context of the globalization of capital markets. In particular, they provide a basis for the consolidated financial statements of multinational corporations based in countries where national GAAP are not considered to provide a basis that satisfies internationally accepted qualitative criteria for financial reporting. Some multinational corporations use U.S. GAAP for a similar reason. In November 2007, the Securities and Exchange Commission (SEC) eliminated the requirement for foreign private issuers using IFRS to reconcile their financial statements to U.S. GAAP. IASs and IFRSs are accepted by the London Stock Exchange and elsewhere in Europe.

Chapter 1, "The International Accounting Standards Board—Past, Present, Future," explains in more detail the role and usage of IASs and IFRSs. It also examines their current status in terms of international acceptance as a basis for financial reporting in the context of cross-border securities listings (including that of foreign registrants in the United States). Their central role in the next phase of accounting harmonization within the European Union is explained. The major restructuring of the IASB, in the light of its intended role as a global accounting standard-setter for listed corporations, is described. More important, these standards are used by virtually all the consolidated accounts of listed companies throughout the European Union for financial periods beginning on or after January 1, 2005, including those in the 12 member states from Eastern Europe that joined since 2004. Australia has also extended the compulsory use of IASs from 2005, and the FASB and the IASB are actively collaborating on a "convergence process" designed to bring IASB and U.S. GAAP closer together. An understanding of IASs and IFRSs is now essential.

How to Use the 2012 IAS/IFRS Guide

Following an introductory section that covers the International Accounting Standards Board, its Framework for the preparation and presentation of financial statements, and the key IAS 1, "Presentation of Financial Statements," the 2012 *IAS/IFRS Guide* organizes IASB accounting pronouncements into three parts (Overview, General Standards, and Industry-Specific Standards) and then alphabetically by topic. So that the authoritative information is immediately accessible, each chapter deals comprehensively with one, or in a few cases two, IASs and IFRSs and the related pronouncements of the IASB's International Financial Reporting Interpretations Committee (IFRIC). Each chapter also indicates the main differences between IASB and U.S. GAAP on the matters dealt with in the chapter. However, the *IAS/IFRS Guide* is not written with the assumption that the reader is familiar with U.S. GAAP.

This edition is fully up to date as of requirements issued by August 2011 relating to financial statements for years beginning on after January 1, 2012. Following the extensive revisions in recent editions, a large number of small, but often significant, amendments to standards are included in the text of this new 2012 edition.

Four new standards were issued during 2011, IFRSs 10, 11, 12, and 13. All are obligatory for financial statements beginning on or after January 1, 2013, but earlier adoption is permitted. IFRSs 10, 11, and 12 all relate to various aspects of group accounts. IFRS 13 is a completely new standard dealing with the operationalization of fair value use and, as such, will have effects on many other standards that permit or require the use of fair value. This standard requires a new chapter, here presented as Chapter 3, "Fair Value Measurement." As a standard with significant general application (once adopted by an entity), its proper place is in Part I of the Guide. Just as we go to press, some amendments have been issued to IAS 1 and the formats of allowed presentations of comprehensive income. These changes are obligatory for financial statements beginning on or after July 1, 2012, and are outlined in Chapter 4, "Presentation of Financial Statements."

Chapters in the *IAS/IFRS Guide* also contain illustrations and examples to demonstrate and clarify specific accounting principles. They also contain **Practice Pointers**, which clarify issues of application, as well as **Observations**, which discuss issues of interpretation and bring apparent inconsistencies to your attention. Material in the *IAS/IFRS Guide* can be located several ways: In addition to the Guide's **Table of Contents,** the **Cross-Reference** shows the chapter in which a particular pronouncement is discussed. The **Index** provides quick, accurate reference to needed information.

For more information about international accounting and auditing standards, search on "International Accounting Library" at **www.CCHGroup.com**.

Acknowledgments

The authors and publisher wish to thank both Susan Harding, formerly Research Manager of the International Accounting Standards Committee, for reviewing the technical content of the *IAS Guide*, and Kurt Ramin, former Commercial Director of the IASB, for making this important addition to professional accounting literature possible. They would also like to thank Sandra Lim, Developmental Editor, and Curt Berkowitz, Senior Production Specialist, of CCH for their indispensable contributions in bringing this edition of the *IAS/IFRS Guide* to press.

About the Authors

David Alexander is former Professor of International Accounting at the Birmingham Business School, The University of Birmingham, England. He has a degree in Economics and Accounting from the University of Bristol, England, and is a Fellow of the Institute of Chartered Accountants in England and Wales.

Simon Archer, a former partner of Price Waterhouse, Paris, has had many years' experience working in Continental Europe. He was until recently Professor of Financial Management at the University of Surrey, Guildford, United Kingdom, and is now Visiting Professor at the ICMA Centre, Henley Business School, University of Reading, United Kingdom. Professor Archer was educated at Oxford University, United Kingdom, and is a Fellow of the Institute of Chartered Accountants in England and Wales.

Contents

PART I
OVERVIEW

CHAPTER 1
THE INTERNATIONAL ACCOUNTING STANDARDS BOARD—PAST, PRESENT, AND FUTURE

CONTENTS

INTRODUCTION

The present International Accounting Standards Board (IASB) is a result of a comprehensive restructuring in 2001 of the former International Accounting Standards Committee (IASC):

> an independent, private sector body, formed in 1973 with the objective of harmonizing the accounting principles which are used by businesses and other organizations for financial reporting around the world.

The IASB's formal objectives, as stated in its International Financial Reporting Standards, are:

(a) to develop, in the public interest, a single set of high quality, understandable and enforceable global accounting standards that require high quality, transparent and comparable information in financial statements and other financial reporting to help participants in the various capital markets of the world and other users of the information to make economic decisions;

(b) to promote the use and rigorous application of those standards; and

(c) to work actively with national standard-setters to bring about convergence of national accounting standards and IFRSs to high quality solutions.

Thus, the original objective of "harmonizing accounting principles" has evolved into the objectives of "develop[ing] . . . a single set of *high quality . . . global accounting standards . . .* to help participants in *capital markets* and others make *decisions,*" "promot[ing] the . . . *rigorous application* of those standards" and "bring[ing] about *convergence . . . [toward] high quality solutions.*"

This evolution of its objectives is associated with its collaboration with the International Organization of Securities Commissions since 1995, which led in 2000 to a comprehensive restructuring of the IASC, which took effect in 2001.

This introductory chapter aims to provide an overview of the IASC's history, its restructuring as the IASB, and the challenges facing it.

HISTORY OF THE IASB

The IASC was created in 1973. Its creation was related to that of the International Federation of Accountants (IFAC). The IFAC is the worldwide umbrella organization of accountancy bodies. It is independent of government or pseudo-government control. Its stated purpose is to develop and enhance a coordinated worldwide accountancy profession with harmonized standards. All members of the IFAC were automatically members of the IASC.

The IASC's description of itself as an "independent private sector body" was accurate and revealing. It was, in essence, a private club, with no formal authority. This is in contrast to national regulatory or standard-setting bodies, which operate within a national jurisdiction and some form of legal and governmental framework that delineates, defines, and provides a level of authority. The IASC, however, operated throughout its existence in the knowledge that in the last resort, it and its standards had no formal authority. It therefore had all along to rely on persuasion and the quality of its analysis and argument. This can be seen to have had two major effects. First, the quality of logic and discussion was generally high, and its conclusions—if sometimes debatable—were feasible and clearly articulated. Second, however, the conclusions and recommendations of many of the earlier published IAS documents often had to accommodate two or more alternative acceptable treatments, simply because both or all were already being practiced in countries that were members of the IASC and were too significant to be ignored.

The disadvantages of this state of affairs are obvious and were well recognized by the IASC itself. Toward the end of the 1980s, the IASC decided it would attempt a more proactive approach, and early in 1989 it published an exposure draft (E32) on the comparability of financial statements. This proposed the elimination of certain treatments permitted by particular IASs and the expression of a clear preference for one particular treatment, even where two alternatives were still to be regarded as acceptable.

This "comparability project" led to a whole raft of revised standards operative from the mid-1990s, which did indeed considerably narrow the degree of optionality compared with the earlier versions of the standards issued in the 1970s and 1980s. The comparability project, therefore, can be said to have made the set of IASs more meaningful and significant. Of course, it did nothing to increase the formal authority of the IASC.

In 1995, as the next stage in its development, the IASC entered into an agreement with the International Organization of Securities Commissions (IOSCO) to complete a "core set" of IASs by 1999. With regard to the agreement, IOSCO's Technical Committee stated that completion of "comprehensive core standards acceptable to the Technical Committee" would allow it to "recommend endorsement" of those standards for "cross-border capital raising in all global markets."

In December 1998, the then IASC completed its "core standards" program with the approval of IAS 39, "Financial Instruments: Recognition and Measurement" (see Chapter 17). Following the publication of the report of the IASC's Strategic Working Party, "Recommendations on Shaping IASC for the Future," in November 1999, the IASC's Board approved proposals in December 1999 to make significant changes to the IASC's structure, in order to prepare it for an enhanced role as a global accounting standard-setter.

Following these preparations, the year 2000 was a momentous one for the IASC. In May 2000, the proposed structural changes were approved by the IASC's membership. (The results of these changes, and of some further relatively minor changes following a constitutional review in 2005, are outlined in "The New Structure," below.) Also in May 2000, IOSCO formally accepted the IASC's "core standards" as a basis for cross-border securities listing purposes worldwide (although for certain countries, notably the United States, reconciliations of items such as earnings and stockholders' equity to national GAAP are still required). In June 2000, the European Commission issued a Communication proposing that all listed companies in the European Union would be required to prepare their consolidated financial statements using IASs, a proposal that has since been adopted.

It is apparent, however, that acceptance of IASs by the SEC, for the financial reporting of foreign registrants for U.S. listings, is a crucial element in the IASB's acceptance as the global accounting standard-setter. The IASB and the Financial Accounting Standards Board (FASB) are collaborating on a phased program of convergence with the ultimate aim of having a single set of standards and a conceptual framework common to both bodies. In this regard, the European Commission has set up an "endorsement mechanism" for the application of IFRSs in the European Union (EU), which is intended, among other things, to provide EU input as a counterbalance to U.S. input. These developments are discussed further in "The Current Position" section below.

CAUSES OF DIFFERENCES

Before we speculate about possible outcomes, it is helpful to think about the context in which this game is being played out. Moving back some 30 years, to the end of the 1970s, financial reporting practices, traditions, and philosophies differed enormously among key countries in the so-called developed world (to say nothing of the situation in developing and third-world countries). Ignorance of these differences was, and indeed in many respects still is, both widespread and deep-seated. The roots of these differences can, to a significant extent, be explained by considering five general factors, as follows.

1. *The relative importance of law.* The point at issue here is the extent to which the "law of the land" determines the details of accounting and financial reporting. Tradition in the Anglo-Saxon countries is that the law specifies general principle only, while in countries heavily influenced by Roman law tradition, the law tends to include more detail. This is largely a difference between systems based on Common Law and those based on Code Law, the latter tending to be more detailed and

prescriptive, while the former relies more on judicial interpretation and precedent. Most of mainland Europe exemplifies the latter approach.

2. *Prescription or flexibility.* If regulation is not specified in full detail in legislation, then there are still two alternatives available. First, regulation might be created in detail by professional accounting bodies. Second, the broad regulation, whether created by legislation or by professional accounting bodies, may be explicitly designed on the assumption that the individual expert, in each unique situation, can and should choose the appropriate course of action within the broad parameters laid down. This was very much the approach in the Anglo-Saxon world before the creation of national standards bodies some 30 years ago.

3. *The role of the accounting profession.* In the Anglo-Saxon countries, the accounting profession plays an influential role in the private sector bodies that set financial accounting standards. In general, this is related to points (1) and (2) above, in that in Common Law jurisdictions there is generally a greater role for private sector bodies in setting accounting standards than in Code Law jurisdictions; an exception to this is The Netherlands, where there is a Roman (Code)Law tradition, but the accounting profession is influential.

4. *The providers of finance.* The national accounting systems developed before the 1970s predate the arguments of recent years that accounting statements must satisfy the needs of a wide variety of users. Generally, the suppliers of finance to business were the only users seriously considered until late in the last century (sometimes quite late). Different countries have very different financial institution structures and finance-raising traditions. It follows that accounting practice will have been adapted to suit the local dominant sources of finance. In some countries, tradition tends to focus on the shareholders and, therefore, on profit and on the reporting of expenses and revenues. Some other countries have more active banking sectors and fewer shareholder investors. Accounting in those countries will tend to focus on creditors, and therefore on the balance sheet and on the convention of prudence. Also, bankers tend to have access to "inside information" in those circumstances and are less reliant on annual reports.

A more obvious, but less often quoted, example of the influence of the finance provision on financial reporting can be seen by considering the systems of eastern Europe as they emerged from a half-century during which all finance was provided by the state.

5. *The influence of taxation.* The general point here is that the scope and extent of the influence of taxation law on financial statements vary considerably. Perceptions of this are often simplistic. In reality, no country can justly claim that tax considerations do not influence published results, and no country can be accused of simply taking tax-based results and publishing them just as they are. Within these nonexistent extremes, however, lies a variety of tradition and practice. It is common in many countries, for instance, for some tax allowances to be claimable only if

the identical figure from the tax computation is also used in the published financial statements.

The most powerful of these causal factors creating and explaining historical differences is almost certainly the sources of finance. It is arguably this same factor that is now driving the move toward internationalism in financial reporting and its regulation. The market for the *supply* of finance for larger enterprises is now a single global market. If our analysis is correct, this means that the *demand* for finance is inevitably forced to operate in a single global market scenario. The demand for globally understood financial reports is therefore logically unstoppable.

As we have already hinted, the above arguments, which in our view are fully justified at the "listed enterprise" level, do not necessarily imply any need to alter national financial reporting as it applies to small businesses. They certainly do not logically apply to the economies of many third-world countries. The implications for possible "two-tier" systems within countries and between economic regions raise significant issues, which both IASB and national regulatory systems have hardly begun to tackle, though discussion of such problems is outside the scope of this book. Historically, IASB GAAP have sought applicability, in general, to all enterprises, in all types of economy. However, the IASB has come under increasing pressure to devote serious effort to assisting the financial reporting needs of both smaller countries and smaller enterprises. On February 15, 2007, the IASB published an exposure draft on its "International Financial Reporting Standard for Small and Medium-sized Entities." The aim of the proposed standard is to provide a simplified, self-contained set of accounting principles that are appropriate for smaller, non-listed companies and are based on full IFRSs, developed primarily for listed companies. Simplifications were proposed in three ways: (1) by removing choices for accounting treatment where they exist in the full IFRS, (2) by eliminating topics that are not generally relevant to small and medium-sized entities (SMEs), and (3) by simplifying methods for recognition and measurement. The IASB has now issued the Standard. Its use, as far as IASB is concerned, is never compulsory, but national governments could make it so within their own jurisdiction. Section P8 clarifies "general purpose financial statements are those directed through general financial information needs of a wide range of users who are not in a position to demand reports tailored to meet their particular information needs". P11 states "SMEs often produce financial statements only for the use of owner-managers or only for the use of tax authorities or other governmental authorities. Financial statements produced solely for those purposes are not necessarily general purpose financial statements". This last point seems to raise doubts about the logical applicability of this Standard.

Given the position and role of the IASB, and the widely differing practices and attitudes of its constituents, is it really valid to talk of generally accepted accounting principles in the IASB context? Is IASB GAAP the same species of animal as, say, U.S. GAAP, distinguished only by relatively minor genetic individualities? Or is it of a different species? How fundamental is the difference between the "principles-based approach," which the IASB endeavors to follow, and the "rules-based approach," which has characterized the FASB's standards?

These issues should be considered in light of the IASB-FASB convergence program and the role of the EU endorsement mechanism (described in "The Current Position" section below). Two sets of concerns have been expressed: (1) that there could be two versions of IFRSs—one that would meet the requirements of the SEC, and another that would meet EU requirements as expressed through the endorsement process; and (2) that if IFRSs need interpretations and this task is undertaken by national standard-setting bodies in Europe, divergent national interpretations might emerge.

However, a suggestion that there might be a need for European interpretations of IFRSs to counter the latter problem has been firmly rejected by the European Financial Reporting Advisory Group (EFRAG). The task of issuing interpretations is to remain with the IASB's International Financial Reporting Interpretations Committee (IFRIC), and steps are being taken to strengthen contacts between the IFRIC and national standard-setters in Europe.

On the one hand, EFRAG has worked hard to ensure that effective European input into the IFRS development process is provided, and there has been a strengthening of contacts between the IFRIC and national standard-setters. The European Union in early 2009 announced that it will substantially increase the resources available to EFRAG by providing direct financial support. On the other hand, from the SEC's perspective, the main concern might be the lack of effective enforcement of compliance with IFRSs in certain countries, rather than differing interpretations of the standards. These issues are discussed in the "Likely Future Developments" section below.

THE NEW STRUCTURE

Like the FASB in 1972, and the U.K. Accounting Standards Board in 1990, which replaced the APB and the ASC, respectively, the new IASB differs from its predecessor by having a two-tier structure, based on an organ of governance not involved in standard-setting (the Trustees), and a standard-setting Board. According to Clause 3 of the IASC Constitution:

> The governance of IASC shall rest with the Trustees and the Board and such other governing organs as may be appointed by the Trustees or the Board in accordance with the provisions of this Constitution. The Trustees shall use their best endeavors to ensure that the requirements of this Constitution are observed; however, they are empowered to make minor variations [in the Constitution] in the interest of feasibility of operation if such variations are agreed by 75% of all the Trustees.

The new structure is broadly the one proposed in the Strategic Working Party's November 1999 report, "Recommendations on Shaping IASC for the Future." There are 22 Trustees of the IASC Foundation, of whom six should be from North America, six from Europe, six from the Asia/Pacific region, and four from any area, subject to establishing an "overall geographical balance." The new Board differs significantly from its predecessor (the Committee) by having 12 full-time members as well as two part-time members. Moreover, its members are to be chosen for their technical expertise and background experience, and (in contrast to the Trustees) not on the basis of geographical representation. The original (2000) constitution contained tightly defined requirements concerning liaison responsibilities with national standard-setters and also as regards the professional backgrounds of the membership. These have now been relaxed (from 2005). Liaison with "national standard setters and other official bodies concerned with standard-setting" is to be maintained, and the IASB membership should provide "an appropriate mix of recent practical experience among auditors, preparers, users and academics" (Constitution, clauses 22 and 21). Each member has one vote and most decisions are to be made by a simple majority of members attending in person or by a telecommunications link, with a quorum being such attendance by "at least 60% of the members" and the Chairman having a casting vote. The publication of an exposure draft, final IFRS, or final interpretation of the IFRIC, which replaced the Standing Interpretations Committee (SIC), requires approval by at least nine members of the Board. This change to majority voting is significant, as the old IASC required a 75% majority.

The first Chairman of the IASC Foundation Trustees was Paul A. Volcker, former Chairman of the U.S. Federal Reserve Board. The first Chairman of the new Board was Sir David Tweedie, who moved from being Chairman of the U.K. Accounting Standards Board and was formerly U.K. technical partner for KPMG, after an academic career in Scotland.

The International Financial Reporting Interpretations Committee has a role similar to that of its predecessor, the SIC. The IFRIC has 12 voting members and a non-voting Chairman, all appointed by the Trustees. An interpretation is approved if no more than three members have voted against it after considering public comments on the draft interpretation.

The Standards Advisory Council, with about 40 members, provides a forum for participation by organizations and individuals with an interest in international financial reporting and having diverse geographic and functional backgrounds, with the objective of giving advice to the Board on agenda decisions and priorities, informing the Board of the view of members of the Council on major standard-setting projects, and giving other advice to the Board or the Trustees. The Chairman of the Standards Advisory Council, from 2005, is appointed by the Trustees and is not to be a member of the IASB or a member of its staff. He or she is invited to attend and participate in the Trustees' meetings.

TRUSTEES

- 20 individuals with diverse geographic and functional backgrounds

- Trustees will:

— Appoint the Members of the Board, the Standing Interpretations Committee, and the Standards Advisory Council

— Monitor IASB's effectiveness

— Raise its funds

— Approve IASB's budget

— Have responsibility for constitutional change

STANDARDS ADVISORY COUNCIL	BOARD 14 members, 12 full-time, 2 part-time	INTERNATIONAL FINANCIAL REPORTING INTERPRETATIONS COMMITTEE

Despite the complicated appointments procedures, the original membership of the Board was widely felt to be excessively "Anglo-Saxon" in its orientation and, in particular, lacking in representation from developing and emerging economies, where the determination of fair value by reference to market prices, among other things required by IASB GAAP, may be particularly problematic. The Standards Advisory Council may have been designed to allow at least some input from such other directions. The IASB has made further revisions to its constitution and membership, the number of members of the Board being increased to 16 in order to provide a wider geographical representation including "emerging market" countries. The name has also been changed to "the IFRS Foundation."

THE CURRENT POSITION

In the report of the Strategic Working Party, "Recommendations on Shaping IASC for the Future," it was stated that:

> The primary attributes [considered desirable to establish the legitimacy of a standard setting organization] identified were the representativeness of the decision making body, the independence of its members, and technical expertise. . . . The proposed structure . . . provides a balanced approach to legitimacy based upon representativeness among members of the Trustees, the Standing Interpretations Committee (SIC), and the Standards Advisory Council, and technical competence and independence among Board Members.

The restructured IASB is undoubtedly much better equipped than its predecessor in these respects, as well as being far better resourced. Yet, the key to the IASB's future as a global accounting standard-setter will be the acceptance of its standards for cross-border listings by securities markets worldwide, by all members of IOSCO, *including the SEC for foreign registrants in the United States*, without the need for reconciliations to national GAAP. One of the watchwords of the IASB is *convergence*. This is a two-way process: national sets of accounting standards are to converge toward one another, with IFRSs as the points of convergence, but IFRSs are also expected to converge toward certain national standards in some cases where the latter are recognized as conceptually or technically superior to existing IASs. On certain particularly important and difficult matters, such as financial instruments, the IASB may look, as it has done in the past, to joint working parties composed of experts from countries such as Australia/New Zealand, Canada, the United Kingdom, and the United States, who with the former IASC formed the so-called G4+1.

The SEC's decision, announced in November 2007, not to require foreign registrants that comply with all applicable IFRSs to file reconciliations to U.S. GAAP is a most important milestone for the IASB.

Of major significance also was the decision of the European Commission to make compliance with IASB GAAP mandatory by 2005 for the consolidated financial statements of all corporations listed on stock exchanges in the EU. In its communication dated June 2000, the Commission set out this policy, but also referred to the need for an "endorsement mechanism" at EU level, "because it would not delegate accounting standard setting unconditionally and irrevocably to a private organization [the IASB] over which the EU has no influence . . . [and] it is important to create legal certainty by identifying the standards which listed companies will have to apply in the future. . . . Because the endorsement mechanism will have an important pro-active role, it can be expected that the new standards adopted by [IASB] will also be acceptable in an EU environment." The reference to "an important pro-active role" suggests an intention to influence the "convergence process" in a "European" direction, as a counterweight to other influences, particularly from the United States and the other countries whose accounting standard-setters made up, with the IASC, the now defunct G4+1 (Australia/New Zealand, Canada, and the U.K.).

As well as pressure from the U.S., therefore, the IASB has to contend with this endorsement mechanism set up by the European Commission. In this connection, a new private sector body, the European Reporting Advisory Group (EFRAG), has been set up, and EFRAG has formed a Technical Expert Group (TEG) to advise the European Commission on the appropriateness of IASB standards for use in the EU. The TEG is composed of representatives from the accounting profession, financial analysts, stock exchange regulators, accounting standard-setters and financial statement preparers. The final component of the endorsement mechanism is the Accounting Regulatory Committee (ARC), which makes the final decision on whether to endorse IASB standards for use in the EU. The ARC is composed of government representatives from all of the EU member states and chaired by a representative of the EC; in other words, it has a political character.

When the endorsement mechanism was first set up, the issue arose of whether it would serve merely to satisfy the considerable body of legal opinion in the EU that does not accept the legitimacy of private sector standard-setting and therefore content itself with performing a purely formal legitimization role, or whether it would seek actively to influence IASB standards and thus provide a forum for lobbying intended to influence them. The experience of the endorsement in November 2004 of the standards extant at that date throws some light on this issue. All of those standards were endorsed, with the exception of IAS 39, "Financial Instruments: Recognition and Measurement," which received only partial endorsement, largely as a result of lobbying by banks in four EU member states: Belgium, France, Germany, and Italy.

In fact, 95% of the text of IAS 39 was endorsed, but there were two significant "carve-outs" involving a number of paragraphs dealing with: (a) the "fair-value option" insofar as it permits the designation of any financial liability as "at fair value through profit and loss" and (b) certain restrictions in hedge accounting on portfolio hedges of interest rate risk (e.g., the prohibition of designating a non-derivative financial asset or liability as a hedging item for interest rate risk). However, but for the first carve-out, the second would have been superfluous, since items accounted for at fair value can act as hedges or hedged items without any need for being so designated, thus making hedge accounting unnecessary. The first carve-out, regarding the fair value option, has now been reversed ("carved back in"). The original fair value option was revised by the IASB, and this revised version (see Chapter 17) was fully endorsed by the EU mechanism, with its application backdated to January 1, 2005. The second carve-out, though of less significance for the reason noted, still remains. It would seem that legalistic objections to the fair-value option (on the grounds that it contravenes the prohibition in the EC Fourth Directive of the recognition of unrealized gains), were overcome by use of the "true and fair override" contained in the Directive.

This experience with IAS 39 both indicates that the operation of the endorsement mechanism can influence the IASB's standard-setting process (the amendments to the fair-value option being a case in point) and suggests that lobbying of the ARC will be part of the picture. It has to be said, however, that IAS 39 has been a particularly controversial standard with respect to its requirements on hedges and hedge accounting. Some future standards may also be controversial.

The endorsement process and, in particular, the phase that consists of approval by the European Parliament, can have the effect of delaying the implementation of an IFRS or an amendment for what appear to be purely "bureaucratic" reasons. Thus, while both the EFRAG and the ARC approved IFRS 8, "Operating Segments" (issued in November 2006), the IFRS did not receive final endorsement until November 2007 (with the effect that the right to early adoption of the IFRS by EU reporting entities was effectively removed). And there are other examples. As the majority of the reporting entities expected to apply IFRSs are domiciled in the EU, these bureaucratic (or political) delays can be tiresome. However, they may turn out to be a price that is worth paying, insofar as the EFRAG brings to bear on the IASB's way of thinking, a well-informed and friendly but critical view, notably on such topics as "fair value measurement" (see, for example, the EFRAG's Comment Letter, dated May 29, 2007, on the IASB's November 2006 Discussion Paper, "Fair Value Measurements").

Nevertheless, there are tensions that result from the fact that the IASB's close cooperation with the FASB in the "convergence program" is quite understandably perceived in the EU to be at the expense of the EU "voice" at the critical stages of the development of a new IFRS or a major revision of an existing one. The EFRAG has a formal say only when a new or revised IFRS is published; and, although it is kept informed of the development of the work, it does not have the same involvement as that of the FASB. During 2008 and 2009 these tensions were manifested in increasing "anti-IASB" feelings in parts of Europe, noticeably France, and a number of highly critical comments were expressed in the European Parliament (which, compared with national parliaments, has little, but gradually increasing, power).

The banking and credit crisis during 2008–2009 has also impacted the work of the IASB, which had to be seen as "doing something" in the face of the crisis. The IASB issued a press release in September 2008 to announce "a range of projects that collectively address issues highlighted by the current dislocation in credit markets." This has opened the door to direct political interference in the IASB standard-setting process, especially regarding IAS 39 and the use of fair values, resulting in the accelerated issuance of Exposure Drafts "Derecognition" in April 2009 and "Fair Value Measurement" in May 2009 (see Chapter 17), mirroring similar political interference in the work of the SEC/FASB in the United States. Moreover, in July 2009, in response to recommendations from the G20 leaders that the IASB should "take action by the end of 2009 to improve and simplify the accounting requirements for financial instruments," the IASB issued a further exposure draft, "Financial Instruments: Classification and Measurement," containing proposals that "would necessitate extensive consequential amendments to IAS 39 and other IFRS and to the guidance on those IFRS." The IASB has been planning for some time to replace IAS 39 by a new IFRS, but following the G20 recommendations the intent is to gain time by doing this in three phases, the first of which is represented by the July 2009 exposure draft. (The quotation marks indicate text from the Introduction to the ED.) Other forces have called strongly for the technical independence of the IASB to be preserved and respected. Conflicting demands seem to be at work.

LIKELY FUTURE DEVELOPMENTS

As discussed above, from January 1, 2005, approximately 7,000 European listed companies were required to use full IASB GAAP in their consolidated financial statements. This now includes 12 member countries largely from Eastern Europe who joined the European Union in 2004–2007 and whose accountants and regulators generally lack experience in operating within a capitalist context.

It is crucial that everyone involved, whether in Europe or in any other relevant countries, such as Australia, is aware of the exact regulations that they are supposed to be trying to follow. In other words, a period of stability regarding the detailed content of IASB GAAP is extremely important. This has created a major problem for the IASB, which both wishes and needs to make many changes to the standards it inherited, if true global convergence, around

IASB GAAP, is to be achievable. The approach it has adopted is to attempt to divide its work into two parts.

Thus, the Board made many changes through to the end of 2004, mostly effective from January 1, 2005, and a number of further important changes as part of the "convergence process" in 2007–2008, to be effective from either January 1 or July 1, 2009.

However, two more general issues are worthy of mention here. The first, although the timing is unclear, is the project on reporting financial performance. The original essence of this initiative was to replace the income statement with, to use the full jargon, a layered matrix structure. Information would be presented vertically analyzed (layered) under various subheadings as well as horizontally so as to separate out the effects of remeasurements (as opposed to transactions). An idea of this proposal, though not the precise final detail, is given in Table 1-1.

Table 1-1: Possible Format for Presenting Information under the Reporting Financial Performance Project

		Total	Profit before Remeasurements	Remeasurements
Business	Revenue	500	Revenue	–
	Cost of sales	(200)	Materials, labour etc	Inventory impairments
	Selling, general, admin expenses	(125)	Depreciation/amortisation Rental/other income	PPE/intangible impairment
			Provision – initial recognition Service cost	Provision – remeasurement Change in pension obligation cash flow assumptions
	Operating Profit	175		
	Disposal gain/loss	50	–	Disposal gain/loss
	PPE revaluation	75	–	PPE revaluation
	Goodwill	(50)	Negative goodwill	Goodwill impairment
	FX gain/loss on net investment	(25)	–	FX gain/loss on net investment
	Investment property		–	Investment property fair value change
	Other Business Profit	**50**		
	Income from associates	25	Income from associates	–
	Write-down of accounts receivable	(5)	–	Write-down of accounts receivable
	Equity investments	(30)	–	Return on equity investments
	Debt investments	10	Interest income	Fair value changes on debt investments
	Pension plan assets	(75)		Return on pension plan assets
	Financial Income	**(75)**		
	Business Profit	150		
Financing	Interest on liabilities	(40)	Interest expenses	Change in provision discount rate
	Pension financing expenses	(60)	Unwinding of discount rate	Change in pension obligation discount rate
	Financing expense	(100)		
Tax		(15)	–	–
Discontinuing activities		(5)	Net discontinuing	Net discontinuing
Cash flow hedges		25	–	Fair value changes in cash flow hedging instruments
	Profit	**55**		

It can easily be seen from Table 1-1 that this new type of analyzed combined statement would be ideally suited to allow transparent reporting of the effects of unrealized revaluation changes (i.e., of remeasurements at fair value). The illustration shows operating profit by function in the total column. Each of the desegregation columns illustrates (1) the columns within which various components of expense would be presented and (2) that related items should be presented on the same line (e.g., depreciation and impairment.) The use of "-" indicates a blank cell; for example, the tax charge is not required to be disaggregated between the columns.

The omission of a total at the bottom of the "Profit Before Remeasurements" column is deliberate. It contains the "realized" items and roughly corresponds to the current income statement. Because *all* the items are included in "Total Profit" for the year of their occurrence, the question of possible recycling automatically disappears. Such a format as illustrated here is thus ideally suited to embrace an increasing emphasis on the use of fair value accounting. At one stage, it looked as though some proposal vaguely on the lines described above would emerge fairly quickly. However, there is clearly some rethinking, and perhaps more fundamental criticism, at work. For more information, check out the IASB web site: http://www.iasb.org.

In September 2007, the IASB issued another revision to IAS 1, "Presentation of Financial Statements," mandatory from January 1, 2009 (see Chapter 4). The major development is a significant expansion of the requirements for performance reporting (as opposed to a statement of position). Titles of several required statements have also been changed, though IAS 1 explicitly accepts that the previous, or indeed other, titles may be used. IAS 1 now requires:

- A statement of financial position as at the end of the period.
- A statement of comprehensive income for the period. The components of profit or loss may be presented as a separate statement, or as part of this single statement of comprehensive income.
- A statement of changes in equity for the period.
- A statement of cash flows.
- Notes.
- An opening statement of financial position as at the *beginning* of the earliest comparative period presented.

The effect of these changes, while not as radical as the proposals of Table 1-1, is to force a visible and transparent presentation of *all* changes in equity over the reporting period.

In May 2010, the IASB issued an exposure draft proposing further developments in "Other Comprehensive Income" reporting under IAS 1. At present, entities have an option in IAS 1 to present either a statement of comprehensive income or two separate statements of profit or loss and other comprehensive income. This exposure draft proposes to require a statement of profit or loss and other comprehensive income containing two distinct sections—profit or loss and items of other comprehensive income.

The exposure draft also proposes a new presentation approach for items of OCI. The Board is proposing to require that items that will never be recognized in profit or loss should be presented separately from those that are subject to subsequent reclassification (recycling).

Other general issues that are being discussed more seriously concern the question of an increasing adoption of fair values. Much of the discussion is at a theoretical stage, and practical outcomes are hard to predict. Suffice to suggest here that:

- The IASB is broadly in favor of an extension of fair value usage;

- Many preparers and regulators in a number of countries are much more cautious; and

- Use of the concept and practicalities of measurement are not yet effectively thought through.

This is a very interesting and important time for the IASB. The outcome in terms of whether or not it achieves its "single set . . . of enforceable global accounting standards" is still unclear. In the short term, as explained above, it had to focus extensively on the 2005 deadline agreed with the EU. Consequently, it had to divide a number of its projects into two parts, generally termed Phase 1 and Phase 2. Good examples are the revision of the Business Combinations requirements (see Chapter 8) and accounting for Insurance Contracts (see Chapter 35). A number of changes had been made and were IASB GAAP requirements from January 1, 2005 (Phase 1). However, further significant developments took place in 2007–2008 or are firmly in the pipeline (Phase 2), and this split has sometimes led to obscurities and oddities in the interregnum.

A further issue still not entirely resolved concerns the level of detail that should be included in financial reporting standards. Convergence is being attempted, inter alia, between the U.S. system, which has become highly detailed and prescriptive in recent years, and the old IASC tradition of a more principles-based approach. The latest new IASB standards do seem to be significantly imbued with a sense that a considerable level of detailed regulation, and sometimes more explicit guidance, is necessary. This is especially true where convergence toward existing U.S. regulation is being pursued. Nevertheless, it is unclear that such a level of prescription will lead to more effective operationalization of letter *and spirit* of IASB GAAP. A recent report to the U.K. Upper House of Parliament has criticized recent IASB standards for being *excessively* rules-based as compared with U.K. national standards, obviously a complaint about American FASB/SEC influence.

The IASB, partly in its own right, and as part of its ongoing convergence project with the FASB, has a large number of projects that are continuing to lead to amendments, often significant ones, to existing Standard requirements. Experience suggests that indications regarding the direction of these changes cannot reliably be assumed to be retained through to the eventual formalization of new Standard requirements. Accordingly, it would be unhelpful to provide much detail, which may be erroneous and therefore confusing. Nevertheless, important likely changes are indicated in the relevant chapters of this book. It is also worth pointing out that the IASB and the FASB are on record as intending complete convergence by 2014.

A final point much heard in Europe, perhaps partly related to the issue discussed in the previous paragraph, is that, at least in the short term, most users of IASB GAAP will be based in Europe, whilst a major influence on the contents of IASB GAAP is coming from the United States. Full U.S. acceptance of IASB GAAP without the need for an additional reconciliation to U.S. GAAP would remove the basis for such concerns. So far, a condition for such full acceptance by the SEC has been full convergence—a worthy objective, but not achievable in the short term. We live in interesting times!

In Spring 2010, the SEC published a work plan that sets out the specific areas and factors that its staff will consider before requiring or permitting U.S.-listed companies to use IFRS instead of U.S. GAAP. The SEC does not expect such a transition to take place before 2016. The work plan lists six key issues, the first two of which are most relevant:

- sufficient development and application of IFRS for the U.S. domestic reporting system;

- the independence of standard-setting for the benefit of investors;

- investor understanding and education regarding IFRS;

- examination of the U.S. regulatory environment that would be affected by a change in accounting standards;

- the impact on issuers, both large and small, including changes to accounting systems, changes to contractual arrangements, corporate governance considerations, and litigation contingencies; and

- human capital readiness.

Reading between the lines, progress is likely to be slow and difficult.

Generally, the dangers of political interference seem to be increasing. As already indicated, political attacks on the IASB from within Europe have increased in intensity, and indeed have directly caused changes in requirements. In the United States the new chairman of the SEC, Mary Schapiro, told Congress in February 2009, that, in relation to the proposal to produce common IASB and FASB standards by 2014, the SEC could not work with a standard-setter that was subject to political interference. Irony of ironies, in March 2009 the SEC and FASB were forced by Congress to change U.S. GAAP on financial instruments in three weeks with, in the words of a respected commentator, "only the merest fig-leaf of due process"! Multiple political interference is a sure way to destroy the effectiveness of global standards.

In this context, it is interesting to note that the new chairman of the Board from July 1, 2011, is Hans Hoogervorst. In some ways, this is a surprising appointment, as he comes from a political and regulatory background, rather than a financial accounting/reporting background. His early comments have indicated no major change in the IASB's focus. He confirms his view that IFRSs are primarily for investors, and that transparency is crucial.

Hoogervorst's comments on legitimacy issues are interesting. He has suggested that standard setters must resist pressure from special interest groups, but that equally the international community must feel a sense of ownership of the international regulator. A similar balancing act is attempted in a Discussion Paper published by EFRAG in January 2011, entitled "Considering the Effects of Accounting Standards." This proposes that an "effects analysis" should be carried out for all proposed standards, defined as: "a systematic process for considering the effects of accounting standards as those standards are developed and implemented." However it goes on to suggest that a standard setter "can only be expected to respond to an effect which is outside of its remit by communicating with the relevant regulator or government body to notify them of the relevant issue . . . " This is in code, of course, but means, for example, that banking regulators should sort out their own problems, which it is not within the IASB's "remit" to solve. Politicians, on both sides of the Atlantic, have a poor record of unhelpful involvement in standard-setting on behalf of special interest groups. It will be interesting to see how this evolves over the next few years.

CHAPTER 2
THE CONCEPTUAL FRAMEWORK FOR FINANCIAL REPORTING

CONTENTS

OVERVIEW

The IASB's Framework belongs to the family of conceptual frameworks for financial reporting that have been developed by accounting standard-setters in a number of countries where accounting standard-setting is carried out by a private sector body. On one level, such conceptual frameworks may be considered attempts to assemble a body of accounting theory (or interrelated concepts) as a guide to standard-setting, so that standards are (as far as possible) formulated on a consistent basis and not in an *ad hoc* manner. On another but complementary level, they may be thought of as devices to confer legitimacy and authority on a private sector standard-setter that lacks the legal authority of a public body. The IASC, as a private sector standard-setter, shared these reasons for developing a conceptual framework.

Conceptual frameworks developed by accounting standard-setters are essentially based on identification of "good practice" from which principles are derived inductively. The criteria for identifying "good practice" are related to the assumed objectives of financial reporting. At the same time, attention is paid to conceptual coherence, and the development process typically involves "conceptual tidying up." Conceptual frameworks may be written in a prescriptive style or a descriptive style, or a mixture of the two. Whatever the style, they are essentially *normative,* since they seek to provide a set of principles as a guide to setting and interpreting accounting standards. Such guidance, however, does not necessarily preclude a standard being issued that, for compelling pragmatic reasons, departs from a principle set out in the applicable conceptual framework.

The IASB's Framework is written in a descriptive style (in fact, it is IASB policy to use the word "shall" only in standards) and seeks to avoid being excessively prescriptive. A principal reason for this is that it needs to have broad international applicability. In the final paragraph of the Framework, the then IASC stated:

> This Framework is applicable to a range of accounting models and provides guidance on preparing and presenting the financial statements constructed under the chosen model. At the present time [1989], it is not the intention of the Board of IASC to prescribe a particular model other than in exceptional circumstances, such as . . . a hyperinflationary economy.

In common with other conceptual frameworks, notably the FASB's set of Statements of Financial Accounting Concepts, the IASB's Framework covers the following topics:

1. *Objective of financial statements.* The Framework takes the position that, because investors are providers of risk capital to an entity, financial statements that meet investors' needs will also meet most of the needs of other users that financial statements can satisfy. On that basis, the objective of financial statements is to provide information about the financial position, performance, and changes in financial position of an entity that is useful to a wide range of users in making economic decisions, including assessment of the stewardship or accountability of management. The Framework states as "underlying assumptions" that, in order to meet their objectives, financial statements are prepared on the accrual basis of accounting and (normally) on the "going concern" basis.

2. *Qualitative characteristics of financial statement information.* The Framework cites four main qualitative characteristics: understandability, relevance, reliability, and comparability. Materiality is mentioned as an aspect of relevance. "Faithful representation," "substance over form," "neutrality"

(freedom from bias), "prudence" (subject to neutrality), and "complete-ness" (within the bounds of materiality and cost) are mentioned as aspects of reliability. The Framework does not deal directly with the concepts of "true and fair view" (TFV) or "fair presentation" (FP), but states that "the application of the principal qualitative characteristics and of appropriate accounting standards normally results in financial statements that convey what is generally understood as [a TFV or FP] of such information." However, IAS 1, "Presentation of Financial State-ments," states fair presentation as a requirement (see below).

3. *Elements of financial statements.* The Framework relates the elements to the measurement of financial position and performance. As elements of financial position, it provides definitions of assets, liabilities, and equity; and as elements of performance, it defines income (including revenue and gains) and expenses (including losses). The definitions given in the section on elements, and especially those of assets and liabilities, are the core of the Framework as a prescriptive basis for standard-setting.

4. *Principles for recognition of the elements.* The Framework states that recog-nition is the process of recording in the financial statements (subject to materiality) an item that meets the definition of an element and satisfies the two criteria for recognition, namely, (a) it is *probable* that any future economic benefit associated with the item will flow to or from the entity and (b) the item has a cost or value that can be measured with reliability. Assessments of the degree of probability of the flow of future economic benefits "are made when the financial statements are prepared."

5. *Bases for measurement of the elements.* Unlike the section in which the elements of financial statements are defined, the treatment of measure-ment in the IASC's Framework avoids being prescriptive. It cites a number of different measurement bases and notes that the basis most commonly adopted is historical cost, usually combined with other bases.

The Framework also covers another topic, which is not necessarily dealt with specifically in other conceptual frameworks:

6. *Concepts of capital and capital maintenance.* The treatment of capital main-tenance in the Framework also avoids being prescriptive. It distin-guishes between (a) *financial* capital maintenance, in two forms, nominal (i.e., monetary units) or real (units of constant purchasing power) and (b) *physical* capital maintenance or operating capability. It states that the physical capital maintenance concept requires the use of a particular measurement basis, namely current cost, whereas neither form of the financial capital maintenance concept requires any particular measure-ment basis. It also states the implications of each concept of capital maintenance for profit measurement.

The IASB's Framework is a succinct document. It is much briefer than the FASB's set of six "Statements of Accounting Concepts," each of which is longer than the Framework. It is also shorter than the U.K. ASB's "Statement of Principles," which runs to some 130 pages. Succinctness is possible because of the limits that the then IASC placed on its prescriptive aims. The IASC also benefited from the trailblazing work of the FASB, thanks to which most of the issues dealt with in the Framework had already been publicized.

BACKGROUND

The origins of the Framework go back to 1982, when the then IASC initiated a limited study on the objectives of financial statements. The IASC stated at that time, however, that it did not intend to prepare an "international conceptual framework." The FASB had already issued in 1978 its SFAC 1, "Objectives of Financial Reporting by Business Enterprises," and in 1980 its SFACs 2 and 3 on "Qualitative Characteristics" and "Elements." In 1982 — 1984, the FASB's conceptual framework project was encountering some difficulties in dealing with issues of recognition and measurement.

In 1984, the then IASC decided to revise IAS 1, "Disclosure of Accounting Policies," published in 1974, and it was also decided to merge the objectives project with this revision. In 1984 and 1985, new projects were started covering liabilities, equity and assets, and expenses. The decision to merge these into a Framework project occurred in November 1986, and the proposed revision of IAS 1 was deferred. The Framework was intended to be separate from the IASs and to avoid binding the IASC to particular accounting treatments in IASs. It was approved and issued in April 1989. Work is in progress on a joint IASB-FASB project to develop a common framework (see below).

The status of the Framework vis-à-vis IASB GAAP may be compared with that of the FASB's SFACs vis-à-vis U.S. GAAP, as follows. As noted above, the IASC did not intend the Framework to be binding on it in its capacity as a standard-setter, just as the SFACs are not binding on the FASB in its standard-setting capacity. However, the Framework has been quite influential in the development of IASs and IFRSs and in major revisions. For example, its definitions (and especially those of assets and liabilities) were highly influential in the preparation of IFRS 3, "Business Combinations"; IAS 37, "Provisions, Contingent Liabilities and Contingent Assets"; IAS 38, "Intangible Assets"; and IAS 39, "Financial Instruments: Recognition and Measurement."

The Framework is not an IAS or IFRS and does not override any specific IAS or IFRS; in case of conflict between it and an IAS, the requirements of the latter prevail. *One may, however, consider the Framework as embodying IASB GAAP in respect of issues that are not dealt with in any IAS.* For example, in the case of topics that have not yet been the subject of an IAS or IFRS, the purpose of the Framework is to assist preparers in dealing with such topics. Moreover, the IASB will be guided by the Framework in the development of future IFRSs and in reviewing existing ones, so that the number of cases of conflict between the Framework and IASs or IFRSs are likely to diminish over time. The Framework itself will be subject to revision in the light of experience.

The relationship between the Framework and IAS 1, "Presentation of Financial Statements," is worthy of comment in the context of the comparison of IASB GAAP with U.S. GAAP. As noted above, originally the start of work on what became the Framework was linked to the revision of IAS 1. This revision was then deferred and not completed until 1997. The revised IAS 1 is a major standard that supersedes the former IASs 1, 5, and 13 (see Chapter 4). Although the Framework does not have the status of a standard, it and IAS 1 (revised) may to some extent be considered as complementary. The Framework itself does not conflict with U.S. GAAP in any important respect, but IAS 1 does. Its paragraphs 16–24 contain a provision to the effect that a specific requirement of an IAS may *need* to be departed from "in extremely rare circumstances . . . when the treatment required by the standard is clearly inappropriate and thus a fair presentation cannot be achieved either by applying the standard or through additional disclosure alone." This is the so-called "override," which is quite alien to U.S. GAAP in practice, if not (according to Rule 203 of the AICPA Code of Ethics) in theory. The override is *mandatory* if the circumstances require it.

While the override represents a major difference between IASB GAAP and U.S. GAAP in principle, the restrictions placed on its use by IAS 1 suggest that there should not be many cases of it in practice.

REVISION OF THE CONCEPTUAL FRAMEWORK

The IASB and FASB are jointly developing a common conceptual framework as part of the process of convergence between the two sets of GAAP. This project is divided into eight phases, A to H, as follows:

(A) Objectives and qualitative characteristics

(B) Elements, recognition, and measurement

(C) Measurement

(D) Reporting entity

(E) Presentation and disclosure

(F) Purpose and status

(G) Application to not-for-profit entities

(H) Finalization

Progress is slow. The conceptual framework as published in the IFRS compendium for 2011 and relevant until further notice, is very obviously a partially revised, indeed hybrid, document. Its structure is as follows:

Introduction (unchanged from 1989), including:

— Purpose and status

— Scope

Chapter 1 The objective of general purpose financial reporting (2010)

Chapter 2 The reporting entity (not yet issued, that is, a blank page)

Chapter 3 Qualitative characteristics of useful information (2010)

Chapter 4 The remaining text from 1989, unchanged but re-numbered, as follows:

— Underlying assumption: 4.1

— The elements of financial statements: 4.2–4.36

— Recognition of the elements of financial statements: 4.37–4.53

— Measurement of the elements of financial statements: 4.54–4.56

— Concepts of capital and capital maintenance: 4.57–4.65

A table of concordance between this (hopefully, temporary) version and the original 1989 Framework is given as follows. In this chapter we use the new reference details throughout.

Table of Concordance

This table shows how the contents of the *Framework* (1989) and the *Conceptual Framework* (2010) correspond.

Framework (1989) paragraphs	*Conceptual Framework* 2010 paragraphs
Preface and introduction paragraphs 1–5	Introduction
6–21	Superseded by Chapter 1
22	Not carried forward
23	4.1
24–46	Superseded by Chapter 3
47–110	Chapter 4
47, 48	4.2, 4.3
49–52	4.4–4.7
53–59	4.8–4.14
60–64	4.15–4.19
65–68	4.20–4.23
69–73	4.24–4.28
74–77	4.29–4.32
78–80	4.33–4.35
81	4.36
82–84	4.37–4.39
85	4.40
86–88	4.41–4.43
89, 90	4.44, 4.45
91	4.46
92, 93	4.47, 4.48
94–98	4.49–4.53
99–101	4.54–4.56
102, 103	4.57, 4.58
104–110	4.59–4.65

Purpose and Status

The Framework does not have the status of an IAS, does not override any specific IAS, and in case of conflict between the Framework and an IAS, the latter prevails. The purpose of the Framework is to:

- Assist the Board in the development of future IASs and in its review of existing IASs;

- Help the Board to promote harmonization of regulations, accounting standards and procedures relating to the presentation of financial statements by providing a basis for reducing the number of alternative accounting treatments permitted by IASs;
- Assist national standard-setting bodies in developing national standards;
- Aid preparers of financial statements in applying IASs and in dealing with topics that have yet to form the subject of an IAS;
- Assist auditors in forming an opinion as to whether financial statements conform with IASs;
- Help users of financial statements to interpret the information contained in financial statements prepared in conformity with IASs;
- Provide those who are interested in the work of the IASC with information about its approach to the formulation of accounting standards.

Scope

The scope of the Framework is to deal with:

- Objectives of financial statements;
- Qualitative characteristics that determine the usefulness of financial statement information;
- Definition, recognition, and measurement of financial statement elements; and
- Concepts of capital and capital maintenance.

THE OBJECTIVE OF GENERAL PURPOSE FINANCIAL REPORTING

In new Chapter 1, "The Objective of General Purpose Financial Reporting," the determined use of the singular in the title is notable. The formal statement (par. OB2) is that the objective of general purpose financial reporting (GPFR) is to provide financial information about the reporting entity that is useful to existing and potential investors, lenders, and other creditors in making decisions about providing resources to the entity. These decisions involve buying, selling, or holding equity and debt instruments, and providing or settling loans and other forms of credit.

These specified users require information to help them assess the prospects for future net cash flows to the entity. This, in turn, requires information about the resources of the entity, claims against the entity, and how efficiently and effectively the entity's management (broadly defined) have discharged their duties to use the entity's resources (pars OB 3-4).

More clearly than in its 1989 document, the IASB spells out the purposes/ users, which are *not* included by the above (pars. OB 5-10). The "primary users" of GPFRs are those "existing and potential investors, lenders and other creditors" who cannot force reporting entities to provide information beyond what is revealed in the GPFRs. However, GPFRs will need to be supplemented from other sources, for example, relating to economic and political developments broadly considered. It is explicitly stated that GPFRs are not designed to show the value of the reporting entity; rather, their purpose is to provide relevant information to help others determine the reporting entity's value. An even more explicit exclusion is in paragraph OB 10.

Other parties, such as regulators and members of the public other than investors, lenders and other creditors, may also find GPFRs useful. However, those reports are not primarily directed to these other groups.

OBSERVATION: This last point is particularly significant, as there has been much criticism from regulators and politicians in recent years (in both Europe and the United States, and against both the IASB and FASB) that published GPFRs have failed regulators, in general, and banking regulators, in particular. This is in one sense factually correct, but the fault lies entirely with the regulators for misusing, perhaps simply not being professionally competent enough to understand, the information contained in the GPFRs.

The remaining part of Chapter 1, pars OB12-OB21, consists of a conventional summary of the ways of providing relevant information. Information about economic resources and claims is provided in a balance sheet/statement of financial position, allowing a focus on liquidity, solvency, and financing. Information about changes in economic resources can focus on an entity's own financial/economic operating performance, through an income statement reflecting accrual accounting, and on external changes, for example, the raising of new external finance by debt or equity. Further, information about cash movements is very important, via a statement of cash flows.

QUALITATIVE CHARACTERISTICS OF USEFUL FINANCIAL INFORMATION

The new Chapter 3, "Qualitative Characteristics of Useful Financial Information," of the Conceptual Framework, finalized in 2010, logically follows the (currently non-existent) Chapter 2, which will discuss the definition of, and, in particular, the boundaries of, the "Reporting Entity." Chapter 3 covers similar ground to pars. 24–46 of the 1989 Framework, but there are several significant changes. These changes have caused much discussion, debate, and criticism during the long gestation period of this material. The most significant changes are of omission: the concepts, or at least the words, of reliability and providence have both disappeared. Reliability is in effect replaced by "faithful representation," which is upgraded in importance, as discussed below.

Two "fundamental" qualitative characteristics are presented: relevance and faithful representation (pars. QC5-16).

Relevant financial information is capable of making a difference in the decisions made by users. Information may be capable of making a difference in a decision even if some users choose not to take advantage of it, or are already aware of it from other sources. Financial information is capable of making a difference in decisions if it has predictive value, confirmatory value, or both.

Financial information has predictive value if it can be used as an input to processes employed by users to predict future outcomes. Financial information need not be a prediction or forecast to have predictive value. Financial information has confirmatory value if it provides feedback about (either confirms or changes) previous evaluations.

The Board notes, regarding materiality, that it is an entity-specific concept, and no proposed "qualitative threshold" would be rational. Information is material if omitting it or misstating it could influence decisions that users make on the basis of financial information about a specific reporting entity.

The Board introduces faithful representation by noting that financial reports represent economic phenomena in words and numbers. To be useful, financial information must not only represent relevant phenomena, but it must also faithfully represent the phenomena that it purports to represent. To be a perfectly faithful representation, a depiction would have three characteristics. It would be *complete, neutral,* and *free from error.* Of course, perfection is seldom, if ever, achievable. The Board's objective is to maximize those qualities to the extent possible. A complete depiction includes all information necessary for a user to understand the phenomenon being depicted, including all necessary descriptions and explanations.

A neutral depiction is without bias in the selection or presentation of financial information. A neutral depiction is not slanted, weighted, emphasised, de-emphasised or otherwise manipulated to increase the probability that financial information will be received favorably by users.

Faithful representation does not mean accurate in all respects. Free from error means there are no errors or omissions in the description of the phenomenon, and the process used to produce the reported information has been selected and applied with no errors. In this context, free from error does not mean perfectly accurate in all respects.

In its "Basis for Conclusions" document issued at the same time as the revised Chapter 3, the IASB discussed and defends the changes made as compared with 1989. Previously, representational faithfulness, verifiability, and neutrality were aspects of (i.e., subservient to) reliability. Verbally, reliability and representational faithfulness have firstly been reversed, and then reliability has been transposed into verifiability (discussed below). The proposition, never quite clearly stated, seems to be that if "information is complete, neutral and free from error" (see above characteristics of faithful representation), then it must automatically be reliable (in the general sense that it "can be depended on" in the words of 1989). Therefore reliability is unnecessary as a separate notion. The proposition seems defensible.

"Substance over form" similarly disappears as being redundant, given faithful representation. Prudence disappears, as being inconsistent with neutrality.

OBSERVATION: It is difficult to disagree with the analytical logic behind all this. But some long-cherished beliefs in some quarters are being ruthlessly assaulted. We would suggest that the real issue is not the dropping of concepts or words. Rather, it is the continued emphasis on external, independent, suppliers of finance to entities, rather than more closely connected sources of finance such as family or banks. The full implications of Chapter 1 of the revised Conceptual Framework, and what it does *not* say, is discussed in Chapter 4.

The Board sums up the implications in practice, as follows (par. QC18):

> The most efficient and effective process for applying the fundamental qualitative characteristics would usually be as follows (subject to the effects of enhancing characteristics and the cost constraint, which are not considered in this example). First, identify an economic phenomenon that has the potential to be useful to users of the reporting entity's financial information. Second, identify the type of information about that phenomenon that would be most relevant if it is available and can be faithfully represented. Third, determine whether that information is available and can be faithfully represented. If so, the process of satisfying the fundamental qualitative, characteristics ends at that point. If not, the process is repeated with the next most relevant type of information.

The remaining paragraphs of Chapter 3 discuss several sub-characteristics, called "enhancing qualitative characteristics" that enhance the usefulness of information that is relevant and faithfully represented. Note that they cannot, by themselves, make information useful if it is not already properly regarded as relevant and faithfully represented. These are comparability, verifiability, timeliness, and understandability.

Comparability is the qualitative characteristic that enables users to identify and understand similarities in, and differences among, items. Unlike the other qualitative characteristics, comparability does not relate to a single item, as a comparison requires at least two items.

Consistency, although related to comparability, is not the same. Consistency refers to the use of the same methods for the same items, either from period to period within a reporting entity or in a single period across entities. Comparability is the goal; consistency helps to achieve that goal.

Comparability is not uniformity. For information to be comparable, similar items must appear similar and different items must appear different. Comparability of financial information is not enhanced by making dissimilar items appear similar any more than it is enhanced by making similar items appear different.

Verifiability helps assure users that information faithfully represents the economic phenomena it purports to represent. Verifiability means that different knowledgeable and independent observers could reach consensus, although not necessarily complete agreement, that a particular depiction is a faithful representation. Quantified information need not be a single point estimate to be verifiable. A range of possible amounts and the related probabilities can also be verified.

Timeliness means having information available to decision-makers in time to be capable of influencing their decisions. Generally, the older the information is, the less useful it is. However, some information may continue to be timely long after the end of a reporting period because, for example, some users may need to identify and assess trends.

Classifying characteristics and presenting information clearly and concisely makes it *understandable*. Some phenomena are inherently complex and cannot be made easily understandable. Excluding this information from financial reports might make the information easier to understand; however, the information would be incomplete and, therefore, potentially misleading.

Financial reports are prepared for users who have a reasonable knowledge of business and economic activities and who review and analyze the information regularly. At times, even well-informed, diligent users may need to seek the aid of an adviser to understand complex economic phenomena.

Finally in this section, the Board notes that cost is a pervasive constraint on the information that can be provided by financial reporting. Reporting financial information imposes costs, and it is important that those costs are justified by the benefits of reporting that information.

Because of the inherent subjectivity, different individuals' assessments of the costs and benefits of reporting particular items of financial information will vary. Therefore, the Board seeks to consider costs and benefits in relation to financial reporting generally, and not solely in relation to individual reporting entities. This does not indicate that assessments of costs and benefits always justify the same reporting requirements for all entities. Differences may be appropriate, for example, because of different sizes of entities, different ways of raising capital (publicly or privately), or different users' needs.

CHAPTER 4, THE REMAINING TEXT

The remaining text of the Conceptual Framework (2010) consists of unaltered material from 1989. Paragraph 4.1 explains the concept of going concern, transposed from an earlier position in 1989.

> The financial statements are normally prepared on the assumption that an entity is a going concern and will continue in operation for the foreseeable future. Hence, it is assumed that the entity has neither the intention nor the need to liquidate or curtail materially the scale of its operations; if such an intention or need exists, the financial statements may have to be prepared on a different basis and, if so, the basis used is disclosed.

The whole of the remainder follows the 1989 version exactly, in content and in sequence.

THE ELEMENTS OF FINANCIAL STATEMENTS

The section of the Framework concerning the elements of financial statements (pars. 4.2–4.35) consists essentially of definitions of the elements of financial statements as identified by the Framework.

OBSERVATION: As noted in the Overview, the definitions given in this section, and especially those of assets and liabilities, are the core of the Framework as a prescriptive basis for standard-setting. The section on Recognition of Elements (pars. 4.37–4.53, see below) acts to reinforce this core. In particular:

1. The Framework defines income and expenses in terms of increases and decreases in economic benefits that are equated with changes in assets and liabilities;

2. The latter are defined in terms of "resources controlled" and "present obligations" to exclude some of the types of items that have been previously recognized as assets or liabilities (accruals and deferrals) in the name of "matching" expenses and revenues; and

3. The effect of these tighter definitions, together with those of the recognition criteria set out in the section on recognition, can be seen particularly in the implications of the definition of a liability for the recognition of provisions (see Chapters 8 and 29 on IFRS 3 and IAS 37), and in the implications of the definition of an asset for the recognition of intangible items (see Chapters 8 and 22 on IFRS 3 and IAS 38).

There is an overlap between definitions and recognition criteria, since satisfying the definition of an element is the principal criterion for recognition. The Framework, however, seeks to distinguish definition issues from recognition issues as far as possible.

The Framework relates the elements of financial statements to the measurement of financial position and performance. As elements of financial position (in the balance sheet), it provides definitions of assets, liabilities, and equity; and as elements of performance (in the income statement), it defines income, including revenue and gains, and expenses, including losses. As for the statement of changes in financial position, this "usually reflects income statement elements and changes in balance sheet elements," and so the Framework does not identify any elements associated uniquely with this statement (par. 4.2).

Financial Position

The elements considered to be "directly related to the measurement of financial position" are assets, liabilities, and equity, which are defined as follows (par. 4.4):

1. An asset is a resource (a) controlled by the enterprise, (b) as a result of past events, and (c) from which future economic benefits are expected to flow to the enterprise. Recognition as an asset thus requires that the three components of the definition, (a), (b), and (c), be satisfied.

2. A liability is (a) a present obligation of the enterprise, (b) arising out of past events, (c) the settlement of which is expected to result in an outflow from the enterprise of resources embodying economic benefits. Recognition as a liability thus requires that the three components of the definition, (a), (b), and (c), be satisfied.

3. Equity is defined as the residual interest in the assets of the enterprise after deducting all its liabilities.

OBSERVATION: Financial position comprises a number of attributes, including liquidity, solvency, leverage, asset structure, reserves available to cover dividends, and so forth. While each of these attributes may be measured, it is not clear what is meant by "measurement" of financial position as such, which is the terminology used in paragraph 4.4. A term such as "evaluation of financial position" would be more usual.

Merely satisfying the above definitions does not entail recognition, since the recognition criteria in pars. 4.37–4.53 must also be satisfied, and also the principle of "substance over form" must be respected. For example, this principle requires fixed assets held under finance leases to be recognized by the lessee as fixed assets (with corresponding leasing liabilities), while the lessor recognizes a financial asset (pars. 4.5–4.6).

Balance sheets drawn up in accordance with "current" IASs may include items the treatment of which does not satisfy the *above* definitions, but the definitions will underlie "future" reviews of existing standards and the formulation of new ones (par. 4.7). As noted above, the IASC acted accordingly, and it would now be unusual to find an item whose treatment according to a current IAS would conflict with the definitions.

Assets

The "future economic benefit embodied in an asset" is defined as "the potential to contribute, directly or indirectly, to the flow of cash and cash equivalents to the enterprise," including "a capability to reduce cash outflows." In case that definition should leave the status of cash itself as an asset unclear, it is stated that cash satisfies this definition, because it "renders a service to the enterprise because of its command over other resources." Assets embody future economic benefits that may flow to the enterprise by having one or more of the following capabilities: (a) being exchanged for other assets; (b) being used to settle a liability; or (c) being distributed to the enterprise's owners (three capabilities that cash conspicuously possesses); as well as that of being used singly or in combination with other assets in the production of goods and services to be sold by the enterprise (pars. 4.8–4.10).

Neither having physical form, nor being the object of a right of ownership, is an essential attribute of an asset. Intangible items such as patents and copyrights may satisfy the definition of an asset, as may a fixed asset held under a finance lease (by virtue of which it is a resource controlled though not owned by, and from which future benefits are expected to flow to, the entity). Moreover, knowledge obtained from development activity may meet the definition of an asset (capitalized development costs) even though neither physical form nor legal ownership is involved, provided there is *de facto* control such that, by keeping the knowledge secret, the enterprise controls the benefits that are expected to flow from it (pars. 4.11–4.12).

Assets may result from various types of past transactions and other past events. Normally, these are purchase transactions and the events associated with production; but they may include donation (for example, by way of a government grant) or discovery (as in the case of mineral deposits). Expected future transactions or events do not give rise to assets; for example, a binding contract by an enterprise to purchase inventory does not cause the inventory in question to meet the definition of an asset of that enterprise until the purchase transaction that fulfils the contract has occurred. While expenditure is a common way to acquire or generate an asset, expenditure undertaken with a view to generating future economic benefits may fail to result in an asset, for example, if the intended economic benefits cannot be expected or are not controlled by the entity (pars. 4.13–4.14).

Liabilities

An essential characteristic of (or necessary condition for) a liability is that the entity should have a "present obligation." An obligation is "a duty or responsibility to act or perform in a certain way." The duty or responsibility may arise from the law, for example, the law of contract; or it may arise from normal business practice, which leads to legitimate expectations that the entity will act or perform in a certain way (that is, a constructive obligation). An example of the latter is a constructive obligation to extend the benefits of a warranty for some period beyond the contractual warranty period, because this is an established practice (par. 4.15).

A present obligation (in the relevant sense) is not the same as a future commitment. An entity may have a commitment to purchase an asset in the future at an agreed price; however, this does not entail a net outflow of resources. The commitment does not give rise to a liability, which arises only when the purchase has actually taken place and title in the asset has passed to the entity, leaving the latter with an obligation to pay for it. In the case of a cash transaction, no liability would arise (par. 4.16).

There are a number of ways in which a liability may be settled or discharged, which include replacement by another obligation, conversion into equity, and the creditor waiving or forfeiting his rights. There are also various types of "past transactions or past events" from which liabilities may result (pars. 4.17–4.18). If a provision involves a present obligation and satisfies the rest of the definition of a liability given in the Framework, it is a liability even if the amount has to be estimated (par. 4.19).

OBSERVATION: Paragraph 4.19 does not emphasize the equally important point that a provision that fails to satisfy the criterion of being an *obligation* arising from a past transaction or past event is not a liability. This point, however, was crucial in arriving at the requirements for recognition of provisions in IAS 37, "Provisions, Contingent Liabilities, and Contingent Assets" (see Chapter 29).

Equity

Paragraphs 4.20–4.23 are concerned with equity. The fact that equity is defined as a residual interest (assets minus liabilities) does not mean that it cannot be meaningfully divided into subclassifications that are shown separately in the balance sheet. Examples are the differences among the following: (a) paid-in capital (capital stock and paid-in surplus); (b) retained earnings; (c) reserves representing appropriations of retained earnings; and (d) reserves representing the amounts required to be retained in order to maintain "real" capital, that is, either real financial capital or (real) physical capital.

There are various legal, tax, and valuation considerations that affect equity, such as requirements for legal reserves, and whether or not the enterprise is incorporated. It is emphasized that transfers to legal, statutory, and tax reserves are appropriations of retained earnings and not expenses. (Likewise, releases from such reserves are credits to retained earnings and not income, but this is not spelled out.) The rather obvious point is made that the amount at which equity is shown in the balance sheet is not intended to be a measure of the market value of the entity, either as a going concern or in a piecemeal disposal. It is stated that the definition and treatment of equity in the Framework are appropriate for unincorporated enterprises, even if the legal considerations are different.

Performance

Paragraphs 4.24–4.36 contain the section of the Framework in which definitions of the financial statement elements relating to performance are given. "Profit is frequently used as a measure of performance or as the basis for other measures, such as return on investment and earnings per share" (par. 4.24). However, this section of the Framework does not discuss the relationship between the elements of performance and the profit measure, except to say that "the recognition and measurement of income and expenses, and hence profit, depends in part on the concepts of capital and capital maintenance used by the entity in preparing its financial statements." The determination of profit and related issues are discussed in a later section of the Framework (pars. 4.57–4.65).

The elements of income and expenses are defined as follows:

1. Income is increases in economic benefits during the accounting period in the form of inflows or enhancements of assets or decreases of liabilities that result in increases in equity, other than those relating to contributions from equity participants.

2. Expenses are decreases in economic benefits during the accounting period in the form of outflows or depletions of assets or incurrences of liabilities that result in decreases in equity, other than those relating to distributions to equity participants (par. 4.25).

These definitions identify the essential features of income and expenses but do not attempt to specify their recognition criteria (par. 4.26).

OBSERVATION: The definitions given above make it clear that the Framework's approach treats the definitions of assets and liabilities as *logically prior to* those of income and expenses. This is sometimes characterized as a "balance sheet approach" to the relationship between financial statements. This term is potentially misleading, however. The Framework's approach should certainly not be understood as implying the subordination of the income statement to the balance sheet from an *informational* perspective.

Income and expenses may be presented in different ways in the income statement in order to provide relevant information. An example given is the distinction between items of income or expense that arise in the course of the ordinary business activities of the particular entity and those that do not (a distinction required by IAS 1, "Presentation of Financial Statements"; see Chapter 4). Combining items of income and expense in different ways also permits different measures of entity performance to be provided. Examples are the alternative income statement formats with different analyses of expenses, by nature and by function (pars. 4.27–4.28). (These different formats are discussed in IAS 1, pars. 102–103; see Chapter 4).

Income

The Framework's definition of income encompasses both revenue and gains. Revenue is described as arising in the course of the ordinary activities of an entity and includes sales, fees, interest, royalties, and rent. Gains may or may not arise in the course of ordinary activities. Gains may arise on the disposal of non-current assets and also include unrealized gains such as those arising on the revaluation of marketable securities and from increases in the carrying amount of long-term assets. Gains, when recognized in the income statement, are usually displayed separately because their economic significance tends to differ from that of revenue, and they are often reported net of related expenses (pars. 4.29–4.32).

The counterpart entry corresponding to a credit for income may be to various asset accounts (not only cash or receivables), or to a liability account such as when a loan is discharged by the provision of goods or services.

Expenses

The Framework's definition of expenses encompasses losses as well as expenses that arise in the course of the ordinary activities of the enterprise. Examples given of expenses that arise in the course of ordinary activities are cost of sales, wages, and depreciation. They usually take the form (that is, are the accounting counterpart) of an outflow or depletion of assets such as cash and cash equivalents, inventory, property, or plant and equipment (par. 4.33).

Losses represent items that may or may not arise in the course of ordinary activities. They include those that result from such disasters as fire or flood, as well as those arising on the disposal of non-current assets, and also encompass unrealized losses, such as those arising from the effects of adverse currency exchange rate movements on financial assets or liabilities. Losses, when recognized in the income statement, are usually displayed separately because their economic significance tends to differ from that of other expenses, and they are often reported net of related income (pars. 4.34–4.35).

OBSERVATION: Paragraphs 4.31 and 4.35 contain the phrases "when gains are recognized in the income statement" and "when losses are recognized in the income statement." IASs require or allow certain unrealized gains to be included directly in equity (for example, certain revaluation surpluses on non-current assets and foreign exchange gains), or to have their recognition deferred until realization occurs. IASs also require or allow certain losses, such as revaluation losses and foreign exchange losses, to be included directly in equity. Thus, the issue of recognition in the income statement needs to be considered in the context of individual IASs.

It is stated in paragraph 4.32 that "various kinds of assets may be received or enhanced by income." Likewise, expenses are described in paragraph 4.33 as "usually tak[ing] the form of an outflow or depletion of assets . . . ." We believe that such points are made more clearly by using the accounting relationships, in virtue of which the income statement effect is the reflection or counterpart of (rather than merely consisting of) the related balance sheet movement. The importance of the accounting relationships in the context of recognition is mentioned in paragraph 4.39 (see below).

Capital Maintenance Adjustments

The effects on equity of revaluations or restatements of assets and liabilities meet the Framework's definitions of income and expenses, but their inclusion in the income statement depends on which concept of capital maintenance is being applied (par. 4.36). This matter is discussed further below.

RECOGNITION OF THE ELEMENTS OF FINANCIAL STATEMENTS

Recognition issues are dealt with in paragraphs 4.37–4.53. Recognition is described as "the process of incorporating in the balance sheet or [the] income statement an item that meets the definition of an element and satisfies the criteria for recognition set out in paragraph 4.38." (The statement of changes in financial position is not mentioned because its elements consist of those that are also elements of financial position or performance.) Failure to recognize *in the main financial statements* items that satisfy the relevant definition and recognition criteria is not rectified by disclosure of the accounting policies used or by use of notes or other explanatory material.

The recognition criteria set out in paragraph 4.38 are that an item which meets the definition of an element should be recognized if:

1. It is probable that any future economic benefit associated with the item will flow to or from the entity; and

2. The item has a cost or value that can be measured with reliability.

Recognition is subject to materiality. Accounting interrelationships are also significant, since recognition in the financial statements of an item that meets the definition and recognition criteria for a particular element, for example an asset, entails the recognition of another (counterpart) element, such as income or a liability (par. 4.39). (This refers, strictly speaking, to the initial recognition of an item. However, a similar point could be made about the implications of remeasurement or valuation adjustments.)

The Probability of Future Economic Benefit

The concept of *probability* is used in the recognition criteria "to refer to the degree of uncertainty [as to whether] the future economic benefits associated with the item will flow to or from the enterprise . . . in keeping with the uncertainty that characterizes the environment in which an enterprise operates." Assessments of such uncertainty are made on the basis of the evidence available when the financial statements are prepared. In regard to receivables, for example, for a large population of accounts, some statistical evidence will usually be available regarding collectibility (par. 4.40).

OBSERVATION: The Framework does not offer any guidance, beyond that mentioned above, on the interpretation of "probable." IAS 37, "Provisions, Contingent Assets and Contingent Liabilities," contains an interpretation of "probable" as "more likely than not," that is, a probability in excess of 50%, but states that this interpretation is not intended to be applied in other contexts. Others have suggested an interpretation of "probable" in the present context as a probability of at least 75%. However, in the case of the receivables example mentioned above, the allowance to be made for probably uncollectible accounts would normally be based on past statistics, perhaps adjusted to take account of the current economic environment.

Reliability of Measurement

Reliability, the second recognition criterion, was discussed in the section "Qualitative Characteristics of Financial Statements" above. If an item does not possess a cost or value that can be measured with reliability (so that the information has that qualitative characteristic), then it is not appropriate to recognize it. However, in many cases, cost or (more particularly) value must be estimated; indeed, the use of reasonable estimates is an essential part of the financial reporting process and need not undermine reliability. In cases where an item satisfies the definition of an element but not the recognition criteria, it will not be recognized in the financial statements themselves, but its relevance is likely to require its disclosure in the notes to the financial statements or in other supplementary disclosures. This applies when the item meets the probability criterion of recognition but not the reliability criterion, but may also apply to an item that meets the definition of an element when neither recognition criterion is met. The key issue here is whether the item is considered to be relevant to the evaluation of financial position, performance, or changes in financial position. An item that does not satisfy the recognition criteria for an asset or a liability at one time may do so later, if more information relevant to estimating its probability, cost, or value becomes available (pars. 4.41–4.43).

OBSERVATION: The concept of a "reasonable estimate" is clearly crucial in the application of the reliability criterion, but the Framework gives no guidance on how it is to be interpreted. While this will not generally be a problematic issue in relation to the ascertainment of cost, estimating value can be problematic. This issue is dealt with in individual IASs, such as the requirement for an active market on which to base estimates in IAS 39, "Financial Instruments: Recognition and Measurement" (see Chapter 17).

On the issue of the retrospective recognition as an asset of an item of expenditure that has previously been recognized as an expense, IAS 38, "Intangible Assets" (see Chapter 22) does not permit the retrospective capitalization of development costs once they have been written off to expense.

Recognition of Assets

An asset is recognized in the balance sheet when it is probable that future economic benefits will flow to the entity (as a result of its control of the asset) and the asset's cost or value can be measured reliably. When expenditure has been incurred but it is not considered probable that economic benefits will flow to the entity beyond the current accounting period, this expenditure will be recognized as an expense, not as an asset. The intention of management in undertaking the expenditure is irrelevant (pars. 4.44–4.45).

Recognition of Liabilities

A liability is recognized in the balance sheet when it is probable that an outflow of resources embodying economic benefits will result from the settlement of a present obligation and the amount of that settlement can be measured reliably. Obligations under executory contracts, that is, non-cancelable contracts that are equally proportionately unperformed (such as the amount that will be a liability when inventory ordered and awaiting delivery is received), are not generally recognized as liabilities in the balance sheet, nor are the related assets recognized in the balance sheet. In some cases, however, recognition may be required (par. 4.46).

OBSERVATION: The treatment of executory contracts is to some extent an open issue in IASB GAAP. Inventory ordered under a non-cancelable contract is not "a resource controlled by" the entity that placed the order until title to the inventory has passed to it, and thus does not satisfy the Framework's definition of an asset of that entity. In such a case, it would be illogical to insist that the price to be paid for the inventory be recognized as a liability of that entity, since there would be no counterpart item to be recognized (recognition of an expense would make no sense).

There may, however, be other types of executory contract (for example, involving financial instruments) in respect of which recognition of an asset (or expense) and a related liability (or income) may be the most appropriate treatment.

Recognition of Income

Recognition of income occurs simultaneously with the recognition of increases in assets or decreases in liabilities (or a combination of the two). The normal recognition procedures used in practice are applications of the Framework's recognition criteria. An example is the requirement that revenue should be earned (that is, it should be associated with a simultaneous increase in assets or decrease in liabilities). These procedures are concerned with restricting the recognition of income to items that, in effect, meet the Framework's recognition criteria of *probability* (a sufficient degree of certainty that an economic benefit has flowed or will flow to the entity) and *reliability* of measurement (pars. 4.47–4.48). (See Chapter 31, "Revenue."

Recognition of Expenses

Recognition of expenses occurs simultaneously with the recognition of an increase in liabilities or a decrease in assets (or a combination of the two). Expenses are commonly recognized in the income statement on the basis of an association (matching) between the incurrence of costs and the earning of specific items of revenue, that result directly and jointly from the same transactions or other events. An example is the matching of the cost of goods sold with the associated sales revenue. However, the Framework does not permit the application of the matching procedure to result in the recognition of items in the balance sheet that do not meet the definition of assets or liabilities (pars. 4.49–4.50).

OBSERVATION: While the last sentence above is true of the Framework, individual IASs may require the recognition of balance sheet items that arguably do not meet the Framework's definitions. Examples include the deferral and amortization of government grants following the matching principle, required by IAS 20 (see Chapter 19); and the similar treatment of gains on certain sale and leaseback transactions, required by IAS 17 (see Chapter 26).

Depreciation and amortization are procedures for dealing with a situation in which a decrease in the future economic benefits embodied in an asset takes place over several accounting periods. It may not be feasible or cost-effective to relate such decreases directly to revenue. In such cases, the expense is recognized in the income statement on the basis of procedures that systematically and rationally allocate it over those accounting periods in which the economic benefits embodied in the asset may be considered to be consumed or to expire (par. 4.51).

An expense is recognized immediately in the income statement in the case of an expenditure that produces no future economic benefits that qualify for recognition as an asset in the balance sheet. An expense is also recognized in the income statement when a liability is incurred without an asset being recognized. An example is the recognition of a liability under a product warranty and of the associated warranty expense (pars. 4.52–4.53).

OBSERVATION: The paragraphs on the recognition of income and expenses use a terminology that we have avoided above. Income is described as being recognized in the income statement "when an increase in the future economic benefits related to an asset or a decrease of a liability has arisen that can be measured reliably." The description of the conditions for recognition of expenses is similar, with "decrease" being substituted for "increase" and vice versa. While logically correct in the Framework's terms, this terminology, with its reference to "future economic benefits," is rather cumbersome and is not essential to clarifying the criteria for recognition of income and expenses.

MEASUREMENT OF THE ELEMENTS OF FINANCIAL STATEMENTS

Paragraphs 4.54–4.56 deal with measurement issues, insofar as these are covered in the Framework. The treatment here is descriptive and avoids being prescriptive. Measurement is described as "the process of determining the monetary amounts at which the elements of the financial statements are to be recognized and carried in the balance sheet and income statement." It involves the selection of a particular basis of measurement.

Four different measurement bases are specifically mentioned and described (without any claim to exhaustiveness): historical cost, current cost (of replacement or settlement), realizable or (for liabilities) settlement value, and present value. Historical cost is mentioned as the measurement basis most commonly adopted by entities in preparing their financial statements, usually in combination with other measurement bases. An example of the latter is the carrying of inventories at the lower of historical cost and net realizable value. Marketable securities may be carried at market value, and pension liabilities are carried at their present value. Current cost may be used as a means of taking account of the effects of changing prices of nonmonetary assets.

CONCEPTS OF CAPITAL AND CAPITAL MAINTENANCE

Concepts of Capital

The Framework identifies two main concepts of capital: the financial concept and the physical concept. The financial concept of capital may take two forms: invested money (nominal financial) capital or invested purchasing power (real financial) capital. In either case, capital is identified with the equity of the entity (in either nominal or real financial terms) and with its net assets measured in those terms. The physical concept of capital is based on the notion of the productive capacity or operating capability of the entity, as embodied in its net assets. Most enterprises adopt a financial concept of capital, normally (in the absence of severe inflation) nominal financial capital (par. 4.57).

> **OBSERVATION:** The Framework does not distinguish clearly between nominal and real financial capital; however, the two are quite distinct and will be treated accordingly below. Physical capital is also a form of "real" capital concept.

Capital Maintenance and the Determination of Profit

Choice of a concept of capital is related to the concept of capital maintenance that is most meaningful, given the implications of the choice for profit measurement and the needs of the users of the financial statements in that regard, as follows:

1. *Maintenance of nominal financial capital.* Under this concept a profit is earned only if the money amount of the net assets at the end of the period exceeds the money amount of the net assets at the beginning of the period, after excluding any distributions to, and contributions from, equity owners during the period.

2. *Maintenance of real financial capital.* Under this concept a profit is earned only if the money amount of the net assets at the end of the period exceeds the money amount of the net assets at the beginning of the period, restated in units of the same purchasing power, after excluding distributions to, and contributions from, owners. Normally, the units of purchasing power employed are those of the currency at the end of the period, into which the net assets at the beginning of the period are restated.

3. *Maintenance of real physical capital.* Under this concept a profit is earned only if the operating capability embodied in the net assets at the end of the period exceeds the operating capability embodied in the net assets at the beginning of the period, after excluding distributions to, and contributions from, owners. Operating capability embodied in assets may, in principle, be measured by employing the current cost basis of measurement (pars. 4.58–4.61).

The main difference among the three concepts of capital maintenance is the treatment of the effects of changes in the carrying amounts of the entity's assets and liabilities. Under nominal financial capital maintenance, increases in the money-carrying amounts of assets held over the period (to the extent that they are recognized as gains) are part of profit.

Under real financial capital maintenance, such increases are part of profit only if they are "real" increases, that is, increases that remain after money-carrying amounts have been restated in units of the same purchasing power. The total amount of the restatement is known as a "capital maintenance adjustment" and is transferred to a capital maintenance reserve, which is part of equity (but not of retained profits). Real financial capital maintenance may be used in conjunction with historical cost as a measurement basis but would more normally be used in conjunction with the current cost basis.

Under real physical capital maintenance, changes in the money prices (current costs) of assets and liabilities held over the period are considered not to affect the amount of operating capability embodied in those items, and therefore the total amount of those changes is treated as a capital maintenance adjustment and excluded from profit.

OBSERVATION: Illustration

Let us assume that a company begins with capital stock of $100 and cash of $100. At the beginning of the year, one item of inventory is bought for $100. The item of inventory is sold at the end of the year for $150, its replacement cost at that time is $120, and general inflation throughout the year is 10%. Profit measured using each of the capital maintenance concepts mentioned earlier would be as shown below.

	Nominal financial capital maintenance	Real financial capital maintenance	Real physical capital maintenance
Sales	$150	$150	$150
Less cost of sales	(100)	(100)	(120)
Operating profit	50	50	30
Less inflation adjustment	—	(10)	—
Total gain	$ 50	$ 40	$ 30
Capital maintenance adjustment	$ 0	$ 10	$ 20

Column 1 shows the gain after ensuring the maintenance of the stockholders' opening capital measured as a sum of money. Column 2 shows the gain after ensuring the maintenance of the stockholders' opening capital measured as a block of purchasing power. Both of these are concerned, under different definitions, with the maintenance of financial capital—in terms either of its money amount or of its general purchasing power. Column 3 shows the gain after ensuring the maintenance of the company's initial operating capacity and is therefore of a completely different nature.

Different combinations of measurement bases and capital maintenance concepts provide different accounting models, between which management should choose, taking into account relevance and reliability. The IASB does not "presently" intend to prescribe a particular model, other than in exceptional circumstances such as when reporting in the currency of a hyperinflationary economy (pars. 4.62–4.65).

OBSERVATION: IAS 29, "Financial Reporting in Hyperinflationary Economies" (see Chapter 10) requires a choice between two different models: real financial capital, together with historical costs restated in units of the same purchasing power by use of a general price index; and real physical capital with adjustments for the purchasing power gain or loss on the net monetary position, together with current costs.

FUTURE DEVELOPMENTS

It is only stating the obvious, to point out that the current (2011) version of the Conceptual Framework is not very satisfactory—partially revised, and partially out of step with some of the thinking behind more recent standards. It is "work-in-progress" that will continue, although it is not being given a high priority. Arguably, given its declared purpose to "assist the Board in its development of future IFRSs," such a low priority is a mistake.

CHAPTER 3
FAIR VALUE MEASUREMENT

CONTENTS

OVERVIEW

Measurement at fair value (FV) has been a major issue in IASB GAAP, especially since the promulgation in 1999 of the original IAS 39, "Financial Instruments:

Recognition and Measurement," which saw a significant shift away from cost or amortized cost as a measurement basis. In the case of derivative instruments, the cost basis is clearly not applicable on subsequent measurement, as the value of the instrument is then independent of its original cost. However, the IASB has favored fair value measurement as the "default" measurement basis for financial assets, that is, the basis that should be used in the absence of a valid reason for using some other basis. In the case of other assets such as investment properties, as well as that of financial liabilities, the use of fair value as the measurement basis in IASB GAAP is an option.

IFRS 13, "Fair Value Measurement," issued in May 2011, does not impose fair value measurement as a requirement. Instead, it:

- Defines fair value; and
- Sets out:
  - A framework for measuring fair value, including the "Fair Value Hierarchy," and
  - Requirements for disclosures when fair value measurement is used.

In other words, it specifies *how* an entity should measure fair value and disclose information about fair value measurement, but not *when* fair value measurement should be used.

Fair value is defined as "the price that would be received to sell an asset or to transfer a liability in an orderly transaction between market participants at the measurement date"—a *market-based exit price*. Both practically and conceptually, fair value measurement is problematic insofar as it requires assumptions about "an orderly transaction between market participants" in situations where there is no active market. The IASB has insisted that fair value measurement is both feasible and meaningful in such circumstances. Its response is the "fair value hierarchy" of inputs into the fair value measurement process. In this three-level hierarchy (passages in quotation marks below are from the text of IFRS 13):

- The unproblematic Level 1 inputs are "quoted prices in active markets for identical assets or liabilities that the entity can access at the measurement date."
- The Level 2 inputs are those which, while not being quoted prices as in Level 1, are *observable*, such as quoted prices for similar assets in active markets, or in markets that are not active, or are not quoted prices but are valuation-relevant information such as interest rates and yield curves, or are *market-corroborated data* derived from or corroborated by *observable* market data by correlation or other means.
- The Level 3 inputs are to be used in the absence of Level 1 or Level 2 inputs (or in some cases to adjust Level 2 inputs) and are *unobservable* inputs that are "used to measure fair value to the extent that relevant observable inputs are not available, . . . [but which] reflect the assumptions that market participants would use when pricing the asset or liability, including assumptions about risk. [Such inputs] might include the entity's own data." Nevertheless, fair value is not an entity-specific value such as net present value, but a market-based value.

It will be clear that it is fair value measurement based on Level 3 inputs that is particularly problematic. IFRS 13 seeks to mitigate this problem by means of disclosure. For both Level 2 and Level 3 inputs, where so-called "marking to model" is involved, IFRS 13 requires a description of the valuation technique and the inputs used, while for Level 3 inputs, assumptions about risk and much more extensive disclosures are required, including the sensitivity of the fair value measurement to changes in unobservable inputs.

BACKGROUND

IFRS 13 is one of the fruits of the collaboration between the IASB and the FASB aimed at achieving convergence between IASB GAAP and U.S. GAAP. The FASB began working on its fair value measurement project in 2003, and in September 2006, it issued FAS-157, now included in FASB Accounting Standards Codification™ (ASC) 820, "Fair Value Measurement," which (like IFRS 13), defines fair value, establishes a framework for measuring fair value, and requires disclosures about fair value measurements. Meanwhile, in September 2005, the IASB initiated a project to clarify the meaning of fair value and to provide guidance for its application, and in November 2005, it published the Discussion Paper, "Fair Value Measurements," which used FAS-157 as a basis for its views at that point. In May 2008, in the context of the global financial crisis and following recommendations from the Financial Stability Forum (i.e., Financial Stability Board), the IASB set up a Fair Value Expert Advisory Panel to address the measurement and disclosure of financial instruments when markets are no longer active.

After analysis of the comments received on the Discussion Paper, the IASB began work on its exposure draft (ED), "Fair Value Measurement," which was, however, not published until May 2009. The ED largely reflected the requirements of FAS-157 but there were a number of differences, as well as differences between the fair value measurement requirements in the other standards in U.S. GAAP and those in IASB GAAP, respectively. In May 2009, the FASB issued FASB Staff Position (FSP) No. FAS 157-4, "Determining Fair Value When the Volume and Level of Activity for the Asset or Liability have Significantly Decreased and Identifying Transactions That Are Not Orderly," which was codified in ASC 820. Among the most prevalent comments received on the ED was a plea that that the IASB and the FASB develop common fair value measurement and disclosure requirements.

In response, the two Boards agreed, in a meeting in October 2009, to work together to develop common requirements, and in January 2010, they began joint discussions with this aim. In June 2010, the IASB published ED/2010/7 "Measurement Uncertainty Analysis for Fair Value Measurement," which was a re-exposure of the parts of the ED, "Fair Value Measurement," that was concerned with disclosure of fair value measurement techniques, and, in particular, for Level 3 inputs the effects of measurements on profit and loss or other comprehensive income. In the same month, the FASB published a proposed Accounting Standards Update (ASU), "Fair Value Measurements and Disclosures (Topic 820): Amendments for Common Fair Value Measurement and Disclosure Requirements in U.S. GAAP and IFRSs."

In September 2010, the two Boards jointly considered the comments received on these two documents, and they concluded their discussions in March 2011. Throughout the process, the IASB also considered inputs from the IFRS Advisory Council, the Analysts' Representative Group and the Fair Value Expert Advisory Panel. The IASB published a "Near Final Draft" of IFRS 13 in April 2011, followed by IFRS 13 itself in May 2011.

OBJECTIVE

Fair value is defined as a market-based, not an entity-specific, measurement. Whether or not observable market transactions or market information is available, the objective of fair value measurement is the same: to estimate the price at which an *orderly transaction* to *sell* the asset or *transfer* the liability would take place between *market participants* at the measurement date under *current market conditions*, that is, an *exit price* from the standpoint of a market participant holding the asset or owing the liability. Because fair value is a market-based measurement, the measurement takes place based on the assumptions that market participants would use when pricing the asset or liability, including *assumptions about risk*. Thus, in such measurement an entity's intention to hold an asset or settle or fulfill a liability is irrelevant. As well as being applied to assets and liabilities, IFRS 13 is to be applied to an entity's own equity instruments. (IFRS 13, pars. 1–4).

SCOPE

IFRS 13 applies, in both initial and subsequent measurement, when another IFRS requires or permits fair value measurements or requires disclosures about such measurements or measurements based on fair value, with the following exceptions:

1. Share-based payment transactions within the scope of IFRS 2, "Share-based Payments";

2. Leasing transactions within the scope of IAS 27, "Leases"; and

3. Measurements that have some similarities to fair value but are not fair value, such as net realizable value in IAS 2, "Inventories," or value in using IAS 36, "Impairment of Assets."

Moreover, the disclosure requirements of IFRS 13 do not apply to:

1. Plan assets measured at fair value in accordance with IAS 19, "Employee Benefits";

2. Retirement benefit plan investments measured at fair value in accordance with IAS 26, "Accounting and Reporting by Retirement Benefit Plans"; and

3. Assets for which a recoverable amount is fair value less costs of disposal in accordance with IAS 36.

On the other hand, the measurement requirements apply when fair value measurements are disclosed by an entity even if they are not used in the entity's financial statements. (IFRS 13 pars. 5–8)

APPLICATION

IFRS 13 (pars. 9–47) sets out or clarifies:

- The definition of fair value,
- The asset or liability,
- The transaction,
- Market participants,
- The price,
- Application to nonfinancial assets, and
- Application to liabilities and to an entity's own equity instruments.

OBSERVATION: IFRS 13 does not always specifically mention an entity's own equity instruments when, for completeness, they should be mentioned but are assumed to be included in liabilities. The English language does not possess a term such as the French word "passif," which includes equity as well as liabilities, but, in substance, IFRS 13 sometimes uses "liability" in this sense. To avoid being prolix, this chapter does likewise.

The Asset or Liability

Fair value measurement applies to a particular asset or liability (or a particular interest in an entity's own equity instruments, for example, an equity interest issued or transferred in a business combination). Depending on its *unit of account*, an asset or liability measured at fair value may be either:

- A stand-alone asset or liability such as a financial instrument,
- A group of assets or a group of liabilities, or
- A group of assets and liabilities such as a business or a cash-generating unit.

The *unit of account* is determined based on the IFRS in accordance with which the fair value measurement is being applied, except where otherwise stated in IFRS 13.

The Transaction

As noted above, a fair value measurement assumes that the asset or liability (or interest in the entity's own equity instruments) is exchanged in an orderly transaction between market participants to sell the asset or transfer the liability or own equity instrument at the measurement date under current market conditions. The market should be either the principal market for the asset, liability or equity interest, or, in the absence of such a market, the most advantageous market. The reporting entity must have access to the market in question at the measurement date. The fair value measurement represents *the price in that market*, whether directly observable or estimated using another valuation technique. *Even when there is no observable market to provide relevant pricing information at the measurement date* (i.e., the fair value measurement is entirely dependent on Level

3 inputs), *a FV measurement assumes that a transaction takes place at that date* considered from the perspective of a market participant that holds the asset or owes the liability (or transfers the equity instrument). *That assumed transaction establishes a basis for estimating the price to sell the asset or transfer the liability* (IFRS 13, pars. 13–21). Guidance is provided on how to carry out fair value measurements of assets based on Level 3 inputs (IFRS 13, pars. 5–30). For liabilities and an entity's own equity instruments, separate guidance is given, as discussed below.

OBSERVATION: There exist professional valuers whose task it may to value assets in the absence of Level 1 or Level 2 inputs, and who have developed valuation techniques for this purpose. However, those preparing or auditing financial statements are generally not able to use valuations provided by professional valuers. Preparers have to apply valuation techniques to obtain fair value measurements, and auditors have to form an opinion as to whether the resultant fair value measurements provide a fair presentation of the entity's financial position and results of operations. These are not new problems, but the 2007-09 financial crisis provided numerous examples of financial assets being grossly overvalued, mainly because of huge underestimations of credit risk (i.e., overestimations of *asset quality*). IFRS 13 aims to mitigate this problem by means of disclosures intended to provide users of financial statements with information on how the valuation process has been carried out and how the resultant fair value measurements are dependent on the values assigned to critical parameters in the valuation models. In other words, *caveat lector*—let the reader beware.

Market Participants and the Price

The hypothetical market price, on the basis of which the fair value of an asset, liability or the entity's own equity instrument is determined, is one between the reporting entity and participants in the principal or most advantageous market for the item in question, *using the same assumptions as those market participants would use* when pricing the acting market price in their economic best interest. *The entity does not need to identify specific market participants*, but considers them generically, with reference to:

- The asset, liability, or equity instrument;
- The principal or most advantageous market for the item in question; and
- Those participants with whom the entity would enter into a transaction in that market.

The price in the principal or most advantageous market is not to be adjusted for transaction costs, which should be accounted for in accordance with other IFRSs. Transaction costs are not considered to be a characteristic of an asset or liability, as they are specific to a transaction and may vary depending on how the transaction is entered into. In contrast, transport costs may be a characteristic of an asset, as they reflect a change in one of its attributes (its location). Hence, in making a fair value measurement, a downward adjustment to the hypothetical price should be made for any transport costs that would be necessary to transport an asset from its current location to the principal or most advantageous market (IFRS 13, pars. 22–26, BC 60–62).

Application to Non-Financial Assets

Apart from the IFRSs dealing with financial assets and liabilities, several IFRSs require or permit measurement at fair value for non-financial assets. These include IAS 16, "Property, Plant and Equipment," IAS 38, "Intangible Assets," IAS 40, "Investment Property," IAS 41, "Agriculture," IFRS 6, "Mineral Resources," and a number of IFRICs.

A fair value measurement of a non-financial asset takes into account a market participant's ability to generate economic benefits by using the asset in its *highest and best use* or by selling it to another market participant that would do so.

Highest and Best Use

Highest and best use (HBU) is a valuation concept used to value many non-financial assets such as real estate. The concept is not relevant to items other than non-financial assets, as they do not have an alternative use without being changed and therefore ceasing to be the same asset or liability.

The HBU of a non-financial asset must be physically possible, financially feasible, and legally permissible. Financial feasibility takes into account whether a physically possible and legally permissible use would generate adequate income or cash flows to produce an investment return that market participants would require, and any costs of converting the asset to that use.

The HBU is determined from the perspective of market participants, even if the reporting entity has a different use in mind. Nevertheless, the entity's current use of a non-financial asset is presumed to be its HBU unless market or other considerations suggest otherwise (e.g., in the case of an intangible asset that the entity plans to use defensively so as to prevent others from using it).

Valuation Premise for Non-Financial Assets

The HBU establishes the *valuation premise* used to measure fair value for a non-financial asset that might be used in combination with other assets as a group, or with other assets and liabilities as a business or business unit, as follows:

- If the HBU is the use of the asset in combination with a group of other assets or other assets and liabilities, the fair value of the asset is the price that would be received in a current transaction to sell the asset assuming that it would be used with that group of other assets or assets and liabilities (its complementary assets and any associated liabilities) and that these would be available to market participants.

- Associated liabilities for this purpose include those that fund working capital but not those that fund assets other than those within the group of complementary assets.

- Assumptions about the HBU must be consistent for all the assets included in the group of complementary assets for which HBU is relevant.

- The HBU might provide maximum value to market participants when the asset is used on a stand-alone basis. In that case, the fair value of the asset is the price that would be received on the assumption that the buyer would use it on a stand-alone basis.

The fair value measurement of a non-financial asset assumes that it is sold consistently with the *unit of account* specified in other applicable IFRSs, which may be an individual asset, even when the fair value measurement assumes that the HBU is to use the asset in combination with other assets or other assets and liabilities. This is because fair value measurement assumes that the hypothetical buyer *already holds the complementary assets and any associated liabilities.*

On the one hand, because the hypothetical buyer is assumed to hold the complementary assets (with any associated liabilities) necessary for the asset to function, the buyer would not be willing to pay more for the asset solely because it was sold as part of a group. However, in the case of specialized assets that may have little value (e.g., only scrap value) for a buyer who did not have the complementary assets, such as work-in-process inventory that is unique, the fair value of the inventory would assume that the buyer would have or would acquire the complementary assets (e.g. specialized machinery) necessary to convert it into finished goods. In effect, the hypothetical buyer takes the place of the entity that holds the asset. (IFRS 13, pars. 27–33, B3 and BC 63–79)

Application to Liabilities and an Entity's Own Equity Instruments

A fair value measurement of a financial or non-financial liability or an entity's own equity instrument (e.g., as issued as consideration in a business combination) assumes that:

- The instrument is transferred to a market participant at the measurement date.

- A liability would remain outstanding and the transferee would be required to fulfill the obligation that would not be settled with the counterparty or otherwise extinguished on the measurement date.

- An entity's own equity instrument would remain outstanding and the transferee would take on the rights and responsibilities associated with the instrument, which would not be cancelled or otherwise extinguished at the measurement date.

Even when there is no observable market to provide pricing information about such a transfer (e.g., because a transfer is prevented by contractual or other legal restrictions), if such items are held by other parties as assets, this may result in an observable market. In all cases, to meet the objective of fair value measurement, which is to estimate the price at which an orderly transaction to transfer the item would take place between market participants under current market conditions at the measurement date, an entity maximizes the use of relevant observable inputs and minimizes the use of unobservable inputs.

Liabilities and Equity Instruments Held as Assets by Other Parties

When a quoted price is not available, and an identical item is held by another party as an asset, the fair value is measured from the perspective of a market participant that holds the item as an asset at the measurement date, according to the fair value hierarchy (see below). A quoted price of an identical or similar item held by another party as an asset should be adjusted only if there are specific factors applicable to the asset that are not applicable to the fair value measurement of the liability or equity instrument, such as:

- A restriction preventing the sale of that asset;
- A difference in credit quality; and
- A difference in the unit of account (e.g., the price of the asset may reflect a combination of the asset and a third party credit enhancement, the effect of which should be excluded).

Liabilities and Equity Instruments Not Held by Other Parties as Assets

When a quoted price is not available, and an identical item is not held by another party as an asset, the fair value of the item is measured using a valuation technique from the perspective of a market participant that owes the liability or has issued the equity instrument. In applying a present value technique, either of the following might be taken into account:

- The future cash outflows that a market participant would expect to incur to fulfill the obligation, including compensation that a market participant would require for taking on the obligation (e.g., for a decommissioning liability); and
- The amount that a market participant would receive to enter into or issue the identical liability or equity instrument, using the assumptions that market participants would use when pricing the identical item (i.e., with the same credit characteristics) in the principal or most advantageous market for issuing an item with the same contractual terms.

Non-Performance Risk

The fair value of a liability reflects the effect of the risk that the entity that owes it may not fulfill that obligation, that is, non-performance risk, which includes, but is not limited to, the entity's own credit risk. Hence, when measuring the fair value of a liability, an entity takes into account the effects of its own credit risk, as well as other factors that may affect the likelihood that the obligation will be fulfilled. Non-performance risk related to a liability is assumed to be the same before and after the transfer of the liability, for various reasons:

- A market participant taking on the obligation would not enter into a transaction that changed the non-performance risk associated with it without reflecting that change in the price;
- Creditors would not knowingly agree to a transfer to a transferee with a lower credit standing; and
- Those who might hold the liability as an asset would consider, when pricing those assets, the effects of the entity's own credit risk, as well as

other factors that may affect the likelihood that the obligation will be fulfilled.

If a liability is issued with an inseparable credit enhancement that is accounted for separately, the fair value of the liability reflects the entity's own credit standing and not that of the guarantor.

Restriction Preventing the Transfer of a Liability or an Entity's Own Equity Instrument

The effect of such a (known) restriction will be included, either implicitly or explicitly, in other inputs to the fair value measurement, such as the transaction price at the transaction date. Hence, no separate input or adjustment to other inputs would be appropriate.

Financial Liability with a Demand Feature

The fair value of such a liability (such as a demand deposit at a bank) cannot be less than the amount payable on demand, discounted from the first date on which payment of the amount could be required (if the effect of such discounting is material).

Application to Financial Assets and Financial Liabilities with Offsetting Positions in Market Risks or Counterparty Credit Risk

If an entity manages a *group of financial assets and financial liabilities* on the basis of its *net exposure* to either market risk or credit risk, IFRS 13 permits, as an exception to its general rule, fair value to be measured for the group on the basis of the price that would be received to sell a net *long* position (an asset) for a particular risk exposure or to transfer a net *short* position (a liability) for a particular risk exposure, as applicable.

This exception applies only to financial assets and financial liabilities that are within the scope of IAS 39/IFRS 9, and is permitted only when all of the following conditions are satisfied. The entity:

- Manages the group of financial assets and financial liabilities on the basis of its exposure to a particular market risk or risks, or to the credit risk of a particular counterparty, in accordance with the entity's documented risk management or investment strategy;

- Provides information on the above basis to the entity's *key management personnel*, as defined in IAS 24; and

- Is required, or has elected, to measure those financial assets and financial liabilities at fair value in its financial statements consistently at the end of each reporting period, in response to an accounting policy decision in accordance with IAS 8.

This exception has no bearing on financial statement presentation.

Exposure to Market Risk

When using the above exception, the entity applies the price within the bid-ask spread that is most representative of fair value in the circumstances, regardless of where the input is categorized within the fair value hierarchy. Bid prices for asset positions and ask prices for liability positions may be used, but are not required. Mid-market pricing or other pricing conventions used by market participants as a practical expedient may be used.

The market risk or risks to which the entity is exposed by the group of items must be substantially of the same kind. For example, interest rate risk may not be combined with commodity price risk, as neither can mitigate exposure to the other. Moreover, for market risks substantially of the same kind, any basis risk from market risk parameters not being identical must be taken into account in measuring fair value. Likewise, differences in duration must be taken into account.

Exposure to the Credit Risk of a Particular Counterparty

When market participants take into account any existing arrangements that mitigate credit risk exposure, such as a master netting agreement with the counterparty or an agreement that requires an exchange of collateral on the basis of each party's net exposure to the credit risk of the other, the effects of such net exposure are included in the fair value measurement, subject to it reflecting market participants' expectations about the legal enforceability of any such agreement in the event of default. (IFRS 13, pars. 34–56)

Fair Value at Initial Recognition

When as asset is acquired or a liability is assumed in an exchange transaction, the transaction price is an *entry* price, whereas fair value is defined as an *exit* price. Nevertheless, in many cases the transaction price will be equal to fair value, for example, when on the transaction date the transaction to buy the asset takes place in the market in which the asset would be sold. When this is not the case and fair value measurement is applied in accordance with an IFRS, the difference (gain or loss) between fair value and the transaction price is recognized in profit or loss for the period unless the applicable IFRS specifies otherwise.

There are some cases where the transaction price will differ from fair value:

- The transaction is between related parties, although the transaction price may be used as an input where the entity has evidence that the transaction was entered into at market terms;

- The transaction takes place under duress or in a forced sale (e.g., in financial distress of the seller);

- There is a difference in the units of account between the buyer and the seller, for example, in a business combination where the transaction includes unstated rights and privileges that are to be measured separately or the transaction price includes transactions costs; and

- The market in which the transaction takes place is not the principal or most advantageous market. This might be the case if the entity is a dealer that enters into transactions in the retail market, whereas the principal or most advantageous market is with other dealers in the wholesale market. If the entity is a dealer, the entry price it will pay for items in the retail market will be lower than the exit price for the same items in the principal or most advantageous market, namely the wholesale market. (IFRS 13, pars. 57–60, B4)

Valuation Techniques

The objective of using a valuation technique is to *estimate* the price at which an orderly transaction to sell the asset or transfer the liability takes place between market participants at the measurement date under current market conditions. Valuation techniques that are used should maximize the use of observable inputs and minimize the use of unobservable inputs. They include the market approach, the cost approach, and the income approach. If a transaction price is used to measure fair value on initial recognition, and a valuation technique that uses unobservable inputs is used to measure fair value in subsequent periods, that valuation technique needs to be *calibrated* so that if applied at initial recognition it would result in the transaction price.

Market Approach

This approach uses prices and other relevant information generated by market transactions in identical or similar assets, liabilities, or groups of assets and liabilities (businesses or cash generating units). Valuation techniques consistent with the market approach include the use of market multiples derived from a set of comparables, and matrix pricing for some types of financial instrument (e.g., debt securities) which, rather than relying exclusively on quoted prices for the securities, uses the relationship of the securities to other benchmark securities.

Cost Approach

This approach reflects the amount that would be required currently to replace the service capacity of an asset, and thus, is applicable to non-financial assets. As such, this is an entry price, rather than an exit price. However, a market participant buyer would not pay more for an asset than the amount for which it could replace the service capacity of that asset. Hence, the price that would be received by a seller (exit price) would be the same as the entry price in the same market.

Income Approach

There are different income approaches but they effectively convert future amounts (cash flows or income and expenses) into a single current (discounted) amount reflecting current market expectations about those future amounts. The different approaches include present value techniques, option pricing models, and *the multi-period excess earnings* method used to value some intangible assets.

Present Value Techniques

A fair value measurement using a present value (PV) technique takes account of the following elements from the perspective of market participants at the measurement date:

- An estimate of future cash flows for the asset or liability being measured;

- Expectations about possible variations in the amount and timing of the cash flows reflecting their inherent uncertainty;

- The time value of money, that is, the risk-free interest rate for the appropriate maturity or duration;

- The price for bearing the uncertainty inherent in the cash flows (risk premium); and

- Other factors that market participants would take into account, including, for liabilities, non-performance risk.

PV techniques include the *discount rate adjustment (DRA) technique* and the expected present value (EPV) technique. The DRA technique uses a single set of cash flows (contractual or most likely) from the range of possible estimated amounts and a discount rate derived from observed rates of return for comparable assets or liabilities traded in the market. In contrast, the EPV technique uses a set of cash flows that is the probability-weighted mean of all the possible cash flows, that is, the *expected* cash flows (not the *most likely* cash flows as in the DRA technique). The expected cash flows may either be discounted using a rate equal to the risk-free rate plus a risk premium, or they may be converted to a certainty equivalent (by subtracting a cash risk premium), which is then discounted using a risk-free rate. In principle, both techniques produce the same result. (IFRS 13, pars. 61–66, B5–B33)

Inputs to Valuation Techniques

Markets in which inputs may be observable include exchange markets, dealer markets, brokered markets, and principal-to-principal markets.

- In an exchange market, closing prices are readily available and generally representative of fair value. Examples are the major stock exchanges.

- In a dealer market, dealers stand ready to trade (to buy or sell for their own account) by holding an inventory of the items for which they *make a market*. Bid and ask prices (at which the dealer is willing to buy and sell, respectively) are more readily available than closing prices. Over-the-counter markets are dealer markets for which prices are publicly reported.

- In a brokered market, brokers attempt to match buyers with sellers but do not stand ready to trade on their own account. A broker knows the price bid by buyer and asked by a seller, but even if an ask price (or a bid price) is advertised, such prices are subject to negotiation and are not a reliable indication of transaction prices. Prices of relevant completed transactions may be available. Examples are markets for property (real estate).

- In a principal-to-principal market, transactions are negotiated directly between the principals with no intermediary. Little public information about such transactions is available.

Inputs are selected that are consistent with the characteristics of the asset or liability that market participants would take into account in a transaction for that asset or liability. This may result in an adjustment, such as a premium (for a controlling interest) or a discount (for a non-controlling interest) being applied, but a fair value measurement must not incorporate a premium or discount that is inconsistent with the unit of account in the applicable IFRS. Any premium or discount must reflect a characteristic of the item for which fair value is being measured. If there is a quoted price in an active market (a Level 1 input), that price should be used without adjustment except as indicated under Level 1 inputs below.

Fair Value Hierarchy

The fair value hierarchy was originally included in IFRS 7 (see Chapter 17), but was transferred to IFRS 13. It classifies the inputs to valuation techniques used to measure fair value into three levels. The fair value hierarchy prioritizes inputs to valuation techniques, not the techniques themselves. Where a combination of inputs from different levels is used, the combined input is classified at the level of the lowest of the inputs. For example, if an observable input requires an adjustment using an unobservable input and the resulting adjustment is a significant amount, then the resulting measurement is a Level 3 measurement. Therefore, the fair value hierarchy is also applied to fair value measurement based on the lowest level of the inputs used in a particular fair value measurement. This then leads to disclosure requirements that are somewhat more onerous for Level 2 measurements than for those at Level 1, and substantially more onerous for Level 3 measurements.

Level 1 Inputs

Level 1 inputs are unadjusted *quoted prices* in active markets for identical assets or liabilities that the entity can access at the measurement date. These prices typically provide the most reliable indication of fair value and should be used to measure fair value whenever available.

Level 2 Inputs

Level 2 inputs are all inputs other than quoted prices included in Level 1 that are *observable*, either directly or indirectly, for the asset or liability, such as quoted prices for similar assets in active markets, or in markets that are not active, or are not quoted prices but are valuation-relevant information, such as interest rates and yield curves or credit spreads, or are *market-corroborated data* derived from or corroborated by *observable* market data by correlation or other means. Such inputs are substantially less subjective than Level 3 inputs.

Adjustments to Level 2 inputs will vary depending on various factors, including:

- The condition or location of the asset (for non-financial assets).
- The extent to which inputs relate to items that are comparable to the asset or liability. There may be differences in characteristics such as credit quality or the unit of account.
- The volume or level of activity in the markets within which the inputs are observed.

Level 3 Inputs

Level 3 inputs are *unobservable* inputs to be used to measure fair value (or in some cases to adjust Level 2 inputs) to the extent that relevant observable inputs are not available, which reflect the assumptions that market participants would use when pricing the asset or liability, *including assumptions about risk*. Such inputs might include the entity's own data. Nevertheless, fair value is not an entity-specific value such as net present value, but a market-based value.

Assumptions about risk include the risk inherent in a particular valuation technique used to measure fair value, such as a pricing model, and the risk inherent in the *inputs* to the valuation technique. A measurement that does not include an adjustment for risk would not be a fair value measurement if market participants would include such an adjustment when pricing the asset or liability. For example, an adjustment might be called for when there is significant measurement uncertainty. This might be the case when there has been a significant decrease in the volume or level of activity when compared to normal market activity for the asset or liability (or similar assets or liabilities) and the entity has determined that a transaction or quoted price does not, as such, represent fair value (e.g., there might be transactions that are not orderly such as forced or - distressed sales).

Where a Level 3 input is used to adjust a Level 2 input and the adjustment is significant, the result is a Level 3 measurement. (IFRS 13, pars. 67–90)

Disclosure

The disclosures required by IFRS 13 are onerous, especially for fair value measurements based on Level 3 inputs. This is intended to mitigate the acknowledged uncertainty and subjectivity of such measurements. Disclosures are intended to help users of an entity's financial statements assess the following:

- For assets and liabilities that are measured at fair value on a recurring or non-recurring basis in the statement of financial position after initial recognition, the valuation techniques and inputs used to develop those measurements; and
- For fair value measurements using significant unobservable inputs (Level 3), the effect of the measurements on profit and loss or other comprehensive income for the period.

To meet these objectives, an entity discloses the following information for each class of assets and liabilities measured at fair value in the statement of financial position (including those based on fair value within the scope of IFRS 13) after initial recognition:

- For recurring and non-recurring fair value measurements, the fair value measurement at the end of the reporting period, and for non-recurring fair value measurements, the reasons for the measurement. Non-recurring fair value measurements are those that are required or permitted in particular circumstances (such as when an entity measures an asset held for sale at fair value less costs to sell in accordance with IFRS 5 because fair value less costs to sell is less than the carrying amount);

- For assets and liabilities held at the reporting date that are measured at fair value on a recurring basis, the amounts of any transfers between Level 1 and Level 2 of the fair value hierarchy, the reasons for those transfers, and the entity's policy for determining when such transfers are considered to have occurred;

- For recurring and non-recurring fair value measurements categorized within Levels 2 and 3, a description of the valuation techniques and inputs used, and disclosure of any change in valuation technique and the reasons for the change;

- For recurring fair value measurements categorized within Level 3:

  — Quantitative information about the significant unobservable inputs used;

  — A reconciliation from the beginning balances to the ending balances, disclosing separately changes during the period attributable to the following:

    ☐ Total gains and losses for the period recognized in profit or loss, and the line item(s) in which they are recognized;

    ☐ Total gains and losses for the period recognized in other comprehensive income, and the line item(s) in which they are recognized;

    ☐ Purchases, sales, issues, and settlements of items so measured (each separately); and

    ☐ The amounts of any transfers into or out of Level 3, the reasons for such transfers, and the entity's policy for determining when such transfers are considered to have occurred. Transfers into and transfers out of Level 3 are to be disclosed separately.

  — For the total gains or losses for the period included in profit or loss, the amount that is attributable to the change in unrealized gains or losses relating to those assets and liabilities held at the end of the period;

- For recurring and non-recurring fair value measurements categorized within Level 3:

  — A description of the valuation processes used by the entity, including how the entity decides its valuation policies and procedures and analyses changes in fair value measurements from period to period;

- For recurring fair value measurements categorized within Level 3:

— A narrative description of the sensitivity of the fair value measurement to changes in unobservable inputs if such a change might result in a significantly different fair value measurement;

— For financial assets and financial liabilities, if changing one or more unobservable input to reflect *reasonably possible* alternative assumptions would change fair value significantly, this is to be stated together with the effect of the change(s) and how that effect was calculated. For this purpose, *significance* is judged in relation to profit or loss and total assets and total liabilities or, where changes in fair value are recognized in other comprehensive income, total equity.

• For all recurring and non-recurring fair value measurements of nonfinancial assets, if the HBU differs from the current use, this is to be disclosed together with the reason why the asset is not being used in its HBU.

Appropriate classes of assets and liabilities for disclosure purposes are to be based on the nature, characteristics, and risks of the asset or liability and the level of the fair value hierarchy within which the fair value measurement of the item is categorized. The number of classes for Level 3 measurements may need to be greater because such measurements are more uncertain and subjective. Additional disaggregation may be required than that of the line items in the financial statements.

The policy for determining when transfers between levels of the hierarchy are considered to have occurred is to be disclosed and consistently followed.

If an accounting policy is adopted by using the exception permitting the measurement of fair value of a group of items on the basis of the price that would be received to sell a net long or a net short position, this is to be disclosed.

For each class of assets and liabilities not measured at fair value in the statement of financial position, but for which fair value is disclosed, a number of the information requirements stated above are applicable, in particular the fair value measurements at the end of the period, the level of the hierarchy in which the measurements are categorized, a description of the valuation techniques and inputs for measurements in Levels 2 and 3, and any differences between current use and HBU.

If a liability measured at fair value is issued with a third party credit enhancement, this fact and whether the credit enhancement is reflected in the fair value are to be disclosed.

The quantitative disclosure required by the above should normally be presented in a tabular format. (IFRS 13, pars. 91–99)

Effective Date and Transition

IFRS 13 is to be applied for annual periods beginning on or after January 1, 2013. Earlier application is permitted. Comparative information is not required for periods before initial application. (IFRS 13, Appendix C)

CHAPTER 4
PRESENTATION OF FINANCIAL STATEMENTS

CONTENTS

OVERVIEW

"Presentation of Financial Statements," the title of the revised IAS 1, represents an attempt to cover several important aspects. The objective of the standard is to prescribe the basis for presentation of general purpose financial statements in order to ensure comparability both with the entity's own financial statements of previous periods and with the financial statements of other entities. To achieve this objective, the standard sets out overall considerations for the presentation of financial statements, guidelines for their structure, and minimum requirements for the content of financial statements.

In principle, therefore, IAS 1 applies to all aspects of all businesses. Many aspects of financial reporting are covered additionally by other more specific standards, as detailed elsewhere in this volume. However, some other aspects are not further developed, and IAS 1, therefore, makes up the IASB GAAP in those respects. For example, disclosure of fixed assets is discussed in IAS 16, "Property, Plant, and Equipment" (see Chapter 28), but disclosure of current assets has no additional standard, except for component parts such as Inventories, covered by IAS 2, "Inventories" (see Chapter 24).

Broadly speaking, IAS 1 consists of two parts. Part 1 discusses a number of "overall considerations," consisting of general principles, conventions, and requirements. Much of Part 1 is a restatement of aspects of the Framework, discussed in Chapter 2. It should be remembered that the Framework does not have the status of a standard, whereas IAS 1 obviously does. Part 2 discusses in some detail the required contents of general purpose financial statements. It is worth noting that most national accounting standards operate, and are designed to operate, within the context of national legislation, especially for corporations. There is, of course, no single international company or corporation statute. To some extent, IAS 1 provides a minimal filling in of this lacuna.

BACKGROUND

To understand how and why IAS 1 as currently constituted came about, it is helpful to look at the chronology involved. The very first standard issued by the IASC was the original IAS 1, "Disclosure of Accounting Policies," effective for accounting periods beginning on or after January 1, 1975. IAS 5, "Information to Be Disclosed in Financial Statements," related to periods beginning on or after January 1, 1977, and IAS 13, "Presentation of Current Assets and Current Liabilities," related to periods beginning on or after January 1, 1981. All three of these were fairly short standards, with limited objectives accurately indicated by their titles.

Later, as its approach became generally more sophisticated, the IASC developed its "Framework for the Preparation and Presentation of Financial Statements." As discussed in detail in Chapter 2, this sets out the concepts that underlie the preparation and presentation of financial statements designed for external users. This document appeared in its agreed-upon form in 1989. It was intended to inform the preparation of standards and so improve consistency over time, but it is of a lower status than the standards, which override the Framework if any conflict occurs.

IAS 1, as revised in 1997, was the next step in this long process of development. It replaced the original IAS 1 and both IAS 5 and IAS 13, but it did a great deal more than merely update the three original standards. In particular, it dealt not only with the disclosure of accounting policies, as did the original IAS 1, but also with the whole issue of policies and conventions, incorporating significant parts of the 1989 Framework (thereby increasing the status of those aspects so incorporated to full standard requirement).

It attempted to provide something approaching a philosophy of financial reporting, together with an overview of the complete required contents of published financial reports. Its gestation was at times fraught with disagreement.

IAS 1 was further revised in 2004, as part of the IASB improvements project. The revised version was formally required for annual periods beginning on or after January 1, 2005, with earlier adoption encouraged. The fundamental approach and structure of the standard was not altered, but a number of changes were made. The requirements relating to the selection and application of accounting policies were transferred *to* IAS 8 (see Chapter 6), and the presentation requirements relating to the income statement for the period were transferred *from* IAS 8. The concept of extraordinary items was eliminated and the phrase was deleted from the IASB Glossary.

The concept of materiality was formally introduced into both IAS 1 and IAS 8. This replaced an earlier statement in the former Preface to IASs; the current Preface to IFRSs makes no mention of materiality. IAS 1 now specifies the application of materiality to disclosures (and IAS 8 now specifies its application to applying accounting policies and to correcting errors and to changes in estimates). Various disclosure requirements were clarified or tightened. In particular, new guidance on the meaning and significance (or lack of significance, see below) of "present fairly" was added. A further small amendment was made in August 2005 and is discussed toward the end of the chapter, in a section titled "Notes to the Financial Statements."

Finally, several significant further amendments were made in a revised version of IAS 1 that was issued in September 2007 (see the Financial Statements section below). These amendments also affect a number of other IASs/IFRSs, mainly with regard to terminology. Compliance with the 2007 version of IAS 1 is required for annual reporting periods beginning on or after January 1, 2009, although earlier adoption is permitted.

This latest version (from January 1, 2009), makes a number of significant amendments summarized below:

- A complete set of financial statements

  —The terms "statement of financial position" and "statement of cash flows" are used in place of "balance sheet" and "cash flow statement."

  —A new requirement is introduced to include in a "complete set of financial statements" a statement of financial position as at the beginning of the earliest comparative period whenever an entity either (i) retrospectively applies an accounting policy or (ii) makes a retrospective restatement or reclassification of items in its financial statements.

- Reporting owner changes in equity and comprehensive income

  —All changes in equity arising from transactions with owners in their capacity as owners (owner changes in equity) are to be presented separately from non-owner changes in equity. Thus, components of comprehensive income (i.e., non-owner changes) must not be presented in the statement of changes in equity.

  —Income and expense are to be presented either in one statement (a statement of comprehensive income) or in two statements (a separate income statement and a statement of comprehensive income), separately from owner changes in equity.

  —Components of "other comprehensive income" are to be displayed in the statement of comprehensive income.

—Total comprehensive income is to be presented in the financial statements.

- Other comprehensive income—reclassification adjustments are related tax effects

    —Income tax relating to each component of comprehensive income is to be disclosed.

    —Reclassification adjustments relating to components of other comprehensive income (i.e., amounts reclassified to profit and loss in the current period that were recognized in other comprehensive income in previous periods) are to be disclosed.

- Presentation of dividends

    —Dividends recognized as distributions to owners and related amounts per share are to be presented in the statement of changes in equity or in the notes, but not in the statement of comprehensive income (which deals only with non-owner changes in equity).

Further minor amendments to this version have been made, as incorporated in our detailed text below.

SCOPE

The scope and applicability of IAS 1 are very wide. IAS 1 should be applied in the presentation of all general purpose financial statements prepared and presented in accordance with International Financial Reporting Standards.

General purpose financial statements are those intended to meet the needs of users who are not in a position to demand reports tailored to meet their specific information needs. They include statements presented separately or those within another public document, such as an annual report or prospectus.

IAS 1 does not apply to condensed interim financial information as regards the structure and content of the statements (see IAS 34, "Interim Financial Reporting" (Chapter 23)), but it does so apply as regards the "general features" discussed in paragraphs 15–35. IAS 1 must be applied in full to all general purpose statements, as described above, that claim to be in accordance with International Accounting Standards. Not-for-profit organizations can also apply the standard (and IASB GAAP generally) by amending item descriptions in the financial statements as appropriate.

DEFINITIONS

IAS 1 contains a set of formal definitions. These are as follows (par. 7):

- *General purpose financial statements.* Referred to as "financial statements," these are intended to meet the needs of users who are not in a position to require an entity to prepare reports tailored to their particular needs.

- *Impracticable.* Applying a requirement is impracticable when the entity cannot apply it after making every reasonable effort to do so.

- *International Financial Reporting Standards (IFRSs).* Standards and Interpretations adopted by the International Accounting Standards Board (IASB). They comprise:

  —International Financial Reporting Standards,

  —International Accounting Standards, and

  —Interpretations originated by the International Financial Reporting Interpretations Committee (IFRIC) or the former Standing Interpretations Committee (SIC).

- *Material.* Omissions or misstatements of items are material if they could, individually or collectively, influence the economic decisions of users taken on the basis of the financial statements. Materiality depends on the size and nature of the omission or misstatement judged in the surrounding circumstances. The size or nature of the item, or a combination of both, could be the determining factor.

- *Notes.* These contain information in addition to that presented in the statement of financial position, statement of comprehensive income, separate income statement (if presented), statement of changes in equity, and statement of cash flows. Notes provide narrative descriptions or disaggregations of items presented in those statements and information about items that do not qualify for recognition in those statements.

- *Other comprehensive income.* This comprises items of income and expense, including reclassification adjustments, that are not recognized in profit or loss as required or permitted by other IFRSs. The components of other comprehensive income include:

  —Changes in revaluation surplus (see IAS 16, "Property, Plant, and Equipment, and IAS 38 Intangible Assets");

  —Actuarial gains and losses on defined benefit plans recognized in accordance with paragraph 93A of IAS 19, "Employee Benefits";

  —Gains and losses arising from translating the financial statements of a foreign operation (see IAS 21, "The Effects of Changes in Foreign Exchange Rates");

  —Gains and losses from investments in equity instruments measured at fair value through other comprehensive income in accordance with paragraph 5.7.5 of IFRS 9, "Financial Instruments";

  —The effective portion of gains and losses on hedging instruments in a cash flow hedge (see IAS 39).

  —For particular liabilities designated as at fair value through profit or loss, the amount of the change in fair value that is attributable to changes in the liability's credit risk (see paragraph 5.7.7 of IFRS 9).

- *Owners.* These are holders of instruments classified as equity.

- *Profit or loss.* This is the total of income less expenses, excluding the components of other comprehensive income.

- *Reclassification adjustments.* These are amounts reclassified to profit or loss in the current period that were recognized in other comprehensive income in the current or previous periods.

- *Total comprehensive income.* This is the change in equity during a period resulting from transactions and other events, other than those changes resulting from transactions with owners in their capacity as owners. Total comprehensive income comprises all components of profit or loss and of other comprehensive income. Although this Standard uses the terms "other comprehensive income," "profit or loss," and "total comprehensive income," an entity may use other terms to describe the totals, as long as the meaning is clear. For example, an entity may use the term "net income" to describe profit or loss.

- The following terms are described in IAS 32, "Financial Instruments: Presentation," and are used in this Standard with the meaning specified in IAS 32:

  —Puttable financial instrument classified as an equity instrument (described in IAS 32, pars. 16A and 16B).

  —An instrument that imposes on the entity an obligation to deliver to another party a pro rata share of the net assets of the entity only on liquidation and is classified as an equity instrument (described in IAS 32, pars. 16C and 16D).

The standard notes, in relation to materiality and possible influences on economic decisions of users, that users are assumed to have reasonable knowledge of business and accounting issues and to apply reasonable diligence. The word "reasonable," as used both in the previous sentence and in the definition of "impracticable," is obviously subjective. The definition of impracticable in IAS 8 goes on to spell out the implications for the purposes of that standard in some detail (see Chapter 6), but IAS 1 contains no corresponding elucidation.

FINANCIAL STATEMENTS

IAS 1 repeats the objective of general purpose financial statements from the Framework, as being to provide information about the financial position, performance, and cash flows of an entity that is useful to a wide range of users in making economic decisions. Financial statements also show the results of management's stewardship of the resources entrusted to it. Financial statements provide information about an entity's (par. 9):

1. Assets,
2. Liabilities,
3. Equity,
4. Income and expenses, including gains and losses,
5. Contributions by and distributions to owners in their capacity as owners, and
6. Cash flows.

A complete set of financial statements, therefore, includes the following components (par. 10):

1. A statement of financial position as at the end of the period;
2. A statement of comprehensive income for the period;
3. A statement of changes in equity for the period;
4. A statement of cash flows for the period;
5. Notes, comprising a summary of significant accounting policies and other explanatory information; and
6. A statement of financial position as at the beginning of the earliest comparative period when an entity applies an accounting policy retrospectively or makes a retrospective restatement of items in its financial statements, or when it reclassifies items in its financial statements.

An entity may use titles for the statements other than those used in this Standard.

An entity shall present with equal prominence all of the financial statements in a complete set of financial statements. The implications of this are discussed and illustrated in more detail later in this chapter.

IAS 1 encourages, but does not require, the additional presentation, "outside the financial statements," of a management report about the financial performance and financial position of the enterprise, and about its environment, risks, and uncertainties. Brief suggestions as to coverage are made in paragraph 13, but none of the suggestions are mandatory. Further additional statements and reports, for example, on environmental matters, are also encouraged.

FAIR PRESENTATION AND COMPLIANCE WITH INTERNATIONAL ACCOUNTING STANDARDS

The first substantive part of IAS 1 concerns the vexed question of the override. The issue at stake is whether the detailed regulations, that is, the standards in this case, are always and automatically both necessary and sufficient conditions for the preparation of adequate financial statements, or whether some more fundamental overriding criterion, such as the provision of a true and fair view, a requirement to present fairly, or a requirement not to mislead users, is, when a clash occurs, the determining requirement (hence "overriding" the standards). IAS 1 recognizes that compliance with the International Standards may be insufficient or inadequate "in extremely rare circumstances."

Enterprises that comply with IASs should say so. This requires that they comply with *all* applicable aspects of all applicable standards and with all applicable interpretations of the Standing Interpretations Committee. However, the overall requirement is that financial statements should present fairly the financial position, financial performance, and cash flows of an entity. Fair presentation requires the faithful representation of the effects of transactions, other events, and conditions in accordance with the definitions and recognition criteria for assets, liabilities, income, and expenses set out in the Framework (see Chapter 2). The appropriate application of International Standards, with additional disclosure when necessary, is presumed to result in financial statements that achieve a fair presentation.

In the extremely rare circumstances in which management concludes that compliance with a requirement in a standard or an interpretation would be so misleading that it would conflict with the objective of financial statements set out in the Framework, the entity should depart from that requirement if the relevant regulatory framework requires, or otherwise does not prohibit, such a departure.

When an entity does so, it must disclose (par. 20):

1. That management has concluded that the financial statements present fairly the entity's financial position, financial performance and cash flows.

2. That it has complied with applicable IFRS, except that it has departed from a particular requirement to achieve a fair presentation.

3. The title of the IFRS from which the entity has departed, the nature of the departure, including the treatment that the standard or interpretation would require, the reason why that treatment would be so misleading in the circumstances that it would conflict with the objective of financial statements, and the treatment adopted.

4. For each period presented, the financial impact of the departure on each item in the financial statements that would have been reported in complying with the requirement.

When an entity has departed from a requirement of a standard or an interpretation in a prior period, and that departure affects the amounts recognized in the financial statements for the current period, it must make the disclosures noted in items 3 and 4, above.

In the extremely rare circumstances in which management concludes that compliance with a requirement in a standard or an interpretation would be so misleading that it would conflict with the objective of financial statements set out in the Framework, but the relevant regulatory framework prohibits departure from the requirement, the entity shall, to the maximum extent possible, reduce the perceived misleading aspects of compliance by disclosing both:

1. The title of the IFRS in question, the nature of the requirement, and the reason management has concluded that complying with that requirement is so misleading in the circumstances that it conflicts with the objective of financial statements; and

2. For each period presented, the adjustments to each item in the financial statements that management has concluded would be necessary to achieve a fair presentation.

OBSERVATION: The question of terminology and national positions here is both important and potentially confusing. The U.S. requirement to present fairly in accordance with (U.S.) GAAP means, in practice if not in theory, to follow (U.S.) GAAP. The U.K. requirement to give a true and fair view equally clearly means to follow standards where suitable but to depart from them if a true and fair view requires it. The U.K. position in essence found its way into the European

Union Fourth Directive and, hence, subject to varying degrees of bastardization, into other European countries. IAS 1 follows the U.S. *wording* but the U.K./EU philosophy. The following table makes this clear. Our categorization of the U.S. in this respect relates to the practice and rhetoric of accounting; auditing theory seems less clear-cut.

Jurisdiction	Terminology	Overriding
U.K.	True and Fair View	Yes
European Union	True and Fair View	Yes
USA	Fair Presentation	No
IASB	Fair Presentation	Yes

This is not to imply that the override is likely to be used in similar ways or in similar volumes in the various jurisdictions where it exists. We predict that its usage under the IASB will indeed be rare. But an important issue of principle is at stake. Can the qualitative characteristics required of financial reporting be ensured by *compliance* with a set of (static) rules, or is some *professional judgment* involved that may, in principle, entail departure from one or more rules?

Although no attempt to define "fair presentation" is provided (rightly in our view), the presumption "in virtually all circumstances" is that a fair presentation is achieved by compliance in all material respects with applicable International Standards. A fair presentation requires (par. 17):

1. Selecting and applying accounting policies as described in IAS 8 (see Chapter 6).

2. Presenting information, including accounting policies, in a manner that provides relevant, reliable, comparable, and understandable information.

3. Providing additional disclosures when the requirements in International Standards are insufficient to enable users to understand the impact of particular transactions or events on the entity's financial position and financial performance.

In extremely rare circumstances, application of a specific requirement in an International Standard might result in misleading financial statements. In such circumstances departure from the standard is *required*. The IASB is at pains to minimize the likelihood of this happening. The override can be applied only when following the standard plus providing additional information would not give a fair presentation (i.e., presumably, would mislead). IAS 1 requires, in addition, if the override is employed, that full details of the departure be given in the financial statements, sufficient to enable users to make an informed judgment on whether the departure is necessary and to calculate the adjustments that would be required to comply with the standard.

OBSERVATION: It is clear that there is a faction in the IASB, including an American influence, which dislikes the whole concept of an override. Paradoxically (compared with attitudes of a decade or two ago), the European Union is broadly in favor of its retention. The possible "get-out clause" because of national regulations (the "relevant regulatory framework") restrictions is a direct reversal of a statement in the 1997 version of IAS 1. It surely represents the possible acceptance of unwarranted interference in the process of maximizing the usefulness of international financial statements.

ASSUMPTIONS AND QUALITATIVE CHARACTERISTICS

As already indicated, the IASB requirements as regards the *choice* of accounting policy have been transferred to IAS 8, "Accounting Policies, Changes in Accounting Estimates and Errors" (see Chapter 6). However, IAS 1 proceeds to incorporate and discuss some, but not all, of the assumptions and qualitative characteristics of financial statements included in the Framework (see Chapter 2). The two "underlying assumptions" are going concern and the accrual basis of accounting. The going concern assumption means that it is assumed that the enterprise will continue in operation for the foreseeable future. Financial statements should be prepared on a going concern basis unless management either intends to liquidate the enterprise or to cease trading or has no realistic alternative but to do so. When management is aware, in making its assessment, of material uncertainties related to events or conditions that may cast significant doubt on the enterprise's ability to continue as a going concern, those uncertainties should be disclosed. When the financial statements are not prepared on a going concern basis, that fact should be disclosed, together with the basis on which the financial statements are prepared and the reason why the enterprise is not considered to be a going concern. When the financial statements are prepared on the going concern basis, it is not necessary to say so. Judgment and, in uncertain cases, detailed investigation may be required.

The accrual basis of accounting (except for cash flow statements) is also an automatic assumption that need not be explicitly stated. Under the accrual basis of accounting, transactions and events are recognized when they occur (and not as cash or its equivalent is received or paid), and they are recorded in the accounting records and reported in the financial statements of the periods to which they relate.

IAS 1 notes that the application of the accruals concept in IASB GAAP does not allow the recognition of items in the balance sheet that do not meet the IAS definition of assets or liabilities. The Framework states, however, that financial statements may include items not falling within these definitions if specific standards require their recognition. Some other standards do so require, for example, with regard to the deferral of government grants (IAS 20, see Chapter 19) and the deferral of income and expenses relating to operating leases (IAS 17, Chapter 26). Although there seems to be conflict between the Framework and IAS 1 on this point, standards, explicitly, override the Framework.

IAS 1 also incorporates the principle of consistency from paragraph QC22 of the Framework, but, oddly, only regarding presentation. A change in presentation and classification of items in financial statements between one period and another is permitted only when it results in a more appropriate presentation (which is expected to continue) or is required by a specific International Standard or interpretation. The Framework principle continues to relate, of course, to recognition and measurement.

The issue of materiality and aggregation raises some important considerations. Each material item should be presented separately in the financial statements. Immaterial amounts should be aggregated with amounts of a similar nature or function and need not be presented separately. In this context, information is material if its nondisclosure could influence the economic decisions of users taken on the basis of the financial statements. Materiality depends on the size and nature of the item judged in the particular circumstances of its omission. In deciding whether an item or an aggregate of items is material, the nature and the size of the item are evaluated together. Depending on the circumstances, either the nature or the size of the item could be the determining factor as the new definition given earlier makes clear. For example, evidence of breaking the law causing a fine could be significant in principle, even if the amount is small. Similar items should be aggregated together however large they or the resulting total are in relation to the enterprise as a whole.

It is important that both assets and liabilities and income and expenses, when material, be reported separately. Offsetting in either the income statement or the balance sheet, except when offsetting reflects the substance of the transaction or event, would detract from the ability of users to understand the transactions undertaken and to assess the future cash flows of the enterprise. Assets and liabilities as well as income and expenses should not be offset except when offsetting is required or permitted by another International Standard.

→ **PRACTICE POINTER:** It is often not fully appreciated that the prevention of offsetting between assets and liabilities, and between income and expenses, is not at all the same thing as the prevention of netting out between debits and credits in a bookkeeping sense. Receipts and payments in relation to the purchase of one asset, for example, involve the netting out of debits and credits and are not examples of offsetting as discussed in IAS 1. We discuss this example in more detail in Chapter 19 relating to government grants.

It should also be noted that there are several examples where other International Standards do "require or permit" offsetting. One such example is IAS 11 (see Chapter 12), where contract costs plus recognized profits less losses are offset against progress billings to give a net figure of amount due from customers.

It is explicitly stated that the specific disclosure requirements of International Standards need not be met if the resulting information is not material. It thus follows that full compliance with IASB GAAP requires the following of complete IASB GAAP except for immaterial disclosure requirements, not the following of complete IASB GAAP period.

IAS 1 (par. 36) states that an entity "shall" present a complete set of financial statements "at least annually." It then recognizes the possibility of a period "longer or shorter than one year," which hardly seems consistent. In this latter case, reasons for the longer or shorter period and the fact that there is a lack of comparability between reporting periods must be disclosed.

The "presentation" section of IAS 1 concludes with requirements about comparative figures. Unless an International Standard permits or requires otherwise, comparative information should be disclosed in respect of the previous period for all amounts in the financial statements. Note that this includes the need for an opening comparative statement of financial position (balance sheet). Comparative narrative and descriptive information should be included when it is relevant to an understanding of the current period's financial statements.

Comparative information should be restated if necessary if the presentation or classification of items in the current financial statements is altered, unless it is impractical to do so, in which case the reason for not reclassifying should be disclosed together with "the nature of the adjustments that would have been made if the amounts had been reclassified." Five- or ten-year summaries should logically be changed as well, although IAS 1 does not consider this point.

It should be noted that IAS 8 applies if changes constitute a change in accounting policy as discussed in that standard (see Chapter 6).

STRUCTURE AND CONTENT

The whole of the remainder of IAS 1 is concerned with the structure and content of financial statements. The standard requires certain disclosures on the face of the financial statements, requires other line items to be disclosed either on the face of the financial statements or in the notes, and provides illustrative formats that an enterprise *may* follow as appropriate in its own circumstances.

IAS 1 requires that "financial statements" (to which IASB GAAP applies) be clearly distinguished from other information, of whatever kind and source, which is included in the same published document. Figures, components, and separate pages must be fully and clearly described.

STATEMENTS OF FINANCIAL POSITION (BALANCE SHEETS)

An entity is required to present current and non-current assets, and current and non-current liabilities, as separate classifications on the face of its balance sheet except when a presentation based on liquidity provides information that is reliable and more relevant. When that exception applies, all assets and liabilities are to be presented broadly in order of liquidity. Whichever method of presentation is adopted, an enterprise should disclose, for each asset and liability item that combines amounts expected to be recovered or settled both before and after 12 months from the balance sheet date, the amount that is expected to be recovered or settled after more than 12 months.

If a business does not have a clearly defined operating cycle or has an operating cycle typically longer than 12 months, a balance sheet classified as above may not be appropriate. IFRS 7, "Financial Instruments: Disclosures" (see Chapter 17), requires disclosure of the maturity dates of financial assets and financial liabilities.

Where, as is usually the case, the current/non-current classification is followed, then IASB GAAP specifies the distinctions as described below. IAS 1 deals with assets first, by defining a current asset.

An asset should be classified as current when (par. 66):

(a) It expects to realize the asset, or intends to sell or consume it, in its normal operating cycle;

(b) It holds the asset primarily for the purpose of trading;

(c) It expects to realize the asset within 12 months after the reporting period; or

(d) The asset is cash or a cash equivalent (as defined in IAS 7) unless the asset is restricted from being exchanged or used to settle a liability for at least 12 months after the reporting period.

All other assets shall be classified as non-current.

This definition of a current asset requires careful consideration. Only one of the four conditions needs to be met for classification as a current asset to be required. Thus, an asset that meets condition 1 in a business that has a two-year operating cycle is a current asset.

→ **PRACTICE POINTER:** The question arises of how to apply this definition to a non-current asset such as a machine, when it is near the end of its useful life and is scheduled for disposal within 12 months. Situation 2 above definitely does not apply, as the machine is not "held primarily for trading purpose. However, does situation 1 or 3 above apply and require reclassification as a current asset? It could be argued that (in most cases) it is "expected to be realized in the normal operating cycle."

In our view, this would be a misreading of the wording and logic of IAS 1. It is clear that purpose rather than degree of market liquidity is the guiding factor in the current/non-current distinction.

The standard confirms that the currently due portion of a long-term nontrading receivable is to be reclassified as current.

The classification of liabilities, when undertaken by the reporting enterprise, must follow a comparable distinction. An entity shall classify a liability as current when (par. 69):

(a) It expects to settle the liability in its normal operating cycle;

(b) It holds the liability primarily for the purpose of trading;

(c) The liability is due to be settled within 12 months after the reporting period; or

(d) The entity does not have an unconditional right to defer settlement of the liability for at least 12 months after the reporting period.

(e) An entity shall classify all other liabilities as non-current.

Again, only one of these criteria needs to apply, so a long operating cycle could lead to the classification as current liabilities of items due to be settled in more than 12 months. The "current" (i.e., due within 12 months) portion of long-term interest-bearing liabilities *is* to be classified as "current" in most cases. However, if an entity expects, and has the discretion, to refinance or roll over an obligation for at least 12 months after the balance sheet date under an existing loan facility, it classifies the obligation as non-current, even if the obligation would otherwise be due within a shorter period. However, when refinancing or rolling over the obligation is not at the discretion of the entity (e.g., when there is no agreement to refinance), the potential to refinance is not considered and the obligation is classified as current.

It is common for loan agreements to contain clauses such that, in the event of defined undertakings by the borrower not being satisfied (e.g., maintenance of an agreed minimum leverage ratio), the liability becomes payable on demand. If this happens, then the liability would, in general, immediately become "current" under IASB GAAP. However, the liability is classified as non-current if the lender agreed by the balance sheet date to provide a period of grace ending at least 12 months after the balance sheet date, within which the entity can rectify the breach and during which the lender cannot demand immediate repayment.

OBSERVATION: It is worth repeating that IAS 1 provides a general definitional and disclosure framework. Many of the items in financial statements are the subject of specific and more detailed International Standards, as discussed throughout this book. Some of IAS 1's coverage is somewhat pragmatic. For example, the detailed discussion of the current/non-current distinction given above is included in IAS 1, arising from the withdrawal of IAS 13, "Presentation of Current Assets and Current Liabilities." However, implications of non-current status are not mentioned in IAS 1, because these are covered by other standards, such as IAS 16, "Property, Plant, and Equipment" (see Chapter 28).

INFORMATION TO BE PRESENTED ON THE STATEMENT OF FINANCIAL POSITION

The remainder of IAS 1 consists, in essence, of a checklist and discussion of minimum disclosure requirements in a set of financial statements. We first consider the balance sheet. As a minimum, the face of the balance sheet (i.e., not the notes to the balance sheet) should include separate line items that present the following amounts (par. 54):

1. Property, plant, and equipment.
2. Investment property.
3. Intangible assets.
4. Financial assets (excluding amounts shown under 5, 8, and 9).
5. Investments accounted for using the equity method.
6. Biological assets.
7. Inventories.
8. Trade and other receivables.
9. Cash and cash equivalents.

10. Total of assets classified as held for sale and assets included in disposal groups classified as held for sale in accordance with IFRS 5, "Non-Current Assets Held for Sale and Discontinued Operations."

11. Trade and other payables.

12. Provisions.

13. Financial liabilities (excluding amounts shown under 11 and 12).

14. Liabilities and assets for current tax, as defined in IAS 12, "Income Taxes."

15. Deferred tax liabilities and deferred tax assets, as defined in IAS 12.

16. Liabilities included in disposal groups classified as held for sale in accordance with IFRS 5.

17. Non-controlling interests, presented within equity.

18. Issued capital and reserves attributable to owners of the parent.

Additional line items, headings, and subtotals should be presented on the face of the balance sheet when their presentation is relevant to an understanding of the entity's financial position. When an entity presents current and non-current assets, and current and non-current liabilities, as separate classifications on the face of its balance sheet, it must not classify deferred tax assets (liabilities) as current assets (liabilities). Amounts included in line items in relation to IFRS 5 should not be also included elsewhere.

The necessity or otherwise of additional line items is obviously a subjective matter. Judgment on this should be based on assessment of the nature and liquidity of assets; the function of assets within the entity; and the amounts, nature, and timing of liabilities.

It should be noted that IAS 1 does not prescribe any particular balance sheet format. The so-called horizontal and vertical formats are equally acceptable. The descriptions used and the ordering of items may be amended according to the nature of the enterprise and its transactions, to provide information that is necessary for an overall understanding of the enterprise's financial position. For example, a financial institution amends the above descriptions in order to apply the more specific relevant requirements of financial institutions. Other amendments not prescribed by promulgated IASB GAAP may be necessary in other industrial or commercial situations.

IAS 1 states that the use of different measurement bases for different classes of assets suggests that their nature or function differs and, therefore, that they should be presented as separate line items. It gives as an example the carrying of certain classes of property, plant, and equipment at cost, and other classes at revalued amounts, under IAS 16, "Property, Plant, and Equipment" (see Chapter 28).

OBSERVATION: It seems to us that the above proposition, or at least the example given, is not logical. The recording of different subsets of property, plant, and machinery under different valuation bases does not necessarily suggest any difference in nature or function. Further disclosure in the notes may well be desirable, as discussed below, but that is a separate matter. A more logical example might be the different treatments allowed for investment properties (see Chapter 25), where the function of the property may affect the accounting treatment.

A further category of required disclosure relating to the balance sheet can be presented either on the face of the balance sheet or in the notes. Further subclassifications of the line items should be presented, classified in a manner appropriate to the enterprise's operations.

The detail provided in subclassifications, either on the face of the balance sheet or in the notes, depends on the requirements of International Standards and the size, nature, and function of the amounts involved. In some cases, other International Standards provide requirements (subject always to the materiality consideration). Tangible assets, for example, are classified by class as required by IAS 16, "Property, Plant, and Equipment" (see Chapter 28), and inventories are subclassified in accordance with IAS 2, "Inventories" (see Chapter 24). Other applications will be more subjective. For example, the standard states that receivables are analyzed between amounts receivable from trade customers, receivables from related parties, prepayments, and other amounts and that provisions are analyzed showing separately provisions for employee benefit costs and any other items.

Extensive detailed disclosure regarding owner's equity is required, either on the face of the balance sheet or in the notes, as follows (par. 79):

1. For each class of share capital:

    (a) The number of shares authorized,

    (b) The number of shares issued and fully paid and issued but not fully paid,

    (c) Par value per share or that the shares have no par value,

    (d) A reconciliation of the number of shares outstanding at the beginning and at the end of the period,

    (e) The rights, preferences, and restrictions attaching to that class, including restrictions on the distribution of dividends and the repayment of capital,

    (f) Shares in the entity held by the entity or by its subsidiaries or associates, and

    (g) Shares reserved for issue under options and sales contracts, including the terms and amounts.

2. A description of the nature and purpose of each reserve within equity.

Enterprises without share capital are required to present equivalent information showing details and movements of each category of equity interest.

If an entity has reclassified (1) a puttable financial instrument classified as an equity instrument, or (2) an instrument that imposes on the entity an obligation to deliver to another party a pro rata share of the net assets of the entity only on liquidation and is classified as an equity instrument between financial liabilities and equity, it shall disclose the amount reclassified into and out of each category (financial liabilities or equity), and the timing and reason for that reclassification.

STATEMENT OF COMPREHENSIVE INCOME

As outlined earlier in this chapter, the new version of IAS 1, mandatory from January 1, 2009, has made major changes regarding the reporting of performance over the period (and the corresponding comparatives). See also "Changes During 2012" below. A "statement of comprehensive income" is required, and its specifications are given with precision (pars. 81–87).

An entity shall present all items of income and expense recognized in a period (1) in a single statement of comprehensive income, or (2) in two statements: a statement displaying components of profit or loss (separate income statement) and a statement beginning with profit or loss and displaying components of other comprehensive income (statement of comprehensive income).

INFORMATION TO BE PRESENTED IN THE STATEMENT OF COMPREHENSIVE INCOME

As a minimum, the statement of comprehensive income shall include line items that present the following amounts for the period:

1. Revenue;
2. Gains and losses arising from the derecognition of financial assets measured at amortized cost;
3. Finance costs;
4. Share of the profit or loss of associates and joint ventures accounted for using the equity method;
5. If a financial asset is reclassified so that it is measured at fair value, any gain or loss arising at the reclassification date (as defined in IFRS 9);
6. Tax expense;
7. A single amount comprising the total of:
    (a) The post-tax profit or loss of discontinued operations, and
    (b) The post-tax gain or loss recognized on the measurement to fair value less costs to sell or on the disposal of the assets or disposal group(s) constituting the discontinued operation;
8. Profit or loss;
9. Each component of other comprehensive income classified by nature (excluding amounts in (10));
10. Share of the other comprehensive income of associates and joint ventures accounted for using the equity method; and
11. Total comprehensive income.

An entity shall disclose the following items in the statement of comprehensive income as allocations of profit or loss for the period:

1. Profit or loss for the period attributable to:

(a) Non-controlling interests, and

(b) Owners of the parent.

2. Total comprehensive income for the period attributable to:

(a) Non-controlling interests, and

(b) Owners of the parent.

An entity may present in a separate income statement (see paragraph 81) the line items in paragraph 82(a)–(f) and the disclosures in paragraph 83(a).

An entity shall present additional line items, headings, and subtotals in the statement of comprehensive income and the separate income statement (if presented), when such presentation is relevant to an understanding of the entity's financial performance.

An entity shall not present any items of income or expense as extraordinary items, in the statement of comprehensive income or the separate income statement (if presented), or in the notes.

For profit or loss for the period, an entity shall recognize all items of income and expense in a period in profit or loss unless an IFRS requires or permits otherwise.

For other comprehensive income for the period, an entity shall disclose the amount of income tax relating to each component of other comprehensive income, including reclassification adjustments, either in the statement of comprehensive income or in the notes.

An entity shall disclose reclassification adjustments relating to components of other comprehensive income. Other IFRSs specify whether and when amounts previously recognized in other comprehensive income are reclassified to profit or loss. Such reclassifications are referred to in this Standard as reclassification adjustments. A reclassification adjustment is included with the related component of other comprehensive income in the period that the adjustment is reclassified to profit or loss. These amounts may have been recognized in other comprehensive income as unrealized gains in the current or previous periods. Those unrealized gains must be deducted from other comprehensive income in the period in which the realized gains are reclassified to profit or loss to avoid including them in total comprehensive income twice.

Additional line items, headings, and subtotals should be presented on the face of the income statement when required by an international standard or when such presentation is necessary to understand financial performance. IAS 33, "Earnings per Share," requires the disclosure of earnings per share data on the face of the statement of comprehensive income (see Chapter 13).

IAS 1 explicitly accepts that considerations of materiality and the nature of an enterprise's operations may require addition to, deletions from, or amendments of descriptions within the above list. The ordering of items also may be changed from that given above "when this is necessary to explain the elements of performance" (which seems likely to occur only rarely).

The requirement for further disclosure is drawn widely and in general terms. An enterprise should present, either on the face of the income statement, which is "encouraged" but not obligatory, or in the notes to the income statement, an analysis of expenses using a classification based on either the nature of expenses or their function within the enterprise.

→ **PRACTICE POINTER:** The implications of these two approaches to the classification of expenses are best shown by pro forma examples.

Nature of Expense Classification

Revenue	X
Other income	X
Changes in inventories of finished goods and work in progress (+ or –)	X
Raw materials and consumables used	X
Employee benefit expense	X
Depreciation and amortization expense	X
Other expenses	X
Total expenses	(X)
Profit before tax	X

Function of Expense (or Cost of Sales) Classification

Revenue	X
Cost of sales	(X)
Gross profit	X
Other income	X
Distribution costs	(X)
Administrative expenses	(X)
Other expenses	(X)
Profit before tax	X

Both methods have advantages. The nature of expense method requires less analysis (and judgment) to prepare, but is arguably less informative and has the logical disadvantage that it might seem to imply that changes in inventory are an expense (or a revenue!), which they are not. Because each method of presentation has merit for different types of enterprises, the standard requires a choice between classifications based on that which most fairly presents the elements of an enterprise's performance. Because information on the nature of expenses is useful in predicting future cash flows, however, additional disclosure on the nature of expenses, including depreciation and amortization expenses and employee benefit costs, is required when the cost of sales classification is used.

STATEMENT OF CHANGES IN EQUITY

The radical changes made by IAS 1 regarding the statement of comprehensive income have necessitated changes also in the statement of changes in equity. The effect of all this, in simple terms, is that much of the data previously presented in the separate statement of changes in equity, as required from January 1, 2005, until January 1, 2009, is now presented in the statement of comprehensive income, as discussed above.

The requirements for the statement of changes in equity are as follows (pars. 106–07).

An entity shall present a statement of changes in equity showing in the statement:

- Total comprehensive income for the period, showing separately the total amounts attributable to owners of the parent and to non-controlling interests;
- For each component of equity, the effects of retrospective application or retrospective restatement recognized in accordance with IAS 8; and
- For each component of equity, a reconciliation between the carrying amount at the beginning and the end of the period, separately disclosing changes resulting from:

—Profit or loss;

—Each item of other comprehensive income; and

—Transactions with owners in their capacity as owners, showing separately contributions by and distributions to owners and changes in ownership interests in subsidiaries that do not result in a loss of control.

An entity shall present, either in the statement of changes in equity or in the notes the amount of dividends recognized as distributions to owners during the period, and the related amount per share.

An entity should also present, either in the statement of changes in equity or in the notes, an analysis of other comprehensive income by item, separately for each component of equity.

IAS 1 presents (non-mandatory) illustrations that are useful in showing the implications of these radical and complicated new requirements, with extracts reproduced below. The statement of financial position (balance sheet) is omitted, which is relatively straightforward, as are all comparatives, which of course must be included in practice, and notes.

Illustration of the Presentation of Comprehensive Income in One Statement and the Classification of Expenses within Profit by Function

XYZ Group—Statement of Comprehensive Income for the Year Ended December 31, 20X7

(*in thousands of currency units*)

	20X7
Revenue	390,000
Cost of sales	(245,000)

	20X7
Gross profit	145,000
Other income	20,667
Distribution costs	(9,000)
Administrative expenses	(20,000)
Other expenses	(2,100)
Finance costs	(8,000)
Share of profit of associates	35,100
Profit before tax	161,667
Income tax expense	(40,417)
Profit for the year from continuing operations	121,250
Loss for the year from discontinued operations	–
PROFIT FOR THE YEAR	121,250
Other comprehensive income:	
Exchange differences on translating foreign operations	5,334
Available-for-sale financial assets	(24,000)
Cash flow hedges	667
Gains on property revaluation	933
Actuarial gains (losses) on defined benefit pension plans	(667)
Share of other comprehensive income of associates	400
Income tax relating to components of other comprehensive income	4,667
Other comprehensive income for the year, net of tax	(14,000)
TOTAL COMPREHENSIVE INCOME FOR THE YEAR	107,250
Profit attributable to:	
Owners of the parent	97,000
Non-controlling interests	24,250
	121,250
Total comprehensive income attributable to:	
Owners of the parent	85,800
Non-controlling interests	21,450
	107,250
Earnings per share (in currency units):	
Basic and diluted	0.46
Alternatively, components of other comprehensive income could be presented in the statement of comprehensive income net of tax:	
	20X7
Other comprehensive income for the year, after tax:	
Exchange differences on translating foreign operations	4,000

	20X7
Available-for-sale financial assets	(18,000)
Cash flow hedges	(500)
Gains on property revaluation	600
Actuarial gains (losses) on defined benefit pension plans	(500)
Share of other comprehensive income of associates	400
Other comprehensive income for the year, net of tax	(14,000)

Illustration of the Presentation of Comprehensive Income in Two Statements and the Classification of Expenses within Profit by Nature

XYZ Group—Income Statement for the Year Ended December 31, 20X7

(*in thousands of currency units*)

	20X7
Revenue	390,000
Other income	20,667
Changes in inventories of finished goods and work in progress	(115,100)
Work performed by the entity and capitalized	16,000
Raw material and consumables used	(96,000)
Employee benefits expense	(45,000)
Depreciation and amortization expense	(19,000)
Impairment of property, plant and equipment	(4,000)
Other expenses	(6,000)
Finance costs	(15,000)
Share of profit of associates	35,100
Profit before tax	161,667
Income tax expense	(40,417)
Profit for the year from continuing operations	121,250
Loss for the year from discontinued operations	–
PROFIT FOR THE YEAR	121,250
Profit attributable to:	
Owners of the parent	97,000
Non-controlling interests	24,250
	121,250
Earnings per share (in current units):	
Basic and diluted	0.46
Profit for the year	121,250
Other comprehensive income:	

	20X7
Exchange differences on translating foreign operations	5,334
Available-for-sale financial assets	(24,000)
Cash flow hedges	(667)
Gains on property revaluation	933
Actuarial gains (losses) on defined benefit pension plans	(667)
Share of other comprehensive income of associates	400
Income tax relating to components of other comprehensive income	4,667
Other comprehensive income for the year, net of tax	(14,000)
TOTAL COMPREHENSIVE INCOME FOR THE YEAR	107,250
Total comprehensive income attributable to:	
Owners of the parent	85,800
Non-controlling interests	21,450
	107,250

Alternatively, components of other comprehensive income could be presented, net of tax. Refer to the statement of comprehensive income illustrating the presentation of income and expenses in one statement.

XYZ Group—Disclosure of Components of Other Comprehensive Income—Notes for the Year Ended December 31, 20X7

(*in thousands of currency units*)

		20X7
Other comprehensive income:		
Exchange differences on translating foreign operations		5,334
Available-for-sale financial assets:		
Gains arising during the year	1,333	
Less: Reclassification adjustments for gains included in profit or loss	(25,333)	(24,000)
Cash flow hedges:		
Gains (losses) arising during the year	(4,667)	
Less: Reclassification adjustments for gains (losses) included in profit or loss	3,333	
Less: Adjustments for amounts transferred to initial carrying amount of hedged items	667	(667)
Gains on property revaluation		933
Actuarial gains (losses) on defined benefit pension plans		(667)
Share of other comprehensive income of associates		400
Other comprehensive income		(18,667)
Income tax relating to components of other comprehensive income		4,667
Other comprehensive income for the year		(14,000)

XYZ Group—Disclosure of Tax Effects Relating to Each Component of Other Comprehensive Income—Notes for the Year Ended December 31, 20X7

20X7

(in thousands of currency units)

	Before-Tax Amount	Tax (Expense) Benefit	Net-of-Tax Amount
Exchange differences on translating foreign operations	5,334	(1,334)	4,000
Available-for-sale financial assets	(24,000)	6,000	(18,000)
Cash flow hedges	(667)	167	(500)
Gains on property revaluation	933	(333)	600
Actuarial gains (losses) on defined benefit pension plans	(667)	167	(500)
Share of other comprehensive income of associates	400	–	400
Other comprehensive income	(18,667)	4,667	(14,000)

CASH FLOW STATEMENTS

IAS 1 says nothing about cash flow statements, merely referring to IAS 7, "Statement of Cash Flows." The reader is, in turn, referred to our full discussion in Chapter 9.

NOTES TO THE FINANCIAL STATEMENTS

In one sense, the notes to the financial statements are "where everything else goes." IAS 1 summarizes the functions of the notes as being to (par. 112):

1. Present information about the basis of preparation of the financial statements and the specific accounting policies used.

2. Disclose the information required by International Standards that is not presented elsewhere in the financial statements.

3. Provide additional information that is not presented on the face of the financial statements but that is relevant to an understanding of them.

Notes to the financial statements should be presented in a systematic manner. Each item on the face of the balance sheet, statement of comprehensive income, separate income statement (if presented), and cash flow statement should be cross-referenced to any related information in the notes.

The standard suggests that notes "are normally" presented in the following order:

1. A statement of compliance with IFRSs.

2. A summary of significant accounting policies applied.

3. Supporting information for items presented in the key statements in the order in which each statement and each line item is presented.

4. Other disclosures, including:

(a) Contingent liabilities (see IAS 37, Chapter 29) and unrecognized contractual commitments.

(b) Non-financial disclosures, such as the entity's financial risk management objectives and policies (see IFRS 7, Chapter 17).

IAS 1 goes to considerable length in discussing disclosure requirements in the notes. However, the central requirements are reasonably clear and reasonably succinct—an entity must disclose the following:

- *In the summary of significant accounting policies*—the measurement basis or bases used in preparing the financial statements and the other accounting policies used that are relevant to an understanding of the financial statements.

- *In the summary of significant accounting policies or other notes*—the judgments, apart from those involving estimations (see below), management has made in the process of applying the entity's accounting policies that have the most significant effect on the amounts recognized in the financial statements.

- *In the notes*—information about the key assumptions concerning the future, and other key sources of estimation uncertainty at the balance sheet date, that have a significant risk of causing a material adjustment to the carrying amounts of assets and liabilities within the next financial year. In respect of those assets and liabilities, the notes shall include details of their nature and their carrying amount as at the balance sheet date.

- *In the notes*—the amount of dividends proposed or declared before the financial statements were authorized for issue but not recognized as a distribution to equity holders during the period, and the related amount per share; and the amount of any cumulative preference dividends not recognized.

- *In the notes*—details relating to puttable financial instruments classified as equity instruments (par. 136A, inserted in February 2008).

- *In information published with the financial statements (if not disclosed elsewhere)*:

  —The domicile and legal form of the entity, its country of incorporation, and the address of its registered office (or principal place of business, if different from the registered office).

  —A description of the nature of the entity's operations and its principal activities.

  —The name of the parent and the ultimate parent of the group.

  —If it is a limited life entity, information regarding the length of its life.

An entity shall disclose information that enables users of its financial statements to evaluate the entity's objectives, policies, and processes for managing capital. Therefore, the entity must disclose the following (pars. 134–36):

1. Qualitative information about its objectives, policies, and processes for managing capital, including (but not limited to):

   a. A description of what it manages as capital;

   b. When an entity is subject to externally imposed capital requirements, the nature of those requirements and how those requirements are incorporated into the management of capital; and

   c. How it is meeting its objectives for managing capital.

2. Summary quantitative data about what it manages as capital. Some entities regard some financial liabilities (e.g., some forms of subordinated debt) as part of capital; other entities regard capital as excluding some components of equity (e.g., components arising from cash flow hedges).

3. Any changes in items 1 and 2 from the previous period.

4. Whether, during the period, it complied with any externally imposed capital requirements to which it is subject.

5. When the entity has not complied with such externally imposed capital requirements, the consequences of such noncompliance.

These disclosures shall be based on the information provided internally to the entity's key management personnel.

SIC-29

The IASB has issued a particular extension to IAS 1, by means of SIC-29, "Service Concession Arrangements: Disclosures,," effective from December 31, 2001. A service concession arrangement involves two parties: (1) the concession operator and (2) the concession provider. A typical example might be a motorway service facility. For the period of the concession, the service provider will generally convey to the service operator the right to provide (and charge for) services to the public, and also possibly the right to use various assets. In exchange, the concession operator accepts an obligation to provide the services according to certain terms and conditions, and possibly to return rights and other resources at the end of the concession period. The essential element is that the concession operator both receives a right and issues an obligation to provide public services.

Some aspects of such arrangements will be covered by other standards, for example, property by IAS 16 (see Chapter 28) and leases by IAS 17 (see Chapter 26). Executory contracts that are onerous are covered by IAS 37 (see Chapter 29); but other non-onerous executory contracts, which are probably the general case where service concession arrangements are concerned, will only be covered by SIC-29, which is concerned only with disclosure. The formal requirements are as follows.

All aspects of a service concession arrangement should be considered in determining the appropriate disclosures in the notes to the financial statements. A Concession Operator and a Concession Provider should disclose the following in each period:

1. A description of the arrangement.

2. Significant terms of the arrangement that may affect the amount, timing, and certainty of future cash flows (e.g., the period of the concession, repricing dates and the basis upon which repricing or renegotiation is determined).

3. The nature and extent (e.g., quantity, time period, or amount as appropriate) of:

   (a) Rights to use specified assets;

   (b) Obligations to provide or rights to expect provision of services;

   (c) Obligations to acquire or build items of property, plant, and equipment;

   (d) Obligations to deliver or rights to receive specified assets at the end of the concession period;

   (e) Renewal and termination options; and

   (f) Other rights and obligations (e.g., major overhauls).

4. Changes in the arrangement occurring during the period.

The disclosures required in accordance with this interpretation should be provided individually for each service concession arrangement or in aggregate for each class of service concession arrangements. A class is a grouping of service concession arrangements involving services of a similar nature (e.g., toll collections, telecommunications, and water treatment services).

OBSERVATION: The major revisions to performance reporting introduced from January 1, 2009, have as their fundamental purpose the prevention of information being "hidden away" outside the essential statement of performance, now designated the statement of comprehensive income. The word "comprehensive" is precisely the point. All adjustments and events should be clearly reported in vision. The success of this policy remains to be seen.

CHANGES DURING 2012

There has been much discussion, and even more uncertainty, about precisely how comprehensive income should be reported. The issue relates to the apparently arcane distinction between a single continuous statement, or two separate but explicitly consecutive statements. In May 2010, the IASB (and the FASB) issued an exposure draft that would require a single continuous performance statement showing two indicators of income: the net income (i.e., the traditional profit/loss) as a subtotal and the comprehensive income as the bottom line.

However, in June 2011 the IASB issued a revision to IAS 1 that will give a choice between the two alternative presentations. This revised IAS 1 allows an entity to present either a single statement of comprehensive income (as the IASB would obviously prefer), or both a statement of profit and loss and a following statement of comprehensive income. This revised IAS 1 is mandatory for financial periods beginning on or after July1, 2012. Earlier application is permitted.

CHAPTER 5
FIRST-TIME ADOPTION OF INTERNATIONAL FINANCIAL REPORTING STANDARDS

CONTENTS

OVERVIEW

The reporting of changes in accounting policies, and the implications of such changes, is an important aspect of effective transparency. This has long been covered by IAS 8, "Accounting Policies, Changes in Accounting Estimates, and Errors" (see Chapter 6). Recognizing that the one-off wholesale adoption of International Standards, by switching from a national GAAP system, raised issues of a greater order of magnitude, the IASB first issued an interpretation (SIC-8, "First-Time Application of IAS as the Primary Basis of Accounting") on this matter. However, with the importance of the mass adoptions foreseen in 2005 amongst European listed enterprises and elsewhere, a full-blown standard was deemed desirable, hence IFRS 1, "First-Time Adoption of International Reporting Standards." This became standard with effect from January 1, 2004.

IFRS 1 is regularly updated to take account of new standards as they appear.

The IFRS applies when an entity adopts IFRSs for the first time by an explicit and unreserved statement of compliance with IFRSs. In general, it requires an entity to comply with each IFRS effective at the reporting date for its first IFRS financial statements. In particular, the IFRS requires an entity to do the following in the opening IFRS balance sheet that it prepares as a starting point for its accounting under IFRSs:

- Recognize all assets and liabilities whose recognition is required by IFRSs.

- Not recognize items as assets or liabilities if IFRSs do not permit such recognition.

- Reclassify items that it recognized under previous GAAP as one type of asset, liability, or component of equity but that are a different type of asset, liability, or component of equity under IFRSs.

- Apply IFRSs in measuring all recognized assets and liabilities.

IFRS 1 grants limited exemptions from these requirements in specified areas where the cost of complying with them would be likely to exceed the benefits to users of financial statements. It also prohibits retrospective application of IFRSs in some areas, particularly where retrospective application would require judgments by management about past conditions after the outcome of a particular transaction is already known. IFRS 1 also requires disclosures that explain how the transition from previous GAAP to IFRSs affected the entity's reported financial position, financial performance, and cash flows.

OBSERVATION: Depending on the particular situation and industry involved, the effects on the reported results of an entity of the switch to IFRS could be highly significant. This implies that readers of published financial statements will need to be "educated" about the effects of these accounting changes (which are not "real" changes), in order to receive a realistic impression of the genuine underlying trend of performance. Interim reports issued *during* the year of the transition to IFRS GAAP will particularly require careful explanation by preparers, and careful interpretation by users.

BACKGROUND

As outlined above, a complete switch from one set of regulatory requirements to a different set raises important issues for the preservation of consistency and trend analysis. The objective of IFRS 1 is stated as follows (par. 1):

> The objective of this IFRS is to ensure that an entity's first IFRS financial statements, and its interim financial reports for part of the period covered by those financial statements, contain high quality information that:
>
> (a) Is transparent for users and comparable over all periods presented;
>
> (b) Provides a suitable starting point for accounting under International Financial Reporting Standards (IFRSs); and
>
> (c) Can be generated at a cost that does not exceed the benefits to users.

SCOPE AND DEFINITIONS

The required scope is that an entity should apply IFRS 1 (par. 2) in:

- Its first IFRS financial statements, and

- Each interim financial report, if any, that it presents under IAS 34, "Interim Financial Reporting" (see Chapter 23), for part of the period covered by its first IFRS financial statements.

In a departure from earlier practice, key definitions are given in an appendix (Appendix A), which is defined as an integral part of the IFRS. These definitions are given below.

Date of transition to IFRSs	The beginning of the earliest period for which an entity presents full comparative information under IFRSs in its first IFRS financial statements.
Deemed cost	An amount used as a surrogate for cost or depreciated cost at a given date. Subsequent depreciation or amortization assumes that the entity had initially recognized the asset or liability at the given date and that its cost was equal to the deemed cost.
Fair value	The amount for which an asset could be exchanged or a liability settled, between knowledgeable, willing parties in an arm's length transaction.
First IFRS financial statements	The first annual financial statements in which an entity adopts International Financial Reporting Standards, by an explicit and unreserved statement of compliance with IFRSs.
First IFRS reporting period	The latest reporting period covered by an entity's first IFRS financial statements.
First-time adopter	An entity that presents its first IFRS financial statements.
International Financial Reporting Standards	Standards and Interpretations adopted by the IASB. They comprise: (a) International Financial Reporting Standards; (b) International Accounting Standards; and (c) Interpretations originated by the International Financial Reporting Interpretations Committee (IFRIC) or the former Standing Interpretations Committee (SIC).

Opening IFRS statement of financial position	An entity's statement of financial position at the date of transition to IFRSs.
Previous GAAP	The basis of accounting that a first-time adopter used immediately before adopting IFRSs.

The IASB has had considerable anxiety about what exactly is meant by "first IFRS financial statements." Paragraph 3 gives the essential point:

> An entity's first IFRS financial statements are the first annual financial statements in which the entity adopts IFRSs, by an explicit and unreserved statement in those financial statements of compliance with IFRSs.

It follows from this that any earlier set of financial statements that did not include this explicit and unreserved statement of compliance with International Standards cannot have been the "first IFRS financial statements," *even if they did, in fact, fully comply with IAS requirements as at that time.* It also follows, on the other hand, that a set of financial statements that makes the required statement of compliance, but does not in fact correctly so comply, *is* still the "first IFRS financial statements," in which case IAS 8 would apply to the process of correcting such errors in future years. Despite this surely successful attempt to avoid ambiguity, IFRS 1 gives a number of example situations in both directions in paragraphs 3–5.

RECOGNITION AND MEASUREMENT

Taking as an example an enterprise that has a financial year-end on December 31 and is required to produce its first IFRS financial statements for a reporting date of December 31, 20X5, a number of implications arise. First, it will already have produced and published its financial statements for the reporting date of December 31, 20X4, under its previous GAAP. Second, when the enterprise eventually publishes its first IFRS financial statements with a reporting date of December 31, 20X5, it will need to produce complete comparative figures for the previous year that are fully comparable and consistent with the 20X5 data. It will therefore need to prepare a complete restatement of its 20X4 report under IFRS requirements, as part of the 20X5 reporting package. It follows from this that, third, the enterprise will need to prepare an opening balance sheet as at the opening of business on January 1, 20X4, under IFRS GAAP, in order that the correct changes and adjustments required for the 20X4 IFRS financial statements can be calculated. With effect from January 1, 2009, under the revised version of IAS 1, "Presentation of Financial Statements" (see Chapter 4), this opening balance sheet (statement of financial position) is required to be published.

→ **PRACTICE POINTER:** An enterprise may choose, or may be required by local legislation or regulation, to produce comparative figures on a comparable basis for more than one year. In such a case, the opening IFRS balance sheet, in relation to a reporting date of December 31, 20X5, would need to be prepared as at January 1, 20X3, or even earlier.

There is obviously the theoretical possibility that the content of IASB requirements will have altered over the two or more years dealt with in the first IFRS financial statements. Indeed, given the state of considerable flux and development attending IFRS GAAP, this is extremely likely. The general rule under IFRS 1 for dealing with this problem is very clear (pars. 7 and 8):

> An entity shall use the same accounting policies in its opening IFRS statement of financial position and throughout all periods presented in its first IFRS financial statements. Those accounting policies shall comply with each IFRS effective at the end of its first IFRS reporting period, except as specified in paragraphs 13–19 and Appendices B–E.

> An entity shall not apply different versions of IFRSs that were effective at earlier dates. An entity may apply a new IFRS that is not yet mandatory if it permits early application.

Thus, in the earlier example of a reporting date of December 31, 20X5, the opening IFRS balance sheet as at January 1, 2004, and *all* the published (IFRS) comparatives for 20X4, should as a general rule be prepared under International Standards effective on December 31, 20X5. The purpose and advantage of this, of course, is to maximize consistency and comparability within the 20X5 financial statements considered as a whole. The necessary adjustments to the opening IFRS balance sheet as compared with the version published earlier under the previous GAAP should be recognized directly in equity, usually in retained earnings (par. 11).

It follows from paragraphs 7 and 8 that, subject to the exceptions referred to in paragraph 7 and discussed below, an entity's opening IFRS balance sheet will (par. 10):

- Recognize all assets and liabilities whose recognition is required by IFRSs as at the reporting date.

- Not recognize items as assets or liabilities if IFRSs do not permit such recognition.

- Reclassify items that it recognized under previous GAAP as one type of asset, liability, or component of equity but that are a different type of asset, liability, or component of equity under IFRSs.

- Apply IFRSs in measuring all recognized assets and liabilities.

It is clear from the "Basis of Conclusions" document that Board members deliberated long and hard about arguments for and against the desirability of the above principle, and about possible exceptions to it. It should be noted that in the case, for example, of an asset that has been held for many years but not recognized as an asset under previous GAAP and that now needs to be recognized and measured under IFRSs, it may be necessary to go back in the accounting records for many years to properly meet the requirements for the opening IFRS balance sheet.

The result of all these deliberations is that the IFRS establishes two categories of exceptions to the principle that an entity's opening IFRS balance sheet shall comply with each IFRS:

1. Appendices C–E grant exemptions from some requirements of other IFRSs.

2. Paragraphs 14–17 and Appendix B prohibits retrospective application of some aspects of other IFRSs.

The first type of exception is dealt with first. IFRS 1 allows (but does not require) certain limited exemptions from the general principle of paragraphs 7 and 10, summarized and delimited as follows:

- Business combinations (App. C);

- Share-based payment transactions (pars. D2 and D3);

- Insurance contracts (par. D4);

- Fair value or revaluation as deemed cost (pars. D5–D8);

- Leases (par. D9–D9A);

- Employee benefits (pars. D10 and D11);

- Cumulative translation differences (pars. D12 and D13);

- Investments in subsidiaries, jointly controlled entities, and associates (pars. D14 and D15);

- Assets and liabilities of subsidiaries, associates, and joint ventures (pars. D16 and D17);

- Compound financial instruments (par. D18);

- Designation of previously recognized financial instruments (par. D19);

- Fair value measurement of financial assets or financial liabilities at initial recognition (par. D20);

- Decommissioning liabilities included in the cost of property, plant, and equipment (par. D21);

- Exempt entities using the full cost method from retrospective application of IFRS for oil and gas assets;

- Financial assets or intangible assets accounted for in accordance with IFRIC 12, "Service Concession Arrangements" (par. D22); and

- Borrowing costs (par. D23).

- Transfers of assets from customers (par. D24)

- Extinguishing financial liabilities with equity investments (par. D25)

- Severe hyperinflation (pars. D26–D30).

The rationale behind allowing these optional exemptions is that the Board felt the costs incurred by enterprises if these limited exemptions were not available might well outweigh the informational benefits to users. These optional exemptions are discussed briefly below. There is little point in repeating every nuance of the IFRS 1 details, and reference should be made to the standard if such exemptions are being used in practice.

Business Combinations

A first-time adopter may elect not to apply IFRS 3, "Business Combinations," retrospectively to past business combinations (business combinations that occurred before the date of transition to IFRSs). However, if a first-time adopter restates any business combination to comply with IFRS 3, it shall restate all later business combinations. For example, if a first-time adopter elects to restate a business combination that occurred on June 30, 2012, it shall restate all business combinations that occurred between June 30, 2012, and the date of transition to IFRSs.

If a first-time adopter does not apply IFRS 3 retrospectively to a past business combination, a number of specified consequences follow (par. C4); major points include:

1. The first-time adopter shall keep the same classification (as an acquisition by the legal acquirer, a reverse acquisition by the legal acquiree, or a uniting of interests) as in its previous GAAP financial statements.

2. The first-time adopter shall recognize all its assets and liabilities at the date of transition to IFRSs that were acquired or assumed in a past business combination, other than:

    (a) Assets, including goodwill, and liabilities that were not recognized in the acquirer's consolidated balance sheet under previous GAAP and also would not qualify for recognition under IFRSs in the separate balance sheet of the acquiree.

    (b) Some financial assets and financial liabilities derecognized under previous GAAP. This is because a first-time adopter shall apply the derecognition requirements in IAS 39, "Financial Instruments Recognition and Measurement," prospectively from the effective date of IAS 39. In other words, if a first-time adopter derecognized financial assets or financial liabilities under its previous GAAP in a financial year beginning before January 1, 2004, it shall not recognize those assets and liabilities under IFRSs (unless they qualify for recognition as a result of a later transaction or event). However, notwithstanding the above, an entity may apply the derecognition requirements of IAS 39 retrospectively from a date of its own choosing, provided that the information needed to apply IAS 39 to financial items derecognized as a result of past transactions was obtained at the time of initially accounting for those transactions (pars. B2 and B3).

3. The first-time adopter shall exclude from its opening IFRS balance sheet any item recognized under previous GAAP that does not qualify for recognition as an asset or liability under IFRSs.

4. If an asset acquired, or liability assumed, in a past business combination was not recognized under previous GAAP, it does not have a deemed cost of zero in the opening IFRS balance sheet. Instead, the acquirer shall recognize and measure it in its consolidated balance sheet on the basis that IFRSs would require in the separate balance sheet of the acquiree. To

illustrate, if the acquirer had not, under its previous GAAP, capitalized finance leases acquired in a past business combination, it shall capitalize those leases in its consolidated financial statements, as IAS 17, "Leases," would require the acquiree to do in its separate IFRS balance sheet.

5. Regardless of whether there is any indication that the goodwill may be impaired, the first-time adopter shall apply IAS 36, "Impairment of Assets," in testing the goodwill for impairment at the date of transition to IFRSs and in recognizing any resulting impairment loss in retained earnings (or, if so required by IAS 36, in revaluation surplus). The impairment test shall be based on conditions at the date of transition to IFRSs.

Share-Based Payment Transactions

A first-time adopter is encouraged, but not required, to apply IFRS 2, "Share-Based Payment," to:

- Equity instruments granted on or before November 7, 2002.
- Equity instruments granted after November 7, 2002, that vested before the later of the date of transition to IFRSs and January 1, 2005.
- Liabilities arising from share-based payment transactions that were settled before the date of transition to IFRSs.
- Liabilities that were settled before January 1, 2005.

Certain further detailed conditions apply (pars. D2 and D3).

Insurance Contracts

A first-time adopter may apply the transitional provisions of IFRS 4, "Insurance Contracts" (see Chapter 35).

Fair Value or Revaluation as Deemed Cost

An entity may elect to measure an item of property, plant, and equipment at the date of transition to IFRSs at its fair value and use that fair value as its deemed cost at that date. A first-time adopter may elect to use a previous GAAP revaluation of an item of property, plant, and equipment at, or before, the date of transition to IFRSs as deemed cost at the date of the revaluation, if the revaluation was, at the date of the revaluation, broadly comparable to either of the following:

- Fair value.
- Cost or depreciated cost under IFRSs, adjusted to reflect, for example, changes in a general or specific price index.

These elections are also available for investment property, if an entity elects to use the cost basis in IAS 40, "Investment Property," and for intangible assets that meet the recognition and revaluation criteria set out in IAS 38, "Intangible Assets." It should be noted that any such fair values should reflect conditions that existed at the date for which the fair values were actually determined (rather than conditions existing at the date the determination was carried out).

Leases

A first-time adopter may apply the transitional provisions in IFRIC 4, "Determining Whether an Arrangement Contains a Lease" (see Chapter 26). This means that the determination may be based on the facts and circumstances at the date of transition, not the earlier date of the arrangement.

Exempt entities with existing leasing contracts are exempt from reassessing the classification of those contracts in accordance with IFRIC 4, *Determining Whether an Arrangement Contains a Lease*, when the application of their national accounting requirements produced the same result.

Employee Benefits

A strict application of the "corridor" approach allowed by IAS 19, "Employee Benefits," by a first-time adopter would require retrospective analysis of cumulative actuarial gains and losses from the date of the inception of the plan. To avoid this necessity, a first-time IFRS adopter may recognize (i.e., take immediately to the income statement) all cumulative actuarial gains and losses at the date of transition to IFRS, even if it uses the corridor approach for later actuarial gains and losses. If a first-time adopter uses this election, it shall apply it to all plans.

Cumulative Translation Differences

IAS 21, "The Effects of Changes in Foreign Exchange Rates," requires an entity to classify some cumulative translation differences (CTDs) relating to a net investment in a foreign operation as a separate component of equity. The entity transfers the CTDs to the income statement on subsequent disposal of the foreign operation. A first-time adopter need not identify the CTDs at the date of transition to IFRSs. The first-time adopter need not show that identifying the CTDs would involve undue cost or effort.

Investments in Subsidiaries, Jointly Controlled Entities, and Associates

When an entity prepares separate financial statements, IAS 27, "Consolidated and Separate Financial Statements," requires it to account for its investments in subsidiaries, jointly controlled entities, and associates either:

1. At cost, or
2. In accordance with IFRS 9, "Financial Instruments."

If a first-time adopter measures such an investment at cost, it shall measure that investment at one of the following amounts in its separate opening IFRS statement of financial position:

1. Cost determined in accordance with IAS 27, or
2. Deemed cost. The deemed cost of such an investment shall be its:
   (a) Fair value (determined in accordance with IAS 39) at the entity's date of transition to IFRSs in its separate financial statements, or
   (b) Previous GAAP carrying amount at that date.

A first-time adopter may choose either (a) or (b) above to measure its investment in each subsidiary, jointly controlled entity, or associate that it elects to measure using a deemed cost.

Assets and Liabilities of Subsidiaries, Associates, and Joint Ventures

Potential problems arise if a subsidiary becomes a first-time IFRS adopter later, or earlier, than its parent, as the same items could have two different dates of first-time adoption, one for each "level" of the reporting process. Hence, under IFRS 1, if a subsidiary adopts IFRSs later than the parent (in the subsidiary's own published financial statements), the subsidiary may choose to measure its assets and liabilities at either:

- The carrying amounts that would be included in the parent's consolidated financial statements, based on the parent's date of transition to IFRSs, if no adjustments were made for consolidation procedures and for the effects of the business combination in which the parent acquired the subsidiary; or

- The carrying amounts required by the rest of the IFRS, based on the subsidiary's date of transition to IFRSs.

A similar election is available to an associate or joint venture that becomes a first-time adopter later than an entity that has significant influence or joint control over it.

However, if an entity becomes a first-time adopter later than its subsidiary (or associate or joint venture) the entity shall, in its consolidated financial statements, measure the assets and liabilities of the subsidiary (or associate or joint venture) at the same carrying amounts as in the separate financial statements of the subsidiary (or associate or joint venture), after adjusting for consolidation and equity accounting adjustments and for the effects of the business combination in which the entity acquired the subsidiary.

Compound Financial Instruments

A detailed exemption exists (par. D18) where the original liability component is no longer outstanding.

Designation of Previous Recognized Financial Instruments

IFRS 9 permits the designation of a financial instrument on initial recognition as a financial asset or liability at fair value through profit or loss, or as available for sale. Such designation is, however, alternatively permitted at the date of transition to IFRSs.

Fair Value Measurement of Financial Assets or Financial Liabilities at Initial Recognition

A detailed specific exemption applies (see par. D20).

Decommissioning Liabilities Included in the Cost of Property, Plant, and Equipment

A first-time adopter need not comply with the requirements of IFRIC 1, "Changes in Existing Decommissioning, Restoration, and Similar Liabilities," in respect of changes in such liabilities that occurred before the date of transaction to IFRSs. Conditions apply if the exemption is used, as specified in paragraph D21.

Certain Oil and Gas Exploration Assets

As described in "Business Combinations," an exemption exists in relation to the full cost method for accounting for oil and gas exploration. In addition, with effect from January 1, 2010 (pars. D21A and D8A(b)), detailed exemptions exist related to cost centers involving large geographical areas.

Financial Assets or Intangible Assets Accounted for in Accordance with IFRIC 12

A first-time adopter may apply the transitional provisions of IFRIC 12, "Service Concession Arrangements" (see Chapter 12).

Borrowing Costs

A first-time adopter may apply the transitional provisions of IAS 23, "Borrowing Costs," as revised for mandatory application from January 1, 2009 (see Chapter 7).

Transfers of Assets from Customers

A first-time adopter may apply the transitional provisions in par. 22 of IFRIC 18, "Transfers of Assets from Customers" (see Chapter 30).

Extinguishing Financial Liabilities with Equity Instruments

A first-time adopter may apply the transitional provisions in IFRC 19, "Extinguishing Financial Liabilities with Equity Instruments" (see Chapter 17).

Severe Hyperinflation

A complicated exemption exists (pars. D26–D30) where an entity's functional currency was, but has ceased to be before the date of transition to IFRS, the currency of a hyperinflationary economy (see IAS 29, "Financial Reporting in Hyperinflationary Economies," Chapter 9). In essence, the exemption allows fair values as at the date of transition to IFRS to be used.

Prohibition of Retrospective Application

There are four situations in which the IASB *prohibits* retrospective application (in contrast to the *option* not to apply retrospective application in the circumstances discussed above). These relate to:

- Derecognition of financial assets and financial liabilities (pars. B2 and B3)
- Hedge accounting (pars. B4–B6)

- Estimates (pars. 14–17)
- Some aspects of accounting for non-controlling interests (par. B7).
- Classification and measurement of financial assets (par. B8).
- Embedded derivatives (par. B9).

As regards the first of these, in general a first-time adopter shall apply the derecognition requirements in IFRS 9, "Financial Instruments," prospectively for transactions occurring on or after the date of transition to IFRS. In other words, if a first-time adopter derecognized non-derivative financial assets or non-derivative financial liabilities in accordance with its previous GAAP as a result of a transaction that occurred before the date of transition to IFRS, it shall not recognize those assets and liabilities in accordance with IFRSs (unless they qualify for recognition as a result of a later transaction or event).

However, an entity may apply the derecognition requirements in IFRS 9 retrospectively from a date of the entity's choosing, provided that the information needed to apply IFRS 9 to financial assets and financial liabilities derecognized as a result of past transactions was obtained at the time of initially accounting for those transactions.

As regards hedging, the Board confirms that the transitional provisions of IFRS 9 (see Chapter 17) shall apply to all hedging relationships that existed at the date of transition to IFRS, except that an entity shall not reflect in its opening IFRS balance sheet a hedging relationship of a type that does not qualify for hedge accounting under IAS 39 (e.g., many hedging relationships in which the hedging instrument is a cash instrument or written option, the hedged item is a net position, or the hedge covers interest risk in a held-to-maturity investment). However, if an entity designated a net position as a hedged item under previous GAAP, it may designate an individual item within that net position as a hedged item under IFRSs, provided that it does so no later than the date of transition to IFRSs.

As regards estimates, because the date of transition to IFRSs is later than when the original estimates were made, more recent evidence that has become available may suggest (or as an adjusting event under IAS 10 [see Chapter 16] would require) revision of the estimate. IFRS 1 prohibits the treatment of such additional evidence as an adjusting event (par. 14):

> An entity's estimates under IFRSs at the date of transition to IFRSs shall be consistent with estimates made for the same date in accordance with previous GAAP (after adjustments to reflect any difference in accounting policies), unless there is objective evidence that those estimates were in error.

The implication of this is that an entity shall not reflect such new information in its opening IFRS balance sheet (unless the estimates need adjustment for any differences in accounting policies or there is objective evidence that the estimates were in error). Instead, the entity shall reflect that new information in profit or loss (or, if appropriate, other comprehensive income) for the year in which the information becomes available.

For non-controlling interests, with effect from July 1, 2009, or on earlier adoption of IAS 27, "Consolidated and Separate Financial Statements," as amended in 2008 (see Chapter 11), a first-time adopter shall apply the following requirements of IAS 27, "Consolidated and Separate Financial Statements" (as amended in 2008), prospectively from the date of transition to IFRSs:

1. The requirement in paragraph 28 that total comprehensive income is attributed to the owners of the parent and to the non-controlling interests even if this results in the non-controlling interests having a deficit balance;

2. The requirements in paragraphs 30 and 31 for accounting for changes in the parent's ownership interest in a subsidiary that do not result in a loss of control; and

3. The requirements in paragraphs 34–37 for accounting for a loss of control over a subsidiary, and the related requirements of paragraph 8A of IFRS 5.

However, if a first-time adopter elects to apply IFRS 3 (as revised in 2008) retrospectively to past business combinations, it also shall apply IAS 27 (as amended in 2008) from that same date.

Further exemptions (pars. B8 and B9) allow a recent date to be used in relation to the possibility of measuring a financial asset at amortised cost (see IFRS 9, par. 4.1.2), and to the separation of embedded derivatives (see IFRS 9, par. B4.3.11). See Chapter 17.

PRESENTATION AND DISCLOSURE

The first point to emphasize is that all presentation and disclosure requirements of all IFRSs must be followed in full. This includes at least three statements of financial position, two statements of comprehensive income, two separate income statements (if presented), two statements of cash flows, and two statements of changes in equity and related notes, including comparative information.

The Board notes that many entities choose, or are required by other regulations, to provide either full comparatives for two or more years or historical summaries of selected data for a number of years. In any such event, consistency with IFRS beyond the one-year requirement is not necessary. However, in any financial statements containing historical summaries or comparative information under previous GAAP, an entity shall:

- Label the previous GAAP information prominently as not being prepared under IFRSs; and

- Disclose the nature of the main adjustments that would make it comply with IFRS. The entity need not quantify those adjustments.

As a general tenet (par. 23), an entity shall explain how the transition from previous GAAP to IFRSs affected its reported financial position, financial performance, and cash flows. The implications of this are spelled out by IFRS 1 in detail and, for completeness, this detail is repeated here.

Reconciliations

To comply with paragraph 23, an entity's first IFRS financial statements shall include (par. 24):

1. Reconciliations of its equity reported under previous GAAP to its equity under IFRSs for both of the following dates:

   (a) The date of transition to IFRSs.

   (b) The end of the latest period presented in the entity's most recent annual financial statements under previous GAAP.

2. A reconciliation to its total comprehensive income under IFRSs for the latest period in the entity's most recent annual financial statements. The starting point for that reconciliation shall be total comprehensive income under previous GAAP for the same period or, if an entity did not report such a total, profit or loss under previous GAAP.

3. If the entity recognized or reversed any impairment losses for the first time in preparing its opening IFRS statement of financial position, the disclosures that IAS 36, "Impairment of Assets," would have required if the entity had recognized those impairment losses or reversals in the period beginning with the date of transition to IFRSs.

The reconciliations required by paragraph 24 shall give sufficient detail to enable users to understand the material adjustments to the statement of financial position and statement of comprehensive income. If an entity presented a statement of cash flows under its previous GAAP, it shall also explain the material adjustments to the cash flow statement (par. 25).

If any entity becomes aware of errors made under previous GAAP, the reconciliations required by paragraph 24 shall distinguish the correction of those errors from changes in accounting policies (par. 26).

IAS 8 does not deal with changes in accounting policies that occur when an entity first adopts IFRSs. Therefore, IAS 8's requirements for disclosures about changes in accounting policies do not apply in an entity's first IFRS financial statements. If an entity did not present financial statements for previous periods, its first IFRS financial statements shall disclose that fact.

If during the period covered by its first IFRS financial statements an entity changes its accounting policies or its use of the exemptions contained in this IFRS, it shall explain the changes between its first IFRS interim financial report and its first IFRS financial statements, in accordance with paragraph 23, and it shall update the reconciliations required by paragraph 24(a) and (b).

Designation of Financial Assets or Financial Liabilities (Par. 29)

An entity is permitted to designate a previously recognized financial asset or financial liability as a financial asset or financial liability at fair value through profit or loss or a financial asset as available-for-sale in accordance with paragraph D19. The entity shall disclose the fair value of financial assets or financial liabilities designated into each category at the date of designation and their classification and carrying amount in the previous financial statements.

Use of Fair Value as Deemed Cost

If an entity uses fair value in its opening IFRS statement of financial position as deemed cost for an item of (1) property, plant, and equipment, (2) an investment property, or (3) an intangible asset, the entity's first IFRS financial statements shall disclose, for each line item in the opening IFRS statement of financial position:

- The aggregate of those fair values, and

- The aggregate adjustment to the carrying amounts reported under previous GAAP.

Similarly, if an entity uses a deemed cost in its opening IFRS statement of financial position for an investment in a subsidiary, jointly controlled entity, or associate in its separate financial statements (see par. D15), the entity's first IFRS separate financial statements shall disclose:

- The aggregate deemed cost of those investments for which deemed cost is their previous GAAP carrying amount;

- The aggregate deemed cost of those investments for which deemed cost is fair value; and

- The aggregate adjustment to the carrying amounts reported under previous GAAP.

Use of deemed cost for oil and gas assets. If an entity uses the exemption in paragraph D8A(b) for oil and gas assets, it shall disclose that fact and the basis on which carrying amounts determined under previous GAAP were allocated.

Use of deemed cost for operations subject to rate regulation. If an entity uses the exemption in paragraph D8B for operations subject to rate regulation, it shall disclose that fact and the basis on which carrying amounts were determined under previous GAAP.

Use of deemed cost after severe hyperinflation. If an entity elects to measure assets and liabilities at fair value and to use that fair value as the deemed costs in its opening IFRS statement of financial position because of severe hyperinflation (see paragraphs D26–D30), the entity's first IFRS financial statements shall disclose an explanation of how, and why, the entity had, and then ceased to have, a functional currency that has both of the following characteristics:

- (a) a reliable general price index is not available to all entities with transactions and balances in the currency.

- (b) exchangeability between the currency and a relatively stable foreign currency does not exist.

Interim Financial Reports

To comply with paragraph 23, if an entity presents an interim financial report under IAS 24, "Interim Financial Reporting," for part of the period covered by its first IFRS financial statements, the entity shall satisfy the following requirements in addition to the requirements of IAS 34:

(a) Each such interim financial report shall, if the entity presented an interim financial report for the comparable interim period of the immediately preceding financial year, include:

   (i) A reconciliation of its equity under previous GAAP at the end of that comparable interim period to its equity under IFRSs at that date; and

   (ii) A reconciliation to its total comprehensive income under IFRSs for that comparable interim period (current and year-to-date). The starting point for that reconciliation shall be total comprehensive income under previous GAAP for that period or, if an entity did not report such a total, profit or loss under previous GAAP.

(b) In addition to the reconciliations required by (a), an entity's first interim financial report under IAS 34 for part of the period covered by its first IFRS financial statements shall include the reconciliations described in paragraph 24 (supplemented by the details required by paragraphs 25 and 26) or a cross-reference to another published document that includes these reconciliations.

IAS 34 requires minimum disclosures, which are based on the assumption that users of the interim financial report also have access to the most recent annual financial statements. However, IAS 34 also requires an entity to disclose "any events or transactions that are material to an understanding of the current interim period." Therefore, if a first-time adopter did not, in its most recent annual financial statements under previous GAAP, disclose information material to an understanding of the current interim period, its interim financial report shall disclose that information or include a cross-reference to another published document that includes it.

OBSERVATION: The basic principle of IFRS 1 is simple and sensible; that is, that the first set of full IFRS financial statements should present information over the two (or more) years involved on a fully consistent basis. To do this in full would require some very complex calculations, sometimes based on information from many years earlier, and the IASB has granted a range of detailed exemptions. Unfortunately, the specification of these exemptions, designed to reduce complexity for preparers, has significantly increased the complexity of the Standard itself.

PART II
GENERAL STANDARDS

CHAPTER 6
ACCOUNTING POLICIES, CHANGES IN ACCOUNTING ESTIMATES, AND ERRORS

CONTENTS

OVERVIEW

The IASB seeks to enhance the relevance and reliability of an entity's financial statements and the comparability of those financial statements over time and with the financial statements of other entities. Disclosure requirements for accounting policies, except those for changes in accounting policies, are set out in IAS 1, "Presentation of Financial Statements," (see Chapter 4 of the same name).

IASB GAAP for this area are contained in IAS 8, issued in 2004 with the (rather ungainly) title of this chapter, and effective for annual periods beginning on or after January 1, 2005, with earlier application being encouraged. The history of IAS 8 is long and complicated. It has been revised several times, and the new version contained significant changes from the previous one, discussed in our 2004 edition under its then (even more ungainly) title, "Net Profit or Loss for the Period, Fundamental Errors, and Changes in Accounting Policies."

Note that first-time adoption of IASB GAAP, by changing from an alternative GAAP system, has its own standard, dealt with in Chapter 5.

BACKGROUND

As stated in the overview, the overall purpose of IAS 8 is to enhance the relevance, reliability, and perhaps especially the comparability of published financial statements. As part of its general "improvements project," the IASB set out in revising IAS 8 to reduce the optionality inherent in the older version and generally to clarify its requirements and to increase their precision. The presentation requirements relating to income statements have been transferred *to* IAS 1 (see Chapter 4) and the requirements for the selection and application of accounting policies have been transferred *from* IAS 1. Major changes of requirements compared with the previous version of IAS 8 are to:

- Remove the allowed alternative to retrospective application of voluntary changes in accounting policies and retrospective restatement to correct prior period errors.
- Eliminate the concept of a fundamental error.
- Articulate the hierarchy of guidance to which management refers when selecting accounting policies in the absence of standards and interpretations that specifically apply.
- Define material omissions or misstatements, and describe how to apply the concept of materiality when applying accounting policies and correcting errors.

Rather more quietly, the concept of extraordinary items has disappeared from IASB GAAP. This term no longer appears in the IASB Glossary.

In general, the changes will increase consistency between IAS, U.K. and U.S. requirements, although the concept of extraordinary items may still be found in the U.S., and indeed elsewhere.

SCOPE AND DEFINITIONS

IAS 8 is to be applied in selecting and applying accounting policies and in accounting for changes in accounting policies, changes in accounting estimates, and correction of prior-period errors. The tax effects of corrections of prior-period errors and of retrospective adjustments made to apply changes in accounting policies are accounted for and disclosed in accordance with IAS 12, "Income Taxes," (see Chapter 21 of the same name).

IAS 8 gives several carefully crafted definitions, which are reproduced below and commented on as necessary.

1. *Accounting policies* are the specific principles, bases, conventions, rules, and practices applied by an entity in preparing and presenting financial statements.

2. *Prior-period errors* are omissions from, and misstatements in, the entity's financial statements for one or more prior periods arising from a failure to use, or a misuse of, reliable information that:

   (a) Was available when financial statements for those periods were authorized for issue, and

   (b) Could reasonably be expected to have been obtained and taken into account in the preparation and presentation of those financial statements.

   Such errors include the effects of mathematical mistakes, mistakes in applying accounting policies, oversights or misinterpretations of facts, and fraud.

3. A *change in accounting estimate* is an adjustment of the carrying amount of an asset or a liability, or the amount of the periodic consumption of an asset, that results from the assessment of the present status of, and

expected future benefits and obligations associated with, assets and liabilities. Changes in accounting estimates result from new information or new developments and, accordingly, are not corrections of errors.

4. *International Financial Reporting Standards (IFRSs)* are standards and interpretations adopted by the International Accounting Standards Board (IASB). They comprise:

   (a) International Financial Reporting Standards,

   (b) International Accounting Standards, and

   (c) Interpretations originated by the International Financial Reporting Interpretations Committee (IFRIC) or the former Standing Interpretations Committee (SIC).

5. *Material.* Omissions or misstatements of items are material if they could individually or collectively influence the economic decisions users make on the basis of the financial statements. Materiality depends on the size and nature of the omission or misstatement judged in the surrounding circumstances. The size or nature of the item, or a combination of both, could be the determining factor.

6. *Prospective application* of a change in accounting policy and of recognizing the effect of a change in an accounting estimate, respectively, are:

   (a) Applying the new accounting policy to transactions, other events, and conditions occurring after the date at which the policy is changed; and

   (b) Recognizing the effect of the change in the accounting estimate in the current and future periods affected by the change.

7. *Retrospective application* is applying a new accounting policy to transactions, other events, and conditions as if that policy had always been applied.

8. *Retrospective restatement* is correcting the recognition, measurement, and disclosure of amounts of elements of financial statement elements as if a prior-period error had never occurred.

9. *Impracticable.* Applying a requirement is impracticable when the entity cannot apply it after making every reasonable effort to do so. For a particular prior period, it is impracticable to apply a change in an accounting policy retrospectively or to make a retrospective restatement to correct an error if:

   (a) The effects of the retrospective application or retrospective restatement are not determinable;

   (b) The retrospective application or retrospective restatement requires assumptions about what management's intent would have been in that period; or

   (c) The retrospective application or retrospective restatement requires significant estimates of amounts and it is impossible to objectively distinguish information about those estimates that:

(i) Provides evidence of circumstances that existed on the date(s) at which those amounts are to be recognized, measured or disclosed; and

(ii) Would have been available when the financial statements for that prior period were authorized for issue from other information.

It is perhaps not helpful that IAS 8 defines accounting policies, but *changes in* accounting estimates. Note that prior-period errors may result from "mistakes in applying accounting policies," which is not the same as applying an unacceptable accounting policy. Note particularly, that estimates needing to be subsequently changed because of new information or new developments neither were nor are errors. The convoluted definition of *impracticable* is an attempt to recognize the practical difficulties that may arise in the real world but at the same time to minimize avoidance of the letter and the spirit of the standard.

ACCOUNTING POLICIES

Having defined its scope and terms, IAS 8 divides its coverage of the three topics suggested by its title into separate sections, giving a somewhat episodic appearance. For convenience and clarity, that structure is followed below.

Selection and Application of Accounting Policies

Most of what IAS 8 says in this respect is both sensible and rather obvious. When a standard or an interpretation specifically applies to a situation, the accounting policy or policies applied are to be determined by applying the standard or interpretation and considering any relevant Implementation Guidance (i.e., guidance defined as an integral part of the standard) issued by the IASB for the standard or interpretation. IFRSs set out accounting policies that the IASB has concluded result in financial statements containing relevant and reliable information about the transactions, other events, and conditions to which they apply. Those policies need not be applied when the effect of applying them is immaterial. However, it is inappropriate to make, or leave uncorrected, immaterial departures from IFRSs to achieve a particular presentation of an entity's financial position, financial performance, or cash flows.

> **OBSERVATION:** First of all, it is explicit that Implementation Guidance needs to be *considered*, but it does not need to be *applied*, and it does not contain requirements. Second, the comments about materiality, given also the definition as above, seem designed to confuse. If an "uncorrected departure" would "achieve a particular presentation," how can it be immaterial?

In the absence of a relevant international standard or interpretation, we have essentially to fall back to general principles, as discussed in Chapter 2, "The Conceptual Framework for Financial Reporting." IAS 8 requires management (par. 10) to use its judgment in developing and applying an accounting policy that results in information that is relevant to the economic decision-making needs of users and is reliable in that the financial statements:

- Represent faithfully the financial position, financial performance and cash flows of the entity.
- Reflect the economic substance of transactions, other events and conditions, and not merely the legal form.
- Are neutral, that is, free from bias.
- Are prudent.
- Are complete in all material respects.

No indication is given of how the inevitable tension between relevance and reliability is to be addressed. However, the standard continues, in words that clearly have been carefully crafted after much heart-searching, to state that in making the judgment described in paragraph 10, management shall refer to, and consider the applicability of, the following sources in descending order:

1. The requirements in standards and interpretations dealing with similar and related issues; and

2. The definitions, recognition criteria, and measurement concepts for assets, liabilities, income, and expenses in the Framework.

In making this judgment, management may also consider the most recent pronouncements of other standard-setting bodies that use a similar conceptual framework to develop accounting standards, other accounting literature, and accepted industry practices, to the extent that these do not conflict with the sources specified above. Note the limitations and qualifications included in the previous sentence.

Changes in Accounting Policies

In general, of course, consistency of accounting policy is required. A change in accounting policy is permitted only if the change either is required by a standard or an interpretation or if it results in the financial statements providing *reliable and more relevant* information about the effects of transactions, other events, or conditions on the entity's financial position, financial performance, or cash flows. This wording indicates that a change that would lead to more reliability without more relevance is not permitted. Neither of the following are changes in accounting policy: (1) the application of an accounting policy for transactions, other events, or conditions that differ in substance from those previously occurring, nor (2) the application of a new accounting policy for transactions, other events, or conditions that did not occur previously or were immaterial. However, the initial application of a policy to revalue assets in accordance with IAS 16, "Property, Plant, and Equipment," or IAS 38, "Intangible Assets," is a change in an accounting policy to be dealt with as a revaluation in accordance with IAS 16 or IAS 38, rather than in accordance with IAS 8.

IAS 8 makes accounting for a change in accounting policy extremely difficult (pars. 19-27). When the change in policy arises from the initial application, including voluntary early adoption, of a standard or interpretation, specific transitional requirements of that document are followed, if there are any. In all other circumstances, subject to the impracticability provision discussed below, an entity applies the change retrospectively. This means that the entity adjusts the opening balance of each affected component of equity for the earliest prior period presented and the other comparative amounts disclosed for each prior period presented as if the new accounting policy had always been applied. However, when it is impracticable, as defined and discussed earlier, to determine the period-specific effects of changing an accounting policy on comparative information for one or more prior periods presented, the entity must apply the new accounting policy to the carrying amounts of assets and liabilities as at the beginning of the earliest period for which retrospective application is practicable (which may be the current period), and make a corresponding adjustment to the opening balance of each affected component of equity for that period.

It may, of course, be impracticable to determine the cumulative effect of applying the new policy, even as at the beginning of the current period. In this, relatively rare, situation, the entity applies the new policy *prospectively* from the start of the earliest period practicable. It therefore disregards the portion of the cumulative adjustment to assets, liabilities, and equity arising before that date. Changing an accounting policy is permitted even if it is impracticable to apply the policy prospectively for any prior period. Paragraphs 50–53 provide guidance on when it is impracticable to apply a new accounting policy to one or more prior periods. Hindsight, in the sense of becoming aware of circumstances that could not have been foreseen at the time of the original preparation of financial statements for prior periods, should not be used to change presented amounts.

Disclosure

The disclosure requirements relating to changes in accounting policies are, unfortunately, both lengthy and precise. When initial application of a standard or an interpretation has an effect on the current period or any prior period, would have such an effect except that it is impracticable to determine the amount of the adjustment, or might have an effect on future periods, an entity shall disclose:

- The title of the IFRS.
- When applicable, that the change in accounting policy is made in accordance with its transitional provisions.
- The nature of the change in accounting policy.
- When applicable, a description of the transitional provisions.
- When applicable, the transitional provisions that might have an effect on future periods.
- For the current period and each prior period presented, to the extent practicable (a) the amount of the adjustment for each financial statement line item affected and (b) if IAS 33, "Earnings per Share," applies to the entity, for basic and diluted earnings per share.
- The amount of the adjustment relating to periods before those presented, to the extent practicable.
- If retrospective application is impracticable for a particular prior period, or for periods before those presented, the circumstances that led to the existence of that condition and a description of how and from when the change in accounting policy has been applied.

Financial statements of subsequent periods need not repeat these disclosures.

When a *voluntary* change in accounting policy has an effect on the current period or any prior period, would have an effect on that period except that it is impracticable to determine the amount of the adjustment, or might have an effect on future periods, an entity shall disclose:

- The nature of the change in accounting policy.
- The reasons why applying the new accounting policy provides reliable and more relevant information.
- For the current period and each prior period presented, to the extent practicable (a) the amount of the adjustment for each financial statement line item affected and (b) if IAS 33 applies to the entity, for basic and diluted earnings per share.
- The amount of the adjustment relating to periods before those presented, to the extent practicable.
- If retrospective application is impracticable for a particular prior period, or for periods before those presented, the circumstances that led to the existence of that condition and a description of how and from when the change in accounting policy has been applied.

Financial statements of subsequent periods need not repeat these disclosures.

When an entity has not applied a new standard or interpretation that has been issued but is not yet effective, the entity must disclose this fact and known or reasonably estimable information relevant to assessing the possible impact that application of the new standard or interpretation will have on the entity's financial statements in the period of initial application.

CHANGES IN ACCOUNTING ESTIMATES

As already discussed, changes in accounting estimates are inherent in the day-to-day subjectivity of the business world and must be distinguished from both errors and changes in accounting policy. A change in the measurement basis applied is a change in an accounting policy, and is not a change in an accounting estimate. When it is difficult to distinguish a change in an accounting policy from a change in an accounting estimate, the change is treated as a change in an accounting estimate.

The effect of a change in an accounting estimate should be recognized prospectively by including it in profit or loss in (1) the period of the change, if the change affects that period only or (2) the period of the change and future periods, if the change affects both.

To the extent that a change in an accounting estimate gives rise to changes in assets and liabilities or relates to an item of equity, it should be recognized by adjusting the carrying amount of the related asset, liability, or equity item in the period of the change.

Prospective recognition of the effect of a change in an accounting estimate means that the change is applied to transactions, other events, and conditions from the date of the change in estimate. For example, a change in the estimate of the amount of bad debts affects only the current period's profit or loss and therefore is recognized in the current period. However, a change in the estimated useful life of a depreciable asset affects depreciation expense for the current period and for each future period during the asset's remaining useful life.

Disclosure

IAS 8 requires (pars. 39 and 40) that an entity disclose the nature and amount of a change in an accounting estimate that has an effect in the current period or is expected to have an effect in future periods, except for the disclosure of the effect on future periods when it is impracticable to estimate that effect. If the amount of the effect in future periods is not disclosed because estimating it is impracticable, the entity shall disclose that fact.

OBSERVATION: It may seem strange that there is no mention of materiality in any of the paragraphs of IAS 8 relating to changes in accounting estimates. The disclosure requirement above simply refers to "an effect"! However, the newly revised IAS 1 (in par. 31, see Chapter 4) contains an explicit general statement that IASB GAAP disclosure requirements do not apply to immaterial items. IAS 1 defines materiality identically to IAS 8.

ERRORS

The requirements for the correction of errors (which must be prior-period errors, as defined earlier, as current-period errors would be corrected before the finalization of the financial statements for the period) follow logically and consistently from the earlier parts of IAS 8. The general rule is that an entity should correct material prior-period errors retrospectively in the first set of financial statements authorized for issue after their discovery by:

- Restating the comparative amounts for the prior periods presented in which the error occurred; or

- If the error occurred before the earliest prior period presented, restating the opening balances of assets, liabilities, and equity for the earliest prior period presented.

When it is impracticable to determine the period-specific effects of an error on comparative information for one or more prior periods presented, the entity must restate the opening balances of assets, liabilities and equity for the earliest period for which *retrospective* restatement is practicable (which may be the current period). If it is impracticable to determine the cumulative effect, at the beginning of the current period, of an error on all prior periods, the entity shall restate the comparative information to correct the error *prospectively* from the earliest date practicable. It therefore disregards the portion of the cumulative restatement of assets, liabilities, and equity relating to before that date.

Disclosure of Prior-Period Errors

An entity is required to disclose:

- The nature of a prior-period error.
- For each prior period presented, to the extent practicable, the amount of the correction (a) for each financial statement line item affected and (b) if IAS 33 applies to the entity, for basic and diluted earnings per share.
- The amount of the correction at the beginning of the earliest prior period presented.
- If retrospective restatement is impracticable for a particular prior period, the circumstances that lead to the existence of that condition and a description of how and from when the error has been corrected.

Financial statements of subsequent periods need not repeat these disclosures.

CHAPTER 7
BORROWING COSTS

CONTENTS

OVERVIEW

The accounting treatment of borrowing costs raises two types of issues: (1) the issue of definition, that is, what should be included in borrowing costs; and (2) the issue of recognition, that is, whether borrowing costs should be recognized as part of the expenses of the period or as part of the cost of an asset (capitalization). The former issue is obviously of much less importance if no borrowing costs are to be capitalized.

IASB GAAP take the view that borrowing costs incurred as part of the cost of a "qualifying asset" (i.e., an asset that necessarily takes a substantial period of time to prepare for its intended use or sale) should be capitalized as part of the cost of that asset. A broad view is taken of borrowing costs and includes items such as amortization of discounts, premiums, and ancillary costs incurred in connection with the arrangements of borrowings; finance charges with respect to finance leases; and exchange differences on foreign borrowings that are regarded as adjustments to interest costs. However, it should be noted that the focus on *borrowing costs* excludes any imputed costs of equity.

The "costs attach" principle is an intrinsic feature of the accrual accounting model (see "Cost of Inventory" in Chapter 24). It is, therefore, logical that this principle be applied to borrowing costs in the case of "qualifying assets." However, unless this principle is also applied to the imputed cost of equity, capitalization of financing charges will result in different carrying values of otherwise identical qualifying assets of two entities that have different capital structures; other things being equal, the qualifying assets of the entity with the higher level of debt will have higher carrying values. This may not seem entirely logical, and, as it affects a number of financial ratios, certainly does not facilitate financial comparisons.

BACKGROUND

IASB GAAP on the treatment of borrowing costs are set out in IAS 23, "Borrowing Costs." The above point in the "Overview" helps to explain the number of changes that have occurred to IASB GAAP on this subject over the years. The original 1984 version of the standard permitted a free choice between systematically expensing borrowing costs and capitalizing them when certain conditions were met. In its comparability project in the early 1990s, the IASC proposed in E32 that a "benchmark" treatment should be for borrowing costs to be expensed, with capitalization as an alternative treatment when certain conditions were met. The responses to E32 were divided on this issue; however, the IASC then issued E39, according to which capitalization would be required if certain conditions were met, and expensing would be required otherwise. This position is similar to that in U.S. GAAP (ASC 835). Again, responses to E39 were mixed. In particular, there is the argument that capital structure would lead to different carrying values of "qualifying assets." Hence, IAS 23 "Capitalization of Borrowing Costs," issued in 1994, restored the choice between expensing and capitalization subject to certain conditions being met, but expensing became the "benchmark treatment" and capitalization the "alternative treatment."

In March 2007, as part of the program of convergence between IASB GAAP and U.S. GAAP, a revised IAS 23, "Borrowing Costs," was issued, which reverted to the position proposed in ED 39. In fact, IASB GAAP on "Borrowing Costs" now align in this respect with U.S. GAAP (see ASC 835), with the result that capitalization is required if certain conditions are met and expensing is required otherwise.

CORE PRINCIPLE AND SCOPE

The "core principle" of the revised IAS 23 is that borrowing costs that are directly attributable to the acquisition, construction, or production of a qualifying asset form part of the cost of that asset (i.e., are capitalized). Other borrowing costs are recognized as an expense (IAS 23, par.1).

IAS 23 is to be applied in accounting for borrowing costs. It does not deal with the actual or imputed cost of equity, including that of preferred capital not classified as a liability. Borrowing costs are not required to be capitalized in the case of qualifying assets that are (1) measured at fair value (e.g., biological assets) or (2) inventories manufactured or otherwise produced in large quantities on a repetitive basis (IAS 23, pars. 2–4).

OBSERVATION: The exclusion of (1) qualifying assets measured at fair value, such as biological assets, from the scope of IAS 23, is logical in that, as such assets are not measured on the basis of cost, the cost of borrowings is irrelevant to their measurement. The exclusion of (2) inventories manufactured or otherwise produced in large quantities on a repetitive basis is based on pragmatic reasons.

DEFINITIONS

Borrowing costs are interest and other costs that an entity incurs in connection with the borrowing of funds, and may include:

1. Interest expense calculated using the effective interest rate method, as described in IAS 39, "Financial Instruments: Recognition and Measurement" (see Chapter 17).

2. Finance charges with respect to finance leases recognized in accordance with IAS 17, "Leases" (see Chapter 26).

3. Exchange differences arising from foreign currency borrowings to the extent that they are regarded as an adjustment to interest costs.

For more information on this definition, see "Borrowing Costs Eligible for Capitalization."

→ **PRACTICE POINTER:** Item 3 above, "exchange differences arising from foreign currency borrowings," may cause difficulties since the wording of IAS 23 leaves it open to the entity to determine the extent to which the exchange differences are "regarded as an adjustment to interest costs," and opinions on this matter may differ.

In principle, any exchange loss or gain on foreign currency borrowings is a component (positive or negative) of the cost of those borrowings. The only issues here would appear to concern (1) the recognition of unrealized exchange losses or gains on borrowings, and (2) the treatment of unrealized but hedged exchange losses or gains.

Regarding (1), paragraph 28 of IAS 21, "The Effects of Changes in Foreign Exchange Rates" (see Chapter 18), makes it clear that foreign exchange differences arising on reporting an entity's monetary items (excluding net investments in foreign entities) at rates different from those at which they were initially recorded or reported in previous financial statements, should be recognized as income or expense in the period in which they arise. Because they are to be recognized as income or expense, it would seem logical to recognize them as part of borrowing costs.

Regarding (2), IAS 21 is silent. However, as indicated by IAS 39, "Financial Instruments: Recognition and Measurement," pars. 89 and 95 (see Chapter 17), exchange gains and losses are to be recognized in profit or loss (i.e., as income or expense) only to the extent that they are not hedged or that the hedge is ineffective.

Qualifying assets are assets that necessarily take a substantial period of time to prepare for their intended use or sale, and depending on the circumstances may include:

- Certain inventories (e.g., construction work-in-process).
- Manufacturing plants.
- Power generation facilities.
- Intangible assets (e.g., patents).
- Investment properties.

Qualifying assets do not include:

- Financial assets.

- Inventories that are manufactured or otherwise produced over a short period of time.

- Assets that are ready for their intended use or sale when they are acquired.

(IAS 23, pars. 5–7)

RECOGNITION

Borrowing costs that are directly attributable to the acquisition, construction, or production of a qualifying asset are to be capitalized as part of the cost of that asset. Other borrowing costs are to be recognized as an expense of the period in which they are incurred. Borrowing costs are capitalized by an entity as part of the cost of a qualifying asset when it is *probable that they will result in future economic benefits* to the entity and the costs can be measured reliably.

OBSERVATION: The requirement to capitalize borrowing costs reflects the principle that all costs necessary to bring an asset to the condition and location of its intended use "attach" to that asset. However, this may result in a lack of comparability among reporting entities, depending on whether they use cash, equity, or debt to finance the acquisition of "qualifying assets," since the use of debt normally results in a qualifying asset having a higher total cost and hence a higher carrying amount than would have been the case had debt not been used. It is also difficult to see how the use of debt to finance the acquisition of an asset, leading to the capitalization of interest and other borrowing costs, can result in *greater future economic benefits* to the entity from the asset than would have been obtained had equity or cash been used, since borrowing costs do not add to the *utility* of the asset.

When an entity applies IAS 29, "Financial Reporting in Hyperinflationary Economies" (see Chapter 10), it should recognize as an expense that part of the borrowing costs that compensates for inflation during the same period; i.e., the entity should capitalize only the "real" or deflated interest cost.

BORROWING COSTS ELIGIBLE FOR CAPITALIZATION

Borrowing costs that are directly attributable to the acquisition, construction, or production of a qualifying asset are those borrowing costs that would have been avoided if the expenditure on the qualifying asset had not been made.

When funds are borrowed specifically for the purpose of obtaining a particular qualifying asset, it is clear that these funds are easily identified as directly attributable borrowing costs. If such borrowings are temporarily invested before being expended for the purpose of obtaining the asset, it is likewise clear that any investment income earned is to be deducted from the cost of the borrowings.

In other circumstances, identifying a direct relationship between particular borrowings and a qualifying asset, and determining the borrowings that would otherwise have been avoided, may be difficult, and judgment may have to be exercised. To the extent that funds that have been borrowed for general purposes are used for obtaining a qualifying asset, the amount of borrowing costs that are eligible for capitalization should be determined by applying a capitalization rate to the expenditures on that asset. This capitalization rate is calculated as the weighted average of the borrowing costs applicable to the borrowings that are outstanding during the period excluding any borrowings made specifically for the purpose of obtaining the particular qualifying asset or any other qualifying asset. The amount of borrowing costs capitalized by an entity during a period must not exceed the total amount of borrowing costs that it incurred during that period (IAS 23, pars. 10–15).

→ **PRACTICE POINTER:** Borrowing costs that are capitalizable with respect to a particular qualifying asset should be identified, first, as those of any borrowings made specifically for the purpose of obtaining that asset, less any investment income from the temporary investment of such funds. If there were no specific borrowings, or these account for less than all of the expenditures on the asset, then "general borrowings" should be applied to the balance of expenditures on the asset, and their cost (the capitalization rate) should be calculated on a weighted average basis, as indicated above. Note that "borrowings that are outstanding during the period" may include existing debt secured on property assets. Thus, unless it is already being capitalized in connection with some qualifying asset, the cost of such borrowings should be taken into account in the calculation despite the fact that they were originally made to finance the acquisition of a different asset.

In some circumstances (such as when a group of companies manages borrowings centrally), it may be appropriate to use an overall group capitalization rate. In other circumstances (such as when an entity within a group has substantial financial autonomy), the entity's capitalization rate should be based on its own borrowings.

EXCESS OF THE CARRYING AMOUNT OF THE QUALIFYING ASSET OVER ITS RECOVERABLE AMOUNT

If the effect of capitalizing borrowing costs is that the carrying amount of a qualifying asset exceeds its recoverable amount or net realizable value, other standards may require that the carrying amount be written down to the recoverable amount or net realizable value. In certain circumstances (e.g., if the recoverable amount subsequently increases), those other standards may subsequently require that such write-downs be reversed, partly or totally (IAS 23, par. 16).

COMMENCEMENT, SUSPENSION, AND CESSATION OF CAPITALIZATION

The commencement date for capitalization is that date on which the entity first meets all of the following three conditions:

1. Expenditures on the qualifying assets are being incurred.
2. Borrowing costs are being incurred.

3. Activities that are necessary to prepare the asset for its intended use or sale are in progress.

Expenditures on the qualifying asset should include only those that have resulted in payments of cash, transfers of other assets, or the assumption of interest-bearing liabilities. They are reduced by any progress payments received (for work-in-process) and grants received in connection with the asset. For the application of the capitalization rate, a reasonable approximation of the balance of expenditures to which it should be applied for a period is given by the average carrying amount of the asset during that period including all borrowing costs capitalized in prior periods.

Activities necessary to prepare the asset for its intended use or sale include technical and administrative work prior to the start of physical construction. However, the mere holding of the asset in the absence of such work does not count as an activity, and borrowing costs incurred during such a period of inactivity (e.g., when land acquired for building purposes is held without any associated development activity) do not qualify for capitalization (IAS 23, pars. 17–19).

Moreover, capitalization of borrowing costs is suspended during extended periods in which active development of a qualifying asset is discontinued and no substantial technical or administrative work is carried out, except in the case of a temporary delay that is a necessary part of the process of preparing the asset for its intended use or sale (e.g., suspension of the building of a bridge during an extended period of high water levels) (IAS 23, pars. 20–21).

Capitalization of borrowing costs should cease when substantially all of the activities necessary to prepare the qualifying asset for its intended use or sale are complete. When a qualifying asset is completed in parts, and each part is capable of being sold or used while work continues on the others (e.g., in the case of a business park comprising several buildings), the capitalization of borrowing costs on a substantially completed part should cease.

An asset is normally considered as "ready for its intended use or sale" when its physical construction is complete, even though (1) some routine administrative work may still continue, or (2) minor modifications, such as the decoration of the property to the purchaser's or user's specification, may still be outstanding (IAS 23, pars. 22–25).

OBSERVATION: The stipulation that, once an asset's physical construction is complete, capitalization should cease even if routine administrative work or minor modifications continue, means that an entity cannot intentionally leave the work on an asset slightly unfinished in order to continue the capitalization of borrowing costs until such time as it is sold, leased, or otherwise put to use.

DISCLOSURE

An entity should disclose in the notes to its financial statements:

- The amount of borrowings capitalized during the period.

- The capitalization rate used to determine the amount of borrowing costs eligible for capitalization. (IAS 23, par. 26).

OBSERVATION: IAS 23, par. 26, refers to "rate" in the singular, but in practice more than one rate may be used if (1) subsidiaries are financially autonomous and have different capitalization rates or (2) one qualifying asset is funded by specific borrowings, while another is funded either by different specific borrowings or by "general borrowings."

TRANSITIONAL PROVISIONS AND EFFECTIVE DATE

When the application of IAS 23 (revised) constituted a change of accounting policy (i.e., notably when an entity previously expensed all borrowing costs, which was the "benchmark" treatment under the old version of IAS 23), the entity was required to apply the revised IAS 23 to borrowing costs relating to qualifying assets for which the commencement date for capitalization is on or after the effective date, namely for accounting periods beginning on or after January 1, 2009.

However, earlier application was permitted, and an entity might designate any date prior to January 1, 2009, and apply the revised IAS 23 to borrowing costs relating to all qualifying assets for which the commencement date for capitalization was on or after that date. Such earlier application must be disclosed.

CHAPTER 8
BUSINESS COMBINATIONS

CONTENTS

OVERVIEW

IASB GAAP on business combinations are set out in IFRS 3, "Business Combinations" (which replaced IAS 22 with effect from March 31, 2004), with reference also to the revised (May 2008) versions of IAS 36, "Impairment of Assets," and IAS 38, "Intangible Assets." IFRS 3 was revised in 2008, as described below. IFRS 3 as revised in 2008 requires that:

1. All business combinations within its scope are to be accounted for using the "acquisition" method.

2. An acquirer is to be identified for every such business combination; the acquirer is the combining entity that obtains control of the other combining businesses, identified as such following the guidance in IAS 27, "Consolidated and Separate Financial Statements" (see Chapter 11).

3. An acquirer is to measure the cost of a business combination as the aggregate of (a) the fair values, at the date of exchange, of assets given, liabilities incurred or assumed, and equity instruments issued by the acquirer in exchange for control of the acquiree and (b) any costs directly attributable to the combination.

4. At the acquisition date, an acquirer is to recognize separately from goodwill, the identifiable assets, acquired liabilities assumed, and contingent liabilities of the acquiree, and any non-controlling interest in the acquiree that satisfy the recognition criteria at that date, regardless of whether they had been previously recognized in the acquiree's financial statements, subject to a number of recognition conditions.

5. The identifiable assets, liabilities, and contingent liabilities that meet the recognition conditions are measured initially by the acquirer at their fair values at the acquisition date, except that any non-controlling interest may be measured at the non-controlling interest's share of the acquiree's identifiable net assets.

6. Goodwill acquired in a business combination is to be recognized by the acquirer at the acquisition date, as the excess of (a) over (b) below:

    (a) The aggregate of:

    (i) The consideration transferred measured in accordance with IFRS 3 (i.e., normally at fair value).

    (ii) The amount of any non-controlling interest in the acquiree measured in accordance with IFRS 3.

    (iii) In a business combination achieved in stages, the acquisition-date fair value of the acquirer's previously held equity interest in the acquiree.

(b) The net of the acquisition-date amounts of the identifiable assets acquired and the liabilities assumed measured in accordance with IFRS 3.

7. Goodwill acquired in a business combination is *not to be amortized,* but instead is to be subjected to *impairment tests* (in accordance with IAS 36) annually or more frequently if events or changes in circumstances indicate the possibility of impairment.

8. If the acquirer's interest in the net fair value of the items recognized and measured in accordance with the IFRS 3 recognition and measurement criteria *exceeds* the cost of the combination, the acquirer must *reassess* the identification and measurement of the acquiree's identifiable assets, liabilities, and contingent liabilities and the measurement of the cost of the business combination. Any excess remaining after that reassessment must be recognized by the acquirer immediately in profit or loss as a gain on a "bargain purchase" (i.e., no "negative goodwill" is allowed).

9. In phased or "step" acquisitions, assets acquired and liabilities assumed in previous phases are to be remeasured at their fair values at the acquisition date of the latest phase.

10. Information must be disclosed that enables users of an entity's financial statements to evaluate:

   (a) The nature and financial effect of:

      (i) Business combinations that were affected during the period.

      (ii) Business combinations that were affected after the balance sheet date but before the issuance of the financial statements is authorized.

      (iii) Some business combinations that were affected in previous periods.

   (b) Changes in the carrying amount of goodwill during the period covered by the statements.

OBSERVATION: The revision of IFRS 3 included two terminological changes: (1) the "purchase method" is changed back to the "acquisition method" as in IAS 22, in recognition of the fact that not every "acquisition" is a "purchase"; (2) the term "non-controlling interest" is substituted for "minority interest" in recognition of the fact that a parent may control a subsidiary without holding a majority of its equity.

The main changes from the previous (2003) version of IFRS 3 are:

- The inclusion within the scope of IFRS 3 of business combinations of mutual entities and combinations achieved by contract alone.

- The measurement of non-controlling interests at the acquisition date, which are now to be measured at the fair value of the non-controlling interest, with an alternative measurement method based on the non-controlling interest's proportionate share of the fair value of the identifiable (i.e., excluding goodwill) net assets of the acquiree.

- The treatment of previously acquired interests in a phased or "step" acquisition, which are now to be remeasured at their fair value at the latest acquisition date.

There have also been a number of changes to the disclosure requirements. However, IFRS 3 has been comprehensively restructured and rewritten, so that the 2008 revised version is effectively a new document.

BACKGROUND

The IASB issued a new IFRS in 2003, rather than amending IAS 22, for two main reasons. First, the new IFRS 3 represented the first phase in a multiphase project on business combinations. Issues left to be dealt with in subsequent phases include applying the acquisition method in various problematic situations (to be worked on jointly with the FASB), joint ventures and combinations involving entities under common control, and possible applications for "Fresh start" accounting. Second, IFRS 3 differed from IAS 22 in several important respects, which are discussed below, and it was therefore a new standard.

In 2008, revisions were made to IFRS 3 as the result of Phase 2 of the business combinations project carried out in cooperation with the FASB, in connection with which the two Boards issued a joint exposure draft in 2005. These revisions included the inclusion within the scope of IFRS 3 of business combinations of mutual entities and combinations achieved by contract alone, excluded from the original version of the standard.

The rejection in IFRS 3 of systematic amortization of acquired goodwill as required by IAS 22 is controversial, for two reasons: (1) reliance on annual impairment tests is cumbersome and does not necessarily produce information of higher quality than the IAS 22 approach (systematic amortization backed up by impairment tests, with a rebuttable presumption that the useful life could not exceed 20 years); (2) the reliance on impairment tests allows acquired goodwill to be gradually replaced by internally generated goodwill so that the distinction between the two is progressively lost. As against these points, it may be stated that the financial analyst community does not consider systematic goodwill amortization to be an expense.

The exemption of intangibles such as in-process research and development acquired in a business combination from the asset recognition criteria in the Framework is also controversial. The differences between IASB GAAP as represented by IFRS 3 and U.S. GAAP (ASC 805, "Business Combinations," and ASC 350, "Intangibles—Goodwill and Other") have been substantially reduced by the Phase 2 revisions made to both sets of standards. A number of differences remain (see IFRS 3 IE Appendix), mostly fairly minor concerning recognition and measurement, except for one difference with regard to *measuring non-controlling interests*. Under IFRS 3 as revised, a non-controlling interest is measured either at its fair value at the acquisition date or at its proportionate share of the fair values of the acquiree's net assets. In U.S. GAAP as revised, only the former method is permitted. There also are a number of remaining differences in the disclosure requirements.

SCOPE AND DEFINITIONS

IFRS 3 is to be applied to all transactions or other events that meet the IFRS 3 definition of a business combination. It does not apply to (par. 2):

- The formation of a *joint venture*.

- The acquisition of an asset or group of assets that does not constitute a *business*, in which case the acquirer identifies and recognizes the individual identifiable assets acquired (including those meeting the definition and recognition criteria for intangible assets in IAS 38, "Intangible Assets") (see Chapter 22).

- A combination of entities or businesses *under common control* (i.e., in which all of the combining entities or businesses are *ultimately controlled by the same party or parties* both before and after the combination, and that control is not transitory (IFRS 3, pars. B1–B4).

In the case of joint ventures, which are the subject of IAS 31, "Interests in Joint Ventures" (see Chapter 11), the Board decided to leave to a later phase the issue of how a joint venture should be accounted for upon its formation. However, to reduce the risk of "accounting arbitrage" by reporting entities seeking to avoid the purchase method, the Board tightened up the definition of a joint venture by amending IAS 31. In May 2011, the IASB issued IFRS 13, "Joint Arrangements," which supersedes IAS 31 for annual reporting periods beginning on or after January 1, 2013 (see Chapter 11).

Definition of a Business and Identifying a Business Combination

A business combination, for the purpose of IFRS 3, is a transaction or other event in which an *acquirer* obtains *control* of one or more *businesses*. The word "business" is defined in IFRS 3 (Appendix A) as:

> An integrated set of activities and assets that is capable of being conducted and managed for the purpose of providing a return in the form of dividends, lower costs or other economic benefits directly to investors or other owners, members, or participants.

A business generally consists of inputs, processes applied to those inputs, and resulting outputs that are, or will be, used to generate revenues. An integrated set of activities and assets in the development stage might not yet have outputs, but if it is not in order to be recognized as a business, it should be pursuing a plan to produce them as well as meeting other related criteria. If goodwill is present in a transferred set of activities and assets, the transferred set shall be presumed to be a business; however, a business need not have goodwill (pars. B7–B10).

A business combination may be structured in a variety of ways for legal, tax, or other reasons, which include but are not limited to the following (par. B6):

- One or more businesses become subsidiaries of an acquirer or the net assets of one or more businesses are legally merged into the acquirer.
- One combining entity transfers its net assets, or its owners transfer their equity interests, to another combining entity or its owners.
- All of the combining entities transfer their net assets, or their owners transfer their equity interests, to a newly formed entity.
- A group of former owners of one of the combining entities obtains control of the combined entity.

OBSERVATION: The reasons given in the previous version of IFRS 3 have been rewritten to avoid references to "purchasing," in recognition in the revised IFRS 3 of the fact that the transactions or other events that give rise to a business combination do not necessarily include a purchase transaction. The revised IFRS 3, unlike its predecessor, includes within its scope (a) combinations of mutual entities and (b) those in which separate entities are brought together by contract alone.

METHOD OF ACCOUNTING: APPLICATION OF THE ACQUISITION METHOD

IFRS 3, paragraphs 4–58, describes the acquisition method and explains how it is to be applied to *all* business combinations falling within the scope of the standard.

Under the acquisition method, a business combination is considered from the perspective of the entity that is identified as the *acquirer*, which *acquires* net assets and recognizes the assets acquired and liabilities and contingent liabilities assumed, *including those not previously recognized by the acquiree*. The measurement of the acquirer's assets and liabilities is not affected by the transaction, nor are any additional assets or liabilities of the acquirer recognized as a result.

OBSERVATION: The logic of the acquisition method is that values are determined when (in Adam Smith's words) "goods change masters"; in this case, it is the acquiree's net assets that change masters, whereas those of the acquirer do not. This is logical in a context of strict historical cost measurement. However, now that the IASB is promoting the use of fair values, including remeasurement of assets and liabilities previously acquired in business combinations achieved in stages ("step acquisitions") at fair values at the date of the latest stage when such assets or liabilities do not change owners or obligors, strict historical cost measurement is no longer the context, and so this logic is hardly compelling. "Fresh start accounting" for all business combinations would be more logical in this context, but the IASB does not seem to be heading in this direction, perhaps because fresh start accounting is considered to be onerous to apply in most cases.

Applying the acquisition method involves the following steps (par. 4):

1. Identifying the acquirer.

2. Determining the acquisition date.

3. Recognizing and measuring the identifiable assets acquired, the liabilities assumed, and any non-controlling interests in the acquiree.

4. Recognizing and measuring goodwill or a gain from a bargain purchase.

OBSERVATION: These four steps differ from the previous version of IFRS 3 and also from those in the 2005 Exposure Draft. The main changes are concerned with eliminating the measurement of the fair value of the acquiree *as a whole*, and to add recognizing and measuring goodwill as a separate step. This reflects the decision to focus on measuring the components of the business combination, *including any non-controlling interests in the acquiree*, rather than measuring the fair value of the acquiree as a whole. It was believed that the decision-usefulness of information about a non-controlling interest would be improved if a measurement attribute were specified rather than solely the mechanics for calculating the amount. The approach in the revised IFRS 3 also permits, however, the alternative method of measuring a non-controlling interest on the basis of its proportionate share of the acquiree's identifiable net assets (i.e., excluding goodwill). Goodwill is excluded because it is a residual amount, and including the non-controlling interest's share in goodwill together with their share of the acquiree's identifiable net assets would mean that the amount recognized for a non-controlling interest in the acquiree would have been a residual "after allocating a residual" (IFRS 3, pars. BC205–BC206). At the same time, when non-controlling interests are measured at fair value as at the acquisition date, goodwill is measured as a true residual amount.

Identifying the Acquirer

IFRS 3, paragraphs 6–7, requires that in a business combination one of the combining entities shall be identified as the acquire, following the guidance in IAS 27, "Consolidated and Separate Financial Statements" (see Chapter 11). The acquirer is the combining entity that *obtains control* of the other combining entities or businesses. *Control* is defined in IAS 27, paragraph 4, as the power to govern the financial and operating policies of an entity or business so as to obtain benefits from its activities. There is a presumption that control has been obtained when an entity acquires more than one-half of another entity's voting rights, unless it can be clearly demonstrated that such ownership does not constitute control. Even if more than half of the voting rights are not obtained, control may be obtained if, as a result of the combination, one of the entities obtains one or more of the following powers (IAS 27, pars. 13–15):

- Power over more than one-half of the voting rights of the other entity by virtue of an agreement with other investors.

- Power to govern the financial and operating policies of the other entity under a statute or an agreement.

- Power to appoint or remove the majority of the board of directors or equivalent governing body of the other entity, and that board or body controls the entity.

- Power to cast the majority of votes at meetings of the board of directors or equivalent governing body of the other entity, and that board or body controls the entity.

OBSERVATION: In May 2011, the IASB issued IFRS 10, "Consolidated Financial Statements," which supersedes IAS 27 for annual reporting periods beginning on or after January 1, 2013. IFRS 10 provides a broader definition of control: an investor controls an investee when it is exposed, or has rights, to *variable returns from its involvement with the investee* and has the ability to affect those returns *through its power over the investee* (IFRS 10, par. 6, emphasis supplied). According to IFRS 10, pars. B14–B21, power arises from rights and may include, but is not limited to, the powers mentioned in IAS 27.

Identifying the Acquirer in Difficult Cases

In such cases, there are usually indications allowing an acquirer to be identified (IFRS 3, pars. B14–B18). For example:

- If the business combination effected mainly by transferring cash or other assets or by incurring liabilities, the acquirer is usually the entity that transfers the cash or other assets or incurs the liabilities.

- In a business combination effected through an exchange of equity interests, the entity that issues equity interests (and thereby acquires the equity interests of the other entity) is normally the acquirer. However, this will not be the case in so-called reverse acquisitions, where the entity that becomes the legal subsidiary will be the acquirer if it has the power to govern the financial and operating policies of the legal parent so as to obtain benefits from its activities (see below). Other relevant considerations are as follows:

  1. *Relative voting rights.* The acquirer is usually the combining entity whose owners as a group, retain or receive the largest portion of the voting rights in the combined entity, taking account of any unusual or special voting arrangements and options, warrants, or convertible securities.

  2. *The existence of a large minority voting interest in the combined entity.* If no other owner or organized group of owners has a significant voting interest, the holder of a large minority voting interest in such circumstances is usually the acquirer.

  3. *The composition of the governing body of the combined entity.* The acquirer is usually the combining entity whose owners have the ability to appoint or remove a majority of the members of that governing body.

  4. *The composition of the senior management of the combined entity.* The acquirer is usually the combining entity whose former management dominates the management of the combined entity.

5. *The terms of the exchange of equity interests.* The acquirer is usually the combining entity that pays a premium over the pre-combination fair value of the equity interests of the other combining entity or entities.

6. *The relative size of the combining entities (as measured, for example, by assets, revenues or profits).* If the relative size of one entity is significantly greater than that of the other entity or entities, that entity is likely to be the acquirer.

When a business combination involves more than two combining entities, determining the acquirer shall include consideration of which of the combining entities initiated the combination, as well as the relative sizes of the combining entities.

When a new entity is formed to effect a business combination, that entity is not necessarily the acquirer. If the new entity is formed as a vehicle to issue equity interests in order effect a business combination, one of the pre-existing combining entities shall be identified as the acquirer by applying the guidance given above.

Reverse Acquisitions

IRFS 3, paragraphs B19–B20, provides guidance on the treatment of reverse acquisitions in accounting for business combinations. A necessary condition for a reverse acquisition is that the entity that issues securities, that is, the acquirer from a legal point of view is identified on the basis of the guidance provided above as being for accounting purposes (and *in substance*) the acquiree. Another necessary condition is that the entity whose equity interests are acquired in exchange, that is, the legal acquiree must be the acquirer for accounting purposes. A reverse acquisition takes place when these two conditions are satisfied. A typical reverse acquisition occurs when a private (unlisted) entity arranges for a public (listed) entity to acquire its equity interests in exchange for the equity interests of the public entity, as a cost-effective means of acquiring a stock exchange listing, and the application of the guidance given above leads to the identification of the legal acquiree as the accounting acquirer and the legal acquirer as the accounting acquiree.

In a reverse acquisition, the accounting acquirer does not normally issue any consideration for the accounting acquiree; rather, the latter issues its equity shares to the owners of the accounting acquirer. Hence, the acquisition-date fair value of the consideration transferred by the accounting acquirer for its interest in the accounting acquiree is based on the number of equity interests that the legal subsidiary (the accounting acquirer) *would have had to issue to give the owners of the legal parent (the accounting acquiree) the same percentage equity interest in the combined entity that results from the reverse acquisition.* The fair value of the number of these hypothetical equity interests can be used as the fair value of consideration transferred in exchange for the accounting acquiree.

Determining the Acquisition Date

The acquirer determines the acquisition date as the date on which it effectively obtains control of the acquiree. This is generally the date on which the acquirer legally transfers the consideration, acquires the assets, and assumes the liabilities of the acquiree (i.e., the closing date). However, the acquirer may obtain control on a date before or after the closing date. For example, a written agreement may provide that the acquirer obtains control on a date before the closing date.

Recognizing and Measuring the Identifiable Assets Acquired, the Liabilities Assumed, and Any Non-Controlling Interest in the Acquiree

IFRS 3, paragraphs 10–31, and the related paragraphs of Appendix B deal with the recognition and measurement of the assets acquired, liabilities assumed, and any non-controlling interest in the acquiree. Recognition and measurement of goodwill or a gain from a "bargain purchase" and the measurement of the consideration transferred are dealt with in subsequent paragraphs.

Recognition Principle

The basic recognition principle in IFRS 3 is that as of the acquisition date the acquirer is to recognize, separately from goodwill, the identifiable assets acquired, liabilities assumed, and contingent liabilities of the acquiree, and any non-controlling interest in the acquiree that satisfy the recognition criteria at that date, *regardless of whether they had been previously recognized in the acquiree's financial statements*, subject to the recognition conditions below (IFRS 3, par. 10).

Recognition Conditions

IFRS 3, paragraphs 11–14, states the following conditions for recognition as part of applying the acquisition method:

1. The definitions of assets and liabilities given in the Framework (see Chapter 2) must be satisfied except for acquired in-process research and development (see Intangible Assets below).

2. Identifiable assets acquired and liabilities assumed must be part of what was exchanged in the business combination transaction and not be the result of separate transactions.

3. Contingent liabilities are recognized provided they are *present obligations* arising out of past events and their fair value can be measured reliably (this differs from the requirement of IAS 37, "Provisions, Contingent Liabilities and Contingent Assets," paragraph 27, according to which an entity shall not recognize a contingent liability; (see Chapter 29 and the Observation below).

4. Deferred income tax assets and liabilities and liabilities (or assets) relating to the acquiree's employee benefit arrangements are recognized and measured in accordance with IAS 12, "Income Taxes," and IAS 19, "Employee Benefits," respectively (see Chapters 21 and 14).

OBSERVATION: For contingent liabilities, the main issue for IAS 37 is whether an outflow of resources embodying economic benefits is *probable*. If so, the liability is not contingent and is recognized. Otherwise, it is not recognized but is disclosed unless the possibility of an outflow of resources is *remote*. For IFRS 3, the main issue is whether a contingent liability represents a *present obligation*, whether or not an outflow of resources embodying economic benefits is probable. The IASB intends to align the recognition requirements for contingent liabilities of IAS 37 and IFRS 3 when IAS 37 is revised. Note that IFRS 3 does not permit the recognition of a contingent *asset* unless it meets the Framework definition of an asset (IFRS 3, pars. BC272–276).

Operating Leases

In the case of operating leases, the acquirer recognizes no related assets or liabilities *unless the terms of the lease are measurably favorable or unfavorable relative to market terms* at the acquisition date, in which case the acquirer recognizes an intangible asset (if favorable) or a liability (if unfavorable). An identifiable intangible asset may be associated with an operating lease even though it is at market terms. For example, retail space in a prime shopping area might provide future economic benefits that qualify as intangible assets (see below) (IFRS 3, pars. B28–B30).

Intangible Assets

The acquirer recognizes, separately from goodwill, the identifiable intangible assets acquired in a business combination. An intangible asset is identifiable if it meets either the *separability* criterion or the *contractual-legal* criterion (IFRS 3, pars. B31–B34).

The separability criterion means that an acquired intangible asset is *capable of being separated or divided from the acquiree and sold, transferred, licensed, rented or exchanged, either individually or together with a related contract, identifiable asset, or liability*. This criterion applies whether or not the acquirer has any intention to sell, license, or otherwise exchange the intangible. Customer lists may meet this criterion, but not if terms of confidentiality or other agreements prohibit selling, leasing, or otherwise exchanging the information about customers.

An intangible asset that meets the contractual-legal criterion is identifiable even if it does not meet the separability criterion. For example, intangible assets recognized in connection with operating leases, as described above, meet the contractual-legal criterion and thus are recognized even if the acquirer cannot sell or otherwise transfer the lease contract. The rationale of this criterion is that the acquirer's rights to the future economic benefits from the asset are legally protected (see Chapter 22).

Reacquired Rights

Examples of rights that may be reacquired as part of a business combination are rights to use:

- The acquirer's trade name under a franchise agreement.
- The acquirer's technology under a licensing agreement.

A reacquired right is an identifiable intangible asset that the acquirer recognizes separately from goodwill. The contract with the acquiree is considered as having in effect been settled. If the terms of the contract giving rise to the reacquired right are favorable or unfavorable relative to current market terms for such contracts, the acquirer recognizes a *settlement gain or loss* (IFRS 3, pars. B35–B36).

Classifying or Designating Identifiable Assets Acquired and Liabilities Assumed in a Business Combination

At the acquisition date, the acquirer is to classify or designate the identifiable assets acquired and liabilities assumed, on the basis of the contractual terms, economic conditions, its operating or accounting policies and other pertinent conditions, *as necessary to apply other IFRSs subsequently*, with two exceptions as noted below. Examples of classifications or designations on the basis of pertinent conditions include:

- Classification in accordance with the applicable IFRS on financial instruments (see Chapter 17). IFRS 9, "Financial Instruments," has two categories: (1) measured at fair value or (2) measured at amortized cost. IAS 39, "Financial Instruments: Recognition and Measurement," has three categories as a financial asset or liability: (1) at fair value through profit and loss, (2) as available for sale, or (3) as held to maturity (see Chapter 17).

- Designation of a derivative instrument as a hedging instrument in accordance with IAS 39; and

- Assessment of whether an embedded derivative should be separated from the host contract in accordance with IAS 39.

The two exceptions noted above are:

1. Classification of a lease contract as either an operating or a finance lease in accordance with IAS 27, "Leases"; and

2. Classification of a contract as an insurance contract in accordance with IFRS 4, "Insurance Contracts."

The acquirer classifies these contracts on the basis of the contractual terms and other factors at the inception of the contract, or at the date of any modification that would change its classification, which might be the acquisition date (e.g., a lease contract) (IFRS 3, pars. 15–17 and BC187–BC188).

Determining What Is Part of the Business Combination Transaction

IFRS 3, pars. 51–52, clarifies that the acquirer shall recognize as part of applying the acquisition method only:

- The consideration transferred for the acquiree or the amount used for the consideration in calculating goodwill if no consideration is transferred (see Recognizing and Measuring Goodwill below); and

- The assets acquired and liabilities assumed in exchange for the acquiree.

The acquirer and the acquiree may have a pre-existing relationship or other arrangement before negotiations for the business combination began, or may enter into an arrangement during the negotiations that is separate from the business combination (a *separate transaction*). The acquirer is required to identify and exclude from accounting for the business combination any amounts that are not part of what the acquirer and the acquiree (or its former owners) exchanged in the business combination. These amounts are treated as separate transactions, which shall be accounted for in accordance with the applicable IFRSs.

A transaction entered into before the combination by or on behalf of the acquirer, or primarily for the benefit of the acquirer or the combined entity, rather than for the benefit of the acquiree or its former owners, is likely to be a separate transaction; for example, a transaction that:

- In effect settles pre-existing relationships between the acquirer and acquiree,
- Remunerates employees or former owners of the acquiree for *future* services, or
- Reimburses the acquiree or its former owners for paying the acquirer's *acquisition-* related *costs*.

Acquisition-Related Costs

These are costs incurred by the acquirer to effect a business combination, and include (IFRS 3, par. 53):

- Finder's fees;
- Advisory, legal, accounting, and other professional or consulting fees;
- General administrative costs, including those of maintaining an internal acquisitions department or unit; and
- Costs of registering and issuing debt and equity securities.

The acquirer accounts for acquisition-related costs as expenses in the periods in which they are incurred and the services are received, with one exception. The costs of issuing debt or equity securities are recognized in accordance with IAS 32 and IAS 39/IFRS 9 (see Chapter 17) and thus may not therefore be recognized as expenses in the period in which they are incurred, that is, if they are directly attributable to the issue of an equity instrument (IAS 32, par. 35) or a financial liability not at fair value through profit and loss (IAS 39, par. 43).

Measurement Principle

The basic principle is that the acquirer shall measure the identifiable assets acquired and the liabilities assumed at their fair values as of the acquisition date. Likewise, any non-controlling interest in the acquiree should be measured at its fair value as of the acquisition date, but alternatively may be measured at its proportionate share of the acquiree's identifiable net assets (i.e., excluding goodwill). Other exceptions to this basic principle are discussed below (IFRS 3, pars. 18–31 and B41–B45).

OBSERVATION: The 2005 Exposure Draft proposed that a non-controlling interest in an acquiree should be determined as the sum of the non-controlling interest's proportionate share of the fair values of identifiable assets acquired and liabilities assumed, *plus the non-controlling interest's share of goodwill*. However, this proposal was subsequently seen as undesirable. The proposal specified the mechanics of determining the reported amount of a non-controlling interest but *failed to identify a measurement attribute*. As goodwill is measured as a residual, the amount recognized for a non-controlling interest in an acquiree would also have been a residual. It was seen as desirable to identify a measurement attribute, and it was concluded that this should be fair value. However, there was no consensus within the IASB to adopt a requirement that a non-controlling interest be measured at its acquisition-date fair value. It was therefore decided to allow the alternative described above.

Exceptions to the Recognition or Measurement Principles

Some exceptions to the above principles solely concern the recognition principle, some concern both recognition and measurement, while some concern the measurement principle only.

As noted under "Recognition Conditions" above, there is an exception for *contingent liabilities*. There also are exceptions to both the recognition and the measurement principles of IFRS 3 for *income taxes and employee benefits*, which are to be recognized and measured in accordance with IAS 12 and IAS 19, respectively.

In addition, there are exceptions to both principles for so-called *indemnification assets*, which arise when the seller in a business combination contractually indemnifies the acquirer in respect of the outcome of a contingency or uncertainty related to all or part of a specific asset or liability. For example, the seller may indemnify the acquirer against losses above a specified amount on a liability arising from a particular contingency. As a result, the acquirer obtains an indemnification asset. The acquirer recognizes the indemnification asset simultaneously with recognizing the indemnified item, and measures it on the same basis subject to the need for a valuation allowance for uncollectible amounts if measurement is not at the acquisition-date fair value. Some indemnified items may be measured on a basis other than fair value, such as one that results from an employee benefit. In such circumstances, the indemnification asset is measured using assumptions consistent with those used to measure the indemnified item, taking account of any valuation allowance as noted above and any contractual limitations on the indemnified amount. In some circumstances, the indemnification may relate to an item that is not recognized according to the IFRS 3 recognition and measurement principles, such as a contingent liability that is not recognized because its fair value is not reliably measurable at the acquisition date. In such a case, no indemnification asset will be recognized (IFRS 3, pars. 27–28).

There is also an exception to the measurement principle involving *reacquired rights*. The value of a reacquired right that is recognized as an intangible asset and any related settlement gain or loss that are recognized as indicated above, shall be measured on the basis of the remaining contractual term, regardless of whether market participants would consider potential contractual renewals in determining the fair value of the reacquired right. The right is valued as the amount by which the contract is relatively favorable or unfavorable from the acquirer's perspective *by comparison with the terms for current market transactions* for the same or similar items (IFRS 3, pars. 29, B35–B36, and B52).

Share-Based Payment Awards

When an acquirer replaces an acquiree's share-based payment awards with the acquirer's share-based payment awards, the acquirer measures liabilities or equity instruments resulting from the replacement in accordance with the methods in IFRS 2, "Share-Based Payment" (see Chapter 33, IFRS 2, par. BC24, and IFRS 3, pars. 30 and B56–62).

Assets Held for Sale

An acquired non-current asset or disposal group classified as held for sale at the acquisition date in accordance with IFRS 5, "Non-Current Assets Held for Sale and Discontinued Operations" (see Chapter 27), is measured at fair value less costs to sell in accordance with IFRS 5, paragraphs 15–18 (IFRS 3, par. 31).

Recognizing and Measuring Goodwill or a Gain from a Bargain Purchase

Goodwill acquired in a business combination is conceptualized in IFRS 3 as representing a payment made by the acquirer in anticipation of future economic benefits from assets that cannot be individually identified and separately recognized. It is measured as the excess of 1 over 2 below:

1. The aggregate of:

    (a) The consideration transferred measured in accordance with IFRS 3 (i.e., normally at fair value).

    (b) The amount of any non-controlling interest in the acquiree measured in accordance with IFRS 3.

    (c) In a business combination achieved in stages, the acquisition-date fair value of the acquirer's previously held equity interest in the acquiree.

2. The net of the acquisition-date amounts of the identifiable assets acquired and the liabilities assumed (including contingent liabilities) measured in accordance with IFRS 3.

In a business combination in which the acquirer and the acquiree (or its former owners) exchange only equity interests, the acquisition-date fair value of the acquiree's equity interests may be more readily measurable than that of the acquirer's equity interests. This may be the case when two mutual entities combine.

To determine the amount of goodwill in a business combination in which no consideration is transferred, the acquirer uses in 1(a) above the acquisition-date fair value of the acquirer's interest in the acquiree determined using a valuation technique, in place of the acquisition-date fair value of the (non-existent) consideration transferred (IFRS 3, pars. 32–33 and B46–B49).

Bargain Purchases

IFRS 3 does not permit the recognition of negative goodwill. If the amount in 2 above, namely the net of the acquisition-date amounts of the identifiable assets acquired and the liabilities assumed (including contingent liabilities) measured in accordance with IFRS 3, exceeds the aggregate of the amounts in 1 above, the acquirer is required:

- To reassess whether it has correctly identified all of the assets acquired and the liabilities assumed and to recognize any additional items identified in that review.

- In order to ensure that the measurements appropriately reflect consideration of all relevant information available at the acquisition date, to review the procedures used to measure the amounts to be recognized at the acquisition date for:

  —The identifiable assets acquired and liabilities assumed.

  —Any non-controlling interests in the acquiree.

  —For a business combination achieved in stages, the acquirer's previously held equity interest in the acquiree.

  —The consideration transferred.

If the excess remains after following the above procedures, the resulting gain is recognized immediately in profit or loss by the acquirer as a gain on a bargain purchase (IFRS 3, pars. 34–36).

Consideration Transferred in a Business Combination

The consideration transferred is calculated as the sum of (1) the assets transferred, (2) the liabilities incurred, and (3) the equity interests issued by the acquirer to the former owners of the acquiree, all of these being measured at their acquisition-date fair values, except for any portion of the acquirer's share-based payment awards exchanged for awards held by the acquiree's employees that is included in the consideration. The latter are measured in accordance with IFRS 2, "Share-based Payments," as required by IFRS 3, paragraphs 30 and B56–62.

Consideration may comprise cash, other assets, a business or subsidiary of the acquirer, contingent consideration (see below), common or preferred equity instruments, options, warrants, and, in mutual entities, member interests. It may include assets or liabilities of the acquirer with carrying amounts that differ from their fair values as at the acquisition date. In this case, the acquirer remeasures the items to their acquisition-date fair values and recognizes any remeasurement gain or loss in profit or loss, unless the transferred items remain within the combined entity (e.g., because they were transferred to the acquiree instead of its former owners) so that the acquirer retain control of them. In the latter case, the items continue to be measured at their carrying amounts and no remeasurement takes place.

Contingent Consideration

The consideration transferred by an acquirer in exchange for the acquiree includes any asset or liability resulting from a *contingent consideration arrangement*. The acquirer recognizes the acquisition-date fair value of any contingent consideration as part of the consideration transferred. An obligation to pay a contingent consideration is classified by the acquirer as a liability or an equity on the basis of the definitions given in paragraph 11 of IAS 32, "Financial Instruments: Presentation," or other applicable IFRSs. A right to the return of previously transferred consideration is classified as an asset by the acquirer if specified conditions are met at the acquisition date.

In some circumstances, the acquirer may have to make a payment to the seller subsequent to the acquisition date, as compensation for a reduction in the value of assets given, equity instruments issued, or liabilities assumed or incurred by the acquirer in exchange for control of the acquiree. For example, the acquirer may have guaranteed the market price of a financial instrument issued as part of the consideration. In such cases, *no increase in the cost of the business combination is recognized*. The additional payment is considered to be offset by a reduction in the value of equity instruments initially issued or by an adjustment to the premium or discount on the initial issue of debt instruments.

Business Combinations Achieved in Stages

An acquirer may obtain control of an acquiree in which it held an equity interest immediately prior to the acquisition date on which control is achieved. In a business combination achieved in stages, the acquirer remeasures its previously held equity interest in the acquiree at its acquisition-date fair value and recognizes any resultant gain or loss in profit or loss. If the acquirer has previously recognized changes in the value of the equity interest in the acquiree in other comprehensive income, the amount that was previously recognized in other comprehensive income is recognized at the acquisition date on the same basis as if the acquirer had disposed of the equity interest.

Business Combinations Achieved without the Transfer of Consideration

An acquirer may obtain control of an acquiree without transferring consideration, for example when:

- The acquiree repurchases a sufficient number of its own shares for an existing investor to be left with an interest that gives it control and makes it the acquirer.

- Minority veto rights lapse, which previously kept the acquirer from controlling an acquiree in which it held the majority voting rights.

- The acquirer and the acquiree agree to combine their businesses by contract alone. The acquirer transfers no consideration in exchange for control and holds no equity interests in the acquiree, either on the acquisition date or previously, as in the case of a dual listed corporation.

The acquisition method of accounting for business combinations applies to such combinations. In the case of combinations by contract alone, the acquirer attributes to the owners of the acquiree the amount of the acquiree's net assets recognized in accordance with IFRS 3. Since equity interests in the acquiree held by parties other than the acquirer are a *non-controlling interest* in the acquirer's post-combination financial statements, the amount of equity thus attributed to the owners of the acquiree is a non-controlling interest even if it constitutes all of the equity interests of the acquiree.

Measurement Period

The initial accounting for a business combination may be incomplete at the end of the reporting period in which the combination occurs, because either the fair values to be assigned to the acquiree's identifiable assets, liabilities, and contingent liabilities or the cost of the combination can be determined only provisionally at that time. In that case, the acquirer should account for the combination using the provisional amounts (IFRS 3, pars. 45–50).

The *measurement period* is the period after the acquisition date during which the acquirer is required to adjust these provisional amounts retrospectively to reflect new information obtained about facts that existed as of the acquisition date which, if known at that time, would have affected the measurements of these items. The acquirer is also required to recognize additional assets or liabilities if, in light of new information obtained about facts that existed at the acquisition date, would have been recognized as of that date.

Subject to not exceeding one year from the acquisition date, the measurement period ends as soon as the acquirer has received the information being sought about facts that existed as of the acquisition date or learned that no more information is available. This provides the acquirer with a reasonable time to obtain the information necessary to identify and measure the following as of the acquisition date in accordance with the requirements of IFRS 3:

- The identifiable assets acquired, liabilities assumed, and any non-controlling interest in the acquirer.

- The consideration transferred for the acquiree (or the other amount used in measuring goodwill if no consideration is transferred (see "Recognizing and Measuring Goodwill" above).

- In a business combination achieved in stages, the equity interest in the acquiree previously held by the acquirer.

- The resulting goodwill or gain on a bargain purchase.

During the measurement period, the acquirer recognizes adjustments to the provisional amounts as if the accounting for the business combination had been completed at the acquisition date. Comparative information presented for prior periods is to be revised as needed, including any change in depreciation, amortization, or other items affecting income that are recognized in completing the initial accounting for the business combination.

Any adjustments made after the measurement period should be recognized only to correct an error in accordance with IAS 8, "Accounting Policies, Changes in Accounting Estimates, and Errors" (see Chapter 6). In the absence of a change in accounting policy, IAS 8 requires an entity to adjust its financial statements retrospectively only to correct an error.

Subsequent Measurement and Accounting

Other IFRSs provide guidance on subsequently measuring and accounting for assets acquired and liabilities assumed or incurred in a business combination (IAS 3, par. B63):

- IAS 38 prescribes accounting for identifiable intangible assets acquired in a business combination. The acquirer measures goodwill at the amount recognized at the acquisition date less any accumulated impairment losses. IAS 36 prescribes accounting for impairment losses.

- IFRS 4 provides guidance on the subsequent accounting for an insurance contract acquired in a business combination.

- IAS 12 prescribes the subsequent accounting for deferred tax assets acquired (including those unrecognized in a business combination) and liabilities assumed in a business combination.

- IFRS 2 provides guidance on subsequent measurement and accounting for the portion of replacement share-based payment awards issued by an acquirer that is attributable to employees' future services.

- IAS 27 (as amended in 2008) provides guidance on accounting for changes in a parent's ownership interest in a subsidiary after control is obtained. (IAS 27 will be superseded by IFRS 10, as noted under "Identifying the Acquirer" above.)

IFRS 3, paragraphs 54–58, states some exceptions to the general rule that an acquirer subsequently measures and accounts for assets acquired, liabilities assumed, and equity instruments issued in a business combination in accordance with other applicable IFRSs. These exceptions concern:

- Reacquired rights;
- Contingent liabilities recognized at the acquisition date;
- Indemnification assets; and
- Contingent consideration.

Reacquired Rights

A reacquired right recognized as an intangible asset is amortized over the remaining contractual period of the contract in which the right was granted. If it is subsequently sold to a third party, the acquirer includes the carrying amount of the intangible asset in determining the gain or loss on the sale.

Contingent Liabilities

After initial recognition of a contingent liability recognized in a business combination, and until it is settled, cancelled, or it expires, the acquirer measures it at the higher of:

- The amount that would be recognized in accordance with IAS 37.

- The amount initially recognized less, if appropriate, cumulative amortization recognized in accordance with IAS 18, "Revenue" (see Chapter 31).

This requirement does not apply to contracts accounted for in accordance with IAS 39/IFRS 9.

Indemnification Assets

At the end of each subsequent reporting period, the acquirer measures an indemnification asset that was recognized at the acquisition date on the same basis as the indemnified liability or asset, subject to any contractual limitations on the amount of the indemnity and, for an indemnification asset that is not subsequently measured at its fair value, management's assessment of the collectibility of the indemnification asset. The acquirer derecognizes the indemnification asset only when it collects it, sells it, or otherwise loses the right to it.

Contingent Consideration

Some changes in the fair value of contingent consideration that are recognized by the acquirer after the acquisition date may be the result of additional information that the acquirer obtained after that date about facts that existed at that date. These are *measurement period adjustments* made as described under Measurement Period above. However, changes resulting from events *after the acquisition date*, such as meeting an earnings target, or achieving a specified share price or specified milestone on a research and development project, are *not* measurement period adjustments, and are to be accounted for as follows:

- Contingent consideration classified as equity shall not be remeasured and its subsequent settlement is accounted for within equity.

- Contingent consideration classified as an asset or a liability that is a financial instrument within the scope of IAS 39/IFRS 9 is measured at fair value, with any resulting gain or loss being recognized either in profit or loss or in other comprehensive income in accordance with IAS 39/IFRS 9.

- Contingent consideration classified as an asset or a liability that is not within the scope of IAS 39/IFRS 9 is accounted for in accordance with IAS 37 or other applicable IFRSs.

DISCLOSURE

The IASB identified three main disclosure objectives for IFRS 3 (IFRS 3, par. BC 411), namely to provide users of an acquirer's financial statements with information enabling them to evaluate:

1. The nature and financial effect of business combinations effected during the current reporting period or after the end of the reporting period but before the financial statements are authorized for issue (par. 59).

2. The financial effects of adjustments recognized in the current reporting period that relate to business combinations effected in the current period or previous reporting periods (par. 61).

3. Changes in the carrying amount of goodwill during the period.

The detailed disclosure requirements implied by the above objectives are set out in paragraphs B64–67.

To meet the first requirement of paragraph 59, for business combinations effected during the reporting period, the following information shall be disclosed:

1. The name and description of the acquiree.

2. The acquisition date.

3. The percentage of voting equity instruments acquired.

4. The primary reason for the business combination and a description of how the acquirer obtained control of the acquiree.

5. A qualitative description of the factors that make up the goodwill recognized, such as expected synergies from combining operations of the acquiree and acquirer, intangibles that do not qualify for separate recognition, or other factors.

6. The acquisition-date fair value of the total consideration transferred and the acquisition-date fair value of each major class of consideration, such as:

   (a) Cash.

   (b) Other tangible or intangible assets, including a business or subsidiary of the acquirer.

   (c) Liabilities assumed or incurred, for example, a liability for contingent consideration.

   (d) Equity interests of the acquirer, including the number of instruments or interests issued or issuable and the method of determining their fair value.

7. For contingent consideration arrangements and indemnification assets:

   (a) The amount recognized as of the acquisition date.

   (b) A description of the arrangement and the basis for determining the amount of the payment.

   (c) An estimate of the range of outcomes (undiscounted) or, if a range cannot be estimated, that fact and the reasons why a range cannot be estimated. If the maximum amount of the payment is unlimited, this fact is to be disclosed.

8. For acquired receivables (by major class of receivable):

   (a) The fair value of the receivables.

   (b) The gross contractual amounts receivable.

   (c) The best estimate at the acquisition date of the contractual cash flows not expected to be collected.

9. The amounts recognized as of the acquisition date for each class of assets acquired and liabilities assumed.

10. For each contingent liability recognized in accordance with IFRS 3, the information required in IAS 37, paragraph 85. If a contingent liability is

not recognized because its fair value cannot be measured reliably, the acquirer is to disclose:

    (a) The information required by IAS 37, paragraph 86.

    (b) The reasons why the liability cannot be measured reliably.

11. The total amount of goodwill that is expected to be deductible for tax purposes.

12. For transactions that are recognized separately from the acquisition of assets and liabilities in the business combination in accordance with IFRS 3, paragraph 51 (see "Determining What Is Part of the Business Combination Transaction" above):

    (a) A description of each transaction.

    (b) How the acquirer accounted for each transaction.

    (c) The amounts recognized for each transaction and the line item in the financial statements in which each amount is recognized.

    (d) If the transaction is the effective settlement of a pre-existing relationship, the method used to determine the settlement amount.

13. The disclosures required in item 12 shall include the amount of acquisition-related costs and, separately, the amount of those costs recognized as an expense and the line item or items in the statement of comprehensive income in which those expenses are recognized. The amount of any issue costs not recognized as an expense, and how they were recognized, are also to be disclosed.

14. In a bargain purchase:

    (a) The amount of any gain recognized in accordance with IFRS 3, paragraph 34 (see "Recognizing and Measuring Goodwill or a Gain from a Bargain Purchase" above) and the line item in the statement of comprehensive income where it is recognized.

    (b) A description of the reasons why the transaction resulted in a bargain purchase.

15. For each business combination in which the acquirer holds less than 100% of the equity interests of the acquiree at the acquisition date:

    (a) The amount of the non-controlling interest in the acquiree recognized at the acquisition date and the measurement basis for that amount.

    (b) For each non-controlling interest in an acquiree measured at fair value, the valuation techniques and key model inputs used in determining that value.

16. In a business combination achieved in stages:

    (a) The acquisition-date fair value of the equity interest in the acquiree held by the acquirer immediately before the acquisition date.

    (b) The amount of any gain or loss recognized as a result of remeasuring to fair value the equity interest in the acquiree held by the acquirer before the business combination and the line item in the statement of comprehensive income in which that gain or loss is recognized.

17. The amounts of:

    (a) Revenue and profit or loss of the acquiree since the acquisition date included in the consolidated statement of comprehensive income for the current reporting period.

    (b) Revenue and profit or loss of the combined entity for the current reporting period as though the acquisition date for all business combinations that occurred during the year had been as of the beginning of the annual reporting period unless any of this is impracticable, in which case this fact should be disclosed together with an explanation. IFRS 3 uses the term "impracticable" with the same meaning as IAS 8, paragraphs 50–53.

For business combinations effected during the period that are individually immaterial, the information indicated in items 5–17 above are to be disclosed in aggregate.

If the acquisition date of a business combination is after the end of the reporting period but before the financial statements are authorized for issue, the acquirer discloses the information indicated in items 1–17 above unless the initial accounting for the combination is incomplete at the time when the financial statements are authorized for issue. In that case, the acquirer describes which disclosures could not be made and the reasons why.

To meet the requirements of paragraph 61, the acquirer discloses the following information for each material business combination or in the aggregate for individually immaterial business combinations that are material collectively:

1. If the initial accounting for a business combination is incomplete for particular assets, liabilities, non-controlling interests, or items of consideration and the amounts recognized in the financial statements for the business combination have thus been determined only provisionally:

   (a) The reasons why the initial accounting is incomplete.

   (b) The assets, liabilities, equity interest, or items of consideration for which the initial accounting is incomplete.

   (c) The nature and amount of any measurement period adjustments recognized during the reporting period in accordance with IFRS 3, paragraph 49 (see "Measurement Period" above).

2. In respect to contingent consideration, for each reporting period after the acquisition date until the entity collects, sells, or otherwise loses the right to a contingent consideration asset, or settles a contingent consideration liability or the liability is cancelled or expires:

   (a) Any changes in the recognized amounts, including any differences arising on settlement.

   (b) Any changes in the range of outcomes (undiscounted) and the reasons for those changes.

(c) The valuation techniques and key model inputs used to measure contingent consideration.

3. For contingent liabilities recognized in a business combination, the acquirer discloses the information required by IAS 37, paragraphs 84–85, for each class of provision.

4. A reconciliation of the carrying amount of goodwill at the beginning and end of the reporting period, detailing:

(a) The gross amount and accumulated impairment losses at the beginning and end of the reporting period.

(b) Additional goodwill recognized during the period, except goodwill included in a disposal group that, on acquisition, met the criteria to be classified as held for sale in accordance with IFRS 5.

(c) Adjustments resulting from the subsequent recognition of deferred tax assets during the reporting period in accordance with IFRS 3, paragraph 67, that is, in accordance with IAS 12, paragraph 68.

(d) Goodwill included in a disposal group classified as held for sale in accordance with IFRS 5, and goodwill derecognized during the reporting period without having been previously included in a disposal group classified as held for sale.

(e) Impairment losses recognized during the reporting period in accordance with IAS 36, which also requires disclosure of information about the recoverable amount and impairment of goodwill.

(f) Net exchange rate differences arising during the reporting period in accordance with IAS 21.

(g) Any other changes in the carrying amount of goodwill during the reporting period.

(h) The gross amount and accumulated impairment losses at the end of the reporting period.

5. The amount and an explanation of any gain or loss recognized in the current reporting period that both:

(a) Relates to the identifiable assets acquired or liabilities assumed in a business combination effected in the current or previous reporting period.

(b) Is of such a size, nature, or incidence that disclosure is relevant to understanding the combined entity's financial statements.

EFFECTIVE DATE AND TRANSITION

IFRS 3 is to be applied prospectively to business combinations for which the acquisition date is on or after the beginning of the first reporting period beginning on or after **July 1, 2009**. Earlier application is permitted; however, an entity shall apply IFRS 3 only at the beginning of a reporting period beginning on or after June 30, 2007. If an entity applies IFRS 3 before its effective date of July 1,

2009, it discloses this fact and also applies the revised (2008) version of IAS 27 at the same time (IFRS 3, par. 64).

Assets and liabilities that arose from business combinations whose acquisition dates preceded the application of IFRS 3 shall not be adjusted on application of the standard. An entity such as a mutual entity that has not yet applied IFRS 3 and had one or more business combinations that were accounted for using the purchase method is to apply the transitional provisions below.

Income Taxes

For business combinations in which the acquisition date was before IFRS 3 is applied, the acquirer is to apply prospectively the requirements of IAS 12, paragraph 68 (as amended as a result of the revision of IFRS 3). Thus, the acquirer does not adjust the accounting for *prior* business combinations in respect to previously recognized changes in recognized deferred tax assets, but from the date when IFRS 3 is applied the acquirer recognizes as an adjustment to profit or loss (or, if IAS 12 requires, outside profit or loss) changes in deferred tax assets.

Transitional Provisions for Business Combinations Involving Only Mutual Entities or by Contract Alone (Application of IAS 3, Paragraph 66)

IFRS 3, paragraphs B68–B69, set out the transitional provisions for entities that were excluded from the scope of the previous version of IFRS 3 and thus may have applied accounting policies incompatible with the revised IFRS 3, particularly in regard to goodwill. For such entities, the requirement to apply IFRS 3 *prospectively* has the following effects for a business combination involving only mutual entities or achieved by contract alone, if the acquisition date for that business combination is *prior* to the application of IFRS 3:

1. *Classification.* An entity continues to classify the prior business combination in accordance with its previous accounting policies.

2. *Previously recognized goodwill.* At the beginning of the first annual period for which IFRS 3 is applied, the carrying amount of goodwill arising from the prior business combination shall be its carrying amount at that date in accordance with the entity's previous accounting policies, except that the amount of any accumulated amortization of that goodwill is to be eliminated so that the carrying value of the goodwill is gross of such amortization. No other adjustments are to be made to the carrying value of goodwill.

3. *Goodwill previously recognized as a deduction from equity.* If the entity's previous accounting policies have resulted in goodwill arising from the prior business combination being recognized as a deduction from equity, the entity shall not recognize that goodwill as an asset at the beginning of the first annual period in which IFRS 3 is applied. Moreover, the entity shall not recognize in profit or loss any part of that goodwill when it disposes of all or part of the business to which that goodwill relates or when a cash-generating unit to which the goodwill relates becomes impaired.

4. *Subsequent accounting for goodwill.* From the beginning of the first annual period in which IFRS 3 is applied, an entity discontinues amortizing goodwill arising from the prior business combination and tests the goodwill for impairment in accordance with IAS 36.

5. *Previously recognized negative goodwill.* If an entity has recognized a deferred credit for an excess of its interest in the net fair value of the acquiree's identifiable assets and liabilities over the cost of that interest, the carrying amount of that deferred credit is derecognized at the beginning of the first annual period in which IFRS 3 is applied, with a corresponding adjustment to the opening balance of retained earnings as of that date.

CHAPTER 9
CASH FLOW STATEMENTS

CONTENTS

OVERVIEW

IAS 7, "Cash Flow Statements," requires that all sets of "financial statements" should include such a statement. It is designed to focus attention on cash and liquidity movements, in contrast to the income statement, which focuses on revenues and expenses. Issued in 1992, with minor revisions in 2004, IAS 7 replaced the previous, significantly different IAS 7, called "Statement of Changes in Financial Position." IAS 7, "Cash Flow Statements," specifies processes and formats for the preparation and presentation of cash flow statements, as discussed below. As a result of the terminology changes introduced by the revision to IAS 1, IAS 7 is now titled "Statement of Cash Flows." The original chapter title has been retained, which focuses on the key word.

BACKGROUND

The traditional accounting process is an uncertain and complex process. Not only is profit determination complex, it is potentially misleading. In any accounting year, there will be a mixture of complete and incomplete transactions. Transactions are complete when they have led to a final cash settlement and cause no profit-measurement difficulties.

Considerable problems arise, however, in dealing with incomplete transactions, where the profit or loss figure can be estimated only by means of the accruals concept, whereby revenue and costs are matched with one another as far as their relationship can be established or justifiably assumed and dealt with in the income statement of the period to which they relate.

Some argue that cash is all that matters, and that the cash flow should be the primary measure of corporate success, rather than net income. But cash flow is "lumpy" and the impact of an inventory build or a build up of vendor payables muddies cash flow and the picture of the entity's ongoing operations. Cash flows need to be adjusted for the one-off happenings year-by-year, and accrual accounting should be used to make those adjustments. It is true that accruals can be manipulated by management, but the financial community has said that it will take that risk. Net income remains the primary measure of performance. Nonetheless, a thoughtful analyst will read the income statement and the cash flow statement together, because the ebb and flow of the cash flow statement tells the reader something about the quality of reported net income. A large buildup of receivables may suggest a too-aggressive revenue recognition policy. A large buildup in inventories may suggest a failure to recognize obsolete or returned products.

A statement that focuses on changes in liquidity rather than on profits has two potential advantages. First, it provides different and additional information on movements and changes in net liquid assets, which assists appraisal of an enterprise's progress and prospects, and second, it provides information that is generally more objective (though not necessarily more *useful*) than that contained in the income statement.

Opinion has varied sharply in the past three decades on exactly what aspect of "liquidity" should best be focused on in published financial statements. Consider the following two balance sheet extracts from A Co.

	000s 12/31/X2	000s 12/31/X1
Inventory	4300	4600
Accounts receivable	2600	1300
Cash and bank	1200	2500
	8100	8400
Accounts payable	6500	7900
Working capital	1600	500

Identify the change in position.

If we look solely at cash, we could state that A Co. had experienced a decrease in cash of 1,300,000 over the year. On the other hand, looking at working capital indicates a much better position, an increase of 1,100,000 over the year. Which figure should users of accounts regard when taking decisions?

Practice through the 1970s and beyond was generally focused on working capital, that is, on the current assets and current liabilities. The original IAS 7 reflected this preference. Now, however, the focus is much more closely on cash. More strictly, it is changes in cash plus cash equivalents, that is, those items that are so liquid as to be "nearly cash," that are analyzed. IAS 7 carefully and precisely defines what it means by "nearly," but different national systems still have different views on this element.

IAS 7 is uncompromising in that it applies to all enterprises. It requires that a statement of cash flows be presented as an integral part of all sets of enterprise financial statements. Such statements of cash flow classify and distinguish cash flows under three headings: operating activities, investing activities, and financing activities.

IASB and U.S. GAAP are broadly similar, although there are differences of detail in the required formats. The U.S. definition of cash equivalents is similar to that in IASB GAAP, but under U.S. GAAP changes in the balances of overdrafts are classified as financing cash flows, rather than being included within cash and cash equivalents.

TERMINOLOGY

The standard defines a number of terms, mostly in a straight- forward way, all of them already mentioned above. These are as follows (par. 6):

- *Cash* comprises cash on hand and demand deposits.

- *Cash equivalents* are short-term, highly liquid investments that are readily convertible to known amounts of cash and that are subject to an insignificant risk of changes in value.

- *Cash flows* are inflows and outflows of cash and cash equivalents.

- *Operating activities* are the principal revenue-producing activities of the enterprise and other activities that are not investing or financing activities.

- *Investing activities* are the acquisition and disposal of long-term assets and other investments not included in cash equivalents, provided that they result in a recognized asset in the statement of financial position.

- *Financing activities* are activities that result in changes in the size and composition of the equity capital and borrowings of the entity.

As indicated above, cash equivalents require further clarification. Cash equivalents are held for the purpose of meeting short-term cash commitments rather than for investment or other purposes. For an investment to qualify as a cash equivalent it must be readily convertible to a known amount of cash and be subject to an insignificant risk of changes in value. Therefore, an investment normally qualifies as a cash equivalent only when it has a short maturity of, say, three months or less from the date of acquisition. Equity investments are excluded from cash equivalents unless they are, in substance, cash equivalents, for example, in the case of preferred shares acquired within a short period of their maturity and with a specified redemption date.

This means that cash equivalents must meet both of two criteria (par. 7), that is:

(a) It has a short maturity "of, say, three months or less"; and

(b) It is held to meet short-term cash requirements, not for investment or other purposes.

Bank borrowings are generally considered to be financing activities. In some countries, however, bank overdrafts that are repayable on demand form an integral part of an enterprise's cash management. In these circumstances, bank overdrafts are included as a component of net cash and cash equivalents.

> **OBSERVATION:** Analysts and readers of financial statements should not assume that "cash and cash equivalents" are interpreted identically in different countries. For example, in the United States the definition of cash equivalents is similar to that in IASB GAAP, but under U.S. GAAP changes in the balances of overdrafts are classified as financing cash flows, rather than being included within cash and cash equivalents. Under U.K. GAAP, cash is defined as cash in hand and deposits receivable on demand, less overdrafts repayable on demand. Cash equivalents are not included but are dealt with in liquid resources and financing.
>
> Enterprises from other countries that report under IASB GAAP may interpret the IAS definition, necessarily somewhat subjective as the concept of "cash equivalents" inevitably must be, in accordance with local cultures and characteristics.

PRESENTATION OF CASH FLOW STATEMENTS

The key requirement is that the cash flow statement reports cash flows during the period classified by operating, investing, and financing activities in a manner that is most appropriate to the business.

IAS 7 gives long lists of examples of each of operating, investing, and financing activities (pars. 13–17), which we do not reproduce here. We restrict our discussion to principles and to particular difficulties.

Cash flows from *operating activities* are primarily derived from the principal revenue-producing activities of the entity. Therefore, they generally result from the transactions and other events that enter into the determination of net profit or loss. All cash flows from the sale of productive non-current assets, such as plant, however, are cash flows from investing activities. However, cash payments to manufacture or acquire assets held for rental to others and subsequently held for sale, as described in paragraph 68A of IAS 16, "Property, Plant and Equipment," are cash flows from operating activities. The cash receipts from rents and subsequent sales of such assets are also cash flows from operating activities.

It follows from the above, of course, that the nature of the business, that is, of the "principal revenue-producing activities," may differ significantly from one business to another, in which case the implications of apparently similar transactions may also differ. For example, an enterprise may hold securities and loans for dealing or trading purposes, in which case they are similar to inventory acquired specifically for resale. Therefore, cash flows arising from the purchase and sale of dealing or trading securities are classified as operating activities. Similarly, cash advances and loans made by financial institutions such as banks are usually classified as operating activities since they relate to the main revenue-producing activity of that enterprise.

It is worth emphasizing that reference to the definitions of operating, investing, and financing activities given earlier makes it clear that any "principal revenue-producing activity" that is not a financing or investing activity as defined is automatically an operating activity.

The standard says very little about *investing activities* except to give a list of examples. They consist essentially of cash payments to acquire, and cash receipts from the eventual disposal of, property, plant, and equipment and other long-term productive assets. Cash payments and receipts relating to future, forward, option, and swap contracts are generally investing activities, unless undertaken by a dealer or trader in such contracts. When a contract is accounted for as a hedge of an identifiable position, however, the cash flows of the contract are classified in the same manner as the cash flows of the position being hedged.

→ **PRACTICE POINTER:** It should be noted that if a relevant asset is acquired by incurring debt directly from the seller, then this represents, *pro tem*, a non-cash transaction that, as such, will not appear in a cash flow statement at all. Subsequent payments could be argued, and have been argued by some commentators, to be investing cash outflows. In our view, this is incorrect and would be inconsistent with the substance of the transaction, which is that of a purchase and a loan. It follows that the subsequent payments off the principal of the debt are financing outflows. IAS 7 gives an illustration (in its Appendix 1), which is consistent with our argument, and supports it explicitly in paragraph 17.

Financing activities, those relating to the size of the equity capital whether by capital inflow, capital repayment, or arguably dividend payment, or to borrowings (other than any short-term borrowings accepted as cash equivalents), are in essence a simple concept. Note that while interest paid (and also taxes paid) are definitely operating activity items, dividends paid could be interpreted as either operating or as financing activities. The standard says (par. 33) that dividends paid may be classified as a financing cash flow because they are a cost of obtaining financial resources. Alternatively, dividends paid may be classified as a component of cash flows from operating activities in order to assist users to demonstrate the ability of an entity to pay dividends out of operating cash flows.

IAS 7 implies, but does not explicitly state, a preference for treating dividends as a financing activity. We concur with this view, which is consistent with U.K. and U.S. practice.

Reporting Cash Flows from Operating Activities

Enterprises are allowed to use either of two methods to analyze and report cash flows from operating activities. These are (par. 18):

(a) The direct method, whereby major classes of gross cash receipts and gross cash payments are disclosed; and

(b) The indirect method, whereby net profit or loss is adjusted for the effects of transactions of a non-cash nature, any deferrals or accruals of past or future operating cash receipts or payments, and items of income or expense associated with investing or financing cash flows.

Entities are encouraged to report cash flows from operating activities using the direct method, but this is not a requirement. The indirect method takes reported net profit and adjusts for, in effect removes, non-cash flow items included in the calculation of that profit figure. The direct method, in contrast, is in effect a direct analyzed summary of the cash book. As such, the direct method provides information that may be useful in estimating future cash flows and that is not available under the indirect method.

The workings of, and differences between, the two methods are best shown by an example.

OBSERVATION: Illustration of Calculation of Cash Flow from Operating Activities by the Direct Method

Cash received from customers	144,750
Cash paid to suppliers and employees	(137,600)
Cash dividend received from affiliate	900
Other operating cash receipts	10,000
Interest paid in cash (net of amounts capitalized)	(5,200)
Income taxes paid in cash	(4,500)
Net cash provided (used) by operating activities	8,350

OBSERVATION: Illustration of Calculation of Cash Flow from Operating Activities by the Indirect Method

Net income	8,000
Adjustments to reconcile net income to net cash provided by operating activities:	
Depreciation and amortization	8,600
Provisions for doubtful accounts receivable	750
Provision for deferred income taxes	1,000
Undistributed earnings of affiliate	(2,100)
Gain on sale of equipment	(2,500)
Payment received on installment sale of product	2,500
Changes in operating assets and liabilities net of effects from purchase of XYZ Company:	
Increase in accounts receivable	(7,750)
Increase in inventory	(4,000)
Increase in accounts payable and accrued expenses	3,850
Total adjustments to net income	350
Net cash provided (used) by operating activities	8,350

A comparison of the above two illustrations makes it clear, we suggest, that the indirect method is at the same time more complicated and less informative in terms of actual cash flows than the direct method. U.S. GAAP, like IASB GAAP, encourage but do not require the use of the direct method. U.K. GAAP now require the indirect method, on the grounds that the benefits to users of the direct method are outweighed by the costs of preparing it. If one takes a user rather than a preparer perspective, it is difficult to support the U.K. view on this point.

Reporting Cash Flows from Investing and Financing Activities

The essential requirement is very simple, namely, that an enterprise should report separately major classes of gross cash receipts and gross cash payments. Netting off of cash receipts and payments is allowed (for investing, financing, and operating activities) only in limited circumstances. These are (par. 22):

(a) Cash receipts and payments on behalf of customers when the cash flows reflect the activities of the customer rather than those of the enterprise; and

(b) Cash receipts and payments for items in which the turnover is quick, the amounts are large, and the maturities are short.

Items (b) and (c) above are likely to be restricted in practice to financial institutions such as banks. IAS 7 clarifies this as follows (par. 24).

Cash flows arising from each of the following activities of a financial institution may be reported on a net basis:

(a) Cash receipts and payments for the acceptance and repayment of deposits with a fixed maturity date;

(b) The placement of deposits with and withdrawal of deposits from other financial institutions; and

(c) Cash advances and loans made to customers and the repayment of those advances and loans.

Note that in every respect, reporting cash flows on a net basis is *allowed* in all the above situations. It is never *required*.

A complication arises with the treatment of foreign currency cash flows. This is because IAS 21, "The Effects of Changes in Foreign Exchange Rates"(see Chapter 18), permits the use of an exchange rate that approximates the actual rate. For example, a weighted average exchange rate for a period may be used for recording foreign currency transactions or the translation of the cash flows of a foreign subsidiary. However, IAS 21 does not permit use of this exchange rate at the balance sheet date when translating the cash flows of a foreign subsidiary (par. 27). Unrealized gains and losses arising from changes in foreign currency exchange rates are not cash flows. The effect of exchange rate changes on cash and cash equivalents held or due in a foreign currency, however, is reported in the cash flow statement in order to reconcile cash and cash equivalents at the beginning and the end of the period. This amount is presented separately from cash flows from operating, investing, and financing activities and includes the differences, if any, had those cash flows been reported at end of period exchange rates.

Cash flows from extraordinary items were separately disclosed, within the appropriate classification of operating, investing, or financing activities. However, with the abolition of the category of extraordinary items, this requirement has been deleted. Cash flows from interest and dividends received and paid should each be shown separately, as already discussed. Cash flows arising from taxes on income should be separately disclosed and should be classified as cash flows from operating activities, unless they can be specifically identified with financing and investing activities.

IAS 7 restricts cash flow reporting related to investments in subsidiaries or associates accounted for by use of the equity or cost method to cash flows that have actually moved between the enterprise and the investee. This also applies to a joint venture consolidated by the equity method. However, an enterprise that reports its interest in a jointly controlled entity (see IAS 31, "Financial Reporting of Interests in Joint Ventures," in Chapter 11) using proportionate consolidation, includes in its consolidated cash flow statement its proportionate share of the jointly controlled entity's cash flows.

Other Disclosures

IAS 7 requires that the aggregate cash outflows arising from acquisitions of subsidiaries or other business units and the aggregate cash inflows arising from such disposals should be reported separately, classified as investing activities (pars. 39–40). In addition, an entity should disclose in relation thereto the aggregate amounts during the period of each of the following:

(a) The total consideration paid or received,

(b) The portion of the consideration consisting of cash and cash equivalents,

(c) The amount of cash and cash equivalents in the subsidiaries or other businesses over which control is obtained or lost, and

(d) The amount of the assets and liabilities other than cash or cash equivalents in the subsidiaries or other businesses over which control is obtained or lost, summarized by each major category.

Arising from changes in IAS 27, "Consolidated and Separate Financial Statements," mandatory from July 1, 2009 (see Chapter 11), IAS 7 now confirms that cash flows relating to changes in ownership interests in a subsidiary that do not result in a loss of control are classified as cash flows from financing activities.

Paragraph 44 makes it clear that investing and financing transactions, such as the creation of a finance lease or the conversion of debt to equity, which do not result in movements in cash or cash equivalents, are not included in a cash flow statement. They must, however, be disclosed elsewhere "in a way that provides all the relevant information about these investing and financing activities"—by narrative, note, or separate schedule.

OBSERVATION: As we pointed out earlier, the substance of a finance lease transaction is that of a purchase and a loan. A purchase implies a payment, financed from the receipt of the loan. Similarly, the conversion of debt to equity is arguably, in substance, the receipt of cash from equity holders and the payment of cash to previous creditors.

Because the IASB supports the principle of substance over form (Framework, par. 35; see Chapter 2), it could be argued that such situations should be reflected by equal and opposite in-substance "cash flows," on opposite sides of the cash flow statement. Paragraphs 43 and 44, without discussion, clearly reject this argument.

Entities are required to disclose the various components of the total cash and cash equivalents (par. 45) and, if necessary, a reconciliation of any differences between the amounts of cash and cash equivalents in the cash flow statement and the amounts in the balance sheet. The policy adopted in determining the figures for cash and cash equivalents must be clearly stated in the appropriate place. An entity should also disclose, together with appropriate explanations (par. 48), the amount of cash and cash equivalent balances, if material, that are not available for immediate use "by the group," for example because of exchange controls (why "by the group" rather than "by the entity" is not clear). The standard concludes by suggesting several non-mandatory disclosures.

Reference may need to be made to several other International Accounting Standards in relation to matters possibly relevant to cash flow statements. These include:

- IAS 14, "Segment Reporting" (Chapter 32)
- IAS 34, "Interim Financial Reporting" (Chapter 23)
- IFRS 5, "Non-Current Assets Held for Sale and Discontinued Operations" (Chapter 27)

CHAPTER 10
CHANGING PRICES AND HYPERINFLATIONARY ECONOMIES

CONTENTS

OVERVIEW

In IASB GAAP, the use of adjustments or restatement to reflect the effects of changing prices on an entity's financial position and result is not a requirement unless the reporting currency is that of a country with a hyperinflationary economy. Hyperinflation is not defined in IASB GAAP, but a cumulative rate of inflation that approaches or exceeds 100% over three years is given as an important indicator. When the rate of inflation affecting the reporting currency is lower than this but significant, IASB GAAP encourage, but do not require, reporting entities to adopt a method of restatement based on either the general purchasing power approach or the current cost approach. In a hyperinflationary situation, IASB GAAP require the use of restatement in terms of general purchasing power, even in the case of financial statements prepared on the basis of current costs.

IASB GAAP on financial reporting in hyperinflationary economies are set out in IAS 29, "Financial Reporting in Hyperinflationary Economies," and the International Financial Reporting Interpretations Committee's IFRIC 7, "Applying the Restatement Approach under IAS 29."

BACKGROUND

In 1977, the IASC issued IAS 6, "Accounting Responses to Changing Prices," which required the disclosure of the effect of any procedures applied to reflect the impact of specific or general price changes. Subsequently, the IASC replaced IAS 6 with IAS 15, "Information Reflecting the Effects of Changing Prices," which required the use of restatement on the basis of either the general price level or current costs when the reporting currency was subject to a significant (but unspecified) degree of inflation. In 1989, the IASC followed an approach similar to that of the FASB, by making IAS 15 optional. In the same year, the IASC issued IAS 29, which requires general price level restatement when the reporting currency is subject to hyperinflation. It is worth noting, however, that IASB GAAP are applied in a number of countries with less developed economies, where significant inflation (but not necessarily hyperinflation) may be prevalent. However, IAS 15 was little used in practice and was withdrawn by the IASB with effect from January 1, 2005.

The main differences between IASB GAAP and U.S. GAAP on accounting for the effects of changing prices and hyperinflation are:

1. IAS 29 uses the measuring unit current at the balance sheet date (end-of-year units of general purchasing power) to express financial statements that are the result of general price-level restatement. For comprehensive restatement, FASB Accounting Standards Codification™ (ASC) 255, "Changing Prices," uses end-of-year units of general purchasing power; for partial restatement, either average-for-year units, or units of general purchasing power of the base period used to calculate the Consumer Price Index, may be used.

2. IAS 29 is applied not merely by entities whose reporting currency is subject to hyperinflation but also (in accordance with IAS 21, "The Effects of Changes in Foreign Exchange Rates") to the financial statements of foreign entities that report in such a currency, prior to their translation into the group reporting currency for the purpose of consolidation or equitization. ASC 830 does not permit this "re-state and translate" approach. Instead, the group reporting currency should be considered the "functional currency" of a foreign operation in a hyperinflationary economy, and the financial statement items should be remeasured in the functional currency.

SCOPE

IAS 29, "Financial Reporting in Hyperinflationary Economies," should be applied to the primary financial statements, including the consolidated financial statements, of any entity whose functional currency is in a hyperinflationary economy (IAS 29, par. 1). See Chapter 18, "Foreign Currency Translation," for a definition of "functional currency" and a further discussion of this issue.

IAS 29, paragraph 3, sets out five characteristics of the economic environment as indicators of hyperinflation, of which the fifth is the most frequently cited:

1. The general population prefers to keep its wealth in nonmonetary assets or in a relatively stable foreign currency.

2. The general population regards monetary amounts not in terms of the local currency but in terms of a relatively stable foreign currency.

3. Sales and purchases on credit take place at prices that compensate for the expected loss of purchasing power during the credit period even when it is short.

4. Interest rates, wages, and prices are linked to a price index.

5. The cumulative inflation rate over three years is approaching or exceeds 100%.

THE RESTATEMENT OF FINANCIAL STATEMENTS

IAS 29 requires that if the measurement currency used by an entity is the currency of a hyperinflationary economy, then the entity's financial statements should be restated in units of the same purchasing power, using the measuring unit current at the balance sheet dates (units of current purchasing power). The general purchasing power approach is related to the concept of maintaining real financial capital (see Chapter 2, "The Conceptual Framework for Financial Reporting"), and reflects the effects of changes in the general purchasing power of the monetary unit, as measured by some general price index. The financial statements are restated in monetary units of the same general purchasing power, using the measuring unit current at the balance sheet date. This approach is described further below. According to IAS 29, paragraph 37, this restatement should be made using "a general price index that reflects changes in general purchasing power," and it is preferable that the same index be used by all enterprises that report in the currency of the same economy. IFRIC 6 requires that, in the reporting period in which an entity identifies the existence of hyperinflation in the economy of its functional currency, it should apply IAS 29 as if it had always applied the standard, and therefore restate its opening balance sheet at the beginning of the earliest period presented in its financial statements. The deferred tax items in the opening balance sheet of any of the comparative periods presented in the restated financial statements (remeasured in accordance with IAS 12, "Income Taxes") should be restated for the change in the measuring unit.

OBSERVATION: As stated in IAS 29, paragraph 7: "In a hyperinflationary economy, financial statements, whether they are based on a historical cost approach or a current cost approach, are useful only if they are expressed in terms of the measuring unit current at the balance sheet date." The concern here goes beyond capital maintenance to the use of a meaningful measuring unit. The measuring unit employed, the unit that is "current at the balance sheet date," is sometimes called a "unit of current purchasing power" or "current purchasing power unit."(This useful term is not used in IASB GAAP but will be employed in this chapter.)

→ **PRACTICE POINTER:** It should be noted that official price indexes sometimes deliberately understate the erosion of the purchasing power of the monetary unit. We may also note that for foreign currency translation in the consolidation process, U.S. GAAP do not permit the "restate and translate" approach of IAS 29, which is vulnerable to this problem.

One method of verifying the accuracy of an official price index is to compare the percentage change in it with the percentage change in the exchange rates of the national currency into "hard" currencies. In the presence of exchange controls and "official" rates of exchange that do not give a fair reflection of the relative loss of purchasing power of the national currency, changes in the "unofficial" rates of exchange into hard currencies may be used for the purposes of verifying the official price indexes. While this may identify a problem, however, it does not provide a solution. The "functional currency" approach of U.S. GAAP, whereby in such a situation the entity would report in a "hard" functional currency other than the national currency, such as the group reporting currency, offers a better chance of finding a solution.

The restated financial statements should be presented as the primary financial statements, and separate presentation of the unrestated financial statements is discouraged. The corresponding figures for the previous period required by IAS 1, "Presentation of Financial Statements" (see Chapter 4) and any information in respect of earlier periods should also be restated in terms of units of current purchasing power at the balance sheet date (IAS 29, pars. 7 – 8).

The gain or loss on net monetary position (see below) should be separately disclosed as part of net income (IAS 29, par. 9).

If the entity is a foreign operation (as defined in IAS 21 paragraph 8; see Chapter 18) and is included in the financial statements or consolidated financial statements of another reporting entity, and its functional currency is that of a hyperinflationary economy, the entity's financial statements are restated in accordance with IAS 29. An entity cannot avoid such a restatement by, for example, adopting as its functional currency a currency other that one determined in accordance with IAS 21, paragraphs 9–12, for example its parent's functional currency (IAS 21, par. 14).

Historical Cost Financial Statements

End-of-Period Balance Sheet

Monetary items are not restated because they are already expressed in terms of the monetary unit current at the balance sheet date (current purchasing power unit). In the case of monetary items that are linked by agreement to changes in prices, such as index-linked bonds and loans, their carrying amounts adjusted in accordance with the agreement are used in the restated balance sheet. Other balance sheet amounts are restated to amounts in units of current purchasing power by applying a general price index, unless they are already carried at amounts in units of current purchasing power, such as current market value or net realizable value (IAS 29, pars. 11– 14).

For items carried at cost or cost less depreciation, the restated cost or cost less depreciation is determined by applying to the historical cost and accumulated depreciation (if any) the change in a selected general price index from the date of acquisition to the balance sheet date. For items carried at revalued amounts, the revalued amount and accumulated depreciation (if any) are restated by applying the change in the price index from the date of the latest revaluation to the balance sheet date.

If records of the acquisition of property, plant, and equipment do not permit the ascertainment or estimation of the acquisition dates, it may be necessary, when the standard is first applied, to use an independent professional valuation of the items concerned as a basis for their restatement. If no general price index is available to cover the period between acquisition and the balance sheet date, an estimate of the changes in general purchasing power of the reporting currency over that period may be made by using the changes in the exchange rate between the reporting currency and a relatively stable foreign currency (IAS 29, pars. 11–18).

The restated amount of a nonmonetary item is reduced (in accordance with the appropriate IFRSs) when it exceeds its recoverable amount (IAS 29, par. 19).

It is not appropriate both to restate capital expenditure (fixed assets) financed by borrowing and to capitalize that part of the borrowing costs that compensates for inflation.

OBSERVATION: The part of borrowing costs that compensates for inflation is the difference between borrowing costs on a nominal or money basis and borrowing costs on a real (inflation-adjusted) basis. For example, if the nominal borrowing cost for a year is 45% and annual inflation is 35%, the real annual borrowing cost is:

$$(1.45/1.35 - 1) \times 100 = 7.407\%$$

While the income statement will show the nominal borrowing cost, it will also show the gain or loss on net monetary position, which includes the effect of inflation on borrowings (see below). Thus, in effect, it is borrowing costs on a real basis that impact net income.

At the beginning of the first period of application of IAS 29, the components of owners' equity are restated by applying a general price index from the dates on which the components were contributed or otherwise arose, except for retained earnings and any revaluation surplus. Any revaluation surplus from prior periods is eliminated, and restated retained earnings is the residual amount (balancing figure) in the restated balance sheet. Subsequently, all components of owners' equity are restated by applying a general price index from the beginning of the period (or the date of contribution, if later). The movements for the period in owners' equity should be disclosed in accordance with IAS 1, "Presentation of Financial Statements" (see Chapter 4) (IAS 29, pars. 24– 25).

Income Statement for the Period

All items in the income statement should be expressed in terms of end-of-year current purchasing power units. Hence, all income statement amounts need to be restated by applying the change in the general price index between the dates at which the amounts were recorded and the balance sheet date.

→ **PRACTICE POINTER:** In practice, average index values for sub-periods, such as months, would normally be used, as in the case of average exchange rates used for the translation of foreign currency amounts under IAS 21 (see Chapter 18). General price-level restatement has been likened to currency translation.

Gain or Loss on Net Monetary Position

According to IAS 29, paragraph 27, the gain or loss on the entity's net monetary position may be estimated by applying the change in the general price index to the weighted average for the period of the difference between monetary assets and monetary liabilities.

OBSERVATION: IAS 29 is not very explicit on this point. The method described in the *GAAP Guide*, Chapter 6, is slightly different but quite explicit and is used in the Illustration in the Appendix to this chapter.

Alternatively, the gain or loss on net monetary position could be derived as the balancing figure in the restated balance sheet, after the inclusion of net income (less any dividend paid) in retained earnings but before the inclusion of the net gain or loss on net monetary position in net income.

The gain or loss on the net monetary position should be included in net income. Any adjustment to index-linked assets or liabilities (as mentioned above in the section on the balance sheet) is offset against the gain or loss on net monetary position. It is suggested that the gain or loss in net monetary position should be presented in the income statement together with interest income and expense (see the Observation above) and foreign exchange differences related to invested or borrowed funds (IAS 29, pars. 27–28).

Investees Accounted for under the Equity Method

If an investee accounted for under the equity method reports in the currency of a hyperinflationary country, the financial statements of the investee are restated in accordance with IAS 29 in order to calculate the investor's share of its net assets and results of operations (IAS 29, par. 20).

Current Cost Financial Statements

End-of-Period Balance Sheet

Items stated at current cost are already expressed in units of current purchasing power and so are not restated. Other items are restated as described for historical cost balance sheets above (IAS 29, par. 29).

Income Statement for the Period

The current cost income statement reports items in terms of the purchasing power of the monetary unit at the times when the underlying transactions or events occurred. For example, cost of goods sold and depreciation are recorded at their current costs at the time of consumption. Therefore, all amounts need to be restated into current purchasing power units at the balance sheet date (IAS 29, par. 30).

Gain or Loss on Net Monetary Position

Gain or loss on net monetary position should be calculated and accounted for as already described above (IAS 29, par. 31).

Cash Flow Statement

All items in the cash flow statement should be restated in terms of current purchasing power units at the balance sheet date (IAS 29, par. 33).

Corresponding Figures

Comparative figures from the previous reporting period, and other comparative information that is disclosed in respect of prior periods, should be restated in terms of units of current purchasing power at the balance sheet date (IAS 29, par. 34).

Consolidated Financial Statements

A parent that reports in the currency of a hyperinflationary economy may have subsidiaries that also report in currencies of hyperinflationary economies. The financial statements of such subsidiaries should be restated in accordance with IAS 29 as described above, before being included in the process of consolidation. In the case of foreign subsidiaries, financial statements (restated as described above if they are in the currency of a hyperinflationary economy) should be translated into the reporting currency at closing rates as required by IAS 21.

If financial statements with different reporting dates are consolidated, all items, whether monetary or nonmonetary, should be restated into units of current purchasing power at the date of the consolidated financial statements (IAS 29, pars. 35–36).

ECONOMIES CEASING TO BE HYPERINFLATIONARY

When an entity discontinues the preparation and presentation of financial statements in accordance with IAS 29 because the economy of its reporting currency is no longer hyperinflationary, the amounts that are expressed in current purchasing power units as at the end of the previous reporting period should be treated as the basis for the carrying amounts in its subsequent financial statements (IAS 29, par. 38).

DISCLOSURES

The following disclosures should be made:

1. The fact that the financial statements and the comparative figures have been restated for changes in the general purchasing power of the reporting currency and are stated in terms of the unit of purchasing power current at the balance sheet date.

2. Whether the underlying financial statements are based on historical costs or current costs.

3. The identity and level of the general price index used at the balance sheet date and the movement in this index during the current and previous reporting periods (IAS 29, par. 39).

APPENDIX:
ILLUSTRATION OF GENERAL PRICE-LEVEL RESTATEMENT

XYZ Company was established on January 1, 2006. Its beginning balance sheet on that date was as follows:

	$
Land	6,000
Plant and equipment	4,000
Inventories	2,000
	12,000
Stockholders' equity	12,000

Gain or Loss on Net Monetary Items

The gain or loss on net monetary items may be calculated in five steps. Note that throughout, a positive figure denotes a net monetary asset position, a negative figure denotes a net monetary liability position, and that if a minus sign is applied to an amount that is already negative, the operation becomes an addition.

1. Calculate the net monetary position at the beginning of the year, and restate it to end-of-year current purchasing power units using the change in the general price-level index.

2. Assemble all increases and decreases in net monetary position during the year and restate them to end-of-year current purchasing power units (as indicated above for income statement items).

3. Calculate an estimated end-of-year net monetary position as the sum of the restated amounts in current purchasing power units obtained in steps 1 and 2.

4. Calculate the actual net monetary position at the balance sheet date.

5. The gain or loss on net monetary position is the amount calculated in step 4 minus the amount calculated in step 3.

Illustration of General Price-Level Restatement

During the year 2006, the company made the following transactions:
1. Purchased extra inventory for $10,000
2. Sold inventory for $11,000 cash, which had a historical cost of $9,000
3. Ending inventory on December 31, 2006, had a historical cost of $3,000 and was bought when the general price index was 115 (average)

4. The plant and equipment have an expected life of 4 years, and nil residual value. The straight-line method of depreciation is used

5. The general price index stood at:

   100 on January 1, 2006

   110 on June 30, 2006

   120 on December 31, 2006

Note: The symbol $CPP is used to indicate the measuring unit, namely dollars of current purchasing power as at December 31, 2006.

General Price-Level Restated Income Statement for the Year 2006

	$	$CPP	$CPP
Sales	11,000 × 120/110		12,000
Beginning inventory	2,000 × 120/100	2,400	
Add purchases	10,000 × 120/110	10,909	
		13,309	
(Less) ending inventory	3,000 × 120/115	(3,310)	
			10,179
			1,821
(Less) depreciation			(1,200)
			621
(Less) loss on net monetary assets items			(91)
Net income after general price-level restatement			530

Calculation of loss on net monetary items:

	$	$CPP
Beginning balance of net monetary items	Nil	Nil
Sales	11,000 × 120/110	12,000
Purchases	10,000 × 120/110	(10,909)
Estimated ending balance of monetary items		1,091
Actual ending balance of net monetary items		(1,000)
Difference = loss		91

The net income before price-level restatement ($11,000 − $9,000 − $1,000 for depreciation = $1,000) and after price-level restatement can be reconciled as follows:

Historical cost net income	$1,000

Inventories

Additional charge based on restating the cost of inventories at the beginning and end of the year in dollars of current purchasing power, thus taking the inflationary element out of the profit on the sale of inventory Beginning inventory + 400 minus ending inventory — 130   (270)

Depreciation

Additional depreciation based on restated cost, measured in dollars of
current purchasing power of plant and equipment $1,200 – $1,000   (200)

Monetary items

Net loss in purchasing power resulting from the effects of inflation on the
company's net monetary assets   (91)

Effect of restatement of sales, purchases, and all other costs

These are increased by the change in the index between the average date at
which they occurred and the end of the year. This restatement increases
profit as sales exceed the costs included in this heading   91

Net income after general price-level restatement $530

Value of stockholders' equity, January 1, 2006 $ 12,000
Restated in terms of $_{CPP} at December 31, 2006   (12,000 × 120/100) $_{CPP} 14,400

General Price-Level Restated Balance Sheet as at December 31, 2006

	$	$_{CPP}	$_{CPP}
Land	6,000 × 120/100		7,200
Plant and equipment	4,000 × 120/100	4,800	
(less) depreciation	1,000 × 120/100	(1,200)	
			3,600
			10,800
Inventories	3,000 × 120/100	3,130	
Cash	(11,000 – 10,000)	1,000	4,130
Stockholders' equity	($_{CPP} 14,400 + 530)		14,930
			14,930

CHAPTER 11
CONSOLIDATED FINANCIAL STATEMENTS AND DISCLOSURE OF INTERESTS IN OTHER ENTITIES

CONTENTS

OVERVIEW

Consolidated financial statements represent the results of operations (income statement), cash flow statement, and financial position (balance sheet) of a single entity (the group) that comprises more than one separate legal entity. Because of the relationships between the entities making up the group, consolidated financial statements are considered to provide a more meaningful picture than the financial statements of the separate entities. The concept of a group in IASB GAAP is based on the concept of *control*, as exercised by a parent company (investor) over an investee, in virtue of which the latter is a subsidiary company of the former.

The definition of *control* in IASB GAAP has evolved in response to the problems of financial reporting revealed by the financial and economic crisis of 2007–2009, and in particular the "creative accounting" that was used to avoid recognizing certain special purpose or "structured" entities as subsidiaries in order to omit them from consolidation. Thus, in IFRSs issued in May 2011, the IASB broadened the definition of control, which was originally set out in IAS 27, "Consolidated and Separate Financial Statements," as having two essential components, namely (1) the power to govern the financial and operating policies of an entity and, therefore, (2) the ability to obtain benefits from the entity's activities. This broader definition of control omits reference to "govern[ing]the financial and operating policies of an entity," and is based on the following three essential components:

1. Power of the investor over the investee;

2. The investor's exposure, or rights, to variable returns from its involvement with the investee; and

3. The investor's ability to use power over the investee to affect the amount of the investor's returns.

A parent should issue consolidated financial statements in which it consolidates its investments in subsidiaries (excluding only those in respect of which there is evidence that they were acquired with the intention to dispose of them within 12 months and that management is actively seeking a buyer), unless (1) it is itself a wholly owned subsidiary or a partially owned subsidiary of another entity and its other owners have been informed about and do not object to it not issuing consolidated financial statements; (2) its debt or equity instruments are not traded in a public market; (3) it did not file and is not in the process of filing its financial statements with a regulatory body for the purpose of issuing financial instruments in a public market; and (4) the ultimate or an intermediate parent of the parent issues consolidated financial statements that comply with IFRSs. A parent that does not issue consolidated financial statements for these reasons should present separate financial statements as required by the revised IAS 27, "Separate Financial Statements." Similar requirements, as set out in IAS 31, "Interest in Joint Ventures," apply to a (joint) venturer in respect of the recognition of its interest in a jointly controlled entity, using proportionate consolidation or the (less preferred alternative) equity method according to IAS 28, "Investments in Associates." However, IAS 31 will be superseded by new IFRSs issued in May 2011 (see below).

The relevant IASB GAAP have been promulgated in:

- IAS 27, "Consolidated and Separate Financial Statements," as revised in December 2003 and amended in 2008 in conjunction with the revision of IFRS 3, "Business Combinations,", to be superseded by IAS 27, "Separate

Financial Statements," for annual periods beginning on or after January 1, 2013.

- IAS 31, "Interests in Joint Ventures," as revised in December 2003, to be superseded by IFRS 11, "Joint Arrangements," and IFRS 12, "Disclosure of Interests in Other Entities," for annual periods beginning on or after January 1, 2013.

- IAS 28, "Investments in Associates," as revised in December 2003, to be superseded by the revised IAS 28, "Investments in Associates and Joint Ventures."

- IAS 39, "Financial Instruments: Recognition and Measurement," as revised in March 2004, December 2004, April 2004, June 2005 and August 2005, being gradually superseded by IFRS 9, "Financial Instruments."

- SIC-12, "Consolidation—Special-Purpose Entities," as amended by IAS 27 in December 2003 and an International Financial Reporting Interpretations Committee (IFRIC) amendment in November 2004. SIC-12 will be superseded by IFRS 10.

- SIC 13 "Jointly Controlled Entities—Non-Monetary Contributions by Venturers," to be superseded by IFRS 11.

- IFRIC 5, "Rights to Interests Arising from Decommissioning, Restoration and Environmental Rehabilitation Funds."

The new and revised standards issued in May 2011 do not become mandatory until annual reporting periods beginning on or after January 1, 2013, although earlier adoption is permitted. Hence, the texts of IASs 27, 28, and 31 as at January 1, 2011, are applicable until that time. Accordingly, this chapter covers IASs 27 and 31, but also includes summaries of IFRSs 10, 11, and 12.

BACKGROUND

The IASB originally issued separate standards for consolidated financial statements (IAS 27), for the equity method (IAS 28), and for business combinations (IAS 22). Consolidated financial statements and the equity method were originally covered by IAS 3, which was then superseded when IAS 27 and IAS 28 were issued. Proportionate consolidation in the case of joint ventures is also dealt with separately in IAS 31.

IAS 27 and IAS 31 were addressed in the IASB's May 2002 exposure draft, "Improvements to International Accounting Standards." Significant changes proposed include (1) tightening up the exemptions from the requirements to prepare consolidated financial statements and to include subsidiaries in the consolidation, and (2) the elimination of the allowed alternative of using the equity method to account, in an investor's *separate* financial statements, for investments in subsidiaries, jointly controlled entities and associates that are consolidated, proportionately consolidated, or accounted for by the equity method in the investor's consolidated financial statements. In the investor's separate financial statements, such investments would be either carried at cost or accounted for in accordance with IAS 39, "Financial Instruments: Recognition and Measurement." In April 2003, the IASB confirmed its general support for the changes proposed in the exposure draft, and revised standards incorporating these changes were scheduled for the third quarter of 2003. The revised standards were in fact issued in December 2003 and were mandatory from January 1, 2005. In 2008, IAS 27 was amended as part of the second phase of the business combinations project undertaken jointly with the FASB. The amendments relate mainly to accounting for non-controlling interests (formerly termed minority interests) and the loss of control of a subsidiary. Further amendments to IAS 27 and minor amendments to IAS 31 were issued in May 2008 and are incorporated below.

In May 2011, as part of its convergence program with U.S. GAAP, the IASB issued a set of new IFRSs dealing with consolidated financial statements (IFRS 10), joint arrangements (a term introduced to replace "joint ventures" (IFRS 11)) and disclosures of interests in other entities (IFRS 12), as well as revised versions of IAS 27 and IAS 28. These new and revised standards are to be adopted for annual reporting periods beginning on or after January 1, 2013, with earlier adoption permitted. When adopted, IFRSs 11 and 12 will supersede IAS 31.

For interests in jointly controlled operations, as part of the convergence with U.S. GAAP, the IASB intended to disallow proportionate consolidation and to require the equity method. A proposal to this effect, and to withdraw IAS 31 and SIC 13, was included in ED 9, "Joint Arrangements," issued in September 2007. The comments received on ED 9 were still under discussion in May 2009, with a view to issuing a new IFRS by the end of 2009. In fact, this was achieved when IFRSs 11 and 12 were issued in May 2011.

A main objective of IFRSs 10 and 12, with a redefinition of "control," is to tighten up the treatment of special-purpose entities, renamed "structured entities." (IFRS 12, par. 2 (b) (iii))

DEFINITIONS

The following terms are used in IAS 27 and IAS 31, with the meanings indicated (IAS 27, par. 4; IAS 31, par. 3; and IAS 28, par. 2):

- *Consolidated financial statements* are the financial statements of a group presented as those of a single economic entity.
- *Control* is the power to govern the financial and operating policies of an entity so as to obtain benefits from its activities.
- *Joint control* is the contractually agreed sharing of control over an economic activity.
- *Significant influence* is the power to participate in the financial and operating policy decisions of an entity but is neither control nor joint control over those policies.
- *A joint venture* is a contractual arrangement whereby two or more parties undertake an economic activity that is subject to joint control.
- *A venturer* is a party to a joint venture that has joint control over that joint venture.
- *An investor in a joint venture* is a party to a joint venture that does not have joint control over that joint venture.

- *The cost method* is a method of accounting for an investment whereby the investment is recognized at cost and the investor recognizes income from the investment only to the extent that the investor receives distributions from accumulated profits of the investee arising after the date of acquisition. Distributions received in excess of such profits are considered to be a recovery of the investment and as such are recognized as a reduction of its cost.

- *The equity method* is a method of accounting whereby an interest in a jointly controlled entity is initially recorded at cost and adjusted thereafter for post-acquisition changes in the venturer's share of net assets of the jointly controlled entity. The venturer's profit or loss includes its share of the profit or loss of the jointly controlled entity.

- *A parent* is an entity that one or more subsidiaries.

- *A subsidiary* is an entity, including an unincorporated entity, such as a partnership, that is controlled by another entity known as the parent.

- *A group* is a parent and all of its subsidiaries.

- *Non-controlling interest* is that portion of the profit or loss and net assets of a subsidiary attributable to equity interests that are not owned, directly or indirectly through subsidiaries, by the parent.

- *Proportionate consolidation* is a method of accounting whereby a venturer's share of each of the assets, liabilities, income, and expenses of a jointly controlled entity is either combined line by line with similar items or reported as separate line items in the venturer's financial statements.

- *An associate* is an entity, including an unincorporated entity such as a partnership, over which the investor has significant influence and that is neither a subsidiary nor an interest in a joint venture.

- *Separate financial statements* are those issued by a parent, an investor in an associate, or a venturer in a jointly controlled entity, in which the investments are accounted for on the basis of the direct equity interest rather than of the reported results and net assets of the investee.

Separate financial statements may be required by law or tax regulations to be produced in addition to consolidated financial statements or financial statements in which investments are accounted for using the equity method or in which venturer's interests in joint ventures are proportionately consolidated. They may also be issued in lieu of consolidated financial statements if the conditions indicated under section addressing scope, below, are satisfied.

SCOPE

Consolidated Financial Statements

According to IASB GAAP, any parent having one or more subsidiaries that do not meet the criteria for exclusion from consolidation is required to issue consolidated financial statements (IAS 27, par. 9).

However, a parent that meets all the following conditions need not issue consolidated financial statements:

1. The parent is itself a wholly owned subsidiary, or is a partially owned subsidiary, of another entity, and its other owners (including those not otherwise entitled to vote) have been informed about, and do not object to, the parent not issuing consolidated financial statements;

2. The parent's debt or equity instruments are not traded in a public market, a domestic or foreign stock exchange or an over-the-counter market, including local and regional markets;

3. The parent did not file and is not is the process of filing its financial statements with a securities commission or other regulator for the purpose of issuing any class of instruments in a public market; and

4. The ultimate or any intermediary parent of the parent issues consolidated financial statements available for public use that comply with IFRSs.

A parent or venturer that elects not to issue consolidated financial statements on the grounds stated above, and issues only separate financial statements, must do so in accordance with IAS 27, paragraphs 38–43 (IAS 27, pars. 10–11).

Interests in Joint Ventures

Any entity having an investment in a jointly controlled entity should issue financial statements in which the investment is recognized using either proportionate consolidation or the equity method; and any entity having an investment in a jointly controlled operation that is not an entity must recognize in its financial statements the assets that it controls, the liabilities and expenses that it incurs, and its share of the income that it earns from the sale of goods or services by the joint venture (IAS 31, par. 15). The conditions for excluding a subsidiary from consolidation also apply to the exclusion of a jointly controlled entity from proportionate consolidation.

However, these requirements do not apply to venturers' interests in jointly controlled entities held by:

- Venture capital organizations; or

- Mutual funds, unit trusts, and similar entities including investment-linked insurance funds that, on initial recognition, are designated as at fair value through profit or loss or are classified as held for trading and accounted for in accordance with IAS 39. A venturer holding such an interest is required to make the disclosures set out in IAS 31, paragraphs 55–56 (see below).

SCOPE OF CONSOLIDATED FINANCIAL STATEMENTS

Criteria for Inclusion: The Concept of Control

IAS 27, paragraph 12, states that consolidated financial statements must include all subsidiaries of the parent. However, if on acquisition a subsidiary meets the criteria for classification as held for sale in accordance with IFRS 5, "Non-current Assets Held for Sale and Discontinued Operations" (see Chapter 27), it is accounted for in the consolidated financial statements in accordance with that IFRS (see IFRS 5, pars. BC52–BC55).

A subsidiary is defined as an entity that is controlled by another entity, the parent. Control is presumed to exist when the parent owns, directly or indirectly through subsidiaries, more than half of the voting power of an entity unless, in exceptional circumstances, it can be clearly demonstrated that such ownership does not constitute control. Control also exists when the parent owns half or less of the voting power of an entity when there is:

- Power over more than half of the voting rights by virtue of an agreement with other investors.

- Power to govern the financial and operating policies of the entity under a statute or an agreement.

- Power to appoint or remove the majority of the members of the board of directors or equivalent governing body and control of the entity is by that board or body.

- Power to cast the majority of votes at meetings of the board or equivalent governing body and control of the entity is by that board or body.

The existence and effect of potential voting rights (e.g., share warrants, call options, or instruments convertible into ordinary shares) that are currently exercisable or convertible need to be considered when assessing whether an entity has control (IAS 27, pars. 14–15). Further guidance on the consideration of potential voting rights is given in the Implementation Guidance published with IASs 27, 28, and 31.

Power to appoint or remove a majority of the board or other governing body raises some problems of interpretation in countries where a two-tier board structure (supervisory board and management board) may be used for some companies. The interpretation generally given is that control exists where one party can appoint or dismiss the majority of either board.

The power to cast a majority of votes at board meetings also requires interpretation if some directors have the right to vote on some issues but not on others. Control would presumably depend on power over directors having the right to vote on substantially all significant matters.

In deciding whether the power to cast a majority of votes exists, any right held by a director to a casting vote must be taken into account. Where the chairman has this right, and two 50% owners each have the right to appoint the chairman in alternate years, then control may be considered to be exercised jointly.

An investor may exercise control by virtue of being the most powerful shareholder, but if there is another potentially dominant shareholder, then control is exercised only subject to the acquiescence of the latter. In that case, the entity may not be effectively controlled in such a way as to make it a subsidiary.

Exercise of control over an entity by virtue of points 1 to 4, above, will result in it being a subsidiary of the company exercising that control only if the latter has the ability to obtain benefits from the entity's activities. Benefits could have a wider interpretation than income in the narrow sense and include the reduction of competition, the avoidance of costs, and so on.

When assessing whether an entity controls another entity, the existence and effect of potential voting rights that are presently or currently exercisable or convertible should be considered. All potential voting rights, including those held by other entities, should be taken into account. Potential voting rights do not meet the criteria of being *currently* exercisable or convertible when they cannot be exercised or converted until a *future* date or upon the occurrence of a *future* event. Other facts that should be considered in determining whether the criteria are met include: (1) the terms of exercise of the potential voting rights and (2) possible linked transactions and positions such as options. However, management's intentions and the financial capability to exercise or convert are not relevant (SIC-33, pars. 3 and 4).

A special-purpose entity (SPE), in the form of a corporation, trust, partnership, or unincorporated entity, may be set up to accomplish a narrow and well-defined objective (e.g., to effect a lease, research and development activities, or a securitization of financial assets), such that in substance the entity has the right to obtain the majority of the benefits from the SPE or retains the majority of the residual risks related to the SPE or its assets in order to obtain benefits from its activities. In such circumstances, the entity should consolidate the SPE, even if it owns little or none of the SPE's equity and the SPE operates in a predetermined way so that no entity has explicit decision-making authority over it (i.e., it operates on "autopilot") (SIC-12).

Illustration

P has percentage holdings in S_1 and S_2, and S_1 S_2 have holdings in S_3, as shown below:

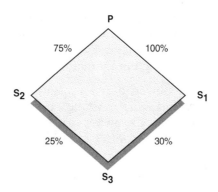

S_1 and S_2 are subsidiaries of P. P's percentage ownership of S_3 is 30% (via S_1) plus 18.75% (via S_2), totaling 48.75%. But P *controls* S_3 because it controls S_1

and S_2, which between them control 55% of the voting rights in S_3. Hence, S_3 is a subsidiary of P.

A subsidiary should not be excluded from consolidation on the grounds that its business activities are dissimilar from those of the other entities within the group. Instead, additional information should be disclosed about the different business activities of subsidiaries, for example, in accordance with IFRS 8, "Operating Segments" (IAS 27, par. 17).

> **OBSERVATION:** As noted in the "Overview" above, the concept of control in IASB GAAP has been broadened by IFRS 10 (see the summary of IFRS 10 below).

CONSOLIDATION PROCEDURES AND ISSUES

Full versus Proportionate Consolidation

In preparing consolidated financial statements, the financial statements of the parent and its subsidiaries are combined on a line-by-line basis by adding together like items of assets, liabilities, equity, income, and expenses (IAS 27, par. 22). This is sometimes referred to as full consolidation. In proportionate consolidation, the venturer's shares of each of the assets, liabilities, income, and expenses of a jointly controlled entity are combined on a line-by-line basis with similar items in the venturer's financial statements. Or, they may be reported as separate line items in the venturer's financial statements (IAS 31, par 34). The Equity Method (see Chapter 15) is allowed as an alternative treatment to proportionate consolidation (IAS 31, pars. 38–40).

The carrying amount of the parent's investment in each subsidiary and the parent's portion of the equity of each subsidiary are eliminated as set out in IFRS 3, "Business Combinations," which also describes the treatment of any resultant goodwill (see Chapter 8).

Illustration

Company I holds 50% of the voting equity shares of company J jointly with another company, Q. Unless I controls J, for example by virtue of a contract with Q, I has joint control of J and the benchmark treatment is to use proportionate consolidation. If I has a contract with Q by virtue of which Q passes its control rights over to I, then J is a subsidiary of I and full consolidation will be used.

The balance sheets immediately following the acquisition of the 50% holding are as follows:

	I	J	Consolidated Full	Consolidated Proportionate
Sundry current assets	$28,600	$6,000	$34,600	$31,600
Investment in J:				

	I	J	Consolidated Full	Consolidated Proportionate
(4000 shares acquired at $1.50n per share)	6,000			
Property, plant, and equipment	50,000	4,000	54,000	52,000
Goodwill on consolidation ($6000 — 50% of $10,000)			1,000	1,000
	$84,600	$10,000	$89,600	$84,600
Shares of $1	$40,000	$ 8,000	$40,000	$40,000
Reserves	44,600	2,000	44,600	44,600
	$84,600	$10,000	$84,600	$84,600
Minority interest (50% of $10,000)			5,000	
	$84,600	$10,000	$89,600	$84,600

Note that the goodwill is the same under both full and proportionate consolidation, but that there is no minority interest in proportionate consolidation.

OBSERVATION: Proportionate consolidation will no longer be an option when IFRS 10, IFRS 11, and the revised IAS 28 are adopted. Instead, the equity method will be applicable.

Calculation and Disclosure of Non-Controlling Interests in Full Consolidation

A non-controlling interest is that part of the net results of operations and of the net assets of a subsidiary attributable to interests that are not owned, directly of indirectly, by the parent (IAS 27, par. 4).

Non-controlling interests in the net income of consolidated subsidiaries are identified and adjusted against the income of the group in order to arrive at the net income attributable to the owners of the parent.

Non-controlling interests in the profit or loss of consolidated subsidiaries for the reporting period are identified, and non-controlling interests in the net assets of consolidated subsidiaries are identified separately from the parent shareholders' equity in them. Non-controlling interests in the net assets consist of:

- The amount of those non-controlling interests at the date of the original combination calculated in accordance with IFRS 3, and

- The non-controlling interest's share of changes in equity since the date of the business combination.

When potential voting rights exist, the proportions of profit or loss and changes in equity allocated to the parent and non-controlling interests are determined on the basis of present ownership interests and do not reflect the possible exercise or conversion of potential voting rights (IAS 27, pars. 22–23).

Intragroup Balances

Intragroup balances and intragroup transactions and any resultant unrealized profits included in the carrying values of assets (e.g., inventory or fixed assets) should be eliminated in full. Unrealized losses reflected in carrying values should also be eliminated, except insofar as this would result in the carrying value of the asset exceeding the recoverable amount (IAS 27, par. 26). Timing differences resulting from such eliminations are to be dealt with in accordance with IAS 12 (see Chapter 21).

Unrealized profit on an "upstream" sale to the parent by a subsidiary with a minority interest, as well as on a "downstream" sale by the parent to a subsidiary with a minority interest, must therefore be fully eliminated. There is no requirement that the elimination of the profit on an "upstream" sale be allocated between the group and the minority interest.

The following illustration is adapted from the *GAAP Guide*.

Illustration of Profit in Inventory

P Company purchased $20,000 and $250,000 of merchandise in 20X1 and 20X2, respectively, from its 80% owned subsidiary S at 25% above cost. As of December 31, 20X1 and 20X2, P had on hand $25,000 and $30,000 of merchandise purchased from S. The following is the computation of intragroup profits:

In beginning inventory	25/125 of $25,000	=	$5,000
In ending inventory	25/125 of $30,000	=	$6,000

Consolidating adjustments at 12/31/X2:

1. Consolidated sales	$250,000	
Consolidated cost of sales		$250,000

To eliminate intragroup sales for the year 20X2.

2. Consolidated retained earnings	$5,000	
Consolidated cost of sales	$1,000	
Inventory		$6,000

To eliminate the intragroup profit in beginning and ending inventory.

Because consolidating adjustments are not booked, the intragroup profit in beginning inventory must again be eliminated in arriving at consolidated retained earnings. The additional unrealized intragroup profit arising in 20X2 is $1,000, and this is adjusted against consolidated cost of sales.

The two debit adjustments in 2 could be apportioned between the majority and minority interests in S in the proportions 80:20. In that case, the beginning balances of consolidated retained earnings and the minority interest would be adjusted downward by $4,000 and $1,000, respectively, and the parent company's and the minority interest's share of profit for 20X2 would be adjusted downward by $800 and $200, respectively. Since the whole $1,000 has been charged to consolidated cost of sales, the deduction of $200 from the minority interest's share of profit would reduce the amount borne by the majority interest (in arriving at the net income attributable to the parent company's shareholders) to $800.

These adjustments assume that the investment in the subsidiary has been accounted for in the parent company's financial statements on the basis of cost or revalued amounts.

Different Reporting Dates

The financial statements of the parent and its subsidiaries used in the preparation of the consolidated financial statements should be prepared as of the same reporting date. If the reporting dates of the parent and a subsidiary are different, for consolidation purposes the subsidiary should prepare additional financial statements as of the same date as those of the parent unless this is impracticable. If the financial statements of a subsidiary used in the consolidation are prepared as of a reporting date different from that of the parent, the difference between the two reporting dates must not be more than three months, and adjustments must be made for the effects of any significant transactions or events occurring between the two reporting dates. The length of the reporting periods and any difference in the reporting dates must be the same from period to period (IAS 27, pars. 22–23).

The same time limit of three months applies to any difference between the reporting dates of a venturer and a venture when the former applies proportionate consolidation or the equity method.

Uniform Accounting Policies

Consolidated financial statements should be prepared by using uniform accounting policies for like transactions and other events in similar circumstances. If a member of the group uses accounting policies other than those adopted in the consolidated financial statements for like transactions and events in similar circumstances, appropriate adjustments must be made to its financial statements in preparing the consolidated financial statements (IAS 27, pars. 24–25).

The income and expenses of a subsidiary are included in the consolidated financial statements from the acquisition date, as defined in IFRS 3. Income and expenses of the subsidiary are based on the values of its assets and liabilities that are recognized in the parent's consolidated financial statements as of the acquisition date (e.g., in the case of depreciation of depreciable assets). The income and expenses of a subsidiary are included in the consolidated financial statements until the date at which the parent ceases to control the subsidiary.

Non-Controlling Interests

In full consolidation, non-controlling interests are disclosed in the consolidated balance sheet within equity, separately from the parent shareholders' equity; and non-controlling interests in the profit or loss of the group should also be disclosed separately. The total comprehensive income is attributed to the parent shareholders and non-controlling interests, even if this results in the non-controlling interests having a debit balance (IAS 27, par. 28).

A subsidiary may have cumulative preference shares outstanding that are classified as equity and held by non-controlling interests. In that case, the parent should deduct the dividends on such shares, whether or not they have been declared, in calculating its share of the profits or losses (IAS 27, par. 29).

Changes in a parent's ownership interest in a subsidiary that do not result in a loss of control are accounted for as equity transactions (i.e., transactions with owners in their capacity as owners). The carrying amounts of the controlling and non-controlling interests are adjusted to reflect the changes in their relative interests in the subsidiary. If there is a difference between the amount by which the non-controlling interests are adjusted and the fair value of the consideration paid or received, this difference is recognized directly in equity and attributed to the owners of the parent (IAS 27, pars. 30–31).

Loss of Control

IFRS 3, as revised in 2008, provides more guidance on the treatment of loss of control than the previous (2003) version. This is set out in paragraphs 32–37.

A parent loses control when it loses the power to govern the financial and operating policies of the investee in order to benefit from the latter's activities. Loss of control may occur with or without a change in absolute or relative ownership levels, for example, when a subsidiary becomes subject to the control of a government, court, administrator, or regulator or as the result of a contractual arrangement.

A parent might lose control of a subsidiary in two or more transactions or arrangements. However, in some cases it is appropriate that such multiple arrangements be accounted for as a single transaction. This may be indicated by one or more of the following:

- The arrangements are entered into at the same time or in contemplation of one another.

- The arrangements form a single transaction designed to achieve an overall commercial effect.

- The occurrence of one arrangement is dependent on the occurrence of at least one other arrangement.

- One arrangement on its own is not economically justified, but is justified when considered together with other arrangements, for example, when one disposal of shares is priced below market and is compensated for by a subsequent disposal priced above market.

If a parent loses control of a subsidiary, it:

1. Derecognizes the assets (including any goodwill) and liabilities of the former subsidiary at their carrying amounts at the date when control is lost.

2. Derecognizes the carrying amount of any non-controlling interests in the former subsidiary at the date when control is lost, including any components of other comprehensive income attributable to them.

3. Recognizes:

   (a) The fair value of the consideration received, if any, from the transaction, event, or circumstances that resulted in the loss of control.

   (b) Any related distribution of shares, if the transaction that resulted in the loss of control involves a distribution of shares of the subsidiary to owners in their capacity as owners.

4. Recognizes any investment retained in the former subsidiary at its fair value as at the date when control was lost; however, from the date of the loss of control, any retained investment in, and any amounts owed by or to, the former subsidiary are to be accounted for in accordance with other IFRSs. Thus, the fair value of any investment retained shall be regarded as the fair value on initial recognition of a financial asset in accordance with IAS 39, or, where appropriate, the cost on initial recognition of an investment in an associate or a jointly controlled entity.

5. Reclassifies to profit or loss, or transfers directly to retained earnings if required by other IFRSs, the amounts identified below.

6. Recognizes any resulting difference as a gain or loss in profit or loss attributable to the parent.

The parent accounts for all amounts recognized in other comprehensive income in relation to a subsidiary over which control has been lost, on the same basis as would be required if the parent had directly disposed of the related assets or liabilities. Thus, if a gain or loss previously recognized in other comprehensive income would be reclassified to profit or loss on the disposal of the related assets or liabilities, the parent reclassifies the gain or loss from equity to profit or loss when it loses control of the subsidiary.

An investment in a jointly controlled entity should be excluded from proportionate consolidation if the joint venturer ceases to exercise joint control over the entity. This may happen when the venturer disposes of its interest or when external restrictions are placed on the jointly controlled entity such that it can no longer achieve its goals (IAS 31, pars. 36–37).

When a venturer discontinues the use of proportionate consolidation (or the equity method) as from the date on which it ceases to have joint control over (or in the case of the equity method, significant influence in) a jointly controlled entity, the carrying amount of the investment at that date is regarded as the cost on initial measurement of a financial asset as per IAS 39. An investor in a joint venture that does not have joint control must account for that investment in accordance with IAS 39 or, if it has significant influence in the joint venture, with IAS 28 (IAS 31, par. 51).

Accounting for Investments in Subsidiaries, Jointly Controlled Entities, and Associates in Separate Financial Statements

When an entity prepares separate financial statements, it accounts for investments in subsidiaries, jointly controlled entities, and associates either at cost or in accordance with IAS 39. The entity applies the same accounting for each category of investments. Investments accounted for at cost shall be accounted for in accordance with IFRS 5 when they are classified as held for sale or included in a disposal group that is so classified in accordance with IFRS 5. The measurement of investments accounted for in accordance with IAS 39 is not changed in such circumstances.

An entity recognizes a dividend from a subsidiary, jointly controlled entity, or associate in profit or loss in its separate financial statements when its right to receive the dividend is established.

A parent may reorganize the structure of its group by establishing a new entity as its parent in a manner that meets the following criteria:

- The new parent obtains control of the original parent by issuing equity instruments in exchange for existing equity instruments of the original parent.

- The assets and liabilities of the new group and the original group are the same immediately before and after the reorganization.

- The owners of the original parent before the reorganization have the same absolute and relative interests in the assets of the original group and the new group immediately before and after the reorganization.

If the new parent accounts for its investment in the original parent in its separate financial statements as indicated above, then it measures cost as being the carrying amount of its share of the equity items shown in the separate financial statements of the original parent at the date of the reorganization.

An entity that is not a parent might similarly establish a new entity as its parent in a manner that meets the above criteria. In that case, the same requirements apply, as references to "original parent" and "original group" are replaced by "original entity" (IAS 27, pars. 38 and 38A–38C).

An interest in a jointly controlled entity is accounted for in a venturer's separate financial statements as indicated above. Investments in jointly controlled entities and associates that are accounted for in accordance with IAS 39 in the consolidated financial statements are accounted for in the same way in the investor's separate financial statements (IAS 31, par. 46).

IAS 27 and IAS 31 do not mandate which entities produce separate financial statements available for public use. However, the relevant provisions of IAS 27 apply when an entity produces separate financial statements that comply with IFRSs. The entity will also produce consolidated financial statements available for public use as required by IAS 27, paragraph 9, unless the exemption in paragraph 10 is applicable.

> **OBSERVATION:** The revised IAS 27, "Separate Financial Statements," as issued in May 2011 does not significantly modify the above requirements. However, the references to IAS 39 and IAS 31 need to be read because IAS 39 is being gradually replaced by IFRS 9 (see Chapter 17) and, as from annual reporting periods beginning on or after January 1, 2013, IFRS 11, "Joint Arrangements," will replace IAS 31 and may be adopted earlier. IFRS 11 is summarized below.

Transactions between a Venturer and a Joint Venture

When a venturer contributes or sells assets to a joint venture, recognition of any portion of a gain or loss from the transaction must reflect the substance of the transaction. Whereas the assets contributed or sold to it are retained by the joint venture, and provided the venturer has transferred the significant risks and rewards of ownership, the venturer recognizes only that portion of the gain or loss that is attributable to the interests of the other investors in the joint venture. The venturer should also recognize the full amount of any loss when the contribution or sale provides evidence of a reduction in the net realizable value of current assets or an impairment loss. When a venturer purchases assets from a joint venture, the venturer should not recognize its share of the profits of the joint venture from the transaction until it resells the assets to an independent party. The same applies to a share of losses, except that losses must be recognized immediately when they represent a reduction in the net realizable value of current assets or an impairment loss.

To assess whether a transaction between a venturer and a joint venture provides evidence of impairment of an asset, the venturer determines the recoverable amount of the asset in accordance with IAS 36. In determining value in use, the venturer estimates future cash flows from the asset on the basis of its continuing use and ultimate disposal by the joint venture (IAS 31, pars. 48–50).

> **OBSERVATION:** As noted above, IAS 31 will be replaced by IFRS 11 for annual reporting periods beginning on or after January 1, 2013, and may be adopted earlier. According to IFRS 11, requirements similar to those above will apply to *joint operators* in joint arrangements. Joint *venturers* will be required to apply the equity method.

Shareholdings by a Subsidiary in Its Parent

IAS 27 does not deal with shareholdings by a subsidiary in its parent or with changes in these. IAS 1 (revised) requires disclosure, in either the balance sheet or the notes, of shares in the enterprise held either by itself or by its subsidiaries or associates. SIC-16, "Share Capital—Reacquired Own Equity Instruments," requires that when an entity holds its own equity instruments ("treasury shares") or when these are held by one or more of its consolidated subsidiaries, and these are legally available for re-issue or resale (whether or not there is an intention to do so), such shares should be presented in the consolidated balance sheet of the issuer as a deduction from equity; in the event of resale, any difference between the purchase cost and the resale price is treated as a change in equity, not as part of net income for the period. Shares held by a subsidiary in its parent may be considered from the perspective of the group as a form of treasury stock, and the appropriate presentation in the consolidated balance sheet would be as a deduction from equity.

This situation should be distinguished from that which occurs after a *reverse acquisition*, as discussed in Chapter 8.

In a situation in which a subsidiary owns shares in its parent, consolidated net income may be found algebraically. The following example is adapted from the *GAAP Guide*.

Company	Unconsolidated net income (excluding income from investees)	
A	$40,000	A (parent) owns 80% of B
B	20,000	B owns 70% of C
C	10,000	C owns 20% of A
	$70,000	

Let a, b, and c = the *consolidated basis* net income of A, B, and C, respectively.

We have:
$$a = 40{,}000 + 0.8b$$
$$b = 20{,}000 + 0.7c$$
$$c = 10{,}000 + 0.2a$$

Solving for a:

$$
\begin{aligned}
a &= 40{,}000 + 0.8(20{,}000 + 0.7c) \\
&= 40{,}000 + 16{,}000 + 0.56(10{,}000 + 0.2a) \\
&= 56{,}000 + 5{,}600 + 0.112a \\
(1 - 0.112)a &= 61{,}600 \\
a &= 61{,}600/0.888 = 69{,}369.4
\end{aligned}
$$

Consolidated (equity) net income of A = $0.8 \times \$69{,}369.4 = \$55{,}496$

The net income of C = $\$10{,}000 + 0.2 \times 69{,}369 = \$23{,}874$, of which the 30% minority interest = $7,162

B's share of the net income of C = $0.7 \times \$23{,}847 = \$16{,}712$

B's net income = $\$20{,}000 + 16{,}712 = \$36{,}712$, of which the 20% minority interest = $7,342

Consolidated net income = $\$70{,}000 - (7{,}162 + 7{,}342) = \$55{,}496$

DISCLOSURE

IAS 27 (pars. 41–43) requires the following disclosures:

1. When a parent does not own, directly or indirectly though subsidiaries, more than half the voting power of a subsidiary, the nature of the relationship between the parent and the subsidiary.

2. If the ownership, directly or indirectly though subsidiaries, of more than half of the actual or potential voting power of an investee does not constitute control, the reasons why it does not.

3. The reporting date of the financial statements of a subsidiary when these are used to prepare consolidated financial statements and areas of a reporting date or for a period that is different from that of the parent, and the reason for using a different reporting date or period.

4. The nature and extent of any significant restrictions (such as those resulting from borrowing arrangements or regulatory requirements) on the ability of a subsidiary to transfer funds to the parent as cash dividends or repayments of loans or advances.

5. A schedule showing the effects of any changes in a parent's ownership interest in a subsidiary that do not result in a loss of control.

6. In the case of a loss of control, the (former) parent discloses the gain or loss, if any, recognized in accordance with IAS 27, paragraph 34 (see "Loss of Control" above), and:

   (a) The portion of that gain or loss attributable to recognizing any investment retained in the former subsidiary at its fair value at the date of the loss of control.

   (b) The line item(s) in the statement of comprehensive income in which the gain or loss is recognized (if not presented separately in the statement of comprehensive income).

When separate financial statements are prepared for a parent that is exempt according to IAS 27 from preparing consolidated financial statements and has elected not to do so, the separate financial statements should disclose the fact that the financial statements are separate financial statements and that the exemption from the consolidation requirement has been used; the name and country of incorporation of the entity whose consolidated financial statements complying with IFRS have been produced for public use; and the address where these financial statements are obtainable. The separate financial statements should also disclose a list of significant investments in subsidiaries, jointly controlled entities, and associates, including the name, country of incorporation or residence, proportion of ownership interest, and, if different, proportion of voting power held as well as a description of the method used to account for these investments.

When a parent other than one that is exempted as above, a venturer with an interest in a jointly controlled entity or an investor in an associate prepares separate financial statements, these should disclose (1) the fact that they are separate financial statements and the reasons why they are prepared if not required by law and (2) a list of significant investments in subsidiaries, jointly controlled entities, and associates, including the name, country of incorporation or residence, proportion of ownership interest, and, if different, proportion of voting power held, along with a description of the method used to account for these investments. The separate financial statements should also identify the consolidated financial statements, or financial statements prepared using proportionate consolidation or the equity method, to which the separate financial statements relate.

IAS 31 states the following disclosure requirements (pars. 54–57). A venturer is required to disclose:

1. The aggregate amount of the following contingent liabilities, unless the probability of loss is remote, separately from the amount of other contingent liabilities:

   (a) Any contingencies that the venturer has incurred in relation to its interests in joint ventures and its share in each of the contingencies that have been incurred jointly with other venturers;

   (b) Its share of the contingencies of the joint ventures themselves for which it is contingently liable; and

   (c) Those contingencies that arise because the venturer is contingently liable for the liabilities of the other venturers of a joint venture.

2. The aggregate amount of the following commitments in respect of its interests in joint ventures separately from other commitments:

   (a) Any capital commitments of the venturer in relation to its interests in joint ventures and its share in the capital commitments that have been incurred jointly with other venturers, and

   (b) Its share of the capital commitments of the joint ventures themselves.

3. A listing and description of interests in significant joint ventures and the proportion of ownership interest held in jointly controlled entities. A venturer that reports its interests in jointly controlled entities using the line-by-line reporting format for proportionate consolidation or the equity method should disclose the aggregate amounts of each of current assets, long-term assets, current liabilities, long-term liabilities, income and expenses related to its interests in joint ventures.

4. The method it uses to recognize its interests in jointly controlled entities.

EFFECTIVE DATE

An entity should apply the revised IAS 27, "Consolidated and Separate Financial Statements," or IAS 31, "Interests in Joint Ventures," as appropriate, for annual periods beginning on or after January 1, 2009. Earlier application is permitted, but in that case the fact of earlier application is to be disclosed.

IFRSs 10, 11 AND 12

The following paragraphs provide a summary of IFRSs 10, 11 and 12, as issued in May 2011.

IFRS 10, "Consolidated Financial Statements": Summary

IFRS 10, "Consolidated Financial Statements," sets out to make it very difficult for an investor in an entity to avoid consolidating that investee if, in substance, it controls the investee. The IFRS provides a new definition of control, broader than that in IAS 27, which is the basis for determining which investees are consolidated. An investor controls an investee when it: (a) has power over the investee; (b) is exposed, or has rights, to variable returns from its involvement with the investee; and (c) has the ability to use its power over the investee to affect the amount of those returns.

The IFRS sets out requirements for applying this principle of control in circumstances when:

- Voting or similar rights give an investor power, including situations where the investor holds less than a majority of voting rights and where potential voting rights are involved;

- An investee is designed so that voting rights are not the dominant factor in deciding who controls the investee (e.g., when voting rights relate only to administrative tasks and the relevant activities are directed through contractual arrangements;

- Agency relationships are involved (e.g., an investor should treat decision-making rights delegated to its agent as being held directly by the investor); and

- The investor has rights over specific assets of an investee, which may constitute a "deemed separate entity" over which the investor may have control.

The greater part of IFRS 10, including the 37 pages of Appendix B, "Application Guidance," is devoted to explicating the principle of control. Control requires power, and power arises from rights. An investor may have control, for example, even if another investor has *significant influence* over an investee.

However, an investor that is an agent with delegated decision-making rights to be exercised on behalf and for the benefit of another party, the principal(s), does not control the investee, though one of the principals may do so if, in substance, the conditions for control as defined above are satisfied in its case.

Appendix B contains 16 application examples designed to elucidate different situations in which the existence of control should or should not be inferred.

When preparing consolidated financial statements, an investor must use uniform accounting policies and must eliminate intragroup balances and transactions. Non-controlling interests in subsidiaries must be included in the consolidated statement of financial position within equity separately from the equity owned by the parent. These requirements are the same as those in IAS 27.

IFRS 11, "Joint Arrangements": Summary

IFRS 11, "Joint Arrangements," is to be applied by all entities that are a party to a *joint arrangement*, that is, an arrangement of which two or more parties have joint control. Joint control is defined as *the contractually agreed sharing of control of an arrangement*, which exists only when decisions about the *relevant activities* (i.e., activities that significantly affect the returns of the arrangement) require the *unanimous consent* of the parties sharing control.

IFRS 11 classifies joint arrangements into two categories: joint operations and joint ventures.

- A joint operation is a joint arrangement such that the parties that have joint control of it (i.e., the joint operators) have *rights to the assets*, and *obligations for the liabilities*, relating to the arrangement.

- A joint venture is a joint arrangement such that the parties that have joint control (i.e., the joint venturers) have *rights to the net assets* of the arrangement.

The IFRS requires a *joint operator* to recognize and measure the assets and liabilities (and to recognize the related revenues and expenses) in relation to its interest in the arrangement in accordance with relevant IFRSs applicable to the particular assets, liabilities, revenues, and expenses.

It requires a *joint venturer* to recognize an *investment* and to account for that investment using the equity method in accordance with IAS 28, unless IAS 28 exempts the entity from applying the equity method. Thus, the option to use proportionate consolidation, as permitted by IAS 31, is removed.

The disclosure requirements for parties that have joint control of a joint arrangement are specified in IFRS 12, as summarized below.

IFRS 12, "Disclosure of Interests in Other Entities": Summary

IFRS 12, "Disclosure of Interests in Other Entities," does not apply to:

- Post-employment or other long-term employee benefit plans to which IAS 19 applies (see Chapter 14); and

- Separate financial statements to which IAS 27 applies (see above).

The IFRS is applicable to entities that have an interest in a subsidiary, a joint arrangement, an associate or an unconsolidated structured entity. It is intended to provide for better information about subsidiaries that are consolidated, as well as interests in joint arrangements and associates that are not consolidated but with which the entity has a special relationship. In particular, IFRS 12 is concerned with the treatment of interests in and dealings with *structured entities*, which are defined as follows:

- *Interest in another entity:* Refers to contractual and non-contractual involvement that exposes an entity to *variability or returns from the performance of the other entity.*

- *Structured entity:* An entity that has been designed so that voting or similar rights are not the dominant factor in deciding who controls the entity, such as when voting rights relate to administrative tasks only and the relevant activities are directed by means of contractual arrangements.

- *Income from a structrured entity:* Includes, but is not limited to:
  — Recurring and non-recurring fees;
  — Interest and dividends; and
  — Gains or losses on the remeasurement or derecognition of interests in the structured entity, or from the transfer of assets or liabilities to it.

The objective of the IFRS is to require an entity to disclose information that permits users of financial statements to evaluate the nature of, and risks associated with, its interests in other entities and the effects of those interests on its financial position, financial performance, and cash flows. In particular, the disclosures should enable users to:

- Understand:
  - The significant judgments and assumptions (and changes to them) made in determining (a) the nature of its interest in another entity or arrangement (i.e., control, joint control, or significant influence) and (b) the type of joint arrangement in which it has an interest;
  - The interest that non-controlling interests have in the group's activities and cash flows; and
- Evaluate:
  - The nature and extent of significant restrictions on its ability to access or use assets, and settle liabilities, of the group;
  - The nature of, and changes in, the risks associated with its interests in consolidated structured entities;
  - The nature and extent of its interests in unconsolidated structured entities, and the nature of, and changes in, the risks associated with those interests;
  - The nature, extent, and financial effects of its interests in joint arrangements and associates, and the nature of the risks associated with those interests; and
  - The consequences of:
    - ☐ Changes in a parent's ownership interest in a subsidiary that do not result in a loss of control, and
    - ☐ Losing control of a subsidiary during the reporting period.

IFRS 12 specifies minimum disclosures to be provided, and if these (together with disclosures required by other IFRSs) are not sufficient to meet the objectives stated above, the entity discloses any additional information that is necessary in order to do so. The IFRS requires an entity to consider the level of detail, and to aggregate or disaggregate disclosures, as necessary, to maximize the usefulness of the information.

The IFRS places emphasis on disclosures in connection with *unconsolidated structured entities*. If an entity has interests in *unconsolidated structured entities*, it must disclose qualitative and quantitative information that enables users of its financial statements to understand the nature and extent of those interests and to evaluate the nature of and changes in the associated risks. In particular, it must disclose:

1. The carrying amounts of the assets and liabilities recognized in its financial statements relating to its interests in such entities;
2. The line items in its statement of financial position in which these items are recognized;

3. The amount that best represents the entity's *maximum exposure to loss* from its interests in such entities, and how that exposure is determined; and

4. A comparison of the carrying amounts in 1. above with the maximum exposures in 3. above.

If during a reporting period an entity has provided, without having any contractual obligation to do so, financial or other support to an unconsolidated entity in which it currently has, or previously had, an interest, it must disclose the type and amount of such support and the reasons for providing it. It must also disclose any current intentions to provide financial or other support to an unconsolidated structured entity.

If it has sponsored such an entity for which it does not provide such information (e.g., because it had no interest in it at the reporting date), the following disclosures are required:

- How it has determined which structures entities it has sponsored;

- Income from those structured entities during the reporting period, and a description of the types of such income; and

- The carrying amount (at the time of the transfer) of all assets transferred to those structured entities during the reporting period.

CHAPTER 12
CONSTRUCTION CONTRACTS

CONTENTS

OVERVIEW

It is in the nature of construction contracts that they last over a long period of time, in general over more than one accounting period. The issue of determining the *total* profit on such a contract raises no new accounting problems over and above those of cost determination and allocation discussed in Chapter 24 in relation to inventory.

There is one important and difficult additional issue, however, which is the question of allocation of the total profit over the various accounting periods. If a contract extends over, say, three years, should the contribution to profits be 0%, 0%, and 100%, respectively, for the three years? Can we make profits on something before we have finished it? The realization convention might seem to argue against doing so, and the prudence convention would certainly argue against it, too. But would this give a "fair presentation" of the results for each period? And would it be of any use? The various users want *regular* information on business progress. Can we not argue that we can be "reasonably certain," during the contract, of at least some profit—and if we can, then surely the matching principle is more important than an excessive slavishness to prudence?

Two alternative approaches have emerged over the years. These are the completed-contract method, which delays profit recognition until the end, and the percentage-of-completion method, which in defined conditions requires allocation of revenues and expenses over the accounting periods concerned. IASB GAAP are given in IAS 11, "Construction Contracts," as revised in 1993, and require the percentage-of-completion method. IFRIC 15, "Agreements for the Construction of Real Estate," is also discussed in this chapter.

BACKGROUND

The primary issue in accounting for construction contracts is the allocation of contract revenue, and of the contract costs to be matched against that revenue, between accounting periods. IAS 11 says that the problem is the allocation of these items to the "accounting periods in which construction work is performed," but this slightly begs the question. The key general accounting criteria such as relevance, reliability, matching, prudence, and usefulness, discussed in the IASC Framework (see Chapter 2), have to be applied, which of course means that the tensions and inconsistencies between them need to be resolved.

The effects of the two generally advanced methods of dealing with this problem, the completed-contract method and the percentage-of-completion method, are best shown by the comparative example below.

Illustration of Accounting for the Completed-Contract and Percentage-of-Completion Methods

The following data pertain to a $2,000,000 long-term construction contract:

	20X5	20X6	20X7
Costs incurred during the year	$500,000	$700,000	$300,000
Year-ended estimated costs to complete	1,000,000	300,000	—
Billing during the year	400,000	700,000	900,000
Collections during the year	200,000	500,000	1,200,000

The computation of realized gross profit under the percentage-of-completion method, assuming for simplicity that the degree of completion is determined on the basis of costs incurred, will be as follows.

The total expected profit is total revenue minus total expected costs at the end of year 1, that is, 2,000,000 − (500,000 + 1,000,000) = 500,000.

This is allocated over the three years as shown.

20X5

$$\frac{\$500,000}{\$1,500,000} \times \$500,000 - 0 = \qquad\qquad \$166,667$$

20X6

$$\frac{\$1,200,000}{\$1,500,000} \times \$500,000 - \$166,667 = \qquad\qquad \$233,333$$

20X7

$$\frac{\$1,500,000}{\$1,500,000} \times \$500,000 - (\$166,667 + \$233,333) = \$100,000$$

Total gross profit $\underline{\$500,000}$

The journal entries for both the completed-contract method and the percentage-of-completion method for the three years are as follows:

20X5	Completed Contract		% of Completion	
Construction in progress	$500,000		$500,000	
Cash or liability		$500,000		$500,000
Accounts receivable	400,000		400,000	
Advance billings		400,000		400,000
Cash	200,000		200,000	
Accounts receivable		200,000		200,000
Construction in progress	no entry		166,667	
Realized gross profit				
(P&L)				166,667

20X6	Completed Contract		% of Completion	
Construction in progress	$700,000		$700,000	
Cash or liability		$700,000		$700,000
Accounts receivable	700,000		700,000	
Advance billings		700,000		700,000
Cash	500,000		500,000	
Accounts receivable		500,000		500,000
Construction in progress	no entry		233,333	
Realized gross profit				
(P&L)				233,333

20X7	Completed Contract		% of Completion	
Construction in progress	$300,000		$300,000	
Cash or liability		$300,000		$300,000
Accounts receivable	900,000		900,000	
Advance billings		900,000		900,000
Cash	1,200,000		1,200,000	
Accounts receivable		1,200,000		1,200,000
Construction in progress	no entry		100,000	
Realized gross profit (P&L)				100,000
Advance billings	2,000,000		2,000,000	
Construction in progress		1,500,000		2,000,000
Realized gross profit (P&L)		500,000		—

At the end of each year during which the contract is in progress, the excess of the construction-in-progress account over the advance billings account is presented as a current asset:

20X5:   ($500,000 + $166,667) − $400,000 = $266,667

20X6:   ($500,000 + $166,667 + $700,000 + $233,333)
            − ($400,000 + $700,000) = $500,000

In this illustration, the estimated gross profit of $500,000 was the actual gross profit on the contract. If changes in the estimated cost to complete the contract had been appropriate at the end of 20X5 and/or 20X6, or if the actual costs to complete had been determined to be different when the contract was completed in 20X7, those changes would have been incorporated into revised estimates during the contract period. For example, if at the end of 20X6 the costs to complete were estimated to be $400,000 instead of $300,000, the 20X6 gross profit would have been determined as follows:

$$\frac{\$1,200,000}{\$1,600,000} \times (2,000,000 - \$1,6000,000) = \$300,000$$

$$\$300,000 - \$166,667 = \$133,333$$

The 20X7 profit, assuming that the revised estimate of $400,000 for cost-of-completion turns out to be accurate, would be

$$\$400,000 - (\$166,667 + \$133,333) = \$100,000$$

The reason why, on these numbers, the 20X7 profit calculates to $100,000 in each circumstance is that (300/1,500) x 500 (circumstance 1)

$$= (400/1,600) \times 400 \text{ (circumstance 2)}$$

> **OBSERVATION:** Looking at the above illustration, under the revised total contract cost figure of $1,600,000, it is clear that, with the advantage of hindsight, too high a proportion of the total profit (i.e., of $400,000) was allocated to 20X5, and too low a proportion to 20X6. Was this imprudent in 20X5? Was there a failure to fairly present in 20X5?
>
> In one sense, yes it was imprudent. Clearly, the completed-contract method carries no such risks. But there was no failure of fair presentation in 20X5 under the percentage-of-completion method. The reality is that work had been done in 20X5 toward a profitable overall outcome. Estimates turned out to be imprecise. But to follow the completed-contract method and automatically report a profit of nil in 20X5 would arguably be the very negation of fair presentation. The amount $166,667 for 20X5 gross profit turned out to be subjectively inaccurate. A gross profit of $0 would be objective (reliable) but downright wrong! IAS 11, as we shall see below, attempts a reasonable path through the tensions inherent in the situation.

In practice, U.S. GAAP is usually similar to IASB GAAP. While under U.S. GAAP both the percentage-of-completion method and the completed-contract method are permitted (ASC 605), the percentage-of-completion method is cited as the preferred method and generally used; the completed-contract method is used only in circumstances when estimates of costs to completion and the extent of progress toward completion are not reasonably dependable.

SCOPE AND DEFINITIONS

IAS 11 is to be applied when accounting for construction contracts in the financial statements of contractors. We are given definitions of different types of contracts (par. 3).

- A *construction contract* is a contract specifically negotiated for the construction of an asset or a combination of assets that are closely interrelated or interdependent in terms of their design, technology, and function or their ultimate purpose or use.

- A *fixed price contract* is a construction contract in which the contractor agrees to a fixed contract price, or a fixed rate per unit of output, which in some cases is subject to cost escalation clauses.

- A *cost-plus contract* is a construction contract in which the contractor is reimbursed for allowable or otherwise defined costs, plus a percentage of these costs or a fixed fee.

Contractor is not defined. The word appears to be used in the general sense, that is, any enterprise that contracts. It is specifically stated (par. 5) that construction contracts are to include contracts for the rendering of services that are directly related to the construction of the asset, for example, those for the services of project managers and architects, and contracts for the destruction or restoration of assets, and the restoration of the environment after the demolition of assets.

It should be noted, however, that IAS 11 applies only to contracts "specifically negotiated." This seems to imply that only customized production is included. Also noteworthy is that the given definition implies no particular length of the construction period. We are talking about contracts, not long-term contracts. In practice, however, if no accounting period-ends are crossed, then no problems of revenue and expense recognition exist, so nothing remains to be resolved.

Sometimes one contract covers the construction of a number of assets. If three conditions are met, then each asset is required to be treated as a separate construction contract. These conditions are (par. 8):

1. Separate proposals have been submitted for each asset.
2. Each asset has been subject to separate negotiation, and the contractor and customer have been able to accept or reject that part of the contract relating to each asset.
3. The costs and revenues of each asset can be identified.

Conversely, a group of contracts, whether with one or with several different customers, may be in substance a single construction contract, and required to be treated as a single contract when, again, three conditions are met. These are (par. 9):

1. The group of contracts is negotiated as a single package.
2. The contracts are so closely interrelated that they are, in effect, part of a single project with an overall profit margin.
3. The contracts are performed concurrently or in a continuous sequence.

A typical example of this last case would be contracts for the design, and then building, of a particular project. Contracts may allow "add-on" options subject to further agreement. Such an add-on should be treated as part of the original contract unless either the asset differs significantly in design, technology, or function from the asset or assets covered by the original contract or the price of the asset is negotiated without regard to the original contract price.

SERVICE CONCESSION ARRANGEMENTS

Service concession arrangements are arrangements in which a government or some other public body grants contracts for the supply of public services, such as roads, energy distribution, prisons, or hospitals, to private operators. IFRIC 12, "Service Concession Arrangements," (issued in November 2006 and mandatory for accounting periods beginning on or after January 1, 2008, with early application permitted) addresses the accounting implications of such arrangements. An arrangement within the scope of this Interpretation typically involves a private sector entity (an operator) constructing the infrastructure used to provide the public service or upgrading it (e.g., by its capacity) and operating and maintaining that infrastructure for a specified period of time. The operator is paid for its services over the period of the arrangement. The arrangement is governed by a contract that sets out performance standards, mechanisms for adjusting prices, and arrangements for arbitrating disputes. Such an arrangement is often described as a "public-to-private" service concession arrangement.

The service arrangement contractually obliges the operator to provide the services to the public on behalf of the public sector entity. Other common features are:

- The party that grants the service arrangement (the grantor) is a public sector entity, including a governmental body, or a private sector entity to which the responsibility for the service has been devolved.
- The operator is responsible for at least some of the management of the infrastructure and related services and does not merely act as an agent on behalf of the grantor.
- The contract sets the initial prices to be levied by the operator and regulates price revisions over the period of the service arrangement.
- The operator is obliged to hand over the infrastructure to the grantor in a specified condition at the end of the period of the arrangement, for little or no incremental consideration, irrespective of which party initially financed it.

IFRIC 12 applies to public-to-private service concession arrangements if:

1. The grantor controls or regulates what services the operator must provide with the infrastructure, to whom it must provide them, and at what price.
2. The grantor controls—through ownership, beneficial entitlement, or otherwise—any significant residual interest in the infrastructure at the end of the term of the arrangement.

It applies to both:

1. Infrastructure that the operator constructs or acquires from a third party for the purpose of the service arrangement.
2. Existing infrastructure to which the grantor gives the operator access for the purpose of the service arrangement.

The Interpretation sets out general principles on recognizing and measuring the obligations and related rights in service concession arrangements. Requirements for disclosing information about service concession arrangements under SIC-29 are discussed in Chapter 4. The issues addressed in IFRIC 12 are outlined below.

- *Treatment of the operator's rights over the infrastructure.* Infrastructure within the scope of this Interpretation shall not be recognized as property, plant, and equipment of the operator because the contractual service arrangement does not convey the right to control the use of the public service infrastructure to the operator.
- *Recognition and measurement of arrangement consideration.* The operator recognizes and measures revenue in accordance with IAS 11 and IAS 18 for the services it performs. If the operator performs more than one service (e.g., construction or upgrade services and operation services) under a single contract or arrangement, consideration received or receivable shall be allocated by reference to the relative fair values of the services delivered, when the amounts are separately identifiable.

- *Construction or upgrade services.* The operator shall account for revenue and costs relating to construction or upgrade services in accordance with IAS 11.

- *Consideration given by the grantor to the operator.* If the operator provides construction or upgrade services, the consideration received or receivable by the operator shall be recognized at its fair value. The consideration may be rights to:

  — A financial asset.

  — An intangible asset.

The operator shall recognize a financial asset to the extent that it has an unconditional contractual right to receive cash or another financial asset from or at the direction of the grantor for the construction services; the grantor has little, if any, discretion to avoid payment, usually because the agreement is enforceable by law.

The operator shall recognize an intangible asset to the extent that it receives a right (a license) to charge users of the public service. A right to charge users of the public service is not an unconditional right to receive cash because the amounts are contingent on the extent that the public uses the service.

- *Operation services.* The operator shall account for revenue and costs relating to operation services in accordance with IAS 18.

- *Contractual obligations to restore the infrastructure to a specified level of serviceability.* The operator may have contractual obligations it must fulfill as a condition of its license (a) to maintain the infrastructure to a specified level of serviceability or (b) to restore the infrastructure to a specified condition before it is handed over to the grantor at the end of the service arrangement. These contractual obligations to maintain or restore infrastructure, except for any upgrade element, shall be recognized and measured in accordance with IAS 37, that is, at the best estimate of the expenditure that would be required to settle this present obligation at the balance sheet date.

- *Borrowing costs incurred by the operator.* These shall be dealt with in accordance with IAS 23.

- *Financial asset.* IASs 32 and 39 and IFRS 7 apply to financial assets that are recognized.

- *Intangible asset.* IAS 38 applies to intangible assets that are recognized.

- *Items provided to the operator by the grantor.* Infrastructure items to which the operator is given access by the grantor for the purposes of the service arrangement are not recognized as property, plant, and equipment of the operator. The grantor may also provide other items to the operator that the operator can retain or deal with as it wishes. If such assets form part of the consideration payable by the grantor for the services, they are not government grants, as defined in IAS 20, but are recognized as assets of the operator, measured at fair value upon initial recognition. The operator shall recognize a liability in respect of unfulfilled obligations it has assumed in exchange for the assets.

- *Transition.* Changes in accounting policies are accounted for in accordance with IAS 8, that is, retrospectively, subject to impracticality exemptions.

AGREEMENTS FOR THE CONSTRUCTION OF REAL ESTATE

A practical problem began to arise, as to whether agreements for the construction of real estate should be considered as covered by IAS 11, or IAS 18, "Revenues." To clarify this problem, IFRIC 15, "Agreements for the Construction of Real Estate," was issued in July 2008, applicable from January 1, 2009.

IFRIC 15 applies to the accounting for revenues and associated expenses by entities that undertake the construction of real estate directly or through subcontractors. Agreements in its scope are those for the construction of real estate. In addition to the construction of real estate, such agreements may include the delivery of other goods or services.

The Interpretation addresses two issues:

1. Is the agreement within the scope of IAS 11 or IAS 18?
2. When should revenue from the construction of real estate be recognized?

Determining whether an agreement for the construction of real estate is within the scope of IAS 11 or IAS 18 depends on the terms of the agreement and all the surrounding facts and circumstances. Such a determination requires judgment with respect to each agreement. IAS 11 applies when the agreement meets the definition of a construction contract set out in paragraph 3 of IAS 11: "a contract specifically negotiated for the construction of an asset or a combination of assets . . . ." An agreement for the construction of real estate meets the definition of a construction contract when the buyer is able to specify the major structural elements of the design of the real estate before construction begins and/or specify major structural changes once construction is in progress (whether or not it exercises that ability). When IAS 11 applies, the construction contract also includes any contracts or components for the rendering of services that are directly related to the construction of the real estate. In contrast, an agreement for the construction of real estate in which buyers have only limited ability to influence the design of the real estate (e.g., to select a design from a range of options specified by the entity, or to specify only minor variations to the basic design) is an agreement for the sale of goods within the scope of IAS 18.

When the agreement is within the scope of IAS 11 and its outcome can be estimated reliably, the entity shall recognize revenue by reference to the stage of completion of the contract activity in accordance with IAS 11.

However, the agreement may not meet the definition of a construction contract, and therefore be within the scope of IAS 18 (see Chapter 31). In this case, the entity shall determine whether the agreement is for the rendering of services or for the sale of goods.

If the entity is not required to acquire and supply construction materials, the agreement may be only an agreement for the tendering of services in accordance with IAS 18. In this case, if the criteria in paragraph 20 of IAS 18 are met, IAS 18 requires revenue to be recognized by reference to the stage of completion of the transaction using the percentage of completion method. The requirements of IAS 11 are generally applicable to the recognition of revenue and the associated expenses for such a transaction (IAS 18, par. 21).

If the entity is required to provide services together with construction materials in order to perform its contractual obligation to deliver the real estate to the buyer, the agreement is an agreement for the sale of goods and the criteria for recognition of revenue set out in paragraph 14 of IAS 18 apply.

When an entity recognizes revenue using the percentage-of-completion method for agreements that meet all the criteria in paragraph 14 of IAS 18 continuously as construction progresses, it shall disclose:

1. How it determines which agreements meet all the criteria in paragraph 14 of IAS 18 continuously as construction progresses;

2. The amount of revenue arising from such agreements in the period; and

3. The methods used to determine the stage of completion of agreements in progress.

For the agreements described above that are in progress at the reporting date, the entity shall also disclose:

1. The aggregate amount of costs incurred and recognized profits (less recognized losses) to date; and

2. The amount of advances received.

CONTRACT REVENUE

The standard takes its time in arriving at the heart of the whole matter, which is, of course, the question of profit recognition. Consistent with the general logical progression of definition before measurement, we first need to define and consider contract revenues and contract costs. Naturally enough, the starting point for quantifying gross revenue is the "price" agreed in the contract. More fully, contract revenue should comprise (par. 11) the initial amount of revenue agreed in the contract and variations in contract work, claims, and incentive payments to the extent that it is probable that they will result in revenue and that they are capable of being reliably measured. Contract revenue is measured at the fair value of the consideration received or receivable.

It is in the nature of long-term and unique customized projects that changes and unforeseen events are likely to occur. A variation is an instruction by the customer for a change in the work to be performed under the contract. The revenue from a variation is included in contract revenue when it is probable that the customer will approve the variation and the amount of revenue arising from the variation and the amount of revenue can be reliably measured.

A claim is an amount that the contractor seeks to collect from the customer or another party as reimbursement for costs not included in the contract price. A claim may arise from, for example, customer-caused delays, errors in specifications or design, and disputed variations in contract work. Claims are included in contract revenue only when negotiations have reached an advanced stage such that it is probable that the customer will accept the claim and the amount that the customer will probably accept can be measured reliably.

Incentive payments are additional amounts paid to the contractor if specified performance standards are met or exceeded, for example, for early completion of the contract. Incentive payments are included in contract revenue when the contract is sufficiently advanced and it is probable that the specified performance standards will be met or exceeded so that the amount of the incentive payment can be measured reliably.

It should be noted that there are, in theory, no options included in any of the above detail. Adjustments for variations, claims, and so on are required when the stated conditions are met and cannot be omitted on the grounds, for example, of conservatism. In practice, however, there are of course a large number of "probables" included in the specifications, so a degree of subjectivity and human or cultural bias is inevitably involved.

CONTRACT COSTS

The standard considers contract costs under three aspects. Contract costs should comprise (par. 16):

1. Costs that relate directly to the specific contract,

2. Costs that are attributable to contract activity in general and can be allocated to the contract, and

3. Such other costs as are specifically chargeable to the customer under the terms of the contract.

IAS 11 gives examples, and some sometimes pedantic detail, about each part in paragraphs 17–21. Allocatable costs, essentially design and construction overheads, are allocated using methods that are systematic and rational and are applied consistently to all costs having similar characteristics. The allocation is based on the normal level of construction activity. Construction overheads include such costs as the preparation and processing of construction personnel payroll. Costs that may be attributable to contract activity in general and can be allocated to specific contracts also include borrowing costs when the contractor capitalizes interest under the 2007 revision of IAS 23 (see Chapter 7).

Expenditures that one would not expect to be allowed to be charged to contract costs, such as general administration costs or research costs, "may" be included in contract costs when they are specifically chargeable to the customer under the terms of the contract. This is only sensible, as they will be included in revenues automatically. Costs incurred in securing a contract, that is, pre-contract costs, "are" included as part of the contract costs if they can be separately identified and measured reliably and it is probable that the contract will be obtained. When costs incurred in securing a contract are recognized as an expense in the period in which they are incurred, they are not included in contract costs when the contract is obtained in a subsequent period.

RECOGNITION OF CONTRACT REVENUE AND EXPENSES

Recognition of contract revenue and expenses, of course, is fundamentally what IAS 11 is all about. When profits are expected, the standard requires the percentage-of-completion method and does not allow the completed-contract method. This does not automatically mean, however, that profits are recognized in the early stages of a long-term construction contract.

The formal statement of the position is as follows (par. 22). When the outcome of a construction contract can be estimated reliably, contract revenue and contract costs associated with the construction contract should be recognized as revenue and expenses, respectively, by reference to the stage of completion of the contract activity at the balance sheet date. An expected loss on the construction contract should be recognized as an expense immediately when it becomes probable that total contract costs will exceed total contract revenue. Any such loss is determined and recognized irrespective of (par. 37):

1. Whether or not work has commenced on the contract,

2. The stage of completion of contract activity, or

3. The amount of profits expected to arise on other contracts that are not treated as a single construction contract.

The standard specifies, separately for fixed price and cost-plus contracts (as defined earlier in this chapter), when reliable estimation is possible. For a fixed price contract, it says that the outcome of a construction contract can be estimated reliably when all the following conditions are satisfied (par. 23):

1. Total contract revenue can be measured reliably.

2. It is probable that the economic benefits associated with the contract will flow to the entity.

3. Both the contract costs to complete the contract and the stage of contract completion at the balance sheet date can be measured reliably.

4. The contract costs attributable to the contract can be clearly identified and measured reliably so that actual contract costs incurred can be compared with prior estimates.

In the case of a cost-plus contract, the outcome of a construction contract can be estimated reliably when both the following conditions are satisfied (par. 24):

1. It is probable that the economic benefits associated with the contract will flow to the entity.

2. The contract costs attributable to the contract, whether or not specifically reimbursable, can be clearly identified and measured reliably.

It is important to understand and accept that "reliable estimation" is not the same as objective fact. As IAS 11 puts it (par. 29), an

> enterprise reviews and, when necessary, revises the estimates of contract revenue and contract costs as the contract progresses. The need for such revisions does not necessarily indicate that the outcome of the contract cannot be estimated reliably.

Clearly it is essential for the enterprise to have an efficient budgeting and costing system. The stage of completion is to be determined consistently in a manner appropriate to the contract, for example, proportion of cost basis, as used in our earlier illustration, by survey of work performed or by physical proportion. Proportion of cash received to a total contract price would not be appropriate, as it would not reflect the work performed.

It is, of course, highly likely that during the early stages of a long-term contract the outcome of the contract cannot be measured reliably under the required conditions stated above. When the outcome of a construction contract cannot be estimated reliably (par. 32):

1. Revenue should be recognized only to the extent of contract costs incurred that it is probable will be recoverable.

2. Contract costs should be recognized as an expense in the period in which they are incurred.

An expected loss on the construction contract should, of course, be recognized as an expense immediately.

The effect of this is that no profit is recognized when the outcome cannot be "estimated reliably," but also that a loss or net expense is recorded only if it is "expected." In other words, revenue equals expenses. Expenditures and costs are recorded, at cost, as assets until the later stages of the contract are reached.

OBSERVATION: When the "early stage" treatment is being applied, the effect is identical to the effect of applying the completed-contract method, that is, no profits are recorded, but losses are recorded only if expected. Given also that the interpretation of words used in IAS 11 like "estimated reliably" and "probable" is inherently subjective and likely to be influenced by national norms and cultures, the way is open for national systems that would prefer, perhaps on the grounds of prudence, to use the completed-contract method, to interpret these subjective expressions in a way that would delay profit recognition, relative to other national norms. This is an inevitable part of international accounting. National cultural characteristics cannot be standardized by regulation.

The effect of a material change in estimates part way through the life of a construction contract is treated in accordance with IAS 8, "Accounting Policies, Changes in Accounting Estimates, and Errors" (see Chapter 6). The effects of the change in estimates are included in the net profit or loss for the period in which the change occurs, or if appropriate partly in that year and partly in future years.

DISCLOSURE

An entity should disclose (pars. 39–42):

1. The amount of contract revenue recognized as revenue in the period,

2. The methods used to determine the contract revenue recognized in the period, and

3. The methods used to determine the stage of completion of contracts in progress.

An entity should disclose each of the following for contracts in progress at the balance sheet date:

1. The aggregate amount of costs incurred and recognized profits (less recognized losses) to date,

2. The amount of advances received, and

3. The amount of retentions.

An entity should present:

1. The gross amount due from customers for contract work as an asset, and

2. The gross amount due to customers for contract work as a liability.

IAS 37, "Provisions, Contingent Liabilities, and Contingent Assets" (see Chapter 29), should also be applied if appropriate.

IAS 11 gives, as an appendix, a long example and illustration that is worthy of study.

POSSIBLE FUTURE DEVELOPMENTS

In the summer of 2010, the IASB issued an exposure draft called "Revenue from Contracts with Customers." If confirmed, it would be a replacement for both IAS 11, "Construction Contracts," and IAS 18, "Revenues." A key proposal is that no revenue could be recognized from a good or service until control of that good or service has passed to the buyer. In the context of construction contracts this could imply a delay in revenue recognition in some cases, as compared with IAS 11.

A fuller note is given at the end of Chapter 31 "Revenue."

CHAPTER 13
EARNINGS PER SHARE

CONTENTS

OVERVIEW

Earnings per share (EPS) is an important summary indicator of corporate performance for investors and other users of financial statements, relating the total earnings of the enterprise to the number of shares issued. It is an essential component in the Price/earnings (PE) ratio, which provides a basis of comparison between listed enterprises, and an indicator of market confidence, calculated as market price per share divided by EPS. High expectations of future performance lead to, and are indicated by, a higher share price and therefore a higher PE ratio.

Earnings per share figures are required by IASB GAAP to be presented in published financial statements in two forms. The basic EPS reports the EPS essentially as achieved in current circumstances. The diluted EPS calculates the EPS as if the dilutive effect of "potential" ordinary or common shares currently foreseeable had already taken place, that is, it assumes that a likely future increase in the number of shares has already happened. Intuitively, diluted EPS will be lower than basic EPS, but this need not be the case universally as the numerator may be increased as well as the denominator.

IAS 33, "Earnings per Share," became operative from January 1, 1998. There was considerable cooperation in this area between the IASC, the U.S. FASB, and the U.K. ASB. IAS 33, FAS-128 (i.e., ASC 260) in the United States, and FRS-14 in the United Kingdom were developed in cooperation and were consistent in all significant respects with each other.

A revised version of IAS 33 was issued in March 2004, applicable for annual periods beginning on or after January 1, 2005, with earlier application encouraged. The changes in this revision were of some importance but are of a technical rather than fundamental nature.

BACKGROUND

EPS is widely regarded as an important and convenient indicator of enterprise performance. In many ways, this is an unsatisfactory state of affairs. Accountants and regulators nationally and internationally have made enormous efforts to prescribe and increase transparency and clarity of reporting, but EPS goes out of its way to seek to reduce a voluminous and complex set of information to a single statistic. While in one sense wishing to downgrade the importance attached to EPS, regulators have inevitably found it necessary to make the EPS figure as reliable and consistent as possible. The earnings figure is relatively easy to regulate in terms of "which figure off the income statement to use," and impossible to regulate in terms of the inherent subjectivity involved in some aspects of revenue and expense calculation. Most of the detail of IAS 33, "Earnings per Share," is concerned with the calculation of the denominator in the EPS ratio, that is, with the actual or imputed number of shares.

SCOPE AND DEFINITIONS

IAS 33 must be applied by entities whose ordinary shares or potential ordinary shares are publicly traded and by entities that are in the process of issuing ordinary shares or potential ordinary shares in public markets. Any other entity that discloses earnings per share should calculate and disclose earnings per share in accordance with the standard.

When an entity presents both consolidated financial statements and separate financial statements prepared in accordance with IAS 27, "Consolidated and Separate Financial Statements," the disclosures required by IAS 33 need be presented only on the basis of the consolidated information. An entity that chooses to disclose earnings per share based on its separate financial statements must present such EPS information only on the face of its separate income statement. An entity shall not present such EPS information in the consolidated financial statements. This last prohibition, a new introduction compared with the previous version, is to avoid confusion for the readers of the consolidated financial statements. In a similar vein, if an entity presents the components of profit or loss in a separate income statement, following paragraph 81 of IAS 1, "Presentation of Financial Statements," as revised in 2007 (see Chapter 4), it presents its EPS information only in that separate statement. Note that the revision of IAS 1 is mandatory only from January 1, 2009.

The standard notes that the IAS 32 definitions of financial instrument, financial asset, financial liability, equity instrument, and fair value should be assumed to apply (see Chapter 17). Other definitions are given in IAS 33 as follow (par. 5):

- *Dilution* is a reduction in earnings per share or an increase in loss per share resulting from the assumption that convertible instruments are converted, that options or warrants are exercised, or that ordinary shares are issued upon the satisfaction of specified conditions.

- *Options, warrants, and their equivalents* are financial instruments that give the holder the right to purchase ordinary shares.

- An *ordinary share* is an equity instrument that is subordinate to all other classes of equity instruments.

- A *potential ordinary share* is a financial instrument or other contract that may entitle its holder to ordinary shares.

- *Put options* on ordinary shares are contracts that give the holder the right to sell ordinary shares at a specified price for a given period.

- *Antidilution* is an increase in earnings per share or a reduction in loss per share resulting from the assumption that convertible instruments are converted, that options or warrants are exercised, or that ordinary shares are issued upon the satisfaction of specified conditions.

- A *contingent share agreement* is an agreement to issue shares that is dependent on the satisfaction of specified conditions.

- *Contingently issuable ordinary shares* are ordinary shares issuable for little or no cash or other consideration upon the satisfaction of specified conditions in a contingent share agreement.

The definition of an ordinary share as "subordinate to all other classes" implies that there is only one class of ordinary shares and, conversely, that all ordinary shares are of the same class. However, this is not in general the case. The standard states explicitly (par. 6) as follows.

> Ordinary shares participate in profit for the period only after other types of shares, such as preference shares, have participated. An entity may have more than one class of ordinary shares. Ordinary shares of the same class have the same rights to receive dividends.

Further ambiguity arises from a comparison of the above statement, which distinguishes ordinary shares in terms of their rights to participate in net profit, with the definition of an equity instrument in IAS 32, which is couched purely in terms of rights to participate in a residual interest in net assets. The one need not automatically embrace the other.

It is possible to envisage complex equity structures creating apparently anomalous situations. For example, two types of shares could exist, A and B, both participating in residual net profits and having an interest in residual net assets, but with A also having an additional fixed preferential dividend entitlement. Clearly A, as a participating preference share, has some preference over B, so therefore B is subordinate to A. The definition of an ordinary share in IAS 33 would then clearly indicate that only B is an ordinary share, despite the fact that A also participates in residual net profit. On the other hand, two types of share could exist where the dividend entitlement of one, while neither fixed nor preferential, is stated as having a fixed proportional relationship to that of the other. Both types meet the definition (provided they also participate, whether equally or otherwise, in the residual net assets on dissolution also), so both are ordinary shares, but they are clearly distinguishable and would be expected to have different market values.

BASIC EARNINGS PER SHARE

Basic earnings per share should be calculated by dividing the net profit or loss for the period attributable to ordinary shareholders, the numerator, by the weighted average number of ordinary shares outstanding during the period, the denominator. Note that the numerator is the net result after deducting preference dividends (and in principle after deducting the returns to any other share class other than the ordinary shares). An entity should calculate basic EPS amounts for profit or loss attributable to ordinary equity holders of the parent entity and, if presented, profit or loss from continuing operations attributable to those equity holders.

The amount of preference dividends that is deducted from the net profit for the period is the amount of any preference dividends on noncumulative preference shares declared in respect of the period, and the full amount of the required preference dividends for cumulative preference shares for the period, whether or not the dividends have been declared. It follows that any dividends paid or declared during the current year in relation to cumulative preference shares in respect of previous period have been dealt with in earlier years, and should not be deducted in the current period EPS calculation.

OBSERVATION: This simple definition of earnings for EPS purposes masks two issues that had caused some controversy in earlier years: tax considerations and unusual items. Under a number of jurisdictions the distribution policy affects the total taxation payable by a company on its income. Because "earnings" are supposed to be gross of dividends to ordinary shareholders and any effects thereof, it has been suggested that in such circumstances tax effects should be adjusted to give theoretical comparability between enterprises with different dividend policies. IAS 33 ignores this issue, simply requiring earnings to be calculated after all tax effects of the actual activities have been taken into account.

Unusual items are likewise not discussed in IAS 33. There had been much discussion in earlier years to the effect that EPS, as an indicator of likely repeatable performance, should exclude the effects of extraordinary items. However, the subjectivity of definition caused considerable difficulty and distortion (if not creativity) where this was tried. IAS 33 sweeps this issue, too, into oblivion by automatically requiring earnings to be calculated after the effects of all such items.

The denominator in the basic EPS calculation is potentially more difficult to calculate. It should be the weighted average number of ordinary shares outstanding during the period. This is the number of ordinary shares outstanding at the beginning of the period, adjusted by the number of ordinary shares bought back or issued during the period multiplied by a time-weighting factor. The time-weighting factor is the number of days that the specific shares are outstanding as a proportion of the total number of days in the period; a reasonable approximation of the weighted average is adequate in many circumstances. In most cases, shares are included in the weighted average number of shares from the date consideration is receivable (which is generally the date of their issue).

Some simple illustrations may be useful. Consider first the situation where an enterprise issues shares partway through the year at full market price.

I. Fullmar had total issued share capital on December 31, 20X1, as follows:

500,000 7% $1 preference shares

4,000,000 25¢ ordinary shares

Profit after tax for the year ended December 31, 20X1, was $435,000. On October 1, 20X1, Fullmar had issued 1 million 25¢ ordinary shares at full market price

The EPS for the year ended December 31, 20X1, would be calculated as follows.

The number of ordinary shares in issue on January 1, 20X1, was 3 million, and 1 million were issued on October 1, 20X1. Thus, the time weighted average number of ordinary shares in issue for the year was

$3,000,000 \times (9/12) + 4,000,000 \times (3/12) = 3,250,000$

The earnings for the year attributable to the ordinary shareholders is $435,000 – 35,000 preference dividend = $400,000. Therefore,

EPS = $(40,000,000/3,250,000)$¢ per share = 12.3¢ per share.

A second situation is when the number of shares is increased by a capitalization or bonus issue, that is, the shares are issued for zero consideration, leading of course to no change in the resources available to the enterprise.

The standard (par. 26) logically requires that the weighted average number of ordinary shares outstanding during the period and for all periods presented should be adjusted for events, other than the conversion of potential ordinary shares, that have changed the number of ordinary shares outstanding without a corresponding change in resources.

II. Using the same data as above, except that Fullmar issued the shares on October 1, 20X1, as bonus shares, EPS for 20X1 would be as follows.

We now have a capitalization issue, not a full market price issue, of shares and therefore we assume 4 million shares in issue for the whole of the year. (Note: This assumption would be the same no matter at what point during the year the capitalization was made.)

The number of shares in issue can also be calculated using the following:

$3,000,000 \times (9/12) \, (4/3) + 4,000,000 \times (3/12)$

(bonus factor)

$= 3,000,000 + 1,000,000 = 4,000,000$

EPS = $(40,000,000/4,000,000) = 10$¢ per share

The above calculation gives the EPS figure for the year 20X1. However, comparability (and paragraph 26 as quoted) requires the adjustment of all prior period EPS figures presented in the 20X1 financial statements.

If the EPS for the year ended December 31, 20X0, for Fullmar was 8¢, how would this figure have to be adjusted for the bonus issue for the 20XI financial statements?

The bonus issue represents a 1 for 3 share issue, that is, the number of shares has increased by one-third; therefore, we must have four-thirds times the original number of shares and the EPS will be multiplied by three-quarters, that is:

$$8¢ \times (3/4) = 6¢$$

The third situation is where shares are issued partway through the year for consideration but at less than the full market price, as is likely to be the case with a "rights issue." In a rights issue, the exercise price is often less than the fair value of the shares. Therefore, such a rights issue includes a bonus element. The number of ordinary shares to be used in calculating basic earnings per share for all periods prior to the rights issue is the number of ordinary shares outstanding prior to the issue, multiplied by the following factor:

Theoretical ex-rights fair value per share/Fair value per share immediately prior to the exercise of rights

The theoretical ex-rights fair value per share is calculated by adding the aggregate fair value of the shares immediately prior to the exercise of the rights to the proceeds from the exercise of the rights and dividing by the number of shares outstanding after the exercise of the rights. Where the rights themselves are to be publicly traded separately from the shares prior to the exercise date, fair value for the purposes of this calculation is established at the close of the last day on which the shares are traded together with the rights.

Thus, a rights issue combines the characteristics of a capitalization issue and a full market price issue. New resources are passing into the business, so a higher earnings figure, related to these new resources, should be expected. At the same time, however, there is a bonus element in the new shares, which should be treated like a capitalization issue. To the extent that the rights issue provides new resources, that is, equates to an issue at full market price, we need to calculate the average number of shares weighted on a time basis. To the extent that the rights issue includes a discount or bonus element, we need to increase the number of shares deemed to have been in issue for the whole period.

III. Illustration of effect of a rights issue:

On June 30, 20X1, Trig has 6,000,000 $1 ordinary shares in issue with a current market value of $2 per share. On July 1, 20X1, Trig makes a four for six rights issue at $1.75, and all rights are taken up. Earnings for the year after tax and preference dividends are $81,579 and the previous year's EPS was declared as 9¢. Calculate the EPS figure that should be shown in the financial statements for the year ended December 31, 20X1.

We first need to calculate the theoretical ex-rights price of the shares:

Market value of equity before rights	=	600,000 × $2	=	$1,200,000
Proceeds from rights issue	=	400,000 × $1.75	=	700,000
		1,000,000		$1,900,000

Theoretical ex-rights price = (1,900,000/1,000,000) = $1.90
Secondly, we calculate the weighted average number of shares:

$600,000 \times (1/2) \times (2/1.9) + 1,000,000 \times (1/2) = 815,789$
(time weighting) (time weighting)

Therefore, EPS for year ending December 31, 20X1 = (8,157,900/815,789) = 10¢ per share

Third, we need to recalculate the previous year's EPS in order to make the comparative figure comparable with the current figure as reported.

$9 \times (1.9/2) = 8.55¢$ per share

A reduction has occurred in the previous year's EPS as we have retrospectively inserted the bonus element of the rights issue.

There are some exceptions to the general rule that shares are to be included in the weighted average number from the date consideration is receivable.

Ordinary shares issued as part of the purchase consideration of a business combination that is treated as an acquisition are included in the weighted average number of shares as of the date of the acquisition, because the acquirer incorporates the results of the operations of the acquiree into its income statement from the date of acquisition.

Where ordinary shares are issued in partly paid form, these partly paid shares are treated as a fraction of an ordinary share (i.e., the proportion of payments received to date over the full subscription price) to the extent that they were entitled to participate in dividends relative to a fully paid ordinary share during the financial period.

Ordinary shares that are issuable upon the satisfaction of certain conditions (contingently issuable shares) are considered outstanding and included in the computation of basic earnings per share from the date when all necessary conditions have been satisfied. Outstanding ordinary shares that are contingently returnable (that is, subject to recall) are excluded from the calculation of basic EPS until the date the shares are no longer subject to recall.

Any different types of unusual share transaction should be treated in accordance with the substance of the situation and consistently with the principles outlined in the above text and illustrations. Further illustrations are given in IAS 33, Appendix A.

DILUTED EARNINGS PER SHARE

Where there are securities existing at the year-end that will have a claim on equity earnings from some time in the future, then it is clear that at this future time the claim of each currently existing share will, other things equal, be reduced (or diluted). It is likely to be useful information to current shareholders and others to give them a picture of what the EPS would be if this dilution takes place. This is done by recalculating the current year's EPS as if the dilution had already occurred.

For the purpose of calculating diluted earnings per share, the net profit attributable to ordinary shareholders and the weighted average number of shares outstanding both should be adjusted for the effects of all dilutive potential ordinary shares. This means that:

1. The net profit for the period attributable to ordinary shares is increased by the after-tax amount of dividends and interest recognized in the period in respect of the dilutive potential ordinary shares and adjusted for any other changes in income or expense that would result from the conversion of the dilutive potential ordinary shares, and

2. The weighted average number of ordinary shares outstanding is increased by the weighted average number of additional ordinary shares that would have been outstanding assuming the conversion of all dilutive potential ordinary shares.

Although this situation is by its nature more complicated than the calculation of basic earnings per share, the adjustments for the numerator, the earnings figure, are relatively straightforward, provided all aspects of the changes are considered. For example, if a convertible debenture exists, then the diluted EPS calculation requires the assumption that the conversion has already taken place. This assumption leads not only to an increase in the number of (assumed) shares, it also leads to the necessity to remove the interest charge on the debentures from the net profit calculation (after tax).

Formally, the net profit or loss attributable to ordinary shareholders is adjusted for the after-tax effect of the following (par. 33):

1. Any dividends on dilutive potential ordinary shares that have been deducted in arriving at the net profit attributable to ordinary shareholders as calculated for the basic EPS,

2. Interest recognized in the period for the dilutive potential ordinary shares, and

3. Any other changes in income or expense that would result from the conversion of the dilutive potential ordinary shares, such as bonus or profit-sharing schemes based on reported earnings.

Regarding the denominator in the diluted EPS calculation, that is, the number of shares, the number of ordinary shares should be the weighted average number of ordinary shares calculated as for the basic EPS, plus the weighted average number of ordinary shares that would be issued on the conversion of all the dilutive potential ordinary shares into ordinary shares. Dilutive potential ordinary shares should be deemed to have been converted into ordinary shares at the beginning of the period or, if later, the date of the issue of the potential ordinary shares. The calculation should be based on the terms of issue of the potential ordinary shares and should assume the most advantageous conversion rate or exercise price from the viewpoint of the holder.

Illustration of Calculation of Basic and Diluted EPS

The summarized income statement for the year ended 20X1 is as follows:

	$000	$000
Profit before taxation		1,000
Taxation		400
		600
Preference dividend	50	
Ordinary dividend	100	
		150
		450

The number of ordinary shares in issue is 2 million.

Calculate the basic EPS.

Basic EPS   = (Profit after tax less preference dividend/Number of ordinary shares)

= (60,000,000 – 5,000,000)/2,000,000

= 27.5¢ per share

Assume now that, in addition to the 2 million ordinary shares already in issue, however, there exists convertible loan stock of $500,000 bearing interest at 10%. This may be converted into ordinary shares between 20X3 and 20X6 at a rate of one ordinary share for every $2 of loan stock. Taxation is taken for convenience as 50%.

The fully diluted EPS is found as follows. If the conversion is fully completed, then there will be two effects:

1. The share capital will increase by 250,000 shares (1 share for every $2 of the $500,000 loans).

2. The profit after tax will increase by the interest on the loan no longer payable less the extra tax on this increase. The interest at 10% on $500,000 is $50,000, but the extra tax on this profit increase would be 50% of $50,000, that is, $25,000.

So profit after tax, and therefore "earnings," will increase by 50,000 – 25,000 = $25,000. Fully diluted EPS will therefore be:

$(600{,}000 + 25{,}000 - 50{,}000)/(2{,}000{,}000 + 250{,}000)$

$= (57{,}500{,}000/2{,}250{,}000)¢$

$= 25.6¢$ per share

IAS 33 discusses a number of possible complications in some detail, in paragraphs 41–63.

As in the computation of basic earnings per share, ordinary shares whose issue is contingent upon the occurrence of certain events are considered outstanding and included in the computation of diluted earnings per share if the conditions have been met. Contingently issuable shares should be included as of the beginning of the period (or as of the date of the contingent share agreement, if later). If the conditions have not been met, the number of contingently issuable shares included in the diluted earnings per share computation is based on the number of shares that would be issuable if the end of the reporting period was the end of the contingency period (which, of course, could be zero).

If a group company other than the parent issues instruments that are potentially convertible into ordinary shares of the parent, then they should be included in the calculation of consolidated diluted EPS.

Options and other share purchase arrangements are dilutive when they would result in the issue of ordinary shares for less than fair value. The amount of the dilution is fair value less the issue price. Fair value for this purpose is calculated on the basis of the average price of the ordinary shares during the period. For the purpose of calculating diluted earnings per share, an enterprise should assume the exercise of dilutive options and other dilutive potential ordinary shares of the enterprise. The assumed proceeds from these issues should be considered to have been received from the issue of shares at fair value. The difference between the number of shares issued and the number of shares that would have been issued at fair value should be treated as an issue of ordinary shares for no consideration. Such ordinary shares generate no proceeds and have no effect on the net profit attributable to ordinary shares outstanding. Therefore, such shares are dilutive, and they are added to the number of ordinary shares outstanding in the computation of diluted earnings per share.

The illustration of the calculation of diluted EPS given above showed the common situation where, compared with the calculation of basic EPS, both the numerator and the denominator are increased. The effect in that case was a lower EPS figure, and indeed that is what the word *diluted* indicates. It is clearly possible, however, depending on the relative effect of the adjustments to numerator and denominator, for the effects to be antidilutive. Potential ordinary shares are antidilutive when their conversion to ordinary shares would increase earnings per share from continuing ordinary operations or decrease loss per share from continuing ordinary operations. The effects of antidilutive potential ordinary shares are ignored in calculating diluted earnings per share.

In considering whether potential ordinary shares are dilutive or antidilutive, each issue or series of potential ordinary shares is considered separately rather than in aggregate. The sequence in which potential ordinary shares are considered may affect whether or not they are dilutive. Therefore, in order to maximize the dilution of basic earnings per share, each issue or series of potential ordinary shares is considered in sequence from the most dilutive to the least dilutive.

It is important to note that, while EPS is based on net profit or loss, the determination of whether potential ordinary shares are dilutive or antidilutive is based on net profit from continuing operations.

The inclusion of potential ordinary shares in the denominator of a diluted EPS calculation when the enterprise has a loss from continuing ordinary activities as defined above would automatically have an antidilutive effect (as it would decrease loss per share). Such shares would therefore be ignored for calculating diluted EPS, even if the net profit (as opposed to net profit from continuing ordinary activities) is positive.

Potential ordinary shares are weighted for the period they were outstanding. Potential ordinary shares that were canceled or allowed to lapse during the reporting period are included in the computation of diluted earnings per share only for the portion of the period during which they were outstanding. Potential ordinary shares that have been converted into ordinary shares during the reporting period are included in the calculation of diluted earnings per share from the beginning of the period to the date of conversion; from the date of conversion, the resulting ordinary shares are included in both basic and diluted earnings per share.

When an entity has issued a contract that may be settled in ordinary shares or cash at the entity's option, the entity must presume that the contract will be settled in ordinary shares, and the resulting potential ordinary shares are included in diluted EPS if the effect is dilutive. For contracts that may be settled in ordinary shares or cash at the holder's option, the more dilutive of cash settlement and share settlement should be used in calculating diluted EPS.

Contracts such as purchased put options and purchased call options (i.e., options held by the entity on its own ordinary shares) are not included in the calculation of diluted EPS, because including them would be antidilutive. This is because a put option would be exercised only if the exercise price were higher than the market price and the call option would be exercised only if the exercise price were lower than the market price.

Contracts that require the entity to repurchase its own shares, such as written put options and forward purchase contracts, are reflected in the calculation of diluted EPS if the effect is dilutive. If these contracts are "in the money" during the period (i.e., the exercise or settlement price is above the average market price for that period), the potential dilutive effect on EPS should be calculated as follows:

1. It should be assumed that at the beginning of the period sufficient ordinary shares will be issued (at the average market price during the period) to raise proceeds to satisfy the contract.

2. It should be assumed that the proceeds from the issue are used to satisfy the contract (i.e., to buy back ordinary shares).

3. The incremental ordinary shares (the difference between the number of ordinary shares assumed issued and the number of ordinary shares received from satisfying the contract) should be included in the calculation of diluted EPS.

RETROSPECTIVE ADJUSTMENTS

As discussed above in relation to IAS 33, paragraph 26, and as shown in Illustration II above, if the number of ordinary or potential ordinary shares outstanding increases as a result of a capitalization or bonus issue or share split or decreases as a result of a reverse share split, the calculation of basic and diluted earnings per share for all periods presented should be adjusted retrospectively (par. 64). If these changes occur after the balance sheet date but before issue of the financial statements, the per share calculations for those and any prior period financial statements presented should be based on the new number of shares. When per share calculations reflect such changes in the number of shares, that fact should be disclosed. In addition, basic and diluted earnings per share of all periods presented should be adjusted for the effects of errors and adjustments resulting from changes in accounting policies accounted for retrospectively.

Restatement of prior period diluted EPS to reflect a change in assumptions used is not allowed.

PRESENTATION AND DISCLOSURE

An entity must present in the statement of comprehensive income basic and diluted EPS for profit or loss from continuing operations attributable to the ordinary equity holders of the parent entity and for profit or loss attributable to the ordinary equity holders of the parent entity, for the period, for each class of ordinary shares that has a different right to share in profit for the period. Basic and diluted EPS must be given equal prominence for all periods presented. These requirements apply even if basic and diluted EPS are identical (in which case a one-line presentation is acceptable), and even if the amounts are negative. An entity that reports a discontinued operation must disclose the basic and diluted amounts per share for the discontinued operation either in the statement of comprehensive income or in the notes to the financial statements. If an entity presents the components of profit or loss in a separate income statement, as described in paragraph 81 of IAS 1, "Presentation of Financial Statements," and as revised in 2007 (see Chapter 4), it presents the basic and diluted EPS figures in that separate statement or the notes.

An entity shall disclose the following:

1. The amounts used as the numerators in calculating basic and diluted EPS, and a reconciliation of those amounts to profit or loss attributable to the parent entity for the period. The reconciliation must include the individual effect of each class of instruments that affects earnings per share.

2. The weighted average number of ordinary shares used as the denominator in calculating basic and diluted EPS and a reconciliation of these denominators to each other. The reconciliation should include the individual effect of each class of instruments that affects earnings per share.

3. Instruments (including contingently issuable shares) that could potentially dilute basic EPS in the future but were not included in the calculation of diluted EPS because they are antidilutive for the periods presented.

4. A description of ordinary share transactions or potential ordinary share transactions, other than those accounted for in accordance with paragraph 64, that occur after the balance sheet date and that would have

changed significantly the number of ordinary shares or potential ordinary shares outstanding at the end of the period if those transactions had occurred before the end of the reporting period.

Examples of transactions in item 4 include:

- An issue of shares for cash;
- An issue of shares when the proceeds are used to repay debt or preference shares outstanding at the balance sheet date;
- The redemption of ordinary shares outstanding;
- The conversion or exercise of potential ordinary shares outstanding at the balance sheet date into ordinary shares;
- An issue of options, warrants, or convertible instruments; and
- The achievement of conditions that would result in the issue of contingently issuable shares.

IAS 33 does not prevent the disclosure of *additional* calculations of performance-per-share ratios beyond those specified in the standard, but it is concerned with preventing either obfuscation of the "official" ratios or confusion by the reader of the financial statements. Accordingly, if an entity discloses, in addition to basic and diluted EPS, amounts per share using a reported component of the income statement other than one required by the standard, such amounts shall be calculated using the weighted-average number of ordinary shares determined in accordance with the standard. Basic and diluted amounts per share relating to such a component are to be disclosed with equal prominence and presented in the notes to the financial statements. An entity should indicate the basis on which the numerators are determined, including whether amounts per share are before tax or after tax. If a component of the income statement is used that is not reported as a line item in the income statement, a reconciliation must be provided between the component used and a line item that is reported in the income statement.

CHAPTER 14
EMPLOYEE BENEFITS

CONTENTS

OVERVIEW

Employee benefits take a variety of forms. Many of them are paid or provided concomitant with, or very shortly after, the provision of the service by the employee, and no particular accounting problems arise. However, important elements of the employee benefit package are likely to be significantly deferred—possibly by up to 50 years or more, and the treatment of pension rights is particularly problematic.

Many, though not all, pension plans are defined benefit plans, meaning that the amount the employee will be entitled to receive is predetermined (by formula, not usually by actual amount). This means that the employing entity is likely to be liable to make up any shortfall necessary to ensure that all relevant (ex-) employees can be fully provided for according to their rights. In other words, the risks, which are considerable given the inherent uncertainty of planning and investing decades in advance, fall on the employer. These risks must be estimated, and provided for, by the employer.

IASB GAAP in this area is provided in IAS 19, "Employee Benefits," issued in a revised—and significantly altered—form in 1998, effective from January 1, 1999; revised again in 2000, effective from January 1, 2001; again in 2002, effective May 31, 2002; and yet again in March 2004, effective January 1, 2005. A further amendment was issued in December 2004, effective from accounting periods beginning on or after January 1, 2006, with earlier adoption being encouraged. This is discussed below at the end of the "Defined Benefit Plans" section. Yet another revision has been issued as we go to press, effective from 2013. This is discussed briefly below. A separate standard, IAS 26, "Accounting and Reporting by Retirement Benefit Plans," deals with reporting by pension funds themselves. IFRIC 14, "IAS 19—The Limit on a Defined Benefit Asset, Minimum Funding Requirements and their Interaction," is also relevant.

BACKGROUND

Employment is based on an exchange agreement. The employee agrees to provide services for the employer; in exchange, the employer agrees to provide a current wage, a pension benefit, and possibly other benefits. Although pension benefits and some other benefits are not paid currently and may not be due for many years, they represent deferred compensation that must be accounted for as part of the employee's total compensation package. The deferred payments relate to current employment and must therefore be accounted for in the current period.

The major difficulties of accounting for employee benefits relate to the deferred elements. The IASB has had five relevant standards over the years (all numbered IAS 19). The first two, approved in 1983 and 1993, both had titles concerning "retirement benefit costs." The remainder was given the broader title of this chapter. IAS 19 now identifies four categories of employee benefits, as follows:

1. Short-term employee benefits, such as wages, salaries, and social security contributions, paid annual leave and paid sick leave, profit sharing and bonuses (if payable within 12 months of the end of the period), and non-monetary benefits (such as medical care, housing, cars, and free or subsidized goods or services) for current employees;

2. Post-employment benefits such as pensions, other retirement benefits, postemployment life insurance, and postemployment medical care;

3. Other long-term employee benefits, including long-service leave or sabbatical leave, jubilee or other long-service benefits, long-term disability benefits, and, if they are payable 12 months or more after the end of the period, profit sharing, bonuses, and deferred compensation; and

4. Termination benefits.

Until the creation of IFRS 2, "Share-Based Payment," issued in March 2004 and effective from January 1, 2005, or earlier adoption (see Chapter 33, "Share-Based Payment"), IAS 19 also attempted to address the issue of equity compensation benefits for employees. The requirements were incomplete and unsatisfactory, being limited to disclosures and ignoring recognition and measurement matters.

Item 2 takes up much of the length of the standard. Pension plans can take a variety of different forms; they can be either funded or unfunded, defined contribution or defined benefit.

An unfunded pension plan is one in which the employer business itself undertakes to pay the pensions directly from its own resources as they fall due. With a funded plan, resources are accumulated in a separate legal entity (i.e., there is a separate fund). This separate fund may be a unique creation for the one employer or it may be operated by a specialist assurance company running many such plans. The two types of plan have obvious differences in terms of financial management and in terms of the bookkeeping entries. With a funded plan, money leaves the employer over the years of the employment and goes into the external fund. With an unfunded plan, no pension money leaves the employer at all until the employment has ceased and the actual pension begins to be paid.

Another distinction between different types of pension plans relates to the way in which the legal obligations under the plan are defined. In a defined contribution plan, the employer will normally discharge its obligation by making agreed contributions to a pension plan and the benefits paid will depend upon the funds available from these contributions and investment earnings thereon. The cost to the employer can, therefore, be measured with reasonable certainty.

In a defined benefit plan, however, the benefits to be paid will usually depend upon either the average pay of the employee during his or her career or, more typically, the final pay of the employee. In these circumstances, it is impossible to be certain in advance that the contributions to the pension plan, together with the investment return thereon, will equal the benefits to be paid. The employer may have a legal obligation to provide any unforeseen shortfalls in funds or, if not, may find it necessary to meet the shortfall in the interests of maintaining good employee relations. Conversely, if a surplus arises, the employer may be entitled to a refund of, or reduction in, contributions paid or payable into the pension plan. Thus, in this type of plan the employer's commitment is generally more open than with defined contribution plans, and the final cost is subject to considerable uncertainty.

There are no major differences of principle between IASB GAAP and U.S. GAAP, although U.S. GAAP do not allow the option of immediate recognition of all material gains and losses.

SCOPE AND DEFINITIONS

The scope of IAS 19 is wide. It should be applied by all employers in accounting for all employee benefits, except those to which IFRS 2 applies. It does not, however, deal with the preparation of financial reports by the actual employee benefit plans themselves. This highly specialized issue is covered by IAS 26, "Accounting and Reporting by Retirement Benefit Plans" (see the Appendix to this chapter).

The standard, as befits the complexity of the area and the variety of different types of employee benefit and pension plan likely to be found, finds it necessary to give a large number of definitions. Most are reasonably comprehensible, but all need to be clearly understood in order to apply the standard.

- *Employee benefits* are all forms of consideration given by an entity in exchange for service rendered by employees.

- *Short-term employee benefits* are employee benefits (other than termination benefits) that are due to be settled within 12 months after the end of the period in which the employees render the related service.

- *Post-employment benefits* are employee benefits (other than termination benefits) that are payable after the completion of employment.

- *Post-employment benefit plans* are formal or informal arrangements under which an entity provides post-employment benefits for one or more employees.

- *Defined contribution plans* are post-employment benefit plans under which an enterprise pays fixed contributions into a separate entity (a fund) and will have no legal or constructive obligation to pay further contributions if the fund does not hold sufficient assets to pay all employee benefits relating to employee service in the current and prior periods.

- *Defined benefit plans* are post employment benefit plans other than defined contribution plans.

- *Multi-employer plans* are defined contribution plans (other than state plans) or defined benefit plans (other than state plans) that:

  (a) Pool the assets contributed by various entities that are not under common control; and

  (b) Use those assets to provide benefits to employees of more than one entity, on the basis that contribution and benefit levels are determined without regard to the identity of the entity that employs the employees concerned.

- *Other long-term employee benefits* are employee benefits (other than post-employment benefits and termination benefits that are not due to be settled within 12 months after the end of the period in which the employees render the related service.

- *Termination benefits* are employee benefits payable as a result of either:

  (a) An entity's decision to terminate an employee's employment before the normal retirement date, or

  (b) An employee's decision to accept voluntary redundancy in exchange for those benefits.

- *Vested* employee benefits are employee benefits that are not conditional on future employment.

- The *present value of a defined benefit obligation* is the present value, without deducting any plan assets, of expected future payments required to settle the obligation resulting from employee service in the current and prior periods.

- *Current service cost* is the increase in the present value of the defined benefit obligation resulting from employee service in the current period.

- *Interest cost* is the increase during a period in the present value of a defined benefit obligation that arises because the benefits are one period closer to settlement.

- *Plan assets* comprise:

  (a) Assets held by a long-term employee benefit fund; and

  (b) Qualifying insurance policies.

- *Assets held by a long-term employee benefit fund* are assets (other than non-transferable financial instruments issued by the reporting entity) that:

(a) Are held by an entity (a fund) that is legally separate from the reporting entity and exists solely to pay or fund employee benefits; and

(b) Are available to be used only to pay or fund employee benefits, are not available to the reporting entity's own creditors (even in bankruptcy), and cannot be returned to the reporting entity, unless either:

(i) The remaining assets of the fund are sufficient to meet all the related employee benefit obligations of the plan or the reporting entity, or

(ii) The assets are returned to the reporting entity to reimburse it for the employee benefits already paid.

- *A qualifying insurance policy* is an insurance policy issued by an insurer that is not a related party (as defined in IAS 24, "Related Party Disclosures") of the reporting entity, if the proceeds of the policy:

(a) Can be used only to pay or fund employee benefits under a defined benefit plan;

(b) Are not available to the reporting entity's own creditors (even in bankruptcy) and cannot be paid to the reporting entity, unless either:

(i) The proceeds represent surplus assets that are not needed for the policy to meet all the related employee benefit obligations, or

(ii) The proceeds are returned to the reporting entity to reimburse it for employee benefits already paid.

- *Fair value* is the amount for which an asset could be exchanged or a liability settled between knowledgeable, willing parties in an arm's-length transaction.

- The *return on plan assets* is interest, dividends, and other revenue derived from the plan assets, together with realized and unrealized gains or losses on the plan assets, less any costs of administering the plan (other than those included in the actuarial assumptions used to measure the defined benefit obligation) and less any tax payable by the plan itself.

- *Actuarial gains and losses* comprise:

(a) Experience adjustments (the effects of differences between the previous actuarial assumptions and what has actually occurred), and

(b) The effects of changes in actuarial assumptions.

- *Past service cost* is the change in the present value of the defined benefit obligation for employee service in prior periods, resulting in the current period from the introduction of, or changes to, post-employment benefits or other long-term employee benefits. Past service cost may be either positive (when benefits are introduced or changed so that the present value of the defined benefit obligation increases) or negative (when existing benefits are changed so that the present value of the defined benefit obligation decreases).

SHORT-TERM EMPLOYEE BENEFITS

The treatment of short-term employee benefits is straightforward. Paragraph 10 requires that where an employee has rendered service to an entity during an accounting period, the entity should recognize the undiscounted amount of short-term employee benefits expected to be paid in exchange for that service:

1. As a liability (accrued expense), after deducting any amount already paid, and

2. As an expense, unless another international standard requires or permits the inclusion of the benefits in the cost of an asset (see, for example, IAS 2, "Inventories," Chapter 24, and IAS 16, "Property, Plant, and Equipment," Chapter 28).

There are no specific disclosure requirements in this respect in IAS 19. Other standards may be relevant, such as the requirement to show employee benefits for key management personnel under IAS 24, "Related Party Disclosures" (see Chapter 30) and the general requirement to disclose staff costs under IAS 1, "Presentation of Financial Statements" (see Chapter 4).

The standard addresses two particular applications, short-term compensated absences and profit sharing and bonus plans. In the former case, IAS 19 gives an illustration that is worthy of comment.

An entity has 100 employees, who are each entitled to 5 working days of paid sick leave for each year. Unused sick leave may be carried forward for one calendar year. Sick leave is taken first out of the current year's entitlement and then out of any balance brought forward from the previous year (a LIFO basis). At December 31, 20X1, the average unused entitlement is 2 days per employee. The entity expects, based on past experience, that 92 employees will take no more than 5 days of paid sick leave in 20X2 and that the remaining 8 employees will take an average of 6-1/2 days each.

The entity expects that it will pay an additional 12 days of sick pay as a result of the unused entitlement that has accumulated at December 31, 20X1 (1-1/2 days each, for 8 employees). Therefore, the entity recognizes a liability equal to 12 days of sick pay.

OBSERVATION: The creation of this liability of 12 days of sick pay creates an expense, in the year to December 31, 20X1, additional to that already recorded. There is, of course, a much greater "entitlement," carried forward into 20X2, giving a total of 2 days of sick pay for each of the 100 employees. In effect, this additional entitlement is valued at nil because, on the basis of past experience, it is not expected to be taken up. If the liability, as calculated above, is obviously going to be immaterial, then IAS 19 notes (par. 15) that the calculations will not need to be made.

The second issue addressed specifically by IAS 19 is the treatment of profit sharing and bonus plans. An entity should recognize the expected cost of profit sharing and bonus payments as a short-term employee benefit when, and only when:

1. The entity has a present legal or constructive obligation to make such payments as a result of past events, and

2. A reliable estimate of the obligation can be made.

A present obligation exists when, and only when, the entity has no realistic alternative but to make the payments.

A problem arises if the employees are entitled to a payment in the future related to the current year's profits, but only if they remain with the entity for a specified period. Such plans create a constructive obligation as employees render service that increases the amount to be paid if they remain in service until the end of the specified period. The measurement of such constructive obligations reflects the possibility that some employees may leave without receiving profit sharing payments, that is, it is likely to be measured at less than the entire theoretical entitlement. Note that if a "reliable estimate" of the obligation cannot be made, then no provision can be recognized at all.

POST-EMPLOYMENT BENEFITS

We have already discussed the important distinction between defined contribution plans and defined benefit plans, and given the formal IAS 19 definitions. The major distinction, as the names accurately indicate, is that with a defined contribution plan the employer's obligations are fixed, and the employee takes the risk of the eventual pension being inadequate; with a defined benefit plan, the eventual pension payments are fixed (by formula, not necessarily by amount), and the employer takes the risk of the pension fund being inadequate and is responsible for making up any shortfall.

IAS 19 goes into some length (pars. 29–42) to "explain" the distinction between defined contribution plans and defined benefit plans in the context of multi-employer plans, state plans, and insured benefits.

With a multi-employer plan that is a defined benefit plan, the entity should account for its proportionate share of the defined benefit obligation, plan assets, and cost associated with the plan in the same way as for any other defined benefit plan. If sufficient information is not available to use defined benefit accounting for a multi-employer plan that is a defined benefit plan, an entity should account for the plan as if it were a defined contribution plan and disclose:

1. The fact that the plan is a defined benefit plan, and

2. The reason why sufficient information is not available to enable the entity to account for the plan as a defined benefit plan.

To the extent that a surplus or deficit in the plan may affect the amount of future contributions, additional disclosure is required of:

1. Any available information about that surplus or deficit,

2. The basis used to determine that surplus or deficit, and

3. The implications, if any, for the enterprise.

→ **PRACTICE POINTER:** With a multi-employer defined benefit plan, an entity may in certain circumstances incur an obligation in respect of other employers involved within the plan. This could create a contingent liability (see IAS 37, "Provisions, Contingent Liabilities, and Contingent Assets," Chapter 29).

State plans are established by legislation to cover all enterprises (or all entities in a particular category, for example, a specific industry) and are operated by national or local government or by another body (for example, an autonomous agency created specifically for this purpose) that is not subject to control or influence by the reporting entity.

Despite the fact that the IASB definition of multi-employer plans (given above) explicitly excludes state plans, IAS 19 requires that an entity account for a state plan in the same way as for a multi-employer plan. The standard notes that state plans are usually defined contribution plans.

An entity may fund a post-employment benefit plan indirectly by means of the regular payment of insurance premiums. In such circumstances, the entity should treat such a plan as a defined contribution plan unless the entity will have (either directly or indirectly through the plan) a legal or constructive obligation to either:

1. Pay the employee benefits directly when they fall due, or

2. Pay further contributions if the insurer does not pay all future employee benefits relating to employee service in the current and prior periods.

If the entity retains such a legal or constructive obligation, the entity should treat the plan as a defined benefit plan. Whether or not there is a legal or constructive obligation is a question of fact.

DEFINED CONTRIBUTION PLANS

As implied above, there are no major difficulties involved in measuring the obligation or the expense as far as the reporting employer enterprise is concerned. The entity recognizes the contribution payable to the plan in relation to service rendered to the entity by an employee during the period as a liability, net of payments already made (which could lead to a net asset) and as an expense, unless another standard requires or permits the inclusion of the contribution in the cost of an asset (see, for example, IAS 2, "Inventories" (Chapter 24), and IAS 16, "Property, Plant, and Equipment" (Chapter 28). Where contributions to a defined contribution plan do not fall due wholly within 12 months after the end of the period in which the employees render the related service, they should be discounted as described below. The expense should be disclosed separately.

DEFINED BENEFIT PLANS

Accounting for defined benefit plans is much more complex because actuarial assumptions are required to measure the obligation and the expense, and there is a possibility of actuarial gains and losses. The obligations are measured on a discounted basis because they may be settled many years after the employees render the related service. IAS 19 takes no fewer than 78 paragraphs to cover this area. We attempt to provide a thorough coverage of the important aspects, without becoming too immersed in the detail.

In summary, the following steps are typically necessary in accounting by an entity for each defined benefit plan.

- Using actuarial techniques to make a reliable estimate of the amount of benefit that employees have earned in return for their service in the current and prior periods. This requires an entity to determine how much benefit is attributable to the current and prior periods and to make estimates (actuarial assumptions) about demographic variables (such as employee turnover and mortality) and financial variables (such as future increases in salaries and medical costs) that will influence the cost of the benefit.

- Discounting that benefit using the projected unit credit method (described below) in order to determine the present value of the defined benefit obligation and the current service cost.

- Determining the total amount of actuarial gains and losses and the amount of those actuarial gains and losses that should be recognized.

- Where a plan has been introduced or changed, determining the resulting past service cost.

- Determining the fair value of any plan assets.

- Where a plan has been curtailed or settled, determining the resulting gain or loss.

The amount recognized in the balance sheet as a defined benefit liability should be the net total of the following amounts (par. 54):

1. The present value of the defined benefit obligation (both legal and constructive) at the end of the reporting period,

2. Plus any actuarial gains (less any actuarial losses) not recognized because of the "corridor" treatment set out below,

3. Minus any past service cost not yet recognized,

4. Minus the fair value at the balance sheet date of plan assets (if any) out of which the obligations are to be settled directly.

The present value of the defined benefit obligation is the present value of the total obligation less the fair value of plan assets (if any). Both these amounts should be determined regularly so that the proper estimates at balance sheet date are not materially departed from. The involvement of a qualified actuary is "encouraged."

One of the purposes of the 2000 revision of IAS 19 was to clarify the treatment of insurance policies. The definition of asset plans, given earlier in this chapter, was revised to make it clear that qualifying insurance policies, as defined, *are* plan assets for all purposes, as under them the insurer will pay some or all of the defined benefit obligation.

When an insurance policy is not "qualifying," it is not a plan asset. However, it is still an asset, and the entity recognizes its rights to reimbursement under the insurance policy as a separate asset, and not as a deduction in calculating the net defined benefit liability under paragraph 54. More formally, IAS 19 now states (par. 104A) that when, and only when, it is virtually certain that another party will reimburse some or all of the expenditure required to settle a defined benefit obligation, an enterprise should recognize its right to reimbursement as a separate asset. The entity should measure the asset at fair value. In all other respects, an entity should treat that asset in the same way as plan assets. In the statement of comprehensive income, the expense relating to a defined benefit plan may be presented net of the amount recognized for a reimbursement.

In essence, therefore, qualifying insurance policies are valued at fair value and treated as a deduction in calculating the net defined benefit liability under paragraph 54, through their inclusion in plan assets. Non-qualifying insurance policies are valued at fair value and treated separately as assets.

The amount determined under paragraph 54 may be negative. An entity should measure the resulting asset at the lower of:

1. The amount determined under paragraph 54.

2. The cumulative total of

    (a) Any unrecognized net actuarial losses and past service cost, and

    (b) The present value of any economic benefits available in the form of refunds from the plan or reductions in future contributions to the plan.

It was this point that caused the 2002 revision of IAS 19. Alternative 2 above includes, in part, the cumulative unrecognized actuarial losses and past service costs, as an asset, although they are not of value as a separable item. They are merely a deferred expense. If, over a period of years, the cumulative unrecognized (un-expensed) losses get bigger, and alternative 2 for the asset measurement is applicable, then the increase in "assets" would lead to reported gains. In other words, an *increase* in the unrecognized (un-expensed) *loss* would lead directly to a reported *gain*, which is arguably absurd.

New and complicated paragraphs (58A and B) were inserted by the 2002 revision of IAS 19. Their effect is to prevent the above situation, by requiring the recognition of sufficient actuarial losses and past service costs to ensure that no increase in such unrecognized items could arise. Paragraph 58A only applies when actually necessary to prevent such a situation as described above.

OBSERVATION: This 2002 amendment is a classic example of a minor repair to stop the effect, but not the cause, of what is in fact a major problem. The new IASB, which issued the revision, has explicitly recognized that fact. IASB (and U.S.) GAAP are seriously deficient in this whole area, and major revision can be expected eventually.

However, further complexity has recently been introduced, in relation to 2(b) above, by the issue of IFRIC 14, "The Limit on a Defined Benefit Asset, Minimum Funding Requirements and their Interactions," mandatory for annual periods beginning on or after January 1, 2008, earlier application being permitted.

IFRIC 14 provides guidance on the determination of refunds and reductions in future contributions. A refund is available to an entity only if it has an unconditional right to the refund during the life of the plan, on the gradual settlement of the plan liabilities, or on the full settlement of the plan liabilities. The amount of the economic benefit available in the form of reduced contributions depends on whether there is a minimum funding requirement for the plan. If there is such a requirement, the reduction in future contributions is the present value of:

- The estimated future service cost in each year, less
- The estimated minimum funding contributions required in respect of the future accrual of benefits in that year.

IFRIC 14 also deals with the possibility that minimum funding requirements may be onerous when the contributions that are payable under the minimum funding requirement cannot be returned to the company. When the requirements are onerous, the entity may be required to recognize an additional liability, but only if both of the following conditions exist:

- The entity has a statutory or contractual obligation to pay additional amounts to the plan.
- The entity's ability to recover those amounts in the future, by refund or otherwise, is restricted.

In the income statement (profit or loss), the entity should recognize the net total of the following amounts as expense (or income), except to the extent that another international standard requires or permits their inclusion in the cost of an asset:

1. Current service cost,
2. Interest cost,
3. The expected return on any plan assets,
4. Actuarial gains and losses, to the extent that they are recognized,
5. Past service cost, to the extent required,
6. The effect of any curtailments or settlements, and
7. Any adjustments to profit or loss arising from paragraphs 58A and B.

The entity needs to calculate the present value of its defined benefit obligations. The increase in this figure over that of the previous year gives the current service cost to the extent that the increase results from employee service in the current period and gives the past service cost to the extent that it results from employee service in past periods (this increase—or decrease—being caused by changes in eventual benefit rights).

The method of calculation required by IAS 19 is the projected unit credit method. Each period of service increases the eventual benefit (by a "unit"), and the total obligation builds up period by period. The detailed procedure is much more effectively illustrated than described. The following example shows the general principles.

Illustration of Projected Unit Credit Method

A lump sum benefit is payable on termination of service and equal to 1% of final salary for each year of service. The salary in year 1 is 10,000 and is assumed to increase at 7% (compound) each year. The discount rate used is 10% per annum. The following table shows how the obligation builds up for an employee who is expected to leave at the end of year 5, assuming that there are no changes in actuarial assumptions.

Year	1	2	3	4	5
Benefit attributed to:					
Prior years	0	131	262	393	524
Current year (1% of final salary)	131	131	131	131	131
Current and prior years	131	262	393	524	655
Opening obligation	—	89	196	324	476
Interest cost at 10%	—	9	20	33	48
Current service cost	89	98	108	119	131
Closing obligation	89	196	324	476	655

Note:

1. The opening obligation is the present value of benefit attributed to prior years.

2. The current service cost is the present value of benefit attributed to the current year (i.e., discounted at 10% per annum).

3. The closing obligation is the present value of benefit attributed to current and prior years.

The calculations are likely to be significantly affected by actuarial assumptions and by the discount rate used. The actuarial assumptions, for example, regarding life expectancy, are largely outside the accounting domain. They must be unbiased and mutually compatible. Regarding the discount rate, however, IAS 19 is specific (par. 78). The rate used to discount post-employment benefit obligations (both funded and unfunded) should be determined by reference to market yields at the balance sheet date on high-quality corporate bonds. In countries where there is no deep market in such bonds, the market yields (at the balance sheet date) on government bonds should be used. The currency and term of the corporate bonds or government bonds should be consistent with the currency and estimated term of the post-employment benefit obligations.

OBSERVATION: There has been considerable debate and controversy over the appropriate discount rate to use. A number of commentators on the discussions and the exposure draft leading up to the standard argued that the discount rate used should reflect the expected long-term return on plan assets. The IASB has rejected this argument, essentially on the grounds that the measurement of an obligation should be independent of the measurement of the plan assets that happen to be held by a plan. The IASB position seems correct in principle.

The issue of whether, when, and how to recognize actuarial gains and losses is another aspect that has been extremely trouble some to the IASB (and to other regulatory authorities). The formal requirements (pars. 92 and 93) are convoluted and are quoted here verbatim.

> In measuring its defined benefit liability under paragraph 54, an entity should, subject to paragraph 58A, recognize a portion of its actuarial gains and losses as income or expense if the net cumulative unrecognized actuarial gains and losses at the end of the previous reporting period exceeded the greater of:
>
> 1. 10% of the present value of the defined benefit obligation at that date (before deducting plan assets); and
>
> 2. 10% of the fair value of any plan assets at that date.
>
> These limits should be calculated and applied separately for each defined benefit plan.

The portion of actuarial gains and losses to be recognized for each defined benefit plan is the excess determined as above, divided by the expected average remaining working lives of the employees participating in that plan. There is a 10% "corridor" inside which nothing need be recognized. However, an entity may adopt any systematic method that results in faster recognition of actuarial gains and losses, provided that the same basis is applied to both gains and losses and the basis is applied consistently from period to period. An entity may apply such systematic methods to actuarial gains and losses even if they fall within the limits specified above. Thus, if the net cumulative unrecognized actuarial gains at the end of the previous reporting period are 140, the present value of the defined benefit obligation is 1,000, the fair value of plan assets is 900, and the expected average remaining working lives of the participating employees is 10 years, then the minimum actuarial gain to be recognized as income in the year is:

$$[140 - (10\% \times 1,000)] \times 10\% = 4$$

The entity can choose any faster method of income (and expense) recognition up to, and including, immediate recognition of all actuarial gains and losses, provided of course that the chosen method is used consistently.

OBSERVATION: This matter is discussed at some length in the standard and in an explanatory appendix issued with the standard. It is clear that a good deal of pragmatic compromise has taken place. The point of the 10% "corridor" seems to be to accept that the estimates of post-employment benefit obligations are at best approximate shots at an uncertain target, and that to alter reported earnings directly by the effects of these uncertainties might be misleading. If this is accepted (and the 10% figure is arbitrary, apparently selected for consistency with U.S. GAAP—itself equally arbitrary, of course), it seems less clear why *all* the gains or losses outside this "corridor" should not be recognized immediately. This does seem like income smoothing on a fairly heroic scale.

A further problem is the treatment of the unrecognized actuarial gain or loss. This has to appear on the balance sheet. In the case of the example given immediately above, the unrecognized gain of 140 − 4 = 136 (probably combined with further adjustments relating to the current reporting year) will appear on the balance sheet as a liability. But according to the IASB definition of a liability in the Framework (see Chapter 2), the 136 simply is not a liability, as the above-mentioned explanatory appendix explicitly confirms. Similarly, an unrecognized loss, recorded as an asset, fails to meet the Framework definition of asset.

It is clear that the IASB Board prefers, in principle, a requirement to recognize the complete actuarial gains and losses immediately as income or expense in each and every annual financial statement but considered that some important issues remained to be resolved. An expectation of a decision to "revisit the treatment of actuarial gains and losses" is signaled (appendix, par. 41). As we write, there are signs of a change in U.S. and U.K. thinking toward immediate recognition, as discussed in the section "Likely Future Developments."

As already explained, past service cost arises when an entity introduces a defined benefit plan that attributes benefits to past service, or changes the benefits payable for past service under an existing defined benefit plan. Such changes are in return for employee service over the period until the benefits concerned are vested. Therefore, the entity recognizes past service cost over that period, regardless of the fact that the cost refers to employee service in previous periods. The entity measures past service cost as the change in the liability resulting from the amendment. Negative past service cost arises when an entity changes the benefits attributable to past service so that the present value of the defined benefit obligation decreases. To the extent that the benefits are already vested immediately following the introduction of, or changes to, a defined benefit plan, an entity should recognize past service cost immediately. Thus, if employees have unequivocal pension rights after three years of service, all past service costs arising in relation to employees who have served their three-year period are an immediate expense. If the average period until vesting for certain employees is two years, then past service costs in relation to them are expensed on a straight-line basis over the following two years.

In principle, the fair value of plan assets is the market value. When no market price is available, the fair value of plan assets is estimated, for example, by discounting expected future cash flows by using a discount rate that reflects both the risk associated with the plan assets and the maturity or expected disposal date of those assets (or, if they have no maturity, the expected period until the settlement of the related obligation). The immediately preceding sentence is deleted from the date the entity adopts IFRS 13, "Fair Value Measurement" (see Chapter 3).

Plan assets exclude unpaid contributions due from the reporting entity to the fund, as well as any non-transferable financial instruments issued by the entity and held by the fund. Where plan assets include "qualifying insurance policies" that exactly match the amount and timing of some or all of the benefits payable under the plan, the plan's rights under those insurance policies are measured at the same amount as the related obligations.

When, and only when, it is virtually certain that another party will reimburse some or all of the expenditure required to settle a defined benefit obligation through an arrangement that is not a "qualifying insurance policy," an entity shall recognize its right to reimbursement as a separate asset, measured at fair value (par. 104A).

The expected return on plan assets is based on market expectations, at the beginning of the period, for returns over the entire life of the related obligation. The expected return on plan assets reflects changes in the fair value of plan assets held during the period as a result of actual contributions paid into the fund and actual benefits paid out of the fund. Such expected returns are, of course, likely to involve significant subjectivity.

The difference between the expected return on plan assets and the actual return on plan assets is an actuarial gain or loss. It is included with the actuarial gains and losses on the defined benefit obligation in determining the net amount that is compared with the limits of the 10% "corridor" specified in paragraph 92.

In a business combination that is an acquisition, an entity recognizes assets and liabilities arising from post-employment benefits at the present value of the obligation less the fair value of any plan assets. The present value of the obligation includes all of the following, even if the acquiree had not yet recognized them at the date of the acquisition:

1. Actuarial gains and losses that arose before the date of the acquisition (whether or not they fell inside the 10% "corridor"),

2. Past service cost that arose from benefit changes, or the introduction of a plan, before the date of the acquisition, and

3. Amounts that, under the transitional provisions of IAS 19, the acquiree had not recognized.

An entity should recognize gains or losses on the curtailment or settlement of a defined benefit plan when the curtailment or settlement occurs. A curtailment occurs when the entity is committed to a significant reduction in the scope of the plan, either by reducing the number of employees included, or by reducing the benefits per employee. A settlement occurs when an entity enters into a transaction that eliminates all further legal or constructive obligation for part or all of the benefits provided under a defined benefit plan, for example, when a lump-sum cash payment is made to, or on behalf of, plan participants in exchange for their rights to receive specified post-employment benefits.

Presentation and disclosure requirements regarding the treatment of defined benefit plans are extensive, and are as follows.

An entity should offset an asset relating to one plan against a liability relating to another plan when, and only when, the entity:

1. Has a legally enforceable right to use a surplus in one plan to settle obligations under the other plan; and

2. Intends either to settle the obligations on a net basis, or to realize the surplus in one plan and settle its obligation under the other plan simultaneously.

When making the December 2004 amendment, the IASB took the opportunity to significantly extend the disclosure requirements relating to defined benefit plans beyond the already detailed requirements of the earlier version.

An entity shall disclose information that enables users of financial statements to evaluate the nature of its defined benefit plans and the financial effects of changes in those plans during the period (par. 120).

An entity shall disclose the following information about defined benefit plans (par. 120A):

1. The entity's accounting policy for recognizing actuarial gains and losses.

2. A general description of the type of plan.

3. A reconciliation of opening and closing balances of the present value of the defined benefit obligation showing separately, if applicable, the effects during the period attributable to each of the following:

   (a) Current service cost;

   (b) Interest cost;

   (c) Contributions by plan participants;

   (d) Actuarial gains and losses;

   (e) Foreign currency exchange rate changes on plans measured in a currency different from the entity's presentation currency;

   (f) Benefits paid;

   (g) Past service cost;

   (h) Business combinations;

   (i) Curtailments; and

   (j) Settlements.

4. An analysis of the defined benefit obligation into amounts arising from plans that are wholly unfunded and amounts arising from plans that are wholly or partly funded.

5. A reconciliation of the opening and closing balances of the fair value of plan assets and of the opening and closing balances of any reimbursement right recognized as an asset in accordance with paragraph 104A showing separately, if applicable, the effects during the period attributable to each of the following:

   (a) Expected return on plan assets;

   (b) Actuarial gains and losses;

   (c) Foreign currency exchange rate changes on plans measured in a currency different from the entity's presentation currency;

   (d) Contributions by the employer;

   (e) Contributions by plan participants;

    (f) Benefits paid;

    (g) Business combinations; and

    (h) Settlements.

6. A reconciliation of the present value of the defined benefit obligation in (3) and the fair value of the plan assets in (5) to the assets and liabilities recognized in the balance sheet, showing at least:

    (a) The net actuarial gains or losses not recognized in the balance sheet (see paragraph 92);

    (b) The past service cost not recognized in the balance sheet (see paragraph 96);

    (c) Any amount not recognized as an asset, because of the limit in paragraph 58(b);

    (d) The fair value at the balance sheet date of any reimbursement right recognized as an asset in accordance with paragraph 104A (with a brief description of the link between the reimbursement right and the related obligation); and

    (e) The other amounts recognized in the balance sheet.

7. The total expense recognized in profit or loss for each of the following, and the line item(s) in which they are included:

    (a) Current service cost;

    (b) Interest cost;

    (c) Expected return on plan assets;

    (d) Expected return on any reimbursement right recognized as an asset in accordance with paragraph 104A;

    (e) Actuarial gains and losses;

    (f) Past service cost;

    (g) The effect of any curtailment or settlement; and

    (h) The effect of the limit in paragraph 58(b).

8. The total amount recognized in other comprehensive income for each of the following:

    (a) Actuarial gains and losses; and

    (b) The effect of the limit in paragraph 58(b).

9. For entities that recognize actuarial gains and losses in other comprehensive income.

10. For each major category of plan assets, which shall include, but is not limited to, equity instruments, debt instruments, property, and all other assets, the percentage or amount that each major category constitutes of the fair value of the total plan assets.

11. The amounts included in the fair value of plan assets for:

    (a) Each category of the entity's own financial instruments; and

    (b) Any property occupied by, or other assets used by, the entity.

12. A narrative description of the basis used to determine the overall expected rate of return on assets, including the effect of the major categories of plan assets.

13. The actual return on plan assets, as well as the actual return on any reimbursement right recognized as an asset in accordance with paragraph 104A.

14. The principal actuarial assumptions used at the balance sheet date, including, when applicable:

   (a) The discount rates;

   (b) The expected rates of return on any plan assets for the periods presented in the financial statements;

   (c) The expected rates of return for the periods presented in the financial statements on any reimbursement right recognized as an asset in accordance with paragraph 104A;

   (d) The expected rates of salary increases (and of changes in an index or other variable specified in the formal or constructive terms of a plan as the basis for future benefit increases);

   (e) Medical cost trend rates; and

   (f) Any other material actuarial assumptions used. An entity shall disclose each actuarial assumption in absolute terms (e.g., as an absolute percentage) and not just as a margin between different percentages or other variables.

15. The effect of an increase of one percentage point and the effect of a decrease of one percentage point in the assumed medical cost trend rates on:

   (a) The aggregate of the current service cost and interest cost components of net periodic post-employment medical costs; and

   (b) The accumulated post-employment benefit obligation for medical costs. For the purposes of this disclosure, all other assumptions shall be held constant. For plans operating in a high inflation environment, the disclosure shall be the effect of a percentage increase or decrease in the assumed medical cost trend rate of a significance similar to one percentage point in a low inflation environment.

16. The amounts for the current annual period and previous four annual periods of:

   (a) The present value of the defined benefit obligation, the fair value of the plan assets and the surplus or deficit in the plan; and

   (b) The experience adjustments arising on:

      (i) The plan liabilities expressed either as an amount or a percentage of the plan liabilities at the balance sheet date, and

      (ii) The plan assets expressed either as an amount or a percentage of the plan assets at the balance sheet date.

17. The employer's best estimate, as soon as it can reasonably be determined, of contributions expected to be paid to the plan during the annual period beginning after the balance sheet date.

OBSERVATION: These new disclosure requirements are an example of the tendency of the IASB in recent years to provide greater detail. Indeed, given the contents of the new paragraph 120A, what is the point of the new paragraph 120?

December 2004 Amendments to IAS 19

As indicated above, the IASB (and U.S.) requirements relating to defined benefit pension plans are problematic, indeed illogical. The IASB wishes to change them, by moving to compulsory immediate recognition of actuarial gains and losses, but is unable to do so quickly. There are probably two reasons for this delay. The first is the pragmatic one that preparers are likely to argue against such a proposed change, necessitating an extensive period of discussion and exposure. The second is that the issue of precisely how such gains and losses should be reported—that is, whether or not they should actually be included as part of "earnings"—is intimately tied up with the outcome of the Reporting Financial Performance project discussed above and at the end of Chapter 1, which is, itself, clearly subject to delay.

The December 2004 amendment was regarded as very much a short-term stopgap, but it does send a clear signal about the IASB's intended direction, and of its commitment to such change. The amendment applied from January 1, 2006, but earlier adoption was encouraged. The key point is that it allows the U.K.'s required treatment under FRS-17, "Retirement Benefits," to be followed, as an option under IASB GAAP, in addition to the considerable flexibility in the existing version of the standard. The opportunity has been taken to make some further amendments. In summary, the amendment requirements are as follows (pars. 93A–93D).

IAS 19's existing requirements for defined benefit plans were similar to those in Canadian, Japanese, and U.S. standards in that some gains and losses in the plan (actuarial gains and losses) do not have to be recognized in the period in which they occur but can be spread forward over the service lives of the employees. In contrast, the U.K. standard FRS-17 requires actuarial gains and losses to be recognized immediately outside profit or loss in a statement of total recognized gains and losses.

Pending further work on post-employment benefits and on reporting comprehensive income, the IASB believes that the approach in FRS-17 should be available as an option to preparers of financial statements using international standards. The result of applying this option is that the amount recognized in the balance sheet (statement of financial position) is the surplus or deficit in the plan at the balance sheet date, and the amount recognized in profit and loss is the best estimate of the cost for the period.

The amendment also requires a group entity that participates in a defined benefit plan that shares risks between entities under common control (i.e., a parent and subsidiaries) to obtain information about the plan as a whole. If there is a contractual agreement or stated policy for charging the cost for the plan as a whole measured in accordance with IAS 19 to individual group entities, the group entity, in its separate or individual financial statements, will recognize the cost so charged. If there is no such agreement or policy, the cost will be recognized in the separate or individual financial statements of the group entity that is legally the sponsoring employer for the plan. The other group entities will, in their separate or individual financial statements, recognize a cost equal to their contribution payable for the period.

Lastly, the amendment requires additional disclosures that:

- Provide information about trends in the assets and liabilities in a defined benefit plan and the assumptions underlying the components of the defined benefit cost; and

- Bring the disclosures in IAS 19 closer to those required by the U.S. standard FASB Accounting Standards Codification™ (ASC) 715, "Compensation—Retirement Benefits."

OBSERVATION: In practice, the option to follow the U.K. FRS-17 treatment will be rarely used, except in the U.K. Note also that the "short-term stopgap" nature of this amendment seems to be getting increasingly long!

ACCOUNTING FOR OTHER LONG-TERM EMPLOYEE BENEFITS

A variety of items could be included under this heading, such as bonuses or profit-sharing payments payable 12 months or more after the period of the related service, or long-service or sabbatical leave. There is usually little uncertainty of calculation, and little or no past service cost. For these reasons, actuarial gains and losses are recognized immediately and no "corridor" is applied, and all past service cost is recognized immediately.

The amount recognized as a liability for other long-term employee benefits should be the net total of the present value of the defined benefit obligation at the balance sheet date minus the fair value at the balance sheet date of plan assets (if any) out of which the obligations are to be settled directly.

TERMINATION BENEFITS

The point about termination, as the definition given earlier in the chapter makes clear, is that it is not related to employee service. Indeed, it arises because of a cessation of employee service. It follows that termination benefits do not provide an entity with future economic benefits and they must therefore be recognized as an expense immediately.

The IASB, however, is obviously as concerned to prevent the creation of excessive provisions as to prevent the non-reporting of expenses. An entity should immediately recognize termination benefits as a liability and an expense when, and only when, the entity is demonstrably committed to either

1. Terminate the employment of an employee or group of employees before the normal retirement date, or

2. Provide termination benefits as a result of an offer made in order to encourage voluntary redundancy.

Demonstrable commitment requires a detailed formal plan and that the entity, either for legal or constructive reasons, is "without realistic possibility of withdrawal." Where termination benefits fall due more than 12 months after the balance sheet date, they should be discounted by using the discount rate specified in paragraph 78. In the case of an offer made to encourage voluntary redundancy, the measurement of termination benefits should be based on the number of employees expected to accept the offer.

→ **PRACTICE POINTER:** Other international standards may require disclosures relating to termination benefits, such as IAS 37, "Provisions, Contingent Liabilities, and Contingent Assets" (see Chapter 29), if a non-remote contingency arises; IAS 8, "Accounting Policies, Changes in Accounting Estimates, and Errors" (see Chapter 6), if the "size, nature or incidence" requires it; and IAS 24, "Related Party Disclosures" (see Chapter 30), in the case of key management personnel.

EQUITY COMPENSATION BENEFITS

As already indicated, the paltry and inadequate requirements (limited to disclosure considerations only) in IAS 19 were deleted with effect from the adoption of IFRS 2, "Share-Based Payment," required from January 1, 2005 (see Chapter 33).

FURTHER REVISIONS FROM 2013

For some time, the IASB (and the FASB) has wanted to remove the corridor method completely. In the summer of 2011, the IASB issued yet another revision to IAS 19. This removes the corridor method relating to defined benefit schemes, and any other method of smoothing the recognition of actual gains and losses in comprehensive income and the statement of financial position. The new version will require an entity to recognize all changes in a net defined benefit liability or asset immediately in the statement of comprehensive income and the statement of financial position in the period in which the changes occur.

A number of detailed changes to the measurement and reporting of expected and actual returns on plan assets are incorporated. The whole of the return on plan assets will be included in comprehensive income, but only the part of that return relating to the passage of time will be included in profit or loss.

This revised version of IAS 19 will be mandatory from January 1, 2013, with earlier application permitted.

APPENDIX:
ACCOUNTING AND REPORTING BY
RETIREMENT BENEFIT PLANS

The IASB has issued a separate standard, IAS 26, "Accounting and Reporting by Retirement Benefit Plans," dealing with this matter. It was effective on January 1, 1988, and thus predates IAS 19 in its current version, and indeed many of the standards in their current versions. Its subject matter is clearly highly specialized, applying to retirement plans, not to employers of potential retirees. Note, however, that IAS 26 applies to retirement plans even if they are not legally separate from the employer. IAS 26 does not require the preparation of reports by retirement benefit plans. Rather, it specifies how such reports should be prepared when they are prepared.

Readers involved in the preparation of such reports should read the whole standard. The major disclosure requirements are summarized below. A series of definitions are given in paragraph 8, generally consistent with, though different in detail from, those in IAS 19.

For defined contribution plans the report should contain a statement of the net assets available for the benefits and a description of the funding policy. The retirement benefit plan investments, for both defined contribution and defined benefit plans, should be carried at fair value. In the case of marketable securities, fair value is market value. Where plan investments are held for which an estimate of fair value is not possible, disclosure should be made of the reason why fair value is not used.

The report of a defined benefit plan should contain either:

1. A statement that shows:

    (a) The net assets available for benefits;

    (b) The actuarial present value of promised retirement benefits, distinguishing between vested benefits and non-vested benefits; and

    (c) The resulting excess or deficit; or

2. A statement of net assets available for benefits including either:

    (a) A note disclosing the actuarial present value of promised retirement benefits, distinguishing between vested benefits and nonvested benefits; or

    (b) A reference to this information in an accompanying actuarial report.

If an actuarial valuation has not been prepared at the date of the report, the most recent valuation should be used as a base and the date of the valuation disclosed. The actuarial present value of promised retirement benefits should be based on the benefits promised under the terms of the plan on service rendered to date by using either current salary levels or projected salary levels with disclosure of the basis used. The effect of any changes in actuarial assumptions that have had a significant effect on the actuarial present value of promised retirement benefits should also be disclosed. The report should explain the relationship between the actuarial present value of promised retirement benefits and the net assets available for benefits, and the policy for the funding of promised benefits.

IAS 26 discusses advantages and disadvantages of the two alternative salary levels—current or projected, in paragraphs 24 and 25. The advantages of using projected salary levels appear greater, being more relevant to the likely outcome, but IAS 26 is careful not to state a clear preference (probably a function of the standard having had no update since 1988).

Three different "formats" for reports on defined benefit plans are given. Again, all are acceptable, but it should be noted that all three require information about the net assets available for benefits and a quantification of the actuarial present value of the promised retirement benefits.

The report of a retirement benefit plan, whether defined benefit or defined contribution, should also contain the following information:

1. A statement of changes in net assets available for benefits.

2. A summary of significant accounting policies.

3. A description of the plan and the effect of any changes in the plan during the period.

CHAPTER 15
THE EQUITY METHOD

Contents

OVERVIEW

The equity method is a method of accounting by an entity for an investment in the equity capital (typically, voting shares) of another entity. The method is considered in IASB GAAP to be appropriate in cases where the investment enables the investor to exercise significant influence over the investee, with the power to participate in its financial and operating policy decisions but not to exercise control over it. In these circumstances, the investor has some responsibility for the return on its investment, and it is considered appropriate to include in the investor's results of operations its share of the profits or losses of the investor. In IASB GAAP, such an investee is referred to as an "associate." The equity method should be used in the consolidated financial statements of the investee, but not in its separate financial statements.

The equity method is not a substitute for full consolidation when the criteria for the use of the latter method are met. It is allowed as an alternative treatment to proportionate consolidation in the case of joint control.

In May 2011, the IASB issued a number of new and revised standards that are relevant, as indicated below. These new and revised standards will be applicable for annual reporting periods beginning on or after January 1, 2013, but earlier adoption is permitted.

The relevant IASB GAAP have been promulgated in:

- IAS 28, "Investments in Associates," revised in May 2011 and reissued as IAS 28, "Investments in Associates and Joint Ventures";

- IAS 31, "Interests in Joint Ventures," to be superseded by the revised IAS 28 and the new IFRS 11, "Joint Arrangements," issued in May 2011;
- IAS 27, "Consolidated and Separate Financial Statements," revised in May 2011 and reissued as IAS 27, "Separate Financial Statements";
- IFRS 3, "Business Combinations";
- IAS 36, "Impairment of Assets";
- IAS 39, "Financial Instruments: Recognition and Measurement," being gradually replaced by IFRS 9, "Financial Instruments"; and
- IFRIC 5, "Rights to Interests Arising from Decommissioning, Restoration and Environmental Rehabilitation Funds."

The main effect of the May 2011 revisions of IAS 28 was to extend the scope of IAS 28 to joint ventures (i.e., investments where the investors have joint control over the investee), with IAS 31 being withdrawn together with the option to use proportionate consolidation for joint ventures. In addition, entities must apply IFRS 11 to distinguish between "joint ventures" and "joint operations". In the case of joint ventures, the investors that have joint control of the arrangement have rights to its net assets, but unlike joint operators, do not have rights to its assets or obligations for its liabilities.

BACKGROUND

IAS 28 was originally issued in 1988, following the issue of IAS 27. It was reformatted in 1994 without substantial changes to its contents. In 1998, it was amended twice, first to reflect the requirements of IAS 36 and again to reflect those of IAS 39. Improvements to international standards and references in this chapter are to the version of IAS 28 issued in December 2003. The effects of the May 2011 revisions are indicated at the end of the chapter.

In May 2011, the IASB published IFRS 10, "Consolidated Financial Statements," which replaces the parts of IAS 27 that deal with consolidated financial statements and SIC 12. IFRS 10 introduces a new definition of *control*, which also entails changes to IAS 28. The main objectives of IFRS 10, together with IFRS 12, "Disclosures of Interests in Other Entities," include redefining *control* and tightening up the treatment of special-purpose entities, renamed "structured entities." The new and revised standards issued in May 2011, including the revised IAS 28, are applicable for annual reporting periods beginning on or after January 1, 2013, with earlier adoption permitted.

In the text below, references to IAS 39 also mention IFRS 9 in cases where the treatment under the latter is similar. The revised IAS 28, par.46, states that if an entity applies the revised IAS 28 before adopting IFRS 9, references to IFRS 9 should be read in relation to IAS 39.

SCOPE

Significant Influence and the Definition of an *Associate*

An associate is an entity over which the investor has significant influence and which is neither a subsidiary nor an interest in a joint venture (IAS 28, par. 2).

According to IAS 28, paragraphs 1, 13, and 14, the equity method is to be applied in accounting for investments in associates, with the following exceptions:

1. When they are held by venture capital organizations or mutual funds, unit trusts, and similar entities including investment-linked insurance funds and are upon initial recognition designated as "at fair value through profit and loss" (FVPL) or "held for trading" and accounted for in accordance with IAS 39. (IFRS 9 abolishes the "held for trading" category, so the FVPL category would be used.) In this case, such investments are accounted for in accordance with IAS 39/IFRS 9, at fair value through profit and loss. An entity holding such an investment shall disclose the nature and extent of any significant restrictions on its ability to transfer funds to the investor in the form of cash dividends, or repayment of loans or advances.

2. When the investment is classified as held for sale in accordance with IFRS 5, "Non-Current Assets Held for Sale and Discontinued Operations" (see Chapter 27), in which case the accounting treatment laid down by IFRS 5 applies.

3. In the case of a parent that meets the criteria in IAS 27 that allow a parent that has an investment in an associate not to present consolidated financial statements.

4. When *all* of the following conditions are met:

   (a) The investor is a wholly owned subsidiary, or it is a partly owned subsidiary and its other owners (including those not otherwise entitled to vote) have been informed about, and do not object to, the non-application of the equity method.

   (b) The investor's debt or equity instruments are not traded in a public market (a domestic or foreign stock exchange or an over-the-counter market, including local and regional markets).

   (c) The investor did not file, and is not in the process of filing, its financial statements with a securities commission or other regulator for the purpose of issuing any class of instruments in a public market.

   (d) The ultimate or any intermediate parent of the investor produces consolidated financial statements available for public use that comply with IFRS.

If all of these four conditions are met, the investor may present its separate financial statements as its only financial statements.

If an investor holds, either directly or indirectly through subsidiaries, 20% or more of the voting power of the investee, there is a rebuttable presumption that the investor has significant influence. Conversely, if the investor holds, either directly or indirectly through subsidiaries, less than 20% of the voting power of the investee, there is a rebuttable presumption that the investor does not have significant influence. The existence of a substantial or majority ownership by another investor does not of itself serve to rebut the presumption of significant influence (IAS 28, par. 6).

Conditions that provide evidence of "significant influence" are set out in paragraphs 7–9 of IAS 28, as follows:

1. Representation on the board of directors or other governing body of the investee,

2. Participation in policy-making processes,

3. Material transactions between the investor and the investee,

4. Interchange of managerial personnel between the investor and the investee, and

5. Provision of essential technical information.

When assessing whether an entity significantly influences another entity, the existence and effect of potential voting rights that are presently or currently exercisable or convertible should be considered. All potential voting rights, including those held by other entities, should be taken into account. Potential voting rights do not meet the criteria of being *currently* exercisable or convertible when they cannot be exercised or converted until a *future* date or upon the occurrence of a *future* event. Other facts that should be considered in determining whether the criteria are met include the terms of exercise of the potential voting rights and possible linked transactions and positions, such as options. However, management's intentions and the financial capability to exercise or convert are not relevant.

The proportion of net assets and net income of an associate that is allocated to an investor that accounts for its investment in the associate using the equity method should be determined solely on the basis of present ownership interests, which should be determined on the basis of substance not form. A present ownership interest may exist in substance when an entity has sold and simultaneously agreed to repurchase, *but has not lost control of*, access to economic benefits associated with an ownership interest. In such a case, the proportion allocated should be determined taking account of the *eventual exercise of potential voting rights, options and other derivatives* that, in substance, *presently* give access to the economic benefits associated with ownership.

When applying the equity method of accounting, instruments containing potential voting rights should be accounted for as part of the investment in an associate only when the proportion of ownership interests is allocated taking into account the *eventual exercise* of those potential voting rights as indicated above. In all other circumstances, instruments containing potential voting rights should be accounted for as required by IAS 39/IFRS 9 (see Chapter 17).

→ **PRACTICE POINTER:** In the case where the investor holds 20% or more of the voting power of the investee, if neither of the conditions 1 and 2 above is met, this would be likely to constitute a rebuttal of the presumption of significant influence. In particular, this would be the case if the investee had successfully resisted the investor's attempts to gain board representation or its equivalent, or a "standstill agreement" had been signed between the investor and the investee that provided evidence of a lack of significant influence. If the investor could be shown to exercise significant influence because conditions 3 to 5 were met, however, the rebuttal could be rejected.

Conversely, in the case where the investor holds less than 20% of the voting power of the investee, if conditions 1 and 2 or most of the conditions 1 to 5 above were met, the presumption of no significant influence could be rebutted, especially if the investee publicly acknowledges the significant influence.

An entity loses significant influence over an investee when it loses the power to participate in the financial and operating policy decisions of that investee. This can occur with or without a change in absolute or relative ownership levels, for example when an associate becomes subject to the control of a government, court, administrator, or regulator or as the result of a contractual arrangement (IAS 28, par. 10).

An investor should discontinue the use of the equity method from the date on which it ceases to have significant influence over an associate and should account for the investment in accordance with IAS 39/IFRS 9 from that date unless the investment becomes a subsidiary or a joint venture as defined in IAS 31. The carrying amount of the investment at that date is taken to be its cost on initial measurement as a financial asset in accordance with IAS 39/IFRS 9 (IAS 28, pars. 18–19).

EQUITY ACCOUNTING PROCEDURES

The accounting procedures for the equity method are largely similar to those required for consolidation (IAS 28, par. 20). In fact, the equity method is sometimes referred to as "one-line consolidation."

Under the equity method, the investment is initially recorded at cost, with a distinction being made between the investor's share of the net fair value of the identifiable assets and liabilities acquired and any goodwill (positive or negative). Subsequently, the carrying amount is increased or decreased to recognize the investor's share of changes in the investee's net assets. Such changes will result from profits retained or losses of the investee but may also be from other sources, as follows. Adjustments to the carrying amount may be needed to reflect changes in the investee's equity that have not been included in its income statement. These include revaluations or remeasurement at fair value of property, plant, and equipment and of investments; foreign exchange translation differences; and adjustments for the differences arising on business combinations, such as those for goodwill and its amortization and for depreciation based on fair values (IAS 28, pars. 11 and 23).

A group's share in an associate is the aggregate of the holdings in that associate by the parent and its subsidiaries. The holdings of other associates or joint ventures are not taken into account for this purpose. When an associate itself has subsidiaries, associates, or joint ventures, the profits or losses and net assets taken into account in applying the equity method are those recognized in the associate's financial statements, including its share of the profits or losses and net assets of its associates and joint ventures, *after any adjustments needed to apply uniform accounting policies* (IAS 28, par. 21).

Unrealized profits and losses resulting from "upstream" transactions (e.g., sales of assets by the associate to the investor) or "downstream" transactions (e.g., sales of assets by the investor to the associate) between an investor or its consolidated subsidiaries and an associate are recognized in the investor's financial statements only to the extent of unrelated third-party investors' interests in the associate. The investor's share in the associate's profits or losses resulting from such transactions is eliminated (IAS 28, par. 22).

Illustration of "Downstream" and "Upstream" Transactions

An investor sells inventory "downstream" to an associate during a financial reporting period. At the end of the period, the associate's inventory includes an amount of $50,000, which is the investor's profit on the sales. The investor's share of the equity capital of the associate is 40%. The entries for the elimination of inter-enterprise profits are as follows:

Share of income of associate (40% of $50,000)	$20,000	
Investment in associate		$20,000

If the inter-enterprise sales were "upstream," the entries would be as follows:

Share of income from associate	$20,000	
Inventory		$20,000

An investment in an associate is accounted for using the equity method as from the date on which it becomes an associate. On acquisition, any difference between the cost of the investment and the investor's share of the fair values of the net identifiable assets is treated as goodwill as per IFRS 3, "Business Combinations" (see Chapter 8). Goodwill relating to an associate is included in the carrying amount of the investment (IAS 28, par. 23).

Illustration of the Equity Method

On December 31, 20X1, X Company acquired 600 common shares in Y Company (out of a total of 2,000 common shares outstanding) at a cost of $1.50 per share, that is, a 30% interest. Because the common shares are voting equity, X has significant influence over Y and is required to account for Y as an associate. At that date, Y's stockholders' equity was $2,800, comprising share capital of $2,000 and retained earnings of $800. Goodwill in Y is thus:

$900 – 30% of $2,800 = $840. This will be amortized over (say) 10 years, that is, $84 per year.

X has no subsidiaries and is not exempt from the requirement to apply equity accounting to Y. The balance sheets of X (before and after equity accounting for Y) and of Y at December 31, 20X2 are given below. The retained earnings of Y increased by $2,200 in the period between the acquisition and the financial year end.

X Company's income statement would include its share of Y's net income (after adjusting for goodwill amortization) under the caption "Income from associates" after "Profit from operations" and before "Income tax expense" (IAS 1, par. 75). Assuming that Y had paid no dividend, this share would be $1,476; X's share of any dividend would be added to this.

As "Income from associates" is reported before "Income tax expense," it would seem preferable to report it gross of income tax and to include the applicable income tax under the caption "Income tax expense." However, neither IAS 1 nor IAS 28 requires this.

	X *Before Equity Accounting*	*Y*	*X* *After Equity Accounting*
Net current assets	$ 1,000	$1,800	$1,000
Property, plant, and equipment	15,000	3,200	15,000
Investment in Y:			
At cost 600 × 1.50 = 900			
Investment in associate:			
Equity 900 + 30% of 2,200 = 1,560, less goodwill amortization of 84 =			1,476
	$16,900	$5,000	$17,476
Share capital	$ 8,000	$2,000	$8,000
Reserves:	8,900	3,000	
8,900 + 30% of 2,200 − 84			9,476
	$16,900	$5,000	$17,476

If an associate has outstanding cumulative preferred shares held by outside interests, the investor's share of the associate's net income or loss should be calculated after adjusting for the preferred dividends, whether declared or not (IAS 28, par. 28).

When applying the equity method, the investor should use the associate's most recent available financial statements. If the reporting dates differ, the associate should prepare financial statements as of the same date as the investor's, unless this is impracticable, in which case the investor's existing financial statements may be used provided the difference in the reporting dates does not exceed three months. In that case, adjustments must be made to reflect appropriately the effects of any significant transactions or events occurring between the two reporting dates. The lengths of the reporting periods and any difference in the reporting dates should be the same from period to period. The investor's financial statements prepared using the equity method should apply uniform accounting policies for like transactions and events in similar circumstances. If an associate uses accounting policies that do not conform to those of the investor, adjustments must be made to achieve conformity when applying the equity method (IAS 28, pars. 24–27).

If an associate has outstanding cumulative preference shares that are held by parties other than the investor and are classified as equity, dividends on such preference shares must be deducted by the investor in calculating its share of the associate's profits or losses, whether or not the dividends have been declared (IAS 28, par. 28).

The Treatment of Loss-Making Associates and Impairment Losses

Loss-Making Associates

If an investor's share of losses of an associate is equal to, or exceeds, the total amount of its interest in the associate, the investor discontinues recognizing its share of further losses. The interest in the associate is the carrying amount of the investment under the equity method plus any long-term interests that, in substance, form part of the investor's net investment in the associate. Such items may include preference shares and long-term receivables, but they do not include trade receivables or any long-term receivables for which adequate collateral exists, such as secured loans.

Losses recognized under the equity method that exceed carrying amount of the investor's investment in the associate's common shares are applied to the other components of its interest in the associate in the reverse order of their seniority (priority in liquidation). After the investor's total interest is reduced to zero, additional losses are provided for, and a liability is recognized, only to the extent that the investor has incurred legal or constructive obligations or made payments on behalf of the associate. If the associate subsequently reports profits, the investor should resume recognizing its shares of those profits only after the total of these equals the total of any previously unrecognized shares of the associate's losses (IAS 28, pars. 29–30).

Impairment Losses

After applying the equity method, including the treatment of an associate's losses as above, the investor applies IAS 39 to determine whether any additional impairment loss needs to be recognized with respect to (1) its net investment in the associate and (2) any other component of its total interest in the associate. If this results in an indication that the investment may be impaired, the investor must apply IAS 36, "Impairment of Assets" (see Chapter 20).

Because goodwill included in the carrying amount of an investment in an associate is not separately recognized, it is not tested for impairment separately by applying the IAS 36 requirements for goodwill. Instead, whenever the IAS 39 criteria indicate that the investment may be impaired, the entire carrying amount of the investment is tested for impairment under IAS 36 as a single asset, by comparing its recoverable amount (higher of value in use and fair value less costs to sell) with its carrying amount. An impairment loss recognized in these circumstances is not allocated to any asset, including goodwill, that forms part of the carrying amount of the investment in the associate. Hence, any reversal of that impairment is recognized in accordance with IAS 36 to the extent that the recoverable amount of the investment subsequently increases.

In determining the value in use of the investment, the investor estimates either one or the other of the following (under appropriate assumptions, both will produce the same result):

- Its share of the present value of the estimated future cash flows expected to be generated by the associate, including both its operating cash flows and the proceeds of its ultimate disposal.

- The present value of the estimated future cash flows expected to arise from dividends to be received from the investment and from its ultimate disposal.

The "recoverable amount" of an investment in an associate is assessed for each associate, except in the case of an associate that does not generate cash inflows from continuing use that are largely independent from the other assets of the investor.

Separate Financial Statements of the Investor

The requirements in respect of the treatment of an investment in an associate in the investor's separate financial statements are set out in IAS 27, "Separate Financial Statements," paragraphs 37–42 (see Chapter 11). In general, such investments should be accounted for either at cost or in accordance with IAS 39/IFRS 9 (not using the equity method). If they are accounted for in accordance with IAS 39/IFRS 9 in the investor's consolidated financial statements, the same treatment should be applied in the separate financial statements.

DISCLOSURE

The revised IAS 28 requires more disclosures than the previous version. They are as follows (par. 37):

1. The fair value of investments in associates for which there are published price quotations.

2. Summarized financial information of associates, including the aggregated amounts of assets, liabilities, revenues, and profit or loss.

3. If an investor holds, directly or through subsidiaries, less than 20% of the actual or potential voting power of an investee but concludes that it nevertheless has "significant influence," the reasons why the presumption that it does not have significant influence has been overcome.

4. If an investor holds, directly or through subsidiaries, 20% or more of the actual or potential voting power of an investee but concludes that it does not have "significant influence," the reasons why the presumption that it has significant influence has been overcome.

5. When the financial statements of an associate that are used in applying the equity method are as of a different reporting date or for a different reporting period from those of the investor, the associate's reporting date or period and the reasons why a different reporting date or period was used.

6. The nature and extent of any significant restrictions (such as those resulting from borrowing arrangements or regulatory requirements) on the ability of associates to transfer funds to the investor in the form of cash dividends or repayments or loans or advances.

7. If an investor has discontinued recognition of its share of losses of an associate, the amounts of such unrecognized share of losses, both for the period and cumulatively.

8. If any associate is not accounted for using the equity method, that fact and summarized financial information, either individually or in groups, of such associates including the amounts of total assets, total liabilities, revenues, and profit or loss.

9. Summarized financial information of associates either individually or in groups that are not accounted for using the equity method, including the amounts of total assets, total liabilities, revenues, and profit or loss.

Other requirements are set out in IAS 28, paragraphs 38–40, as follows:

- Investments in associates accounted for using the equity method are to be classified as non-current assets. The investor's share of the profit or loss of such associates and the carrying amount of the investments are to be separately disclosed, as must the investor's share of any discontinuing operations of such associates.

- The investor's share of changes recognized directly in the associate's equity are to be recognized directly in equity by the investor and disclosed in its statement of changes in equity as required by IAS 1, "Presentation of Financial Statements" (see Chapter 4).

- In accordance with IAS 37, "Provisions, Contingent Liabilities, and Contingent Assets" (see Chapter 29), the investor must disclose:

  — Its share of the contingent liabilities of an associated incurred jointly with other investors.

  — Those contingent liabilities that arise because the investor is severally liable for all or part of the liabilities of the associate.

EFFECTIVE DATE

IAS 28 is to be applied for annual periods beginning on or after January 1, 2005. Earlier application is encouraged, but if an entity does so it must disclose the fact. Paragraphs 1 and 33 were amended in May 2008, and these amendments are to be applied for annual periods beginning on or after January 1, 2009, with earlier application permitted, provided the fact is disclosed and the amendments to paragraph 3 of IFRS 7, paragraph 1 of IAS 31, and paragraph 4 of IAS 32, issued in May 2008, are also applied. IAS 27, as amended in 2008, resulted in amendments to paragraphs 18, 19, and 35 of IAS 28, and these are to be applied for annual periods beginning on or after July 1, 2009, or together with the amended IAS 27 if the latter is applied earlier. The effective date for IAS 28 as revised in May 2011 is for annual periods beginning on or after January 1, 2013.

SUMMARY OF THE MAIN CHANGES IN THE MAY 2011 REVISION OF IAS 28

The revised IAS 28:

1. Incorporates accounting for joint ventures.

2. Does not address disclosure requirements for entities with joint control of, or significant influence over, an investee, which are included in the new IFRS 12, "Disclosure on Interests in Other Entities."

3. Replaces the scope exception for venture capital organizations, or mutual funds, unit trusts, or similar entities including investment-linked insurance funds, by a measurement exemption from the requirement to measure investments in associates and joint ventures using the equity method, if the entity elects to measure such investments at FVPL. The same applies to a *portion* of an investment in an associate when that portion is held indirectly through a venture capital organization, or mutual fund, unit trust, or a similar entity including investment-linked insurance funds, regardless of whether the latter has significant influence over that portion of the investment. The equity method must be applied to any remaining portion of the investment.

4. Requires a portion of an investment in an associate or joint venture to be classified as held for sale if the disposal of that portion would meet the IFRS 5 criteria for being so classified (see Chapter 27).

5. Incorporates and supersedes SIC-13, to the effect that gains and losses resulting from a contribution of a non-monetary asset to an associate or a joint venture in exchange for an equity interest are recognized only to the extent of unrelated investors' interests in the associate or joint venture, except when the transaction lacks commercial substance, as described in IAS 16 (see Chapter 28).

6. Does not include disclosure requirements, now included in IFRS 12, as noted in 2. above.

CHAPTER 16
EVENTS AFTER THE REPORTING PERIOD

CONTENTS

OVERVIEW

The purpose of the published financial statements of an enterprise is to give information about its results for the financial year under review and about its position at the balance sheet date. In principle, therefore, the financial statements should reflect those events that occurred during that year, and only those events. However, the financial statements are obviously not finalized until a considerable period after the actual balance sheet date, and events that occur between the balance sheet date and the date of the finalization of the financial statements may have implications for the information in those financial statements.

IAS 10, "Events after the Reporting Period," deals with the appropriate treatment of these events. In broad terms, three situations can be distinguished, each with its own implications, as follows.

1. The event between balance sheet date and finalization date may provide new evidence or information about a situation that already existed on or before the balance sheet date, that is, the new event provides information concerning an earlier event. Because the effects of the earlier event are to be reported in the financial statements for the year under review, the accounts *should* be adjusted to take account of the new evidence or information.

2. The event between balance sheet date and finalization date may relate to a situation or condition that is new and that did not exist at the date of the balance sheet. This is a matter, therefore, for the following year, and the financial statements currently under preparation should *not* be adjusted to reflect the new situation, although disclosure may be required in the notes.

3. There is one exception to 2 above, in that if the new event seems likely to render the going concern assumption invalid (i.e., to suggest that the enterprise is shortly to be liquidated, see the discussion in Chapter 2),

then this would be so fundamental that the basis of the preparation of the accounts *would* be changed, to reflect the likelihood of imminent liquidation.

IAS 10 was originally issued in 1978 under the title "Contingencies and Events Occurring after the Balance Sheet Date." Much of the content of this standard was replaced by IAS 37, "Provisions, Contingent Liabilities, and Contingent Assets," which was effective for accounting periods beginning on or after July 1, 1999 (fully discussed in Chapter 28). The remainder, very confusingly in terms of the numbering system, was replaced by a new IAS 10 (revised 1999), called "Events after the Balance Sheet Date," effective for accounting periods beginning on or after January 1, 2000. With one exception, the new IAS 10 did not involve major changes from the post-balance-sheet event parts of the old IAS 10. Minor amendments to IAS 10 were made by the revisions to IAS 1, issued in 2007. These included an unhelpful change in the title from "Events after the Balance Sheet Date," to "Events after the Reporting Period."

BACKGROUND

As outlined above in the "Overview," IAS 10 seeks to ensure logical consistency in the extent to which events occurring in an enterprise between the date of the annual financial statements and the date of the finalization of those statements are, or are not, taken into account in the published annual financial statements. The standard should be applied in accounting for, and to the disclosure of, all events occurring after the reporting balance sheet date. IAS 10 is on the whole simple, clear, and succinct.

There are no differences of principle between IASB GAAP and U.S. GAAP. However, IAS 10 now requires that dividends, proposed or declared after the balance sheet date, are not adjusting events. Under U.S. GAAP the declaration of a cash dividend is non-adjusting, but the declaration of a stock dividend is adjusting. A further revision was issued for IAS 10 (revised 2004), effective from January 1, 2005, with earlier application encouraged. The only further change of substance was actually minor, relating to the declaration of dividends, and is discussed below.

DEFINITIONS

The definitions of the two types of post-balance sheet events can be simply stated (par. 3).

Events after the reporting period are those events, both favorable and unfavorable, that occur between the end of the reporting period and the date when the financial statements are authorized for issue. Two types of events can be identified:

1. Those that provide evidence of conditions that existed at the balance sheet date (*adjusting events after the reporting period*); and

2. Those that are indicative of conditions that arose after the balance sheet date (*non-adjusting events after the reporting period*).

Events after the balance sheet date include all events up to the date when the financial statements are authorized for issue, even if those events occur after the publication of a profit announcement or of other selected financial information.

Care may need to be taken in determining the date of "authorization" for this purpose. Inevitably, the standard has to allow for a variety of different national systems of corporate governance and of management structure. As a general rule, the date of authorization is the date on which the executive directors approve the financial statements. If the financial statements are, for example, required to be submitted to the shareholders for approval after issue or required to be approved by a non-executive supervisory board after acceptance by the executive management of the enterprise, then these later dates are not relevant for IAS 10 purposes. IAS 10 gives two simple examples illustrating these points (pars. 5–6).

The standard gives some indicative illustrations of adjusting and non-adjusting events, which require logical application of the above definitions (pars. 9 and 11). For example, the resolution after the balance sheet date of a court case that, if it confirms that an entity already had a present obligation at the balance sheet date, may require the entity to adjust a provision already recognized or to recognize a provision instead of merely disclosing a contingent liability. This would, therefore, be an adjusting event. Similarly, information about the realizability of accounts receivable in existence at the balance sheet date, or about the net realizable value of items held in inventory at the balance sheet date, would be regarded as adjusting events. The discovery of errors, or the results of fraud, that show that the draft financial statements were incorrect is also specifically stated to be an adjusting event.

On the other hand, an example of a non-adjusting event after the balance sheet date is a decline in market (= "fair," from the date of adopting IFRS 13) value of investments between the balance sheet date and the date when the financial statements are authorized for issue. The fall in market (= "fair," from the date of adopting IFRS 13) value would not normally relate to the condition of the investments at the balance sheet date but would reflect circumstances that had arisen in the following period. Therefore, an entity would not adjust the amounts recognized in its financial statements for the investment, except in the rare situation of the going concern assumption being put at risk (see "Going Concern," below).

RECOGNITION AND MEASUREMENT

Now obvious, the formal requirements can be very briefly stated (pars. 8 and 10). An entity should adjust the amounts recognized in its financial statements to reflect adjusting events after the reporting period. It should not adjust the amounts recognized in its financial statements to reflect non-adjusting events after the reporting period.

The one major change introduced by the 1999 revision to IAS 10, further amended by the 2004 revision, concerns the treatment of dividends. IAS 10 now states that if dividends to holders of equity instruments (as defined in IAS 32, "Financial Instruments: Disclosure and Presentation," see Chapter 17) are declared after the balance sheet date, then an entity should not recognize those dividends as liabilities at the balance sheet date (par. 12). This reflects the normal existing treatment in some countries, Germany for example, but was a significant change from previous practice in other countries, for example, the United Kingdom.

The issue is as follows. It is common practice for an enterprise to announce dividends that are stated to be in respect of the period covered by the financial statements but that are proposed or declared after the balance sheet date and before the financial statements are authorized for issue. This leads to the question as to whether or not such announcements create a liability as of the balance sheet date. The definition of a liability given in IAS 1 (see Chapter 4) and in the IASB Framework (see Chapter 2) needs to be applied. Does an obligation exist as of the balance sheet date?

The logical answer to this question is no. At the balance sheet date the enterprise was under no contractual obligation, express or constructive, to declare any dividend at all. Even an announcement to seek formal approval for the payment of a certain dividend does not, of itself, create an obligation. It is only the formal declaration of the dividend itself that creates the obligation. It therefore follows that only a dividend already formally declared (and, of course, not paid) by the balance sheet date would create an obligation on that date.

OBSERVATION: The above argument is entirely logical. The alternative, more pragmatic argument previously followed by many countries was that the dividend related to the reporting period and was an intended payment, thereby creating an in-substance liability. The choice between these two arguments, allowed by the previous international standard, is now withdrawn, as indicated above. No liability should be recognized for dividends not formally declared by the balance sheet date.

It should be noted that IAS 1, "Presentation of Financial Statements," requires an entity to *disclose* the amount of dividends that were proposed after the balance sheet date but before the financial statements were authorized for issue. IAS 1 permits an entity to make this disclosure either on the face of the balance sheet *as a separate component of equity* (i.e., not among the liabilities) or in the notes to the financial statements.

GOING CONCERN

As already discussed in the "Overview" at the beginning of this chapter, if the going concern assumption is no longer appropriate, the effect is so pervasive that IAS 10 requires a fundamental change in the basis of accounting, rather than an adjustment to the amounts recognized within the original basis of accounting.

In effect, therefore, if management determines after the balance sheet date either that it intends to liquidate the entity or to cease trading, or that it has no realistic alternative but to do so, then the accounts are to be completely redrawn on a non-going-concern basis. As stated in Chapter 4, IAS 1, "Presentation of Financial Statements," requires specified disclosures in such circumstances.

DISCLOSURE

It is important for users to know when the financial statements were authorized for issue, as the financial statements do not reflect events after this date. An entity should, therefore, disclose the date when the financial statements were authorized for issue and who gave that authorization. If the entity's owners or others have the power to amend the financial statements after issuance, the entity should disclose that fact.

Disclosure requirements contained in other standards, concerning conditions that existed at the balance sheet date, may themselves need to be updated. One example is when evidence becomes available after the balance sheet date about a contingent liability that existed at the balance sheet date. In addition to considering whether it should now recognize a provision under IAS 37, "Provisions, Contingent Liabilities, and Contingent Assets," an entity should update its disclosures about the contingent liability in light of that evidence.

NON-ADJUSTING EVENTS AFTER THE REPORTING PERIOD

Although, by definition, non-adjusting events should not have any effect on the numbers included in the financial statements for the reporting year, some non-adjusting events after the balance sheet date may be of such importance that non-disclosure would affect the ability of users of the financial statements to make proper evaluations and decisions (par. 21). In such cases, the entity should disclose in the Notes the following information for each significant category of non-adjusting event after the balance sheet date:

1. The nature of the event, and
2. An estimate of its financial effect, or a statement that such an estimate cannot be made.

This is clearly likely in some cases to be a subjective matter. The standard gives a list of examples, reproduced below (par. 22):

1. A major business combination after the balance sheet date (IFRS 3, "Business Combinations," requires specific disclosures in such cases, see Chapter 8) or disposing of a major subsidiary.

2. Announcing a plan to discontinue an operation.

3. Major purchases and disposals of assets or expropriation of major assets by government, classification of assets as held for sale in accordance with IFRS 5, "Non-Current Assets Held for Sale and Discontinued Operations" (see Chapter 27).

4. The destruction of a major production plant by a fire after the balance sheet date.

5. Announcing, or commencing the implementation of, a major restructuring (see IAS 37, "Provisions, Contingent Liabilities, and Contingent Assets," discussed in Chapter 29).

6. Major ordinary share transactions and potential ordinary share transactions after the balance sheet date (IAS 33, "Earnings per Share," encour-

ages an entity to disclose a description of such transactions, other than capitalization issues and share splits, see Chapter 13).

7. Abnormally large changes after the balance sheet date in asset prices or foreign exchange rates.

8. Changes in tax rates or tax laws enacted or announced after the balance sheet date that have a significant effect on current and deferred tax assets and liabilities (see IAS 12, "Income Taxes," discussed in Chapter 21).

9. Entering into significant commitments or contingent liabilities, for example, by issuing significant guarantees.

10. Commencing major litigation arising solely out of events that occurred after the balance sheet date.

It should not be assumed that this list is in any way exhaustive.

→ **PRACTICE POINTER:** The subjectivity inherent in this question of possible disclosure of non-adjusting events is not removed by the inclusion in IAS 10 of this list of examples. Words like *major* or *significant* appear in nearly all the examples given, so the expert subjective judgment of the accountants responsible for the preparation of the financial statement package remains crucial.

CHAPTER 17
FINANCIAL INSTRUMENTS

Contents

OVERVIEW

Current IASB GAAP is set out in three standards: (1) IAS 32, "Financial Instruments: Presentation," (2) IAS 39, "Financial Instruments: Recognition and Measurement" (as last revised in 2005), and (3) IFRS 9, "Financial Instruments: Disclosure," together with a number of applicable Interpretations. However, the IASB is currently revising all of its standards dealing with financial instruments. Ultimately, IASB GAAP on financial instruments will replace IAS 39, namely IFRS 9, "Financial Instruments," together with IFRS 7 supplemented by IAS 32, and the applicable sections of IFRS 13, "Fair Value Measurement" (issued in May 2011; see Chapter 3). The completion of IFRS 9 is taking considerable time, because of the IASB's attempts to establish a consensus on a number of contentious issues (see "Background" below) together with the requirements of the Convergence project with the FASB (see Chapter 1).

Consequently, IFRS 9 is being issued in phases or installments. The three phases are:

1. *Classification and measurement.* The relevant exposure draft (ED), "Financial Instruments: Classification and Measurement," was issued in July 2009.

2. *Impairment methodology.* The relevant ED, "Financial Instruments: Amortized Cost and Impairment," was published in November 2009 with a supplemental ED issued in January 2011.

3. *Hedge accounting.* An ED was published in December 2010.

Although this process is supposed to conclude in 2011, it may continue into 2012, as both hedge accounting and impairment provisioning are particularly contentious topics (see below).

The version of IFRS 9, issued in October 2010, covers the classification and measurement of financial assets and financial liabilities, replacing the relevant paragraphs of IAS 39. However, not all aspects of measurement are included in this version. Further chapters dealing with assets measured at amortized cost and hedge accounting have been published as EDs (see below), while issues of fair value measurement will be dealt with in the new IFRS 13, which will supersede the relevant paragraphs of IFRS 9, as well incorporate contents applicable to non-financial assets. IFRS 13 and IFRS 9, together with the consequentially amended version of IFRS 7, will be applicable for financial statements for annual periods beginning on or after January 1, 2013, with earlier adoption permitted. IFRS 13 does not change when an entity is required to use fair value, but rather, describes how to measure fair value under IFRS when it is required or permitted by IFRS.

The paragraphs of IAS 39 that are due to be superseded by IFRS 9 and IFRS 13, appear in this chapter. As earlier application of IFRS 9 is permitted, the requirements of the latter are also included.

In May 2009, the IASB issued an ED of a proposed new IFRS, ED/2009/5, "Fair Value Measurement," which led to the publication of a Near Final Draft in April 2011 followed by IFRS 13 in May 2011. The "Fair Value Hierarchy" proposed in the ED and in IFRS 13 has been included in the 2010 version of IFRS 7 and in this chapter.

As of May 2011, as well as IFRS 13, the IASB had issued a lengthy ED on hedge accounting and another two EDs on amortized cost and impairment. As noted above, these EDs are due to be included in a subsequent version of IFRS 9. On hedge accounting, it may be noted that in March 2011, the European Financial Reporting Advisory Group (EFRAG) made a submission in response to the ED in which it advised the IASB to make certain revisions and then to re-expose the ED. In August 2011, the IASB issued an ED in which it proposes to delay the mandatory effective date of IFRS 9 until January 1, 2015. The reasons given for this were: (i) the delays in finalizing the impairment and hedge accounting provisions of IFRS 9; and (ii) the fact that any new requirements for the accounting for insurance contracts will have a mandatory effective date later than January 1, 2013.

Financial instruments are defined broadly in IASB GAAP, a financial instrument is any contract (written or oral) that gives rise both to a financial asset of one entity and to a financial liability or an equity instrument of another entity. Financial instruments thus include all financial assets and financial liabilities, whether securitized or not, as well as derivatives.

In addition to their broad scope in terms of the recognition of financial instruments, IASB GAAP broke new ground in the application of fair value accounting to such instruments. Fair value is stated to be "a more appropriate measure for most financial assets than amortized cost," but in fact IASB GAAP require certain items to be accounted for at cost or amortized cost. Moreover, in the case of items that after initial recognition are remeasured at fair value, some may be classified so that gains and losses on their remeasurement are recognized in other comprehensive income, rather than in profit and loss. Hedging instruments that are derivatives are measured at fair values, whereas the measurement basis for the hedged items may be cost or amortized cost. This hybrid approach gives rise to a need for hedge accounting (see "Background" below). However, the restrictive rules for hedge accounting in IAS 39 were the object of protests from preparers and were amended to make them less restrictive. In addition, IAS 39 incorporates a *fair value option,* that is, a category to which *any* financial asset or liability may be designated (but not reclassified) and for which remeasurement gains or losses are recognized in profit and loss.

Recognition and Derecognition

An entity recognizes a financial instrument when the entity becomes a party to the financial instrument contract. It derecognizes a financial liability when its obligation is extinguished. It derecognizes a financial asset when:

- Its contractual rights to the asset's cash flows expire;
- It has transferred the asset and substantially all the risks and rewards of ownership; or
- It has transferred the asset, and has retained some substantial risks and rewards of ownership, but the transferee may sell the asset. In that case, the retained risks and rewards are recognized as an asset.

Categories of Financial Instruments

IAS 39 (as last revised in 2005) incorporates five categories of financial instruments, which are measured as indicated below:

1. *Held-to-maturity investments,* measured at amortized cost, are non-derivative financial assets with fixed or determinable payments and fixed maturity that an entity intends and is able to hold to maturity. These investments are not designated on initial recognition as "at fair value through profit or loss" or "available for sale" and do not meet the definition of "loans and receivables."

2. *Loans and receivables,* measured at amortized cost, are non-derivative financial assets with fixed or determinable payments that are not quoted in an active market and do not fall within the following categories:

   (a) Those that the entity intends to sell immediately in the near future and that are thus held for trading.

   (b) Those designated on initial recognition as being available for sale.

   (c) Those for which the holder may not recover substantially all of its initial investment for reasons other than credit deterioration, which should be classified as available for sale.

3. *Financial liabilities,* unless held for trading or designated as "at fair value through profit and loss," measured at amortized cost.

4. *Financial assets or financial liabilities "at fair value through profit or loss,"* measured at fair value, must either be classified as held for trading or designated upon initial recognition as being at fair value through profit or loss.

5. *Available-for-sale financial assets,* measured at fair value, are non-derivative financial assets that either are designated as available for sale or are not classified in any of the other categories. Fair value remeasurement gains or losses on these assets are recognized in other comprehensive income, not in profit and loss, pending realization.

OBSERVATION: In contrast, IFRS 9 incorporates two measurement bases for financial assets, reflecting the "business model" in accordance with which they are managed by the entity and their contractual cash flow characteristics; fair value and amortized cost (see below). In general, for items measured at fair value, remeasurement gains and losses are presented in profit and loss. For equity instruments, however, an entity may make an irrevocable election on initial recognition to present remeasurement gains and losses in other comprehensive income.

After initial recognition, the measurement basis for financial assets is fair value, except for loans and receivables and held-to-maturity investments (measured at amortized cost) and investments in equity instruments that do not have a quoted market price in an active market. For financial liabilities, subsequent measurement is at amortized cost, except for:

- Financial liabilities designated as "at fair value through profit and loss" that are measured at fair value, except for derivatives that are liabilities and are linked to, and needing to be settled by, the delivery of such instruments (measured at amortized cost).

- Financial liabilities that arise when a transfer of a financial asset does not qualify for derecognition and that are measured on a basis that reflects the rights and obligations that the entity has retained.

Hedge Accounting

Considerable attention is given in IASB GAAP to accounting for hedging relationships (see "Background" below). Hedge accounting recognizes the offsetting effects of changes in the fair values (fair value hedge) or the cash flows (cash flow hedge) of the hedging instrument and the hedged item, subject in the original IAS 39 to strict conditions, some of which have met with objections from preparers, and which have been somewhat relaxed in revisions of IAS 39 and in the current EDs:

- There must be formal designation and documentation of a hedge *up front,* including the related risk management strategy.

- The hedging instrument must be expected to offset *almost fully* changes in the fair value or cash flows of the hedged item that constitute the hedged risk.

- Any forecast transaction being hedged must be *highly probable.*

- Hedge effectiveness must be *reliably measurable*, in other words the fair values or cash flows of the hedged item and the hedging instrument can be reliably measured.

- The hedge must be assessed on an ongoing basis and shown to be *highly effective*.

IAS 39 includes Appendix A, which contains application guidance (AG). Some of the issues dealt with in the main text of the earlier version of the standard are dealt with in the AG.

The following interpretations apply to IAS 39:

- SIC 27, "Evaluating the Substance of Transactions Involving the Legal Form of a Lease";

- IFRIC 2, "Members' Shares in Co-operative Entities and Similar Instruments";

- IFRIC 5, "Rights to Interests Arising from Decommissioning, Restoration and Environmental Rehabilitation Funds";

- IFRIC 9, "Reassessment of Embedded Derivatives";

- IFRIC 10, "Interim Financial Reporting and Impairment";

- IFRIC 12, "Service Concession Arrangements";

- IFRIC 16, "Hedges of a Net Investment in a Foreign Operation";

- IFRIC 17, "Distributions of Non-cash Assets to Owners"; and

- IFRIC 19, "Extinguishing Financial Liabilities with Equity Instruments."

BACKGROUND

As noted above, the IASB is approaching the finalization of its GAAP on financial instruments, an enterprise that will have taken the IASB a decade, after replacing its predecessor the IASC in 2001. The length of time taken may be attributed largely to the difficulties encountered in operationalizing the concept of fair value measurement, together with related difficulties in accounting for hedging relationships (i.e., hedge accounting).

Fair value is of necessity used in measuring derivative financial instruments, as measurement at cost would, in general, not provide a fair presentation of a derivative as an element of an entity's financial position. Fair value is defined as "the price that would be received to sell an asset or paid to transfer a liability in an orderly transaction between market participants at the measurement date." Therefore, in principle, a precondition of fair value measurement of an item is the existence of an active secondary market in that type of item. When that precondition is not satisfied, fair value measurement is problematic, as it requires an estimate of the price that would be received or paid in a hypothetical market situation. Derivatives apart, the question then arises of whether such an estimate is accurate enough to provide a fairer presentation of the item than cost (amortized cost). The position taken consistently by the IASB has been to prefer such estimates to the use of amortized cost, on the basis that fair value, even if estimated, is more useful information than amortized cost.

Fair value measurement gives rise to remeasurement gains and losses, which, if recognized in profit or loss, increase the volatility of earnings. Hence, financial institutions have resisted any requirement to apply fair value measurement to items not held for trading, arguing that remeasurement gains and losses are not relevant information for such items. The IASB (together with the FASB) finally proposes to permit the use of amortized cost for assets that are "held within a business model whose objective is to hold assets in order to collect contractual cash flows [provided] . . . such cash flows are solely payments of principal and interest on the principal amount outstanding" (i.e., in banking jargon, assets that are held in the "banking book"). In the case of financial liabilities, the proposal is that amortized cost (using the "effective interest rate" method) be the measurement basis, with certain exceptions, unless the entity elects on initial recognition to classify the liability as at fair value through profit and loss (FVPL).

The rationale for hedge accounting is clearest in the case of fair value hedges. In such hedges, the *hedging* items are typically measured at fair value, whereas the related *hedged* items may be measured at amortized cost. In this case, the remeasurement gains and losses on the hedging item may not be matched by any offsetting remeasurement gains and losses on the related hedged item, although in economic substance such offsetting value changes (the reason for the hedge) have occurred. Thus, recognition in profit and loss of only the remeasurement gains or losses on the hedging instrument does not provide a fair presentation. Hedge accounting allows the symmetrical recognition in profit and loss of the gain or loss on the hedging item and the loss or gain on the hedged item attributable to the hedged risk, the latter being reflected in an adjustment to the carrying amount of the hedged item. In the case of cash flow hedges, hedge accounting permits remeasurement gains and losses on hedging items to be recognized in other comprehensive income rather than in profit and loss.

Hedge accounting may provide opportunities for entities to conceal remeasurement losses, and therefore, as mentioned, the hedge accounting provisions of IASB GAAP (and U.S. GAAP) contained quite onerous restrictions intended to remove such opportunities. Reporting entities have found such restrictions to be excessive, and in successive versions of IAS 39, they have been gradually relaxed.

However, at the time of writing the IASB's latest ED on hedge accounting is still under discussion (the exposure period ended on March 9, 2011), while a comprehensive standard on fair value measurement has recently been issued as IFRS 13. An ED on amortized cost and impairment had an exposure period that ended on April 1, 2011.

IASB GAAP on financial instruments arose originally out of the then IASC's financial instruments project, which started in 1988 following an Organization for Economic Cooperation and Development (OECD) symposium in which accounting for financial instruments had been discussed. The history of the Financial Instruments project was to be marked by difficulties concerning, in particular, the extent to which fair values should be used as a basis for measurement and related issues. As noted above, more than 20 years later, the IASC's successor, the IASB, is still wrestling with some of these issues. These efforts are being affected by the IASB's commitment to a joint program with the FASB intended to produce convergence between IASB GAAP and U.S. GAAP.

In November 1994, following review of comments on earlier exposure drafts, and consideration of input from representatives of standard-setting bodies in 20 countries, the past IASC took the decision to split its Financial Instruments project into two stages. The first stage would deal with presentation and disclosure and would aim to produce a standard by March 1995. The second stage would deal with the more controversial issues of recognition and measurement, with the hope of producing a standard by 1996 at the latest. The first of these target dates was met with the approval of IAS 32 in March 1995. The other target date, however, was not to be achieved.

E62, "Financial Instruments: Recognition and Measurement," was issued in April 1998 and the first version of IAS 39 was approved in December 1998 and published in March 1999. It was largely based on the FASB's FAS-133 (ASC 815). By so doing, the IASC embarked on a treatment of financial instruments that was rule-based (similar to U.S. GAAP at the time) rather than principle-based as generally intended by the IASC. Its successor, the IASB, while aiming to pursue a principle-based approach in its standards, has taken more than ten years to develop a principle-based approach in IFRS 9, which is still incomplete, and the "Near Final" l new standard on fair value measurement.

The IASC made a number of revisions to IAS 39 before handing it over to the IASB in 2001. In turn, the IASB has made revisions in 2004 and 2005.

In 2001, the IASB appointed a Financial Activities Advisory Council (FAAC) based on the IAS 30 steering committee set up by the IASC in 1999 to advise on a new standard to replace the increasingly obsolete IAS 30. It became clear to the FAAC that for various reasons it would be preferable for the scope of the new standard to be more comprehensive so as to apply to disclosures about risks arising from financial instruments in all entities and to make certain simplifications and other improvements to the disclosure provisions of IAS 32. This led, in July 2004, to the publication of an exposure draft, ED 7, "Financial Instruments: Disclosures." The resultant standard, IFRS 7, was issued in August 2005.

Since 2005, the IASB and the FASB have been cooperating with a long-term objective to improve and simplify the reporting for financial instruments. In addition, in April 2009 the input received from the conclusions of the G20 and the recommendations of the Financial Stability Board led the IASB to announce an accelerated timetable for replacing IAS 39 in three main phases that were intended to be concluded by the end of 2010 (see "Overview" above).

In April 2009, the IASB issued an exposure draft ED/2009/3, "Derecognition: Proposed Amendments to IAS 39 and IFRS 7." However, on the basis of the comments received, these proposals were abandoned, and the derecognition provisions of IAS 39 have been carried forward into IFRS 9.

The responses to the July 2009 ED, and to the Board's June 2009 Discussion Paper, "Credit Risk in Liability Measurement," on the matter of the measurement of financial liabilities (namely the recognition of the effects of changes in the entity's own credit risk) were such that the IASB decided that this matter needed further consideration before being included in the new standard. Accordingly, in November 2009 the Board issued only those chapters of IFRS 9 that relate to the classification and measurement of financial assets. The paragraphs dealing with the treatment of financial liabilities were added in the version of IFRS 9 issued in October 2010, which is summarized in this chapter.

Entities are not required to apply IFRS 9 until annual periods beginning on or after January 1, 2013 (or, if the proposal in the August 2011 ED is retained, January 1, 2015), although earlier application is permitted. IFRS 9 makes a number of consequential changes to other standards, set out in Appendix C to IFRS 9. In case of earlier application of IFRS 9, these other changes will also need to be made at the same time.

The IASB and the FASB are committed to achieving a comprehensive and improved treatment of financial instruments that provides comparability internationally in financial reporting for such instruments. In their joint meeting in October 2009, the Boards reached agreement on a set of core principles designed to achieve comparability and transparency in reporting, consistency in accounting for credit impairments and reduced complexity. As a result, only minor differences, at most, are to be expected between IASB GAAP and U.S. GAAP for financial instruments.

The 2011 Bound Volume of IASB Standards includes IFRS 9, as issued in October 2010 and all the consequential changes to IAS 39 and other standards. Hence, in particular, the paragraphs of IAS 39 relating to the classification and measurement of financial assets and financial liabilities have been removed from the version of IAS 39 that appears in the volume. Finally, given that the application date for IFRS 9 is not until January 2013, in this edition of the *IAS/IFRS Guide*, we refer to the text of IAS 39 and the other standards as they stood before making the consequential changes required by IFRS 9, but we also include in this chapter a summary of those parts of IFRS 9 that were issued in October 2010, as well as summaries of the exposure drafts on hedge accounting and amortized cost and impairment. References are also made to the relevant paragraphs of IFRS 13.

SCOPE

The scope of IASB GAAP on financial instruments is set out in IAS 39, paragraphs 2–7, for recognition and measurement; IAS 32, paragraphs 4–10, for presentation; and IFRS 7, paragraphs 3–5, for disclosure. As noted above, IFRS 9 as issued in October 2010 will replace the paragraphs of IAS 39 dealing with the classification and measurement of assets, leaving the treatment of liabilities as set out in IAS 39 pending the extension of IFRS 9 to include them. An outline and summary of IFRS 9 are provided at the end of this chapter. The scope of IAS 39 excludes rights and obligations under leases (see step 2 below), financial instruments issued by the entity that are mentioned in step 4 below, and some loan commitments (see step 8 below), but these exclusions do not apply to IAS 32 and IFRS 7. Thus, the scope of the standards for presentation and disclosure includes certain financial instruments whose recognition and measurement are covered by standards other than IAS 39. IASB GAAP on financial instruments apply to all entities, including banks and insurance companies, and to all financial instruments, *with the following exclusions*:

1. Interests in subsidiaries, associates, and joint ventures that are accounted for under IAS 27, "Consolidated Financial Statements and Accounting for Investments in Subsidiaries"; IAS 28, "Accounting for Investments in Associates"; and IAS 31, "Financial Reporting of Interests in Joint Ventures" (see Chapter 11). However, an entity should apply IAS 39 in its consolidated financial statements to account for an interest in a subsidiary, associate, or joint venture that, according to IAS 27, IAS 28, or IAS 31 is to be accounted for under IAS 39 (i.e., not consolidated or accounted for using the equity method). In these cases, the disclosure requirements of IAS 32 apply. An entity should also apply IAS 39 to derivatives on an interest in a subsidiary, associate, or joint venture unless the derivative meets the IAS 32 definition of an equity instrument of the entity.

2. For IAS 39, rights and obligations under leases, to which IAS 17, "Leases," applies. However, lease receivables recognized by a lessor are subject to the derecognition and impairment provisions of IAS 39, and IAS 39 also applies to derivatives that are embedded in leases (see Chapter 26). Finance lease payables recognized by a lessee are subject to the derecognition provisions of IAS 39. Derivatives that are embedded in leases are subject to the derecognition provisions of IAS 39.

3. Employers' assets and obligations under employee benefit plans, to which IAS 19, "Employee Benefits," applies (see Chapter 14).

4. For IAS 39, financial instruments issued by the entity that meet the IAS 32 definition of an equity instrument, including options and warrants. However, the *holder* of such equity instruments should apply IAS 39 to those instruments unless they are covered by the exception in item 1, above.

5. Rights and obligations arising under either of the following:

   (a) An insurance contract as defined in IFRS 4, "Insurance Contracts," (see Chapter 35) other than an issuer's rights and obligations that arise under an insurance contract that meets the definition of a *financial guarantee contract* given in IAS 39, paragraph 9 (see below), which should be accounted for according to IAS 39. However, if an issuer of financial guarantee contracts has previously stated explicitly that it regards such contracts as insurance contracts and has accounted for them accordingly, such an issuer may elect to apply either IAS 39 or IFRS 4 to such contracts; this election may be made separately for each such contract, but once made for a particular contract, may not be changed for that contract. If the issuer elects to apply IAS 39 to such a contract, it should also apply IFRS 7 to that contract (IFRS 7, par. 3[d]).

   (b) A contract that falls within the scope of IFRS 4 because it contains a discretionary participation feature. However, IAS 39 applies to a derivative embedded in such a contract unless the derivative is itself a contract falling within the scope of IFRS 4.

6. Contracts between an acquirer and a vendor in a business combination to buy or sell an acquiree at a future date.

7. For IAS 39, loan commitments that cannot be settled in cash or another financial instrument, except for those that an entity designates as "financial liabilities at fair value through profit or loss." The issuer of a commitment to provide a loan at a below-market interest rate must initially recognize it at fair value and subsequently measure it at the higher of the amount recognized under IAS 37 and the amount initially recognized less, where appropriate, cumulative amortization in accordance with IAS 18, "Revenue Recognition." An issuer of loan commitments should apply IAS 37 to other loan commitments that are not within the scope of IAS 39. However, loan commitments are subject to the derecognition provisions of IAS 39.

8. Financial instruments, contracts and obligations under share-based payment transaction to which IFRS 2, "Share-Based Payment," applies, except for the contracts mentioned below.

9. Rights to payments to reimburse the entity for an expenditure it is required to make to settle a liability that it recognizes, or recognized in an earlier period, as a provision in accordance with IAS 37.

IAS 39 applies to the following loan commitments:

1. Loan commitments designated as financial liabilities at fair value through profit and loss. If an entity has a past practice of selling the assets resulting from its loan commitments shortly after origination, it applies IAS 39 to all of its loan commitments in the same class.

2. Loan commitments that can be settled net in cash or by delivering or issuing another financial instrument. These loan commitments are derivatives. A loan commitment is not recognized as settled net merely because the loan is paid out in installments, as in the case of a mortgage construction loan that is paid out in installments in line with the progress of construction.

3. Commitments to provide a loan at a below-market interest rate (for subsequent measurement of such items, see "Subsequent Measurement of Financial Liabilities" below).

IASB GAAP on financial instruments apply to contracts to buy or sell a nonfinancial item that can be settled net in cash or another financial instrument, or by exchanging financial instruments, as if the contracts were financial instruments, except for contracts entered into and continuing to be held for the purpose of receipt or delivery of a non-financial item in accordance with the entity's expected requirements for purchase, sale or use. It also applies to a written option to buy or sell a non-financial item that can be settled net in cash or another financial instrument, or by exchanging financial instruments; such a contract cannot be entered into held for the purpose of receipt or delivery of a non-financial item in accordance with the entity's expected requirements for purchase, sale, or use.

DEFINITIONS

The definitions given in IAS 32, paragraphs 11–14, and further clarified in IAS 32, paragraphs AG3–AG23, are used in IAS 39, and a considerable number of additional definitions are given in IAS 39, paragraphs 9–13.

OBSERVATION: Paragraphs 10–13 do not appear in the current IFRS Bound Volume, as they are to be superseded by definitions given in Appendix A of IFRS 9. The number of definitions of categories used in classifying financial assets given below is reduced by IFRS 9, which recognizes only one category measured at Fair Value and another category measured at Amortized Cost. Apart from that, the definitions in IFRS 9 are the same as those in IAS 9.

---

1. A *financial instrument* is any contract that gives rise to a financial asset of one entity and a financial liability of another entity.

2. A *financial asset* is any asset that is any of the following:

   (a) Cash (but not gold bullion, which is a commodity).

   (b) An equity instrument of another entity.

   (c) A contractual right either to receive cash or another financial asset from another entity or to exchange financial instruments with another entity under conditions that are potentially favorable to the entity having the right.

   (d) A contract that will or may be settled in the entity's own equity instruments and is either (i) a non-derivative for which the entity is or may be obliged to receive a variable number of the entity's own equity instruments, or (ii) a derivative that will or may be settled other than by the exchange of a fixed amount of cash or another financial asset for a fixed number of the entity's own equity instruments (which for this purpose do not include instruments that are themselves contracts for the future receipt or delivery of the entity's own equity instruments). For this purpose, the entity's own equity instruments do not include puttable financial instruments classified as equity instruments in accordance with IAS 32, paragraphs 16A–16B (see "Puttable Instruments" below), instruments that impose on the entity to deliver to another party a *pro rata* share of the net assets of the entity only upon liquidation and are classified as equity instruments in accordance with IAS 32, paragraphs 16C–16D (see below), or instruments that are contracts for the future receipt or delivery of the entity's own equity instruments.

3. A *financial liability* is any liability that is either:

   (a) A contractual obligation to deliver cash or another financial asset to another entity or a contractual obligation to exchange financial assets or financial liabilities with another entity under conditions that are potentially unfavorable to the entity having the obligation; or

(b) A contract that will or may be settled in the equity's own equity instruments and is (i) a non-derivative derivative for which the entity is or may be obliged to deliver a variable number of the entity's own equity instruments or (ii) a derivative that will or may be settled other than by the exchange of a fixed amount of cash or another financial asset for a fixed number of the entity's own equity instruments. For this purpose the entity's own equity instruments do not include puttable financial instruments that are classified as equity instruments in accordance with IAS 32, paragraphs 16A–16B, instruments that impose on the entity to deliver to another party a *pro rata* share of the net assets of the entity only upon liquidation and are classified as equity instruments in accordance with IAS 32, paragraphs 16C–16D, or instruments that are contracts for the future receipt or delivery of the entity's own equity instruments.

As an exception, an instrument that meets the definition of a financial liability is classified as an equity instrument if it has all the features and meets the conditions in IAS 32, paragraphs 16A–16B or 16C–16D.

4. An *equity instrument* is any contract that is evidence of a residual interest in the assets of an entity after deducting all of its liabilities.

5. A *puttable instrument* is a financial instrument that gives the holder the right to put the instrument back to the issuer for cash or another financial asset or is automatically put back to the issuer on the occurrence of an uncertain future event or the death or retirement of the instrument holder.

6. *Fair value* is the amount for which an asset could be exchanged, or a liability settled, between knowledgeable, willing parties in an arms length transaction.

IAS 39, paragraph 9, provides the further definitions given below:

1. A *derivative* is a financial instrument or other contract within the scope of IAS 39 with all three of the following characteristics:

   (a) Its value changes in response to the change in a specified underlying variable (the "underlying"), such as an interest rate, financial instrument price, commodity price, foreign exchange rate, index of prices or rates, credit rating or credit index, or any other variable, provided that, in the case of a non-financial variable, that variable is not specific to a party to the contract;

   (b) It requires no, or little, initial net investment relative to other types of contracts that have a similar response to changes in market conditions; and

   (c) It is settled at a future date.

→ **PRACTICE POINTER:** The prepayment on a prepaid pay-fixed, receive-variable interest rate swap is not considered as an initial net investment for this purpose, so that the swap contract is a derivative. However, the prepayment on a prepaid pay-variable, receive-fixed interest rate swap *is* considered as an initial net investment, and the swap contract is not a derivative. Margin accounts do not constitute an initial net investment, as they are a form of collateral, not a prepayment (IAS 39 IG B.5).

---

2. A *financial asset or financial liability at fair value through profit or loss* (FVPL) is one that meets either of the following conditions:

   (a) It is classified as held for trading. It is so classified if:

      (i) It is acquired (or incurred) principally for the purpose of selling or repurchasing it in the near term;

      (ii) On initial recognition it is part of a portfolio of identical financial instruments that are managed together and for which there is evidence of a recent actual pattern of short-term profit taking; or

      (iii) It is a derivative (except for a derivative that is a designated and effective hedging instrument).

   (b) Upon initial recognition, it was irrevocably designated as "at fair value through profit and loss" (FVPL). This designation may be used only when the financial instrument is a host contract containing one or more embedded derivatives subject to the restrictions set out in IAS 39, paragraph 11A (see below), are satisfied or when doing so results in *more relevant information* by either:

- Eliminating an inconsistency in recognition or measurement (accounting mismatch), examples of which are given in IAS 39, paragraph AG4E, or

- Treating a group of financial instruments in a manner consistent with the use of fair value for managing and evaluating its performance *in accordance with a documented risk management or investment strategy* and in the entity's internal information system for senior management.

IAS 39, paragraph 11A, sets out that a host contract containing one or more embedded derivatives that is not an asset within the scope of the standard may be designated in its entirety as at FVPL *unless* the embedded derivative does not significantly modify the cash flows that would otherwise be required by the contract, or it is clear when such a hybrid instrument is first considered that the embedded derivative(s) cannot be separated from the host contract, as in the case of a prepayment option in a loan, whereby the holder may prepay the loan for approximately its amortized cost.

An entity may not reclassify financial assets or liabilities in or out of the FVPL category.

OBSERVATION: The above is the amended version of the fair value option that, in its original version, was carved out of IAS 39 as endorsed by the EU

Commission in November 2004. However, in April 2004, the IASB issued an exposure draft setting out a number of restrictions to designation at FVPL; and in March 2005, it held a series of roundtable discussions to meet the concerns of prudential supervisors of banks, among others, namely that:

- The FVPL designation might be applied to financial instruments whose fair value is not verifiable, thus leaving open a possibility of "earnings management."

- The use of the option might lead to increased income volatility.

- The application of the option to financial liabilities might result in gains or losses being recognized by an entity associated with changes in its own creditworthiness.

The amended fair value option was issued in June 2005 and is incorporated in the text of IAS 39. The restrictions on the use of the FVPL designation led to the endorsement of the amended version by the EU Commission in November 2005, but made the application of the option more complex. IFRS 9, with its different basis for determining how items are to be classified for measurement purposes as between fair value and amortized cost, has superseded the above.

3. *Held-to-maturity (HTM) investments* are non-derivative financial assets with fixed or determinable payments and fixed maturity that an entity has the positive intent and ability to hold to maturity, other than:

   (a) Those that the entity upon initial recognition designates as at FVPL.

   (b) Those that the entity designates as available for sale (AFS).

   (c) Those that meet the definition of loans and receivables.

An entity shall not classify any financial assets as HTM if the entity has, during the current or two preceding financial years, sold or reclassified more than an insignificant amount of HTM investments before maturity other than those that:

— Are so close to maturity or call date (for example, less than three months) that changes in the market rate of interest would not have a significant effect on the financial asset's fair value,

— Occur after the entity has collected substantially all of the financial asset's original principal through scheduled payments or prepayments, or

— Are attributable to an isolated event that is beyond the entity's control, is non-recurring, and could not have been reasonably anticipated by the entity.

OBSERVATION: This restriction is known as the "tainting rule," as the sale before maturity or the reclassification of HTM assets "taints" the HTM category. This rule has met with objections from preparers and has been removed in IFRS 9.

4. *Loans and receivables* are non-derivative financial assets with fixed or determinable payments that are not quoted in an active market, other than:

   (a) Those that the entity intends to sell immediately or in the near term, which should be classified as held for trading, and those that the entity on initial recognition designates as at FVPL.

   (b) Those designated at AFS on initial recognition.

   (c) Those for which the holder may not recover substantially all of its initial investment, other than because of credit deterioration, which should be classified as AFS.

An interest acquired in a pool of assets that are not loans or receivables (e.g., in interest in a mutual fund) is not a loan or receivable.

5. *Available-for-sale financial assets* are those non-derivative financial assets that are designated as AFS or are not classified in any of the other three categories described above.

6. A *financial guarantee contract* is a contract that requires the issuer to make specified payments to reimburse the holder for a loss that it incurs because a *specified* debtor fails to make payment when due in accordance with the original or modified terms of a debt instrument.

7. The *amortized cost of a financial asset or financial liability* is the amount at which the item was measured on its initial recognition, minus any repayments of principal, plus or minus the cumulative amortization of any difference between that initial amount and the amount due on maturity, and minus any write-down (directly or by using an allowance account) for impairment or uncollectibility.

8. The *effective interest method* is a method of calculating the amortized cost of a financial asset or financial liability (or group of such items) and of allocating the interest income or expense over the relevant period. The *effective interest rate* of a financial instrument is that rate that exactly discounts estimated future cash payments or receipts through the expected life of the instrument or, where appropriate, a shorter period, to the net carrying amount of the instrument. The effective interest rate is thus the internal rate of return on the instrument for that period, sometimes known as the yield to maturity (or to the next repricing date). In the calculation, the entity should estimate cash flows considering all contractual terms of the instrument such as prepayment, call and similar options, but should not consider future credit losses. The computation should include all fees and points paid or received between the contracting parties that are an integral part of the effective interest rate, transaction costs and all other premiums or discounts.

9. *Derecognition* is the removal of a previously recognized financial asset or financial liability from an entity's statement of financial position.

10. *Fair value* is the amount for which an asset could be exchanged, or a liability settled, between knowledgeable, willing parties in an arm's-length transaction.

11. A *regular-way purchase or sale* is a purchase or sale of a financial asset under a contract whose terms require delivery of the asset within the time frame established generally by regulation or convention in the market concerned.

12. *Transaction costs* are incremental costs that are directly attributable to the acquisition, issue, or disposal of a financial instrument. They include fees and commissions paid to agents, advisers, brokers, and dealers; levies by regulatory agencies and securities exchanges; and transfer taxes and duties. They do not include debt premium or discount, financing costs, or allocations of internal administrative or holding costs.

13. A *firm commitment* is a binding agreement for the exchange of a specified quantity of resources at a specified price on a specified date or dates.

14. A *forecast transaction* is an uncommitted but anticipated future transaction.

15. A *hedging instrument* is a designated derivative or (for a hedge of the risk of changes in foreign currency exchange rates) a designated non-derivative financial asset or financial liability whose fair value or cash flows are expected to offset changes in the fair value or cash flows of a designated hedged item.

16. A *hedged item* is an asset, liability, firm commitment, highly probable forecast future transaction, or net investment in a foreign operation that (a) exposes the entity to risk of changes in fair value or in future cash flows and (b) for hedge accounting purposes is designated as being hedged.

17. *Hedge effectiveness* is the degree to which changes in the fair value or cash flows attributable to a hedged risk are offset by changes in the fair value or cash flows of the hedging instrument.

18. An *embedded derivative* is a component of a hybrid (combined) financial instrument that also includes a non-derivative "host contract," with the effect that some of the cash flows of the combined instrument vary like those of a stand-alone derivative. It causes some or all of the cash flows that would otherwise be required by the host contract to be modified, based on the behavior of a specified variable such as an interest rate, security price, commodity price, foreign exchange rate, index of prices or rates, or other variable. A separately transferable derivative that is attached to a non-derivative financial instrument (such as a transferable call option) is not an embedded derivative, but a separate financial instrument (IAS 39, par. 10–11, IFRS 9, par. 4.3.1).

An embedded derivative should be separated from the host contract and treated as a derivative only if all of the following conditions are met:

- The economic characteristics and risks of the embedded derivative are not closely related to those of the host contract.

- A separate instrument with the same terms as the embedded derivative would meet the definition of a derivative.

- The hybrid instrument is not itself measured at fair value with changes in fair value being recognized in profit or loss (i.e., a derivative that is embedded in a financial asset or financial liability at FVPL is not separated).

If an embedded derivative is separated, the host contract should be accounted for, either under IAS 39 if it is a financial instrument, or under the applicable standard if it is not, unless the entity is unable to measure the embedded derivative separately either initially or at a subsequent reporting date. In case of such inability, the entity should designate the entire combined (hybrid) contract as at FVPL.

The fair value of an embedded derivative, if it cannot be determined reliably on the basis of its terms and conditions, may be estimated as the difference between the fair value of the hybrid (combined) contract and the fair value of the host instrument, if these can be determined under IAS 39. If IAS 39 requires the separation of an embedded derivative but this cannot be done either at acquisition or at a subsequent financial reporting date, then the entire hybrid (combined) contract must be designated as at FVPL, unless the embedded derivative does not significantly modify the cash flows that would otherwise be required by the contract.

RECOGNITION AND DERECOGNITION

Initial Recognition

The basic rule for initial recognition is that an entity should recognize a financial asset or a financial liability on its balance sheet when, and only when, the entity becomes a party to the contractual provisions of the instrument (IAS 39, par. 14). See below for regular-way purchases of financial assets.

"Regular Way" Contracts: Trade Date versus Settlement Date

Regular-way contracts are dealt with in Appendix A to IAS 39, paragraphs AG53–AG56. A regular-way contract is a contract for the purchase or sale of financial assets that requires delivery of the assets *within the time frame generally established* by regulation or convention in the market concerned. The fixed price commitment between the *trade date* (on which the contract is derivative but the duration established) and the *settlement date* (on which the asset is delivered) is similar to that under a forward contract and meets the definition of a derivative. However, the duration of the commitment is short, and therefore such a contract is not recognized as a derivative in IASB GAAP.

→ **PRACTICE POINTER:** A bank's commitment to make a loan at a specified rate of interest during a fixed period is a derivative (an option issued by the bank); but if the commitment allows draw-down of the loan within the time frame generally established (the period expected to be needed for the bank to perform the underwriting, and for the transaction that is the subject of the loan to be scheduled and executed), then the regular-way exemption applies.

For purchases or sales of financial assets under regular-way contracts, IAS 39 allows a choice between a policy of *trade date accounting* and a policy of *settlement date accounting*. The policy chosen should be applied consistently for all purchases and sales of financial assets that belong to the same category of financial assets defined in IAS 39, paragraph 9.

Under trade date accounting, the asset to be received and the liability to pay for it are both recognized by the buyer, and the asset to be delivered is derecognized and the receivable from the buyer is recognized by the seller, on the trade date; however, interest generally does not start to accrue on either the asset or the liability until the settlement date.

Under settlement date accounting, the asset and the corresponding liability are not recognized by the buyer, and the asset is not derecognized and the receivable is not recognized by the seller, until the settlement date. When settlement date accounting is used for purchases under regular-way contracts, the issue arises of how any change in the fair value of the purchased asset during the period between trade date and settlement date should be treated. In IASB GAAP, the treatment of value changes that occur during this period (the settlement period) depends on the classification of the related asset. Thus, value changes that occur during the settlement period are not recognized for assets carried at cost or amortized cost. For assets classified as held for trading, value changes that occur during the settlement period are recognized in net profit or loss, and for assets classified as AVS, they are recognized either in net profit or loss or in other comprehensive income.

In IASB GAAP, the treatment of a change in fair value during this period follows that of the asset itself, depending on its classification. That is, the value change is not recognized for assets carried at cost or amortized cost; it is recognized in profit or loss for assets classified as FVPL; and it is recognized in other comprehensive income for assets classified as AFS.

Illustration of Trade Date vs. Settlement Date Accounting

On December 29, 20X1, an entity commits to purchase a financial asset for $1,000 (including transaction costs), which is its fair value on the trade (commitment) date. On December 31, 20X1 (fiscal year-end), and on January 4, 20X2 (settlement date), the fair value of the asset is $1,002 and $1,003, respectively. The amounts to be recorded in respect of the asset will depend on how it is classified and whether trade date accounting or settlement date accounting is used. This is illustrated in the two tables below. (Note: Parentheses denote credits.)

SETTLEMENT DATE ACCOUNTING

Balances	Held-to-Maturity Investments— Carried at Amortized Cost	Available-for-Sale Assets— Remeasured to Fair Value with Changes in Other Comprehensive Income	Assets at Fair Value through Profit or Loss

December 29, 20X1			
Financial asset	—	—	—
Liability	—	—	—
December 31, 20X1			
Receivable	—	$2	$2
Financial asset	—	—	—
Liability	—	—	—
Equity (fair value adjustment)	—	(2)	—
Retained earnings (through net profit or loss)	—	—	(2)
January 4, 20X2			
Receivable	$1,000	$1,003	$1,003
Financial asset	—	—	—
Liability	—	—	—
Equity (fair value adjustment)	—	(3)	—
Retained earnings (through net profit or loss)	—	—	(3)

TRADE DATE ACCOUNTING

Balances	Held-to-Maturity Investments— Carried at Amortized Cost	Available-for-Sale Assets— Remeasured to Fair Value with Changes in Other Comprehensive Income	Assets at Fair Value through Profit or Loss
December 29, 20X1			
Financial asset	$1,000	$1,000	$1,000
Liability	(1,000)	(1,000)	(1,000)
December 31, 20X1			
Receivable	—	—	—
Financial asset	$1,000	$1,002	$1,002
Liability	(1,000)	(1,000)	(1,000)
Equity (fair value adjustment)	—	(2)	—
Retained earnings (through net profit or loss)	—	—	(2)
January 4, 20X2			
Receivable	—	—	—
Financial asset	$1,000	$1,003	$1,003
Liability	—	—	—

Equity (fair value adjustment)	—	(3)	—
Retained earnings (through net profit or loss)	—	—	(3)

Derecognition

> **OBSERVATION:** The derecognition rules given below have been carried forward to IFRS 9, Sections 3.2 and 3.3.

Derecognition of a Financial Asset

IAS 39 devotes approximately 38 pages to derecognizing financial assets (pars. 15–37 and AG36–AG52), reflecting the importance of this issue for risk measurement purposes and when assessing the capital adequacy of financial institutions. In consolidated financial statements, the contents of these paragraphs are applied at the consolidated level.

Before evaluating whether, and to what extent, derecognition is appropriate as set out below, an entity must first determine whether those derecognition rules should be applied to part of a financial asset (or of a group of similar assets) or to a financial asset (or group of similar assets) in its entirety, as follows. The derecognition rules are applied to part of a financial asset (or of a group of similar assets) if, and only if, the part being considered for derecognition meets one of the following three conditions:

1. The part comprises only *specifically identified cash flows* from a financial asset (or of a group of similar assets). For example, in the case of an interest rate strip, the counterparty obtains the right to the interest cash flows but not the principal cash flows.

2. The part comprises only a *fully proportionate share* of the cash flows from a financial asset (or of a group of similar assets). For example, when an entity enters into an arrangement whereby the counterparty obtains the right to a 90% share of all cash flows from a debt instrument, the derecognition rules are applied to 90% of those cash flows. If there is more than one counterparty, each is not required to have a proportionate share of the cash flows, provided the transferring entity has a fully proportionate share.

3. The part comprises only a *fully proportionate share of specifically identified cash flows* from a financial asset (or of a group of similar assets). In that case, the derecognition rules are applied to that proportionate share of the specifically identified cash flows (e.g., to 90% of an interest rate strip). Again, if there is more than one counterparty, each is not required to have a proportionate share of the specifically identified cash flows, provided the transferring entity has a fully proportionate share.

In all other cases, the derecognition rules are applied to the financial asset (or group of similar assets) in its entirety.

An entity derecognizes a financial asset when, and only when the contractual rights to the cash flows from the financial asset expire; or the entity transfers the financial asset, and the transfer qualifies for derecognition, as set out below (see above for regular-way sales of financial assets).

An entity transfers a financial asset only if it either transfers the contractual rights to receive the cash flows of the financial asset; or retains the contractual rights to receive the cash flows of the financial asset (the original asset) but assumes a contractual obligation to pay the cash flows to one or more entities (the eventual recipients) in an *arrangement* that meets the following *three conditions*:

1. The entity has no obligation to pay amounts to the eventual recipients unless it collects equivalent amounts from the original asset.

2. The entity is prohibited by the terms of the transfer contract from selling or pledging the original asset other than as security to the eventual recipients for the obligation to pay them cash flows.

3. The entity has an obligation to remit any cash flows it collects on behalf of the eventual recipients without material delay, and is not entitled to invest those cash flows, except for investments in cash or cash equivalents as defined in IAS 7, "Cash Flow Statements," during a short settlement period, with any interest earned being passed on to the eventual recipients.

When an entity transfers a financial asset, it must evaluate the extent to which it retains the risks and rewards of ownership of that asset:

- If the entity transfers substantially all the risks and rewards of ownership, it derecognizes the financial asset and recognizes separately as assets or liabilities any rights and obligations created or retained in the transfer.

- If the entity retains substantially all the risks and rewards of ownership, it continues to recognize the financial asset.

- If the entity neither transfers nor retains substantially all the risks and rewards of ownership of the financial asset, it determines whether it has retained control of the asset. If it has not retained control, it derecognizes the financial asset and recognizes separately as assets or liabilities any rights and obligations created or retained in the transfer. If it has retained control, it continues to recognize the financial asset to the extent of its continuing involvement in the asset, as described below under "Continuing Involvement in Transferred Assets."

Derecognition in IASB GAAP thus involves a combination of criteria. IAS 39, paragraph AG36, presents a helpful flowchart (reproduced with some modifications below) with cross-references to the text of IAS 39, which summarizes, in two preliminary steps and six questions, the process of evaluating whether and to what extent a financial asset can be derecognized, according to the above criteria, as follows:

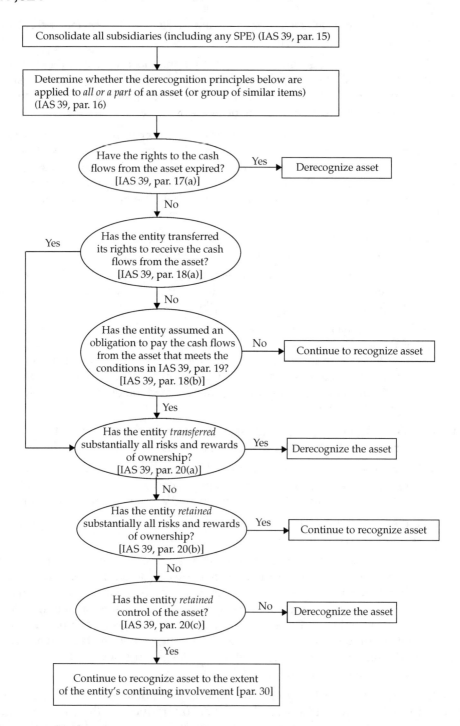

The transfer of risks and rewards as described above is evaluated by comparing the entity's exposure, before and after the transfer, with reference to the variability in the amounts and timing of the net cash flows of the transferred asset. The entity has retained substantially all the risks and rewards of ownership of a financial asset if its exposure to the variability in the present value of the future net cash flows from the asset does not change significantly as a result of the transfer (e.g., if it has sold the asset subject to a buy-back agreement at a fixed price or the sale price plus a lender's return). The entity has transferred substantially all the risks and rewards of ownership of a financial asset if its exposure to such variability is no longer significant in relation to the total variability in the present value of the future net cash flows associated with the asset—for example, if it has sold a financial asset subject only to an option to buy it back at fair value at the time of repurchase or has transferred a fully proportionate share of the cash flows from a larger financial asset in an arrangement (such as a loan subparticipation) that meets the three conditions for treating such an arrangement as a transfer that were set out above. Whether an entity has retained control of a transferred asset depends on the transferee's ability to sell the asset. If the transferee has the practical ability to sell the asset in its entirety to an unrelated third party and is able to exercise that ability unilaterally and without needing to impose further restrictions on that transfer, the entity has not retained control. Otherwise, it has.

Transfers That Qualify for Derecognition

If a transfer of a financial asset qualifies for derecognition in its entirety, and the entity retains the right to service the asset for a fee, the entity recognizes either a servicing asset or a servicing liability for the servicing contract, depending on whether the fee to be received is or is not expected to provide adequate compensation for performing the servicing. A servicing liability is recognized at its fair value. A servicing asset is recognized at an amount determined on the basis of an allocation of the carrying amount of the larger (transferred) asset as described below.

If a transferred asset is part of a larger financial asset and the part transferred qualifies for derecognition in its entirety, the previous carrying amount of the larger asset is to be allocated between the part that continues to be recognized and the part that is derecognized based on the relative fair values of those parts at the date of the transfer. For this purpose, a servicing asset is treated as a part that continues to be recognized. Any difference between (a) the carrying amount of the part derecognized and (b) the sum of (i) the consideration received for it (including any new asset obtained less any liability assumed) and (ii) any cumulative gain or loss allocated to it previously recognized directly in equity is to be recognized in profit or loss.

If, as a result of a transfer, a financial asset is derecognized in its entirety but the transfer results in the entity obtaining a new financial asset or assuming a new financial liability or a servicing liability, the new asset, liability, or servicing liability is to be recognized at fair value.

On derecognition of a financial asset in its entirety, the difference between (a) the carrying amount of the part derecognized and (b) the sum of (i) the consideration received for it (including any new asset obtained less any liability assumed) and (ii) any cumulative gain or loss allocated to it previously recognized directly in equity is to be recognized in profit or loss.

Transfers That Do Not Qualify for Derecognition

In the case of a transfer that does not qualify for derecognition because the entity has retained substantially all the risks and rewards of ownership of the transferred asset, the transferred asset must continue to be recognized in its entirety and a financial liability is recognized for the consideration received. Subsequently, the entity recognizes any income on the transferred asset and any expense incurred on the liability. Examples of such transfers are:

- Sale and repurchase transactions where the repurchase price is a fixed price plus a lender's return.
- A securities lending agreement.
- A sale of a financial asset together with a total return swap that transfers the market risk exposure back to the entity.
- A sale of a financial asset together with a "deep-in-the-money" put or call option.
- A sale of short-term receivables in which the entity guarantees to compensate the transferee for likely credit losses.

Continuing Involvement in Transferred Assets

If an entity neither transfers nor retains substantially all of the risks and rewards of ownership of a transferred asset and retains control of the transferred asset, the entity continues to recognize the asset to the extent of its continuing involvement, that is to the extent to which it remains exposed to changes in the value of the transferred asset (see IAS 39, pars. 30–35).

Such involvement may take the form of a guarantee of, or an option on, the transferred asset. When an asset is recognized to the extent of the entity's continuing involvement, an associated liability is also recognized and is measured in such a way that the *net carrying amount* of the transferred asset and the associated liability is one of the following:

- If the transferred asset is measured at amortized cost, the amortized cost of the rights and obligations retained by the entity; or
- If the transferred asset is measured at fair value, the fair value of the rights and obligations retained by the entity when measured on a stand-alone basis.

For the purpose of subsequent measurement, recognized changes in the fair value of the transferred asset and the associated liability are accounted for consistently with each other (see below under "Gains and Losses") and should not be offset.

All Transfers

If a transferred asset continues to be recognized, the asset and any associated liability should not be offset, nor should any income arising from the asset and any expense incurred on the associated liability (see IAS 32, par. 42, under "Offsetting of a Financial Asset and a Financial Liability" below).

If non-cash collateral is provided by the transferor to the transferee, the collateral should be accounted for as follows. If the transferee has the right by contract or market custom to sell or repledge the collateral, the transferor reclassifies the asset separately from other assets (e.g., as a loaned asset, pledged equity instrument, or repurchase receivable). If the transferee sells collateral pledged to it, the transferee recognizes the proceeds from the sale and a liability measured at fair value for its obligation to return the collateral. If the transferor defaults under the terms of the contract and is no longer entitled to redeem the collateral, it derecognizes the collateral, and the transferee recognizes the collateral as its asset initially measured at fair value or, if it has already sold the asset, derecognize its obligation to return the collateral. In the event of no such default, the transferor continues to carry the collateral as its asset and the transferee does not recognize it as an asset.

Illustration of a Transferor's Accounting for a Sale or Securitization When Servicing Is Retained

An entity originates $1,000 of loans that yield 10% interest for their estimated lives of nine years. The entity sells the $1,000 principal plus the right to receive interest income of 8% of another entity for $1,000. The transferor will continue to service the loans, and the contract stipulates that its compensation for performing the servicing is the right to receive half of the interest income not sold (that is, 100 of the 200 basis points). The remaining half of the interest income not sold is considered an interest-only strip receivable. At the date of the transfer, the fair value of the loans, including servicing, is $1,100, of which the fair value of the servicing asset is $40 and the fair value of the interest-only strip receivable is $60. Allocation of the $1,000 carrying amount of the loan is computed as follows:

	Fair Value	Percentage of Total Fair Value	Allocated Carrying Amount
Loans sold	$1,000	91.0%	$910
Servicing asset	40	3.6	36
Interest-only strip receivable	60	5.4	54
Total	$1,100	100.0%	$1,000

The transferor will recognize a gain of $90 on the sale of the loan—the difference between the net proceeds of $1,000 and the allocated carrying amount of $910. Its balance sheet will also report a servicing asset of $36 and an interest-only strip receivable of $54. The servicing asset is an intangible asset subject to the provisions of IAS 38, "Intangible Assets."

Illustration of a Transfer of Receivables Subject to a Guarantee against Default Loss

Company A transfers certain receivables to Company B for a single, fixed cash payment. A is not obligated to make future payments of interest on the cash it has received from B. However, A guarantees B against default loss on the receivables up to a specified amount. Actual losses in excess of the amount guaranteed will be borne by B. As a result of the transaction, A has lost control over the receivables and B has obtained control. B now has the contractual right to receive cash inherent in the receivables, as well as a guarantee from A. Hence, under IAS 39:

1. The receivables are recognized by B on its balance sheet, and are derecognized (removed from its balance sheet) by A.

2. The guarantee is treated as a separate financial instrument, created as a result of the transfer. It is recognized as a financial liability by A, and as a financial asset by B (which, for practical purposes, might include the guarantee with the receivables). Note that this illustration assumes that the fair value of A's guarantee to B can be reliably estimated or measured.

Derecognition of a Financial Liability

A financial liability (or part of a financial liability) should be derecognized when, and only when, it is extinguished by the obligation specified in the contract being discharged or cancelled, or expiring.

An exchange between an existing borrower and a lender of debt instruments with substantially different terms should be accounted for as an extinguishment of the original financial liability and the recognition of a new financial liability. Likewise, a substantial modification of the terms of all or part of an existing financial liability (whether or not attributable to financial difficulties of the debtor) should be accounted for as an extinguishment of the original financial liability and the recognition of a new financial liability.

The difference between (a) the carrying amount of a financial liability (or part of it) extinguished or transferred to another party and (b) the consideration paid, including any non-cash assets transferred or liabilities assumed, should be recognized in profit or loss.

MEASUREMENT

Initial Measurement of Financial Assets and Financial Liabilities

When a financial asset or financial liability is initially recognized, an entity should measure it at its fair value *plus*, in the case of an item *not at FVPL*, transaction costs that are directly attributable to the acquisition or issue of the item.

In the case of settlement date accounting for an asset that is subsequently measured at cost or amortized cost, the asset is initially recognized at its fair value on the *trade date* (IAS 39, pars. 42–43).

OBSERVATION: For the measurement of financial assets and financial liabilities, IFRS 9 will supersede the relevant paragraphs of IAS 39 except that the methods for determining fair value when fair value is required or permitted by the applicable IFRS are provided by IFRS 13 (see Chapter 3).

In the case of initial measurement of financial assets, the requirements of IFRS 9 have similar results to those of IAS 39. Where the fair value at initial recognition differs from the transaction price, if the market for a financial instrument is not active, its fair value is estimated using a valuation technique, as required by IAS 39 (see "No Active Market: Valuation Technique"). However, the best evidence of fair value on initial recognition is normally the transaction price (i.e., fair value of the consideration given or received). If a valuation technique is applied instead, a gain or loss should be recognized after initial recognition only to the extent to which it arises from a factor (including time) that market participants would consider relevant in setting a price (IAS 39, par. AG76A). Thus, there could be a difference between the fair value based on the transaction price at initial recognition and the fair value that would be estimated at that date using the valuation technique. The requirements set out below under "Fair Value Measurement Considerations" apply.

IFRS 9, paragraph B5.1, considers the case in which part of the consideration given is for something other than the financial instrument being acquired, so that the difference provides no reason for not using fair value at initial recognition. IFRS 9, paragraph B5.6, addresses a different issue, indicating seven circumstances in which cost may not be representative of fair value for unquoted equity instruments, in which case fair value must be estimated.

These matters are also dealt with in IFRS 13, pars. 57-60 and B4 (see Chapter 3).

Subsequent Measurement of Financial Assets

For measurement subsequent to initial recognition, IAS 39, paragraph 45, classifies financial assets into the four categories mentioned under "Definitions," namely:

1. Financial assets at fair value through profit or loss (FVPL).
2. Held-to-maturity (HTM) investments.
3. Loans and receivables, and
4. Available-for-sale (AFS) financial assets.

The general requirement (IAS 39, par. 46) is that, after initial recognition, an entity should measure financial assets, including derivatives, at their fair value without any deduction for transaction costs. Assets in categories 2 and 3 are exempt from this general requirement and are instead required to be measured at cost or amortized cost, as indicated below.

Investments in equity instruments without a quoted market price in an active market and whose fair value cannot be reliably measured, and derivatives that are linked to and must be settled by delivery of such equity instruments, are to be measured at cost.

Financial assets that are designated as hedged items are subject to measurement under the hedge accounting requirements described under "Hedge Accounting" below.

All financial assets except those measured at FVPL are subject to review for impairment as described below under "Impairment and Uncollectibility of Financial Assets."

Subsequent Measurement of Financial Liabilities

After initial recognition, all financial liabilities are measured at amortized cost, except for:

- Financial liabilities at FVPL. These (including derivative liabilities) are measured at fair value, except for derivative liabilities that are linked to and must be settled by delivery of equity instruments without a quoted market price in an active market and whose fair value cannot be reliably measured, which are to be measured at cost.

- Financial liabilities that arise when a transfer of a financial asset does not qualify for derecognition or is accounted for using the continuing involvement approach. The latter are measured in such a way that measurement of the net carrying amount of the transferred asset and the associated liability follows the measurement method applied to the transferred asset (amortized cost or fair value).

- Financial guarantee contracts, as defined in IAS 39, paragraph 9. After initial recognition, the issuer of such a contract shall (unless either of the two previous points applies) measure it at the higher of (a) the amount determined in accordance with IAS 37, "Provisions, Contingent Liabilities, and Contingent Assets" (see Chapter 29), and (b) the amount initially recognized less, when appropriate, cumulative amortization.

OBSERVATION: The exceptions should also include forms of share capital in which the issuer does not have an unconditional right to avoid delivering cash or another financial asset to settle a contractual obligation, for example, puttable instruments and share capital in open-ended investment companies that are classified as liabilities, as required by IAS 32 (see below). Such items cannot be measured at amortized cost, but some other measurement basis reflecting the underlying net asset value would be appropriate.

Financial liabilities that are designated as hedged items are subject to measurement under the hedge accounting requirements described under "Hedge Accounting" below.

Illustration of Valuation at Amortized Cost

On January 1, 2004, an entity acquires $100,000 par value 9% bonds of Paper Co. priced to yield 10%, with a maturity date of 12/31/2008. The value of the bonds on acquisition is:

Present value of interest payments 9% of $100,000 × annuity factor for $1 at 10% p.a. for 5 years (= 3.79079)	$ 34,117
Present value of maturity value $100,000 × present value factor for $1 in 5 years at 10% p.a. (= 0.62092)	62,092
Market value	$ 96,209
Discount from par value	3,791
Par value	$100,000

In the present example, the discount from par value reflects the fact that the coupon rate is 9% p.a. whereas the market interest rate on such an instrument on the acquisition date was 10% p.a. and the bond was priced accordingly.

AC using the effective interest method is as shown in column E below. The effect of this method is to amortize any discount from, or premium over, par value over the periods to maturity, and to recognize as periodic interest income (column A) the market rate (i.e., the periodic yield rate to maturity) at acquisition on the market value at acquisition. The periodic difference between the cash received, based on the coupon rate of 9%, and the interest income (effective yield) recognized, constitutes the periodic amortization of the discount.

Year	(A) Interest Income (E*×10%) $	(B) Cash Received $	(C) Discount Amortization (A — B) $	(D) Remaining Discount (D* — C) $	(E) Carrying Amount $
01/01/04				3,791	96,209
12/31/04	9,621	9,000	621	3,170	96,830
12/31/05	9,683	9,000	683	2,487	97,513
12/31/06	9,951	9,000	751	1,736	98,264
12/31/07	9,826	9,000	826	910	99,090
12/31/08	9,910	9,000	910	—	100,000

Note: D* and E* are the previous year's values in columns D and E, respectively.

Fair Value Measurement Considerations

These are dealt with in IAS 39, paragraphs 48–49 and AG69–AG82. Underlying the definition of *fair value* is a presumption that the entity is a going concern without any intention or need to liquidate, to curtail materially the scale of its operations, or to undertake a transaction on adverse terms. However, fair value reflects the credit quality of the instrument.

OBSERVATION: Fair value measurement considerations are now covered by IFRS 13 (issued in May 2011 for application in 2013 with earlier application permitted). IFRS 13 amends the relevant paragraphs of IAS 39, IFRS 7, IFRS 9, and the applicable IFRICs.

Active Market: Quoted Price

If a financial instrument is quoted in an active market, the published price quotations are the best evidence of fair value; and when they exist, they are used to measure the financial asset or financial liability.

The appropriate market price for an asset held or a liability to be issued is usually the current bid price and, for an asset to be acquired or a liability held, the current asking (offer) price. When current prices are unavailable, the price of the most recent transaction provides evidence of fair value, subject to adjustments for changes in conditions such as a change in the risk-free rate.

No Active Market: Valuation Technique

The objective of using a valuation technique is to establish what the transaction price would have been on the measurement date in an arm's-length exchange motivated by normal business considerations (IAS 39, par. AG75). The valuation technique should make maximum use of market inputs and minimum use of entity-specific inputs.

Valuation techniques include using recent arm's-length transactions between knowledgeable, willing parties, if available; reference to the current value of another instrument that is substantially the same; discounted cash flow (DCF) analysis; and option pricing models.

In applying DCF analysis, the discount rates used are those equal to the prevailing rates of return for financial instruments that have substantially the same characteristics, including credit quality, remaining term to repricing or maturity, and currency of payments.

For equity instruments with no active markets, and derivatives linked to and needing to be settled by delivery of such instruments, the fair value is reliably measurable if the variability in the range of reasonable fair value estimates is not significant or if the probabilities of the various estimates within the range can be reasonably assessed and used in estimating fair value.

Inputs to Valuation Techniques

The following market inputs are likely to be relevant, depending on the characteristics of the instrument (IAS 39, par. AG82):

- The risk-free interest rate or rates (from the yield curve).
- Credit risk.
- Foreign currency exchange rates.
- Commodity prices.

- Equity prices.

- Volatility.

- Prepayment risk and surrender risk.

- Servicing costs for a financial asset or liability.

The fair value of a financial liability with a demand feature (such as demand deposit) cannot be less than the amount payable on demand, discounted from the first date on which payment of the amount could be required.

OBSERVATION: IFRS 13 brings in substantial modifications to these fair value measurement considerations. Some of these have been reflected in requirements that appear in the 2010 version of IFRS 7. In particular, IFRS 13 now incorporates the "Fair Value Hierarchy" originally proposed in ED/2009/5, "Fair Value Measurements," and subsequently included in IFRS 7, as covered in this chapter (see "Other Disclosures" (IFRS 7, pars. 21–30)).

Reclassifications

IAS 39, paragraphs 50–54 (as amended in October 2008), states a number of restrictions and other requirements regarding reclassification:

- A derivative instrument may not be reclassified into or out of the FVPL category while it is held or issued.

- A financial instrument may not be reclassified out of the FVPL category if upon initial recognition it was designated as at FVPL.

- If a financial asset is no longer held for the purpose of selling or repurchasing it in the near future (even if it may originally have been acquired principally for this purpose), it may be reclassified out of the FVPL category if the requirements stated below are met.

The following changes in circumstances are not considered as reclassifications for this purpose:

— A derivative that was previously a designated and effective hedging instrument in a cash flow hedge or net investment hedge no longer qualifies as such.

— A derivative becomes a designated and effective hedging instrument in a cash flow hedge or net investment hedge.

— Financial assets are reclassified when an insurance company changes its accounting policies in accordance with IFRS 4, paragraph 45.

- If a financial asset is reclassified out of the FVPL category, it is reclassified at its fair value on the date of reclassification, which becomes its new amortized cost. Any gain or loss already recognized in profit or loss is not reversed. If the financial asset in question would have met the definition of loans and receivables had it not been required to be classified as HFT on initial recognition, it may be classified out of the FVPL category provided the entity holding it has the intention and ability to hold it for the foreseeable future or until maturity. If this condition does not apply, such a reclassification should be made only in rare circumstances.

- A financial asset classified as AFS that would have met the definition of loans and receivables had it not been designated as AFS may be reclassified out of the AFS category to the loans and receivables category provided the entity holding it has the intention and ability to hold it for the foreseeable future or until maturity.

- If a financial asset is reclassified out of the FVPL category or the AFS category in accordance with the above, it is reclassified at its fair value on the date of reclassification, which becomes its new amortized cost. In the case of reclassification out of the HFT category, any gain or loss on the asset already recognized in profit or loss is not reversed. In the case of reclassification out of the AFS category, any previous gain or loss on the asset that has been recognized in other comprehensive income is reclassified from equity to profit and loss as a reclassification adjustment.

- If it is no longer appropriate to classify an investment as HTM (because of a change in intention or ability), it should be reclassified as AFS and remeasured at fair value, and the resultant remeasurement gain or loss should be recognized in other comprehensive income.

- For items that are required to be measured at fair value if a reliable measure of fair value is available; if a reliable measure becomes available for an item for which it was previously unavailable, the item is remeasured at fair value and the resultant remeasurement gain or loss recognized as appropriate for its category (i.e., through profit and loss for FVPL or in comprehensive income for AFS), except in the case of impairment losses and foreign exchange gains and losses (see under "Gains and Losses" below).

- If for any acceptable reason it becomes appropriate to carry a financial asset or financial liability at amortized cost instead of at fair value, its fair value carrying amount on the relevant date is treated as its new amortized cost, as applicable. Any previous gain or loss on that item that has been recognized in comprehensive income is accounted for as follows:

  — For a financial asset with a fixed maturity, the gain or loss is to be amortized over the remaining life of the HTM investment using the effective interest method. Any difference between the "new" amortized cost and the maturity amount should be similarly amortized. If the asset is subsequently impaired, any cumulative gain or loss that has been recognized in comprehensive income (i.e., if it was previously classified as AFS) is recognized in profit or loss.

  — For a financial asset with no fixed maturity, the gain or loss remains in equity until the asset is sold, at which time it is recognized in profit or loss. If the asset is subsequently impaired, any gain or loss that has been recognized in other comprehensive income is recognized in profit or loss.

> **OBSERVATION:** Because IFRS 9 reduces the number of financial asset categories to two, which depend on the business model applied for managing them, it does not contain such a lengthy list of provisions on reclassification (see below).

Gains and Losses

A gain or loss arising from a change in the fair value of a financial asset or liability *that is not part of a hedging relationship* (see below) is to be recognized as follows (IAS 39, pars. 55–57 and AG83):

- If the financial asset or liability is classified as at FVPL, the gain or loss is recognized in profit or loss

- If the financial asset or liability is classified as AFS, the gain or loss is recognized in other comprehensive income, except for:

  — impairment losses (see below);

  — foreign exchange gains and losses, which, unless they are designated as a hedging instrument in a cash flow hedge or a hedge of a net investment, are recognized in profit and loss in accordance with IAS 21, "The Effects of Changes in Foreign Exchange Rates" (see Chapter 18).

until the financial asset is derecognized, at which time the cumulative amount previously recognized in other comprehensive income is reclassified from equity to profit or loss. However, interest calculated using the effective interest method is recognized in profit or loss in accordance with IAS 18, "Revenue Recognition," and dividends on AFS equity instruments are recognized in profit or loss when the entity's right to receive payment is established.

For financial assets and financial liabilities carried at amortized cost, a gain or loss is recognized in profit or loss when the item is derecognized or impaired, through the amortization process, except if the item is hedged (see "Hedging").

Impairment and Uncollectibility of Financial Assets

For financial assets carried at amortized cost (i.e., HTM assets and loans and receivables), an asset is impaired if its carrying value is in excess of its estimated recoverable amount. At each balance sheet date, an entity should assess whether there is any *objective evidence* of the impairment of any of its financial assets or groups of such assets in these categories as a result of one or more events that occurred after the initial recognition of the asset (a loss event) and that this loss event (or events) has an impact on the estimated future cash flows of the financial asset or group of assets that can be reliably estimated. Losses expected as a result of future events, no matter how likely, are not recognized. If any such evidence exists, the relevant recoverable amount should be estimated, and any resultant impairment loss should be recognized in accordance with the requirements for the relevant category of asset (IAS 39, pars. 58–59).

IAS 39, paragraphs 59–62, enumerates various types of objective evidence that may indicate the possible impairment of a financial asset or group of assets. These include (a) significant financial difficulty, or a high probability of bankruptcy or other financial reorganization, of the issuer or obligor (but not, of itself, the downgrading of the issuer's or obligor's credit rating); (b) default or delinquency in payments, or other breach of contract; (c) a concession granted by the lender to the borrower, which the lender would not otherwise consider, for reasons relating to the borrower's financial difficulties; (d) previous recognition of an impairment loss on the asset in a prior period; (e) disappearance of an active market for the asset owing to financial difficulties (but not just because the asset is a security that has ceased to be publicly traded); and (f) observable data indicating that there is a measureable decrease in the estimated future cash flows from a group of financial assets since the initial recognition of those assets, although the decrease cannot yet be identified with the individual assets in the group.

Financial Assets Carried at Amortized Cost

The amount of the impairment loss is the difference between the asset's carrying amount and the present value of the expected future cash flows from the asset (excluding future credit losses that have not been incurred) discounted at its original effective interest rate as computed at initial recognition. The current interest rate is not used, as this would equate to measurement at fair value of an asset carried at amortized cost. (Discounting of cash flows from short-term receivables is normally not practiced because of its immaterial effect.)

The carrying amount of the asset should be reduced to its estimated recoverable amount either by direct deduction or through the use of an allowance (contra-asset) account. The amount of the loss should be recognized in profit or loss for the period. Impairment and uncollectibility are measured and recognized individually for financial assets that are individually significant, and they may be measured and recognized on a portfolio basis for a group of similar financial assets *that are not individually identified as impaired* (IAS 39, pars. 63–65).

For loans, receivables, or HTM investments with a variable or floating interest rate, the discount rate for estimating recoverable amount is the current effective interest rate or rates as determined under the contract. This will effectively result in an estimate of fair value, and the holder may use the observable market price of the instrument instead. If an asset is collateralized and foreclosure is probable, then the holder should measure impairment on the basis of the fair value of the collateral.

An impairment or bad debt loss may be partly or entirely made good in a subsequent period. Provided the reversal can be objectively related to an event occurring after the write-down (which provides evidence that the once probable loss will not occur or will be significantly smaller), the write-down of the financial asset should be reversed. This should be effected either by directly adjusting the carrying amount of the asset on the date of the reversal if the impairment had not been or by adjusting the allowance (contra-asset) account. The reversal should not result in a carrying amount in excess of what the amortized cost would have been at the date of the reversal, had the impairment not been recognized. The amount of the reversal should be recognized in net profit or loss for the period (IAS 39, par. 65).

OBSERVATION: The model used in IAS 39 for recognition and measurement of impairment losses on assets carried at amortized cost is an "incurred loss" model. This model does not recognize expected losses; the rationale is that expectations of losses are subjective and can be manipulated to allow excessive loss provisions to be set aside (and subsequently released) as a form of "hidden reserve" with resultant manipulation of reported profits. This incurred loss model has been strongly criticized in the wake of the 2007-2009 financial crisis on the basis that it fails to give sufficient timely recognition to asset impairment. The IASB has been under pressure from the report of the G20 and the Financial Stability Forum (FSF), now the Financial Stability Board (FSB), to adopt a "counter-cyclical" or "through-the-cycle" (TTC) approach to provisions for impairments of financial assets, in which default probabilities are estimated though the economic cycle, rather than a "point-in-time" (PiT) approach in which the probability of impairment is estimated at a point in time and, therefore, is pro-cyclical because it is influenced by the economic outlook. The TTC approaches take a statistical or insurance view of expected credit losses on a portfolio of financial assets through the economic cycle (or relevant portion of the cycle), rather than a judgmental view at a point in time. The IASB and FASB have taken the view that the TTC approaches rely excessively on historical events rather than using statistical information to forecast credit losses. (It is not clear every TTC approach necessarily has this defect.)

Subsequently, the IASB (and the FASB) moved to a form of "expected loss" model. In November 2009, the IASB issued ED/2009/12, "Financial Instruments: Amortized Cost and Impairment," followed by a supplemental exposure draft, "Financial Instruments: Impairment," in March 2011. In the "Basis to Conclusions" in ED/2009/12 (BC 22-24), the IASB stated that for the reason given above it was not prepared to adopt a TTC approach for its expected loss model. The main difference from the existing model is in the interest rate used to determine amortized cost. Under the incurred loss model, the original market interest rate is used and is not adjusted to reflect subsequent changes in estimates of expected credit losses (probabilities of default multiplied by expected losses given default). In the IASB's expected loss model, amortized cost is the present value calculated using the following inputs: (a) the expected cash flows over the remaining life of the financial instrument and (b) the effective interest rate as the discount rate. The effective interest rate reflects how the contract sets the interest payments for the financial instrument. It is the effective interest rate as at initial recognition to the extent that it is not contractually reset to current conditions; this is intended to maintain a (conceptually desirable) link between the pricing of financial assets and expected credit losses.

However, in its supplemental exposure draft of December 2011, the IASB (jointly with the FASB) set out a modified model with two sub-models under which substantially the above IASB approach would be adopted for financial assets in a "good book," while for financial assets placed in a "bad book" because the entity's credit management objective has changed from receiving regular contractual payments to recovery of the financial asset, in accordance with the FASB's approach, the entire amount of expected credit losses in the foreseeable future is to be recognized in an allowance (contra-asset) account. Both of these sub-models are PiT, and the proposed model may thus be criticized for being "pro-cyclical."

Financial Assets Carried at Cost

In the case of a unquoted equity instrument that is not carried at fair value because this cannot be reliably measure (or a derivative asset that is linked to it and must be settled by delivery of it), its carrying amount should be reviewed for impairment at each balance sheet date on the basis of an analysis of expected net cash inflows. In such a case, the amount of any impairment loss is the difference between the carrying amount and the recoverable amount, which for such assets is equal to the present value of the expected future cash flows discounted at the current market rate of return for a similar instrument (IAS 39, par. 66).

Available-for-Sale Financial Assets

In case of impairment loss, any cumulative net loss from remeasurement at fair value that has previously been recognized in other comprehensive income should be removed from equity and recognized in profit or loss for the period, even though the asset has not been derecognized. The amount of the loss that should be treated as just described is the excess of the asset's original acquisition cost (net of any principal repayment or amortization) over the asset's current fair value) less any impairment loss on that asset already recognized in profit or loss. The recoverable amount of a debt instrument remeasured to fair value is the present value of expected future cash flows from the asset discounted at the current market rate of interest for a similar asset (IAS 39, pars. 67–69).

Subsequently, there may be objective evidence that the fair value of a debt instrument classified as AFS has increased, making good the impairment loss entirely or in part. In such a case, the impairment write-down should be reversed (entirely or in part), and the amount of the reversal should be recognized in profit or loss for the period (IAS 39, par. 70).

HEDGING

IAS 39 devotes paragraphs 71–102 and AG94–132 to the implications of hedging in accounting for financial instruments. First, the criteria for identifying items as hedging instruments and hedged items within a hedging relationship are given; then the provisions for hedge accounting, to be applied to items so identified are set out. Hedging relationships are analyzed for accounting purposes into three categories: (a) fair value hedges, where the hedged exposure is to changes in fair value; (b) cash flow hedges, where the hedged exposure is to variability in cash flows; and (c) hedges of a net investment in a foreign operation.

OBSERVATION: In December 2010, the IASB issued an exposure draft, "Hedge Accounting", which is intended to become Chapter 6 of IFRS 9. The ED proposes significant changes to the general hedge accounting requirements in IAS 39 in order: (a) to align hedge accounting more closely with hedging as actually practiced as part of risk management; and (b) to establish a more objective-based and principle-based approach (as opposed to the somewhat rule-based approach of IAS 39). At the time of this writing, there is some doubt as to whether the exposure draft will be adopted for inclusion into IFRS 9. Comments from respondents to the exposure draft, notably EFRAG, take the view that the approach in the exposure draft is still too restrictive (in terms of at least the first of its stated objectives) in regard to eligibility of items as hedging instruments or as hedged items.

Hedging Instruments

Hedging involves a proportionate income offset between changes in the fair value of, or the cash flows attributable to, the hedging instrument and the hedged item. For hedge accounting purposes, this proportionate income offset constitutes the essence of the hedging relationship. In the case of cash flow hedges, in addition to its offsetting effect with regard to variations in cash flows from or to the hedged item, there may be changes in the fair value of the hedging instrument.

Qualifying Instruments

Under IASB GAAP, any derivative may be designated as a hedging instrument for hedge accounting purposes, with the following exception: a *written option* is a hedging instrument *only* when designated as an offset to a purchased option, including an embedded one (such as a written option used to hedge callable debt). The reason for the exception is that, otherwise, a written option may entail a loss to the writer significantly greater than the potential gain on the item that it is supposed to hedge. Non-derivative instruments may not be designated as hedging instruments, except in hedges of foreign currency risk.

OBSERVATION: The exclusion of non-derivatives from designation as hedging instruments except in hedges of foreign currency risk in IAS 39 (as in U.S. GAAP) has the apparently illogical effect that in the case of non-derivative asset and liability positions that offset each other, neither can be designated as a hedge of the other for hedge accounting purposes, and the net position cannot be designated as a hedged item. This was a major reason for objections to IAS 39 by European banks.

The December 2010 exposure draft, "Hedge Accounting," would allow non-derivative financial assets and financial liabilities *measured at FVPL in their entirety* to be designated as hedging items. EFRAG, in its response to the exposure draft, suggests that the exclusion of other items, such as equity instruments designated as at fair value through other comprehensive income (FVOCI) and financial instruments at amortized cost, should be reconsidered, especially as according to IFRS 9 (par. 4.1.5) the option to designate as at FVPL a financial asset *which meets the criteria for measurement at amortized cost* is irrevocable.

Only instruments that involve a party external to the reporting entity can be designated as hedging instruments (with the exception noted below). Individual entities within a consolidated group may enter into hedging transactions with one another, but any such intra-group transactions are eliminated on consolidation and do not qualify for hedge accounting in the consolidated financial statements. As an exception, the foreign currency risk of an intra-group monetary item (e.g., a payable/receivable between two subsidiaries) may qualify as a hedged item in the consolidated financial statements if it results in an exposure to foreign exchange rate gains or losses that are not fully eliminated on consolidation in accordance with IAS 21 (see Chapter 18)—that is, they have different functional currencies.

The foreign currency risk of a *highly probable* forecast intra-group transaction may qualify as a hedged item in consolidated financial statements provided that the transaction is denominated in a currency other than the functional currency of the entity entering into that transaction and the foreign currency risk will affect consolidated profit or loss.

→ **PRACTICE POINTER:** However, a parent company in country A, for example, can hedge a foreign currency exposure of a subsidiary in country B to a payable in the currency of a supplier in country C, and that hedge can qualify for hedge accounting in the consolidated financial statements. IAS 39 does not require that the operating unit that is exposed to the risk being hedged be a party to the hedging instrument. Also, an intra-group monetary item that is eliminated on consolidation can be designated as the hedged item in a foreign currency fair value hedge or cash flow hedge at the consolidated level, but only if the item results in an exposure to exchange differences that cannot be eliminated on consolidation in accordance with IAS 21 (i.e., when the two group entities have different functional currencies).

A non-derivative financial asset or liability may be designated as a hedging instrument for hedge accounting purposes only when used to hedge foreign currency risk. This is because, unlike derivatives, under IASB GAAP non-derivatives are not systematically measured at fair value with resultant remeasurement gains and losses being systematically recognized in profit or loss (unless they are designated as at FVPL on initial recognition). Therefore, the designation of non-derivatives as hedging instruments, except in limited circumstances, would lead to inconsistencies in measurement. As an example of such limited circumstances, HTM investments carried at amortized cost may be effective hedging instruments against foreign currency exchange rate risk.

An entity's own equity securities are not financial assets or financial liabilities of the entity and thus cannot be designated as hedging instruments.

An investment in an unquoted equity instrument that is not carried at fair value because this cannot be reliably measured, or a derivative linked to and needing to be settled by delivery of such an instrument cannot be designated as a hedging instrument.

Designation of Hedging Instruments

In principle, a hedging relationship must be designated by an entity for a hedging instrument in its entirety, with the following exceptions: separating the intrinsic value and time value of an option contract and designating as the hedging instrument only the change in its intrinsic value, and separating the interest element and the spot price of a forward contract.

A proportion of the entire hedging instrument (e.g., 50% of the notional amount) may be designated as the hedging instrument in a hedging relationship. However, a hedging relationship may not be designated for only a portion of the time period during which a hedging instrument remains outstanding.

A single hedging instrument may be designated as a hedge of more than one type of risk provided the following conditions are satisfied:

- The risks hedged can be identified clearly.
- The effectiveness of the hedge can be demonstrated.
- It is possible to ensure that there is specific designation of the hedging instrument and different risk positions.

Two or more derivatives or proportions of them (or in the case of a hedge of currency risk, non-derivatives or proportions of them or a combination of derivatives and non-derivatives or proportions of them) may be jointly designated as the hedging instrument. However, an interest rate collar or other derivative that combines a written option and a purchased option does not qualify as a hedging instrument if it is in effect a net written option for which a net premium is received.

Hedged Items

The last-minute amendments to the revised IAS 39 made in March 2004 affected the treatment of portfolio hedges of interest rate risk and, more generally, the designation of financial items as hedged items.

Qualifying Items

A hedged item may be any of the following:

- A recognized asset or liability.
- In the case of a portfolio hedge of interest rate risk only, a portion of the portfolio consisting of items that share the risk being hedged.
- A firm commitment not recognized in the balance sheet.
- An uncommitted but highly probable future (forecast) transaction.
- A net investment in a foreign operation.

These may be considered as hedged either singly or as a group of like items with similar risk characteristics.

In July 2008, the IASB issued amendments to IAS 39 clarifying the eligibility for designation in a hedging relationship of certain separately identifiable risks arising from a hedged item, including one-sided risks.

Unlike loans and receivables, HTM investments cannot be hedged with respect to interest rate risk or prepayment risk, because their designation as HTM entails a requirement to hold them until maturity without regard to changes in their fair values or cash flows attributable to changes in interest rates. However, HTM investments can be hedged items with respect to other risks, namely credit risk and foreign currency exchange rate risk.

→ **PRACTICE POINTER:** If an entity forecasts that it will purchase a financial asset that will be classified as held to maturity when it is acquired, enters into a derivative contract with the intent to lock in the current interest rate, and designates the derivative as a hedge of the forecasted purchase of the financial asset, then the hedging relationship can qualify for hedge accounting, because although the financial asset will be classified as held-to-maturity, it is not yet so classified.

Hedge accounting cannot be applied to transactions between entities or segments in the same group in the consolidated financial statements of the group, with the following exception: the foreign currency risk of an intra-group monetary item may qualify as a hedged item if it results in an exposure to foreign exchange rate gains or losses that are not fully eliminated on consolidation under IAS 21, "The Effects of Changes in Foreign Exchange Rates" (see Chapter 18), because the two entities in the group have different functional currencies.

Designation of Financial Items as Hedged Items

A hedged item that is a financial asset or financial liability may be a hedged item with respect to the risks associated with only a portion of its cash flows or fair value, provided the effectiveness of a partial hedge can be measured.

In a fair value hedge of the interest rate exposure of a portfolio of financial assets or liabilities (and only in such a hedge), the hedged portion may be designated in terms of an amount of money (i.e., a currency) rather than as individual asset or liability items. However, designation of a *net amount* of assets less liabilities (or vice versa) is not permitted. The entity may hedge only a portion of the interest rate risk of this designated amount, such as, for example, in the case of a portfolio containing prepayable assets, the change in fair value attributable to changes in the hedged interest rate on expected, rather than contractual, repricing dates. However, hedge effectiveness may be affected if such a portfolio is hedged with a non-prepayable derivative and the prepayment dates are revised or are different from those expected.

Designation of Non-Financial Items as Hedged Items

In contrast, a hedged non-financial asset or non-financial liability should be designated as a hedged item either (a) for foreign currency risks or (b) in its entirety for all risks. This is because changes in the price of a component of a non-financial asset generally do not have a predictable and separately measurable effect on the price of the item itself, unlike (for example) the effect of a change in market interest rates on the price of a bond.

Designation of Groups of Items as Hedged Items

If similar assets or liabilities are aggregated and hedged as a group, the individual assets or liabilities in the group will share in the designated risk exposure. Any change in fair value of an individual item in the group that is attributable to the hedged risk will be expected to be approximately proportional to the overall change in fair value of the group attributable to the hedged risk of the group.

→ **PRACTICE POINTER:** If an entity acquires a portfolio of shares to replicate a stock index and also a put option on the index to hedge against fair value losses on the portfolio, the put may not be designated as a hedging instrument in a hedge of the portfolio. This is because the changes in the individual fair values of the shares in the portfolio cannot be expected to be approximately proportional to the overall change in fair value of the portfolio.

A firm commitment to acquire a business in a business combination cannot be a hedged item (except with respect to exchange risk, if applicable), since no other risks can be specifically identified and measured.

OBSERVATION: The exposure draft, "Hedge Accounting," allows more flexibility in designating hedged items. Thus, the following may be designated as hedged items: (a) "synthetic exposures," that is, aggregated exposures that are combinations of a non-derivative instrument and a derivative; (b) changes in the cash flows or the fair value of an item attributable to a specific risk component in a hedging relationship, provided the risk component is separately identifiable and measurable; and (c) a "layer" component of the nominal amount of an item (except for contracts with a pre-payment option). Hence, *risk components of non-financial items* may be designated as hedged items.

Hedge Accounting

By virtue of hedge accounting, there is symmetrical recognition of the offsetting effects on net profit or loss of changes in the fair values of the hedging instrument and the related hedged item within a hedging relationship. Hedging relationships are of three types:

1. A *fair value hedge* is a hedge of the exposure to changes in the fair value of a recognized asset or liability, or of an identified portion of such an asset or liability, that is attributable to a particular risk and will affect profit or loss.

2. A *cash flow hedge* is a hedge of the exposure to variability in cash flows that (a) is attributable to a particular risk associated with (i) a recognized asset or liability, such as interest payments on variable rate debt, or (ii) a forecasted transaction, such as an anticipated purchase or sale; and (b) could affect profit or loss.

3. A *hedge of a net investment in a foreign operation* is as defined in IAS 21, "The Effects of Changes in Foreign Exchange Rates" (see Chapter 18). Under IAS 21, all foreign exchange differences that result from translat-

ing the financial statements of a foreign entity are recognized directly in equity until disposal of the net investment.

A hedge of the foreign currency risk of a firm commitment may be accounted for either as a fair value hedge or as a cash flow hedge.

A hedging relationship qualifies for hedge accounting only if all of the following conditions are met (IAS 39, par. 88):

1. The hedging relationship and the entity's risk management objective and strategy in undertaking the hedge should be formally documented from the inception of the hedge, which must be formally designated, providing identification of the hedging instrument and the related hedged item or transaction, the nature of the hedged risk, and the manner in which the effectiveness of the hedging instrument's effectiveness will be assessed.

2. The hedge is expected to be "highly effective" (see "Assessing Hedge Effectiveness") in a manner consistent with the risk management strategy documented as required in item 1, above.

3. For cash flow hedges, the forecast transaction that is hedged must be *highly probable* and must present exposure to variations in cash flows that could ultimately affect profit or loss.

4. The effectiveness of the hedge can be reliably measured, that is, the fair value or cash flows of the hedged item that are attributable to the hedged risk and the fair value of the hedging instrument can be reliably measured.

5. The hedge is assessed on an ongoing basis and determined actually to have been highly effective throughout the financial reporting periods for which it was designated.

Assessing Hedge Effectiveness

A hedge is considered as "highly effective" only if both of the following conditions are satisfied:

1. At its inception and subsequently, the hedge is expected to be highly effective in achieving offsetting changes in the fair value or cash flows attributable to the hedged risk during the period for which the hedge is designated.

2. The actual results of the hedge are within a range of 80-125%, using the ratio of the gain/loss on the hedge and the loss/gain on the hedged item.

Further detailed requirements for *fair value hedge accounting for portfolio hedges of interest rate risk* are set out in IAS 39, paragraphs AG114–AG132.

Fair Value Hedges

If a fair value hedge meets the five conditions set out above during the period, it is accounted for as follows:

- The gain or loss from remeasuring the hedging instrument at fair value (for a derivative hedging instrument) or the foreign currency component of its carrying amount measured in accordance with IAS 21 (for a non-derivative hedging instrument) is recognized in profit or loss.

- The gain or loss on the hedged item attributable to the hedged risk adjusts the carrying amount of the hedged item and is recognized in profit and loss. This applies if the hedged item is otherwise measured at cost.

In the case of a portfolio hedge of interest rate risk, the requirements set out in IAS 39, paragraphs AG114–AG132, also apply.

In the case of a fair value hedge of the *interest rate exposure* of a portion of a portfolio of financial assets or liabilities (and only in that case), the requirement above may be met by presenting the gain or loss attributable to the hedged item in a separate line item within assets or liabilities, as appropriate, for those repricing time periods for which the hedged item is an asset or a liability. The separate line item is to be presented next to financial assets or financial liabilities, as appropriate, and removed from the balance sheet as and when the assets or liabilities to which they relate are derecognized.

Any adjustment, arising from the above, to the carrying amount of a hedged item for which the effective interest method is used (or, in the case of a portfolio hedge of interest rate risk, to the separate line item just described), should be amortized to profit or loss fully by the maturity of the hedged item (or, in the case of a portfolio hedge of interest rate risk, by the expiry of the relevant repricing time period).

If a firm commitment that is not recognized is designated as a hedged item, the subsequent cumulative change in its fair value that is attributable to the hedged risk is recognized as an asset or liability with a corresponding gain or loss recognized in profit or loss, together with the changes in the fair value of the hedging instrument. In the case of a firm commitment to acquire an asset or assume a liability that is a hedged item in a fair value hedge, the initial amount of the asset or liability that results from meeting the commitment is adjusted to include the cumulative change in the fair value of the firm commitment attributable to the hedged risk that was recognized in the balance sheet.

If only particular risks attributable to a hedged item are hedged, recognized changes in the fair value of the hedged item unrelated to the hedged risk are recognized as set out above under "Gains and Losses."

An entity must discontinue prospectively the hedge accounting specified above if:

- The hedging instrument expires or is sold, terminated, or exercised (for the purpose, this replacement or rollover of a hedging instrument into another hedging instrument is not an expiration or termination if it is part of the entity's documented hedging strategy);

- The hedge no longer meets the hedge accounting criteria set out above; or

- The entity revokes the designation

Illustration of a Fair Value Hedge. The following example illustrates hedge accounting for a hedge of exposure to changes in the fair value of an investment in fixed rate debt from changes in market interest rates (market risk), by the holder of the investment. The investor classifies such investments as AFS.

On January 1, 2006, an investor purchases a fixed interest debt security for $100. At December 31, 2006, its current fair value is $110. The carrying amount in the balance sheet is increased to $110, and the remeasurement gain of $10 is recognized in other comprehensive income (OCI).

To protect the value of $110, the holder enters into a hedge by acquiring a derivative. By December 31, 2007, the fair value of the derivative has increased by $5, while the fair value of the hedged debt security has declined by the same amount to $105. Note that the illustrative joined entries below do not include that recording the acquisition of the derivative asset.

Investor's Journal Entries for the Year 2006

1/1		
Investment in debt security	$100	
Cash		$100
12/31		
Investment in debt security	$ 10	
Equity (increase in fair value)		$ 10

Investor's Journal for the Year 2007

12/31		
Derivative asset	$ 5	
Gain included in net profit/loss		$ 5
Loss included in net profit/loss	$ 5	
Investment in debt security		$ 5

The entries for the year 2007 illustrate the effect of hedge accounting: (a) the remeasurement gain and loss are included in net profit/loss (this was not the case for the unhedged remeasurement gain of $10 in 2006, which was recognized in OCI); (b) both the fair value remeasurement gain on the hedging instrument and the fair value remeasurement loss on the hedged asset are included in net profit/loss. The fair value remeasurement loss is exactly offset by the fair value remeasurement gain.

At December 31, 2007, the carrying amount of the investment in the debt security is $105, and the carrying amount of the derivative is $5.

The gain of $10 recognized directly in equity at December 31, 2006, is reported as part of equity until the asset is disposed of but is amortized to profit and loss over the remaining term to maturity of the asset, as from the date on which the asset ceases to be hedged, if not earlier.

Cash Flow Hedges

If a cash flow hedge is, during a financial reporting period, a hedging relationship that meets the conditions for hedge accounting set out above, it should be accounted for as follows:

- That portion of the gain or loss on the hedging instrument that is determined to be an effective hedge is recognized directly in OCI.

- Any ineffective portion of the gain or loss on the hedging instrument is recognized in profit or loss.

- The separate component of equity associated with the hedged item is adjusted to the lesser of:

  — The cumulative gain or loss on the hedging instrument from the inception of the hedge.

  — The cumulative change in fair value (present value) of the expected future cash flows on the hedged item from the inception of the hedge.

- Any remaining gain or loss on the hedging instrument or designated component of it that is not an effective hedge is recognized in profit or loss.

- If an entity's documented risk management strategy for a particular hedging relationship excludes from the assessment of hedge effectiveness a specific component of the gain or loss or related cash flows on the hedging instrument, that excluded component is recognized as a gain or loss on a financial asset or liability that is not part of a hedging relationship as set out under "Gains and Losses".

A hedged firm commitment or forecasted transaction may result in the recognition of a financial asset or liability. In that case, any associated gains or losses on the hedging instrument that had been recognized directly in equity as indicated above should be reclassified into profit or loss in the same period or periods during which the asset acquired or liability assumed affects profit or loss. However, if an entity 'expects that all or a portion of a loss recognized in OCI will not be recovered in one or more future periods, it reclassifies the amount that is expected not to be recovered into profit or loss.

In the case where a hedge of a forecast transaction subsequently results in the recognition of a non-financial asset or a non-financial liability, or a forecast transaction for a non-financial asset or a non-financial liability becomes a firm commitment for which fair value hedge accounting is applied, one of the two following treatments must be consistently followed:

- The entity reclassifies the associated gains and losses that were recognized in OCI into profit and loss in the same period or periods during which the asset acquired or liability assumed affects profit or loss. Any loss or portion of a loss previously recognized directly in equity that an entity expects not to recover in one or more future periods is reclassified into profit or loss.

- The entity removes the associated gains and losses that were recognized in OCI and includes them in the initial cost or other carrying amount of the asset or liability.

For other cash flow hedges, amounts that had been recognized in OCI are recognized in profit or loss in the same period or periods during which the hedged forecast transaction affects profit or loss (e.g., when a forecast sale occurs).

Hedge accounting as just specified should be discontinued prospectively if any of the following occurs:

- The hedging instrument expires or is sold, terminated, or exercised, or the hedge no longer meets the criteria for hedge accounting. In these cases, the cumulative gain or loss on the hedging instrument that had been reported in OCI when the hedge was effective (or met the criteria) should remain separately in equity until the forecasted transaction occurs, at which time it should be accounted for as described above. For this purpose, a replacement or rollover of a hedging instrument, provided it is part of the entity's documented hedging strategy, does not count as an expiration or termination.

- The hedge no longer meets the IAS 39 criteria for hedge accounting. In this case, the cumulative gain or loss on the hedging instrument that remains directly in equity from the period when the hedge was effective continues to remain in equity until the forecast transaction occurs.

- The forecast transaction is no longer expected to occur, in which case any related cumulative gain or loss that has been recognized in OCI from the period when the hedge was effective should be recognized in profit or loss. A forecast transaction that is no longer *highly probable* may still be *expected to occur.*

- The entity revokes the designation. For hedges of a forecast transaction, the cumulative gain or loss on the hedging instrument that remains recognized in OCI from the period when the hedge was effective should remain separately recognized in equity until the forecast transaction either occurs or is no longer expected to occur. When the transaction occurs, the accounting treatments described above for hedges of forecast transactions are applied. If it is no longer expected to occur, the cumulative gain or loss that has been recognized in OCI is recognized in profit or loss.

Hedges of a Net Investment

Hedges of a net investment in a foreign operation, including a hedge of a monetary item that is accounted for as part of the net investment (see IAS 21), are accounted for similarly to cash flow hedges. The portion of gain or loss on the hedging instrument that is determined to be an effective hedge should be recognized directly in equity. Any gain or loss on the ineffective portion should be recognized in profit or loss. On disposal of the foreign operation, the gain or loss on the hedging instrument relating to the effective portion of the hedge that has been recognized directly in equity should be recognized in profit or loss. The required treatment of such items has been clarified by IFRIC 16, issued in July 2008, which *inter alia* makes it clear that when the group presentation currency differs from the parent's functional currency, it is the latter that needs to be considered in hedging the net investment in a foreign operation.

PRESENTATION

Liabilities and Equity

The issuer of a financial instrument should classify the instrument, or its component parts, on initial recognition as a financial liability, a financial asset, or an an equity instrument in accordance with the substance of the contractual arrangement and the definitions of a financial liability, a financial asset, and an equity instrument (IAS 32, pars. 15–20 and AG25–AG29).

When an issuer applies the definitions from IAS 32 (paragraphs 11–14), given at the beginning of this chapter, to determine whether a financial instrument is an equity instrument rather than a financial liability, the instrument is an equity instrument only if both conditions 1 and 2 below are met.

1. The instrument includes no contractual obligation either to deliver cash or another financial asset to another entity, or to exchange financial assets or financial liabilities with another entity under conditions that are potentially unfavorable to the issuer.

2. If the instrument will or may be settled in the issuer's own equity instruments, it is either:

   (a) A non-derivative that includes no contractual obligation for the issuer to deliver a variable number of its own equity instruments, or

   (b) A derivative that will be settled only by the issuer exchanging a fixed amount of cash or another financial asset for a fixed number of its own equity instruments. For this purpose the issuer's own equity instruments do not include instruments that are contracts for the future receipt or delivery of the issuer's own equity instruments.

A contractual obligation, including one arising from a derivative financial instrument, that will or may result in the future receipt or delivery of the issuer's own equity instruments, but does not meet conditions 1 and 2 above, is not an equity instrument.

IAS 32, as revised in February 2008, contains new paragraphs 16A–16F that are concerned with the classification as equity or as financial liabilities of puttable instruments and instruments that impose on the entity an obligation to deliver to another party a *pro rata* share of the net assets of the entity only upon liquidation.

Puttable Instruments

A puttable instrument includes a contractual right for the issuer to repurchase or redeem that instrument for cash or another financial asset on exercise of the put. *As an exception to the definition of a financial liability,* an instrument that includes such an obligation is classified as an *equity instrument* if it has *all* of the following features:

1. It entitles the holder to a *pro rata* share of the entity's net assets in the event of liquidation. The entity's net assets are those assets that remain

after deducting all other claims on its assets. A *pro rata* share is determined by:

    (a) Dividing the entity's net assets on liquidation into units of equal amount, and

    (b) Multiplying that amount by the number of units held by the holder of the financial instrument.

2. The instrument is in the class of instruments that is subordinate to all other classes of instruments. To be in such a class, the instrument:

    (a) Has no priority over other claims to the assets of the entity on liquidation, and

    (b) Does not need to be converted into another instrument before it is in the class of instruments that is subordinate to all other classes of instruments.

3. All financial instruments in the class of instruments in item 2 above have identical features.

4. Apart from the contractual obligation for the issuer to repurchase or redeem the instrument for cash or another financial asset, the instrument does not include any contractual obligation to deliver cash or another financial asset to another entity, or to exchange financial assets or financial liabilities with another entity under conditions that are potentially unfavorable to the entity, and it is not a contract that will or may be settled in the entity's own instruments as set out in sub-paragraph (b) of the definition of a financial liability given under Definitions above.

5. The total expected cash flows attributable to the instrument over the life of the instrument are based substantially on the profit or loss, the change in recognized net assets or the change in the fair value of the recognized and unrecognized net assets of the entity over the life of the instrument (excluding any effects of the instrument itself).

For an instrument to be classified as an equity instrument, in addition to its having all of the above features, the issuer must have *no other financial instrument or contract* that has:

1. Total cash flows based substantially on the profit or loss, the change in recognized net assets, or the change in the fair value of the recognized and unrecognized net assets of the entity over the life of the instrument (excluding any effects of the instrument or contract), and

2. The effect of substantially restricting or fixing the residual returns to the puttable instrument holders.

For the purposes of this condition, the entity does not consider *non-financial* contracts with a holder of an instrument having the features described in items 1–5 above that have contractual terms and conditions similar to those of an equivalent contract that might occur between a non-instrument holder and the issuing entity. If the entity cannot determine that the above condition is met, it does not classify the puttable instrument as an equity instrument.

Instruments, or components of instruments, that impose on the entity an obligation to deliver to another party a pro rata share of the entity's net assets only upon liquidation. Some financial instruments include a contractual obligation for the issuing entity to deliver to another entity a *pro rata* share of its net assets *only on liquidation.* The obligation arises because liquidation is either certain to occur and outside the control of the entity, or is uncertain to occur but is at the option of the instrument holder. *As an exception to the definition of a financial liability,* an instrument that includes such an obligation is classified as an equity instrument if it has *all* of the following features:

1. It entitles the holder to a *pro rata* share of the entity's net assets in the event of liquidation. The entity's net assets are those assets that remain after deducting all other claims on its assets. A *pro rata* share is determined by:

   (a) Dividing the entity's net assets on liquidation into units of equal amount, and

   (b) Multiplying that amount by the number of the units held by the holder of the financial instrument.

2. The instrument is in the class of instruments that is subordinate to all other classes of instruments. To be in such a class, the instrument:

   (a) Has no priority over other claims to the assets of the entity on liquidation, and

   (b) Does not need to be converted into another instrument before it is in the class of instruments that is subordinate to all other classes of instruments.

3. All financial instruments in the class of instruments in item 2 above have an identical contractual obligation for the issuing entity to deliver a *pro rata* share of its net assets on liquidation.

For an instrument to be classed as an equity instrument, in addition to its having all of the above features, the issuer must have *no other financial instrument or contract* that has:

1. Total cash flows based substantially on the profit or loss, the change in recognized net assets, or the change in the fair value of the recognized and unrecognized net assets of the entity over the life of the instrument (excluding any effects of the instrument or contract), and

2. The effect of substantially restricting or fixing the residual returns to the puttable instrument holders.

For the purposes of this condition, the entity does not consider *non-financial* contracts with a holder of an instrument having the features described in items 1–5 above that have contractual terms and conditions similar to those of an equivalent contract that might occur between a non-instrument holder and the issuing entity. If the entity cannot determine that the above condition is met, it does not classify the puttable instrument as an equity instrument.

Reclassification of puttable instruments and instruments that impose on the entity an obligation to deliver to another party a pro rata share of the entity's net assets only upon liquidation. An entity classifies a financial instrument as an equity instrument in accordance with the paragraphs above from the date when the instrument has all the features and meets the conditions set out in those paragraphs. An entity reclassifies a financial instrument from the date when the instrument ceases to have all of the features or meet all of the conditions set out above.

If an entity reclassifies an instrument in accordance with the above:

1. It reclassifies an equity instrument as a financial liability from the date when the instrument ceases to have all of the features or meet all of the conditions above. The financial liability is measured at the instrument's fair value at the date of reclassification. Any difference between this amount and the carrying value of the equity instrument is recognized in profit or loss.

2. It reclassifies a financial liability as equity from the date when the instrument has all of the features and meets the conditions stated above. The equity instrument is measured at the carrying value of the financial liability at the date of reclassification.

With the exception of the circumstances described above, a critical feature in differentiating a financial liability from an equity instrument is the existence of a contractual obligation on one party to the financial instrument (the issuer) either to deliver cash or another financial asset to the other party (the holder) or to exchange another financial instrument with the holder under conditions that are potentially unfavorable to the issuer. When such a contractual obligation exists, that instrument meets the definition of a financial liability regardless of the manner in which the contractual obligation will be settled. A restriction on the ability of the issuer to satisfy an obligation, such as a lack of access to foreign currency or the need to obtain approval for payment from a regulatory authority, does not negate the issuer's obligation or the holder's right under the instrument.

When a financial instrument does not give rise to a contractual obligation on the part of the issuer to deliver cash or another financial asset or to exchange another financial instrument under conditions that are potentially unfavorable, it is an equity instrument. Although the holder of an equity instrument may be entitled to receive a pro rata share of any dividends or other distributions out of equity, the issuer does not have a contractual obligation to make such distributions.

The substance of a financial instrument, rather than its legal form, governs its classification on the issuer's balance sheet. Whereas substance and legal form are commonly consistent, this is not always the case. For example, some financial instruments take the legal form of equity but are liabilities in substance and others may combine features associated with equity instruments and features associated with financial liabilities. The classification of an instrument is made on the basis of an assessment of its substance when it is first recognized. That classification continues at each subsequent reporting date until the financial instrument is removed from the entity's balance sheet.

When a preferred share provides for mandatory redemption by the issuer for a fixed or determinable amount at a fixed or determinable future date or gives the holder the right to require the issuer to redeem the share at or after a particular date for a fixed or determinable amount, the instrument meets the definition of a financial liability and is classified as such. A preferred share that does not establish such a contractual obligation explicitly may establish it indirectly through its terms and conditions. For example, a preferred share that does not provide for mandatory redemption or redemption at the option of the holder may have a contractually provided accelerating dividend such that, within the foreseeable future, the dividend yield is scheduled to be so high that the issuer will be economically compelled to redeem the instrument. In these circumstances, classification as a financial liability is appropriate because the issuer has little, if any, discretion to avoid redeeming the instrument. Similarly, if a financial instrument labeled as a share gives the holder an option to require redemption upon the occurrence of a future event that is highly likely to occur, classification as a financial liability on initial recognition reflects the substance of the instrument.

A puttable instrument, that is, a financial instrument that gives the holder the right to put it back to the issuer for cash or another financial asset, is a *financial liability* of the issuer, except for those instruments classified as equity instruments in accordance with IAS 32, paragraphs 16A–16D, as indicated above. For example, issuers such as open-ended mutual funds, unit trusts, partnerships, and some financial cooperatives may provide their unit holders or members with the right to redeem their interests in the issuer at any time for cash, which results in the unit holders' or members' interests being classified as financial liabilities, except for those that meet the criteria and conditions for classification as equity instruments set out above. However, classification of such interests as financial liabilities does rule out the use of balance sheet headings for them such as "net assets attributable to unit holders" or "share capital repayable on demand." Such issuers may have no contributed equity, or no paid-in equity but some reserves that are not part of share capital repayable on demand (such as revaluation surplus) and that are classified as equity.

→ **PRACTICE POINTER:** In the balance sheet of an entity having no equity "Total assets" would be equal, for example, to "Current and non-current liabilities excluding net assets attributable to unit holders" plus "Net assets attributable to unit holders" (IAS 32, par. IE32). In the balance sheet of an entity in which total members' interests include, for example, items such as reserves that meet the definition of equity (e.g., revaluation reserves), as well as puttable instruments, the term "Share capital repayable on demand" may be used to designate the latter, and "Total assets" will be equal to "Share capital repayable on demand" plus other current and non-current liabilities plus "Reserves." "Total members' interests" consisting of "Share capital repayable on demand" plus "Reserves" may be shown as a memorandum note at the foot of the balance sheet (IAS 32, par. IE33).

OBSERVATION: Unrestricted profit-sharing investment accounts (UPSIA) in Islamic banks, which do not accept interest-bearing deposits but offer UPSIA instead, are instruments which are redeemable at net asset value, either on demand or subject to a notice period. It is quite clear that such instruments are not part of the Islamic bank's equity. The revised IAS 32, by including the guidance previously contained in draft SIC Interpretation 34, "Financial Instruments—Instruments Redeemable by the Holder," clarifies that such instruments are to be classified (under a separate heading) among the liabilities in the balance sheet of the Islamic bank. A descriptor for a commonly found form of such instruments is "Equity of Unrestricted Investment Account Holders."

Settlement in the Entity's Own Equity Instruments

A contractual right or obligation of an entity to deliver to receive or deliver a number of its own shares that varies so that the fair value to be delivered is a fixed amount or an amount that fluctuates in response to changes in a variable other than the market price of the entity's own equity instruments (e.g., an interest rate or commodity price) is a *financial liability* of the entity (IAS 32, pars. 21–24).

A contract that contains an obligation for an entity to purchase (or redeem) its own equity instruments for cash or another financial asset gives rise to a financial liability for the present value of the redemption amount, even if the contract itself is an equity instrument. An example is an entity's obligation under a forward contract or a written put option to purchase its own equity instruments for cash. When the financial liability is initially recognized, its fair value (the present value of the redemption amount) is reclassified from equity. If the contract expires without delivery, the carrying amount of the financial liability is reclassified back to equity.

Except as stated below, a contract that will be settled by the entity receiving or delivering a fixed number of its own equity instruments in exchange for a fixed amount of cash or another financial asset is an equity instrument. For example, a share (call) option issued by the entity that gives the counterparty a right to buy a fixed number of the entity's shares for a fixed consideration is an equity instrument. Any consideration received (e.g., a premium for an issued option) is added directly to equity, and any consideration paid (e.g., a premium paid for a purchased option) is deducted directly from equity. Changes in the fair value of an equity instrument are not recognized in the financial statements.

If the entity's own equity instruments to be received, or delivered, by the entity upon settlement of a contract are puttable financial instruments with all of the features and meeting the conditions described in IAS 32, paragraphs 16A–16B, as indicated above, or instruments that impose on the entity an obligation to deliver to another party a *pro rata* share of the net assets of the entity only on liquidation with all of the features and meeting the conditions described in IAS 32, paragraphs 16C–16D, as indicated above, the contract is a financial asset or a financial liability. This includes a contract that will be settled by the entity receiving or delivering a fixed number of such instruments in exchange for a fixed amount of cash or another financial asset.

When a derivative financial instrument gives one party a choice over how it is to be settled, it is a financial liability unless *all* of the settlement alternatives would result in it being an equity instrument.

Contingent Settlement Provisions

A financial instrument may require an entity to deliver cash or another financial asset, or otherwise to settle it in such a way that it would be a financial liability, in the event of the occurrence or non-occurrence of uncertain future events (or on the outcome of uncertain circumstances) that are beyond the control of both the issuer and the holder of the instrument. The instrument is a financial liability of the issuer unless:

1. The part of the contingent settlement provision that could require settlement in such a way that it would be a financial liability is not genuine;
2. The issuer can be required to settle it in this way only in the event of the issuer's liquidation (IAS 32, pars. 25–27); or
3. The instrument has all of the features and meets the conditions in IAS 32, paragraphs 16A–16B, as indicated above.

Compound Financial Instruments

The issuer of a financial instrument that contains both a liability and an equity element should classify the instrument's component parts separately (IAS 32, pars. 28–32 and AG30–AG35).

IASB GAAP requires the separate presentation on an issuer's balance sheet of liability and equity elements created by a single financial instrument. It is more a matter of form than substance that both liabilities and equity interests are created by a single financial instrument rather than two or more separate instruments. An issuer's financial position is more faithfully represented by separate presentation of liability and equity components contained in a single instrument according to their nature.

For purposes of balance sheet presentation, an issuer recognizes separately the component parts of a financial instrument that creates a primary financial liability of the issuer and grants an option to the holder of the instrument to convert it into an equity instrument of the issuer. A bond or similar instrument convertible by the holder into common shares of the issuer is an common example of such an instrument. From the perspective of the issuer, such an instrument comprises two components: a financial liability (a contractual arrangement to deliver cash or other financial assets), and an equity instrument (a call option granting the holder the right, for a specified period of time, to convert into common shares of the issuer). The economic effect of issuing such an instrument is substantially the same as issuing simultaneously a debt instrument with an early settlement provision and warrants to purchase common shares or issuing a debt instrument with detachable share purchase warrants. Accordingly, in all such cases, the issuer presents the liability and equity elements separately on its balance sheet.

Classification of the liability and equity components of a convertible instrument is not revised as a result of a change in the likelihood that a conversion option will be exercised, even when exercise of the option may appear to have become economically advantageous to some holders. Holders may not always act in the manner that might be expected because, for example, the tax consequences resulting from conversion may differ among holders. Furthermore, the likelihood of conversion will change from time to time. The issuer's obligation to make future payments remains outstanding until it is extinguished through conversion, the maturity of the instrument or some other transaction.

A financial instrument may contain components that are neither financial liabilities nor equity instruments of the issuer. For example, an instrument may give the holder the right to receive a non-financial asset such as a commodity in settlement and an option to exchange that right for shares of the issuer. The issuer recognizes and presents the equity instrument (the exchange option) separately from the liability components of the compound instrument, whether the liabilities are financial or non-financial.

Treasury Shares

If an entity reacquires its own equity instruments, those instruments (treasury shares) are deducted from equity. No gain or loss shall be recognized by an entity in profit or loss on the purchase, sale, issue, or cancellation of its own equity instruments. Such shares may be acquired and held by the entity or by other members of the consolidated group. Consideration paid or received is recognized directly in equity. The amount of treasury shares held is disclosed separately either on the face of the balance sheet or in the notes, in accordance with IAS 1, "Presentation of Financial Statements." If an entity reacquires its own equity instruments from related parties, it must provide disclosure in accordance with IAS 24, "Related Party Disclosures" (IAS 32, pars. 33–34 and AG36).

Interest, Dividends, Losses, and Gains

Interest, dividends, losses, and gains relating to a financial instrument, or a component part, classified as a financial liability should be recognized as income or expense in profit or loss. Distributions to holders of equity instruments should be charged by the issuer directly to equity, net of any related income tax benefit (IAS 32, pars. 35–41 and AG37).

The classification of a financial instrument in the balance sheet determines whether interest, dividends, losses, and gains relating to that instrument are classified as expenses or income and recognized in profit or loss. Thus, dividend payments on shares classified as liabilities are classified as expenses in the same way as interest on a bond and recognized in profit or loss. Similarly, gains and losses associated with redemptions or refinancings of instruments classified as liabilities are recognized in profit or loss, whereas redemptions or refinancings of instruments classified as equity of the issuer are recognized directly in equity.

Dividends classified as an expense may be presented in the income statement either with interest on other liabilities or as a separate item. Disclosure of interest and dividends is subject to the requirements of IAS 1, "Presentation of Financial Statements," and IAS 32, "Financial Instruments: Presentation." In some circumstances, because of significant differences between interest and dividends with respect to matters such as tax deductibility, it is desirable to disclose them separately within the income statement. Disclosures of the amounts of tax effects are made in accordance with IAS 12, "Income Taxes."

Offsetting of a Financial Asset and a Financial Liability

A financial asset and a financial liability should be offset and the net amount reported in the balance sheet when an entity either currently has a legally enforceable right to set off the recognized amounts or intends either to settle on a net basis, or to realize the asset and settle the liability simultaneously (IAS 32, pars. 42–50 and AG38–AG39).

IASB GAAP require the presentation of financial assets and financial liabilities on a net basis when this reflects an entity's expected future cash flows from settling two or more separate financial instruments. When an entity has the right to receive or pay a single net amount and intends to do so, it has, in effect, only a single financial asset or financial liability. In other circumstances, financial assets and financial liabilities are presented separately from each other consistent with their characteristics as resources or obligations of the entity.

In accounting for a transfer of a financial asset that does not qualify for derecognition, an entity may not offset the transferred asset and the associated liability.

Offsetting a recognized financial asset and a recognized financial liability and presenting the net amount differs from ceasing to recognize a financial asset or a financial liability. Although offsetting does not give rise to recognition of a gain or a loss, ceasing to recognize a financial instrument not only results in the removal of the previously recognized item from the balance sheet but may also result in recognition of a gain or a loss.

Simultaneous settlement of two financial instruments may occur through, for example, the operation of a clearinghouse in an organized financial market or a face-to-face exchange. In these circumstances the cash flows are, in effect, equivalent to a single net amount and there is no exposure to credit or liquidity risk. In other circumstances, an entity may settle two instruments by receiving and paying separate amounts, becoming exposed to credit risk for the full amount of the asset or liquidity risk for the full amount of the liability. Such risk exposures may be significant even though relatively brief. Accordingly, realization of a financial asset and settlement of a financial liability are considered simultaneous only when the transactions occur at the same moment.

Offsetting is usually inappropriate when:

- Several different financial instruments are used to emulate the features of a single financial instrument (i.e., a "synthetic instrument");

- Financial assets and financial liabilities arise from financial instruments having the same primary risk exposure (e.g., assets and liabilities within a portfolio of forward contracts or other derivative instruments) but involve different counter parties;

- Financial or other assets are pledged as collateral for non-recourse financial liabilities;

- Financial assets are set aside in trust by a debtor for the purpose of discharging an obligation without those assets having been accepted by the creditor in settlement of the obligation (for example, a sinking fund arrangement); or

- Obligations incurred as a result of events giving rise to losses are expected to be recovered from a third party by virtue of a claim made under an insurance policy.

An entity that undertakes a number of financial instrument transactions with a single counterparty may enter into a *master netting arrangement* with that counterparty. Such an agreement provides for a single net settlement of all financial instruments covered by the agreement in the event of default on, or termination of, any one contract. These arrangements are commonly used by financial institutions to provide protection against loss in the event of bankruptcy or other events that result in a counterparty being unable to meet its obligations. A master netting arrangement commonly creates a right of set-off that becomes enforceable and affects the realization or settlement of individual financial assets and financial liabilities only following a specified event of default or in other circumstances not expected to arise in the normal course of business. A master netting arrangement does not provide a basis for offsetting unless the entity has a legally enforceable right of set-off and intends to use it.

OBSERVATION: In January 2011, the IASB published ED2011/1, "Offsetting Financial Assets and Financial Liabilities," which, if adopted, would modify the above provisions as well as the related disclosure requirements. The exposure draft would restrict offsetting to cases where the entity has a right or obligation for only the net amount (i.e., it has a single financial asset or financial liability) and the resultant amount represents the entity's expected future cash flows from the settlement of two or more separate financial instruments. Offsetting has been used to reduce the reported leverage of entities, and the exposure draft is intended, among other things, to mitigate this problem.

DISCLOSURE

The disclosures required by IFRS 7 are intended to enable users of financial statements to evaluate:

- The significance of financial instruments for the entity's *financial position and performance*; and

- The nature and extent of *risks* arising from financial instruments to which the entity is exposed during the period covered by the financial statements and at the reporting date, and how the entity *manages* those risks.

There are some consequential amendments resulting from IFRS 9.

SIGNIFICANCE OF FINANCIAL INSTRUMENTS FOR FINANCIAL POSITION AND PERFORMANCE

This section covers disclosures in the balance sheet, income statement, and statement of changes in equity, and other disclosures.

Balance Sheet (IFRS 7, pars. 8–19)

Enterprises are required to disclose the *carrying amounts* of each category of financial assets and financial liabilities, as defined in IAS 39 (see the "Definitions" section above).

The categories, as amended by IFRS 9, are as follows:

1. Financial assets measured as at FVPL, showing separately those so *designated* upon initial recognition and those *mandatorily* measured at fair value in accordance with IFRS 9;

2. Financial liabilities at FVPL, showing separately those so designated upon initial recognition and those that meet the definition of held for trading in IFRS 9;

3. Financial assets measured at amortized cost;

4. Financial liabilities measured at amortized cost; and

5. Financial assets measured at FVOCI.

Financial Assets and Financial Liabilities Designated at FVPL

Further disclosures are required, as follows:

1. *For financial assets at FVPL:*

    (a) The maximum exposure to *credit risk* of the loan or receivable (or group thereof) at the reporting date.

    (b) The amount by which any related credit derivatives or similar instruments *mitigate* that maximum disclosure.

    (c) The amount of any change, during the period and cumulatively, in the fair value of the financial asset (or group thereof) that is attributable to *changes in the credit risk* of the financial asset. This amount may be determined either as the amount of the change in its fair value that is *not* attributable to changes in *market conditions* that give rise to *market risk,* or using an alternative method if the entity believes that it gives a more faithful representation of the change in fair value attributable to changes in credit risk.

(d) The amount of the change in the fair value of any related credit derivatives or similar instruments that have occurred during the period and cumulatively.

2. *For financial liabilities at FVPL:*

(a) The amount of any change, during the period and cumulatively, in the fair value of the loan or receivable (or group thereof) that is attributable to *changes in the credit risk* of that financial liability. This amount may be determined either as the amount of the change in its fair value that is *not* attributable to changes in *market conditions* that give rise to *market risk,* or using an alternative method if the entity believes that it gives a more faithful representation of the change in fair value attributable to changes in credit risk.

(b) The difference between the financial liability's carrying amount and the amount that the entity would be contractually required to pay at maturity to the holder.

(c) Any transfers of the cumulative gain or loss within equity during the period and the reasons for such transfers.

(d) If a liability is derecognized during the period, the amount (if any) presented in OCI that was realized at recognition.

For both financial assets and financial liabilities, the methods used to calculate the amount of the change in fair value that is attributable to changes in credit risk are to be disclosed. If the entity believes that the resultant disclosures do not faithfully represent the changes in the fair value that are attributable to credit risk, it should disclose the reasons for this belief and the factors it believes are relevant. In particular:

1. A detailed description is required of the methods used to comply with the above requirements in regard to changes in fair value attributable to changes in credit risk, and if following those requirements is not considered to represent faithfully such changes in fair value, the entity must provide the reasons why it believes this to be the case.

2. For financial liabilities at FVPL, a detailed description is required of the methodology used to determine whether presenting the effects of changes in a liability's credit risk in OCI would create or enlarge an accounting mismatch in profit and loss.

OBSERVATION: A major objection to the application of the fair value option in IAS 39 to financial liabilities has been the apparently perverse effect of the option, whereby a *deterioration of the credit risk* of a financial liability of an entity results in a remeasurement *gain* for that entity; and conversely, an improvement of the credit risk of a liability results in a remeasurement *loss.* IFRS 39 incorporates the option to designate financial liabilities as at FVPL. The above provisions of IFRS 7, with consequential amendments from IFRS 9, are intended to make such changes in fair value transparent.

Financial Assets Measured at Fair Value through Other Comprehensive Income

For equity instruments not held for trading that have been irrevocably elected for designation as at financial assets measured at fair value through other comprehensive income (FVOCI), the following disclosures are required::

1. Which investments in equity instruments have been so designated;

2. The reasons for this election;

3. The fair value of each such investment at the end of the reporting period;

4. Dividends recognized during the period, showing separately those related (a) to investments derecognized during the reporting period and (b) to investments held at the end of the period;

5. Any transfers of the cumulative gain or loss within equity during the period, including the reason for such transfers; and

6. If the entity has derecognized investments in equity instruments measured at FVOCI during the reporting period, it should disclose:

   • The reasons for the disposals,

   • The fair value of the investments at the date of derecognition, and

   • The cumulative gain or loss on disposal.

Reclassification

If a financial asset has been reclassified (in accordance with IAS 39, pars. 51–54) from being measured at fair value to being measured at cost or amortized cost, the amount reclassified into and out of each category and the reasons for the reclassification are to be disclosed.

If a financial asset has been reclassified out of the FVPL category in accordance with paragraphs 50B or 50D of IAS 39, or out of the AFS category in accordance with paragraph 50E of IAS 39, the entity shall disclose:

• The amount reclassified into and out of each category;

• For each reporting period until derecognition, the carrying amounts and fair values of all financial assets that have been reclassified in the current and previous reporting periods;

• If a financial asset was reclassified that should have been reclassified only in rare circumstances, what those circumstances were and why they should be considered as rare;

• For the reporting period in which the financial asset was reclassified, the fair value gain or loss on the financial asset recognized in that and the previous reporting periods;

• For each reporting period following the reclassification, including that in which the reclassification was made, until derecognition, the fair value gain or loss that would have been recognized in profit or loss or other comprehensive income if the asset had not been reclassified and the gain, loss, income; or expense had been recognized in profit and loss; and

- The effective interest rate and estimated cash flows that the entity expects to recover, as at the date of reclassification.

OBSERVATION: Paragraphs 50B, 50D, and 50E of IAS 39 were added by the amendments to IAS 39 and IFRS 7 made in October 2008.

IFRS 9 resulted in some consequential amendments to the above, to reflect the new classification scheme based on the concept of the business model for managing financial assets. Accordingly, reclassifications of financial assets take place only if the business model for managing such assets changes. The required disclosures are:

- The date of reclassification;
- A detailed explanation of the change in business model and a description of its effects on the entity's financial statements;
- The amount reclassified out of each category;
- For *financial assets reclassified to amortized cost,* for each reporting period following reclassification until derecognition:
  - The effective interest rate determined on the date of reclassification,
  - The interest income or expense recognized, and
  - If such assets have been reclassified to amortized cost since the entity's last reporting date:
    - ☐ The fair value of the financial assets at the end of the reporting period, and
    - ☐ The fair value gain or loss that would have been recognized in profit or loss during the reporting period if the financial assets had not been reclassified.

Derecognition

(**Note:** This section has been removed from IFRS 7 following the promulgation of IFRS 9. See the OBSERVATION below.)

If an entity has transferred financial assets in such a way that part or all of the assets do not qualify for derecognition (see the "Derecognition of a Financial Asset" section above), it shall disclose for each class of such assets:

1. The nature of the assets;
2. The nature of the risks and rewards of ownership to which the entity remains exposed;
3. If the entity continues to recognize all of the assets, their carrying amounts, and that of any associated liabilities; and
4. If the entity continues to recognize the assets to the extent of its continuing involvement, the total carrying amount of the original assets, the

amount of those assets that the entity continues to recognize, and the carrying amount of any associated liabilities.

OBSERVATION: ED/2009/3, "Derecognition—Proposed Amendments to IAS 39 and IFRS 7," contains proposed deletions and insertions to IFRS 7. Paragraph 13 (cited above) would be deleted and a new section containing six paragraphs would be added (see "Market Risk" below). These amendments have been made in the 2011 version of IFRS 7.

Collateral Pledged or Held

An entity shall disclose the carrying amount of financial assets *that it has pledged* as collateral for liabilities or contingent liabilities, including amounts of non-cash collateral that have been reclassified by the entity as transferor, as indicated under "All Transfers" and the terms and conditions relating to the pledge.

When an entity *holds* collateral (of financial or non-financial assets) and is permitted to sell or re-pledge the collateral in the absence of default by the owner of the collateral, the following should be disclosed:

1. The fair value of the collateral held;
2. The fair value of any such collateral sold or repledged and whether the entity has an obligation to return it; and
3. The terms and conditions associated with its use of the collateral.

Allowance for Credit Losses

When financial assets are impaired by credit losses, the impairment may be recognized by recording its amount in a separate account or a collective account for impairments (an allowance account) rather than directly reducing the carrying amount of the asset. In this case, a reconciliation of changes in that account for each class of financial assets affected is to be disclosed.

Compound Financial Instruments with Multiple Embedded Derivatives

In the case of instruments issued with both a liability and an equity component such that it has multiple embedded derivatives whose values are interdependent (such as a debt instrument that is both convertible and callable), these features are to be disclosed.

Defaults and Breaches

For loans payable that are recognized at the reporting date, the following must be disclosed:

1. Details of any defaults during the period in respect of:
    (a) Principal,
    (b) Interest,
    (c) Sinking fund payments, and
    (d) Redemption terms;

2. The carrying amount of loans payable in default at the reporting date; and

3. Whether the default was remedied or the terms of the loans renegotiated before the financial statements were authorized for issue.

Income Statement and Statement of Comprehensive Income (IFRS 7, par. 20)

The following items of income, expense, and gains or losses are to be disclosed either on the face of the financial statements or in the notes:

1. Net gains or losses on:

    (a) Financial assets or liabilities at FVPL, showing separately those on financial assets and financial liabilities:

        (i) Designated at FVPL upon initial recognition and

        (ii) Mandatorily measured at fair value in accordance with IFRS 9 (or "held for trading" in accordance with IAS 39);

    (b) AFS financial assets, showing separately the amount of gains or losses recognized directly in equity during the period and the amount removed from equity and recognized in profit and loss for the period (this is deleted in the 2011 version of IFRS 7, as IFRS 9 abolishes the AFS category);

    (c) HTM investments in IAS 39 or financial assets measured at FVOCI in IFRS 9 (IFRS 9 replaces the HTM category by the FVOCI category);

    (d) Loans and receivables in IAS 39 (this is deleted in the 2011 version of IFRS 7, as IFRS 9 abolishes the Loans and Receivables category); and

    (e) Financial liabilities measured at amortized cost;

2. Total interest income and total interest expense (calculated using the effective interest rate method (see (8) under the "Definitions" section above for a description) for financial assets or financial liabilities that are not at FVPL.

3. Fee income and expense (other than amounts included in determining the effective interest rate) arising from:

    (a) Financial assets or financial liabilities that are not at FVPL; and

    (b) Trust and other fiduciary activities that result in the holding or investment of assets on behalf of individuals, trusts, retirement benefit plans, and other institutions.

4. Interest income on impaired financial assets accrued using the rate of interest that was used to discount the future cash flows for the purpose of measuring the impairment loss.

5. The amount of any impairment loss for each class of financial asset.

Other Disclosures (IFRS 7, pars. 21–30)

The "other disclosures" that are required relating to financial position and performance are concerned with accounting policies, hedge accounting, and fair value.

Accounting Policies

IAS 1, paragraph 108, requires the disclosure by an entity, in its summary of significant accounting policies, of the measurement basis or bases used in preparing its financial statements and the other accounting policies that are relevant to an understanding of the financial statements. IFRS 7, paragraph 21, reiterates this requirement.

Hedge Accounting

Three types of hedges are described in IAS 39—fair value hedges, cash flow hedges, and hedges of net investments in foreign operations (see "Hedge Accounting"). IFRS 7 requires disclosure, separately for each type of hedge, of the following:

- A description of
  - The type of hedge, and
  - The financial instruments designated as hedging instruments;
- The fair values of those financial instruments at the reporting date; and
- The nature of the risks being hedged.

For cash flow hedges, the following should also be disclosed:

- The periods when cash flows are expected to occur and when they are expected to affect profit and loss;
- A description of any forecast transactions for which hedge accounting had previously been used, but which are no longer expected to occur;
- The total amount that was recognized directly in equity in the period in respect of gains or losses on hedging instruments;
- The total amount that was removed from equity and included in profit or loss during the period, showing the amount included in each line of the income statement; and
- The total amount that was removed from equity during the period and included in the initial cost or other carrying amount of a non-financial asset or liability whose acquisition or incurrence was a *hedged highly probable forecast transaction.*

For fair value hedges, an entity should disclose separately gains or losses on the hedging instrument and on the hedged item attributable to the hedged risk.

For hedge ineffectiveness, the amounts recognized in profit and loss arising from ineffectiveness of cash flow hedges and from hedges of net investments in foreign operations should be disclosed separately.

Fair Value

Except as indicated below, the fair value of each class of financial assets and financial liabilities should be disclosed so that the fair value may be compared to the carrying amount. For this purpose, the financial assets and financial liabilities are to be grouped into classes but should be offset only to the extent to which their carrying amounts are offset in the balance sheet. The methods and (when a valuation technique is used) the assumptions applied in determining the fair value of each class of financial assets and financial liabilities should also be disclosed, as should whether fair values are (1) determined in whole or in part by reference to published price quotations in an active market or (2) estimated using a valuation technique.

When the fair values recognized or disclosed in the financial statements are determined in whole or in part using a valuation technique based on assumptions that are not supported by prices from observable current market transactions in the same instrument and are not based on available and observable market data, this fact should be disclosed. For fair values *recognized* in the financial statements, if changing one or more of these assumptions to other assumptions that are reasonably possible would change fair value significantly (in relation to profit or loss, total assets or total liabilities, or equity, as applicable), this and the effect of such changes should be disclosed, as should the total amount of the change in fair value estimated using the valuation technique that was recognized in profit or loss during the period.

The Fair Value Hierarchy

The fair value hierarchy proposed in the May 2009 exposure draft, "Fair Value Measurement," is included in the 2010 version of IFRS 7 (par. 27A). Fair value measurements are to be classified according to a hierarchy that reflects the significance of the inputs used in making measurements. The hierarchy has the following three levels:

Level 1: Quoted prices (unadjusted) in active markets for identical assets or liabilities;

Level 2: Inputs other than quoted prices included within Level 1 that are observable for the asset or liability, either directly (i.e., as prices) or indirectly (i.e., derived from prices (Level 2);

Level 3: Inputs for the asset or liability that are not based on observable market data.

A fair value measurement is categorized within the hierarchy on the basis of the lowest level input that is significant to the measurement in its entirety. For example, if a fair value measurement uses observable inputs that require significant adjustment based on unobservable inputs, the measurement is a Level 3 measurement.

The following disclosures are to be made for each class of financial instruments recognized in the statement of financial position:

- The level in the hierarchy into which each fair value measurement is categorized in its entirety.

- Any significant transfers between Level 1 and Level 2 and the reasons therefor.

- For Level 3 measurements, a reconciliation from the beginning balances to the ending balances, disclosing separately changes during the period attributable to

  — Total gains or losses in the period recognized in profit or loss, and a description of where they are presented;

  — Total gains or losses recognized in other comprehensive income;

  — Purchases, sales, issues and settlements (each type being disclosed separately); or

  — Transfers into or out of Level 3 (e.g., transfers attributable to changes in the observability of market data) and the reasons therefor. For significant transfers, transfers into Level 3 and transfers out of Level 3 are to be disclosed and discussed separately.

- The amount of total gains or losses for the period included in profit or loss that are attributable to gains or losses relating to those assets and liabilities held at the end of the reporting period and a description of where those gains or losses are presented.

- For fair value measurements in Level 3, a type of sensitivity analysis as follows: If changing one or more of the inputs to reasonably possible alternative assumptions would change the fair value significantly, this fact is to be stated and the effects of the changes and how they were calculated are to be disclosed. (IFRS 7, pars. 27A and 27B).

If the market for a financial instrument is not active, a valuation technique is used to establish its fair value (a Level 3 measurement). Nevertheless, the best evidence of fair value at initial recognition is normally the transaction price, unless the fair value is evidenced by other observable current transactions in the same instrument without modification or repackaging, or based on a valuation technique whose variables include only data from observable markets. If fair value as so determined differs from the transaction price, the following should be disclosed:

- The entity's accounting policy for recognizing that difference in profit or loss to reflect a change in factors (including time) that market participants would consider relevant in setting a price; and

- The aggregate difference yet to be recognized in profit or loss at the beginning and end of the period and a reconciliation of changes in the balance of this difference.

OBSERVATION: One may note from the above: (a) that contentious issues in fair value measurement with which the May 2009 exposure draft, "Fair Value Measurement," was concerned and which are dealt with in IFRS 13 (see Chapter 3) have been addressed primarily (a) by extensive disclosure requirements with reference to the fair value hierarchy; and (b) the attention given to fair value measurements at Level 3 of the hierarchy, which are in principle the least reliable.

Disclosures of fair value are not required:

- When the carrying amount is a reasonable approximation of fair value;
- For an investment in equity instruments that do not have a quoted market price in an active market, or derivatives linked to such instruments, measured at cost in accordance with IAS 39 because the value of the investment cannot be measured reliably (this point has been deleted from the 2011 version of IFRS 7 as amended in consequence of IFRS 9); and
- For a contract containing a discretionary participation feature (as described in IFRS 4—see Chapter 35) if the fair value of that feature cannot be measured reliably.

In the cases described, information should be disclosed to assist users of the financial statements to make their own judgments about the extent of possible differences between the carrying amount of the financial assets or financial liabilities in question and their fair value, including:

- The fact that fair value has not been disclosed for these instruments because it cannot be measured reliably, and an explanation of why it cannot be measured reliably.
- A description of the instruments and their carrying amounts.
- Information about the market for the instruments.
- Whether the entity intends to dispose of the instruments, and if so, how.
- If financial instruments whose fair value previously could not be reliably measured are derecognized, that fact and their carrying amount at the time of derecognition and the amount of the gain or loss recognized.

NATURE AND EXTENT OF RISKS ARISING FROM FINANCIAL INSTRUMENTS

IFRS 7 requires disclosures that focus on the risks that arise from financial instruments and how they have been managed. The types of risk specifically mentioned in the standard are credit risk, liquidity risk, and market risk. Certain disclosures are required for each type of risk arising from financial instruments, whereas others are specific to a particular type of risk.

Qualitative Disclosures (IFRS 7, par. 33)

For each type of risk arising from financial instruments, the following should be disclosed:

- The exposures and how they arise.
- The entity's objectives, policies, and processes for managing the risk and the methods used to measure it.
- Any changes in the above from the previous period.

Quantitative Disclosures (IFRS 7, pars. 34–35)

For each type of risk arising from financial instruments, the following should be disclosed:

- Summary quantitative data on its exposure to that risk at the reporting date, based on information provided internally to key management personnel.
- Disclosures for particular types of risk as indicated under credit, liquidity, and market risk below.
- Concentrations of risk unless disclosed under the two previous headings.

Credit Risk (IFRS 7, pars. 36–38)

The following disclosures are required by class of financial instrument:

- The amount that best represents the entity's maximum exposure to credit risk at the reporting date without taking account of any collateral held or other credit enhancements (e.g., netting agreements that do not qualify for offsetting under IASB GAAP).
- Regarding the above, a description of collateral held as security and other credit enhancements.
- Information about the credit quality of financial assets that are neither past due nor impaired.
- The carrying amount of financial assets that would otherwise be past due or impaired had their terms not been renegotiated.

Financial Assets That Are Either Past Due or Impaired

The following disclosures are required by class of such financial asset:

- An analysis of the age of financial assets that are past due at the reporting date but not impaired.
- An analysis of financial assets that are individually determined to be impaired at the reporting date, including the factors considered in determining that they are impaired.
- For the amounts disclosed in accordance with the above, a description of collateral held as security and other credit enhancements and, unless impracticable, an estimate of their fair value.

Collateral and Other Credit Enhancements Obtained

If an entity obtains assets (financial or non-financial) during the period by taking possession of collateral that it holds as security or by calling on other credit enhancements such as guarantees, and such assets meet the recognition criteria in IASB GAAP, it should disclose the nature and carrying amount of the assets obtained and, if the assets are not readily convertible into cash, its policies for disposing of such assets or for using them in its operations.

Liquidity Risk (IFRS 7, par. 39)

The following information is required to be disclosed:

- A maturity analysis for financial liabilities showing the remaining contractual maturities.
- A description of how the entity manages the liquidity risk implied by the above.

Market Risk (IFRS 7, pars. 40–42)

The required disclosures consist of those relating to sensitivity analysis and other market risk disclosures.

Sensitivity Analysis

Unless an entity prepares a sensitivity analysis, such as a value-at-risk analysis, that reflects interdependencies between risk variables, such as interest rates and exchange rates, and uses it to manage risks, it should disclose the following:

- A sensitivity analysis for each type of market risk to which it is exposed at the reporting date, indicating how profit or loss and equity would have been affected by reasonably possible changes in the relevant risk variable.
- The methods and assumptions used in the above.
- Changes in the methods and assumptions from the previous period and the reasons for these changes.

If an entity prepares a sensitivity analysis, such as a value-at-risk analysis, that reflects interdependencies between risk variables, such as interest rates and exchange rates, and uses it to manage risks, it may use this sensitivity analysis in place of those indicated above. In that case, it should also disclose:

- An explanation of the method used and of the main parameters and assumptions underlying the data provided; and
- An explanation of the objective of the method used and any limitations that might result in the information not fairly reflecting the fair value of the assets and liabilities involved.

Other Market Risk Disclosures

If the sensitivity analyses disclosed in accordance with the above requirements are considered to be unrepresentative of a risk inherent in a financial instrument (e.g., because the exposure at the reporting date does not reflect that during the year), the entity is required to disclose this fact and its reason for considering that the sensitivity analyses are unrepresentative.

Transfers of Financial Assets

ED/2009/3, "Derecognition-Proposed Amendments to IAS 39 and IFRS 7," proposed the insertion of six paragraphs at this point setting out new disclosures to be made in a single note to the financial statements. These, together with two additional paragraphs, are included in the 2011 version of IFRS 7. They relate to information that an entity needs to disclose in order to meet the requirements of enabling users of its financial statements: (a) to understand the relationship between transferred financial assets that are not derecognized in their entirety and the associated liabilities, and (b) to evaluate the nature of, and risks associated with, the entity's continuing involvement in derecognized financial assets. They also relate to:

- *Transferred financial assets that are not derecognized in their entirety.* The disclosures should enable users of the financial statements to understand the relationship between those assets and associated liabilities after the transfer.

- *Transferred financial assets that are derecognized in their entirety.* The disclosures should enable users of the financial statements to evaluate the nature of and risks associated with the entity's continuing involvement in those derecognized assets.

In both cases, the entity should disclose:

- The gain or loss recognized at the date of the transfer;

- Income and expense, gains and losses recognized, both in the reporting period and cumulatively, from the entity's continuing involvement in the derecognized financial instruments (e.g. fair value changes in derivatives); and

- Further information if the total amount of proceeds from transfer activity that qualifies for derecognition in a reporting period is not evenly distributed throughout the period.

An entity should also disclose any additional information that it considers necessary to meet the objectives (a) and (b) stated above.

EFFECTIVE DATE AND TRANSITION

As covered by this chapter, the presentation requirements of IAS 32, "Financial Instruments: Presentation," are applicable for fiscal years beginning on or after January 1, 2009. In the amended version covered in this chapter, IAS 39, "Financial Instruments: Recognition and Measurement," is applicable for fiscal years beginning on or after January 1, 2009, and the chapters of IFRS 9 included here are applicable for fiscal years beginning on or after January 1, 2013, with an option for earlier adoption. IFRS 7, "Financial Instruments: Disclosures," as included here, is applicable for fiscal years beginning on or after January 1, 2007, with indications of amendments to be adopted when an entity adopts IFRS 9, as issued in October 1, 2010.

The 2008 amendments to these standards, included in this chapter, are to be applied for fiscal years beginning on or after January 1, 2009.

IFRS 9

The following paragraphs provide an outline and summary of IFRS 9 as expanded and amended in October 2010, to be applied for annual periods beginning on or after January 1, 2013, with early application permitted. As IFRS 9 is less restrictive than, and incorporates the IASB's attempts to meet a number of preparer objections to, IAS 39, it is to be expected that the option of earlier application will be popular.

One of the main objectives of the IASB in developing IFRS 9 has been to align accounting for financial instruments better with the risk management practices employed by entities with respect to such items. This applies particularly to hedge accounting, the chapter on which was, however, still at the exposure draft stage at the time of writing.

IFRS 9 has a different structure from the earlier IFRSs, having a number of "chapters" and a different system for numbering paragraphs. At present, IFRS 9, Chapter 6, "Hedge Accounting," and the section of IFRS 9, Chapter 3, "Measurement," that covers measurement at amortized cost and impairment, are pending, waiting final acceptance of the related exposure drafts.

Outline: Main Features

Chapters 4 and 5 of IFRS 9 specify the requirements for the classification and measurement of financial assets and financial liabilities, including some hybrid contracts (but at the time of writing, excluding financial assets measured at amortized cost). These provisions are intended to improve and simplify the approach compared to that in IAS 39, by applying a consistent approach and reducing the number of categories of financial instruments to two, according to the measurement method to be applied after initial recognition as set out below, namely fair value or amortized cost.

All financial assets are to be:

- Classified on the basis of the entity's business model for managing the financial asset and the cash flow characteristics of the financial asset;

- Initially measured at fair value plus, in the case of a financial asset not at FVPL, particular transactions costs; and

- Subsequently measured at either:
  — Amortized cost, or
  — Fair value.

All financial liabilities are to be classified as subsequently measured at amortized cost using the effective interest rate method, with the exceptions noted below.

Summary

Chapter 1: Objective

The objective of IFRS 9 is to establish principles for the financial reporting of *financial assets* and *financial liabilities* that will present relevant and useful information to users of financial statements for their assessment of the amounts, timing, and uncertainty of an entity's future cash flows.

OBSERVATION: This wording echoes the Conceptual Framework (see Chapter 2).

Chapter 2: Scope

IFRS 9 is to be applied to all assets within the scope of IAS 39, and is to replace those paragraphs of the latter that are concerned with assets.

Chapter 3: Recognition and Derecognition

An entity shall recognize a financial asset in its statement of financial position when and only when it becomes party to the contractual provisions of that instrument. On initial recognition a financial asset is to be classified and measured as indicated in Chapters 4 and 5 below. However, in *regular way purchases or sales* of financial assets, trade date or settlement date accounting will be used as applicable (see the illustration given in "Recognition and Derecognition" in IAS 39 above).

Chapter 4: Classification

This chapter sets out the requirements for classifying financial instruments, including the option to designate them as at FVPL.

4.1 Classification of financial assets. Unless the option to designate a financial asset at FVPL on initial recognition (see below) is exercised, a financial asset is to be classified based on how it is to be subsequently measured, that is, at either amortized cost or fair value on the basis of both:

- The business model applied for managing the financial asset; and
- The contractual cash flow characteristics of the financial asset.

If both of the following conditions are met, a *set or portfolio of financial assets* is measured at amortized cost:

- The set of assets is held within a business model the objective of which is to hold assets to collect contractual cash flows (e.g., assets held in the "banking book" of a bank); and
- The contractual cash flows give rise on specified dates to cash flows that consist only of principal and/or interest on the principal.

If the conditions for measurement at amortized cost are not met, then a financial asset is to be measured at fair value.

OBSERVATION: The above requirement is applicable to a set or portfolio of assets and should not be applied to assets individually. In contrast to the classifications in IAS 39, there is no requirement that all assets classified as at amortized cost are supposed to be held to maturity. Hence, the tiresome "tainting" rule applicable to HTM assets in IAS 39 is removed. However, if sales of assets in a portfolio are not infrequent, then IFRS 9 requires a reassessment of the business model to be applied, that is, possibly the portfolio should be classified as held for trading, which implies measurement at fair value.

4.2 Classification of financial liabilities. A financial liability is to be classified as subsequently measured at amortized cost using the effective interest method, except for:

- Financial liabilities measured at FVPL following an election to do so on initial recognition;
- Financial liabilities that arise when a transfer of a financial asset does not qualify for derecognition or when the "continuing involvement" approach applies; and
- Financial guarantee contracts and commitments to provide a loan at a below-market interest rate, the requirements for the measurement of which are laid down by other IFRSs.

Option to Designate a Financial Asset or a Financial Liability as at FVPL

Notwithstanding the above, a financial asset or financial liability may, at initial recognition, be irrevocably designated as measured at FVPL if so doing eliminates or significantly reduces an accounting mismatch (i.e., an inconsistency in measurement or recognition) that would otherwise arise. Designation at FVPL may allow a hedged asset or liability to be measured consistently with an item (e.g., a derivative) held to hedge it.

OBSERVATION: Making the option irrevocable is intended to prevent the "creative accounting" that might arise from shifting items that qualify for measurement at amortized cost between the two measurement categories. However, as pointed out by EFRAG, if an entity elects to exercise the option to designate such an instrument as at FVPL on initial recognition in order for it to serve as a hedging instrument in accordance with its risk management strategy, it would not be possible for it subsequently to revoke this election in case of a change in the risk management strategy.

4.3 Embedded Derivatives. An embedded derivative is a derivative component of a hybrid contract such that the derivative is *embedded* in a non-derivative host, with the effect that some of the cash flows of the combined instrument vary like those of a stand-alone derivative. Thus, some or all of the cash flows that would otherwise be required by the contract are modified according to a specified variable (e.g., interest rate, financial instrument price, commodity price, foreign exchange rate, index of prices or rates credit rating or index), excluding any non-financial variable that is specific to a party to the contract. If a derivative attached to a financial instrument is contractually transferable independently of that instrument, or has a different counterparty, it is not an embedded derivative but a separate financial instrument.

A hybrid contract with a host that is within the scope of IFRS 9 is to be treated in its entirety in accordance with the requirements of IFRS 9 as set out above. If the host is not within the scope of IFRS 9, the requirements of IAS 39 are applied to determine whether the embedded derivative is to be separated from the host. If it must be separated, then

- a derivative *asset* is to be classified according to IFRS 9 as indicated above,
- a derivative that is not an asset is to be classified in accordance with IAS 39, and
- the host is to be accounted for in accordance with other applicable IFRSs.

4.4 Reclassification. When, but only when, an entity changes its business model for managing a portfolio of financial assets, the latter must be reclassified in accordance with the criteria set out above.

If a financial asset is reclassified, the reclassification is applied prospectively from the reclassification date so that previously recognized gains, losses or interest are not restated. If an item is reclassified from amortized cost to fair value, the fair value is determined at the reclassification date, and any gain or loss resulting from a difference between fair value and the previous carrying amount is recognized in profit or loss. If an item is reclassified from fair value to amortized cost, the fair value at the reclassification date is the new carrying amount.

Chapter 5: Measurement

5.1 Initial measurement. At initial recognition, a financial asset or financial liability is to be measured at its fair value plus, in the case of a financial asset or financial liability not at FVPL, transaction costs directly attributable to its acquisition or issue.

OBSERVATION: In the case of an financial asset not at FVPL, if on subsequent measurement the total of the fair value at acquisition plus the transaction costs directly attributable exceeds the fair value at the subsequent date, the excess is written off and recognized as a loss in other comprehensive income.

5.2 Subsequent measurement of financial assets. After initial recognition, a financial asset is measured either at fair value or at amortized cost in accordance with the above. In the case of assets measured at amortized cost, the impairment requirements set out in IAS 39 (see above) are applicable. If a financial asset is designated as a hedged item, the hedge accounting requirements in IAS 39 as set out above apply.

5.3 Subsequent measurement of financial liabilities. After initial recognition, a financial liability is measured at amortized cost using the effective interest method, except for:

- Financial liabilities measured at FVPL following an election to do so on initial recognition;

- Financial liabilities that arise when a transfer of a financial asset does not qualify for derecognition or when the "continuing involvement" approach applies; and

- Financial guarantee contracts and commitments to provide a loan at a below-market interest rate, the requirements for the measurement of which are laid down by other IFRSs.

For a financial liability that is designated as a hedged item, the hedge accounting requirements of IAS 39, as set out above, apply.

5.4 Fair value measurement. The guidance on fair value measurement in IFRS 9 is contained in Appendix B to the IFRS, pars. B5.4.1–B5.4.17. This does not differ substantially from that in IAS 39.

OBSERVATION: Extensive guidance on fair value measurement is provided by IFRS 13, issued in May 2011; see Chapter 3.

5.5 Amortized cost measurement. This section of IFRS 9 was absent at the time of writing pending acceptance of the exposure draft," Financial Instruments: Impairment," as an IFRS.

5.6 Reclassification of financial assets. If an entity reclassifies a financial asset in accordance with 4.4 above, it applies the reclassification *prospectively* from the *reclassification date*. Previously recognized gains, losses, or interest are not restated.

If a financial asset is reclassified so that it is measured at fair value, the fair value is determined at the reclassification date, and any difference between this fair value and the previous carrying value is recognized in profit or loss.

If a financial asset is reclassified so that it is measured at amortized cost, its fair value at the reclassification date becomes its new carrying amount.

5.7 Gains and losses. *Financial assets or financial liabilities measured at fair value.* For items not part of a hedging relationship, gains or losses are recognized immediately in profit or loss unless:

(a) In the case of an asset, (i) it is an investment in an equity instrument (see below) and (ii) the entity has elected to present gains and losses on that investment in other comprehensive income;

(b) In the case of a liability, it has been designated as at FVPL and the entity is required to present the effects of changes in the liability's *credit risk* separately in OCI, in which case only the remainder of the change in fair value is recognized in profit or loss.

Financial assets measured at amortized cost. For assets not part of a hedging relationship, gains or losses are recognized in profit or loss when the item is derecognized, impaired or reclassified as set out in "Reclassification" above, and through the amortization process.

Hedged items. Gains or losses on financial assets that are hedged items are recognized in accordance with IAS 39.

Settlement date accounting. Changes in the fair value of financial assets that are recognized using settlement date accounting any change in the fair value of the asset to be received during the period between the trade date and the settlement date is not recognized for assets measured at amortized cost (except for impairment losses). For assets measured at FVPL, the change in fair value is recognized in profit or loss unless (a) it is part of a hedging relationship or (b) it is an investment in an equity instrument and the entity has elected to present gains and losses in OCI, in which case the change in fair value is recognized in OCI.

Investments in Equity Instruments

For an equity instrument that is *not held for trading* and is within the scope of IFRS 9, an *irrevocable* decision may be made at initial recognition that subsequent changes in its fair value will be presented in other comprehensive income.

OBSERVATION: This treatment is the same as that for AFS financial assets according to IAS 39. Hence the claim that IFRS 9 reduces the number of measurement categories of financial assets from four to two is perhaps slightly exaggerated, since financial assets measured at fair value may be accounted for either (a) at FVPL, or (b) if equity instruments are not held for trading, in such a way that changes in fair value are presented in OCI.

Liabilities Designated as at FVPL

Gains or losses on financial liabilities designated as at FVPL are presented as follows: (a) the amount of the change in the fair value that is attributable to changes in the *credit risk* of that liability is presented in OCI; (b) the remainder is presented in profit or loss, unless the treatment under (a) would create or enlarge an accounting mismatch in profit or loss. In the latter case, the entire amount of the gain or loss is presented in profit or loss. Such an accounting mismatch could be caused by the existence of another financial instrument designated as at FVPL, the gains or losses on which offset the losses or gains on the financial liability (IFRS 9, pars. B5.7.7–B5.7.10).

Chapter 6: Hedge Accounting

This chapter was missing at the time of writing, as the related exposure draft had not yet completed the process of becoming an IFRS. In the meantime, the provisions of IAS 39 apply (see under "Hedging" in IAS 39 above, including the "Observations," which indicate the main respects in which the exposure draft differs from IAS 39).

Chapter 7: Date and Transition

IFRS 9 is intended to be applicable for annual periods beginning on or after January 1, 2013, but earlier adoption is permitted. There are a number of transitional requirements relating to classification and measurement.

As IFRS 9 is in general more aligned to preparers' methods for managing financial instruments and the attendant risks, early adoption is to be expected. This will also apply to the new provisions in the exposure drafts on hedge accounting and amortized cost when they have completed the process of becoming part of the IFRS.

CHAPTER 18
FOREIGN CURRENCY TRANSLATION

CONTENTS

OVERVIEW

Changes in foreign currency exchange rates affect financial reporting in two ways. There are effects on:

1. Accounting for transactions in foreign currencies and the carrying amounts in the reporting currency of financial assets and liabilities denominated in foreign currencies and of the net investment in a foreign entity; and

2. Translating the financial statements of foreign operations that are included in the financial statements of a reporting entity through full or proportionate consolidation or the equity method. A foreign operation may be a subsidiary, joint venture, or branch of the reporting entity.

IASB GAAP for foreign currency translation are set out in IAS 21, "The Effects of Changes in Foreign Exchange Rates" (as revised and amended in 2004, 2005, and 2008). SIC-7, "Introduction of the Euro," clarifies the application of IAS 21 when EU member states adopt the euro in place of their national currency. IASB GAAP require foreign currency transactions to be accounted for by applying the spot exchange rate in effect at the transaction date. An average rate for the period (e.g., week or month) in which the transaction occurred may be used, in the absence of significant fluctuations in the spot rate. Foreign currency monetary items should be translated at the closing (spot) rate at the balance sheet date. Nonmonetary items carried at historical cost continue to be translated at the historical rate originally used, while those carried at fair value denominated in foreign currency are carried at the spot rate on the date on which the fair value was determined. For monetary items, exchange differences between the closing rate and the rate previously used should be recognized immediately in income, except in certain situations involving hedge accounting or in the case of unavoidable exchange losses on a liability incurred in the recent acquisition of an asset invoiced in foreign currency, where an allowed alternative treatment is permitted.

A net investment in a foreign entity should be translated at the closing rate, and exchange differences (gains or losses) arising on the translation should generally be recognized in other comprehensive income (OCI) until the investment is disposed of and the gain or loss on disposal is recognized, at which time the exchange gains or losses should be included in the calculation of the gain or loss on disposal.

BACKGROUND

The main problem areas in accounting for the effects of changes in foreign exchange rates have been (a) the translation into the reporting currency of the financial statements of foreign entities in the consolidation process and (b) the particular problem when a foreign entity reports in the currency of a hyperinflationary economy (dealt with in IAS 29; see Chapter 10).

Historically, several methods have existed for translating the financial statements of a foreign entity into the reporting currency, with distinctions being made between those balance sheet items to be translated at closing rates and those to be translated at historic rates. Thus, there were distinctions between monetary and nonmonetary items, or between current and non-current items, or between items (including monetary items) carried at current fair values and those carried at historical costs; with the first-named of each pair being translated at closing rates and the second at historical rates. A major issue was the treatment of gains or losses arising on translation because of exchange rate changes: should these be included in income or not?

ASC 830 in the United States resolved most of these issues by requiring that all balance sheet items be translated at current (closing) rates and that the resultant translation gains and losses be recognized in OCI, bypassing net income. Essentially, this represented a recognition that, in the consolidation or equitization of an independent foreign entity, such gains and losses are merely artifacts of the accounting process of translation and do not necessarily reflect any value changes that are relevant to the measurement of consolidated net income.

Ostensibly, major changes have been made in the revised IAS 21 as compared with the previous revision, but in practice, as explained below, the effects are likely to be less than first appearances would suggest. The previous IAS 21, effective from 1995, contained an explicit distinction between a foreign operation and a foreign entity. The definitions were as follows. A *foreign operation* is a subsidiary, associate, joint venture, or branch of the reporting entity, the activities of which are based or conducted in a different country from that of the reporting entity. A *foreign entity* is a foreign operation, the activities of which are not an integral part of those of the reporting entity.

The implication was that two types of foreign organization could be distinguished: (a) a foreign operation that was not an integral part of the activities of the reporting entity, called a foreign entity and (b) a foreign operation that was an integral part of these activities. The first type would be run as an independent operation, and the second as a branch that happened to be abroad. The old IAS 21 required that, for foreign entities, the assets and liabilities be translated at closing rates and income statements be translated at a reasonable approximation to actual rates (such as monthly average rates). However, goodwill and fair value adjustments to non-monetary items arising on an acquisition could, alternatively, be translated at the historical rate at the acquisition date. Exchange differences were recognized in OCI. If the foreign entity's reporting currency was that of a hyperinflationary economy, its financial statements should be restated in accordance with IAS 29, "Financial Reporting in Hyperinflationary Economies" (see Chapter 10), before translation at the closing rate. The financial statements of foreign operations that were an integral part of the parent's operations were translated as if their transactions had been those of the parent. This implies in general the use of historical rates (i.e., the rate ruling when the transaction took place by the presumed singly economic and operating entity)—an approach often referred to, though not in the old IAS 21 itself, as the temporal method.

At the same time, the previous notion of a reporting currency has been replaced with two notions:

- *Functional currency*—the currency of the primary economic environment in which the entity operates. The term "functional currency" is used in place of "measurement currency" (the term used in SIC-19) because it is the more commonly used term, but with essentially the same meaning.

- *Presentation currency*—the currency in which financial statements are presented.

The new IAS 21 revises the provisions on distinguishing between foreign operations that are integral to the operations of the reporting entity (referred to below as "integral foreign operations") and foreign entities, to become part of the indicators of what is an entity's functional currency. As a result:

- No distinction is made between integral foreign operations and foreign entities. Rather, an entity that was previously classified as an integral foreign operation will have the same functional currency as the reporting entity.

- Only one translation method is needed for foreign operations, namely that previously described in IAS 21 as applying to foreign entities.

In most cases, the effect of this apparently major change of principle will not be very great. As the functional currency of a foreign operation whose activities are an integral part of those of the reporting entity will be the same as the functional currency of the reporting entity, by definition, no year-end currency differences can arise.

The functional currency will usually be obvious. Suppose a parent in the U.K. runs a foreign operation in France. If the foreign operation is an integral part of the U.K. parent's operations then the functional currency of the foreign operation must be the currency of the U.K. parent (i.e., sterling). If the foreign operation is an independent operation (in France), then its functional currency must be that of France (i.e., euro).

A further by-product of this revised approach is that the IASB has extricated itself from the mess it had previously got into relating to IAS 29, "Financial Reporting in Hyperinflationary Economies" (see Chapter 10), as developed by SIC-19, "Reporting Currency—Measurement and Presentation of Financial Statements under IAS 21 and IAS 29," now withdrawn. The effect of all these previous requirements, without going into details now, was that an entity could often avoid applying IAS 29, against the intentions of IASB GAAP. The new material in the new IAS 21 on functional currency incorporates some of the guidance previously included in SIC-19 on how to determine a measurement currency. However, the standard gives greater emphasis than SIC-19 gave to the currency of the economy that determines the pricing of transactions, as opposed to the currency in which transactions are denominated. As a result of these changes and the incorporation of guidance previously in SIC-19:

- An entity (whether a stand-alone entity or a foreign operation) does not have a free choice of functional currency.

- An entity cannot avoid restatement in accordance with IAS 29, "Financial Reporting in Hyperinflationary Economies," by, for example, adopting a stable currency (such as the functional currency of its parent) as its functional currency.

In May 2008, in conjunction with amendments to IAS 27 (replacement of the cost method), IAS 21 was amended to remove the stipulation that the payment of a dividend is part of a disposal only when it constitutes a return of the investment.

The main differences from U.S. GAAP (ASC 830) are:

1. IAS 21 requires the financial statements of a foreign entity that reports using the currency of a hyperinflationary country to be restated for general price-level changes prior to translation into the reporting entity's currency. ASC 830 requires remeasurement of the elements of the entity's financial statements into the reporting entity's currency, as though the latter were its functional currency. Whether the two methods produce similar results depends on how closely the change in the general price-level in the hyperinflationary economy is reflected in the change in the exchange rate between the two currencies.

2. IAS 21 does not deal with foreign currency hedges, which are dealt with in IAS 39. There are some differences between the treatment of foreign currency hedges in IAS 39 and in ASC 830 (see Chapter 17).

SCOPE

The objective of IAS 21 is to prescribe how to include foreign currency transactions and foreign operations in the financial statements of an entity and how to translate financial statements into a presentation currency. The standard applies:

- In accounting for transactions and balances in foreign currencies, except for those derivative transactions and balances that are within the scope of IAS 39/IFRS 9 "Financial Instruments";
- In translating the results and financial position of foreign operations that are included in the financial statements of the entity by consolidation, proportionate consolidation or the equity method; and
- In translating an entity's results and financial position into a presentation currency.

IAS 21 does not deal with the following:

1. Hedge accounting for foreign currency items, dealt with in IAS 39 (see Chapter 17).
2. Specifying the currency in which financial statements are presented.
3. "Convenience translations" of financial statements from the reporting currency into another currency for the benefit of some users.
4. Presentation of foreign exchange difference in cash flow statements arising from transactions in a foreign currency, which are dealt with in IAS 7, "Cash Flow Statements" (see Chapter 9) (IAS 21, pars. 4–7).

DEFINITIONS

The following terms are used in the standard with the meanings specified (par 8):

- *Foreign operation* is an entity that is a subsidiary, associate, joint venture or branch of a reporting entity, the activities of which are based or conducted in a country or currency other than those of the reporting entity.
- *Functional currency* is the currency of the primary economic environment in which the entity operates.
- *Foreign currency* is a currency other than the functional currency of the entity.
- *Presentation currency* is the currency in which the financial statements are presented.
- *Exchange rate* is the ratio of exchange for two currencies.
- *Spot exchange rate* is the exchange rate for immediate delivery.
- *Exchange difference* is the difference resulting from translating a given number of units of one currency into another currency at different exchange rates.
- *Closing rate* is the spot exchange rate at the balance sheet date.
- *Net investment in a foreign operation* is the amount of the reporting entity's interest in the net assets of that operation.
- A *group* is a parent and all its subsidiaries.

- *Monetary items* are units of currency held and assets and liabilities to be received or paid in a fixed or determinable number of units of currency.

- *Fair value* is the amount for which an asset could be exchanged, or a liability settled, between knowledgeable, willing parties in an arm's-length transaction.

IAS 21 elaborates on the determination of the functional currency at considerable length (pars. 9-14). The primary indicators as to the functional currency for an entity are twofold. It will be:

1. The currency (a) that mainly influences sales prices for goods and services (this will often be the currency in which sales prices for its goods and services are denominated and settled); and (b) of the country whose competitive forces and regulations mainly determine the sales prices of its goods and services.

2. The currency that mainly influences labor, material, and other costs of providing goods or services (this will often be the currency in which such costs are denominated and settled).

The standard then lists a series of factors that may also provide evidence of an entity's functional currency (making it explicit that the two primary indicators given above have priority in the decision if doubts arise):

- The currency in which funds from financing activities (i.e., issuing debt and equity instruments) are generated.

- The currency in which receipts from operating activities are usually retained.

- Whether the activities of a foreign operation are carried out as an extension of the reporting entity, rather than being carried out with a significant degree of autonomy. An example of the former is when the foreign operation sells only goods imported from the reporting entity and remits the proceeds to it. An example of the latter is when the operation accumulates cash and other monetary items, incurs expenses, generates income, and arranges borrowings, all substantially in its local currency.

- Whether transactions with the reporting entity are a high or a low proportion of the foreign operation's activities.

- Whether cash flows from the activities of the foreign operation directly affect the cash flows of the reporting entity and are readily available for remittance to it.

- Whether cash flows from the activities of the foreign operation are sufficient to service existing and normally expected debt obligations with funds being made available by the reporting entity.

In the end, if uncertainty continues, judgment is necessary, the functional currency being that which most faithfully represents the economic effects of the underlying transactions, events, and conditions. It follows that a change in functional currency over time is generally unlikely. If the functional currency is the currency of a hyperinflationary economy, the entity's financial statements are restated in accordance with IAS 29.

Note that the net investment in a foreign operation again needs to be evaluated in accordance with economic realities. Thus a long-term monetary item receivable from or payable to a foreign operation may be part of net investment, rather than a receivable or payable in the usual sense.

REPORTING FOREIGN CURRENCY TRANSACTIONS IN THE FUNCTIONAL CURRENCY

As previously discussed, any particular entity has one functional currency, which, once established, will not be expected to change unless the operations of the entity change in some particularly fundamental way. This functional currency then becomes the basis of the recording and translation activities of the entity. This functional currency will often be, but need not be, the currency used as the reporting currency in published financial statements–an alternative"presentation currency" may be used, as discussed below. However, *in all cases*, recording first takes place in the functional currency.

Initial Recognition

A foreign currency transaction is one that is denominated or requires settlement in a foreign currency, including:

1. Buying or selling goods or services at a price denominated in a foreign currency.

2. Borrowing or lending funds if the amounts payable or receivable are denominated in a foreign currency.

3. Otherwise acquiring or disposing of assets and incurring or settling of liabilities denominated in a foreign currency (IAS 21, par. 20).

A foreign currency transaction should be recorded, on initial recognition in the functional currency, by applying to the foreign currency amount the exchange rate between the foreign currency and the reporting currency at the date of the transaction. This exchange rate should in principle be the spot rate. For practical reasons, however, where there is a large number of transactions during a relatively short period such as a week or a month, a reasonable approximation of it may be used, such as the average rate over the period, provided the fluctuations in the exchange rate are not such as to make such an approximation unreliable (IAS 21, pars. 21–22).

Reporting at Subsequent Balance Sheet Dates

Monetary items should be translated into the reporting currency at the closing rate. Nonmonetary items carried at fair value *in the foreign currency* should be translated at the rate prevailing on the date when the fair values were determined; there will be no subsequent retranslation unless a new fair value in the foreign currency is subsequently determined. Nonmonetary items carried at historical cost in the foreign currency should be translated at the rate prevailing at the date of the transaction; there is no subsequent retranslation (IAS 21, par. 23).

A complication recognized in the latest version of IAS 21 (par. 25) is that some assets are carried at a mixture of different types of valuation, or more accurately, some units within a class of assets may be carried at, say, cost and other units within the same class at, say, net realizable value (under IAS 2, "Inventories," see Chapter 24) or at recoverable amount (under IAS 36, "Impairment of Assets," see Chapter 20). When such an asset is non-monetary and is measured in a foreign currency, the carrying amount is determined by comparing:

1. The cost or carrying amount, as appropriate, translated at the exchange rate at the date when that amount was determined (i.e., the rate at the date of the transaction for an item measured in terms of historical cost); and

2. The net realizable value or recoverable amount, as appropriate, translated at the exchange rate at the date when that value was determined (i.e., the closing rate at the balance sheet date).

The effect of this comparison may be that an impairment loss is recognized in the functional currency but would not be recognized in the foreign currency, or vice versa.

Recognition of Exchange Differences

IAS 21 does not deal with hedge accounting. Hedge accounting is dealt with in IAS 39, "Financial Instruments" (see Chapter 17). The requirements set out below may be modified by IAS 39 (or ultimately by the new chapter of IFRS 9 on hedge accounting) when the requirements for hedge accounting are met.

Exchange differences arising on the settlement of monetary items, or on translating monetary items at rates different from those at which they were previously translated, should be recognized in profit or loss in the period in which they arise, with the exception of the items described below under "Net Investment in a Foreign Entity." When a transaction is settled in a subsequent accounting period, an exchange difference will be recognized on translation or retranslation at each balance sheet date, and at settlement the difference to be recognized will be that between the rate on settlement and that at the previous balance sheet date (IAS 21, pars. 28–29).

However, note that when a gain or loss on a non-monetary item is recognized in OCI, any exchange component of that gain or loss also must be recognized in OCI. Conversely, when a gain or loss on a non-monetary item is recognized in profit or loss, any exchange component of that gain or loss also must be recognized in profit or loss. For example, IAS 16 requires some gains and losses arising on a revaluation of property, plant, and equipment to be recognized in OCI. When such an asset is measured in a foreign currency, IAS 21 requires the revalued amount to be translated using the rate at the date the value is determined, resulting in an exchange difference that is also recognized in equity.

Net Investment in a Foreign Operation

An entity or any of its subsidiaries may have a monetary item that is receivable from, or payable to, a foreign operation, settlement of which is neither planned nor likely to occur in the foreseeable future. Such an item does not include trade receivables or trade payables (IAS 21, par. 15). Such an item is, in substance, an extension to or deduction from the entity's net investment in that foreign operation, and IASB GAAP require exchange differences arising on such items to be recognized in OCI until the net investment in the foreign operation is disposed of, at which time they should be taken into account as part of the overall gain or loss on disposal (IAS 21, pars. 32–33).

Change in Functional Currency

As previously discussed, such changes are likely to be rare. Equally clearly, because of the relationship between an entity's functional currency and its operating environment, such changes can happen. When they do, the effect of a change in functional currency is accounted for prospectively. In other words, an entity translates all items into the new functional currency from the old one using the exchange rate at the date of the change. The resulting translated amounts for non-monetary items are treated as their historical cost. Exchange differences arising from the translation of a foreign operation previously classified in equity are not recognized in profit or loss until the disposal of the operation.

USE OF A PRESENTATION CURRENCY OTHER THAN THE FUNCTIONAL CURRENCY

IAS 21 recognizes that an entity may choose to publish its financial statements using a presentation currency that is different from its functional currency. As regards the functional currency requirements discussed above, when an entity keeps its permanent accounting records in a currency that is not its functional currency, the translation into the functional currency when the financial statements are prepared produces the same amounts in the functional currency as would have occurred had the items been recorded initially in the functional currency. For example, monetary items are translated into the functional currency using the closing rate, and non-monetary items that are measured on a historical cost basis are translated using the exchange rate at the date of the transaction that resulted in their recognition.

Any further translation into a different presentation currency is prepared so as to minimize as far as possible any changes in the *relative* relationships between the various items in the financial statements. In the general case, when the functional currency is not that of a hyperinflationary economy (as defined in IAS 29, "Financial Reporting in Hyperinflationary Economies," see Chapter 10), the financial statements are to be translated into a different presentation currency using the following procedures:

1. Assets and liabilities for each balance sheet presented (i.e., including comparatives) are translated at the closing rate at the date of that balance sheet.

2. Income and expenses for each income statement (i.e., including comparatives) are translated at exchange rates at the dates of the transactions.

3. All resulting exchange differences are recognized as a separate component of equity.

Consistent with comparable situations described earlier, an average exchange rate may be used regarding point 2 when differences will be insignificant.

→ **PRACTICE POINTER:** The exchange differences referred to above result from:

(a) Translating income and expenses at the exchange rates at the dates of the transactions and assets and liabilities at the closing rate. Such exchange differences arise both on income and expense items recognized in profit or loss and on those recognized in OCI.

(b) Translating the opening net assets at a closing rate that differs from the previous closing rate.

These exchange differences are not recognized in profit or loss because the changes in exchange rates have little or no direct effect on the present and future cash flows from operations. When the exchange differences relate to a foreign operation that is consolidated but not wholly owned, accumulated exchange differences arising from translation and attributable to minority interests are allocated to, and recognized as part of minority interest in, the consolidated balance sheet.

If the functional currency is that of a hyperinflationary economy, further considerations apply. As discussed earlier, the IASB was at pains, in drafting the new version of IAS 21, to extricate itself from the previous position in which entities could often avoid the application of purchasing power (general inflation) adjustments through a judicious, and arguably artificial, choice of reporting currency. Through the enforced application of a functional currency, as defined and applied above, whether or not a separate presentation currency is used, such avoidance is now impossible. Accordingly (for pars. 42–43), the results and financial position of an entity whose functional currency is the currency of a hyperinflationary economy are translated into a different presentation currency using the following procedures:

1. All amounts (i.e., assets, liabilities, equity items, and income and expenses, including comparatives) are translated at the closing rate at the date of the most recent balance sheet, except that

2. When amounts are translated into the currency of a non-hyperinflationary economy, comparative amounts are those that were presented as current year amounts in the relevant prior-year financial statements (i.e., not adjusted for subsequent changes in the price level or subsequent changes in exchange rates).

When an entity's functional currency is the currency of a hyperinflationary economy, the entity restates its financial statements in accordance with IAS 29, "Financial Reporting in Hyperinflationary Economies," before applying this translation method, except for comparative amounts that are translated into a currency of a non-hyperinflationary economy. When the economy ceases to be hyperinflationary and the entity no longer restates its financial statements in accordance with IAS 29, it must use as the "historical costs" for translation into the presentation currency the amounts restated to the price level at the date the entity ceased restating its financial statements.

OBSERVATION: Note that we have put quotation marks, unlike the IASB, around the words "historical cost" in the last sentence above. Strictly, they are neither historical costs (i.e., amounts of currency units expended) nor fully adjusted "current purchasing power costs"(as they only contain adjustments relating to hyperinflationary years as defined). They are somewhere in between, the precise position being indeterminate as far as a financial statement user is concerned.

Whether or not a hyperinflationary economy is involved, certain additional considerations apply when the results and financial position of a foreign operation are translated into a presentation currency so that the foreign operation can be included in the financial statements of the reporting entity by consolidation, proportionate consolidation, or the equity method (pars. 44–47)—in particular, differences in year-end between foreign operation and reporting entity may arise. In such a case, the assets and liabilities of the foreign operation are translated at the exchange rate at the balance sheet date of the foreign operation. Adjustments are made for significant changes in exchange rates up to the balance sheet date of the reporting entity, in accordance with IAS 27. The same approach is used in applying the equity method to associates and joint ventures and in applying proportionate consolidation to joint ventures in accordance with IAS 28 and IAS 31 (see Chapters 8 and 15). Note that proportionate consolidation ceases to be part of IASB GAAP when IFRS 11, "Joint Arrangements," is adopted.

Any goodwill arising on the acquisition of a foreign operation and any fair value adjustments to the carrying amounts of assets and liabilities arising on the acquisition of that foreign operation should be treated as assets and liabilities of the foreign operation. Thus they are expressed in the functional currency of the foreign operation and translated at the closing rate in accordance with the general requirements of IAS 21 (par. 47).

DISPOSAL OF A FOREIGN OPERATION

On the disposal of a foreign operation, the cumulative amount of any exchange differences relating to that foreign operation that were recognized in other comprehensive income and accumulated in the separate component of equity, is reclassified from equity to profit or loss by a reclassification adjustment when the gain or loss is recognized (see IAS 1, "Presentation of Financial Statements," Chapter 4). In the case of a partial disposal, the relevant proportion of the cumulative amount of exchange differences should be included in the gain or loss on disposal.

In addition to the disposal of an entity's entire interest in a foreign operation, the following are counted as disposals even if the entity retains an interest in the former subsidiary, associate, or jointly controlled entity:

- The loss of control of a subsidiary that includes a foreign operation.

- The loss of significant influence over an associate that includes a foreign operation.

- The loss of joint control over a jointly controlled entity that includes a foreign operation.

With the exception of the above, any reduction in an entity's ownership interest in a foreign operation is a *partial* disposal.

On disposal of a subsidiary that includes a foreign operation, the cumulative amount of the exchange differences relating to the foreign operation that have been attributed to the non-controlling interests are derecognized but not reclassified to profit or loss. On the *partial* disposal of a subsidiary that includes a foreign operation, the entity reattributes the proportionate share of the cumulative amount of the exchange differences recognized in other comprehensive income to the non-controlling interests in that operation. In any other *partial* disposal of a foreign operation, the entity reclassifies to profit or loss only the proportionate share of the cumulative amount of the exchange differences recognized in other comprehensive income.

An entity may dispose or partially dispose of its interest in a foreign operation through sale, liquidation, repayment of share capital, or abandonment of all or part of that entity. A write-down in the carrying amount of a foreign operation either because of its own losses or because of an impairment recognized by the investor is not a partial disposal and does not result in any cumulative exchange differences, previously recognized directly in other comprehensive income, being reclassified to profit or loss of the period (IAS 21, pars. 48–49).

TAX EFFECTS OF EXCHANGE DIFFERENCES

Gains and losses on foreign currency transactions, and exchange differences arising on the translation of financial statements of foreign operations, may have tax effects, which should be dealt with according to IAS 12, "Income Taxes" (see Chapter 21).

> **OBSERVATION:** In fact, IASB GAAP have little to say about this matter, which is addressed briefly in IAS 12, paragraphs 41 and 62–63. One problem for an international standard on such a topic is the different tax treatment of such items in different jurisdictions.

DISCLOSURE

An entity (which may be an enterprise or a group) should disclose:

- The amount of exchange differences recognized in profit or loss except for those arising on financial instruments measured at fair value through profit or loss in accordance with IAS 39.
- Net exchange differences classified in a separate component of equity and a reconciliation of the amount of such exchange differences at the beginning and end of the period.

When the presentation currency is different from the functional currency, that fact should be stated, together with disclosure of the functional currency and the reason for using a different presentation currency.

When there is a change in the functional currency of either the reporting entity or a significant foreign operation, that fact and the reason for the change in functional currency shall be disclosed. When an entity presents its financial statements in a currency that is different from its functional currency, it describes the financial statements as complying with International Financial Reporting Standards only if the statements comply with all the requirements of each applicable standard and each applicable interpretation of those standards, including the translation method set out in IAS 21.

When an entity displays its financial statements or other financial information in a currency that is different from either its functional currency or its presentation currency and the requirements of the preceding paragraph are not met in full, it must:

1. Clearly identify the information as supplementary information to distinguish it from the information that complies with International Financial Reporting Standards;
2. Disclose the currency in which the supplementary information is displayed; and
3. Disclose the entity's functional currency and the method of translation used to determine the supplementary information.

OBSERVATION: This last point is intended to deal with various so-called convenience translations. IASB does not wish to outlaw such practices, but it is determined that readers of financial statements be absolutely clear in their own minds that any such statements are additional to, and in no sense part of, fair presentation under IASB GAAP.

TRANSITIONAL PROVISIONS

In general, IAS 8, "Accounting Policies, Changes in Accounting Estimates, and Errors," applies when the revised IAS 21 is first used. A complicated requirement relates to the goodwill requirement in par. 47, as discussed above. This is as follows (par. 59):

> An entity shall apply paragraph 47 prospectively to all acquisitions occurring after the beginning of the financial reporting period in which IAS 21 is first applied. Retrospective application of paragraph 47 to earlier acquisitions is permitted. For an acquisition of a foreign operation treated prospectively but which occurred before the date on which the standard is first applied, the

entity does not restate prior years and accordingly may, when appropriate, treat goodwill and fair value adjustments arising on that acquisition as assets and liabilities of the entity rather than as assets and liabilities of the foreign operation. Therefore, those goodwill and fair value adjustments either are already expressed in the entity's functional currency or are non-monetary foreign currency items, which are reported using the exchange rate at the date of the acquisition.

OBSERVATION: It is perhaps worth repeating our earlier point that, although the whole theoretical approach to foreign currency translation under IASB GAAP appears to have—and indeed has—changed significantly with the introduction of the newly revised version of IAS 21, the practical differences as compared with the previous IAS 21 are much less than a cursory consideration might suggest. The introduction of the notion of a functional currency, derived (and developed) from U.S. GAAP, has in fact led to a simplification of the basic principles and to a much greater consistency of basic approach.

SIC-7, "INTRODUCTION OF THE EURO"

Although in one sense historical, this Interpretion will be applicable when further countries join the Euro system. Essentially, it merely confirms that the full requirements of IAS 21 should be strictly applied when the changeover takes place.

CHAPTER 19
GOVERNMENT GRANTS AND GOVERNMENT ASSISTANCE

CONTENTS

OVERVIEW

Entities that receive a material amount of assistance from government or state sources are clearly in a different economic position from otherwise comparable entities that receive no such assistance. In order to allow proper appraisal of the results of the enterprise activities, and to facilitate comparisons, disclosure of this government assistance in as much detail as practicable is necessary.

More specifically, government *grants* are usually easily quantifiable, and the general principle of transparency requires that they be both properly accounted for and clearly disclosed. Government grants typically represent a reduction in net cash outflows, and therefore, at least ultimately, an increase in entity earnings. Some interesting issues of definition and alternative treatments arise, which need to be addressed and regulated. IASB GAAP are given in IAS 20, "Accounting for Government Grants and Disclosure of Government Assistance," effective from 1984. SIC-10, "Government Assistance—No Specific Relation to Operating Activities," is also relevant.

BACKGROUND

The issues of disclosure have already been summarized in the overview given above. The issues of measurement and definition are more complex, particularly in respect of grants related to the purchase of non-current assets. Under historical cost accounting, cost is obviously the basis of carrying value. IAS 16, "Property, Plant, and Equipment," for example, requires that an item of property, plant, and equipment that qualifies for recognition as an asset should initially be measured at its cost (see Chapter 28). The question is, what *is* its cost?

Suppose a government grant is paid to an entity because, and under the condition that, the entity purchases a depreciable non-current asset. The figures concerned are as follows:

Purchase price of asset	$12,000
Expected useful life	4 years
Expected residual value	Nil
Government grant	$2,000
Annual profits before depreciation, and grants relating to the asset	$20,000

It is possible to suggest at least four possible different ways of treating the grant.

1. To credit the total amount of the grant immediately to the income statement.

2. To credit the amount of the grant to a nondistributable reserve.

3. To credit the amount of the grant to revenue over the useful life of the asset by:

   (a) Reducing the cost of the acquisition of the non-current asset by the amount of the grant, or

   (b) Treating the amount of the grant as a deferred credit, a portion of which is transferred to revenue annually.

The first two methods may be rejected on the ground that they provide no correlation between the accounting treatment of the grant and the accounting treatment of the expenditure to which the grant relates. The first method would increase the profits in the first year by the entire amount of the grant, failing to associate the grant with the useful life of the asset. It thus ignores both the prudence convention and the matching convention. The second method means that the grant will *never* affect the profit figure. It also, therefore, ignores the matching convention and additionally leaves the "nondistributable reserve" in the balance sheet, presumably forever, that is, it is treated as paid-in surplus.

The third and fourth methods both follow and apply the matching convention. They both have exactly the same effect on reported annual profits, the differences being concerned only with balance sheet presentation.

Illustration of Different Accounting Treatments

Using the data given above, the two "acceptable" methods give the following results.

Method 3(a)

Profit before depreciation, etc.	$20,000	$20,000	$20,000	$20,000
Depreciation	(2,500)	(2,500)	(2,500)	(2,500)
Profit	$17,500	$17,500	$17,500	$17,500

Balance sheet extract at year-end				
Non-current asset at (net) cost	$10,000	$10,000	$10,000	$10,000

Depreciation	2,500	5,000	7,500	10,000
Carrying amount	$ 7,500	$ 5,000	$ 2,500	$ 0

Method 3(b)

Profit before depreciation, etc.	$20,000	$20,000	$20,000	$20,000
Depreciation	(3,000)	(3,000)	(3,000)	(3,000)
Grant released	500	500	500	500
Profit	$17,500	$17,500	$17,500	$17,500

Balance sheet extract at year-end

Non-current asset at cost	$12,000	$12,000	$12,000	$12,000
Depreciation	3,000	6,000	9,000	12,000
Carrying amount	$ 9,000	$ 6,000	$ 3,000	$ 0

Deferred credit

Government grant	$ 1,500	$ 1,000	$ 500	$0

Thus, method (a) shows assets of 7,500, 5,000, 2,500, and 0 over the four years, and method (b) shows assets of 9,000, 6,000, 3,000, and 0, together with "liabilities" of 1,500, 1,000, 500, and 0.

From a pragmatic point of view, method (a) has the obvious advantage of simplicity. No entries, and no thought, are required in the second and subsequent years. Method (b), however, has the advantage that assets acquired at different times and locations are recorded on a uniform basis, regardless of changes in governmental policy. But what *is* the cost of the asset? Is it 12,000 or is it 10,000? IAS 16, "Property, Plant, and Equipment" (see Chapter 28), states that cost is the amount of cash or cash equivalents paid, net of any trade discounts and rebates. This statement does not seem to categorically resolve the question. The government grant is not a trade discount. It is not a *trade* rebate, but it is a rebate. This would seem to imply that the cost in the sense of IAS 16 is 10,000. This is surely the net outflow arising because of the purchase. Yet, IAS 20, as discussed in detail below, allows both methods.

OBSERVATION: A difficult conceptual problem arises with the deferred credit under method (b), for example, the 1,500 at the end of year 1. We described it above as a "liability." As discussed in Chapter 2, the IASB defines a liability as a present obligation of the entity arising from past events, the settlement of which is expected to result in an outflow of resources embodying economic benefits. On the assumption that the grant cannot be reclaimed by the governmental body concerned (the usual situation), the 1,500 is clearly *not* a liability, as no outflow of resources is foreseeable. It is more logically either a reserve (not yet realized), or a contra-asset. It could be suggested that this leads to a different possible treatment, that is, regular inclusion in the balance sheet as a visible contra-asset (i.e., included as a negative balance among the "assets" instead of as a positive balance amongst the liabilities). This would raise its own problems—not least the lack of user-friendliness involved in the concept of a negative asset. Such conceptual difficulties do not appear to worry either the IASB or other national regulators.

U.S. GAAP, or at least promulgated U.S. GAAP, appear to be silent on this whole area. ASC 958, "Not for Profit Entities," applies to not-for-profit organizations and explicitly excludes transfer of assets from governments to businesses.

U.K. GAAP, in SSAP 4, does not permit the netting out of capital grants in the balance sheet and allows only the treatment retaining a separate deferred income balance. This is under the stated, but mistaken, belief that U.K. law, following European Directive wording, prohibits such setting off. U.K. (and European) legal requirements forbid the netting out of assets and liabilities, but of course deferred income is not a liability, as already discussed, so therefore netting would be perfectly legal!

SCOPE AND DEFINITIONS

IAS 20, "Accounting for Government Grants and Disclosure of Government Assistance," should be applied in accounting for, and in the disclosure of, government grants and in the disclosure of other forms of government assistance.

It does not deal with:

1. The special problems arising in accounting for government grants in financial statements reflecting the effects of changing prices or in supplementary information of a similar nature;

2. Government assistance that is provided for an enterprise in the form of benefits that are available in determining taxable income or are determined or limited on the basis of income tax liability (such as income tax holidays, investment tax credits, accelerated depreciation allowances, and reduced income tax rates);

3. Government participation in the ownership of the enterprise; and

4. Government grants covered by IAS 41, "Agriculture" (see Chapter 34).

Government assistance is action by government designed to provide an economic benefit specific to an entity or range of entities qualifying under certain criteria. Government assistance for the purpose of this standard does not include benefits provided only indirectly through action affecting general trading conditions, such as the provision of infrastructure in development areas or the imposition of trading constraints on competitors.

A specific subset of government assistance is government grants. *Government grants* are assistance by government in the form of transfers of resources to an enterprise in return for past or future compliance with certain conditions relating to the operating activities of the entity. They exclude those forms of government assistance that cannot reasonably have a value placed upon them and transactions with government that cannot be distinguished from the normal trading transactions of the entity.

The notion of government is to be interpreted broadly. *Government* refers to government, government agencies, and similar bodies, whether local, national, or international.

Government grants may be related to revenue/expense items, such as repayment of 10% of the wages bill, or to capital/asset items, such as repayment of 10% of the cost of a machine. These two types are formally distinguished by IAS 20:

- *Grants related to assets* are government grants whose primary condition is that an entity qualifying for them should purchase, construct, or otherwise acquire long-term assets. Subsidiary conditions may also be attached restricting the type or location of the assets or the periods during which they are to be acquired or held.

- *Grants related to income* are government grants other than those related to assets.

The standard gives two other definitions, including the familiar *fair value*:

- *Forgivable loans* are loans of which the lender undertakes to waive repayment under certain prescribed conditions.

- *Fair value* is the amount for which an asset could be exchanged between a knowledgeable, willing buyer and a knowledgeable, willing seller in an arm's-length transaction. (See also Chapter 3.)

GOVERNMENT ASSISTANCE

Despite the inclusion of government assistance in the title of IAS 20, the statements about it are brief and rather obscure. The definitions given above suggest, in effect, that government grants are government assistance that is distinguishable and quantifiable. Turning this around, references to government assistance in the standard are to government activities that cannot be quantified or clearly distinguished. It follows, of course, that government assistance in this sense cannot be included numerically in the financial statements.

Examples of assistance that cannot reasonably have a value placed upon it are free technical or marketing advice and the provision of guarantees. An example of assistance that cannot be distinguished from the normal trading transactions of the entity is a government procurement policy that is responsible for a portion of the entity's sales. The existence of the benefit might be unquestioned, but any attempt to segregate the trading activities from government assistance could well be arbitrary.

The significance of the benefit in the above examples may be such that disclosure of the nature, extent, and duration of the assistance is necessary in order that the financial statements may not be misleading (par. 36). The standard explicitly, and very oddly, stated (par. 37) that while loans at nil or low interest rates are a form of government assistance, the "benefit is not quantified by the imputation of interest." However, from January 1, 2009, this statement is withdrawn and indeed reversed by new paragraph 10A (see below).

The disclosure requirement implied in the above seems rather weakly stated. Nonquantified government support need not be disclosed at all unless its omission would be so serious as to be "misleading."

GOVERNMENT GRANTS

The major portion of IAS 20 is concerned with the treatment of government grants. The first issue to deal with is the timing of recognition. The IAS requirement (par. 7) is that government grants, including nonmonetary grants at fair value, should not be recognized until there is reasonable assurance that the enterprise will comply with the conditions attaching to them and that the grants will be received. Receipt of a grant does not of itself provide conclusive evidence that the conditions attaching to the grant have been or will be fulfilled.

"Reasonable assurance" is not, of course, definable or defined, but it is clearly less rigorous or demanding than, for example, "virtual certainty" or "beyond all reasonable doubt." The standard confirms (par. 10) that a forgivable loan (as defined earlier) is treated as a government grant when there is reasonable assurance that the entity will meet the terms for forgiveness of the loan. Once a government grant is recognized, any related contingency would be treated in accordance with IAS 37, "Provisions, Contingent Liabilities, and Contingent Assets" (see Chapter 29).

The benefit of a government loan at a below-market rate of interest is treated as a government grant. The loan shall be recognized and measured in accordance with IAS 39, "Financial Instruments: Recognition and Measurement." The benefit of the below-market rate of interest shall be measured as the difference between the initial carrying value of the loan determined in accordance with IFRS 9 and the proceeds received. The benefit is accounted for in accordance with this Standard. The entry shall consider the conditions and obligations that have been, or must be, met when identifying the costs for which the benefit of the loan is intended to compensate (par. 10A, inserted in 2008).

Perhaps rather surprisingly, IAS 20 discusses at some length (pars. 13 – 16) the ostensible advantages of two alternative approaches to the accounting treatment of government grants after recognition, namely the capital approach, under which a grant is credited directly to shareholders' interests, and the income approach, under which a grant is taken to income over one or more periods. Presumably there were members of the Board at the time who felt some sympathy with the "capital approach," but by implication most Board members must have tended toward the "net cost" argument of IAS 16, discussed above, as use of the capital approach is not permitted. The standard requires (par. 12) that government grants be recognized as income over the periods necessary to match them with the related costs that they are intended to compensate, on a systematic basis, that is, following method 3(a) or 3(b) as discussed at the beginning of this chapter. They should not be credited directly to shareholders' interests. SIC-10, "Government Assistance—No Specific Relation to Operating Activities," effective from August 1, 1998, has confirmed that government assistance to enterprises is a grant under IAS 20, even if granted generally to all entities within certain regions or industry sectors.

The matching principle will usually be simple to apply, as illustrated earlier in this chapter. Grants related to non-depreciable assets may also require the fulfillment of certain obligations and would then be recognized as income over the periods that bear the cost of meeting the obligations. As an example, a grant of land may be conditional upon the erection of a building on the site, and it may be appropriate to recognize it as income over the life of the building. A government grant that becomes receivable as compensation for expenses or losses already incurred or for the purpose of giving immediate financial support to the entity with no future related costs should be recognized as income of the period in which it becomes receivable. Separate disclosure and explanation may be required.

Usually, a careful reading of the contract with the governmental body will determine the appropriate accounting treatment, although an intelligent appraisal of the in-substance thrust of the contract may be required. For example a grant toward building a factory that stipulates that the factory must remain operating and employing at least 30 people for at least 3 years is clearly in essence a grant toward building a factory, not a revenue grant toward reducing net wage costs. However, where a grant clearly relates in material terms to both specific capital and specific revenue items, the standard is silent on appropriate treatment. Accounting common sense obviously requires an apportionment in such cases.

The standard is surprisingly vague about nonmonetary government grants, such as land donated by a government. IAS 20 merely notes (par. 23) that:

> it is usual to assess the fair value of the non-monetary asset and to account for both grant and asset at that fair value. An alternative course that is sometimes followed is to record both asset and grant at a nominal amount.

This is worded as a description, not as a requirement, although the preference is clear enough. Our view is that merely to record the event at nominal amount lacks transparency to an unacceptable degree. Also, it is not consistent with the substance over form principle and would lead to an inconsistent treatment of assets affecting both inter-entity and intra-entity comparisons.

Emission Rights

In December 2004, the IASB issued IFRIC 3, "Emission Rights." This issue arises because a number of governments are giving financial encouragement to companies to reduce undesirable emissions (greenhouse gases). The interpretation focused on so-called cap-and-trade schemes, but its principles applied more generally where relevant to other forms of incentive scheme to reduce such emissions.

Typically in cap-and-trade schemes, a government agency issues rights (allowances) to participating entities to emit a specified level of emissions. The government may issue the allowances free of charge or the participant may be required to pay for them. Participants in the scheme are able to buy and sell allowances and, therefore, in many schemes there is an active market for the allowances. At the end of a specified period, participants are required to deliver allowances equal to their actual emissions.

The interpretation specified that:

- Rights (allowances) are intangible assets that should be recognized in the financial statements in accordance with IAS 38, "Intangible Assets" (see Chapter 22).

- When allowances are issued to a participant by government (or government agency) for less than their fair value, the difference between the amount paid (if any) and their fair value is a government grant that is accounted for in accordance with IAS 20.

- As a participant produces emissions, it recognizes a provision for its obligation to deliver allowances in accordance with IAS 37, "Provisions, Contingent Liabilities, and Contingent Assets" (see Chapter 29). This provision is normally measured at the market value of the allowances needed to settle it.

IFRIC 3 was not well received, and was withdrawn in June 2005. The question of emission rights has been subsumed into a wider ongoing reappraisal of IAS 38, "Intangible Assets." In May 2011, the IASB decided not to proceed with the broad reappraisal of IAS 38 until further notice.

PRESENTATION OF GOVERNMENT GRANTS

Regarding the presentation of grants related to assets, IAS 20 allows both methods (a) and (b) as discussed and illustrated earlier in this chapter. Thus, government grants related to assets, including nonmonetary grants at fair value, should (pars. 24 – 28) be presented in the balance sheet either by setting up the grant as deferred income or by deducting the grant in arriving at the carrying amount of the asset. The standard spells out that separate disclosure of the gross cash flows in the cash flow statement is likely to be necessary, whatever treatment is followed in the balance sheet. IAS 7, "Statement of Cash Flows" (see Chapter 9), is more explicit in making this grossing up of cash flows a requirement.

Regarding the presentation of grants related to income, the standard again accepts either of two alternatives (pars. 29 – 31). It states, with approval, that grants related to income are sometimes presented as a credit in the income statement, either separately or under a general heading such as "Other income": alternatively, they are deducted in reporting the related expense.

A proper understanding of the financial statements may require separate disclosure of the grant and of its effects on particular items of income or expense. If an entity presents the components of profit or loss in a separate income statement, following paragraph 81 of IAS 1, "Presentation of Financial Statements," as revised in 2007 (see Chapter 4), it presents grants related to income in that separate statement.

REPAYMENT OF GOVERNMENT GRANTS

A grant to which conditions were attached may have been properly recognized under the "reasonable assurance" criterion discussed above. It may still become repayable in whole or in part, however, if, in fact, the conditions are not met. IAS 20 requires (par. 32) that such a grant, as soon as the repayment becomes foreseeable (which might be significantly earlier than when the repayment actually occurs), should be accounted for as a revision to an accounting estimate, under IAS 8, "Accounting Policies, Changes in Accounting Estimates, and Errors," see Chapter 6. This essentially requires that the entries be made in the financial statements of the year concerned. Repayment of a grant related to income should be applied first against any unamortized deferred credit set up in respect of the grant. To the extent that the repayment exceeds any such deferred credit, or where no deferred credit exists, the repayment should be recognized immediately as an expense. Repayment of a grant related to an asset should be recorded by increasing the carrying amount of the asset or reducing the deferred balance by the amount repayable. The cumulative additional depreciation that would have been recognized to date as an expense in the absence of the grant should be recognized immediately as an expense. Circumstances giving rise to repayment of a grant related to an asset may require consideration to be given to the possible impairment of the new carrying amount of the asset (see IAS 36, "Impairment of Assets," discussed in Chapter 20).

DISCLOSURE

The following matters should be disclosed:

1. The accounting policy adopted for government grants, including the methods of presentation adopted in the financial statements,

2. The nature and extent of government grants recognized in the financial statements and an indication of other forms of government assistance from which the entity has directly benefited, and

3. Unfulfilled conditions and other contingencies attaching to government assistance that has been recognized.

CHAPTER 20
IMPAIRMENT OF ASSETS

CONTENTS

OVERVIEW

Very broadly speaking, purchase transactions are recorded in accounting terms first by including the purchased item as an asset at its cost price, then by expensing the item over one or a number of accounting periods according to its usage or consumption pattern. The going concern convention supports this treatment, as it explicitly assumes that there will be future operational accounting periods in which present assets can be transferred to expenses.

Strictly, this means that there is no need, at an intermediate stage in this process, to compare the temporary balance sheet number with any form of value—using the word *value* in its proper sense of monetary benefit to be derived. This would not be in accordance with the prudence convention, however, and would arguably be dangerously misleading to creditors and lenders. Over the years accounting has dealt with the inherent tension and conflict here in a variety of ways, all more or less *ad hoc*, depending on the accounting issue involved (and often depending also on the country involved).

The IASB has quite properly attempted to provide a general standard, IAS 36, "Impairment of Assets," to provide consistency and coherence to this whole matter. The principle of the standard is clear and simple. First, the carrying amount of an asset is determined in accordance with accounting principles and other relevant international standards. Second, the "recoverable amount" of the asset is determined as of that date, being the *higher* of fair value less costs to sell and the asset's value in use (to the existing entity). If the recoverable amount is lower than the carrying value as recorded, then an impairment loss must be recognized immediately, that is, the carrying value is lowered to the recoverable amount. Otherwise, no impairment loss is required. It is important to emphasize that recoverable amount is a very different concept from fair value and, for non-current assets, will often be significantly higher than fair value. IAS 36 does not require assets within its scope to be recorded at the lower of cost and market or fair value.

The question of which assets IAS 36 applies is rather complicated, and the "Scope" section below should be read carefully. Unfortunately, although the principle of IAS 36 is simply stated, the IASB, perhaps influenced by tradition in the U.S., found it necessary to specify considerable operational detail in relation to its application. We consider these details below.

BACKGROUND

The essential objective of IAS 36 is to ensure that assets are not carried at a figure greater than their recoverable amount. The standard itself says nothing about possible or normal methods of arriving at carrying value. The standard applies whatever the underlying basis of valuation of the asset is. It explicitly states (par. 5) that it applies to assets carried at revalued amount (e.g., under IAS 16, see Chapter 28), as well as to assets recorded on a cost basis. It will also apply to relevant assets where the carrying value has been arrived at in accordance with IAS 29, "Financial Reporting in Hyperinflationary Economies" (see Chapter 10).

The general principles of IAS 36, although the standard itself was only formally operative for accounting periods beginning on or after July 1, 1999, were already well established in IAS 16, "Property, Plant, and Equipment," in its 1993 version and can be traced back at least as far as IAS 15, issued in 1981. IAS 36 is essentially a set of "how-to" instructions. A revised version of IAS 36 was effective from March 31, 2004. The only major changes of principle relate to impairment tests for goodwill and are linked with contemporaneous changes introduced by IFRS 3, "Business Combinations" (see Chapter 8). Further minor amendments have been made through recent revisions to IAS 1, "Presentation of Financial Statements" (see Chapter 4), mandatory from January 1, 2009, and to IFRS 3, "Business Combinations" (see Chapter 8), mandatory from July 1, 2009. A further more fundamental reconsideration of the whole impairment area is ongoing; any resulting changes are not likely to appear in the short term.

IASB GAAP require first of all an investigation for indications of impairment. If such exist, then the assets should be tested for impairment and, if necessary, written down to their recoverable amount—the higher of fair value less costs to sell or value in use, calculated on the basis of discounted future pretax cash flows related to the asset or the income-generating unit. Impairment losses are recognized in the income statement unless they relate to revalued assets. Under IAS such losses are accounted for in accordance with the standard relating to that asset.

U.S. GAAP requires a numerical calculation. An entity assesses whether impairment has occurred on the basis of the future cash flows (undiscounted and excluding interest) expected to result from use and eventual disposal of the asset. An impairment loss exists if the sum of these cash flows is less than the carrying amount of the asset.

The impairment loss recognized in the income statement is based on the asset's fair value, being either market value or the sum of discounted future cash flows. IASB GAAP requires the reversal of impairment losses when the change is due to changes in estimates of the asset's recoverable amount for most assets. In a straight reversal of previous requirements, however, such reversal was prohibited in respect of goodwill as of March 31, 2004. U.S. GAAP does not allow reversals of impairment losses.

SCOPE

The standard begins by saying that it applies to all assets except . . . , and then gives a significant number of exceptions (par. 2). These are generally items that are covered in detail by other international standards. Thus, IAS 36 does not apply to:

1. Inventories (see IAS 2, "Inventories," discussed in Chapter 24);

2. Assets arising from construction contracts (see IAS 11, "Construction Contracts," discussed in Chapter 12);

3. Deferred tax assets (see IAS 12, "Income Taxes," discussed in Chapter 21);

4. Assets arising from employee benefits (see IAS 19, "Employee Benefits," discussed in Chapter 14);

5. Financial assets that are within the scope of IFRS 9, "Financial Instruments" (see Chapter 17);

6. Investment property that is measured at fair value (see IAS 40, "Investment Property," Chapter 25);

7. Biological assets related to agricultural activities that are measured at fair value less costs to sell (see IAS 40, "Agriculture," Chapter 34);

8. Deferred acquisition costs, and intangible assets, arising from an insurer's contractual rights under insurance contracts within the scope of IFRS 4, "Insurance Contracts" (see Chapter 35); and

9. Non-current assets (or disposal groups) classified as held for sale in accordance with IFRS 5, "Non-Current Assets Held for Sale and Discontinued Operations" (see Chapter 27).

In relation to point 5, it must be noted that financial assets which are excluded from IFRS 9, which are the same as those excluded from IAS 39, are automatically excluded from the exclusion! Thus, investments in:

1. Subsidiaries, as defined in IAS 27, "Consolidated Financial Statements and Accounting for Investments in Subsidiaries";

2. Associates, as defined in IAS 28, "Accounting for Investments in Associates"; and

3. Joint ventures, as defined in IAS 31, "Financial Reporting of Interests in Joint Ventures."

are financial assets but are excluded from the scope of IFRS 9. Therefore, IAS 36 applies to such investments.

> **OBSERVATION:** The standard very deliberately describes itself as dealing with impairment of assets, not with impairment of non-current assets. However, it then excludes inventories and construction contracts (IAS 2 and IAS 11) and accounts receivable and cash (both covered by IFRS 9). In many if not most businesses, this will mean that all current assets are excluded from consideration under IAS 36. However, the IAS definition of current assets (discussed in Chapter 4) is more generally expressed, and IAS 36 could be applicable to certain current assets in special cases.

TERMINOLOGY

IAS 36 gives a number of definitions of key terms, many of which are interrelated, one term being used in the definition of another (par. 6):

- An *impairment loss* is the amount by which the carrying amount of an asset or a cash-generating unit exceeds its recoverable amount.

- *Carrying amount* is the amount at which an asset is recognized after deducting any accumulated depreciation (amortization) and accumulated impairment losses thereon.

- *Depreciation (amortization)* is the systematic allocation of the depreciable amount of an asset over its useful life.

- *Depreciable amount* is the cost of an asset, or other amount substituted for cost in the financial statements, less its residual value.

- *Useful life* is either:
    - The period of time over which an asset is expected to be used by the entity; or
    - The number of production or similar units expected to be obtained from the asset by the entity.

- *Fair value less costs to sell* is the amount obtainable from the sale of an asset or cash-generating unit in an arm's-length transaction between knowledgeable, willing parties, less the costs of disposal.

- *Costs of disposal* are incremental costs directly attributable to the disposal of an asset or cash-generating unit, excluding finance costs and income tax expense.

- *Value in use* is the present value of the future cash flows expected to be derived from an asset or cash-generating unit.

- The *agreement date* for a business combination is the date that a substantive agreement between the combining parties is reached and, in the case of publicly listed entities, announced to the public. In the case of a hostile takeover, the earliest date that a substantive agreement between the combining parties is reached is the date that a sufficient number of the acquiree's owners have accepted the acquirer's offer for the acquirer to obtain control of the acquiree.

- An *active market* is a market in which all the following conditions exist:

(a) The items traded within the market are homogeneous;

(b) Willing buyers and sellers can normally be found at any time; and

(c) Prices are available to the public.

Most of these terms should be fairly easy to understand, but they can be difficult to calculate. Two further definitions are given, as follows:

- A *cash-generating unit* is the smallest identifiable group of assets that generates cash inflows that are largely independent of the cash inflows from other assets or groups of assets.

- *Corporate assets* are assets other than goodwill that contribute to the future cash flows of both the cash-generating unit under review and other cash-generating units.

When several assets are interrelated in their usage in a way that makes it impossible to meaningfully attribute cash inflows to each individual asset, they are to be considered together as a single cash-generating unit as defined above. In effect, therefore, a cash-generating unit is *"an* asset" for the purposes of IAS 36. Corporate assets do not generate their own cash flows, but, as described above, are necessary for the generation of cash flows by other units. Special considerations, discussed below, apply to such assets.

OBSERVATION: An interesting little oddity concerns the use of the two phases "costs to sell" and "costs of disposal" in the preceding series of definitions. The trail of finding a formal distinction is convoluted: costs of disposal relate to "an asset or cash-generating unit," as above, or to "an asset," as in the IASB 2008 Glossary whereas costs to sell relate to "an asset (or disposal group)," as in both IFRS 5, Appendix A, and the 2008 Glossary. To ordinary human beings (which presumably excludes lawyers), costs to sell and costs of disposal can be regarded as operationally identical. To us this sort of complication just illustrates the dangers of trying to be excessively legalistic, instead of sticking to a principles approach.

As discussed in Chapter 3, the IASB has introduced a completely new standard known as IFRS 13, "Fair Value Measurement." The new standard is not a requirement of IFRS GAAP until January 1, 2013, but earlier application is "permitted." This standard, when applied, obviously changes the definition of fair value in IAS 36 and there are a number of consequential amendments, mainly of terminology and none of fundamental principles.

But on IFRS 13 application there will be implications regarding the "costs to sell/costs of disposal" point discussed in the above "Observation." Fair value will then be defined as the "price received to sell an asset" in the relevant market without taking account of *transaction costs*, but after taking account of *transport costs*. The notion of "fair value less costs to sell" will then disappear, being replaced throughout IAS 36 by "fair value less costs of disposal." It is not obvious that this clarifies the situation.

IDENTIFYING AN ASSET THAT MAY BE IMPAIRED

It is important to be clear that IAS 36 does not require that the recoverable amount of all assets must be determined annually in order to test for impairment. Rather, it postulates a two-stage process. The first stage is to assess, at each balance sheet date, whether there is any indication that an asset may be impaired. If any such indication exists, the entity should estimate the recoverable amount of the asset. There are two different formal requirements. The first requirement relates to all assets (par. 9) and states that an entity should assess at each reporting date whether there is any indication that an asset may be impaired. If such an indication exists, the entity should estimate the recoverable amount of the asset. The second requirement is more stringent but relates only to certain intangible assets. It stipulates that (par. 10), irrespective of whether there is any indication of impairment, an entity must also:

1. Test an intangible asset with an indefinite useful life, or an intangible asset not yet available for use, for impairment annually by comparing its carrying amount with its recoverable amount. This impairment test may be performed at any time during an annual period, provided it is performed at the same time every year. Different intangible assets may be tested for impairment at different times. However, if such an intangible asset was initially recognized during the current annual period, that intangible asset must be tested for impairment before the end of the current annual period.

2. Test goodwill acquired in a business combination for impairment annually in accordance with paragraphs 80 – 99, as described below.

The concept of materiality applies to the general requirement in paragraph 9 but not to the specific requirement of paragraph 10, which, in its defined circumstances, is absolute.

In assessing whether there is any indication that an asset may be impaired, an entity should consider, *as a minimum*, the following indications (par. 12):

External sources of information:

1. During the period, an asset's market value has declined significantly more than would be expected as a result of the passage of time or normal use.

2. Significant changes with an adverse effect on the entity have taken place during the period, or will take place in the near future, in the technological, market, economic, or legal environment in which the entity operates or in the market to which an asset is dedicated.

3. Market interest rates or other market rates of return on investments have increased during the period, and those increases are likely to affect the discount rate used in calculating an asset's value in use and decrease the asset's recoverable amount materially.

4. The carrying amount of the net assets of the reporting entity is more than its market capitalization.

Internal sources of information:

1. Evidence is available of obsolescence or physical damage of an asset.

2. Significant changes with an adverse effect on the entity have taken place during the period, or are expected to take place in the near future, in the extent to which, or manner in which, an asset is used or is expected to be used. These changes include the asset becoming idle, plans to discontinue or restructure the operation to which an asset belongs, plans to dispose of an asset before the previously expected date, and reassessing the useful life of an asset as finite rather than indefinite.

3. Evidence is available from internal reporting that indicates that the economic performance of an asset is, or will be, worse than expected.

4. For an investment in a subsidiary, jointly controlled entity or associate, the investor recognizes a dividend from the investment and evidence is available that:

   (a) The carrying amount of the investment in the separate financial statements exceeds the carrying amounts in the consolidated financial statements of the investee's net assets, including associated goodwill; or

   (b) The dividend exceeds the total comprehensive income of the subsidiary, jointly controlled entity, or associate in the period the dividend is declared.

Only if such an indication of likely impairment exists do we need, in the general case, to move on to the second stage and actually measure the recoverable amount.

Several of the above considerations require some comment. Items 1 and 2 (under "External sources of information") are fairly obviously indicators of a possible fall in recoverable amount, relating directly to fair value less costs to sell and value in use, respectively. In neither case, however, does a low recoverable amount *necessarily* follow, as recoverable amount is the *higher* of fair value less costs to sell and value in use. The relevance of item 3 is that value in use, as defined above, is the *present value* of future cash flows. Discounting is thus central to the calculation of recoverable amount, and an increase in discount rate may significantly reduce the value in use of an asset, as defined, if the new discount rate is regarded as relevant in the long term. Item 4, again, is a fairly obvious indicator that something is widely perceived as being wrong somewhere, though not, of course, that every, or any one particular, asset is impaired.

MEASUREMENT OF RECOVERABLE AMOUNT

IAS 36 devotes no less than 39 paragraphs to the measurement of recoverable amount, not including another 42 paragraphs on cash-generating units, and sets out what it describes as "detailed computations." Nevertheless, a number of simplifications may be justified. If either fair value less costs to sell or value in use exceeds the asset's carrying amount, then the other figure need not be determined at all. If fair value less costs to sell is unobtainable even by a reliable estimate, because of the absence of an active market, the recoverable amount can be taken as equal to value in use. Conversely, the recoverable amount may be taken or given by the fair value less costs to sell if the nature of the asset or the nature of its usage by the entity is such that value in use is unlikely to differ materially from fair value less costs to sell, which will usually be the case with active and competitive factor markets (i.e., in developed economies).

Fair Value Less Costs to Sell

Fair value less costs to sell will often be straightforward to determine, being fair value less any incremental costs that would be directly attributable to the disposal of the asset. Fair value may need to be estimated by reference to comparable transactions. Costs of disposal, other than those that have already been recognized as liabilities, are deducted in determining fair value by costs to sell. Examples of such costs are legal costs, stamp duty and similar transaction taxes, costs of removing the asset, and direct incremental costs to bring an asset into condition for its sale. However, termination benefits (as defined in IAS 19, "Employee Benefits," see Chapter 14) and costs associated with reducing or reorganizing a business after the disposal of an asset are not direct incremental costs to dispose of the asset (see IAS 37, "Provisions, Contingent Liabilities, and Contingent Assets," discussed in Chapter 29).

Value in Use

Estimating the value in use in a realistic way is often likely to be rather more difficult. It involves the following steps (par. 31):

1. Estimating the future cash inflows and outflows to be derived from continuing use of the asset and from its ultimate disposal; and

2. Applying the appropriate discount rate to these future cash flows.

In measuring value in use:

1. Cash flow projections should be based on reasonable and supportable assumptions that represent management's best estimate of the set of economic conditions that will exist over the remaining useful life of the asset. Greater weight should be given to external evidence.

2. Cash flow projections should be based on the most recent financial budgets/forecasts that have been approved by management for the asset in its currently existing state. Projections based on these budgets/forecasts should cover a maximum period of five years, unless a longer period can be justified.

3. Cash flow projections beyond the period covered by the most recent budgets/forecasts should be estimated by extrapolating the projections on the basis of the budget/forecasts by using a steady or declining growth rate for subsequent years, unless an increasing rate can be justified.

This is all common sense stuff, although inevitably somewhat subjective.

Estimates of future cash flows should include:

1. Projections of cash inflows from the continuing use of the asset, net of projections of cash outflows that are necessarily incurred to generate the cash inflows (including cash outflows to prepare the asset for use) and that can be directly attributed, or allocated on a reasonable and consistent basis, to the asset; and

2. Net cash flows, if any, to be received (or paid) for the disposal of the asset at the end of its useful life.

→ **PRACTICE POINTER:** Two practical points need to be observed in relation to the above. First, it is essential that estimates of future cash flows, and the discount rate used, be consistent regarding the treatment of inflation. It is consistent to estimate future cash flows in real terms (i.e., including specific price increases or decreases but excluding the effect of price increases due to general inflation) and to use a real discount rate (again, excluding the effects of general inflation). It is also consistent to estimate future cash flows in nominal terms (i.e., in number of inflated currency units) and then use a nominal discount rate, (i.e., a discount rate that includes inflation effects). No other pairing would be acceptable.

The second point is that double counting must be avoided. For example, if a physical asset creates cash inflows via receivables, we cannot count the cash inflow from the asset *and* the cash inflow from the receivable. Cash outflows via purchases and via payables would involve a similar double-counting.

Future cash flows should be estimated for the asset in its current condition. It follows that estimates of future cash flows should not include estimated future cash inflows or outflows that are expected to arise from:

1. A future restructuring to which an entity is not yet committed, or

2. Future (uncommitted) capital expenditure that will improve or enhance the asset in excess of its originally assessed standard of performance.

The issue of when an entity is "committed to a future restructuring" is discussed in IAS 37, "Provisions, Contingent Liabilities, and Contingent Assets" (see Chapter 29). If it is so committed, then obviously the related cash inflows and outflows *are* to be included.

The estimate of net cash flows to be received (or paid) for the disposal of an asset at the end of its useful life is determined in a similar way to an asset's fair value less costs to sell, except that, in estimating those net cash flows:

1. An entity uses prices prevailing at the date of the estimate for similar assets that have reached the end of their useful life and that have operated under conditions similar to those in which the asset will be used.

2. Those prices are adjusted for the effect of both future price increases due to general inflation and specific future price increases (decreases). However, if estimates of future cash flows from the asset's continuing use and the discount rate exclude the effect of general inflation, this effect is also excluded from the estimate of net cash flows on disposal.

The standard briefly mentions the treatment of foreign currency cash flows (par. 54). This is that they are estimated in the foreign currency, discounted at a rate appropriate to that currency, and then the resulting figure is translated into the reporting currency at the spot rate ruling at the balance sheet date (i.e., the closing rate, see IAS 21, "The Effects of Changes in Foreign Exchange Rates," discussed in Chapter 18).

Discount Rate

The key points can be briefly stated. The discount rate (or rates) should be a pretax rate (or rates) that reflect(s) current market assessments of the time value of money and risks specific to the asset (par. 55). The discount rate(s) should not reflect risks for which future cash flow estimates have been adjusted, as this would involve double-counting. The standard rightly makes no attempt to argue that this process is other than subjective. It does try to suggest a suitable thought process (Appendix A).

As a starting point, the entity may take into account the following rates:

1. The entity's weighted average cost of capital determined using techniques such as the Capital Asset Pricing Model;
2. The entity's incremental borrowing rate; and
3. Other market borrowing rates.

These rates are adjusted:

1. To reflect the way that the market would assess the specific risks associated with the projected cash flows, and
2. To exclude risks that are not relevant to the projected cash flows.

Consideration is given to such risks as country risk, currency risk, price risk, and cash flow risk.

This makes it clear, for example, that the appropriate discount rate may be different for different types of asset or different circumstances within the same entity. What is crucial, above all else except basic rationality and common sense, is that the method used should be applied consistently.

RECOGNITION AND MEASUREMENT OF IMPAIRMENT LOSSES

After all the subjectivity, complexity, and detail of earlier sections of IAS 36, it is easy to lose sight of the importance of those paragraphs dealing with recognition and measurement of impairment losses. This is the point and purpose of the entire standard. The standard requires that if, and only if, the recoverable amount of an asset is less than its carrying amount, the carrying amount of the asset should be reduced to its recoverable amount. That reduction is an impairment loss (par. 59).

An impairment loss should be recognized immediately as an expense in the income statement, unless the asset is carried at revalued amount under another international standard (for example, under the allowed alternative treatment in IAS 16, "Property, Plant, and Equipment," see Chapter 28). Any impairment loss of a revalued asset should be treated as a revaluation decrease under the other international standard.

In the general case, if the estimated impairment loss is greater than the carrying value of the relevant asset, the asset is simply reduced to nil, with a corresponding expense. Only if so required by another international standard should a liability be recognized.

Common sense indicates, but the standard feels it necessary to state, that after the impairment loss has been recognized, the depreciation charge for the asset should be adjusted to allocate the revised carrying amount, net of any expected residual value, on a systematic basis over its remaining useful life.

This is all very well when "an asset" means "an asset." But when "an asset" means "a cash-generating unit," as discussed earlier, the treatment is not so easy in practice—as the standard's need for more than 40 paragraphs on the topic would suggest. If it is not possible to estimate the recoverable amount of an individual asset, an entity should determine the recoverable amount of the cash-generating unit to which the asset belongs (the asset's cash-generating unit) (par. 66). Identification of an asset's cash-generating unit involves judgment. If the recoverable amount cannot be determined for an individual asset, an entity identifies the lowest aggregation of assets that generate largely independent cash inflows from continuing use.

In other words, an asset's cash-generating unit is the smallest group of assets that includes the asset and that generates cash inflows from continuing use that are largely independent of the cash inflows from other assets or groups of assets.

Perhaps inevitably, the standard resorts to a series of examples in order to try and indicate more precisely how the analysis of any particular situation should proceed. Common sense and economic substance are perhaps the key watchwords. Thus, if an active market exists for the output produced by an asset or a group of assets, this asset or group of assets should be identified as a cash-generating unit, even if some or all of the output is used internally. If this is the case, management's best estimate of future arm's-length market prices for the output should be used (par. 70):

1. In determining the value in use of this cash-generating unit, when estimating the future cash inflows that relate to the internal use of the output; and

2. In determining the value in use of other cash-generating units of the reporting entity, when estimating the future cash outflows that relate to the internal use of the output.

As an indicative illustration, we quote below an example given by IAS 36 in relation to this specification.

Illustration

A significant raw material used for plant Y's final production is an intermediate product bought from plant X of the same entity. X's products are sold to Y at a transfer price that passes all margins to X. Eighty percent of Y's final production is sold to customers outside of the reporting entity, 60% of X's final production is sold to Y, and the remaining 40% is sold to customers outside of the reporting entity.

For each of the following cases, what are the cash-generating units for X and Y?

Case 1: X could sell the products it sells to Y in an active market. Internal transfer prices are higher than market prices.

Case 2: There is no active market for the products X sells to Y.

Case 1

X could sell its products on an active market and, so, generate cash inflows that would be largely independent of the cash inflows from Y. Therefore, it is likely that X is a separate cash-generating unit, although part of its production is used by Y.

It is likely that Y is also a separate cash-generating unit. Y sells 80% of its products to customers outside of the reporting entity. Therefore, its cash inflows can be considered to be largely independent.

Internal transfer prices do not reflect market prices for X's output. Therefore, in determining value in use of both X and Y, the entity adjusts financial budgets/forecasts to reflect management's best estimate of future arm's-length market prices for those of X's products that are used internally (see IAS 36, par. 70).

Case 2

It is likely that the recoverable amount of each plant cannot be assessed independently of the recoverable amount of the other plant because:

1. The majority of X's production is used internally and could not be sold in an active market. So, cash inflows of X depend on demand for Y's products. Therefore, X cannot be considered to generate cash inflows that are largely independent of those of Y.

2. The two plants are managed together.

As a consequence, it is likely that X and Y together is the smallest group of assets that generates cash inflows that are largely independent.

Readers who are actually engaged in the process of defining cash-generating units in real entities are advised to read all the illustrative examples given in IAS 36 carefully.

OBSERVATION: In the context of Case 1 of this illustration, one might wonder why Y pays *more* than the market price. Economics might suggest that paying *less* than the market price is more likely, though other considerations such as multinational tax optimization could point either way. The issue is unimportant here as, either way, if internal transfer prices do not reflect market prices for X's output, then adjustment to estimated future *market* prices is required.

Once the cash-generating unit has been defined, the next step is to determine, and compare, the recoverable amount and carrying amount of that unit. It should go without saying, but the standard reminds us, that the carrying amount of a cash-generating unit should be determined consistently with the way the recoverable amount of the cash-generating unit is determined.

This means, for example, that the carrying amount of a cash-generating unit includes the carrying amount of only those assets (1) that can be attributed directly, or allocated on a reasonable and consistent basis, to the cash-generating unit and (2) that will generate the future cash inflows estimated in determining the cash-generating unit's value in use. It does not include the carrying amount of any recognized liability, unless the recoverable amount of the cash-generating unit cannot be determined without consideration of this liability. However, the standard notes that in practice the recoverable amount of a cash-generating unit may be considered either including or excluding assets or liabilities that are not part of the cash-generating unit—for example a net selling price of a business segment might be determined on the assumption that either the vendor or the purchaser accepts certain obligations. Consistency requires that if the obligation is included in the evaluation of the recoverable amount, it is the *net* carrying value with which this recoverable amount must be compared in determining whether an impairment loss exists.

There are two problems that need special consideration, namely goodwill and corporate assets (as already defined). In essence, these two problems are related. Goodwill, by definition, does not generate cash flows independently from other assets or groups of assets and, therefore, the recoverable amount of goodwill as an individual asset cannot be determined. As a consequence, if there is an indication that goodwill may be impaired, the recoverable amount is determined for the cash-generating unit to which the goodwill belongs. This amount is then compared to the carrying amount of this cash-generating unit, and any impairment loss is recognized, attributed first to the goodwill, as discussed below.

It is particularly in relation to the treatment of possible impairment of goodwill that the new version of IAS 36 has been made much more detailed (and therefore, at least apparently, more complex). The previous version of IAS 36 required goodwill acquired in a business combination to be tested for impairment as part of impairment testing of the cash-generating unit(s) to which it related. It employed a "bottom-up/top-down" approach under which the goodwill was, in effect, tested for impairment by allocating its carrying amount to each cash-generating unit or smallest group of cash-generating units to which a portion of that carrying amount could be allocated on a reasonable and consistent basis. The standard now similarly requires goodwill acquired in a business combination to be tested for impairment as part of impairment testing the cash-generating units to which it relates. However, IAS 36 now clarifies that:

1. The goodwill should, from the acquisition date, be allocated to each of the acquirer's cash-generating units or groups of cash-generating units that are expected to benefit from the synergies of the business combination, irrespective of whether other assets or liabilities of the acquiree are assigned to those units or groups of units.

2. Each unit or group of units to which the goodwill is allocated should:

(a) Represent the lowest level within the entity at which the goodwill is monitored for internal management purposes; and

(b) Not be larger than an operating segment, as defined by paragraph 5 of IFRS 8, "Operating Segments," before aggregation.

3. If the initial allocation of goodwill acquired in a business combination cannot be completed before the end of the annual period in which the business combination occurs, that initial allocation should be completed before the end of the annual period beginning after the acquisition date.

4. When an entity disposes of an operation within a cash-generating unit or group of units to which goodwill has been allocated, the goodwill associated with that operation should be:

(a) Included in the carrying amount of the operation when determining the gain or loss on disposal; and

(b) Measured on the basis of the relative values of the operation disposed of and the portion of the cash-generating unit or group of units retained, unless the entity can demonstrate that some other method better reflects the goodwill associated with the operation disposed of.

5. When an entity reorganizes its reporting structure in a manner that changes the composition of cash-generating units or groups of units to which goodwill has been allocated, the goodwill should be reallocated to the units or groups of units affected. This reallocation should be performed using a relative value approach similar to that used when an entity disposes of an operation within a cash-generating unit or group of units, unless the entity can demonstrate that some other method better reflects the goodwill associated with the reorganized units or groups of units.

By way of example, to illustrate point 4 above, suppose that an entity sells for $100 an operation that was part of a cash-generating unit to which goodwill has been allocated. The goodwill allocated to the unit cannot be identified or associated with an asset group at a level lower than that unit, except arbitrarily. The recoverable amount of the portion of the cash-generating unit retained is $300. Because the goodwill allocated to the cash-generating unit cannot be non-arbitrarily identified or associated with an asset group at a level lower than that unit, the goodwill associated with the operation disposed of is measured on the basis of the relative values of the operation disposed of and the portion of the unit retained. Therefore 25% of the goodwill allocated to the cash-generating unit is included in the carrying amount of the operation that is sold, and 75% is left in the retained portion.

The standard permits (not requires) the annual impairment test for a cash-generation unit or group of units to which the goodwill has been allocated to be performed at any time during an annual reporting period, provided that the test is performed at the same time every year, and different cash-generating units or groups of units to be tested for impairment at different times. If, however, some of the goodwill allocated to a cash-generating unit or group of units was acquired in a business combination during the current annual period, the standard requires that unit or group of units to be tested for impairment before the end of the current period.

The standard also permits the most recent detailed calculation made in a preceding period of the recoverable amount of a cash-generating unit (group of units) to which goodwill has been allocated to be used in the impairment test for that unit or group of units in the current period, provided specified criteria are met, as follows:

1. The assets and liabilities making up the unit have not changed significantly since the most recent recoverable amount calculation;

2. The most recent recoverable amount calculation resulted in an amount that exceeded the carrying amount of the unit by a substantial margin; and

3. Based on an analysis of events that have occurred and circumstances that have changed since the most recent recoverable amount calculation, the likelihood that a current recoverable amount determination would be less than the current carrying amount of the unit is remote.

Similarly, corporate assets, also by definition, do not generate independent cash flows, and, again, the recoverable amount is determined by reference to the cash-generating unit to which the corporate asset belongs. In testing a cash-generating unit for impairment, an entity must identify all the corporate assets that relate to the cash-generating unit under review. If a portion of the carrying amount of a corporate asset can be allocated on a reasonable and consistent basis to that unit, the entity should compare the carrying amount of the unit, including the portion of the carrying amount of the corporate asset allocated to the unit, with its recoverable amount. Any impairment loss is to be recognized in accordance with paragraph 104, discussed below. If a portion cannot be allocated on a reasonable and consistent basis to that unit, the entity should then:

1. Compare the carrying amount of the unit, excluding the corporate asset, with its recoverable amount and recognize any impairment loss in accordance with paragraph 104;

2. Identify the smallest group of cash-generating units that includes the cash-generating unit under review and to which a portion of the carrying amount of the corporate asset can be allocated in a reasonable and consistent basis; and

3. Compare the carrying amount of that group of cash-generating units, including the portion of the carrying amount of the corporate asset allocated to that group of units, with the recoverable amount of the group of units. Any impairment loss should be recognized in accordance with paragraph 104.

An amazingly lengthy illustrative example (no. 8) is given in an accompaniment to the standard.

Once the impairment loss for a cash-generating unit has been determined, it has to be deducted from the carrying amounts of specific assets that are part of that unit, in some systematic manner. IAS 36 specifies its requirements with precision (pars. 104 – 105).

An impairment loss should be recognized for a cash-generating unit if, and only if, its recoverable amount is less that its carrying amount. The impairment loss should be allocated to reduce the carrying amount of the assets of the unit in the following order:

1. First, to goodwill allocated to the cash-generating unit (if any); and

2. Then, to the other assets of the unit on a pro rata basis, based on the carrying amount of each asset in the unit.

In allocating an impairment loss, the carrying amount of an asset should not be reduced below the *highest* of:

1. Its fair value less costs to sell (if determinable),

2. Its value in use (if determinable), or

3. Zero.

The amount of the impairment loss that would otherwise have been allocated to the asset should be allocated to the other assets of the unit on a pro rata basis. A liability should be recognized for any remaining amount of an impairment loss for a cash-generating unit, if, and only if, that is required by other international standards.

The effect of this is, first, to eliminate goodwill, but then to ensure that the carrying amount of any individual asset is not reduced so far as to produce a figure not economically relevant to that asset.

REVERSAL OF AN IMPAIRMENT LOSS

The whole point, in a sense, of impairment losses is that they represent unusual or "extra" reductions in asset numbers (carrying values) as used in financial statements. If regular depreciation is a downward slope, then an impairment loss is a step downward. The basic cause of this downward step is something unusual and/or extraneous to the asset and its regular accounting treatment. It follows that this cause, this unusual or extraneous factor, may be removed over time. In such a situation, as explained and defined in IAS 36, the original impairment loss *must* be reversed, except for goodwill.

We again, as with impairment losses, have a two-stage process. An enterprise first checks to see whether there is any *indication* that an impairment loss recognized in earlier years may have decreased significantly. IAS 36 spells out a series of likely indicators (par. 111) that mirror those discussed earlier under "Identifying an Asset That May Be Impaired."

The formal requirement for reversing impairment losses for an asset other than goodwill (par. 114) is that an impairment loss recognized for an asset in prior years must be reversed if, and only if, there has been a change in the estimates used to determine the asset's recoverable amount since the last impairment loss was recognized. If this is the case, the carrying amount of the asset should be increased to its recoverable amount. That increase is a reversal of an impairment loss. It is important to note that an asset's value in use may become greater than the asset's carrying amount simply because the present value of future cash inflows increases as they become closer. However, the service potential of the asset has not increased. Therefore, such an impairment loss is not reversed, even if the recoverable amount of the asset becomes higher than its carrying amount.

The reversal of an impairment loss should in no circumstances increase the carrying value of an asset above what it would have been at this balance sheet date if no impairment loss had been recognized in prior years. This means, in particular, that the carrying value of assets subject to depreciation cannot be increased above the figure that the pre-impairment depreciation policy applied to the pre-impairment recoverable amount would have given at this balance sheet date, that is, the amount of the reversal will be less than the amount of the original impairment. The new carrying value forms the basis for a systematic depreciation policy to allocate the carrying value, less estimated residual value if any, over the remaining useful life.

A reversal of an impairment loss for an asset as above should be recognized as income immediately in the income statement, unless the asset is carried at revalued amount under another international standard (for example, under the allowed alternative treatment in IAS 16, "Property, Plant, and Equipment"; see Chapter 28). Any reversal of an impairment loss on a revalued asset should be treated as a revaluation increase under that other international standard.

A reversal of an impairment loss for a cash-generating unit should be allocated to increase the carrying amount of the assets of the unit on a pro rata basis based on the carrying amount of each asset in the unit.

In allocating a reversal of an impairment loss for a cash-generating unit, the carrying amount of an asset should not be increased above the *lower* of:

1. Its recoverable amount (if determinable); and
2. The carrying amount that would have been determined (net of amortization or depreciation) had no impairment loss been recognized for the asset in prior years.

The amount of the reversal of the impairment loss that would otherwise have been allocated to the asset should be allocated to the other assets of the unit, except for goodwill, on a pro rata basis.

The treatment of a reversal of an impairment loss for goodwill has changed significantly in the new version of IAS 36 (i.e., with effect from March 31, 2004) as compared with the earlier version. The previous version of IAS 36 required an impairment loss recognized for goodwill in a previous period to be reversed when (1) the impairment loss was caused by a specific external event of an exceptional nature that was not expected to recur and (2) subsequent external events have occurred that reverse the effect of that event. The standard now completely prohibits the recognition of reversals of impairment losses for goodwill.

OBSERVATION: The rationale for prohibiting the reversal of impairment losses for goodwill is presented by the IASB as follows. The key point is that IAS

38, "Intangible Assets" (see Chapter 22), prohibits the recognition of internally generated goodwill. This prohibition is theoretically debatable but is undoubtedly widely supported and is consistent with national laws in many countries, including the whole of the European Union, following the Fourth Directive.

Given this prohibition, there is still no *theoretical* problem in arguing, supported by analogy with other assets, that *previously purchased* goodwill that has been subsequently impaired because of a circumstance now reversed should have the impairment loss reversed. However, there is a *practical* problem in distinguishing, numerically as well as conceptually, between a reversal of a previous impairment to previously purchased goodwill, on the one hand, and the appearance of new internally generated goodwill, which cannot be recognized, on the other. It is because of this practical impossibility and the resulting "danger" of effectively capitalizing internally generated goodwill that the change to an outright prohibition of the recognition of a reversal of an impairment loss for goodwill has been introduced.

The IASB notes that internally generated goodwill may in fact be involved at an earlier stage in the whole impairment process, in that purchased goodwill may not be impaired in the first place because its recoverable amount is kept up through the creation of new goodwill to replace the old; however, it also notes that, again on purely practical grounds, such a position cannot be numerically demonstrated and therefore cannot be prevented.

DISCLOSURE

The disclosure requirements of IAS 36, like much else in the standard, are extensive. They are also quite straightforward, and we simply repeat them here.

For each class of assets, the financial statements should disclose:

1. The amount of impairment losses recognized in profit or loss during the period and the line item(s) of the statement of comprehensive income in which those impairment losses are included;

2. The amount of reversals of impairment losses recognized in profit or loss during the period and the line item(s) of the statement of comprehensive income in which those impairment losses are reversed;

3. The amount of impairment losses on revalued assets recognized in other comprehensive income during the period; and

4. The amount of reversals of impairment losses on revalued assets recognized in other comprehensive income during the period.

An entity that reports segment information in accordance with IFRS 8, "Operating Segments" (see Chapter 32), shall disclose the following for each reportable segment:

1. The amount of impairment losses recognized in profit or loss and in other comprehensive income during the period; and

2. The amount of reversals of impairment losses recognized in profit or loss and in other comprehensive income during the period.

If an impairment loss for an individual asset, including goodwill, or a cash-generating unit is recognized or reversed during the period and is material to the financial statements of the reporting entity as a whole, an entity should disclose:

1. The events and circumstances that led to the recognition or reversal of the impairment loss;

2. The amount of the impairment loss recognized or reversed;

3. For an individual asset:

    (a) The nature of the asset, and

    (b) If the entity reports segment information in accordance with IFRS 8, the reportable segment to which the asset belongs;

4. For a cash-generating unit:

    (a) A description of the cash-generating unit (such as whether it is a product line, a plant, a business operation, a geographical area, or a reportable segment as defined in IFRS 8),

    (b) The amount of the impairment loss recognized or reversed by class of assets and, if the entity reports segment information in accordance with IFRS 8, by reportable segment, and

    (c) If the aggregation of assets for identifying the cash-generating unit has changed since the previous estimate of the cash-generating unit's recoverable amount (if any), the entity should describe the current and former way of aggregating assets and the reasons for changing the way the cash-generating unit is identified;

5. Whether the recoverable amount of the asset (cash-generating unit) is its fair value less costs to sell or its value in use;

6. If recoverable amount is fair value less costs to sell, the basis used to determine fair value less costs to sell (such as whether fair value was determined by reference to an active market or in some other way); and

7. If recoverable amount is value in use, the discount rate(s) used in the current estimate and previous estimate (if any) of value in use.

If impairment losses recognized (reversed) during the period are material in aggregate to the financial statements of the reporting entity as a whole, an entity should disclose a brief description of the following:

1. The main classes of assets affected by impairment losses (reversals of impairment losses) for which no information is disclosed as above; and

2. The main events and circumstances that led to the recognition (reversal) of these impairment losses for which no information is disclosed as above.

The new version of the standard continues to require that if any portion of the goodwill acquired in a business combination during the period has not been allocated to a cash-generating unit at the reporting date, an entity should disclose the amount of the unallocated goodwill together with the reasons that amount remains unallocated. The standard requires disclosure of information for each cash-generating unit or group of units for which the carrying amount of goodwill or intangible assets with indefinite useful lives allocated to that unit or group of units is significant in comparison with the entity's total carrying amount of goodwill or intangible assets with indefinite lives. That information is concerned primarily with the key assumptions used to measure the recoverable amounts of such units or groups of units.

The standard also requires specified information to be disclosed if some or all of the carrying amount of goodwill or intangible assets with indefinite lives is allocated across multiple cash-generating units or groups of units and the amount so allocated to each unit or group of units is not significant in comparison with the total carrying amount of goodwill or intangible assets with indefinite lives. Further disclosures are required if, in such circumstances, the recoverable amounts of any of those units or groups of units are based on the same key assumptions and the aggregate carrying amount of goodwill or intangible assets with indefinite lives allocated to them is significant in comparison with the entity's total carrying amount of goodwill or intangible assets with indefinite lives.

These disclosure requirements are likely to be somewhat specialist in application, and are very, perhaps excessively, detailed. If necessary, the reader is referred to paragraphs 134–137 of the standard.

CHAPTER 21
INCOME TAXES

CONTENTS

OVERVIEW

In the case of many transactions, the accounting treatment is likely to be the same as the tax treatment. This means that the effect on taxable net income is the same as the effect on reported accounting income in the particular period under consideration. The current year's current liability for taxes on income will, in such cases, be what one would expect from the reported accounting profit. Sometimes, however, the recognition and measurement requirements of tax laws differ from the recognition and measurement requirements of relevant accounting GAAP. Differences arise between the tax bases of assets and liabilities and their carrying amounts in the annual financial statements.

These differences are temporary, and they give rise to deferred tax assets and liabilities. Such temporary differences will generally reverse in later years when the related asset is used or the related liability is settled. A deferred tax liability or deferred tax asset represents the increase or decrease in taxes payable or refundable in future years as a result of temporary differences arising in, and carryforwards at the end of, the current year.

The principle applied is that full provision in the current financial statements should be made for the tax effects of the year's transactions and events, whether these effects are current or postponed (deferred) into the future.

IASB GAAP are contained in IAS 12, "Income Taxes." The original IAS 12 was replaced by a revised version, effective for accounting periods beginning on or after January 1, 1998. There were significant differences between the two versions. Although the basic issue is a simple one, the area has created a number of theoretical controversies over the years. Broadly speaking, IAS and U.S. GAAP are now reasonably consistent. The U.S. standard, ASC 740, "Income Taxes," is similar to IAS 12 in all essential details. SIC-25, "Income Taxes—Changes in the Tax Status of an Enterprise or Its Shareholders," is also part of IASB GAAP.

It must be remembered that taxation is generally regarded as very much a national issue. Tax systems and tax rates differ significantly among different countries. It follows that if countries with different tax regimes all implement IASB GAAP, the differences between tax and accounting effects are themselves likely to be different among the countries.

For many years, the IASB and the FASB have been considering proposals for convergence between FAS-109 (ASC 740) and IAS 12, and the IASB published an exposure draft in 2009. However as of April 2011, this project has been reassessed as "lower priority" and early action is not to be expected. There have been the usual crop of minor amendments in recent years, and in December 2010, some more substantive amendments were made, developing, and replacing, a previous interpretation: SIC-21. This change is obligatory from January 1, 2012, with earlier application permitted. This chapter is fully up to date in the context of the above

BACKGROUND

As outlined above, there is an accounting problem arising when, in any particular year, the tax effects of transactions differ from the accounting effects in a manner that is temporary, that is, expected to reverse in later years. There are many possible causes of this, as, depending on national tax regulations, there are many possible differences between tax and accounting effects. As an example of major significance in many countries, consider non-current assets.

It is common to apply the straight-line method of depreciation to non-current assets in financial statements. It is common in national tax systems, as part of governmental economic control, to regulate the tax allowance for such non-current assets in a precise way, often based on the reducing balance basis, applying a given percentage to the net tax written down value brought forward.

Timing differences are differences between taxable profit and accounting profit that originate in one period and reverse in one or more subsequent periods. Temporary differences are differences between the tax base of an asset or liability and its carrying amount in the balance sheet. The tax base of an asset or liability is the amount attributed to that asset or liability for tax purposes.

All timing differences are temporary differences. Temporary differences also arise in the following circumstances, which do not give rise to timing differences, although the original IAS 12 treated them in the same way as transactions that do give rise to timing differences:

1. Subsidiaries, associates, or joint ventures have not distributed their entire profits to the parent or investor.

2. Assets are revalued, and no equivalent adjustment is made for tax purposes.

3. The cost of a business combination that is an acquisition is allocated to the identifiable assets and liabilities acquired, by reference to their fair values, but no equivalent adjustment is made for tax purposes.

The principle followed by the revised IAS 12 is that it requires an entity to account for the tax consequences of transactions and other events in the same way that it accounts for the transactions and other events themselves. Thus, for transactions and other events recognized in the income statement, any related tax effects are also recognized in the income statement. For transactions and other events recognized directly in equity, any related tax effects are also recognized directly in equity. Similarly, the recognition of deferred tax assets and liabilities in a business combination affects the amount of goodwill or negative goodwill arising in that business combination.

There are no major differences in accounting principles between IASB GAAP and U.S. GAAP regarding the treatment of deferred tax assets and liabilities. However, all national tax systems have their own characteristics, and the effects of the relationship between national tax systems and IASB GAAP may well be different in various countries.

Illustration of Fundamental Issues

Consider a non-current asset costing $100. It has an expected life of five years, at the end of which it is estimated it can be sold for $25. Straight-line depreciation is applied in the financial statements. For tax purposes the asset attracts an annual allowance of 25% on the reducing balance basis. Assume that the company concerned has a constant accounting profit (i.e., after charging the depreciation) of $100 per annum. For the calculation of taxable profit, the depreciation effect is removed and replaced by the tax allowances. Assume that taxation is payable at the rate of 33% of the taxable profit. In terms of the taxation payable as a current liability in respect of each of the five years, this would lead to the following results.

	Year				
	1	2	3	4	5
Accounting profit (after depreciation charge)	100	100	100	100	100
+ Depreciation	15	15	15	15	15
Taxation allowance	(25)	(18)	(14)	(11)	(8)
Taxable profit	90	97	101	104	107
Profit before tax	100	100	100	100	100
Taxation 33% of taxable profit	(30)	(32)	(33)	(34)	(36)
Profit after tax	70	68	67	66	64

The implication of a falling profit (i.e., earnings) figure is false, as the reality is that management has produced an identical profit each year using identical resources. Inspection indicates that the reality of the situation is that total tax payable over the five years is $165, and intuitively this should be spread equally each year, in proportion to the (equal) accounting results (i.e., $33 each year). The income effect of the taxation regulations should be equalized.

Consideration of balance sheet effects is also important. The illustration shows that in relation to the earnings of year 1, two tax effects follow, that is,

1. There is a current tax liability of $30.

2. There is an eventual further tax liability of $3 (33 – 30), which becomes current in years 4 or 5. Under the accruals principle (see Chapter 2), it is clear that this $3 arises as a result of the activities and earnings of year 1 and is therefore a liability at the end of year 1 (see the definition of liability in Chapter 2). Because it is not a current liability (the current taxation creditor being $30), it must be a deferred liability, which is settled by the end of year five. The amount to be transferred to the credit of the deferred tax account can be formally calculated as follows.

Amount equals:

Tax rate × (taxation allowances given – depreciation disallowed)

Thus for year 1:

$33\% \times (25 - 15) = 3$

and year 2:

$33\% \times (18 - 15) = 1$

	Year					
	1	2	3	4	5	Total
Profit before tax	$100	$100	$100	$100	$100	$500
Taxation: payable for year	30	32	33	34	36	165
Additional charge (credit) to deferred tax account	3	1	0	(1)	(3)	0
Total tax charge	33	33	33	33	33	165
Profit after tax	$67	$67	$67	$67	$67	$335

In this simple situation, it seems to make no difference whether we make the argument in terms of the income statement (equalizing the tax charge) or in terms of the balance sheet (recording all liabilities—or possibly assets) according to the general definitions of IASB GAAP. In the general case, as discussed later, it can make a difference. The original version of IAS 12 focused essentially on the income statement; the revised version now in force focuses on the balance sheet.

One practical consideration much argued by businesses in some jurisdictions is that, given (*a*) a stable tax regime, (*b*) a tendency for rising price levels, and (*c*) a tendency toward capital intensive expansion, it follows that the deferred tax account is likely to grow and grow, as the reversal of earlier temporary differences is more than counterbalanced by the originating temporary differences on new non-current assets. Formally, three approaches can be distinguished to this consideration:

1. *The flow-through approach*, which accounts only for that tax payable in respect of the period in question, that is, temporary differences are ignored.

2. *Full deferral*, which accounts for the full tax effects of differences, that is, tax is shown in the published accounts based on the full accounting

profit, and the element not immediately payable is recorded as a liability until reversal.

3. *Partial deferral*, which accounts only for those differences where reversal is likely to occur in aggregate terms (because, for example, replacement of assets and expansion is expected to exceed depreciation).

Approach 1, which ignores deferred tax considerations altogether, is the old system before the 1970s. Approach 2 is that required by IAS 12 and in the United States. Approach 3, for many years, was required in the United Kingdom, but full deferral is now required there, from 2002.

Another issue of principle arises because it is quite likely that, over the years during which a tax liability is deferred, tax rates are likely to change. Two approaches can be distinguished, known as the deferral method and the liability method. Under the *deferral method* of provision for deferred tax, the tax effects of temporary differences are calculated by using the tax rates current when the differences arise. No adjustments are made subsequently if tax rates change. Reversals are accounted for by using the tax rates in force when the temporary differences originated, although in practice the effects of reversal and new temporary differences are sometimes accounted for as one item.

Those who support this method recognize that, when tax rates change, this method will not give an indication of the amount of tax payable or recoverable. Any deferred tax balance will, therefore, be a deferred charge or credit rather than a liability or asset. When tax rates change, there is no need to revise the deferred tax already provided. Thus the tax charge or credit for the period relates solely to that period and is not distorted by any adjustments relating to prior periods.

Alternatively, it could be argued that the balances on the deferred tax account should be regarded as liabilities payable in the future or as assets receivable in the future. The best available estimate of the tax rate ruling in the future when the amount is to be paid or received will generally be the current tax rate. This means that the liability balance will need to be continually revised whenever the current tax rate changes. This is known as the *liability method*. Thus, the tax charge or credit for the period may include adjustments of accounting estimates relating to prior periods. The deferred tax provision represents the best estimate of the amount that would be payable or receivable if the relevant differences reversed.

The original IAS 12 had, in broad terms, an income statement focus, although with considerable optionality. It permitted either full or partial deferral using either the deferral method or a version of the liability method that focused on temporary differences between various income statement years. The revised IAS 12 requires full deferral, using a different variant of the liability method, which it terms the balance sheet liability method, described in detail below, which takes account of all temporary differences. The distinction is again one of income statement versus balance sheet.

SCOPE

IAS 12 applies to accounting for taxes on income, that is, taxes based on taxable profit. This includes all domestic and foreign income taxes, including taxes, such as withholding taxes, which are payable by a subsidiary, associate, or joint venture on distributions to the reporting entity. The 1998 version of IAS 12 did not, however, deal with the tax consequences of dividends and other distributions made by the reporting entity itself, which in some jurisdictions can have a significant effect on the amount of tax payable. Additional paragraphs dealing with this matter were, as discussed below, effective January 1, 2001.

DEFINITIONS

The definitions given in IAS 12 (par. 5) are reproduced below.

- *Accounting profit* is profit or loss for a period before deducting tax expense.

- *Taxable profit* (*tax loss*) is the profit (loss) for a period, determined in accordance with the rules established by the taxation authorities, upon which income taxes are payable (recoverable).

- *Tax expense* (*tax income*) is the aggregate amount included in the determination of profit or loss for the period in respect of current tax and deferred tax.

- *Current tax* is the amount of income taxes payable (recoverable) in respect of the taxable profit (tax loss) for a period.

- *Deferred tax liabilities* are the amounts of income taxes payable in future periods in respect of taxable temporary differences.

- *Deferred tax assets* are the amounts of income taxes recoverable in future periods in respect of:
  — Deductible temporary differences,
  — The carryforward of unused tax losses, and
  — The carryforward of unused tax credits.

- *Temporary differences* are differences between the carrying amount of an asset or liability in the balance sheet and its tax base. Temporary differences may be either:
  — *Taxable temporary differences*, which are temporary differences that will result in taxable amounts in determining taxable profit (tax loss) of future periods when the carrying amount of the asset or liability is recovered or settled; or
  — *Deductible temporary differences*, which are temporary differences that will result in amounts that are deductible in determining taxable profit (tax loss) of future periods when the carrying amount of the asset or liability is recovered or settled.

- The *tax base* of an asset or liability is the amount attributed to that asset or liability for tax purposes.

Most of these definitions are straightforward. The distinction between taxable temporary differences and deductible temporary differences is made to sound complicated, but it is not. Taxable temporary differences lead in principle to a deferred tax liability, whereas deductible temporary differences lead to a deferred tax asset.

The standard discusses and illustrates the concept of the tax base at some length (pars. 7 – 11). The tax base of an asset is the amount that will be deductible for tax purposes against any taxable economic benefits (revenues or gains) that will flow to an entity when it recovers the carrying amount of the asset. If those economic benefits will not be taxable, the tax base of the asset is equal to its carrying amount.

Thus, for example, an entity shows interest receivable in its balance sheet with a carrying amount of 200 and dividends receivable with a carrying amount of 300. The revenue from the interest to be received will be taxed in full on a cash basis. The dividends receivable are from a subsidiary and are not taxable. The interest receivable has a tax base of nil, and the dividends receivable have a tax base of 300. The effect, as the above definitions make clear, is to create a taxable temporary difference of 200 in respect of the interest receivable and zero temporary difference (300 – 300) in respect of the dividends receivable.

The tax base of a liability is its carrying amount, less any amount that will be deductible for tax purposes in respect of that liability in future periods. In the case of revenue that is received in advance, the tax base of the resulting liability is its carrying amount, less any amount of the revenue that will not be taxable in future periods. Thus, if current liabilities include accrued expenses with a carrying amount of 1,000, and if the related expenses are deductible for tax purposes on a cash basis (i.e., in future years), then the tax base of the accrued expenses is nil, but if the related expense has already been deducted for tax purposes, then the tax base of the accrued expenses is 1,000. If current liabilities include interest revenue received in advance with a carrying amount of 400, and the related interest revenue has already been taxed on a cash basis, the tax base is the carrying amount of 400, reduced by the revenue not taxable in future periods, which is all of the 400. In this case the tax base of the current liability of interest received in advance is therefore nil.

Some items may have a tax base but will not be recognized as assets or liabilities in the balance sheet, that is, they have a carrying amount of nil. In such circumstances, a temporary difference will necessarily result. Business start-up costs and some types of research costs are examples that may occur in some jurisdictions of items that create tax assets but not accounting assets. A deductible temporary difference leading to a deferred tax asset would logically result.

→ **PRACTICE POINTER:** In the case of consolidated financial statements, it is the consolidated carrying amount that needs to be compared with the corresponding tax base. The tax base is determined by reference to a consolidated tax return in those jurisdictions in which such a return is filed. In other jurisdictions, the tax base is determined by reference to the tax returns of each entity in the group.

RECOGNITION OF CURRENT TAX LIABILITIES AND ASSETS

Recognition of current tax liabilities and assets is perfectly straightforward. Unpaid current tax relating to current or earlier periods should be recognized as a liability. If the amount already paid in respect of current and prior periods exceeds the amount due for those periods, the excess should be recognized as an asset. The benefit relating to a tax loss that can be carried back to recover current tax of a previous period should be recognized as an asset.

RECOGNITION OF DEFERRED TAX LIABILITIES

The principle is again simple, in that a deferred tax liability should be recognized for all taxable temporary differences, as defined above. IAS 12 gives two exceptions, however, and then an exception to one of the exceptions. In summary, a deferred tax liability should not be recognized (i.e., there is no liability), if it arises from (par. 15):

1. The initial recognition of goodwill;

2. Goodwill for which amortization is not deductible for tax purposes; or

3. The initial recognition of an asset or liability in a transaction that:

   (a) Is not a business combination; and

   (b) At the time of the transaction, affects neither accounting profit nor taxable profit (tax loss).

However, for taxable temporary differences associated with investments in subsidiaries, branches, and associates, and interests in joint ventures, a deferred tax liability should be recognized in certain circumstances. All this is discussed in more detail below.

It is important not to lose sight of the general principle, which is that if the carrying amount of an asset (in the financial statements) is greater than the tax base, then a taxable temporary difference arises and a deferred tax liability must be recognized. Thus, in the example given earlier (see "Illustration of Fundamental Issues"), the cost of the asset is $100, and at the end of year 1 the carrying amount is $85 (100–15) and the tax base is $75 (100–25). IAS 12 requires the recognition (and recording) of the resulting deferred tax liability of $10 multiplied by the tax rate (25% in the example).

The standard discusses a number of differently caused temporary differences at some length. The most common cause of temporary differences in most jurisdictions will be timing differences, that is, differences that arise when income or expense is included in accounting profit in one reporting period but is included in taxable profit in a different period. Common examples are depreciation, as already illustrated, interest revenues, which may be assessed on a cash basis for tax purposes but not for accounting purposes, and development costs, which may be capitalized for accounting purposes but not for tax purposes.

IAS 12 does not explicitly refer to timing differences as a subset of temporary differences. It discusses five circumstances, however, where temporary differences arise that are not timing differences, which we address below.

1. The cost of a business combination that is an acquisition is allocated to the identifiable assets and liabilities acquired by reference to their fair values, but no equivalent adjustment is made for tax purposes. For example, when the carrying amount of an asset is increased to fair value at the date of acquisition but the tax base of the asset remains at the original figure with the previous entity, then a taxable temporary difference arises resulting in the recognition of a deferred tax liability. The amount of this recognized liability would affect the calculation of goodwill on acquisition on a dollar-for-dollar basis.

2. Assets are revalued and no equivalent adjustment is made for tax purposes. In some jurisdictions, when the carrying amount of an asset is changed to fair value or revalued amount, the difference is effective for tax purposes also, in which event the tax base of the asset will be altered correspondingly and no temporary difference will arise. In other jurisdictions, there would be no tax effects and the tax base for the asset is not adjusted. In the latter case, there is a temporary difference between the carrying value (which has altered) and the tax base (which has not), and so a deferred tax liability or asset appears to arise. The standard explicitly states that such a deferred tax effect should be recognized. This temporary difference exists even if (par. 20):

   (a) The enterprise does not intend to dispose of the asset. In such cases, the revalued carrying amount of the asset will be recovered through use, and this will generate taxable income that exceeds the depreciation that will be allowable for tax purposes in future periods (i.e., the asset increase does logically create a corresponding deferred tax liability); or

   (b) Tax on capital gains is deferred if the proceeds of the disposal of the asset are invested in similar assets by virtue of "rollover" relief. In such cases, the tax will ultimately become payable on sale or use of the similar assets (i.e., when the "rolling-over" ceases).

OBSERVATION: The logic of the IAS 12 position on this revaluation issue can be criticized. Given the explicit claims by the IASB that a balance sheet approach is being taken, the definition of a liability seems crucial. Since by definition in the relevant jurisdictions a revaluation has no tax effects, it seems extremely difficult to argue that a further tax obligation (or benefit) can arise. The IAS 12 statement in (a) immediately above that usage "will generate" taxable income is correct, but it is also logically irrelevant, as the future taxable income cannot be the "past event" required by the definition of a liability accepted and used by the IASB (see Chapter 2).

---

3. Goodwill or negative goodwill arises on consolidation. In many jurisdictions, the amortization of goodwill is not regarded as a deductible expense in calculating taxable profit, and the cost of goodwill is not

deductible for taxation purposes when a subsidiary disposes of its underlying business. In such jurisdictions, goodwill has a tax base of nil, leading to a possibly large difference between carrying value and tax base, and therefore to a large taxable temporary difference. However, IAS 12 explicitly forbids the recognition of the deferred tax amount arising. The justification given is as follows (par. 21).

However, this standard does not permit the recognition of the resulting deferred tax liability because goodwill is a residual and the recognition of the deferred tax liability would increase the carrying amount of goodwill.

OBSERVATION: At first glance, this rationale again seems suspect. But it is correct to say that recognizing the calculated deferred tax liability would increase the carrying amount of the goodwill, calculated as a residual. This would then lead to an increase in the taxable temporary difference arising, leading to some extra deferred tax liability that, if recorded, would further increase the carrying amount of the goodwill. And so ad infinitum! Perhaps the fundamental point is that goodwill is seen as "a residual" rather than as an asset. Nevertheless, in an environment where fair value accounting is practiced, it is difficult to disagree with the suggestion that goodwill as calculated on acquisition is the fair value of the cost of acquisition, that is, something with economic meaning. The whole issue is more complicated than IAS 12 implies.

---

4. The tax base of an asset or liability on initial recognition differs from its initial carrying amount. In the case of a business combination, the resulting deferred tax number is recognized as discussed in point 1, above. If the transaction affects either accounting profit or taxable profit, an entity recognizes any deferred tax liability or asset and recognizes the resulting deferred tax expense or income in the income statement. If neither of these circumstances exists, that is, neither accounting profit nor tax profit are immediately affected, then the general rule would suggest the recognition of the resulting deferred tax liability or asset, and the adjustment of the carrying amount of the asset or liability by the same amount. However, as already summarized above, this is neither required nor allowed. Paragraph 22(c) explains this as follows.

Such adjustments would make the financial statements less transparent. Therefore, this standard does not permit an enterprise to recognize the resulting deferred tax liability or asset, either on initial recognition or subsequently. Furthermore, an enterprise does not recognize subsequent changes in the unrecognized deferred tax liability or asset as the asset is depreciated.

IAS 12 gives an example, with explanation, which we reproduce below.

Example Illustrating Paragraph 22(c)

An enterprise intends to use an asset that costs 1,000 throughout its useful life of five years and then dispose of it for a residual value of nil. The tax rate is 40%. Depreciation of the asset is not deductible for tax purposes. On disposal, any capital gain would not be taxable and any capital loss would not be deductible.

As it recovers the carrying amount of the asset, the enterprise will earn taxable income of 1,000 and pay tax of 400. The enterprise does not recognize the resulting deferred tax liability of 400 because it results from the initial recognition of the asset.

In the following year, the carrying amount of the asset is 800. In earning taxable income of 800, the enterprise will pay tax of 320. The enterprise does not recognize the deferred tax liability of 320 because it results from the initial recognition of the asset.

The tax base of the asset referred to, that is, the amount deductible for tax purposes against taxable economic benefits from the asset's use, is nil. It is the difference between carrying value and tax base, that is, 1,000–nil = 1,000, which would lead to the theoretical deferred tax liability of 400. However, this 400 is not recognized because it results "from the initial recognition of the asset," and this in turn arises because the (deferred tax) "adjustments would make the financial statements less transparent."

OBSERVATION: Taking the figures of the IASB example, there are two possible presentations on the initial recognition of the asset. The asset could be recorded at 1,000 and deferred tax not recorded. Second, the asset could be recorded at its "gross" cost of 1,400, together with a deferred tax liability of 400. This latter is the version stated to be "less transparent." Because it provides more information, this seems a peculiar comment. More fundamentally, *is* there a liability? A sum of 1,000 has been spent that has no tax effects. If it has no tax effects, how can it increase the liabilities for taxation? This, surely, is both a clearer and a simpler justification for not recognizing deferred taxation than the statements of IAS 12. More pragmatically, it seems unlikely that, apart from goodwill, expenditures will arise that create assets that are not recognized for tax purposes either as capital expenditure or as allowable expenses.

---

5. The carrying amount of investments in subsidiaries, branches, and associates or interests in joint ventures becomes different from the tax base of the investment or interest. In many cases the tax base will be cost, but the carrying amount may change, for example because of:

   (a) The existence of undistributed profits of subsidiaries, branches, associates, and joint ventures;

   (b) Changes in foreign exchange rates when a parent and its subsidiary are based in different countries; and

   (c) A reduction in the carrying amount of an investment in an associate to its recoverable amount.

6. The general rule is that deferred tax should be recognized as a liability for all such taxable temporary differences except (par. 39) to the extent that *both* of the following conditions are satisfied:

   (a) The parent, investor, or venturer is able to control the timing of the reversal of the temporary difference; and

(b) It is probable that the temporary difference will not reverse in the foreseeable future.

Regarding subsidiaries (and also branches), the parent will, by definition, normally be able to control the dividend policy of the foreign entity and therefore to control the timing of the reversal of temporary differences relating to its investment. If the parent has determined that the profits will not be distributed in the foreseeable future, then no deferred tax liability is to be recognized. In the general case, an investor in a foreign associate (see Chapter 18) will not be in a position to control the dividend policy, so the above argument would not apply (although the issue of whether or not control exists is in the end a pragmatic matter). In the case of, for example, changes in foreign exchange rates, the timing of the reversal of temporary differences is obviously outside the control of the investor, and recognition of deferred tax is required.

RECOGNITION OF DEDUCTIBLE TEMPORARY DIFFERENCES

In principle, a deductible temporary difference, which gives rise to a deferred asset, is the exact mirror image of a taxable temporary difference, so it should arguably be treated as such. The difficulty, however, is that the "asset" is not in general repayable by the taxation authorities. Rather, it is deductible from the taxation charges relating to later years, if there are any. If future taxable profits do not in fact arise, then the "asset" will have no beneficial value, in which case of, course, it is not an asset at all and should not be recognized. Given the inherent uncertainty, at least in the case of unprofitable entities, of future taxable profits, a degree of caution and prudence is required.

The general requirement of IAS 12 (pars. 24 and 28) is that a deferred tax asset should be recognized for all deductible temporary differences to the extent that it is probable that taxable profit will be available against which the deductible temporary difference can be utilized. It is probable that taxable profit will be available against which a deductible temporary difference can be utilized when there are sufficient taxable temporary differences relating to the same taxation authority and the same taxable entity which are expected to reverse:

1. In the same period as the expected reversal of the deductible temporary difference, or

2. In periods into which a tax loss arising from the deferred tax asset can be carried back or forward.

The asset can (and should) be recognized on a partial basis if a positive but inadequate amount of future taxable profit is probable.

→ **PRACTICE POINTER:** The meaning of "probable" is both important and uncertain. In IAS 37, "Provisions, Contingent Liabilities, and Contingent Assets" (see Chapter 29), it is stated (pars. 15 and 23) that an event is "probable" if the probability that the event will occur is greater than the probability that it will not. However, IAS 37 also explicitly states that this interpretation "does not necessarily apply in other international standards." It should also be noted that the IAS 37 statement is presented in the context of liabilities, not of assets.

It is in our view inevitable that "probable" in the IAS 12 context, and indeed in many contexts, is likely to be interpreted differently in different countries and cultures. For an "expectation" of reversal in the context of IAS 12, we suggest that significantly more than a 50-50 likelihood is required.

There are two circumstances in which, notwithstanding the above, a deferred tax asset should not be recognized (par. 24). These mirror the exceptions to the recognition of deferred tax liabilities given in paragraph 15 and discussed above. A deferred tax asset should not be recognized if it arises from the initial recognition of an asset or liability in a transaction that:

1. Is not a business combination; and

2. At the time of the transaction, affects neither accounting profit nor taxable profit (tax loss).

The reasons given for this, and the possible doubts about those reasons, are the same as those discussed above in relation to liabilities.

Further, again, consistently with the considerations in respect of deferred liabilities, an entity (par. 44) should recognize a deferred tax asset for all deductible temporary differences arising from investments in subsidiaries, branches, and associates and interests in joint ventures to the extent that, and only to the extent that, it is probable that:

1. The temporary difference will reverse in the foreseeable future, and

2. Taxable profit will be available against which the temporary difference can be utilized.

Deferred tax assets can arise not only through the existence of deductible temporary differences, as discussed at length above, but also through unused tax losses or tax credits that, in many jurisdictions, can be carried forward for a limited period or without limit. The criteria for recognizing deferred tax assets arising from the carryforward of unused tax losses and tax credits are the same as the criteria for recognizing deferred tax assets arising from deductible temporary differences, namely that a deferred tax asset should be recognized for the carryforward of unused tax losses and unused tax credits to the extent that it is probable that future taxable profit will be available against which the unused tax losses and unused tax credits can be utilized.

The implications are likely to be different, however, because the existence of unused tax losses suggests an unprofitable entity. The onus is therefore on the entity to verify and demonstrate that an expectation of future taxable profits is justifiable. When an entity has a history of recent losses, the entity recognizes a deferred tax asset arising from unused tax losses or tax credits only to the extent that the entity has sufficient taxable temporary differences or there is other convincing evidence that sufficient taxable profit will be available against which the unused tax losses or unused tax credits can be utilized by the entity. In such circumstances, disclosure of the amount of the deferred tax asset and the nature of the evidence supporting its recognition is required.

IAS 12 suggests "criteria" for assessing the probability of future taxable profits against which unused tax losses or credits can be utilized, though in truth these are little more than signposts. They are (par. 36):

1. Whether the entity has sufficient taxable temporary differences relating to the same taxation authority and the same taxable entity, which will result in taxable amounts against which the unused tax losses or unused tax credits can be utilized before they expire;

2. Whether it is probable that the entity will have taxable profits before the unused tax losses or unused tax credits expire;

3. Whether the unused tax losses result from identifiable causes that are likely to recur; and

4. Whether tax planning opportunities are available to the entity that will create taxable profit in the period in which the unused tax losses or unused tax credits can be utilized.

Where unrecognized deferred tax assets exist, the situation should be reviewed at each successive balance sheet date. The entity recognizes a previously unrecognized deferred tax asset to the extent that it has now become probable that future taxable profit will allow the deferred tax asset to be recovered.

MEASUREMENT

As discussed in this chapter, the current version of IAS 12 requires, consistent with its focus on the balance sheet rather than on the income statement, the liability method of measurement to be used. This means that, at any particular balance sheet date, the deferred tax assets or liabilities should in principle represent the actual amounts recoverable or payable at the expected relevant date. Current (balance sheet date) tax rates will usually be used as proxies, though announced tax rates should be used in jurisdictions when they "have the substantive effect of actual enactment." The formal statement of the general principle (pars. 46, 47, and 51) is as follows:

> Current tax liabilities (assets) for the current and prior periods shall be measured at the amount expected to be paid to (recovered from) the taxation authorities, using the tax rates (and tax laws) that have been enacted or substantively enacted by the balance sheet date.

> Deferred tax assets and liabilities shall be measured at the tax rates that are expected to apply to the period when the asset is realized or the liability is settled, based on tax rates (and tax laws) that have been enacted or substantively enacted by the balance sheet date.

> The measurement of deferred tax liabilities and deferred tax assets shall reflect the tax consequences that would follow from the manner in which the entity expects, at the balance sheet date, to recover or settle the carrying amount of its assets and liabilities.

This last point means, necessarily, that the reported figure will, in such circumstances, be dependent on management's intentions or stated intentions. IAS 12 gives a series of examples that make this clear, and we produce the simplest one below:

An asset has a carrying amount of 100 and a tax base of 60. A tax rate of 20% would apply if the asset were sold and a tax rate of 30% would apply to other income.

The entity recognizes a deferred tax liability of 8 (40 at 20%) if it expects to sell the asset for its carrying amount without further use and a deferred tax liability of 12 (40 at 30%) if it expects to retain the asset and recover its carrying amount through use.

The 2010 revision of IAS 12 referred to above provides further details and illustrations to emphasize the importance of management's intentions. One example is given in detail here, from par. 51C. Note the specific reference to the "business model," that is, to the intentions of management, and not to the characteristics of the asset, or its available markets.

An investment property has a cost of 100 and a fair value of 150. It is measured using the fair value model in IAS 40. It comprises land with a cost of 40 and a fair value of 60 and a building with a cost of 60 and a fair value of 90. The land has an unlimited useful life.

Cumulative depreciation of the building for tax purposes is 30. Unrealized changes in the fair value of the investment property do not affect taxable profit. If the investment property is sold for more than cost, the reversal of the cumulative tax depreciation of 30 will be included in taxable profit and taxed at an ordinary tax rate of 30%. For sales proceeds in excess of cost, tax law specifies tax rates of 25% for assets held for less than two years and 20% for assets held for two years or more.

Because the investment property is measured using the fair value model in IAS 40, there is a rebuttable presumption that the entity will recover the carrying amount of the investment property entirely through sale. If that presumption is not rebutted, the deferred tax reflects the tax consequence of recovering the carrying amount entirely through sale, even if the entity expects to earn rental income from the property before sale.

The tax base of the land if it is sold is 40 and there is a taxable temporary difference of 20 (60 − 40). The tax base of the building if it is sold is 30 (60 − 30) and there is a taxable temporary difference of 60 (90 − 30). As a result, the total taxable temporary difference relating to the investment property is 80 (20 + 60).

In accordance with paragraph 47, the tax rate is the rate expected to apply to the period when the investment property is realized. Thus, the resulting deferred tax liability is computed as follows, if the entity expects to sell the property after holding it for more than two years.

	Taxable Temporary Difference	Tax Rate	Deferred Tax Liability
Cumulative tax depreciation	30	30%	9
Proceeds in excess of cost	50	20%	10
Total	80		19

If the entity expects to sell the property after holding it for less than two years, the above computation would be amended to apply a tax rate of 25%, rather than 20%, to the proceeds in excess of cost.

If, instead, the entity holds the building within a business model whose objective is to consume substantially all of the economic benefits embodied in the building over time, rather than through sale, this presumption would be rebutted for the building. However, the land is not depreciable. Therefore the presumption of recovery through sale would not be rebutted for the land. It follows that the deferred tax liability would reflect the tax consequences of recovering the carrying amount of the building through use and the carrying amount of the land through sale.

The tax base of the building if it is used is 30 (60 – 30) and there is a taxable temporary difference of 60 (90 – 30), resulting in a deferred tax liability of 18 (60 at 30%).

The tax base of the land if it is sold is 40 and there is a taxable temporary difference of 20 (60 – 40), resulting in a deferred tax liability of 4 (20 at 20%).

As a result, if the presumption of recovery through sale is rebutted for the building, the deferred tax liability relating to the investment property is 22 (18 + 4).

The question of whether or not long-term liabilities and long-term monetary assets should be discounted is a difficult and complex one, which is going to cause world standard-setters much angst over the next few years. It has implications for a number of IASB standards, and the IASB has set up a project team to consider the whole matter. Early results should not be expected.

The major purpose of the revision to IAS 12, operative from January 1, 2001, was to deal with the taxation implications of dividend payments, which had been explicitly excluded from the scope of the previous version. In some jurisdictions, income taxes are payable at a higher or lower rate if part or all of the net profit or retained earnings is paid out as a dividend to shareholders of the entity. In these circumstances, current and deferred tax assets and liabilities are measured at the tax rate applicable to undistributed profits, and the income tax consequences of dividends are recognized when a liability to pay the dividend is recognized. The income tax consequences of dividends are more directly linked to past transactions or events than to distributions to owners. Therefore, the income tax consequences of dividends are recognized in net profit or loss for the same period as the dividend is recognized, as discussed in the next section.

IAS 12 does not allow discounting of deferred tax assets or liabilities. Its stated reasons are distinctly pragmatic (par. 54), namely, in effect,

1. Reliable calculation is impracticable or highly complex.
2. Therefore, discounting should not be *required*.
3. Comparability between enterprises is necessary.
4. Therefore, discounting should not be *permitted*.

After the deferred tax balances have been revised under the liability method as of the balance sheet date, the carrying amount of deferred tax assets must additionally be reviewed and reduced to the extent that it is no longer probable that sufficient taxable profit will be available to allow the benefit of part of all of that deferred tax asset to be utilized. Any such reduction should be reversed to the extent that it becomes probable that sufficient taxable profit will be available.

RECOGNITION OF CURRENT AND DEFERRED TAX

Although the whole focus of IAS 12 is on the balance sheet numbers, it is obviously necessary also to consider the implications of the "other entry." The principle is that current and deferred tax effects should be accounted for consistently with the underlying transactions or events. This means that the tax effect is included:

- In the income statement in most cases,
- In equity if the item is itself recognized directly in equity,
- In other comprehensive income if the item is itself recognized directly in other comprehensive income, and
- In goodwill, for business combinations.

In the majority of cases, deferred tax will arise because of timing differences between years in relation to expense and revenue items. The tax effect of these occurrences will be a part of the current year tax charge in the income statement. We have already noticed that the carrying amount of deferred tax asset or liability balances may change even though there is no change in the amount of the related temporary differences, for example, from a change in tax rates or tax laws, a reassessment of the recoverability of deferred tax assets, or a change in the expected manner of recovery of an asset. The resulting deferred tax is likewise recognized in the income statement except to the extent that it relates to items previously charged or credited to equity.

IFRS require or permit particular items to be recognized in other comprehensive income. Examples of such items are:

1. A change in carrying amount arising from the revaluation of property, plant, and equipment (see IAS 16); and
2. Exchange differences arising on the translation of the financial statements of a foreign operation (see IAS 21).

IFRS require or permit particular items to be credited or charged directly to equity. Examples of such items are:

1. An adjustment to the opening balance of retained earnings resulting from either a change in accounting policy that is applied retrospectively or the correction of an error (see IAS 8, "Accounting Policies, Changes in Accounting Estimates and Errors"); and
2. Amounts arising on initial recognition of the equity component of a compound financial instrument (see paragraph 23).

Where items are charged or credited directly to equity, then current tax and deferred tax should also be so credited or charged, whether it arises in the same or a different accounting period. If it proves impossible to isolate the amount of tax that relates to items put directly to equity or recognized in other comprehensive income, then rational apportionment is permitted (par. 63). When an asset is revalued for tax purposes and that revaluation is related to an accounting revaluation of an earlier period or to one that is expected to be carried out in a future period, the tax effects of both the asset revaluation and the adjustment of the tax base are credited or charged to equity in the periods in which they occur. However, if the revaluation for tax purposes is not related to an accounting revaluation of an earlier period, or to one that is expected to be carried out in a future period, the tax effects of the adjustment of the tax base are recognized in profit or loss.

The IASC has noted, in SIC-25, "Changes in the Tax Status of an Enterprise Its Shareholders," that a change in tax status, such as for a public listing, a restructuring, or a change in domicile of a controlling shareholder, may cause an immediate change in tax liabilities or assets. The SIC confirms that a change in the tax status of an entity or its shareholders does not give rise to increases or decreases in amounts recognized directly in equity. The current and deferred tax consequences of a change in tax status should be included in net profit or loss for the period, unless those consequences relate to transactions and events that result, in the same or a different period, in a direct credit or charge to the recognized amount of equity. Those tax consequences that relate to changes in the recognized amount of equity, in the same or a different period (not included in net profit or loss), should be charged or credited directly to equity.

It is perhaps helpful to summarize the position related to deferred tax arising from a business combination, which requires considerable clarity of thought. A business combination that is an acquisition (as IFRS requires in all cases) is likely to lead to temporary differences, leading in turn (subject to the recognition criteria discussed above) to identifiable deferred tax liabilities or assets that will affect the calculation of goodwill. As also indicated above, however, an entity does not recognize deferred tax liabilities arising from goodwill itself or deferred tax assets arising from nontaxable negative goodwill that is treated as deferred income.

PRESENTATION

Tax assets and tax liabilities should be presented separately from other assets and liabilities in the balance sheet. Deferred tax assets and liabilities should be distinguished from current tax assets and liabilities. If the entity presents a classified balance sheet, all deferred tax assets and liabilities must be classified as non-current.

Current tax assets and current tax liabilities should be offset and shown as a net figure if, but only if, the entity (par. 71):

1. Has a legally enforceable right to set off the recognized amounts; and

2. Intends either to settle on a net basis, or to realize the asset and settle the liability simultaneously.

This requires in effect that offset items all relate to a single taxation authority, and that authority allows the entity to make or receive a single net payment.

The word "entity" in the previous sentence includes a group in the case of consolidated financial statements.

The rules for offsetting deferred tax assets and deferred tax liabilities are broadly similar. An entity is required to offset deferred tax balance sheet items if, but only if (par. 74):

1. The entity has a legally enforceable right to set off current tax assets against current tax liabilities; and

2. The deferred tax assets and the deferred tax liabilities relate to income taxes levied by the same taxation authority on either:

   (a) The same taxable entity; or

   (b) Different taxable entities that intend either to settle current tax liabilities and assets on a net basis or to realize the assets and settle the liabilities simultaneously, in each future period in which significant amounts of deferred tax liabilities or assets are expected to be settled or recovered.

The tax expense (income) related to profit or loss from ordinary activities shall be presented in the statement of comprehensive income. If an entity presents the components of profit or loss in a separate income statement, as described in paragraph 81 of IAS 1, "Presentation of Financial Statements" (as revised in 2007), it presents the tax expense (income) related to profit or loss from ordinary activities in that separate statement. Paragraph 78 notes that IAS 21, "Accounting for the Effects of Changes in Foreign Exchange Rates" (see Chapter 18), is silent as to where exchange differences should be presented in the income statement. IAS 12 states that exchange differences on deferred tax items that are recognized in the income statement may be included as part of the deferred tax expense or income or as part of foreign exchange losses or gains, whichever is "considered to be the most useful to financial statement users."

DISCLOSURE

The standard requires that the "major components" of tax expense or income should be disclosed separately (usually by way of note). Paragraph 80 gives a list of what such components "may include." Transparency should be the watchword, and all major elements should be separately disclosed. In addition, paragraph 81 gives a long and detailed list of additional disclosure requirements, which we reproduce. Disclosure is required of:

1. The aggregate current and deferred tax relating to items that are charged or credited to equity;

2. The amount of income tax relating to each component of other comprehensive income (see paragraph 62 and IAS 1 (as revised in 2007);

3. An explanation of the relationship between tax expense (income) and accounting profit in either or both of the following forms:

   (a) A numerical reconciliation between tax expense (income) and the product of accounting profit multiplied by the applicable tax rate(s), disclosing also the basis on which the applicable tax rate(s) is (are) computed, or

(b) A numerical reconciliation between the average effective tax rate and the applicable tax rate, disclosing also the basis on which the applicable tax rate is computed;

4. An explanation of changes in the applicable tax rate(s) compared to the previous accounting period;

5. The amount (and expiration date, if any) of deductible temporary differences, unused tax losses, and unused tax credits for which no deferred tax asset is recognized in the balance sheet;

6. The aggregate amount of temporary differences associated with investments in subsidiaries, branches, and associates and interests in joint ventures, for which deferred tax liabilities have not been recognized (see par. 39);

7. In respect of each type of temporary difference and in respect of each type of unused tax losses and unused tax credits:

   (a) The amount of the deferred tax assets and liabilities recognized in the balance sheet for each period presented, or

   (b) The amount of the deferred tax income or expense recognized in the income statement, if this is not apparent from the changes in the amounts recognized in the balance sheet;

8. In respect of discontinued operations, the tax expense relating to:

   (a) The gain or loss on discontinuance, and

   (b) The profit or loss from the ordinary activities of the discontinued operation for the period, together with the corresponding amounts for each prior period presented; and

9. The amount of income tax consequences of dividends to shareholders of the entity that were proposed or declared before the financial statements were authorized for issue, but are not recognized as a liability in the financial statements.

10. If a business combination in which the entity is the acquirer causes a change in the amount recognized for its pre-acquisition deferred tax asset, the amount of that change; and

11. If the deferred tax benefits acquired in a business combination are not recognized at the acquisition date but are recognized after the acquisition date, a description of the event or change in circumstances that caused the deferred tax benefits to be recognized.

Further, as already indicated earlier, an entity should disclose the amount of a deferred tax asset and the nature of the evidence supporting its recognition, when:

1. The utilization of the deferred tax asset is dependent on future taxable profits in excess of the profits arising from the reversal of existing taxable temporary differences.

2. The entity has suffered a loss in either the current or preceding period in the tax jurisdiction to which the deferred tax asset relates.

An entity should disclose the nature of any potential income tax consequences that would result from the payment of dividends to its shareholders. In addition, the entity should disclose the amounts of the potential income tax consequences practicably determinable and whether there are any potential income tax consequences not practicably determinable.

OBSERVATION: Deferred taxation is a complex area in principle, and IAS 12 is a complex standard. The emphasis on the balance sheet and the liability method (which is consistent with the Framework) seems to have forced some strained logic in places in order to produce the treatment that the IASB first thought of. It is not obvious that the requirements of IAS 12 are always fully consistent with the Framework criteria for liabilities (see Chapter 2). The discounting ban may be reconsidered in principle. The U.K. ASB has produced a U.K. standard, which broadly swings into line with IAS and U.S. thinking but explicitly permits discounting. Further discussion can be expected.

CHAPTER 22
INTANGIBLE ASSETS

CONTENTS

OVERVIEW

In IASB GAAP, an intangible asset is defined as "an *identifiable* non-monetary asset without physical substance." This excludes goodwill, which is by definition non-identifiable, being the difference between the fair value of the purchase consideration given for, and the aggregate fair values of the *identifiable* assets and liabilities of, an acquired business that are recognized on acquisition.

Identifiability in IASB GAAP does not equal separability, since an asset of an entity is defined as "a *resource* [that is] (a) *controlled* by the enterprise as a result of past events; and (b) from which future economic benefits are expected to flow to the entity." Hence, an asset that is not separable meets the identifiability criterion if the asset arises from contractual or other legal rights whereby the entity *controls* the asset. For an intangible asset to be recognized, the future economic benefits must be "probable," and it must be possible to measure the cost of the asset reliably. "Control" encompasses both the right to obtain the benefits and the ability to restrict access to them by others. It is not considered to imply the ability to sell the item separately from other assets of the enterprise. These criteria thus permit the recognition as assets, in appropriate circumstances, of non-separable items such as development costs that have not been converted into (separable) patents. As well as internally generated goodwill, expenditure on the following is not recognized as an intangible asset: brands, mastheads, publishing titles, customer lists and items similar in substance, start-ups, training, advertising and/or promotion, and relocation or reorganization. These expenditures are not considered to meet the recognition criteria stated in (a) and (b) above, and in particular the requirement that the flow of economic benefits to the entity as a result of such expenditures should be "probable." When such items are reflected in the cost of acquiring a business, they should be included in the amount of goodwill on acquisition. The position taken in IASB GAAP is that intangible assets (not including goodwill) should be accounted for in the same manner whether they are acquired or internally generated.

IASB GAAP require intangible assets to be recognized initially at cost. Thereafter, the entity must chose between applying the *cost model* or the *revaluation model*. Under the cost model, after initial recognition the asset is carried at its cost less any accumulated amortization and impairment losses. Under the revaluation model, it is carried at its fair value as of the date of the revaluation less any subsequent accumulated amortization and impairment losses, fair value being determined by reference to an active market. An entity needs to assess whether the useful life of the asset is finite (and if so, what is the length of that life in time periods or production units) or indefinite (if, based on an analysis of all relevant factors, there is no foreseeable limit to the period over which the asset is expected to generate net cash flows for the entity).

The relevant IASB GAAP have been promulgated in:

- IAS 38, "Intangible Assets" (March 2004), which replaced IAS 38 issued in July 1998 and superseded IAS 9, "Research and Development Costs," from July 1, 1999;
- IFRIC 4, "Determining whether an Arrangement contains a Lease";
- IFRIC 12, "Service Concession Arrangements";
- SIC 29, "Service Concession Arrangements: Disclosures";
- SIC-32, "Intangible Assets—Web Site Costs";
- IAS 36, "Impairment of Assets" (see Chapter 20); and
- IFRS 3, "Business Combinations" (recognition criteria for acquired intangibles, see Chapter 8).

This chapter is concerned with IAS 38 (as amplified by SIC-29, SIC-32 and IFRIC 4 and 12), which restates the relevant provisions of IFRS 3. A revised IAS 38 was issued in March 2004 as part of the IASB's project on business combinations, in conjunction with the new IFRS 3 and the revised IAS 36, "Impairment of Assets" (see Chapter 20). The revisions to IAS 38 were thus not intended to cover all the requirements of the standard, being concerned primarily with clarifying the notion of "identifiability" as it relates to intangible assets, the useful life and amortization of intangibles, and accounting for in-process R&D projects acquired in business combinations. IFRS 6, "Exploration for and Evaluation of Mineral Resources" (see Chapter 36) included a small consequential amendment to the wording of IAS 38, clarifying the exclusion from its scope of the recognition and measurement of exploration and evaluation assets.

BACKGROUND

The treatment of R&D costs has been the subject of particular controversy internationally. While there is general agreement that research does not give rise to intangible values that can be recognized as assets, there is disagreement as to whether development may do so, subject to certain criteria. In its 1993 revision of IAS 9, "Research and Development Costs," later superseded by IAS 38, the IASC changed its preferred (benchmark) treatment from that proposed in its exposure drafts E32 and E47, namely, the immediate expensing of all development costs, to capitalization (i.e., recognition as an asset), provided certain criteria were met. It was thought that this was more consistent with the concept of an asset as set out in the IASC's Framework. In IAS 38, capitalization is maintained, but the criteria for recognition have been tightened up (with further guidance provided in the revised version of IAS 38 issued in March 2004); immediate expensing is not allowed as an alternative treatment if these criteria are met.

Another area of controversy has been the treatment of brands. Here, however, the IASC felt able to take a firm line: internally generated brands are not to be recognized as assets, and brands acquired in a business combination are not considered to be separately identifiable assets and are thus assimilated to goodwill.

IAS 38 was originally issued in 1998, but in March 2004 (following an exposure draft in December 2002) the IASB issued the revised version with which this chapter is concerned, except that a number of fairly minor revisions were made in 2008 in connection with the revision on IFRS 3, which are included in this chapter.

IFRS 13, "Fair Value Measurement," when adopted, will entail consequential amendments to the wording of IAS 38 in regard to measurement at fair value, but not any change of principle.

The main differences between IASB GAAP and U.S. GAAP regarding intangibles are the following:

1. With the exception of certain software development costs, which are required to be capitalized in accordance with ASC 985, "Software" (ASC 985-20-25-2), U.S. GAAP (ASC 730) require all R&D costs to be immedi-

ately expensed. Under IASB GAAP, the required treatment of development costs is that they should be capitalized if certain recognition criteria are met.

2. IASB GAAP permit, as an alternative treatment, the restatement of intangible assets to their fair values, provided fair value can be determined by reference to an active market for that type of asset. This is not permitted by U.S. GAAP.

3. For subsequent expenditure on acquired in-process R&D, IASB GAAP require capitalization if the expenditure meets the IAS 38 recognition criteria for development expenditure, whereas U.S. GAAP always require recognition as an expense.

DEFINITIONS

The following terms are used in the revised IAS 38, with the meanings specified below (IAS 28, par. 8):

- An *active market* is a market in which all of the following conditions are met: (a) the items traded in the market are homogeneous; (b) willing buyers and sellers can normally be found at any time; and (c) prices are available to the public.

- The *agreement date* for a business combination is the date on which a substantive agreement between the combining parties is reached and, in the case of publicly listed entities, announced to the public. For hostile takeovers, the earliest such date is that on which the acquiree's owners have accepted the acquirer's offer in sufficient numbers for the acquirer to obtain control of the acquiree.

- *Amortization* is the systematic allocation of the depreciable amount of an intangible asset over its useful life.

- An *asset* is a resource that is (a) controlled by an entity as a result of past events and (b) from which future economic benefits are expected to flow to the entity.

- *Carrying amount* is the amount at which an asset is recognized in the balance sheet after deducting any accumulated amortization and/or impairment losses thereon.

- *Cost* is the amount of cash or cash equivalents paid or the fair value of other consideration given to acquire an asset at the time of its acquisition or construction or, when applicable, the amount attributed to that asset when initially recognized in accordance with the specific requirements of other IFRSs (e.g., IFRS 2, "Share-Based Payment").

- *Depreciable amount* is the cost of an asset or other amount substituted for cost, less its residual value.

- *Development* is the application of research findings or other knowledge to a plan or design for the production of new or substantially improved materials, devices, products, processes, systems, or services before the start of commercial production or use.

- *Entity-specific value* is the present value of the cash flows that an entity expects (a) to arise from the continuing use of an asset and from its disposal at the end of its useful life or (b) to incur when settling a liability.

- *Fair value of an asset* is the amount for which that asset could be exchanged between knowledgeable, willing parties in an arm's-length transaction.

- An *impairment loss* is the amount by which the carrying amount of an asset exceeds its recoverable amount.

- An *intangible asset* is as identifiable non-monetary asset without physical substance.

- *Monetary assets* are money held and assets to be received in fixed and determinable amounts of money.

- *Research* is original and planned investigation undertaken with the prospect of gaining new scientific or technical knowledge and understanding.

- The *residual value* of an intangible asset is the estimated amount that an entity would currently obtain from disposal of the asset, after deducting the estimated costs of disposal, if the asset were already of the age and in the condition expected at the end of its useful life.

- *Useful life* is (a) the period over which an asset is expected to be available for use by an entity or (b) the number of production or similar units expected to be obtained from the asset by an entity.

SCOPE

The term *intangible assets* raises the major issue of which intangible items should be recognized as assets and which should not. Hence, IAS 38 mentions numerous items of expenditure on what may be termed *intangible resources*, many of which do not meet its asset recognition criteria. These items include expenditure on advertising, training, start-up, research and development activities, and computer software, patents, copyrights, motion picture films, customer lists, mortgage servicing rights, fishing licenses, import quotas, franchises, customer or supplier relationships, customer loyalty, market share, and marketing rights (IAS 38, pars. 9–10). A good number of these do not qualify for recognition as assets in terms of the criteria set out in the IASC's Framework, and one of the main purposes of IAS 38 is to distinguish between those that do and those that do not. The Introduction to IAS 38 cites several of the items mentioned above as examples of expenditure that does not meet these criteria, namely, start-ups, research, training, advertising and/or promotion, and relocation or reorganization. Paragraphs 20 and 63–64 mention externally acquired or internally generated brands, mastheads, publishing titles, customer lists, and items similar in substance as items not qualifying for recognition as assets.

In the case of an intangible asset held by a lessee under a finance lease, IAS 38, paragraph 6, states the requirement that, after initial recognition, the lessee should account for the asset in accordance with IAS 38.

The scope of IAS 38 is clarified in paragraphs 2–3 by stating which categories of item are not included, namely:

1. Intangible assets that are within the scope of another standard, such as the recognition and measurement of exploration and evaluation assets covered by IFRS 6 (see Chapter 36);

2. Financial assets as defined in IAS 39/IFRS 9 (see Chapter 17); and

3. The development and extraction of minerals, oil, natural gas, and similar non-regenerative resources.

In addition, if another standard lays down the accounting rules for a *specific* type of intangible, an entity should apply *that* standard and not IAS 38. Thus, IAS 38 does not apply to:

- Intangible assets held by an enterprise for sale in the ordinary course of business, covered by IAS 2, "Inventories," or IAS 11, "Construction Contracts."

- Deferred tax assets (IAS 12, "Income Taxes").

- Leases falling within the scope of IAS 17, "Leases."

- Assets arising from employee benefits (IAS 19, "Employee Benefits").

- Goodwill acquired in a business combination (see IFRS 3).

- Financial assets as defined in IAS 39/IFRS 9. Also, the recognition and measurement of some financial assets are covered by IAS 27, "Consolidated and Separate Financial Statements"; IAS 28, "Investments in Associates"; and IAS 31, "Interests in Joint Ventures."

- Deferred acquisition costs and intangible assets arising from an insurer's contractual rights under insurance contracts within the scope of IFRS 4, "Insurance Contracts," which sets out specific disclosure requirements for those acquisition costs but not for those intangible assets. Therefore, the IAS 38 disclosure requirements apply to those intangible assets.

- Non-current intangible assets classified as held for sale (or included in a disposal group that is so classified) in accordance with IFRS 5, "Non-Current Assets Held for Sale and Discontinued Assets."

OBSERVATION: The exclusions from the scope of IAS 38 of the recognition and measurement of exploration and evaluation assets covered by IFRS 6 and the development and extraction of minerals, oil, natural gas, and similar non-regenerative resources are explained by the fact that current oil and gas industry accounting practices in certain countries (including the United States) for these types of intangibles would not necessarily meet the requirements of IAS 38. The issues arising from this situation are expected to be dealt with as part of a comprehensive project on accounting and financial reporting in the extractive industries, which will be undertaken at a later stage. With regard to the recognition and measurement of exploration and evaluation assets covered by IFRS 6, the latter standard imposes, *for the time being*, significantly less demanding requirements as set out in Chapter 36. However, whereas the scope of IAS 38 ostensibly excludes the development and extraction of minerals, oil, natural gas, and similar non-regenerative resources, IFRS 6, paragraph 10, states "The 'Framework' and IAS 38, *Intangible Assets*, provide guidance on the recognition of assets arising from development." Presumably, such guidance is not the same as a requirement.

Some intangible assets may be contained in or on a physical substance, such as a compact disc in the case of computer software, legal documentation in the case of a patent or license, or film. Whether an asset that incorporates both intangible and tangible elements should be treated as a physical asset under IAS 16, "Property, Plant, and Equipment," or as an intangible asset under IAS 38 is a matter of judgment as to which element is more significant. For example, computer software may be installed on related hardware that cannot function without it, in which case the software forms an integral part of the physical asset and is treated with it as property, plant, and equipment. Software that is not an integral part of related hardware is treated as an intangible asset.

Definitions

IAS 38, paragraph 8, sets out the following definitions:

- An *active market* is one in which *all* of the following conditions are satisfied:
  - Items traded in the market are homogeneous,
  - Willing buyers and sellers can normally be found at any time, and
  - Prices are available to the public.
- The *agreement date* is, for a business combination, the date on which a substantial agreement between the combining parties is reached; for publicly listed entities, it is the date on which the agreement is publicly announced. In the case of a hostile takeover, the *earliest* date on which a substantive agreement between the combining parties is reached is that on which the number of the acquiree's owners that have accepted the acquirer's offer becomes *sufficient for the acquirer to obtain control* of the acquiree.
- *Amortization* is the systematic allocation of the *depreciable amount* of an intangible asset over its useful life.
- An *asset* is a resource that is *controlled* by an entity as a result of past events and from which *future economic benefits* are expected to flow to the entity.
- The *carrying amount* is the amount at which an asset is recognized in the balance sheet, after deducting any accumulated amortization and accumulated impairment losses.
- *Cost* is the amount of cash or cash equivalents paid, and/or the fair value of other consideration given, to acquire an asset at the time of its acquisition or construction or, when applicable, the amount attributed to that asset when initially recognized in accordance with the specific requirements of other IFRSs.
- *Depreciable amount* is the cost of an asset, or other amount used instead of cost, less the asset's residual value.

- *Development* is the *application of* research findings or other *knowledge to a plan or design for the production of new or substantially improved* materials, devices, products, processes, systems, or services *before the start of commercial production or use.*

- *Entity-specific value* is the present value of the cash flows that an entity expects either (a) to arise from the continuing use of an asset and from its disposal at the end of its useful life or (b) to incur when settling a liability.

- *Fair value of an asset* is the amount for which that asset could be exchanged between knowledgeable, willing parties in an arm's-length transaction.

- *Impairment loss* is the amount by which the carrying amount of an asset exceeds its recoverable amount.

- *Intangible asset is* an identifiable non-monetary asset without physical substance.

- *Monetary assets* are money held and assets to be received in fixed or determinable amounts of money.

- *Research* is original and planned investigation undertaken with the prospect of gaining new scientific or technical knowledge and understanding.

- *Residual value* is for an intangible asset, the estimated amount that an entity would currently obtain from disposal of the asset, after deducting the estimated costs of disposal, if the asset were already of the age and in the condition expected at the end of its useful life.

- *Useful life* is measured either *in time,* and is therefore the total period over which an asset is expected to be available for use by an entity, or *in units of output,* in which case it is the total number of production or similar units expected to be obtained from the asset by an entity.

RECOGNITION AND MEASUREMENT

The main criterion for recognition of an intangible asset separately from goodwill is *identifiability* (IAS 38, pars. 11–17). For intangibles acquired as part of a business combination, recognition as an intangible asset separate from goodwill also depends on meeting the criterion of *reliable measurement.* However, if the intangible asset is separable or arises from contractual or other legal rights, sufficient information exists to measure its fair value reliably (IAS 38, par. 33).

Identifiability is necessary in order to distinguish an intangible asset from goodwill. An asset is identifiable if it is *separable* or *arises from contractual or other legal rights.* Separability is a sufficient condition for identifiability, but in IASB GAAP not a necessary one. An asset is separable if the entity could rent, sell, exchange, or distribute the specific future economic benefits attributable to the asset without also disposing of other assets or future economic benefits that flow from them. (Future economic benefits include both revenues and cost savings.)

An entity, however, may be able to identify an intangible asset in some other way. If an intangible asset is acquired together with a set of other assets, it may be separately identifiable by virtue of separate legal rights attaching to it. An internally generated intangible asset may also result from an internal project that gives rise to legal rights for the entity. Nevertheless, usually legal rights are transferable, so that such assets are separable (an exception is rights resulting from a legal duty on employees to maintain confidentiality). But identifiability in IASB GAAP can be achieved even if an asset generates future economic benefits only in combination with other assets, that is, it is not separable, provided the enterprise can identify the future economic benefits that will flow from the asset. In that case, however, the second criterion, control, is particularly crucial.

An operator in a service concession agreement acquires rights to future benefits under the agreement. These rights may be recognized as either financial assets or intangible assets, as follows. An unconditional contractual right to receive cash or another financial asset is recognized and measured as a *financial asset* in accordance with IAS 39/IFRS 9, "Financial Instruments," IAS 32, "Financial Instruments: Presentation," and IFRS 7, "Financial Instruments: Disclosure," also apply (see Chapter 17). A right or license to charge users of the public service of which the operator is the service provider under the service agreement is recognized and measured as an *intangible asset* in accordance with IAS 38, initial recognition being on the basis of fair value (IFRIC 12, pars. 15–18).

Control (IAS 38, pars. 13–16) is exercised by an entity over an asset if the entity (a) has the power to obtain the future economic benefits flowing from the underlying resource and (b) can also restrict the access of others to such benefits. Note that this is not the same concept as control over another entity in the context of consolidated financial statements. (See Chapter 11.) The reference to the "underlying resource" should be interpreted as indicating that the resource itself is not recognizable as an asset unless the criterion of control (as well as that of identifiability) is met. Control will generally result from legal rights enforceable in law, and such rights provide a sufficient condition for control. But IASB GAAP do not exclude the possibility that control over the future economic benefits could be exercised in some other way.

OBSERVATION: For example, development expenditure may give rise to an intangible asset if the criteria in IAS 38, paragraph 57, are met (see below), even though no legal rights to intellectual property such as a patent or a copyright have been created. However, in such a case another type of legal right, resulting from a legal duty on employees to maintain confidentiality, would presumably exist. It is hard to envisage control in the absence of some kind of related legal right, and IAS 38 provides no examples of this.

In the case of such intangible resources as benefits arising from a team of skilled staff and from training, even if the identifiability criterion can be satisfied, the criterion of controllability will most likely not be met in the absence of protection by legal rights. The same is true for customer lists or market shares. Such intangible resources therefore do not usually qualify for recognition as intangible assets.

IAS 38, paragraph 21, states that an intangible asset (that has met the other recognition criteria) should be recognized only if its cost can be measure reliably, and that it should be measured initially at cost.

The recognition of an item as an intangible asset requires an entity to demonstrate that the item meets (a) the IAS 38 definition of an intangible asset as given above, and (b) the IAS 38 recognition criteria, namely that (i) it is *probable* that the expected future benefits attributable to the asset will flow to the entity and (ii) the *cost* of the asset can be *measured reliably*. This latter requirement applies both to costs incurred initially to acquire or to generate internally an intangible asset and to costs incurred subsequently to add to, replace part of, or service the asset (IAS 38, par. 18).

For the purpose of determining cost, four different modes of acquisition are considered (pars. 25–47): separate acquisition; acquisition as part of a business combination; acquisition by way of a government grant; and acquisition by exchange of assets.

In the case of separate acquisition, the rules for determining cost are the same as those for assets generally and do not call for comment here. The rules for determining cost in the case of acquisition as part of a business combination are given in IFRS 3, "Business Combinations" (see Chapter 8). In the case of acquisition by way of a government grant, the rules in IAS 20 are applicable (see Chapter 19). These permit the following alternatives: (a) both the asset and the grant to be recognized at fair value, with amortization of the asset over its useful life unless it is nondepreciable (e.g., land), and the grant being recognized as income over the periods necessary to match them with related costs; (b) the asset to be recognized at a nominal value plus any expenditure that is directly attributable to preparing it for its intended use.

Separate Acquisition

Normally, the price paid to acquire separately an intangible asset reflects expectations as to the probability that the expected future economic benefits from the asset will flow to the acquiring entity—that is, this probability is reflected in the cost of the asset. Hence, the *probability* recognition criterion mentioned above is always considered to be met for separately acquired intangible assets. In addition, the *cost* of a separately acquired intangible asset can usually be *measured reliably*, especially when the purchase consideration consists of cash or other monetary items. Cost comprises purchase price including import duties and non-refundable taxes, after deducting trade discounts and rebates, plus any directly attributable costs of preparing the asset for its intended use. The following costs are not included in the above: costs of introducing a new product or service; costs of conducting business in a new location or with a new category of customer; administration and other general overhead expenses; expenses incurred in using or redeploying an intangible asset once it is in the condition necessary for it to be able to operate in the intended manner; initial operating losses (e.g., those incurred while demand for the asset's output builds up).

If payment for an intangible asset is deferred beyond normal credit terms, its cost is the cash price equivalent, and the difference between this and the total amount paid is recognized as interest expense unless it is capitalized in accordance with IAS 23, "Borrowing Costs" (see Chapter 7) (IAS 38, pars. 25–32).

Acquisition as Part of a Business Combination

In accordance with IFRS 3, for an intangible asset acquired in a business combination, its cost is considered to be its fair value at the acquisition date. The fair value reflects market expectations regarding the probability that the future economic benefits attributable to the asset will flow to the acquiring entity. Hence, the *probability* recognition criterion in IAS 38 is *always* considered to be met for intangible assets acquired in business combinations.

Thus, at the acquisition date an acquirer recognizes an acquired intangible asset separately from goodwill *if the asset's fair value can be measured reliably*, whether or not the asset was previously recognized by the acquiree. This applies to an in-process R&D project of the acquiree provided the project meets the IAS 38 definition of an intangible asset and its fair value (which is considered to be its cost) can be measured reliably. If the intangible asset meets the criterion of separability or the criterion arising from contractual or other legal rights, sufficient information is available to measure the fair value of the asset reliably. Hence, while in general, expenditure on research is recognized as an expense when incurred (see "Recognition as an Expense" below), when it is acquired as part of a business combination, it is recognized separately from goodwill if it meets the IAS 38 recognition criteria as amplified by IFRS 3 (i.e., it meets the separability or the contractual-legal criterion for identifiability—see IAS 38, pars. BC78–BC82).

When there is a probability distribution of possible reasonable estimates of an intangible asset's fair value, the degree of uncertainty is a factor in the measurement of the fair value, and not an indication that the fair value cannot be measured reliably. In addition, if an intangible asset acquired in a business combination has a *finite useful life*, there is a rebuttable presumption that its fair value can be measured reliably.

If an intangible acquired in a business combination is separable *only together with* a related contract, identifiable asset, or liability (e.g., a trademark for a natural spring water that cannot be sold separately from the spring itself, or a publishing title together with its subscriber database), and the *individual* fair value of the related item cannot be reliably measured, the intangible is recognized separately from goodwill but together with the related item. An acquirer may also recognize a group of complementary intangible assets as a single asset provided the individual assets in the group have similar useful lives. For example, terms such as "brand" are typically used to refer to a group of complementary assets such as a trademark and its related trade name, formulas, and technological expertise.

The presumption that the fair value of an intangible asset acquired in a business combination can be measured reliably is in doubt only when the asset arises from contractual or other legal rights and is either *not separable*, or is separable but there is *no evidence of exchange transactions for the same or similar assets* and *an estimate of fair value would be dependent on variables that are not measurable*. The fact that an intangible asset is unique does not necessarily imply that an estimate of its fair value would be dependent on immeasurable variables, because entities that are regularly involved in dealing in such assets may have developed techniques for measuring their fair values indirectly. If no active market exists for an intangible asset, its fair value is the amount that the acquirer would have paid for it at the acquisition date in an arm's-length transaction between knowledgeable and willing parties on the basis of the best information available. To arrive at this amount, the outcomes of recent transactions in similar assets are considered. Entities that are involved in the purchase and sale of intangible assets may have developed techniques for estimating their fair values indirectly. Such techniques may be used for initial measurement of intangible assets acquired in business combinations if the objective is to estimate fair value and the techniques reflect current transactions and practices in the relevant industry. Examples are: (a) discounting estimated net cash flows from the asset, and (b) a "deprival value" approach such as (i) estimating and discounting the costs avoided by owning the asset and thus not needing to license it from another party, or (ii) estimating the costs avoided by not having to recreate or replace the asset (IAS 38, pars. 33 – 41).

Subsequent Expenditure on an Acquired In-Process Research and Development Project

Research or development expenditure that (1) relates to an in-process research or development project acquired separately or in a business combination and recognized as an intangible asset, and (2) is incurred after the acquisition of that project is accounted for in accordance with the guidance on internally generated intangible assets below.

Acquisition by Way of a Government Grant

An intangible asset may be acquired free of charge or for a nominal consideration as a result of a government grant. In accordance with one treatment permitted by IAS 20, an entity may choose to recognize initially both the intangible asset and the grant at fair value. If the entity chooses the other treatment permitted by IAS 20, it recognizes the asset initially at a nominal amount plus any expenditure directly attributable to preparing it for its intended use (IAS 38, par. 44).

Exchanges of Assets

In general, the cost of an intangible acquired in exchange for one or more non-monetary assets or a combination of monetary and non-monetary assets is measured at fair value, even if the entity cannot immediately derecognize the asset or assets given up in exchange. This is so unless either (a) the exchange transaction lacks *commercial substance* (see below) or (b) the fair value neither of the asset acquired, nor of that or those given up in exchange, is reliably measurable. If an entity can determine reliably the fair value either of the asset received or of that or those given up in exchange, then the fair value of the asset or assets given up is used to measure fair value unless the fair value of the asset received is more clearly evident. If the acquired asset is not measured at fair value, its *cost* is measured as the *carrying amount* of the asset or assets given up.

An exchange transaction has *commercial substance* if one of the two conditions below, and the third condition below, are satisfied: *either* (a) the risk, timing, and amount of the cash flows from the asset received differ from those of the asset or assets given up, *or* (b) the entity-specific value of the portion of the entity's operations affected by the transaction changes as a result of the exchange, *and* (c) the difference in (a) or (b) is significant relative to the fair value of the assets exchanged (IAS 38, pars. 45 – 47).

The fair value of an intangible asset for which comparable market transactions do not exist is *reliably measurable* if (a) the variability in the range of reasonable estimates of fair value for the asset is not significant or (b) the probability distribution of the various estimates within that range can be reasonably assessed and used to estimate fair value (IAS 38, pars. 45 – 47).

INTERNALLY GENERATED INTANGIBLE ASSETS

Internally generated goodwill is not to be recognized as an asset, according to IAS 38, as indicated below. It should be noted, however, that the use of impairment tests instead of systematic amortization for acquired goodwill will in some cases lead to the recognition of internally generated goodwill "through the back door," because when applying IAS 36, paragraph 104, to "cash-generating units" the value recognized for goodwill will include a combination of goodwill acquired and allocated to that unit and internally generated goodwill subsequently built up within the unit.

Internally Generated Goodwill

Expenditure may be incurred to generate future economic benefits without it resulting in the creation of an intangible asset in accordance with the IAS 38 recognition criteria. Such expenditure may be considered as contributing to "internally generated goodwill," which is *not recognized as an asset* because it is not an *identifiable* resource (i.e., it is not separable, nor does it arise from contractual or other legal rights) controlled by the entity and measurable reliably at cost. Likewise, the amount of goodwill, in the sense of a difference between the market value of an entity and the carrying value of its identifiable net assets, does not represent the cost of an intangible asset controlled by the entity (IAS 38, pars. 49– 50).

Internally Generated Intangible Assets

In assessing whether an internally generated intangible qualifies for recognition as an asset, there may be difficulties because of problems in:

- Identifying whether and when there is an identifiable asset that will generate expected future economic benefits.
- Determining the cost of the asset reliably. In some cases, the cost of generating an intangible asset internally cannot be distinguished from the cost of maintaining or enhancing the entity's internally generated goodwill or of day-to-day operations.

In order to assess whether an internally generated intangible resource meets the criteria for recognition as an asset, IAS 38 set out the following methodology (pars. 52– 64):

1. The entity classifies the internal project resulting in the generation of the resource into two phases: a research phase and a development phase. If this distinction cannot be made for the internal project, then the entire project should be considered as a research phase.

2. Research is defined as original and planned investigation undertaken with the prospect of gaining new scientific or technical knowledge and understanding. Development is the application of research findings or other knowledge to a plan or design for the production of new or substantially improved materials, devices, products, processes, systems, or services prior to the commencement of commercial production or use (IAS 38, par. 8). However, the terms "research phase" and "development phase" have somewhat broader meanings, as indicated below. If an entity cannot distinguish between the research and the development phases of an internal project, all expenditure on the project is treated as if it were incurred in the research phase.

3. No intangible asset should be recognized as resulting from research or from the research phase of an internal project. In this phase, an entity cannot demonstrate that an intangible asset exists that will generate probable future economic benefits. Expenditure on research is recognized as an expense when incurred.

4. An intangible resource arising from development (or from the development phase of an internal project) is recognized as an intangible asset if, and only if, an entity can demonstrate all of the following:

   (a) The technical feasibility of completing the intangible asset so that it will be available for use or sale;

   (b) Its intention to complete the intangible asset and use or sell it;

   (c) Its ability to use or sell it;

   (d) How the intangible asset will generate probable future economic benefits. Among other things, the following should be demonstrated: the existence of a market for the intangible asset or its output or, if it is to be used internally, its usefulness to the entity;

   (e) The availability of adequate technical, financial, and other resources to complete the development and to use or sell the intangible asset, which may be demonstrated by an appropriate business plan; and

   (f) The entity's ability to measure reliably the expenditure attributable to the intangible asset during its development, for example, by means of the entity's costing system.

5. To demonstrate how an intangible asset will generate probable future economic benefits, the principles set out in IAS 36, "Impairment of Assets," especially paragraphs 30 – 57 on "Value in Use" (see Chapter 20) should be applied. If the asset will generate economic benefits only in combination with other assets, the principles for "cash generating units" set out in IAS 36 should be followed.

Expenditure on internally generated resources that does not meet these asset recognition criteria includes the following: start-ups, research, training, advertising and/or promotion, relocation or reorganization, internally generated brands, mastheads, publishing titles, customer lists, and items similar in substance.

SIC-32 deals with expenditure on web sites. An entity's web site that arises from internal development, and is for internal or external access, is an internally generated intangible and subject to the recognition criteria of IAS 38. Internal expenditure on a web site involves (a) a planning stage, for which all expenditure should be expensed when incurred, and (b) development stages, for which some of the expenditure may be able to satisfy the IAS 38 recognition criteria for internally generated intangible assets.

In particular, an entity may be able to satisfy the requirement to demonstrate how its web site will generate probable future economic benefits when, for example, the site is able to generate revenues, such as enabling orders to be placed. A web site developed solely or primarily for promoting and advertising the entity's products and services will not meet this criterion, and all expenditure on developing it should be recognized as an expense when incurred.

Cost of an Internally Generated Intangible Asset

The cost of an internally generated asset is the sum of the expenditure incurred from the date when the intangible asset first meets the recognition criteria set out above. Cost includes all expenditure that is either directly attributable to generating the asset or has been allocated on a reasonable and consistent basis to the activity of generating it. Allocations of overheads should follow the principles set out in IAS 2, "Inventories" (see Chapter 24). With regard to the recognition of interest as a cost, IAS 23, "Borrowing Costs" (see Chapter 7), sets out the applicable principles.

Expenditure that is not part of the cost of the intangible asset includes that on selling, administration, and training staff to operate the asset.

Expenditure on an intangible resource that was initially recognized as an expense in previous financial statements or reports (for example, expenditure during the "research phase" of an internal project) should not be recognized as part of the cost of an intangible asset at a later date (IAS 38, par. 71).

Illustration

An entity is developing a new production process. During 20X5, expenditure incurred was 1,000, of which 900 was incurred before December 1, 20X5 and 100 was incurred between December 1, 20X5, and December 31, 20X5. The entity is able to demonstrate that, at December 1, 20X5, the production process met the criteria for recognition as an intangible asset. The recoverable amount of the know-how embodied in the process (including future cash outflows to complete the process before it is available for use) is estimated to be 500.

At the end of 20X5, the production process is recognized as an intangible asset at a cost of 100 (expenditure incurred since the date when the recognition criteria were met, that is, December 1, 20X5). The 900 expenditure incurred before December 1, 20X5, is recognized as an expense because the recognition criteria were not met until December 1, 20X5. This expenditure will never form part of the cost of the production process recognized in the balance sheet.

During 20X6, expenditure incurred is 2,000. At the end of 20X6, the recoverable amount of the know-how embodied in the process (including future cash outflows to complete the process before it is available for use) is estimated to be 1,900.

At the end of 20X6, the cost of the production process is 2,100 (100 expenditure recognized at the end of 20X5 plus 2,000 expenditure recognized in 20X6). The entity recognizes an impairment loss of 200 to adjust the carrying amount of the process before impairment loss (2,100) to its recoverable amount (1,900). This impairment loss will be reversed in a subsequent period if the requirements for the reversal of an impairment loss in IAS 36, "Impairment of Assets," are met.

Recognition as an Expense

Expenditure on an intangible item is recognized as an expense when incurred, unless:

- It forms part of the cost of an intangible asset that meets the IAS 38 recognition criteria, or
- The item is acquired in a business combination and cannot be identified separately as an intangible asset according to either the separability criterion or the contractual-legal criterion in IFRS 3, paragraphs B31–B34 (see Chapter 8). In this case, it forms part of the amount recognized as goodwill.

In some cases, expenditure is incurred to provide future economic benefits to an entity, but no intangible or other asset is acquired or created that can be recognized. In the case of the supply of goods (such as promotional goods or mail order catalogs), the entity recognizes the expenditure as an expense when it has a right to access those goods. In the case of the supply of services, the entity recognizes the expenditure as an expense when it receives the services.

An entity has a right of access to goods when it has ownership title to them, or when they have been constructed by a supplier in accordance with the terms of a supply contract and the entity could demand delivery of them in return for payment. Services are received when they are performed by a supplier in accordance with a contract to deliver them to the entity, and not when the entity uses them to deliver another service, such as to deliver an advertisement to customers. The foregoing does not preclude an entity from recognizing a prepayment as an asset when payment for goods has been made in advance of the entity obtaining a right to access those goods, or when payment for services has been made in advance of the entity receiving those services.

OBSERVATION: Goods and services acquired to be used to undertake advertising or promotional activities have no other purpose than to undertake those activities. The only benefit from those goods or services is to develop or create brands or customer relationships, and internally generated brands or customer relationships are not recognized as intangible assets. Hence, an entity should not recognize as an asset goods or services that it has received in respect to its advertising or promotional activities. However, an entity may recognize as an asset a prepayment that gives it a right to receive such goods or services. The prepayment expires and is recognized as an expense when the entity has gained the right to access the goods (not when they are actually delivered) or has received the service (see IAS 38, BC46A–46F).

MEASUREMENT AFTER RECOGNITION

For its accounting measurement policy applicable to intangible assets, an entity has a choice between two models, a *cost model* and a *revaluation model*. If the revaluation model is chosen for an intangible asset, it must also be applied to all the other assets in the same class, which are to be revalued simultaneously. A class of intangible assets is a grouping of assets of a similar nature and use in an entity's operations (IAS 38, pars. 72 – 73).

In the *cost model*, after initial recognition an intangible asset is carried at its cost less any accumulated amortization and impairment losses (IAS 38, par. 74).

In the *revaluation model*, after initial recognition an intangible asset is carried at a revalued amount, which is its fair value at the date of the revaluation less any subsequent accumulated amortization and accumulated impairment losses. IAS 38 requires that, for revaluation purposes, fair value be determined by reference to an active market and that revaluations be made with sufficient regularity that at the balance sheet date the asset's carrying amount does not differ materially from its fair value. The frequency of revaluation depends on the volatility of the fair value, and if the fair value differs materially from the carrying amount a further revaluation is necessary. Some assets may require annual revaluation, whereas for others such frequent revaluation may be unnecessary. If an intangible asset is revalued, any accumulated amortization at the date of the revaluation is either:

- Restated proportionately with the change in the gross carrying value of the asset so that the (net) carrying amount of the asset after revaluation equals its revalued amount, or
- Eliminated against the gross carrying amount of the asset, and the net amount restated to the revalued amount of the asset.

The revaluation model does not allow:

- The revaluation of intangible assets that have not previously been recognized as assets.
- The initial recognition of intangible assets at amounts other than cost (with the exceptions noted below).

If only part of the cost of an internally generated intangible asset (such as a development project) is recognized as an asset because the asset did not meet the criteria for recognition until part of the way through the process, the revaluation model may be applied to the asset as a whole. It may also be applied to an intangible asset that was received by way of a government grant and recognized at a nominal amount.

If an intangible asset in a class of revalued intangible assets cannot be revalued because there is no active market for it, it must be carried at cost less any accumulated amortization and accumulated impairment losses. If the fair value of a revalued intangible asset can no longer be determined by reference to an active market, the accruing amount of the asset is its revalued amount at the date of the last revaluation by reference to an active market less any subsequent accumulated amortization and accumulated impairment losses. However, the fact that an active market no longer exists for an intangible asset may be a sign that the asset is impaired and needs to be tested in accordance with IAS 36, "Impairment of Assets." If, at a subsequent measurement date, the fair value of the asset can be determined by reference to an active market, the revaluation model is applied from that date.

If an intangible asset's carrying amount is increased as a result of a revaluation, the increase is to be recognized in other comprehensive income under the heading of revaluation surplus, except to the extent that it reverses a revaluation decrease of the same asset previously recognized in profit or loss, in which case it is likewise recognized in profit or loss.

If an intangible asset's carrying amount is decreased as a result of a revaluation, the increase is to be recognized in profit or loss. However, any decrease is recognized in other comprehensive income to the extent of any credit balance in the revaluation surplus in respect of that asset. The decrease recognized in other comprehensive income reduces the amount accumulated in equity under the heading of revaluation surplus.

Any cumulative revaluation surplus included in equity may be transferred directly (i.e., not through the income statement) to retained earnings when the surplus is realized. The whole surplus may be realized on the retirement or disposal of the asset, but some of it may be realized as the asset is used by the entity, in which case the amount realized is the difference between:

- Amortization based on the revalued carrying amount of the asset, and

- Amortization that would have been recognized on the basis of the asset's historical cost.

(IAS 38, pars. 75 – 87).

USEFUL LIFE

The useful life of an intangible asset must be assessed either as being finite or as being indefinite. If it is finite, the length of that useful life must be assessed in terms of either time periods or production or similar units. An intangible asset is regarded as having an indefinite life when, on the basis of an analysis of all relevant factors, there is *no foreseeable limit* to the period during which the asset is expected to generate net cash inflows for the entity. An intangible asset with a finite useful life is amortized over that useful life; an intangible asset with an indefinite useful life is not amortized (IAS 38, pars. 88– 89).

Factors that need to be considered in estimating an intangible asset's useful life include the following (IAS 38, par. 90):

1. The expected usage of the asset by the entity and whether the asset could be efficiently managed by another management team.

2. Typical product life cycles for the type of asset and public information on estimates of useful lives for similar types of assets that are used in a similar way.

3. Technical, technological, or other types of obsolescence.

4. The stability of the industry in which the asset operates and changes in the market demand for the outputs of the asset.

5. Expected actions by competitors or potential competitors.

6. The level of maintenance expenditure required to obtain the expected future economic benefits from the asset and the entity's intent and ability to spend such amounts.

7. The entity's period of control over the asset and legal and similar limits on control or use, such as the expiration dates of related patents, copyrights, or leases. If control over the future economic benefits from the asset is achieved though legal rights that have been granted for a finite period, the useful life of the asset should not exceed the duration of the legal rights unless they are renewable and renewal is virtually certain.

8. Whether the asset's useful life is dependent on that of other assets of the entity.

The term "indefinite" does not mean "infinite." Uncertainty justifies estimating the useful life of an intangible asset prudently, but not choosing a life that is unrealistically short.

The useful life of an intangible asset that arises from contractual or other legal rights shall not exceed the period over which those rights extend, but may be shorter depending on how long the entity expects to use the asset. If the rights are conveyed for a limited term that can be renewed, the useful life includes the renewal period(s) only if there is evidence to support renewal by the entity without significant cost. The useful life of a reacquired right recognized as an intangible asset in a business combination is the remaining period of the contract in which the right was granted and cannot include renewal periods.

INTANGIBLE ASSETS WITH FINITE USEFUL LIVES

When intangible assets have finite useful lives, the following need to be decided:

- The amortization period ("useful life"),
- The method of amortization (time-based or based on units of production), and
- The residual value (zero or non-zero, and if the latter, how it should be estimated).

The requirements of IAS 38 in these regards are as follows.

Amortization Period and Method

The depreciable amount of an intangible asset with a finite useful life is allocated on a systematic basis over its useful life. Amortization begins when the asset is available for use and ceases at the earlier of:

- The date on which the asset is classified as held for sale (or included in a disposal group classified as held for sale) in accordance with IFRS 5, "Non-Current Assets Held for Sale and Discontinued Operations," and
- The date on which the asset is derecognized.

The amortization method used reflects the pattern in which the future economic benefits from the asset are expected to be consumed by the entity. Normally, amortization is recognized as an expense in profit or loss, but sometimes the economic benefits embodied in an asset are absorbed in producing other assets, in which case the amortization charge constitutes part of the cost of the other asset and is included in its carrying amount (e.g., the amortization of an intangible asset used in a production process is included in the carrying amount of inventories in accordance with IAS 2, "Inventories") (IAS 38, pars. 97 — 99).

IAS 38 envisages a variety of amortization methods that may be used to allocate systematically the depreciable amount of an intangible asset over the periods making up its useful life. The standard mentions the straight-line, diminishing balance, and units of production methods. The method used is selected on the basis of the expected time pattern of consumption of the asset's future economic benefits and is applied consistently from period to period unless there is a change in the expected pattern of consumption of those future economic benefits (IAS 38, par. 98).

The amortization period and method should be reviewed at least at each financial year-end, and the amortization period should be changed if the expected useful life of the asset is significantly different from previous estimates (IAS 38, pars. 104 –106). If the expected time pattern of economic benefits has changed, the amortization method should be changed accordingly. Such changes should be accounted for as changes in accounting estimates under IAS 8, "Accounting Policies, Changes in Accounting Estimates, and Errors" (see Chapter 6).

Residual Value

The residual value of an intangible asset with a finite useful life is assumed to be zero, unless there is:

- A commitment by a third party to purchase the asset at the end of its useful life, or
- An active market for the asset: and (i) the residual value can be determined by reference to that market; (ii) it is probable that such a market will exist at the end of the assets useful life.

A non-zero residual value implies that the entity expects to dispose of the asset *before the end of its economic life.* The residual value should be reviewed at least at each financial year-end, and any change in the residual value is accounted for as a change in an accounting estimate in accordance with IAS 8, "Accounting Policies, Changes in Accounting Estimates, and Errors." It is possible that the residual value of an intangible asset may increase to an amount equal to or greater than its carrying amount, in which case the asset's amortization charge is zero unless and until the residual value subsequently decreases to an amount less than the carrying amount (IAS 38, pars. 100 –103).

INTANGIBLE ASSETS WITH INDEFINITE USEFUL LIVES

Intangible assets with indefinite useful lives are not amortized but are subject to impairment testing. In accordance with IAS 36, "Impairment of Assets," an entity is required to test an intangible asset with an indefinite useful life for impairment by comparing its carrying amount with its recoverable amount *annually* and *whenever there is an indication that the asset might be impaired.* The useful life of an intangible asset that is not being amortized is to be reviewed each period to determine whether events and circumstances continue to support the assessment of an indefinite useful life. If they no longer do so, the change to a finite useful life assessment is accounted for as a change in accounting estimate in accordance with IAS 8, "Accounting Policies, Changes in Accounting Estimates, and Errors." Such a reassessment may also be an indication that the asset is impaired, so that the entity should apply an impairment test by comparing its carrying amount with its recoverable amount determined in accordance with IAS 36, and recognizing any excess of the former over the latter as an impairment loss.

Impairment Losses

The method to be used in making a review of an intangible asset's carrying amount for possible impairment (an impairment test) is set out in IAS 36, "Impairment of Assets" (see Chapter 20) (IAS 38, par. 111).

In addition, IAS 38 requires impairment tests to be carried out at least at each financial year-end, even if there is no indication of impairment in value, in the following cases (IAS 38, pars. 99– 102):

- The intangible asset is not yet ready for use (in which case its ability to generate sufficient future economic benefits to recover its cost is considered to be subject to much uncertainty).
- The intangible asset has an estimated useful life exceeding 20 years.

Retirements and Disposals

An intangible asset is derecognized on disposal or when no future economic benefits are expected from its use or disposal. The gain or loss arising from its derecognition is determined as the difference between the net disposal proceeds, if any, and the asset's carrying amount, and should be recognized immediately in profit or loss (*unless, for a sale and leaseback, IAS 1, "Leases," requires otherwise*). Consideration receivable on disposal is recognized initially at its fair value; if settlement is deferred, the consideration is recognized initially at its cash price equivalent, and the difference is recognized as interest revenue in accordance with IAS 18, "Revenue." Except for a sale and leaseback, the entity should apply the IAS 18 criteria for recognizing revenue from a disposal. Gains are not classified as revenue.

In the case of the replacement of part of an intangible asset, an entity recognizes the cost of the replacement in the carrying amount of the asset and derecognizes the carrying amount of the part replaced. If it is not practicable to determine the latter, the cost of the replacement may be used as an indication of what the cost of the replaced part was when it was acquired or internally generated.

In the case of a reacquired right in a business combination, if the right is subsequently reissued or sold to a third party, the related carrying amount, if any, is used in determining the gain or loss.

The consideration receivable on disposal of an intangible asset is recognized initially at its fair value. If payment is deferred, the consideration received is recognized initially at the cash price equivalent. The difference between the nominal amount of the consideration and the cash price equivalent is recognized as interest revenue in accordance with ISA 18 to reflect the effective yield on the receivable.

Amortization of an intangible asset with a finite useful life does not cease when the asset is no longer used, unless it has been fully amortized or is classified as held for sale (or held in a disposal group so classified) in accordance with IFRS 5, "Non-Current Assets Held for Sale and Discontinued Operations" (IAS 38, pars. 112 –117).

DISCLOSURE

The financial statements should disclose the following for each class of intangible assets, distinguishing between internally generated intangible assets and other intangible assets (IAS 38, par. 118):

1. Whether the useful lives are indefinite or finite and, if finite, the useful lives or the amortization rates used;

2. The amortization methods used for intangibles with finite useful lives;

3. The gross carrying amount and the accumulated amortization (aggregated with accumulated impairment losses) at the beginning and end of the period;

4. The line item(s) of the income statement in which the amortization of intangible assets is included; and

5. A reconciliation of the carrying amount at the beginning and end of the period, showing:

    (a) Additions, indicating separately those from internal development and through business combinations,

    (b) Retirements and disposals,

    (c) Increases or decreases during the period resulting from revaluations under paragraphs 75– 87 and from impairment losses recognized or reversed in other comprehensive income under IAS 36, "Impairment of Assets" (if any),

    (d) Impairment losses recognized in the income statement during the period under IAS 36 (if any),

    (e) Impairment losses reversed in the income statement during the period under IAS 36 (if any),

(f) Amortization recognized during the period,

(g) Net exchange differences arising on the translation of the financial statements of a foreign entity, and

(h) Other changes in the carrying amount during the period. Comparative information is not required.

A *class* of intangible assets is a grouping of assets of a similar nature and use in an entity's operations. Examples of separate classes may include:

1. Brand names,

2. Mastheads and publishing titles,

3. Computer software,

4. Licenses and franchises,

5. Copyrights, patents, and other industrial property rights, service and operating rights,

6. Recipes, formulas, models, designs, and prototypes, and

7. Intangible assets under development.

The classes mentioned above are disaggregated (aggregated) into smaller (larger) classes if this results in more relevant information for the users of the financial statements.

OBSERVATION: Note that *internally generated* brand names, mastheads, publishing titles, and similar items are not recognized as assets (IAS 38, par. 64). Such items may be acquired as part of a business combination, in which case they will be recognized separately from goodwill only if the criteria laid down in IFRS 3, "Business Combinations" (see Chapter 8), are met.

An entity discloses information on impaired intangible assets under IAS 36 in addition to the information required as stated in IAS 38, paragraph 118.

An entity discloses the nature and effect of a change in an accounting estimate that has a material effect in the current period or that is expected to have a material effect in subsequent periods, under IAS 8, "Accounting Policies, Changes in Accounting Estimates, and Errors." Such disclosure may arise from changes in:

1. The amortization period,

2. The amortization method, or

3. Residual values.

(IAS 38, pars. 119–121)

The financial statements should also disclose:

1. For an intangible asset assessed as having an indefinite useful life, the carrying amount of that asset and the reasons supporting the assessment of an indefinite useful life, with a description of the factors that played a significant role in determining it.

2. A description, the carrying amount, and remaining amortization period of any individual intangible asset that is material to the financial statements of the entity as a whole.

3. For intangible assets acquired by way of a government grant and initially recognized at fair value (see "Acquisition by Way of a Government Grant," above):

   (a) The fair value initially recognized for these assets,

   (b) Their carrying amount, and

   (c) Whether they are carried under the benchmark or the allowed alternative treatment for subsequent measurement.

4. The existence and carrying amounts of intangible assets whose title is restricted and the carrying amounts of intangible assets pledged as security for liabilities.

5. The amount of commitments for the acquisition of intangible assets.

When an entity describes the factors that played a significant role in determining that the useful life of an intangible asset is indefinite, the entity considers the eight factors listed in the section "Useful Life" above.

Intangible Assets Measured after Recognition Using the Revaluation Model

If intangible assets are carried at revalued amounts, the following should be disclosed:

1. By class of intangible assets:

   (a) The effective date of the revaluation,

   (b) The carrying amount of revalued intangible assets, and

   (c) The carrying amount that would have been included in the financial statements had the revalued intangible assets been carried under the benchmark treatment mentioned in "Measurement after Recognition," above.

2. The amount of the revaluation surplus that relates to intangible assets at the beginning and end of the period, indicating the changes during the period and any restrictions on the distribution of the balance to shareholders.

It may be necessary to aggregate the classes of revalued assets into larger classes for disclosure purposes. However, classes are not aggregated if this would result in the combination of a class of intangible assets that includes amounts measured under both benchmark and allowed alternative treatments for subsequent measurement.

Research and Development Expenditure

The financial statements should disclose the aggregate amount of research and development expenditure recognized as an expense during the period (IAS 38, par. 126).

Research and development expenditure comprises all expenditure that is directly attributable to research or development activities or that can be allocated on a reasonable and consistent basis to such activities (see "Cost of an Internally Generated Intangible Asset," above, for guidance on the type of expenditure to be included for the purpose of the disclosure requirement in paragraph 126).

Other Information

An entity is encouraged, but not required, to give the following information:

1. A description of any fully amortized intangible asset that is still in use; and

2. A brief description of significant intangible assets controlled by the enterprise but not recognized as assets because they did not meet the recognition criteria in the previous version of IAS 38 issued for 1998 or because they were acquired or generated before this standard was effective (IAS 38, par. 128).

TRANSITIONAL PROVISIONS AND EFFECTIVE DATE

IAS 38 is applied to:

- The accounting for intangible assets acquired in business combinations for which the agreement date was on or after March 31, 2004.

- The accounting for all other intangible assets prospectively from the beginning of the first annual period beginning on or after March 31, 2004. The entity does not adjust the carrying amounts of intangible assets recognized at that date but applies IAS 38 to reassess their useful lives, and any resultant changes in the useful lives are accounted for as a change in an accounting estimate in accordance with IAS 8 (IAS 38, par. 130).

A number of amendments were made to IAS 38 in 2008 in conjunction with the revisions of IAS 1 and IFRS 3. These amendments are to be applied for annual periods beginning on or after January 1, 2009, for those made in conjunction with IAS 38 and July 1, 2009, for those made in conjunction with IFRS 3. A minor amendment was made to IAS 38 in April 2009 clarifying the requirements regarding the acquisition of intangibles as part of a business combination and the description of valuation techniques commonly used to measure intangible assets at fair value when such assets are not traded in an active market. These amendments should be applied prospectively for annual periods beginning on or after July 1, 2009. Earlier application is permitted but should be disclosed.

CHAPTER 23
INTERIM FINANCIAL REPORTING

CONTENTS

OVERVIEW

Annual financial statements are something of a blunt instrument. They cover a long period and do not appear until a considerable time after the end of that period. It is helpful to many users of financial statements to receive one or more progress reports at interim times and/or at shorter intervals. This is a requirement of most stock exchanges, which are likely to issue their own regulations on such statements for their own listed companies. It is also good public relations to appear to wish to keep an image of openness and transparency with one's investors, lenders, and customers.

The practice of issuing interim financial information has become more prevalent generally among listed entities in recent years. Clearly, as with the annual financial statements themselves, consistency, clarity of policy, and adherence to fair presentation are essential. IASB GAAP do not *require* the publication of interim financial reports. However, if an entity reporting under IASB GAAP does choose (or is required by other authorities) to issue such reports, then IASB GAAP prescribes the minimum content of an interim financial report, and the principles for recognition and measurement in complete or condensed financial statements for an interim period.

IASB GAAP are contained in IAS 34, "Interim Financial Reporting," effective for accounting periods beginning on or after January 1, 1999. IFRIC 10, "Interim Financial Reporting and Impairment," is also relevant. Further, minor amendments have been made.

BACKGROUND

There are two possible ways of viewing the preparation of interim financial statements. The first, known as the *discrete approach*, views interim periods like any other accounting period, only shorter. The second, known as the *integral approach*, views an interim period as a component, or integral, part of the annual reporting period. Within this second approach, the purpose of interim financial reporting is to provide information over the course of the annual period that helps to anticipate annual results.

To some extent, IASB GAAP follow the second integral philosophy. They do not require that seasonal or cyclical revenues or expenses are smoothed out, as they can be properly interpreted as indicators of annual performance, given proper comparison figures plus further explanation if necessary. IAS 34 seeks to ensure that such meaningful comparison and necessary explanation are provided. There are no major differences between IASB and U.S. GAAP as promulgated in ASC 270. It should be remembered as a general point, however, that many stock exchanges have their own rules in relation to enterprises quoted thereon.

SCOPE AND DEFINITIONS

As already indicated, IASB GAAP do not of themselves require the preparation and publication of interim financial reports by any entity, listed or otherwise. The fact that an entity may not have provided interim financial reports during a particular financial year or may have provided interim financial reports that do not comply with IAS 34 does not prevent the entity's annual financial statements from conforming to international standards if they otherwise do so. However, if an entity's interim financial report is described as complying with international standards, it must comply with all of the requirements of IAS 34. Thus, IAS 34 applies to all entities that are required, or elect, to publish an interim financial report in accordance with international standards. The IASB "encourages" publicly traded (listed) entities (par. 1) to provide interim financial reports at least as of the end of the first half of their financial year and to make their interim financial reports available not later than 60 days after the end of the interim period.

The standard gives two formal definitions, as follows (par. 4):

- *Interim period* is a financial reporting period shorter than a full financial year.

- *Interim financial report* means a financial report containing either a complete set of financial statements (as described in IAS 1, "Presentation of Financial Statements" (see Chapter 4)) or a set of condensed financial statements (as described in this standard) for an interim period.

IAS 34 makes it clear that it does not intend in any way to "discourage" the issue of an interim complete set of financial statements, that is, in full accord with IAS 1 (which requirement automatically embraces all other applicable IASs). The IAS itself, however, specifies the minimum components of an interim financial report as follows (par. 8):

1. A condensed statement of financial position;
2. A condensed statement of comprehensive income, presented as either;
   (a) A condensed single statement, or
   (b) A condensed separate income statement and a condensed statement of comprehensive income;

3. A condensed statement of changes in equity;

4. A condensed statement of cash flows; and

5. Selected explanatory notes.

It is to be assumed that a reader of an interim financial report also has access to the previous full annual financial statements. The interim report, therefore, focuses on new circumstances and need not duplicate information previously reported.

FORM AND CONTENT OF INTERIM FINANCIAL STATEMENTS

As already discussed, an entity may, if it chooses, issue its interim financial statements in full accord with IAS 1. Otherwise, if an entity publishes a set of condensed financial statements in its interim financial report, those condensed statements should include, at a minimum, each of the headings and subtotals that were included in its most recent annual financial statements and the selected explanatory notes as required by IAS 34. Additional line items or notes should be included if their omission would make the condensed interim financial statements misleading. Basic and diluted earnings per share should be presented on the face of each income statement, complete or condensed, for each interim period.

The interim report should be as consistent as possible, for example, regarding consolidation, with the most recent annual financial statements. The condensed changes in equity statement (see component 3, above) should also be consistent with that of the annual statements.

This relatively brief comment deals with components 1–4 of the condensed interim report. The element of subjectivity involvedin the question of "additional line items or notes" should be observed. However, IAS 34 deals with the content of required explanatory notes (note that component 5 does not include the word "condensed") in detail. Again, it is assumed that the previous full financial statements are available to the reader, so the notes in the interim reports should focus on an explanation of events and transactions that are significant to an understanding of the changes in financial position and performance of the enterprise since the last annual reporting date (pars. 15–15C).

As part of its annual "Improvements" project, the IASB in May 2010 issued significantly more detailed disclosure requirements, replacing the previous par. 16 discussed in detail in our last (2011) edition. These details, now presented as paragraph 16A, are provided below. Further with effect from January 1, 2013, or earlier, if IFRS 13 is early-adopted, paragraph 16A is also required.

In addition to disclosing significant events and transactions in accordance with paragraphs 15–15C, an entity shall include the following information in the notes to its interim financial statements if not disclosed elsewhere in the interim financial report. The information shall normally be reported on a financial year-to-date basis as follows:

1. A statement that the same accounting policies and methods of computation are followed in the interim financial statements as compared with the most recent annual financial statements or, if those policies or

methods have been changed, a description of the nature and effect of the change.

2. Explanatory comments about the seasonality or cyclicality of interim operations.

3. The nature and amount of items affecting assets, liabilities, equity, net income, or cash flows that are unusual because of their nature, size, or incidence.

4. The nature and amount of changes in estimates of amounts reported in prior interim periods of the current financial year or changes in estimates of amounts reported in prior years.

5. Issues, repurchases, and repayments of debt and equity securities.

6. Dividends paid (aggregate or per share) separately for ordinary shares and other shares.

7. The following segment information (disclosure of segment information is required in an entity's interim financial report only if IFRS 8, "Operating Segments," requires that entity to disclose segment information in its annual financial statements):

   a. Revenues from external customers, if included in the measure of segment profit or loss reviewed by the chief operating decision maker or otherwise regularly provided to the chief operating decision maker.

   b. Intersegment revenues, if included in the measure of segment profit or loss reviewed by the chief operating decision maker or otherwise regularly provided to the chief operating decision maker.

   c. A measure of segment profit or loss.

   d. Total assets for which there has been a material change from the amount disclosed in the last annual financial statements.

   e. A reconciliation of the total of the reportable segments' measures of profit or loss to the entity's profit or loss before tax expense (tax income) and discontinued operations. However, if an entity allocates to reportable segments items such as tax expense (tax income), the entity may reconcile the total of the segments' measures of profit or loss to profit or loss after those items. Material reconciling items shall be separately identified and described in that reconciliation.

8. Events after the interim period that have not been reflected in the financial statements for the interim period.

9. The effect of changes in the composition of the entity during the interim period, including business combinations; obtaining or losing control of subsidiaries; and long-term investments, restructurings, and discontinued operations. In the case of business combinations, the entity shall disclose the information required by IFRS 3, "Business Combinations."

10. For financial instruments, the disclosures about fair value required by paragraphs 91-96, 98 and 99 of IFRS 13, "Fair Value Measurement," and

paragraphs 25, 26 and 28–30 of IFRS 7, "Financial Instruments: Disclosures."

→ **PRACTICE POINTER:** The requirement to present information on a financial year-to-date basis *and* to ensure an understanding of the current interim period should be noted carefully. It logically has no effect in the context of half-yearly interim statements, but if interim statements are issued quarterly, then its implications could be significant. The notes included must satisfy the requirements of providing an understanding of the latest quarter (and its comparatives) and also an understanding of the year-to-date (and its comparatives).

A clear statement of disclosure of IAS compliance is required. This should specify either that the interim financial statements achieve *full* compliance with IAS 1, with all its implications, or specify that the interim financial statements achieve *full* compliance with IAS 34. No partial or "in all material respects" claims for compliance are permitted.

Interim reports are required to include interim financial statements as follows (par. 20):

1. Statement of financial position as of the end of the current interim period and a comparative statement of financial position as of the end of the immediately preceding financial year.

2. Statements of comprehensive income for the current interim period and cumulatively for the current financial year to date, with comparative statements of comprehensive income for the comparable interim periods (current and year-to-date) of the immediately preceding financial year. As permitted by IAS 1 (as revised in 2007), an interim report may present for each period either a single statement of comprehensive income, or a statement displaying components of profit or loss (separate income statement) and a second statement beginning with profit or loss and displaying components of other comprehensive income (statement of comprehensive income).

3. Statement of changes in equity cumulatively for the current financial year to date, with a comparative statement for the comparable year-to-date period of the immediately preceding financial year.

4. Statement of cash flows cumulatively for the current financial year to date, with a comparative statement for the comparable year-to-date period of the immediately preceding financial year.

Illustration

To illustrate, suppose an entity's financial year ends December 31 (calendar year). The entity will present the following financial statements (condensed or complete) in its quarterly interim financial report as of June 30, 2007:

Statement of Financial Position

At	June 30, 2007	December 31, 2006

Statement of Comprehensive
Income

6 months ending	June 30, 2007	June 30, 2006
3 months ending	June 30, 2007	June 30, 2006

Statement of Cash Flows

6 months ending	June 30, 2007	June 30, 2006

Statement of Changes in Equity:

6 months ending	June 30, 2007	June 30, 2006

EPS figures would be required for each one of the four income statements presented. Entities whose business is highly seasonal are "encouraged to consider reporting," in addition to the above, financial information for the 12 months ending on the interim reporting date and comparative information for the prior 12-month period. Presumably full compliance with IAS 34 does not strictly require this.

The question of materiality needs to be considered carefully. In deciding how to recognize, measure, classify, or disclose an item for interim financial reporting purposes, materiality should be assessed in relation to the interim period financial data. An event affecting an interim period may be material regarding that interim period but not material, or not expected to be material, in the context of a full financial year. Remember that "information is material if its omission or misstatement could influence the economic decisions of users" (Framework, par. 30). If it is material in the context of the interim period, then IAS 34 requires its disclosure.

→ **PRACTICE POINTER:** Logically, if it is material for the interim period but possibly or probably not in the context of the whole year, the disclosure must be sufficiently detailed to make all the implications clear. Disclosure for the interim period, with no further comment, could be taken to imply a continuation of the situation over the remainder of the year, and thus its continuing materiality, which would be misleading. As IAS 34 puts it (par. 25), judgment must be exercised, remembering that the overriding goal is to ensure that an interim financial report includes all information that is relevant to understanding an enterprise's financial position and performance during the interim period.

Paragraph 16 A(d) (given as item 4 in the "Form and Content of Interim Financial Statements" section above) requires, where material, disclosure of changes in estimates used in previous interim periods within the year, in the current interim period. However, IAS 34 does not require the preparation of separate interim reports for the last interim period in the year (i.e., an entity reporting quarterly is required to present three quarterly reports and one annual report, not four quarterly reports and one annual report). This creates a lacuna dealt with by paragraph 26, which requires that if an estimate of an amount reported in an interim period is changed significantly during the final interim period of the financial year but a separate financial report is not published for that final interim period, the nature and amount of that change in estimate should be disclosed in a note to the annual financial statements for that financial year.

RECOGNITION AND MEASUREMENT

The key principle is that consistency of accounting policies is required between the annual statements and the interim statements. However, change in accounting policy is allowed under IAS 8 (see Chapter 6) and may be required by the issue of a new international standard or statement by the International Financial Reporting Interpretations Committee (IFRIC). The implications (par. 28) are that an entity should apply the same accounting policies in its interim financial statements as are applied in its annual financial statements, except for accounting policy changes made after the date of the most recent annual financial statements that are to be reflected in the next annual financial statements. However, the frequency of an entity's reporting (annual, half-yearly, or quarterly) should not affect the measurement of its annual results. To achieve that objective, measurements for interim reporting purposes should be made on a year-to-date basis.

The standard makes rather heavy weather of the implications of this, but the principle is quite simple. This is that the definitions of the elements, in particular, assets, liabilities, revenues, and expenses given in the IASB Framework (see Chapter 2), must be applied absolutely consistently between annual and interim statements. If an expenditure does not create an asset capable of recognition under the Framework as of the end of an interim period, then it must be treated as an expense in those interim results. Similarly, a liability can be recorded as such only if it represents an existing obligation as of the date of the interim period-end.

IAS 34 recognizes, as it must, that estimates and expectations, for example, concerning future benefits, will change as the full reporting year progresses, that is, they will change between interim reporting periods. An entity that reports more frequently than semiannually, measures income and expenses on a year-to-date basis for each interim period, using information available when each set of financial statements is being prepared. Amounts of income and expenses reported in the current interim period will reflect any changes in estimates of amounts reported in prior interim periods of the financial year. The amounts reported in prior interim periods are not retrospectively adjusted. Paragraphs 16(d) and 26 require, however, that the nature and amount of any significant changes in estimates be disclosed. These paragraphs also require, in the case of an entity that reports only semiannually, similar disclosure in the annual financial statements of significant changes in estimates used in the interim statements.

OBSERVATION: Some uncertainties of detail arise. For example, suppose an entity has a policy of remeasuring certain assets to fair value on a frequent and regular basis. Such remeasurements will be reflected in interim reports. Is the base carrying amount, for the calculation of gain or loss on disposal, that of the latest interim report, or that of the last annual report? Logic would suggest the latter, at least as it will be shown in the next full annual report, as an optional interim report should not logically affect the position in and between compulsory annual reports. But the formal position is unclear. Additionally in this situation, and also with provisions, for example, for inventory write-down or doubtful debts, estimates may reverse between interim periods. Disclosure, if material, is of course required under paragraph 16(d)—presumably in the later interim period, but not, if the *net* movement is immaterial, in the eventual annual report. When these mobile interim figures become comparatives in the following year, the spirit of the standard will need to be followed, rather than the (absent) letter, in order to give adequate and non-misleading disclosure.

IAS 34 explicitly confirms that revenues that are seasonal, cyclical, or occasional and costs that are incurred unevenly are (pars. 37 and 39) anticipated or deferred for interim reporting purposes if, and only if, it is also appropriate to anticipate or defer that type of item at the end of the financial year. In general, such items are recognized when they occur (with additional explanation under paragraph 16(b) as stated above as item 2 in the "Form and Content of Interim Financial Statements" section), if appropriate.

IAS 34 notes and effectively accepts that the use of estimation in interim reports is likely to be greater than might be acceptable in full annual financial statements. The trade-off between relevance and reliability, given that the whole point of interim reports is rapid and timely information, is likely to lead to a different balance. Appendix 3 to the standard gives a number of detailed suggestions ("illustrative and not part of the standard") as to what this might mean. For example, the existence of an annual stock-take does not imply the need for interim stock-takes.

The IASB has issued IFRIC 10, "Interim Financial Reporting and Impairment," to deal with a typically obscure point of detail relating to impairment losses recognized in interim financial statements. The essential points are:

- An entity shall not reverse an impairment loss recognized in a previous interim period in respect of goodwill or an investment in either an equity instrument or a financial asset carried at cost.

- An entity shall not extend this consensus by analogy to other areas of potential conflict between IAS 34 and other standards.

It should be noted that the reversal of impairment losses under IFRS GAAP is not necessarily forbidden in the general case.

RESTATEMENT OF PREVIOUSLY REPORTED INTERIM PERIODS

In general, IAS 8 will apply (see Chapter 6). IAS 34, paragraph 43, states that a change in accounting policy, other than one for which the transition is specified by a new standard or interpretation, should be reflected by:

1. Restating the financial statements of prior interim periods of the current financial year and the comparable interim periods of prior financial years that would be restated in the annual financial statements under IAS 8; or

2. When it is impractical to determine the cumulative effect of the new policy, as at the beginning of the financial year, adjusting the financial

statements of prior interim periods of the current financial year and comparable interim periods of prior financial years to apply the new policy prospectively from the earliest date practicable.

The effect of this is to require that the change in accounting policy be applied retrospectively, or if that is not practicable, that it be applied prospectively from no later than the beginning of the financial year.

APPLYING THE RECOGNITION AND MEASUREMENT PRINCIPLES

IAS 34 contains an appendix, which gives a large number of examples of applying the principles of the standard. This appendix is only "illustrative" and not part of the standard. Many of the illustrations, paragraphs 12–22, relate to income taxes and discuss the application of the basic requirement to use the estimated weighted average annual effective tax rate expected for the full financial year. The examples are detailed and should be read in full by those seeking to apply IAS 34 in a complex scenario.

To reflect the nuances of difficulty at a more general level, we reproduce here just two of the examples given (IAS 34, Appendix B, pars. 5–7):

- *Year-End Bonuses.* The nature of year-end bonuses varies widely. Some are earned simply by continued employment during a time period. Some bonuses are earned on the basis of a monthly, quarterly, or annual measure of operating result. They may be purely discretionary, contractual, or based on years of historical precedent. A bonus is anticipated for interim reporting purposes if, and only if, (a) the bonus is a legal obligation, or past practice would make the bonus a constructive obligation for which the entity has no realistic alternative but to make the payments, and (b) a reliable estimate of the obligation can be made. IAS 19, "Employee Benefits," provides guidance.

- *Contingent Lease Payments.* Contingent lease payments can be an example of a legal or constructive obligation that is recognized as a liability. If a lease provides for contingent payments based on the lessee achieving a certain level of annual sales, an obligation can arise in the interim periods of the financial year before the required annual level of sales has been achieved, if that required level of sales is expected to be achieved and the entity, therefore, has no realistic alternative but to make the future lease payment.

It is interesting to observe the strong emphasis on the balance sheet elements in the above arguments—the focus is on the existence and measurement of obligations (liabilities), not on the usage or consumption of resources (expenses). This is consistent with the general approach taken in the IASB Framework (see Chapter 2).

CHAPTER 24
INVENTORIES

CONTENTS

OVERVIEW

The preparation of financial statements requires careful determination of an appropriate monetary amount of inventory. Usually, that amount is presented as a current asset in the balance sheet and is a direct determinant of cost of goods sold in the income statement; as such, it has a significant impact on the amount of net income. Because the matching convention is applied in determining net income, the measurement of inventories is of primary importance.

This measurement is also difficult, however. There is inevitable subjectivity involved in making assumptions about which costs "attach" to inventory items, and which "cost flows" are involved when they are used up or sold. The effect of this subjectivity is reduced, as far as possible, by requiring consistent application of the assumptions chosen.

IASB GAAP are given in IAS 2, "Inventories."

BACKGROUND

Inventory can include a number of different types or stages of item. These can be envisaged as:

- Goods or other assets purchased complete for resale;

- Consumable stores;

- Raw materials and components purchased for incorporation into products for sale;

- Products and services in intermediate stages of completion; and

- Finished products for sale.

The key problem is how to evaluate the "cost" of an item at each and every stage in the production process, how to determine the cost of items sold, and, therefore, the cost of items not yet sold (i.e., still in inventory). The first major difficulty is the appropriate allocation of overhead costs (i.e., indirect costs) to particular items or products. The principle is that the cost of inventories should comprise all costs of purchase, costs of conversion, and other costs incurred in bringing the inventories to their present location and condition.

A moment's reflection will make it obvious that there are practical problems here. "Direct" items should present no difficulties, as figures can be related "directly" by definition. But overhead allocation necessarily introduces assumptions and approximations: What is the normal level of activity taking one year with another? Can overheads be clearly classified according to function? Which other (non-production) overheads are "attributable" to the present condition and location of an item of inventory? So, for any item of inventory that is not still in its original purchased state, it is a problem to determine the cost of a unit or even of a batch. Methods in common use include job, process, batch, and standard costing. All include arbitrary overhead allocations.

Once we have found a figure for unit cost "in its present location and condition," the next difficulty will arise when we have to select an appropriate method for calculating the related cost where several identical items have been purchased or made at different times and therefore at different unit costs.

Consider the following transactions:

Purchases:	January	10 units at $25 each
	February	15 units at $30 each
	April	20 units at $35 each
Sales:	March	15 units at $50 each
	May	18 units at $60 each

How do we calculate inventory, cost of sales, and gross profit? There are several ways of doing this, based on different assumptions as to which unit has been sold, or which unit is deemed to have been sold. These are discussed in the next section.

INVENTORY COST ASSUMPTIONS

Five possible inventory cost assumptions are discussed below.

Unit Cost

Here we assume that we know the actual physical units that have moved in or out. Each unit must be individually distinguishable, for example, by serial numbers. In these circumstances, impractical in most cases, we simply add up the recorded costs of those units sold to give cost of sales and of those units left to give inventory. This needs no detailed illustration.

First-In, First-Out (FIFO)

With the FIFO method it is assumed that the units moving out are the ones that have been in the longest (i.e., came in first). The units remaining will therefore be regarded as representing the latest units purchased.

Illustration of FIFO Calculation

Calculate the cost of sales and gross profit based on FIFO inventory cost assumption from the data given above.

			at			Cost of Sales
January		10	at $25	=	$250	
February		15	at $30	=	450	
February total		25			700	
March	−	10	at $25 (Jan.)	=	250	
	−	5	at $30 (Feb.)	=	150	400
March total		10	at $30	=	300	
April	+	20	at $35	=	700	
April total		30			1000	
May	−	10	at $30 (Feb.)	=	300	
	−	8	at $35 (Apr.)	=	280	580
May total		12	at $35		420	
						$980

Sales are 750 + 1080 = $1830
Purchases are 250 + 450 + 700 = $1400

This gives:	Sales		1830
	Purchases	1400	
	Closing inventory	420	
	Cost of sales		980
	Gross profit		$850

Last-In, Last-Out (LIFO)

With the LIFO method, we reverse the assumption. We act as if the units moving out are the ones that came in most recently. The units remaining will therefore be regarded as representing the latest units purchased.

Illustration of LIFO Calculation

Calculate the cost of sales and gross profit based on LIFO inventory cost assumption using the given data.

						Cost of Sales
January		10	at $25	=	$250	
February		15	at $30	=	450	
February total		25			700	
March	−	15	at $30 (Feb.)	=	450	450
March total		10		=	250	
April	+	20	at $35	=	700	
April total		30			950	
May	−	18	at $30 (Apr.)	=	630	630
		2	at $35 & 10 at $25		320	
						$1080

This gives:	Sales		1830
	Purchases	1400	
	Closing inventory	320	
	Cost of sales		1080
	Gross profit		$750

Weighted Average

With the weighted average method, we apply the average cost, weighted according to the different proportions at the different cost levels, to the items in inventory. The illustration below shows the fully worked out method, involving continuous calculations. In practice, an average cost of purchases figure is often used, particularly in manual systems, rather than an average cost of inventory figure. This approximation reduces the need for calculation to a periodic, maybe even annual, requirement.

Illustration of Weighted Average Calculation

Calculate the cost of sales and gross profit based on a weighted average inventory cost assumption.

						Cost of Sales
January		10	at $25	=	$250	
February		15	at $30	=	450	
February total		25	at $28*		700	
March	−	15	at $28	=	420	420
March total		10	at $28	=	280	
April	+	20	at $35	=	700	
April total		30	at $32²/₃*		980	
May	−	18	at $32²/₃	=	588	588
		12	at $32²/₃		392	
						$1008

*Working:	[(10 x 25) + (15 x 30)] / (10 + 15) = 28	
	[(10 x 28) + (20 x 35)] / (10 + 20) = 32²/₃	

This gives:	Sales		1830
	Purchases	1400	
	Closing inventory	392	
	Cost of sales		1008
	Gross profit		$822

Base Inventory

The base inventory approach is based on the argument that a certain minimum level of inventory is necessary in order to remain in business at all. Thus, it can be argued that some of the inventory, viewed in the aggregate, is not really available for sale and should therefore be regarded as a non-current asset. This minimum level, defined by management, remains at its original cost, and the remainder of the inventory above this level is treated, as inventory, by one of the other methods. In our example, the minimum level might be 10 units.

Illustration of Base Inventory Calculation

Calculate the cost of sales and gross profit based on a minimum inventory level of 10 units and using FIFO.

January purchase of base inventory 10 at $25 = $250

						Cost of Sales
February		15	at $30	=	$450	
March	–	15	at $30	=	450	450
March total		0			0	
April	+	20	at $35	=	700	
April total		20		=	700	
May	–	18	at $35	=	630	630
May total		2	at $35	=	70	
						$1080
This gives:	Sales					1830
	Purchases				1150	
	Closing inventory				70	
	Cost of sales					1080
	Gross profit					$750

INVENTORY SYSTEMS

Periodic System

Inventory is determined by a physical count as of a specific date. As long as the count is made frequently enough for reporting purposes, it is not necessary to maintain extensive inventory records. The inventory shown in the balance sheet is determined by the physical count and is priced in accordance with the inventory method used. The net change between the beginning and ending inventories enters into the computation of the cost of goods sold.

Perpetual System

In a perpetual system, inventory records are maintained and updated continuously as items are purchased and sold. The system has the advantage of providing inventory information on a timely basis but requires the maintenance of a full set of inventory records. Theoretically, physical counts are not necessary, but they are normally taken to verify the inventory records. Audit practice will certainly require that a physical check of perpetual inventory records be made periodically.

The latest version of IAS 2, as discussed below, forbids the use of LIFO. This is in contrast to many national systems, including U.S. GAAP, which often allow it as an option.

IASB GAAP

IASB GAAP for this area are given in IAS 2, "Inventories." This standard was first issued in 1975, revised in 1993, effective January 1, 1995, and again in 2004, effective January 1, 2005, earlier application being encouraged. Major changes between the 1995 and 2005 versions are discussed below.

The scope is that IAS 2 applies to all inventories, except:

1. Work in progress arising under construction contracts, including directly related service contracts (see IAS 11, "Construction Contracts," Chapter 12);

2. Financial instruments (see Chapter 17); and

3. Biological assets related to agricultural activity and agricultural produce at the point of harvest (see IAS 41, "Agriculture," Chapter 34).

The standard does not apply to the *measurement* of inventories held by:

- Producers of agricultural and forest products, agricultural produce after harvest, and minerals and mineral products, to the extent that they are measured at net realizable value in accordance with well-established practices in those industries. When such inventories are measured at net realizable value, changes in that value are recognized in profit or loss in the period of the change.

- Commodity broker-traders who measure their inventories at fair value less costs to sell. When such inventories are measured at fair value less costs to sell, changes in fair value less costs to sell are recognized in profit or loss in the period of the change (pars. 2 and 3).

OBSERVATION: This may seem clear, if not simple, but it masks a major issue. The 1995 version explicitly restricted its application to financial statements prepared in the context of the historical cost system. The new version (par. IN5) states that the objective and scope paragraphs of IAS 2 were amended "by removing the words 'held under the historical cost system,' to clarify that the standard applies to all inventories that are not specifically excluded from its scope." This is not correct, as the previous version did not use the word "held." The essential definition of "cost," given in the IASB glossary, is "the amount of cash or cash equivalents paid or the fair value of other consideration given to acquire an asset at the time of its acquisition or construction." This definition categorically excludes replacement cost, so what cost possibility other than historical cost exists anyway under IASB GAAP?

Note carefully that the two exclusions above apply only to the *measurement* requirements of IAS 2; recognition and disclosure requirements still apply in these cases. The point, in both cases, is that industry practice frequently values such items at net realizable value or at fair value less costs to sell.

DEFINITIONS

IAS 2 gives only three definitions, as follows (par. 6):

1. *Inventories* are assets:

    (a) Held for sale in the ordinary course of business;

    (b) In the process of production for such sale; or

(c) In the form of materials or supplies to be consumed in the production process or in the rendering of services.

2. *Net realizable value* is the estimated selling price in the ordinary course of business less the estimated costs of completion and the estimated costs necessary to make the sale.

3. *Fair value* is the amount for which an asset could be exchanged, or a liability settled, between knowledgeable, willing parties in an arm's-length transaction.

The standard makes a very interesting comment in paragraph 7:

> Net realisable value refers to the net amount that an entity expects to realise from the sale of inventory in the ordinary course of business. Fair value reflects the amount for which the same inventory could be exchanged between knowledgeable and willing buyers and sellers in the marketplace. The former is an entity-specific value; the latter is not. Net realisable value for inventories may not equal fair value less costs to sell.

The concept of fair value, a matter of considerable academic complexity well beyond our scope here, is briefly discussed elsewhere, for example in Chapters 17 and 34.

MEASUREMENT OF INVENTORIES

The basic requirement of the entire standard is very simply stated (par. 9):

> Inventories should be measured at the lower of cost and net realizable value.

So, for each separate item, we need to determine both cost and net realizable value (NRV), as defined above.

The significance of the "separate items" point should be noted. Suppose there are three products, A, B, and C, with figures as shown in Table 24-1.

Table 24-1: Lower of Cost and NRV

Product	Cost	NRV	Lower
A	10	12	10
B	11	15	11
C	12	9	9
Total	33	36	30

The figure for inventory in the accounts is $30, not the lower of $33 and $36. This is, of course, a classic example of the prudence convention. It is also consistent with the requirements of IAS 18, "Revenue" (see Chapter 31).

COST OF INVENTORY

The cost of inventories must comprise all costs of purchase, costs of conversion, and other costs incurred in bringing the inventories to their present location and condition. This embraces the purchase price; import duties and other taxes (other than those subsequently recoverable by the entity from the taxing authorities); and transport, handling, and other costs directly attributable to the acquisition of finished goods, materials, and services. Trade discounts, rebates, and other similar items are deducted in determining the costs of purchase. Although the matter is debatable from a theoretical perspective, a discount for prompt payment (which is not the same as a trade or volume discount) would probably be an "other similar item" in the context of the previous sentence.

In its 1995 version, IAS 2 permitted foreign exchange differences to be included in the cost of inventory in certain circumstances. However, related to the elimination of an alternative treatment allowing the capitalization of certain exchange differences in IAS 21, "The Effects of Changes in Foreign Exchange Rates" (see Chapter 18), the 2005 version does not permit this possibility.

The costs of conversion of inventory items are more problematic. They certainly include costs directly related to the units of production, such as direct labor. They also include a systematic allocation of fixed production overheads, such as depreciation, maintenance and administration of factory buildings and equipment, and of variable production overheads, that is, those indirect costs of production that vary directly, or nearly directly, with the volume of production, such as indirect materials and indirect labor.

OBSERVATION: Although it does not say so in so many words, the standard makes it quite clear that direct or marginal costing methods, which treat overheads as a period cost related to time, rather than as a production cost related to units of product, are not permitted. The items stated above are *required* to be included, as "systematically allocated," in cost of conversion.

The allocation of variable production overheads is on the basis of the "actual use" of the production facilities, implying a machine-hour basis or some similar method. The allocation of fixed production overheads is explicitly required to be "based on the normal capacity of the production facilities." Normal capacity is the production expected to be achieved on average over a number of periods or seasons under normal circumstances, taking into account the loss of capacity resulting from planned maintenance. The actual level of production may be used if it approximates normal capacity. The standard thus makes it clear that normal capacity is to be a realistic expectation of practical outcomes, not an idealistic target or notional full capacity. Unallocated overheads arising as a result of production levels below normal capacity are treated as expenses of the period. In periods of abnormally high production, however, the amount of fixed overhead allocated to each unit of production is decreased so that inventories are not measured above cost.

An additional problem is the treatment of a production process that involves several products. Joint products occur when the production of one product necessarily results in the production of one or more other products. By-products are joint products of low or insignificant value. By-products are by definition immaterial. The standard suggests but does not seem to explicitly require (par. 14), that the net realizable value of by-products (which is obviously small) is deducted from the cost of the main product or products.

With other joint products, where both or all are significant, the costs of conversion of the production process as a whole need to be allocated between the products on a "rational and consistent" basis. The relative sales value of each product is suggested as an appropriate proportional allocation by the standard. Allocation according to gross contribution margin would be a sensible alternative. Once the products reach a stage in the production process where the conversion activities become separately identifiable, then individual allocation is required.

Any costs not covered by the above discussions are to be excluded from inventory costs, unless they are demonstrably incurred in bringing the inventories to their present location and condition. The distinction can sometimes be a fine one. For example, if wine is aged in the barrel prior to bottling, the cost of storing in the barrel is a cost of production. The later cost of storing the finished bottle is not. This still leaves open the issue of aging in the bottle, which in logic is a cost of production until the wine becomes finally "finished." It is explicitly stated that abnormal amounts of wasted materials, labor, or other production costs are to be treated as expenses, not as cost of inventory (thereby confirming that *normal* amounts of such wastages *are* cost of inventory and not expense). Borrowing costs may be included as cost of inventory in limited circumstances as defined in IAS 23, "Borrowing Costs" (see Chapter 7). Selling costs are never part of cost of inventory.

Paragraph 18 notes that an entity may purchase inventories on deferred settlement terms. When the arrangement effectively contains a financing element, that element (e.g., a difference between the purchase price for normal credit terms and the amount paid) is recognized as interest expense over the period of the financing. This confirms that the credit charge is not part of inventory cost.

If the industry under consideration is a service provider rather than a product manufacturer, wholesaler, or retailer, then the same principles discussed above should be applied. In the case of a service provider, costs of inventories include the costs of the service (par. 19), that is, the labor and other costs of personnel directly engaged in providing the service, including supervisory personnel and attributable overheads for which the enterprise has not yet recognized the related revenue in accordance with IAS 18, "Revenue" (see Chapter 31). Broadly speaking, IAS 18 requires the recognition of revenue on a percentage-of-completion basis. Therefore the cost of services not yet recognized, that is, the "inventory" to be included in the closing balance sheet, is not likely to be large.

In the case of agricultural produce harvested from biological assets, the implications of IAS 41, "Agriculture" (see Chapter 34), must be considered. Under IAS 41, inventories comprising agricultural produce that an enterprise has harvested from its biological assets are measured on their initial recognition at their fair value less costs to sell at the point of harvest. It therefore follows that this "net fair value" figure is deemed to be the "cost" of such agricultural produce inventories for the purposes of applying IAS 2.

IAS 2 recognizes that, in practice, cost may be measured by convenience methods such as standard costs, which take into account normal levels of activity and are reviewed regularly and kept up to date, or the retail method. This latter is often used in the retail industry for measuring inventories of large numbers of rapidly changing items that have similar margins and for which it is impracticable to use other costing methods. The cost of the inventory is determined by reducing the sales value of the inventory by the appropriate percentage gross margin. The percentage used takes into consideration inventory that has been marked down to below its original selling price. An average percentage for each retail department is often used.

→ **PRACTICE POINTER:** Readers who work in commerce or industry will be well aware that the detailed discussion above about the calculation of cost of inventory masks some difficult, narrow, and often subjective decisions. The definition and calculation of normal capacity are crucial. What do we include in factory administration? There is no way in which such issues can be resolved in a uniform manner across industries or across national jurisdictions and differing local employment and production methods.

What can be required, however, is consistency of policy and practice over time. It is necessary to be clear about the effect on reported annual earnings of changes in balance sheet inventory valuation. An "error" (i.e., a difference) of one dollar in closing inventory, everything else held constant, means a difference of one dollar in reported earnings. However, a difference of one dollar in opening inventory coupled with a difference of one dollar in the same direction in closing inventory means a difference of nil in reported earnings. For many practical purposes, consistency is quite enough.

FORMULAS FOR UNIT COST DETERMINATION

IAS 2 requires (not permits) the use of the unit cost method, as described earlier in this chapter, in certain circumstances. More formally, the inventory costs of items that are not ordinarily interchangeable and of goods or services produced and segregated for specific projects should be assigned by using specific identification of their individual costs (par. 23).

→ **PRACTICE POINTER:** The above wording clearly indicates that a customized job lot, being by definition not interchangeable with other job lots, should be separately costed. However, it does not imply that identical items that are distinguishable, for example, by individual registration numbers, should be costed separately from each other. The criterion is interchangeability, not distinguishability.

In the majority of situations, individual non-interchangeability will not apply, so one of the more-or-less arbitrary cost formulas will need to be used.

The cost of inventories, other than those dealt with in paragraph 23, should be assigned by using the FIFO or weighted-average cost formula. An entity uses the same cost formula for all inventories having a similar nature and use to the entity. For inventories with a different nature or use, different cost formulas may be justified. For example, inventories used in one business segment may have a use to the entity different from the same type of inventories used in another business segment. However, a difference in geographical location of inventories (or in the respective tax rules), by itself, is not sufficient to justify the use of different cost formulas. This represents a major shift from the 1995 version of IAS 2 in that it outlaws the use of LIFO under IASB GAAP—a change long foreshadowed but never previously achieved.

OBSERVATION: There is undoubtedly a strong general argument in favor of reducing the number of options available in the choice of cost formula. That having been said, the reasons given for eliminating LIFO are significantly spurious. The standard states (par. 27) that FIFO assumes that the items of inventory that were purchased or produced first are sold first, contrasting this favorably with the opposite "assumption" under LIFO (in par. BC10). Nevertheless, this is simply untrue. The formulae are concerned with differing views as to the *economic* resources consumed in the revenue-generation process, not at all with physical movements. If one takes the view that "old" historical costs are less relevant than "newer" historical costs, it can be argued that LIFO is "better" for income calculation (as it tends to use "newer" cost figures as expenses) and FIFO is "better" for balance sheet purposes (as it tends to leave "newer" cost figures in closing inventory).

NET REALIZABLE VALUE

Net realizable value is perhaps easier to define theoretically than cost but obviously contains elements of subjectivity in practice. As already illustrated, net realizable value must be calculated, and the "lower of cost and net realizable value" rule must be applied, on an item-by-item basis (pars. 28–33). Grouping of items is allowed only if they are "similar or related." This is interpreted restrictively to, for example, items from the same product line that have similar purposes or end uses, are produced and marketed in the same geographic area, and cannot be practicably evaluated separately from other items in that product line. It is not appropriate to write inventories down on the basis of a classification of inventory, for example, finished goods, or all the inventories in a particular industry or geographic segment. Service providers generally accumulate costs in respect of each service for which a separate selling price will be charged. Therefore, each such service is treated as a separate item.

Estimates of net realizable value should reflect the conditions existing at the balance sheet date. These estimates take into consideration fluctuations of price or cost directly relating to events occurring after the end of the period only to the extent that such events confirm conditions existing at the end of the period. Estimates of net realizable value also take into consideration the purpose for which the inventory is held. Raw materials are written down below cost only if it is expected that the resulting finished product itself will have a net realizable value less than its costs.

IAS 2 requires that when the circumstances that previously caused inventories to be written down below cost no longer exist, the amount of the write-down is reversed so that the new carrying amount is the lower of the cost and the revised net realizable value. In certain cases such as with commodities subject to significant market price changes, this requirement could, of course, lead to large swings in operating results due to unrealized gains and losses. However, this is arguably acceptable and even desirable if you take the view that management should be called to account for its success, or failure, in predicting price movements in those commodities in which it deals.

EXPENSE RECOGNITION

It is important, amidst all this welter of detail, not to lose sight of the simple central requirements of IAS 2, namely, that inventories should be measured at the lower of cost and net realizable value. When inventories are sold, the carrying amount of those inventories should be recognized as an expense in the period in which the related revenue is recognized (par. 34). The amount of any write-down of inventories to net realizable value, and of other losses of inventories, should be recognized as an expense in the period in which the write-down or loss occurs. The amount of any reversal of any write-down of inventories, arising from an increase in net realizable value, should be recognized as a reduction in the expense charge for inventories in the period in which the reversal occurs.

DISCLOSURE

The financial statements must disclose (par 36):

1. The accounting policies adopted in measuring inventories, including the cost formula used;
2. The total carrying amount of inventories and the carrying amount in classifications appropriate to the entity;
3. The carrying amount of inventories carried at fair value less costs to sell;
4. The amount of inventories recognized as an expense during the period;
5. The amount of any write-down of inventories recognized as an expense in the period in accordance with paragraph 34;
6. The amount of any reversal of any write-down that is recognized as a reduction in the amount of inventories recognized as expense in the period in accordance with paragraph 34;
7. The circumstances or events that led to the reversal of a write-down of inventories in accordance with paragraph 34; and
8. The carrying amount of inventories pledged as security for liabilities.

CHAPTER 25
INVESTMENT PROPERTY

CONTENTS

OVERVIEW

Investment property is real estate (land or buildings) that is held to earn rentals, or for capital appreciation—that is, it is held as an investment rather than for consumption or use. The treatment of investment properties in financial statements has been varied and controversial in recent years, and the debates are not yet over.

The IASB issued an exposure draft on investment properties, E64, in July 1999. This proposed a mandatory fair value model for investment properties. However, in the resulting debate, IAS was forced to backtrack, and the standard, IAS 40, "Investment Property," gives a choice.

Investment property, as defined below, can be treated in either of two ways. The Board has agreed that the standard should permit enterprises to choose between a fair value model and a cost model. The fair value model is the model proposed in E64; investment property should be measured at fair value, and changes in fair value should be recognized in the income statement.

The cost model is the cost treatment in IAS 16, "Property, Plant, and Equipment"; investment property should be measured at depreciated cost (less any accumulated impairment losses). An entity that chooses the cost model should additionally disclose the fair value of its investment property in the notes to the financial statements.

IAS 40 was issued in April 2000, effective for financial statements covering periods beginning on or after January 1, 2001. Before that date, IAS 25, "Accounting for Investments," applied. IAS 40 withdrew IAS 25. A revised version of IAS 40 was issued in 2004. The one significant change was to allow properties held under operating leases to be treated as investment properties, in circumstances described and discussed below. This revised version was applicable for annual periods beginning on or after January 1, 2005, earlier application being encouraged.

BACKGROUND

The classic perception of a non-current asset is that of a long-term resource that is necessary to support the day-to-day operational activities of a business. It is used in production or administration, but is not itself sold. It gradually wears out, as its use-value, or service potential, is consumed, in recognition of which depreciation is charged in the annual profit calculation. The classic perception of an investment is that of an asset held so that the asset itself will earn positive returns, either through regular inflows such as interest, dividend, or rent or through capital appreciation. With an investment, the key issue is impairment, rather than consumption of use-value or service potential.

The specific problem with properties is that they can be held for either purpose or for both purposes at different times. Because of a general tendency, over the long term, for property prices to rise significantly in nominal terms, the distinction in practice is often particularly significant.

Until at least the 1970s, property held as an investment was generally treated for accounting purposes like any other property, with or without the possibility of revaluation and with or without the possibility of non-depreciation, depending on the jurisdiction. This approach began to be challenged, notably in the United Kingdom. It was argued that if a property is held as an investment, then:

1. The matching convention is arguably not relevant, as no service potential is being used up; and

2. The current values of such investments, and any change therein, are of prime importance and relevance.

IAS 25, "Accounting for Investments," effective from January 1, 1987, was constructed to allow, but not to require, the treatment of an investment property as a long-term investment under IAS 25, rather than as property under IAS 16, "Property, Plant, and Equipment" (see Chapter 28). Even under IAS 25, such a property could be carried at either cost or revalued amount. Thus, there was a great deal of choice involved.

The proposals of E64 were designed to regularize this situation. E64 proposed a single required treatment for investment properties as defined, namely, measurement at fair value. As indicated in the overview to this chapter, the Board was forced to backtrack from this position. Its long-term intentions were clear, as the Board's Introduction to the original IAS 40 indicates. We quote the relevant paragraphs in full so that readers can appreciate the nuances for themselves:

> This is the first time that the Board has introduced a fair value accounting model for non-financial assets. The comment letters on Exposure Draft E64 showed that although many support this step, many others still have significant conceptual and practical reservations about extending a fair value model to non-financial assets. Also, some believe that certain property markets are not yet sufficiently mature for a fair value model to work satisfactorily.

Furthermore, some believe that it is impossible to create a rigorous definition of investment property and that this makes it impracticable to require a fair value model at present.

For those reasons, the Board believes that it is impracticable, at this stage, to require a fair value model for investment property. At the same time, the Board believes that it is desirable to permit a fair value model. This evolutionary step forward will allow preparers and users to gain greater experience working with a fair value model and will allow time for certain property markets to achieve greater maturity.

The Standard requires that an enterprise should apply the model chosen to all its investment property. A change from one model to the other model should be made only if the change will result in a more appropriate presentation. The Standard states that this is highly unlikely to be the case for a change from the fair value model to the cost model.

In exceptional cases, there is clear evidence when an enterprise first acquires an investment property (or when an existing property first becomes investment property following the completion of construction or development, or after a change in use) that the enterprise will not be able to determine the fair value of the investment property reliably on a continuing basis. In such cases, the Standard requires an enterprise to measure that investment property using the benchmark treatment in IAS 16 until the disposal of the investment property. The residual value of the investment property should be assumed to be zero. An enterprise that has chosen the fair value model measures all its other investment property at fair value.

U.S. GAAP, as currently constituted (ASC 605, APB-6), require that investment properties be treated the same way as any other properties and are, therefore, squarely inconsistent with the original E64 proposals.

SCOPE

IAS 40 applies to all investment property. This includes investment properties held under a lease accounted for as a finance lease, in the books of the lessee, and those leased out under an operating lease, in the books of the lessor. IAS 40 does not apply to:

- Biological assets related to agricultural activity (see IAS 41, Chapter 34), or

- Mineral rights and mineral reserves such as oil, natural gas, and similar non-regenerative resources (see IFRS 6, Chapter 36).

DEFINITIONS

IAS 40 gives the following definitions, several of them familiar from other standards.

- *Investment property* is property (land or a building or part of a building—or both) held (by the owner or by the lessee under a finance lease) to earn rentals or for capital appreciation or both, rather than for:

  — Use in the production or supply of goods or services or for administrative purposes, or

  — Sale in the ordinary course of business.

- *Owner-occupied property* is property held (by the owner or by the lessee under a finance lease) for use in the production or supply of goods or services or for administrative purposes.
- *Fair value* is the amount for which an asset could be exchanged between knowledgeable, willing parties in an arm's-length transaction.
- *Cost* is the amount of cash or cash equivalents paid or the fair value of other consideration given to acquire an asset at the time of its acquisition or construction or, where applicable, it is the amount attributed to that asset when initially recognized in accordance with the specific requirements of other IFRSs (e.g., IFRS 2, "Share-Based Payment").
- *Carrying amount* is the amount at which an asset is recognized in the statement of financial position.

It follows from the definition of investment property that an investment property will generate cash flows "largely independent" of other assets held by an entity. It is this which distinguishes investment property from owner-occupied property, as owner-occupied property only generates cash flows in conjunction with other operating assets necessary for the production or supply process. Examples of investment property include:

- Land held for long-term capital appreciation rather than for short-term sale in the ordinary course of business;
- Land held for a currently undetermined future use;
- A building owned by the entity (or held by the entity under a finance lease) and leased out under one or more operating leases;
- A building that is vacant but is held to be leased out under one or more operating leases; or
- Property that is being constructed or developed for future use as investment property (only since January 1, 2009).

The following are examples of items that do not meet the definition of investment property.

- Property intended for sale in the ordinary course of business (see IAS 2, "Inventories," discussed in Chapter 24), for example, property held for trading by property traders or for development and resale by property developers;
- Property being constructed for third parties (see IAS 11, "Construction Contracts," discussed in Chapter 12);
- Owner-occupied property (see IAS 16, "Property, Plant, and Equipment," discussed in Chapter 28); and
- Property that is leased to another entity under a finance lease.

OBSERVATION: In marginal cases, judgment will be needed in distinguishing investment properties from owner-occupied properties. For example, an owner-managed hotel is essentially concerned with the provision of services to guests, so it is not an investment property. However, the owner of a building that is managed as a hotel by a third party is in the position of holding an investment, with "largely independent" cash flows arising, hence creating an investment property. In complex intermediate situations, the substance of the situation, and the balance of emphasis, should be followed. Disclosure of the criteria used is required when classification is difficult.

A new introduction in the 2004 version of IAS 40 concerns property interests under operating leases. It was widely suggested that, in substance, given the long life of most property, these should be treatable similarly to finance leases. Accordingly (par. 6), a property interest that is held by a lessee under an operating lease may be classified and accounted for as investment property if, and only if, the property would otherwise meet the definition of an investment property and the lessee uses the fair value model for the asset recognized. This classification alternative is available on a property-by-property basis. However, once this classification alternative is selected for one such property interest held under an operating lease, all property classified as investment property is to be accounted for using the fair value model. When this classification alternative is selected, any interest so classified is included in the disclosures required. Note that this is an option, not a requirement.

An investment property within the definition should be recognized as an asset when, and only when:

1. It is probable that the future economic benefits that are associated with the investment property will flow to the entity, and

2. The cost of the investment property can be measured reliably.

MEASUREMENT

The initial measurement is fairly straightforward. Under IAS 40, an investment property should be measured initially at its cost, which is the fair value of the consideration given for it. Transaction costs are included in the initial measurement. The cost of a purchased investment property comprises its purchase price and any directly attributable expenditure. Directly attributable expenditure includes, for example, professional fees for legal services and property transfer taxes.

When an investment property has already been recognized, subsequent expenditure on that investment property should be recognized as an expense when it is incurred unless:

1. It is probable that this expenditure will enable the asset to generate future economic benefits in excess of its originally assessed standard of performance, and

2. This expenditure can be measured and attributed to the asset reliably.

If these conditions are met, the subsequent expenditure should be added to the carrying amount of the investment property.

The initial cost of a property interest held under a lease and classified as an investment property should be as prescribed for a finance lease by paragraph 20 of IAS 17, "Leases"—that is, the asset should be recognized at the lower of the fair value of the property and the present value of the minimum lease payments. An equivalent amount shall be recognized as a liability in accordance with that same paragraph. Note that this applies both to finance leases, and to property interests under operating leases treated as investment properties under the option introduced in paragraph 6.

The question of measurement subsequent to the initial measurement is more complicated. As already outlined, two models are available: the fair value model and the cost model. An entity has a choice between these two models under IAS, and should apply the chosen model to all of its investment property.

OBSERVATION: Although the choice given in IAS 40 between these two models is a free one, and there is no stated "benchmark" treatment, it is very clear that the preference indicated in E64 for a fair value model remains. Fair value has to be determined in *all* cases—for measurement in the financial statements if the fair value model is used, and for disclosure in the notes if the cost model is used. The standard notes that IAS 8, "Accounting Policies, Changes in Accounting Estimates, and Errors," states that a voluntary change in accounting policy should be made only if the change will result in a more appropriate presentation of events or transactions in the financial statements of the entity. The standard explicitly states that it is highly unlikely that a change from the fair value model to the cost model will result in a more appropriate presentation.

Some insurers and other entities operate an internal property fund that issues notional units, with some units held by investors in linked contracts and others held by the entity. Paragraph 32A states that an entity may:

1. Choose either the fair value model or the cost model for all investment property backing liabilities that pay a return linked directly to the fair value of, or returns from, specified assets including that investment property; and

2. Choose either the fair value model or the cost model for all other investment property, regardless of the choice made in item 1.

Measurement under the Fair Value Model

There is a rebuttable presumption that an entity will be able to determine the fair value of an investment property reliably on a continuing basis. After initial recognition, an entity that chooses the fair value model should measure all of its investment property at its fair value, unless this presumption is not valid.

A gain or loss arising from a change in the fair value of investment property should be included in net profit or loss for the period in which it arises. The standard makes it absolutely explicit that changes in fair value are to be taken directly to earnings, and not taken to or from reserves.

IAS 40 discusses the practicalities of measuring fair value at some length, dissecting the implications of "knowledgeable, willing parties," and "arm's length" in its definition. Much of this discussion is common sense. Note that the fair value figure used in a balance sheet should reflect the actual market state and circumstances as of the balance sheet date, not as of either a past or a future date. It follows, for example, that the cost of any anticipated future capital expenditure that will enhance the property, and any related expected increase in benefits, are both omitted from the estimation of fair value at the current date.

The best evidence of fair value is normally given by current prices on an active market for similar property in the same location and condition and subject to similar lease and other contracts. In the absence of current prices on an active market, an entity considers information from a variety of sources, including:

- Current prices in an active market for properties of different nature, condition or location (or subject to different lease or other contracts), adjusted to reflect those differences;

- Recent prices of similar properties on less active markets, with adjustments to reflect any changes in economic conditions since the date of the transactions that occurred at those prices; and

- Discounted cash flow projections based on reliable estimates of future cash flows, supported by the terms of any existing lease and other contracts and by any external evidence such as current market rents for similar properties in the same location and condition, and using discount rates that reflect current market assessments of the uncertainty in the amount and timing of the cash flows.

IAS 40 recognizes that, in exceptional cases, an entity may not be able to determine the fair value of an investment property reliably on a continuing basis. This arises when comparable market transactions are infrequent and alternative estimates of fair value (e.g., based on discounted cash flow projections) are not available. In such cases, an entity should measure that investment property using the cost treatment in IAS 16, "Property, Plant, and Equipment" (see Chapter 28). The residual value of the investment property should be assumed to be zero. The entity should continue to apply IAS 16 until the disposal of the investment property. In such circumstances, the entity measures all its other investment properties at fair value. Once an entity has begun measuring an investment property at fair value, it should continue to do so, even if the measurements subsequently become less reliable.

OBSERVATION: The IASB, and indeed world accounting thought generally, is moving toward a greater support for the fair value concept, but not yet on a systematic basis. IAS 40 took the thinking a little further by discussing the concept, and we can usefully do the same. Fair value is an actual market price, theoretically identical for buyer and seller. It therefore differs from, and will in practice be greater than, net realizable value, which is net of realization expenses. It also differs from value in use, as defined in IAS 36, "Impairment of Assets" (see Chapter 20). Fair value reflects knowledge and estimates of participants in the market, as well as factors that are relevant to market participants in general. In contrast, value in use reflects the enterprise's knowledge and estimates, as well as entity-specific factors that may be specific to the enterprise and that are not applicable to enterprises in general. For example, fair value does not reflect any:

- Additional value derived from the creation of a portfolio of properties in different locations,
- Synergies between investment property and other assets,
- Legal rights or legal restrictions that are specific only to the current owner, or
- Tax benefits or tax burdens that are specific to the current owner.

It follows from the above that fair value is also not the same as recoverable amount, which is the higher of net realizable value and value in use (see Chapter 28). Further confusion has been caused by the unilateral issue of FAS-157 (i.e., ASC 820, "Fair Value Measurement") in late 2006 changing the definition of fair value for U.S. GAAP purposes to an exit value concept. Note that, as discussed in Chapter 3, the IASB is changing its definition of fair value from January 1, 2013, with earlier application "permitted" (not "encouraged," the word used on the introduction of a number of earlier standards), to an explicitly exit value concept. The change in definition, when IFRS 13 is applied, has a number of detailed textural implications for IAS 40.

Measurement Using the Cost Model

After initial recognition, an entity that chooses the cost model should measure all of its investment property using the cost treatment in IAS 16, "Property, Plant, and Equipment," that is, at cost less any accumulated depreciation and any accumulated impairment losses. In other words, if choosing the cost model, an entity proceeds, in measurement (but not disclosure) terms to follow IAS 16 (see Chapter 28), as if IAS 40 did not exist. However, investment properties that meet the criteria to be classified as held for sale (or are included in a disposal group that is classified as held for sale) must be measured in accordance with IFRS 5, "Non-Current Assets Held for Sale and Discontinued Operations" (see Chapter 27).

TRANSFERS

According to IAS 40, transfers to or from investment property should be made when, and only when, there is a change in use, evidenced by:

- Commencement of owner-occupation, for a transfer from investment property to owner-occupied property,
- Commencement of development with a view to sale, for a transfer from investment property to inventories,
- End of owner-occupation, for a transfer from owner-occupied property to investment property,
- Commencement of an operating lease to another party, for a transfer from inventories to investment property.

The wording indicates that this list is intended to be exhaustive.

→ **PRACTICE POINTER:** When the cost model is being used for investment properties, transfers between investment property, owner-occupied property and inventories do not change the carrying amount of the property transferred and they do not change the cost of that property for measurement or disclosure purposes. The standard does not remind us, but we should note, that the fair value of investment properties measured under the cost model has to be disclosed in the notes, a requirement that does not extend to owner-occupied property or to inventory.

A transfer to or from investment properties that are being carried at fair value obviously has potentially very significant effects on the measurement process and the carrying amount of an asset.

If an investment property carried at fair value becomes an owner-occupied property, or is transferred to inventory, then the property's "cost" for subsequent accounting purposes is its fair value as at the date of the change in use. It will subsequently be dealt with under IAS 16, "Property, Plant, and Equipment" (see Chapter 28), or IAS 2, "Inventories" (see Chapter 24), as appropriate.

If an owner-occupied property becomes an investment property carried at fair value, then IAS 16 should be applied up to the date of the change of use, that is, the entity continues to depreciate the property and to recognize any impairment losses. A difference between the carrying amount of the asset under IAS 16 at the date of the change of use, and the fair value at that date, is dealt with in the same way as a revaluation under IAS 16. This means that:

1. Any resulting decrease in the carrying amount of the property is recognized in profit or loss. However, to the extent that an amount is included in revaluation surplus in respect of that property, the decrease is recognized in other comprehensive income, and reduces the revaluation surplus within equity; and

2. Any resulting increase in the carrying amount is treated as follows:

   (a) To the extent that the increase reverses a previous impairment loss for that property, the increase is recognized in profit or loss. The amount recognized in profit or loss does not exceed the amount needed to restore the carrying amount to the carrying amount that would have been determined (net of depreciation) had no impairment loss been recognized; and

   (b) Any remaining part of the increase is recognized in other comprehensive income, and increases the revaluation surplus within equity. On subsequent disposal of the investment property, the revaluation surplus included in equity may be transferred to retained earnings. The transfer from revaluation surplus to retained earnings is not made through the income statement.

If a property classed as inventory is transferred to become an investment property carried at fair value, then the treatment is consistent with that of a sale of inventory under IAS 2. A difference between the fair value of the property at that date and its previous carrying amount is therefore part of net profit or loss for the period. Similarly, a self-constructed investment property that will be carried at fair value will give rise, on completion, to an effect on reported net profit or loss for the period equal to the difference between the fair value on the completion date and its previous (cost-based) carrying amount.

> **OBSERVATION:** Many readers may be struck by the apparent lack of prudence, and of strict adherence to the realization principle, inherent in the previous paragraph. However, this is the whole point of the fair value concept. There is, by definition, reliable evidence to determine fair value, which is a market-based concept, and therefore it follows logically, and consistently with a true sale, that a gain relating to operating processes has been "made." Anybody who regards only a completed transaction as providing adequate evidence for fair value should reject the whole notion of fair value accounting, not just a small aspect of the standard.

DISPOSALS

An investment property should be eliminated from the balance sheet (derecognized) on disposal. The disposal of an investment property may occur by sale or by entering into a finance lease. In determining the date of disposal for investment property, an entity applies the criteria in IAS 18, "Revenue" (see Chapter 31), for recognizing revenue from the sale of goods. IAS 17, "Leases" (see Chapter 26), applies on a disposal by entering into a finance lease or by a sale and leaseback. An investment property must also be derecognized when it is permanently withdrawn from use and no further economic benefits are expected from its disposal. Gains or losses arising on derecognition, that is, the difference between the net disposal proceeds and the carrying amount, are recognized as income or expense in the income statement, unless IAS 17, "Leases," requires otherwise in the case of a sale and leaseback. This is, of course, consistent with the treatment of annual changes in fair value of a retained investment property.

If payment for an investment property is deferred, the consideration received is recognized initially at the cash price equivalent. The difference between the nominal amount of the consideration and the cash price equivalent is recognized as interest revenue on a time proportion basis under IAS 18, "Revenue" (see Chapter 31).

> **OBSERVATION:** If an investment property is disposed of by means of a finance lease, then there is likely to be a freehold reversion at the end of the lease period. In other words, the property is disposed of now, but may return to the possession and ownership of the disposing party at a known date in the future. This logically means that:
>
> 1. A tangible asset will (re)-appear eventually; and
>
> 2. The right to receive (or re-receive) that tangible asset in the future represents an identifiable intangible asset now.
>
> It would seem that the intangible asset referred to in item (2) above would fall within the scope of IAS 38 "Intangible Assets" (see Chapter 22). This would eventually be replaced by the tangible asset (as in item (1) above) to which IAS 40 or IAS 16 would apply, as appropriate to its use at that time. Under IAS 17,

"Leases" (see Chapter 26), the lessor entity is supposed to include "any un-guaranteed residual value" in its receivable.

DISCLOSURE

The IAS 40 disclosure requirements are extensive and, as usual, incapable of effective summary. The requirements can usefully be considered under three headings, beginning with those requirements that apply in all cases, that is for both the fair value and the cost value models.

Certain requirements of IAS 17, "Leases" (see Chapter 26), may be relevant. Under IAS 17, the owner of an investment property gives a lessor's disclosures about operating leases. An entity that holds an investment property under a finance lease gives a lessee's disclosure about that finance lease and a lessor's disclosure about any operating leases that the entity has entered.

Disclosure requirements specified in all cases under IAS 40 are as follows:

1. An entity shall disclose:

    (a) Whether it applies the fair value model or the cost model.

    (b) If it applies the fair value model, whether, and in what circumstances, property interests held under operating leases are classified and accounted for as investment property.

    (c) When classification is difficult, the criteria it uses to distinguish investment property from owner-occupied property and from property held for sale in the ordinary course of business.

2. The methods and significant assumptions applied in determining the fair value of investment property, including a statement whether the determination of fair value was supported by market evidence or was more heavily based on other factors (which the entity should disclose) because of the nature of the property and lack of comparable market data.

3. The extent to which the fair value of investment property (as measured or disclosed in the financial statements) is based on a valuation by an independent valuer who holds a recognized and relevant professional qualification and who has recent experience in the location and category of the investment property being valued. If there has been no such valuation, that fact should be disclosed.

4. The amounts included in the income statement for:

    (a) Rental income from investment property;

    (b) Direct operating expenses (including repairs and maintenance) arising from investment property that generated rental income during the period;

    (c) Direct operating expenses (including repairs and maintenance) arising from investment property that did not generate rental income during the period; and

> (d) The cumulative change in fair value recognized in profit or loss on a sale of investment property from a pool of assets in which the cost model is used into a pool in which the fair value model is used.

5. The existence and amounts of restrictions on the realizability of investment property or the remittance of income and proceeds of disposal.

6. Material contractual obligations to purchase, construct or develop investment property or for repairs, maintenance, or enhancements.

Additional disclosures required when the fair value model is used are that an enterprise should disclose a reconciliation of the carrying amount of investment property at the beginning and end of the period showing the following:

- Additions, disclosing separately those additions resulting from acquisitions and those resulting from subsequent expenditure recognized in the carrying amount of an asset;
- Additions resulting from acquisitions through business combinations;
- Assets classified as held for sale or included in a disposal group classified as held for sale in accordance with IFRS 5, and other disposals;
- The net exchange differences arising on the translation of the financial statements into a different presentation currency, and on translation of a foreign operation into the presentation currency of the reporting entity;
- Transfers to and from inventories and owner-occupied property; and
- Other changes.

When a valuation obtained for investment property is adjusted significantly for the purpose of the financial statements (e.g., to avoid double-counting of assets or liabilities that are recognized as separate assets and liabilities), the entity has to disclose a reconciliation between the valuation obtained and the adjusted valuation included in the financial statements, showing separately the aggregate amount of any recognized lease obligations that have been added back and any other significant adjustments.

In the exceptional cases when an entity measures investment property using the cost treatment in IAS 16, "Property, Plant, and Equipment" (because of the lack of a reliable fair value), the reconciliation required by the previous paragraph should disclose amounts relating to that investment property separately from amounts relating to other investment property. In addition, an entity should disclose:

- A description of the investment property;
- An explanation of why fair value cannot be reliably measured;
- If possible, the range of estimates within which fair value is highly likely to lie; and
- On disposal of investment property not carried at fair value:
  - The fact that the entity has disposed of investment property not carried at fair value,
  - The carrying amount of that investment property at the time of sale, and

— The amount of gain or loss recognized.

Additional disclosures are also required when the cost model is used. In this situation, an entity should also disclose:

- The depreciation methods used;
- The useful lives or the depreciation rates used;
- The gross carrying amount and the accumulated depreciation (aggregated with accumulated impairment losses) at the beginning and end of the period;
- A reconciliation of the carrying amount of investment property at the beginning and end of the period showing the following:
  - Additions, disclosing separately those additions resulting from acquisitions and those resulting from subsequent expenditure recognized as an asset,
  - Additions resulting from acquisitions through business combinations,
  - Assets classified as held for sale or included in a disposal group classified as held for sale in accordance with IFRS 5, and other disposals,
  - Depreciation,
  - The amount of impairment losses recognized and the amount reversed during the period in accordance with IAS 36, "Impairment of Assets,"
  - The net exchange differences arising on the translation of the financial statements into a different presentation currency, and on translation of a foreign operation into the presentation currency of the reporting entity, and
  - Transfers to and from inventories and owner-occupied property; and other changes; and
- The fair value of investment property. In the exceptional cases when an enterprise cannot determine the fair value of the investment property reliably, the entity should disclose:
  - A description of the investment property,
  - An explanation of why fair value cannot be determined reliably, and
  - If possible, the range of estimates within which fair value is highly likely to lie.

TRANSITIONAL PROVISIONS

An entity choosing the fair value model that has previously applied IAS 40 (2000) and elects for the first time to classify and account for some or all eligible property interests held under operating leases as investment property must recognize the effect of that election as an adjustment to the opening balance of retained earnings for the period in which the election is first made. In addition:

1. If the entity has previously disclosed publicly (in financial statements or otherwise) the fair value of those property interests in earlier periods

(determined on a basis that satisfies the current version of the standard), the entity is encouraged, but not required:

(a) To adjust the opening balance of retained earnings for the earliest period presented for which such fair value was disclosed publicly, and

(b) To restate comparative information for those periods.

2. If the entity has not previously disclosed publicly the information described in item 1, it should not restate comparative information and should disclose that fact.

This is in contrast to the general requirement in IAS 8 to restate comparative information.

DECISION TREE

The following decision tree, reproduced from the appendix to the 2000 version of IAS 40, provides a useful summary of the process of deciding on the appropriate IAS treatment of most property.

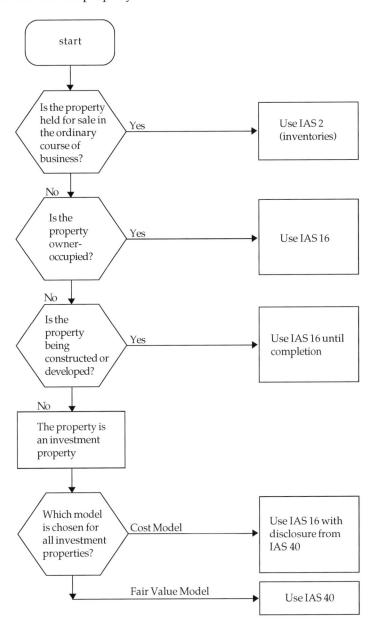

CHAPTER 26
LEASES

CONTENTS

OVERVIEW

A lease is an agreement that conveys to one party (the lessee) the right to use property but does not convey legal ownership of that property. It follows that if an asset is defined as something that is legally owned (i.e., that has been acquired in an exchange transaction), then leases will not give rise to an asset in the financial statements of the lessee. It also follows that if nothing has been "acquired," then nothing is unpaid for, that is, the lease agreement will also not give rise to a liability in the financial statements of the lessee.

If, however, the lease agreement allows the lessee to use the property for all or most of its useful life, requires the lessee to pay total amounts close to and possibly greater than the normal buying price of the item, and requires or assumes that the lessee will look after the item as if the item belonged to it (e.g., insurance, repairs, and maintenance), then it is clear that in substance the lessee would be in the same position, both economically and in terms of production and operating capacity, *as if* the lessee actually owned the asset. Furthermore, a contractual requirement to make future payments greater than the net cost of a straightforward purchase of the item means that the lessee is in the same position *as if* it had taken out a loan under agreed regular repayment terms and at an agreed rate of interest. Thus, in such circumstances, the economic substance of the situation is that the lessee has an asset and a liability, although the legal form of the agreement makes it quite clear that the legal ownership of the item remains with the other party (the lessor).

The general principle of substance over form discussed in Chapter 2 requires that, in such circumstances, the lessee *does* record an asset and a liability in its balance sheet, and the lessor also records a sale and an account receivable in its financial statements.

In broad terms, the whole issue of accounting for leases can be summarized quite simply. If a lease agreement essentially gives the parties rights and obligations similar to those arising from a legal purchase, then the accounting proceeds as if it *were* a legal purchase. This gives rise to a fixed asset and an obligation. If, on the other hand, a lease agreement is, in the context of the particular characteristics of the object in question, essentially a short-term rental, then the accounting treats it as such, giving rise in the books of the lessee to a simple expense, normally allocated on a time basis.

Unfortunately, this simple division masks a considerable amount of practical difficulty. There are problems involved in creating a clear demarcation line between the two situations, and a number of particular issues and problems have arisen over the years that the IASB and various national standards have tried to tackle.

The main GAAP for accounting for leases is in IAS 17. This was originally issued in 1982, as "Accounting for Leases," but was replaced by a new standard, "Leases," agreed to in 1997 and standard from January 1, 1999, but still referred to as IAS 17. A further revision appeared in March 2004, effective for annual periods beginning on or after January 1, 2005, with earlier application encouraged. The main (but limited) objective of this revision was to clarify the classification of a lease of land and buildings and to eliminate accounting alternatives for initial direct costs in the financial statements of lessors. A more fundamental reconsideration of the standard is ongoing, but no time schedule has emerged.

SIC 15, "Incentives in an Operating Lease"; SIC 27, "Evaluating the Substances of Transactions Involving the Legal Form of a Lease"; and IFRIC 4, "Determining Whether an Arrangement Contains a Lease," are also relevant.

BACKGROUND

A lease agreement that puts the parties to the lease (the lessee and the lessor) into a relationship that is, in substance, that of buyer and borrower (the lessee) and of seller and lender (the lessor) is known as a finance lease (sometimes referred to as a capital lease). The accounting treatment of finance leases required by IASB GAAP follows the substance of the situation. All other leases are operating leases. Operating leases are treated as hire or rental contracts on a time basis.

There are no major differences of principle between IASB GAAP and U.S. GAAP regarding leases. There are some detailed differences, however, and U.S. GAAP are distinctly more prescriptive in some respects. IASB GAAP define a finance lease as a lease where the present value of the minimum lease payments is equal to "substantially all" of the fair value of the asset at the date of the lease.

U.S. GAAP require a precise 90% threshold. Alternatively, IASB GAAP specify that a lease is a finance lease if it is for "a major part" of the economic life, whereas U.S. GAAP specify a precise 75%.

Both jurisdictions require the net investment method to allocate gross earnings over time by the lessor of a finance lease, which excludes the effect of cash flows arising from taxes and financing relating to a lease transaction. An exception to this is for leveraged leases under U.S. GAAP where such cash flows are included.

LIKELY FUTURE DEVELOPMENTS

No further material early changes are expected. However, the IASB has signaled its intention to develop an active research project in the leasing area. It intends that this project should have "the objective of developing a single method of accounting for leases that is consistent with the IASB's Framework." This implies that *all* leases, including operating leases as currently defined, would lead to the presentation of an asset and a liability on the balance sheet of a lessee. The final outcome of this project is several years away.

SCOPE AND TERMINOLOGY

The scope of IAS 17 is that it applies to all leases except as stated below. IAS 17 does not apply to:

- Lease agreements to explore for or use minerals, oils, natural gas, and similar non-regenerative resources, or

- Licensing agreements for items such as motion pictures, video recordings, plays, manuscripts, patents, and copyrights.

Additionally, IAS 17 should not be applied to the measurement by:

- Lessees of investment property held under finance leases (see IAS 40, "Investment Property," Chapter 25),

- Lessors of investment property leased out under operating leases (see IAS 40),

- Lessees of biological assets held under finance leases (see IAS 41, "Agriculture," Chapter 34), or

- Lessors of biological assets leased out under operating leases (see IAS 41).

In an attempt to impose a reasonable degree of logic, clarity, and precision on what are inevitably subjective (or arbitrary) distinctions, IASB GAAP, like major national GAAP, have indulged in a certain amount of complication and complexity. A number of terms are defined in paragraph 4 of IAS 17, and an understanding of these definitions and terms is essential in order to appreciate the meaning and significance of the GAAP requirements. Explanations of these terms are given as follows:

- A *lease* is an agreement whereby the lessor conveys to the lessee in return for a payment or series of payments the right to use an asset for an agreed period of time.

- A *finance lease* is a lease that transfers substantially all the risks and rewards incidental to ownership of an asset. Title may or may not eventually be transferred.

- An *operating lease* is a lease other than a finance lease.

The risks of ownership relating to a finance lease are those of breakdown, damage, wear and tear, theft, obsolescence, and so on. The rewards of ownership are extracted by using the asset for substantially all its productive usefulness, that is, its economic life, and by receiving its residual value at the time of its disposal.

1. *Economic life* is either:

    (a) The period over which an asset is expected to be economically usable by one or more users, or

    (b) The number of production or similar units expected to be obtained from the asset by one or more users.

2. *Useful life* is the estimated remaining period, from the commencement of the lease term, without limitation by the lease term, over which the economic benefits embodied in the asset are expected to be consumed by the entity.

Note that the useful life relates to the expected situation *for the lessee.* The economic life relates to the asset, whether or not the current lessee is the only presumed user. Thus, although the useful life can exceed the lease term, the useful life cannot exceed the economic life.

1. The *lease term* is the non-cancelable period for which the lessee has contracted to lease the asset, together with any further terms for which the lessee has the option to continue to lease the asset, with or without further payment, when at the inception of the lease it is reasonably certain that the lessee will exercise the option.

2. A *non-cancelable lease* is a lease that is cancelable only in one of the following circumstances:

    (a) Upon the occurrence of some remote contingency;

    (b) With the permission of the lessor;

    (c) If the lessee enters into a new lease for the same or an equivalent asset with the same lessor; or

    (d) Upon payment by the lessee of an additional amount such that, at inception, continuation of the lease is reasonably certain.

3. The *inception of the lease* is the earlier of the date of the lease agreement and the date of commitment by the parties to the principal provisions of the lease. As of this date:

    (a) A lease is classified as either an operating or a finance lease; and

    (b) In the case of a finance lease, the amounts to be recognized at the commencement of the lease term are determined.

4. The *commencement of the lease term* is the date from which the lessee is entitled to exercise its right to use the leased asset. It is the date of initial

recognition of the lease (i.e., the recognition of the assets, liabilities, income or expenses resulting from the lease, as appropriate).

One of the major criteria for deciding whether or not a finance lease exists is the total amount, or more accurately the total minimum amount, payable under the lease contract. This leads to a set of related terms, as follows:

1. *Minimum lease payments* are the payments over the lease term that the lessee is, or can be, required to make, excluding contingent rent, costs for services, and taxes to be paid by and reimbursed to the lessor, together with:

    (a) In the case of the lessee, any amounts guaranteed by the lessee or by a party related to the lessee; or

    (b) In the case of the lessor, any residual value guaranteed to the lessor by either:

        (i) The lessee,

        (ii) A party related to the lessee, or

        (iii) A third party that is unrelated to the lessor and is financially capable of discharging the obligations under the guarantee.

However, if the lessee has an option to purchase the asset at a price that is expected to be sufficiently lower than the fair value at the date when the option becomes exercisable so that, at the inception of the lease, it is reasonably certain to be exercised, that is, a "bargain purchase option" exists, then the minimum lease payments comprise the minimum payments payable over the lease term and the payment required to exercise this purchase option.

1. *Fair value* is the amount for which an asset could be exchanged or a liability settled, between knowledgeable, willing parties in an arm's-length transaction.

Note that the new IFRS 13, "Fair Value Measurement" (see Chapter 3), does not apply to IFRS 17. An amendment to IAS 17 (par. 6A), relevant from the date of application of IFRS 13, states that "when applying IAS 17 an entity measures fair value in accordance with IAS 17, not IFRS 13." The definition given here, from IAS 17, is not changed by IFRS 13, as par. D1 of that standard confirms by omission.

2. From the viewpoint of the lessee, the *guaranteed residual value* is that part of the residual value that is guaranteed by the lessee or by a party related to the lessee (the amount of the guarantee being the maximum amount that could, in any event, become payable).

3. From the viewpoint of the lessor, the *guaranteed residual value* is that part of the residual value that is guaranteed by the lessee or by a third party unrelated to the lessor who is financially capable of discharging the obligations under the guarantee.

4. *Unguaranteed residual value* is that portion of the residual value of the leased asset, the realization of which by the lessor is not assured or is guaranteed solely by a party related to the lessor.

5. The lessor's *gross investment in the lease* is the aggregate of the minimum lease payments receivable under a finance lease by the lessor, and any unguaranteed residual value accruing to the lessor.

6. *Net investment in the lease* is the gross investment in the lease discounted at the interest rate implicit in the lease.

7. *Unearned finance income* is the difference between:

   (a) The gross investment in the lease; and

   (b) The net investment in the lease.

Some of the greatest technical difficulties are caused by the need, at least theoretically, to calculate backward the interest rates implicitly included in arriving at the total payments under the lease.

- The *interest rate implicit in the lease* is the discount rate that, at the inception of the lease, causes the aggregate present value of (a) the minimum lease payments and (b) the unguaranteed residual value to be equal to the sum of the fair value of the leased asset and any initial direct costs of the lessor.

- The *lessee's incremental borrowing rate of interest* is the rate of interest the lessee would have to pay on a similar lease or, if that is not determinable, the rate that, at the inception of the lease, the lessee would incur to borrow over a similar term, and with a similar security, the funds necessary to purchase the asset.

- *Contingent rent* is that portion of the lease payments that is not fixed in amount but is based on the future amount of a factor that changes with the passage of time (e.g., percentage of sales, amount of usage, future price indices, future market rates of interest).

LEASE CLASSIFICATION

As already indicated, the words that determine the classification of a lease as a finance lease or an operating lease is simple.

A lease is classified as a finance lease if it transfers substantially all the risks and rewards incidental to ownership. A lease is classified as an operating lease if it does not transfer substantially all the risks and rewards incidental to ownership. Because the transaction between a lessor and a lessee is based on a lease agreement common to both parties, it is appropriate to use consistent definitions. The application of these definitions to the differing circumstances of the two parties, however, may sometimes result in the same lease being classified differently by lessor and lessee.

The standard makes no attempt to define "substantially all." Some national GAAP take a much more numerical approach to this question, for example, requiring the present value of the minimum lease payments to be 90% or more of the fair value of the asset at the inception of the lease (e.g., the United States and Germany). Others, such as the United Kingdom, suggest that 90% gives a "presumption" of a finance lease but make it clear that the determining factor is "substantially all," not 90%.

OBSERVATION: The desirability of creating a precise numerical distinction is very much open to question. It has the obvious surface advantage of apparent objectivity and precision. However, the chosen figure is purely arbitrary. More importantly, the creation of a definitive numerical distinction allows, and arguably encourages, business enterprises to structure lease contracts so that they fall just marginally below the chosen criterion, even though the whole purpose may, quite visibly, be, in substance, to finance the "purchase" of major resources by borrowing. The use of a fixed numerical boundary may substantially reduce subjectivity for the accountant and the auditor, but it may at the same time substantially increase creative accounting and the likelihood of misleading or unfair financial statements.

What IAS 17 does do is to give a number of examples of situations that would normally (1–5) or that could (6–8) point to a lease being properly classified as a finance lease. These are as follows (pars. 10 and 11):

1. The lease transfers ownership of the asset to the lessee by the end of the lease term.

2. The lessee has the option to purchase the asset at a price that is expected to be sufficiently lower than the fair value at the date the option becomes exercisable such that, at the inception of the lease, it is reasonably certain that the option will be exercised (i.e., a bargain purchase option exists).

3. The lease term is for the major part of the economic life of the asset even if title is not transferred.

4. At the inception of the lease the present value of the minimum lease payments amounts to at least substantially all of the fair value of the leased asset.

5. The leased assets are of a specialized nature such that only the lessee can use them without major modifications being made.

6. If the lessee cancels the lease, the lessor's losses associated with the cancellation are borne by the lessee.

7. Gains or losses from the fluctuation in the fair value of the residual accrue to the lessee (for example, in the form of a rent rebate equaling most of the residual sales proceeds at the end of the lease).

8. The lessee has the ability to continue the lease for a secondary period at a rent that is substantially lower than market rent (i.e., a bargain rental option).

Because, under situations 1 and 2, the lessee ends up with legal ownership, the validity of a finance lease classification is obvious. Situation 3 assumes, reasonably enough, that a major part of the economic life (measured in years) must imply transfer of substantially all the risks and rewards of ownership (measured in money). Situation 4 argues that payment of substantially all of the purchase price, after discounting to present value, must again imply that the substance of the transaction is a purchase on credit terms, and situation 5 indicates by definition that only the lessee can derive "rewards" from possession of the particular items. The remaining three situations, 6, 7, and 8, while perhaps less definitive, all clearly point to the likelihood of the lessee being in the in-substance ownership position of deriving the benefits and "paying the price." Lease classification is to be made at the inception of the lease.

Illustration of Lease Classification

Costa PLC uses three identical pieces of machinery in its factory. These were all acquired for use on the same date by the following means:

1. Machine 1 rented from Brava Corporation at a cost of $250 per month payable in advance and terminable at any time by either party

2. Machine 2 rented from Blanca Corporation at a cost of eight half-yearly payments in advance of $1,500

3. Machine 3 rented from Sol Corporation at a cost of six half-yearly payment in advance of $1,200

The cash price of this type of machine is $8,000, and its estimated life is 4 years. Are the above machines rented by operating or finance leases?

Machine 1 is held on an operating lease, as there is no transfer of the risks or rewards of ownership. Machine 2 involves a total payment of $12,000. In present value terms this will almost certainly be more than the $8,000 fair value of the asset, and therefore clearly more than "substantially all of the fair value of the leased asset" (see situation 4 above). Machine 2 is therefore held on a finance lease. Machine 3 involves a total payment of $7,200, the present value of which will be significantly less than $8,000, so situation 4 above will not apply. The question is whether or not situation 3 applies, that is, whether or not 3 years is a "major part of the economic life" of the machine (which is 4 years). Under U.S. GAAP, which specifies an arbitrary 75% ratio here, this would be a finance lease under situation 3 (in which circumstance the lease agreement would probably have been changed before signing in order to be a week or two shorter). Under U.K. GAAP, which focuses more exclusively on situation 4, machine 3 would, on the available information, be an operating lease. This example well illustrates the practical difficulties that may arise in lease classification.

The 2004 revision, further amended in 2009, added a number of detailed requirements relating to leases of land and buildings (pars. 14–19). The essential point is that when a lease includes both land and buildings elements, an entity assesses the classification of each element as a finance or an operating lease separately in accordance with paragraphs 7-13. In determining whether the land element is an operating or a finance lease, an important consideration is that land normally has an indefinite economic life. This implies that land is likely, in substance, to be a finance lease if the lease term is a long one. This implication, introduced with effect from January 1, 2010, reverses the previous implicit statement that land is likely to be "normally classified as an operating lease."

Separate measurement of the land and buildings elements is not required when the lessee's interest in both land and buildings is classified as an invest-ment property in accordance with IAS 40 and the fair value model is adopted.

Detailed calculations are required for this assessment only if the classification of one or both elements is otherwise uncertain. In accordance with IAS 40, it is possible for a lessee to classify a property interest held under an operating lease as an investment property. If it does, the property interest is accounted for as a finance lease and, in addition, the fair value model is used for the asset recognized. The lessee should continue to account for the lease as a finance lease, even if a subsequent event changes the nature of the lessee's property interest so that it is no longer classified as investment property.

Yet another attempt to tighten up the requirements for lease capitalization was made by the issue in December 2004 of IFRIC 4, "Determining Whether an Arrangement Contains a Lease." The interpretation notes that in recent years arrangements have developed that do not take the legal form of a lease but convey rights to use assets in return for a payment or series of payments, such as outsourcing arrangements, telecommunication contracts that provide rights to capacity, and take-or-pay and similar contracts, in which purchases must make specified payments, regardless of whether they take delivery of the contracted products or services.

The interpretation specifies that an arrangement that meets both the following criteria is, or contains, a lease that should be accounted for in accordance with IAS 17:

1. Fulfillment of the arrangement depends upon a specific asset. The asset need not be explicitly identified by the contractual provisions of the arrangement. Rather, it may be implicitly specified because it is not economically feasible or practical for the supplier to fulfill the arrangement by providing use of alternative assets.

2. The arrangement conveys a right to control the use of the underlying asset. This is the case if any one of the following conditions is met:

   a. The purchaser in the arrangement has the ability or right to operate the asset or direct others to operate the asset (while obtaining more than an insignificant amounts of the output of the asset).

   b. The purchaser has the ability or right to control physical access to the asset (while obtaining more than an insignificant amount of the output of the asset).

   c. There is only a remote possibility that parties other than the purchaser will take more than an insignificant amount of the output of the asset (and the price that the purchaser will pay is neither fixed per unit of output nor equal to the current market price at the time of delivery).

OBSERVATION: The issue of this interpretation is interesting in two respects. First, it is a further example of the principle of substance over form; if it has an effect similar to a contract that is legally a lease, it should be treated as if it is a lease. Second, it is, however, also a further example of the IASB's perceived need to spell out in detailed operational terms what the implications of that principle are in particular circumstances.

ACCOUNTING AND REPORTING
BY LESSEES—FINANCE LEASES

In the case of finance leases, the substance and financial reality are that the lessee acquires the economic benefits of the use of the leased asset for the major part of its economic life in return for entering into an obligation to pay for that right an amount approximating to the fair value of the asset and the related finance charge.

Lessees should recognize finance leases as assets and liabilities in their balance sheets at amounts equal at the inception of the lease to the fair value of the leased property or, if lower, at the present value of the minimum lease payments (par. 20). In calculating the present value of the minimum lease payments, the discount factor is the interest rate implicit in the lease, if this is practicable to determine; if not, the lessee's incremental borrowing rate should be used. At the inception of the lease, the asset and the liability for the future lease payments are recognized in the balance sheet at the same amounts.

During the lease term, each lease payment should be allocated between a reduction of the obligation and the finance charge to produce a constant periodic rate of interest on the remaining balance of the obligation over the amortization period. The asset initially recorded is depreciated in a manner consistent with that used by the lessee for owned assets.

If the circumstances described in situations 1 or 2 above are present, that is, a transfer of ownership is clearly foreseeable, then depreciation is usually based on the economic life of the leased asset; otherwise, it is based on the shorter of economic life and lease term. Contingent rentals are generally not included in the minimum lease payments and are not accounted for as part of the capitalized lease. They should be charged to expense in the period to which they relate.

Illustration of Finance Lease Accounting by the Lessee

A lessee leases an asset on a non-cancelable lease contract with a primary term of 5 years from January 1, 20X1. The rental is $650 per quarter payable in advance. The lessee has the right to continue to lease the asset after the end of the primary term for as long as it wishes at a nominal rent. In addition, the lessee is required to pay all maintenance and insurance costs as they arise. The leased asset could have been purchased for cash at the start of the lease for $10,000 and has a useful life of 8 years.

The interest rate implicit in the lease can be found as follows:

From the definition of "interest rate implicit in the lease," we can state that:

1. $10,000 (fair value) = the present value at implicit interest rate of 20 quarterly rentals payable in advance of $650.

2. The present value of the first rental payable is $650 as it is paid now.

3. Thus, $9,350 = the present value at implicit interest rate of 19 rentals of $650.

4. Therefore, 9,350/650 = 14.385 = annuity present value factor at implicit interest rate of 19 rentals of $1.

5. Using discount tables and interpolating, we can determine the quarterly interest rate to be 2.95%.

Assuming the asset has a nil residual value and that the asset is to be leased for a further 2 years after the primary period, we can show the accounting entries over the life of the lease required in the lessee's books.

The lease falls within the definition of a finance lease; therefore, the "rights in the lease" will be capitalized at fair value of $10,000 and the obligation under the lease of $10,000 will be shown as a liability, as shown by the following journal.

1/1/X1 Fixed asset	10,000	
Creditors (lessor)		10,000

The minimum lease payments amount to 20 × $650 = $13,000; the cash price was $10,000; hence, the total finance charge will be $3,000.

Remembering that this total finance charge should be allocated to accounting periods during the lease to produce a constant periodic rate of charge on the remaining balance of the obligation for each accounting period, then an appropriate method of allocation would be the actuarial method as follows:

Period	Capital Sum at Start of Period $	Rental Paid $	Capital Sum during Period $	Finance Charge (2.95% per Quarter)* $	Capital Sum at End of Period $
1/X1	10,000	650	9,350	276	9,626
2/X1	9,626	650	8,976	265	9,241
3/X1	9,241	650	8,591	254	8,845
4/X1	8,845	650	8,195	242	8,437
				1,037	
1/X2	8,437	650	7,787	230	8,017
2/X2	8,017	650	7,367	217	7,584
3/X2	7,584	650	6,934	205	7,139
4/X2	7,139	650	6,489	191	6,680
				843	
1/X3	6,680	650	6,030	178	6,208
2/X3	6,208	650	5,558	164	5,722
3/X3	5,722	650	5,072	150	5,222
4/X3	5,222	650	4,572	135	4,707
				627	
1/X4	4,707	650	4,057	120	4,177
2/X4	4,177	650	3,527	104	3,631
3/X4	3,631	650	2,981	88	3,069
4/X4	3,069	650	2,419	71	2,490
				383	
1/X5	2,490	650	1,840	54	1,894

Period	Capital Sum at Start of Period	Rental Paid	Capital Sum during Period	Finance Charge (2.95% per Quarter)*	Capital Sum at End of Period
2/X5	1,894	650	1,244	37	1,281
3/X5	1,281	650	631	19	650
4/X5	650	650	—	—	—
				110	
		13,000		3,000	

We can now apportion the annual rental of $2600 (i.e., 4 × $650) between a finance charge and a capital repayment as follows:

	Total Rental $	Finance Charge $	Capital Repayments $
X1	2,600	1,037*	1,563
X2	2,600	843	1,757
X3	2,600	627	1,973
X4	2,600	383	2,217
X5	2,600	110	2,490
	13,000	3,000	10,000
	(a)	(b)	(a) – (b)

* As calculated using actuarial method

We also need to calculate a depreciation charge. The period for depreciation will be 7 years as this is the lesser of economic life (8 years) and lease period (7 years). The annual depreciation charge on a straight-line basis is, therefore:

$10,000 ÷ 7 = $1,429

The accounting entries in the lessee's books will be as follows, assuming year-end as December 31.

Profit and loss account charges

	Depreciation	Finance Charge	Total
X1	1,429	1,037	2,466
X2	1,429	843	2,272
X3	1,429	627	2,056
X4	1,429	383	1,812
X5	1,428	110	1,538
X6	1,428	—	1,428
X7	1,428	—	1,428
	10,000	3,000	13,000

Balance sheet entries:

Assets held under finance leases

	Cost		Accumulated Depreciation		Net Book Value of Assets Held under Finance Leases
	$		$		$
12/31/X1	10,000	–	1,429	=	8,571
12/31/X2	10,000	–	2,858	=	7,142
12/31/X3	10,000	–	4,287	=	5,713
12/31/X4	10,000	–	5,716	=	4,284
12/31/X5	10,000	–	7,145	=	2,855
12/31/X6	10,000	–	8,574	=	1,426
12/31/X7	10,000	–	10,000	=	—

Obligations under finance leases (i.e., the capital element of future rentals payable)

	Obligations under Finance Leases Outstanding at Start of Year		Capital Repayment		Obligations under Finance Leases Outstanding at Year-End
	$		$		$
12/31/X1	10,000	–	1,563	=	8,437
12/31/X2	8,437	–	1,757	=	6,680
12/31/X3	6,680	–	1,973	=	4,707
12/31/X4	4,707	–	2,217	=	2,490
12/31/X5	2,490	–	2,490	=	—
12/31/X6					—
12/31/X7					—

Note in the above illustration that, after inception, the net asset and net liability figures are different. This will be the usual situation. They are reduced on different bases for different reasons and related to different assumptions.

→ **PRACTICE POINTER:** IAS 36, "Impairment of Assets," applies to finance lease assets. It may be necessary under IAS 36 to recognize, or to reverse, an impairment loss (see Chapter 20).

ACCOUNTING AND REPORTING BY LESSEES—OPERATING LEASES

Lease payments under an operating lease should be recognized as an expense in the income statement on a straight-line basis over the lease term unless another systematic basis is more representative of the time pattern of the user's benefit (par. 33). Note that the pattern of payment is not relevant. Remember that contingent rent, as discussed above, is not included in the original calculations. It therefore follows that the rental expense for any year will consist of:

1. The minimum rent under the lease divided equally over the number of years, plus

2. Any contingent rent relating to that year.

Illustration of Operating Lease Accounting by the Lessee

If the lease given in the earlier illustration were to be treated as an operating lease, then the only entries in the financial statements would be the following annual journal entry:

Rental expense (4 × 650)	2,600	
Creditors (4 × 650)		2,600

OBSERVATION: Consideration of the two illustrations, for finance lease and operating lease, respectively, will quickly suggest the potentially great differences in terms of the shape of the reported performance, and the reported balance sheet structure, that the two methods can give. Note again that these differences, especially in marginal cases, may not be indicative of fundamental realities that are anywhere near as different and distinctive as the accounting numbers might imply.

Lease Incentives in Operating Leases

During the negotiation of a new operating lease or the renewal of an existing one, the lessee may receive incentives to sign the agreement from the lessor. Incentives take many forms, including rent-free periods, reduced rents for a period of time, leasehold improvements on the lessor's account, or a cash signing fee. IAS 17 is silent on this matter, but the Standing Interpretations Committee has clarified the position in SIC-15, "Incentives in an Operating Lease." This requires that the benefit of such incentives be recognized at the inception of the lease and treated as a reduction of rental expense over the term of the lease. The benefit is recognized on a straight-line basis, unless another systematic basis is representative of the time pattern in which benefit is derived from the leased asset.

FINANCIAL STATEMENT DISCLOSURE—LESSEES

It must be remembered that leases are a specific type of financial instrument and, therefore, that the requirements of IAS 32, "Financial Instruments: Presentation," and IFRS 7, "Financial Instruments: Disclosures," apply to leases (see Chapter 17). IAS 39, "Financial Instruments: Recognition and Measurement," does not apply to "rights and obligations under leases, to which IAS 17, Leases, applies."

In addition, the requirements on disclosure under IAS 16, "Property, Plant, and Equipment" (see Chapter 28); IAS 36, "Impairment of Assets" (see Chapter 20); IAS 38, "Intangible Assets" (see Chapter 22); IAS 40, "Investment Property" (see Chapter 25); and IAS 41, "Agriculture" (see Chapter 34), apply to the amounts of leased assets under finance leases that are accounted for by the lessee as acquisitions of assets.

Disclosure requirements specific to IAS 17 for finance leases are as follows (par. 23):

1. For each class of asset, the net carrying amount at the balance sheet date;

2. A reconciliation between the total of minimum lease payments at the balance sheet date and their present value. In addition, an entity should disclose the total of minimum lease payments at the balance sheet date, and their present value, for each of the following periods:

   (a) Not later than one year,

   (b) Later than one year and not later than five years, and

   (c) Later than five years.

3. Contingent rents recognized as an expense in the period;

4. The total of future minimum sublease payments expected to be received under non-cancelable subleases at the balance sheet date; and

5. A general description of the lessee's significant leasing arrangements including, but not limited to, the following:

   (a) The basis on which contingent rent payable is determined,

   (b) The existence and terms of renewal or purchase options and escalation clauses, and

   (c) Restrictions imposed by lease arrangements, such as those concerning dividends, additional debt, and further leasing.

For operating leases, in addition to the general requirements of IAS 32, IAS 17 requires disclosure of the following (par. 35):

1. The total of future minimum lease payments under non-cancelable operating leases for each of the following periods:

   (a) Not later than one year,

   (b) Later than one year and not later than five years, and

   (c) Later than five years;

2. The total of future minimum sublease payments expected to be received under non-cancelable subleases at the balance sheet date;

3. Lease and sublease payments recognized as an expense in the period, with separate amounts for minimum lease payments, contingent rents, and sublease payments; and

4. A general description of the lessee's significant leasing arrangements including, but not limited to, the following:

   (a) The basis on which contingent rent payments are determined,

   (b) The existence and terms of renewal or purchase options and escalation clauses, and

(c) Restrictions imposed by lease arrangements, such as those concerning dividends, additional debt, and further leasing.

ACCOUNTING AND REPORTING BY LESSORS—FINANCE LEASES

As is the case with the financial statements of lessees, the approach is to follow and record the substance of the situation. From the viewpoint of the lessor, the substance is that the lessor has an amount receivable, much of it usually non-current, due from the lessee. In direct relation to the lease contract, the lessor has no other assets or liabilities. The amounts received from the lessee will embrace two elements, that is, a repayment of "loan" and an interest revenue.

Lessors should recognize assets held under a finance lease in their balance sheets and present them as a receivable at an amount equal to the net investment in the lease (pars. 36 — 41). A lessor aims to allocate finance income over the lease term on a systematic and rational basis. This income allocation is based on a pattern reflecting a constant periodic return on the lessor's net investment outstanding in respect of the finance lease. Lease payments relating to the accounting period, excluding costs for services, are applied against the gross investment in the lease to reduce both the principal and the unearned finance income.

Estimated unguaranteed residual values used in computing the lessor's gross investment in a lease are reviewed regularly. If there has been a reduction in the estimated unguaranteed residual value, the income allocation over the lease term is reviewed and any reduction in respect of amounts already accrued is recognized immediately.

Initial direct costs are often incurred by lessors and include amounts such as commissions, legal fees, and internal costs that are incremental and directly attributable to negotiating and arranging a lease. They exclude general over-heads such as those incurred by a sales and marketing team. For finance leases other than those involving manufacturer or dealer lessors, initial direct costs are included in the initial measurement of the finance lease receivable and reduce the amount of income recognized over the lease term. The interest rate implicit in the lease is defined in such a way that the initial direct costs are included automatically in the finance lease receivable; there is no need to add them separately. Costs incurred by manufacturer or dealer lessors in connection with negotiating and arranging a lease are excluded from the definition of initial direct costs. As a result, they are excluded from the net investment in the lease and are recognized as an expense when the selling profit is recognized, which for a finance lease is normally at the commencement of the lease term.

An asset under a finance lease that is classified as held for sale (or included in a disposal group that is classified as held for sale) in accordance with IFRS 5, "Non-Current Assets Held for Sale and Discontinued Operations," is to be accounted for in accordance with that IFRS (see Chapter 27).

Finance Leasing by Manufacturers or Dealers

The manufacturer or dealer may be the person who actually provides the asset, as well as the finance. A finance lease of an asset by a manufacturer or dealer lessor gives rise to two types of income:

1. The profit or loss equivalent to the profit or loss resulting from an outright sale of the asset being leased, at normal selling prices, reflecting any applicable volume or trade discounts; and

2. The finance income over the lease term.

The sales revenue recorded at the commencement of a finance lease term by a manufacturer or dealer lessor is the fair value of the asset, or, if lower, the present value of the minimum lease payments accruing to the lessor, computed at a commercial rate of interest (par. 44). The cost of sale recognized at the commencement of the lease term is the cost, or carrying amount if different, of the leased property less the present value of the unguaranteed residual value. The difference between the sales revenue and the cost of sale is the selling profit or loss, which is recognized in accordance with the policy followed by the enterprise for sales that will be consistent with IAS 18, "Revenue" (see Chapter 31).

Manufacturer or dealer lessors sometimes quote artificially low rates of interest in order to attract customers. The use of such a rate would result in an excessive portion of the total income from the transaction being recognized at the time of sale. If artificially low rates of interest are quoted, selling profit must be restricted to that which would apply if a commercial rate of interest were charged. Initial direct costs should be charged as expenses at the inception of the lease.

Illustration of Finance Lease Accounting by the Lessor

A lessor leases out an asset on terms that constitute a finance lease. The primary period is 5 years commencing July 1, 20X0, and the rental payable is $3,000 per annum (in arrears). The lessee has the right to continue the lease after the 5-year period referred to above for an indefinite period at a nominal rent. The cash price of the asset in question at July 1, 20X0, was $11,372, and one can calculate the rate of interest implicit in the lease to be 10%.

Show the entries in the lessor books.

The finance charge is simply the difference between the fair value of the asset (in this case being the cash price of the new asset) and the rental payments over the lease period, that is, of $15,000 less $11,372, or $3,628. Using the actuarial method with an interest rate of 10%, the allocation of the finance charge will be as follows:

Year-Ended June 30	Balance b/f $		Finance Charge(10%) $	Rental $		Balance c/f (in Year-End Balance Sheet) $
20X1	11,372	+	1,137	(3,000)	=	9,509
20X2	9,509	+	951	(3,000)	=	7,460

Year-Ended June 30	Balance b/f		Finance Charge(10%)	Rental		Balance c/f (in Year-End Balance Sheet)
	$		$	$		$
20X3	7,460	+	746	(3,000)	=	5,206
20X4	5,206	+	521	(3,000)	=	2,727
20X5	2,727	+	273	(3,000)	=	Nil
			$3,628	$15,000		

The relevant extracts from the income statements of the years in question will thus appear as follows:

	20X1	20X2	20X3	20X4	20X5	Total
Rentals	3,000	3,000	3,000	3,000	3,000	15,000
Less capital						
Repayments	1,863	2,049	2,254	2,479	2,727	11,372
Finance charges	1,137	951	746	521	273	3,628
Interest payable	(x)	(x)	(x)	(x)	(x)	
Overheads	(x)	(x)	(x)	(x)	(x)	

The relevant balance sheets will appear as follows:

	Year-Ended June 30			
	20X1	20X2	20X3	20X4
Net investment in finance lease				
Current	2,049	2,254	2,479	2,727
Non-current	7,460	5,206	2,727	—
	9,599	7,460	5,296	2,727

ACCOUNTING AND REPORTING BY LESSORS—OPERATING LEASES

As IAS 17 (par. 49) unsurprisingly says, lessors should present assets subject to operating leases according to the nature of the asset. The asset subject to the operating lease is, in substance as well as in form, a non-current asset of the lessor. Such an asset should be depreciated on a basis consistent with the lessor's policy for similar assets. IAS 16, "Property, Plant, and Equipment," or IAS 38, "Intangible Assets," will apply (see Chapters 28 and 22, respectively). In addition IAS 36, "Impairment of Assets," will need to be considered (see Chapter 20).

Costs, including depreciation, incurred in earning the lease income are recognized as an expense. Lease income (excluding receipts for services provided such as insurance and maintenance) is recognized in income on a straight-line basis over the lease term even if the receipts are not on such a basis, unless another systematic basis is more representative of the time pattern in which use benefit derived from the leased asset is diminished. By definition, no element of selling profit can arise.

Initial direct costs incurred specifically to earn revenues from an operating lease are added to the carrying amount of the leased asset and recognized as an expense over the lease term on the same basis as the lease income.

FINANCIAL STATEMENT DISCLOSURE—LESSORS

As with lessees, IAS 32, "Financial Instruments: Presentation," and IFRS 7, "Financial Instruments: Disclosures," apply to both finance leases and operating leases in the financial statements of the lessor. Additional requirements are given below.

For finance leases (par. 47):

1. A reconciliation between the total gross investment in the lease at the balance sheet date and the present value of minimum lease payments receivable at the balance sheet date. In addition, an enterprise should disclose the total gross investment in the lease and the present value of minimum lease payments receivable at the balance sheet date, for each of the following periods:

   (a) Not later than one year,

   (b) Later than one year and not later than five years, and

   (c) Later than five years;

2. Unearned finance income;

3. The unguaranteed residual values accruing to the benefit of the lessor;

4. The accumulated allowance for uncollectible minimum lease payments receivable;

5. Contingent rents recognized as income in the period; and

6. A general description of the lessor's significant leasing arrangements.

For operating leases (par. 56):

1. The future minimum lease payments under non-cancelable operating leases in the aggregate and for each of the following periods:

   (a) Not later than one year,

   (b) Later than one year and not later than five years, and

   (c) Later than five years;

2. Total contingent rents recognized as income in the period; and

3. A general description of the lessor's significant leasing arrangements.

In addition, the requirements on disclosure under IAS 16, "Property, Plant, and Equipment" (see Chapter 28); IAS 36, "Impairment of Assets" (see Chapter 20); IAS 38, "Intangible Assets" (see Chapter 22); IAS 40, "Investment Property" (see Chapter 25); and IAS 41, "Agriculture" (see Chapter 34), apply to operating leases in the lessor's financial statements.

SALE AND LEASEBACK TRANSACTIONS

A sale and leaseback transaction involves the sale of an asset by the vendor and the leasing of the same asset back to the vendor. The lease payment and the sale price are usually interdependent as they are negotiated as a package. The accounting treatment of a sale and leaseback transaction depends upon the type of lease involved.

If the leaseback is an operating lease and the lease payments and the sale price are established at fair value, there has, in effect, been a normal sale transaction and any profit or loss is recognized immediately. If the sale price is below fair value, any profit or loss should be recognized immediately except that, if the loss is compensated by future lease payments at below market price, it should be deferred and amortized in proportion to the lease payments over the period for which the asset is expected to be used. If the sale price is above fair value, the excess over fair value should be deferred and amortized over the period for which the asset is expected to be used. Also, for operating leases, if the fair value at the time of a sale and leaseback transaction is less than the carrying amount of the asset, a loss equal to the amount of the difference between the carrying amount and fair value should be recognized immediately.

If the leaseback is a finance lease, the transaction is a means whereby the lessor provides finance to the lessee, with the asset as security. For this reason it is not appropriate to regard an excess of sales proceeds over the carrying amount as income because there has, in substance, been no sale. Such excess is deferred and amortized over the lease term. For finance leases, if the fair value at the time of the sale and leaseback transaction is less than the carrying amount of the asset, then no recognition of the difference between the two is necessary (again, because there has in substance not been a sale). However, such a difference might indicate an impairment in accordance with IAS 36, "Impairment of Assets," which standard would then be applied (see Chapter 20).

Uncertainty in this area has led to the issue of SIC-27, "Evaluating the Substance of Transactions Involving the Legal Form of a Lease." The issue is that an entity may create a series of related transactions, involving the legal form of a lease or leases, with an unrelated party or parties. For example, there may be a long-term lease of an asset from A to B and a shorter-term lease of the same asset from B to A. SIC-27 requires, as one would expect, that the substance of the end result is paramount. IAS 17 will apply to the overall arrangement when, but only when, the substance of an arrangement includes the conveyance of the right to use an asset for an agreed period of time. Indicators that individually demonstrate that an arrangement may not, in substance, involve a lease under IAS 17 include:

1. An entity retains all the risks and rewards incident to ownership of an underlying asset and enjoys substantially the same rights to its use as before the arrangement.

2. The primary reason for the arrangement is to achieve a particular tax result and not to convey the right to use an asset.

3. An option is included on terms that make its exercise almost certain (e.g., a put option that is exercisable at a price sufficiently higher than the expected fair value when it becomes exercisable).

A series of examples are given in an appendix to the SIC. In general, such arrangements will not involve an in substance change in the rights to use assets, in which case IAS 17 will not apply. When IAS 17 is not applicable to such arrangements, adequate disclosures to understand the situation and its effects are required.

CHAPTER 27
NON-CURRENT ASSETS HELD FOR SALE AND DISCONTINUED OPERATIONS

CONTENTS

OVERVIEW

A discontinuing operation is a relatively large component of an entity that is either being disposed of completely or substantially or being terminated through abandonment or piecemeal sale. The effects of such discontinuation are likely to be significant both in their own right and in changing likely future results of the remaining components of the entity. The objective of IASB GAAP is to establish a basis for segregating information about a major operation that an entity is discontinuing from information about its continuing operations and to specify minimum disclosures about a discontinuing operation. Distinguishing discontinuing and continuing operations will improve the ability of investors, creditors, and other users of financial statements to make projections of the entity's cash flows, earnings-generating capacity, and financial position.

IASB GAAP from 2005 focuses on two related aspects of this objective, namely on (non-current) assets held for sale and on discontinuing operations. Assets held for sale may be viewed and treated as a coherent group of assets and liabilities to be marketed as a single group, termed a disposal group. Assets or disposal groups held for sale are carried at the lower of:

- Carrying amount, or
- Fair value less costs to sell.

They are not depreciated and are presented separately on the face of the balance sheet. An operation becomes discontinued on the date the operation meets the criteria to be classified as held for sale, or when the entity has disposed of the operation. The results of discontinued operations are disclosed separately on the face of the income statement.

IASB GAAP for these matters are now contained in IFRS 5, "Non-Current Assets Held for Sale and Discontinued Operations," effective for periods beginning on or after January 1, 2005. Transitional issues are discussed at the end of the chapter. Further, minor amendments have been made by revisions to IAS 1, "Presentation of Financial Statements" (see Chapter 4), and IFRS 3, "Business Combinations" (see Chapter 8), mandatory from January 1, 2009, and July 1, 2009, respectively. IFRIC 17, "Distributions of Non-Cash Assets to Owners," is mandatory from July 1, 2009.

BACKGROUND

In essence, the results of entity operations need to be presented in a manner that will satisfy two objectives. First, the activities and results of the year under review must be reported fully and clearly. Second, readers should be able to glean, as effectively as possible, an impression of the implications of current-period results for future periods.

The original IAS requirements relating to discontinuing operations were contained in IAS 8, "Net Profit or Loss for the Period, Fundamental Errors, and Changes in Accounting" (see Chapter 6). These requirements were amended and separated from IAS 8, being presented in IAS 35, "Discontinuing Operations," which was operative from January 1, 1999. IFRS 5 replaced IAS 35. The origins of IFRS 5 lie in the desire to seek convergence between U.S. and IASB GAAP. To that end, the IASB looked in detail at the contents of the U.S. standard FAS-144, "Accounting for the Impairment or Disposal of Long-Lived Assets," issued in 2001. The FASB standard is now codified as ASC 360, "Property, Plant, and Equipment."

ASC 360 addresses three areas: (1) the impairment of long-lived assets to be held and used; (2) the classification, measurement, and presentation of assets held for sale; and (3) the classification and presentation of discontinued operations. The impairment of long-lived assets to be held and used is an area in which there are extensive differences between IFRSs and U.S. GAAP, and those differences were not thought to be capable of resolution in a relatively short time. Convergence on the other two areas, however, was thought to be worth pursuing within the context of the short-term project.

IFRS 5 achieves substantial convergence with the requirements of ASC 360 relating to assets held for sale, the timing of the classification of operations as discontinued, and the presentation of such operations.

SCOPE AND DEFINITIONS

The classification and presentation requirements of IFRS 5 apply to all recognized non-current assets and to all disposal groups of an entity. The measurement requirements apply to all recognized non-current assets and disposal groups, except for those assets listed below that continue to be measured in accordance with the relevant standard.

Assets classified as non-current in accordance with IAS 1, "Presentation of Financial Statements," should not be reclassified as current assets until they meet the criteria to be classified as held for sale in accordance with IFRS 5. Assets of a class that an entity would normally regard as non-current and that are acquired exclusively with a view to resale are not to be classified as current unless they meet the criteria to be classified as held for sale in accordance with this IFRS (pars. 2 and 3).

The standard defines key terms used above as follows (Appendix A):

- *Current asset.* An entity shall classify an asset as current when:

  (a) It expects to realize the asset, or intends to sell or consume it, in its normal operating cycle;

  (b) It holds the asset primarily for the purpose of trading;

  (c) It expects to realize the asset within 12 months after the reporting period; or

  (d) The asset is cash or a cash equivalent, unless the asset is restricted from being exchanged or used to settle a liability for at least 12 months after the reporting period.

- *Non-current asset.* An asset that does not meet the definition of a current asset.

- *Disposal group.* A group of assets to be disposed of, by sale or otherwise, together as a group in a single transaction and liabilities directly associated with those assets that will be transferred in the transaction. The group includes goodwill acquired in a business combination if the group is a cash-generating unit to which goodwill has been allocated in accordance with the requirements of paragraphs 80–87 of IAS 36, "Impairment of Assets," or if it is an operation within such a cash-generating unit.

- *Cash-generating unit.* The smallest identifiable group of assets that generates cash inflows that are largely independent of the cash inflows from other assets or groups of assets.

The measurement provisions of IFRS 5 do not apply to the following assets, that are covered by the standards listed, either as individual assets or as part of a disposal group (par. 5):

- Deferred tax assets (IAS 12, "Income Taxes," see Chapter 21).

- Assets arising from employee benefits (IAS 19, "Employee Benefits," see Chapter 14).

- Financial assets within the scope of IFRS 9, "Financial Instruments" (see Chapter 17).

- Non-current assets that are accounted for in accordance with the fair value model in IAS 40, "Investment Property" (see Chapter 25).

- Non-current assets that are measured at fair value less costs to sell in accordance with IAS 41, "Agriculture" (see Chapter 34).

- Contractual rights under insurance contracts as defined in IFRS 4, "Insurance Contracts" (see Chapter 35).

Notice very carefully that it is the *measurement* provisions of IFRS 5 that do not apply in the stated cases. The remainder of IFRS 5 and, crucially, the disclosure provisions, will still apply.

Paragraph 5A, introduced in 2008 by IFRIC 17, confirms that the classification, presentation, and measurement requirements in IFRS 2 that are applicable to a non-current asset (or disposal group) that is classified as held-for-sale apply also to a non-current asset (or disposal group) that is classified as held for distribution to owners acting in their capacity as owners (held for distribution to owners).

A disposal group may be a group of cash-generating units, a single cash-generating unit, or part of a cash-generating unit. The group may include any assets and liabilities of the entity, including current assets, current liabilities, and assets excluded by paragraph 5 from the measurement requirements of the IFRS. If a non-current asset within the scope of the measurement requirements of the IFRS is part of a disposal group, the measurement requirements of the IFRS apply to the group as a whole, so that the group as an entity is measured at the lower of its carrying amount and fair value less costs to sell.

The standard gives other definitions as follows:

- *Discontinued operation.* A component of an entity that either has been disposed of or is classified as held for sale and:
  — Represents a separate major line of business or geographical area of operations,
  — Is part of a single coordinated plan to dispose of a separate major line of business or geographical area of operations, or
  — Is a subsidiary acquired exclusively with a view to resale.
- *Component of an entity.* Operations and cash flows that can be clearly distinguished, operationally and for financial reporting purposes, from the rest of the entity.
- *Costs to sell.* The incremental costs directly attributable to the disposal of an asset (or disposal group), excluding finance costs and income tax expense.
- *Firm purchase commitment.* An agreement with an unrelated party, binding on both parties and usually legally enforceable, that (a) specifies all significant terms, including the price and timing of the transactions and (b) includes a disincentive for non-performance that is sufficiently large to make performance highly probable.
- *Highly probable.* Significantly more likely than probable.
- *Probable.* More likely than not.
- *Recoverable amount.* The higher of an asset's fair value less costs to sell and its value in use.
- *Value in use.* The present value of estimated future cash flows expected to arise from the continuing use of an asset and from its disposal at the end of its useful life.

- *Fair value.* The amount for which an asset could be exchanged, or a liability settled, between knowledgeable, willing parties in an arm's-length transaction. See Chapter 3 regarding an eventual change in this definition.

CLASSIFICATION OF NON-CURRENT ASSETS AND DISPOSAL GROUPS AS HELD FOR SALE OR HELD FOR DISTRIBUTION TO OWNERS

As indicated in the "Overview" section in the beginning of the chapter, the key question regarding the application of the standard is the determination of when resources are held for sale. It will be noted that this concept is not included in the definitions section; rather it is discussed in the standard (pars. 6–14).

The key requirement is that an entity should classify a non-current asset (or disposal group) as held for sale if its carrying amount will be recovered principally through a sale transaction rather than through continuing use. For this to be the case, the asset (or disposal group) must be available for immediate sale in its present condition subject only to terms that are usual and customary for sales of such assets (or disposal groups) and its sale must be highly probable.

"Highly probable," from the definitions given, means: significantly more likely than not (for the purpose of this standard). This is clearly a stated principle rather than an operational procedure (and none the worse for that). But the IASB feels it necessary to be more specific, as follows (pars. 8 and 9). For the sale to be highly probable, the appropriate level of management must be committed to a plan to sell the asset (or disposal group) and an active program to locate a buyer and complete the plan must have been initiated. Further, the asset (or disposal group) must be actively marketed for sale at a price that is reasonable in relation to its current fair value. In addition, the sale should be expected to qualify for recognition as a completed sale within one year from the date of classification, except as permitted below, and actions required to complete the plan should indicate that it is unlikely that significant changes to the plan will be made or that the plan will be withdrawn.

An entity that is committed to a sale plan involving loss of control of a subsidiary shall classify all the assets and liabilities of that subsidiary as held for sale when the criteria set out above are met, regardless of whether the entity will retain a non-controlling interest in its former subsidiary after the sale (par. 8A, inserted in 2008).

Events or circumstances may extend the period to complete the sale beyond one year. An extension of the period required to complete a sale does not preclude an asset (or disposal group) from being classified as held for sale if the delay is caused by events or circumstances beyond the entity's control and there is sufficient evidence that the entity remains committed to its plan to sell the asset (or disposal group).

In fact, in relation to this last paragraph, the IASB wished to be even more specific. The last sentence in this paragraph is further operationalized in Appendix B, itself "an integral part of the IFRS," that is, not merely illustrative.

Appendix B, does not appear to claim to be exhaustive, however, and is both common sense, and unlikely to be frequently applied.

OBSERVATION: The above few paragraphs represent another example of the tension between a principled requirement and a detailed "rule-book." It is evident in this particular situation that a rule-book approach is in the ascendant. The preparer is likely to seek to establish whether paragraphs 8 and 9 have been satisfied and not to form an opinion on whether or not the sale seems "highly probable" as a concept in its own right. It is noteworthy that IFRS 5 represents convergence toward an existing U.S. standard, rather than the other way round.

Several other points are specifically clarified in the standard. Exchanges of non-current assets for other non-current assets are sale transactions for IFRS 5 purposes if this exchange has commercial substance (as in IAS 16, "Property, Plant, and Equipment," see Chapter 28). A non-current asset or disposal group acquired "exclusively with a view to its current disposal" is accepted as held for sale at the acquisition date only if the criteria stated above are met (for the one-year requirement) or will be met "within a short period (usually within three months)." This specification seems superfluous. If the held-for-sale criteria are met only after the balance sheet date, reclassification is not permitted, but certain disclosures are required if the financial statements have not been finalized. A non-current asset (or disposal group) is classified as held for distribution to owners when the entity is committed to distribute the asset (or disposal group) to the owners. For this to be the case, the assets must be available for immediate distribution in their present condition and the distribution must be highly probable. Finally, a non-current asset or disposal group that is to be abandoned (as opposed to being temporarily taken out of use), is not considered held for sale. This is because, although its carrying value is likely to be low, the carrying value that does remain will be recovered through use up to the date of abandonment. If it is not expected to be sold, it cannot be held for sale.

MEASUREMENT OF NON-CURRENT ASSETS OR DISPOSAL GROUPS CLASSIFIED AS HELD FOR SALE

Here again, the basic rule is easily stated, but complications arise. The basic rule (pars. 15 and 15A) is that an entity shall measure a non-current asset (or disposal group) classified as held for sale, or held for distribution to owners, at the lower of its carrying amount and fair value less costs to sell. The carrying amount of newly acquired resources would be their cost.

→ **PRACTICE POINTER:** Cost of acquisition is assumed to be equal to fair value at date of acquisition. Because fair value less costs to sell is obviously less than fair value, it follows that the lower of carrying amount and fair value less costs to sell, both as at date of acquisition, is always fair value less costs to sell.

When the sale is expected to occur beyond one year, the entity should measure the costs to sell at their present value. Any increase in the present value of the costs to sell that arises from the passage of time should be presented in profit or loss as a financing cost.

Both immediately before the initial classification of a previously acquired non-current asset or disposal group as held for sale, and on each subsequent re-measurement of a disposal group, all the relevant assets and liabilities should be re-measured in accordance with the appropriate IFRS for the item concerned. This gives the carrying value for consideration in accordance with paragraph 15.

It is explicitly stated (par. 25) that an entity should not depreciate (or amortize) a non-current asset while it is classified as held for sale or while it is part of a disposal group classified as held for sale. Interest and other expenses attributable to the liabilities of a disposal group classified as held for sale shall continue to be recognized.

Impairment losses are recognized, however. Regular (presumably annual) calculations of fair value less costs to sell are required, with immediate recognition of differences. Subsequent increases in fair value less costs to sell must (not may) be recognized, to the extent that they do not exceed previously recognized losses (whether those losses were recognized under IFRS 5, or IAS 36, "Impairment of Assets," or some other international standard).

If an entity has classified an asset (or disposal group) as held for sale, but the criteria for this classification are no longer met, the entity must cease to classify the asset (or disposal group) as held for sale. A non-current asset that ceases to be classified as held for sale (or ceases to be included in a disposal group classified as held for sale) is measured at the lower of:

1. Its carrying amount before the asset (or disposal group) was classified as held for sale, adjusted for any depreciation, amortization, or revaluations that would have been recognized had the asset (or disposal group) not been classified as held for sale, and

2. Its recoverable amount at the date of subsequent decision not to sell.

Any measuring adjustment to carrying value arising from such a reclassification is part of income from continuing operations.

IFRIC 17, "Distributions of Non-Cash Assets to Owners," applies from July 1, 2009. Its key points are as follows.

The liability to pay a dividend shall be recognized when the dividend is appropriately authorized and is no longer at the discretion of the entity, which is the date:

1. When declaration of the dividend (e.g., by management or the board of directors) is approved by the relevant authority (e.g., the shareholders), if the jurisdiction requires such approval, or

2. When the dividend is declared (e.g., by management or the board of directors), if the jurisdiction does not require further approval.

An entity shall measure a liability to distribute non-cash assets as a dividend to its owners at the fair value of the assets to be distributed. If an entity gives its owners a choice of receiving either a non-cash asset or a cash alternative, the entity shall estimate the dividend payable by considering both the fair value of each alternative and the associated probability of owners selecting each alternative.

At the end of each reporting period and at the date of settlement, the entity shall review and adjust the carrying amount of the dividend payable, with any changes in the carrying amount of the dividend payable recognized in equity as adjustments to the amount of the distribution. When an entity settles the dividend payable, it shall recognize the difference, if any, between the carrying amount of the assets distributed and the carrying amount of the dividend payable in profit or loss.

OBSERVATION: In its basis for conclusions supporting IFRS 5, the IASB devotes a number of paragraphs to the measurement question. Most of this discussion is concerned with the rationale for not depreciating—essentially that, by definition, the resources are no longer being held for use. Why the "fair value less costs to sell" criterion is used is not really explained, except that it gives consistency with IAS 36, "Impairment of Assets" (see Chapter 20). The fact that it is not consistent with IAS 39, "Financial Instruments: Recognition and Measurement" (see Chapter 17), or IAS 40, "Investment Property" (see Chapter 25), both of which focus on fair value *without* deduction of costs to sell, is not mentioned.

PRESENTATION AND DISCLOSURE

Once again, we are given a statement of principle, printed in bold type in the original IFRS itself (par. 30), requiring an entity to present and disclose information that enables users of the financial statements to evaluate the financial effects of discontinued operations and disposals of non-current assets (or disposal groups). What follows, then, is a considerable degree of detail, as expected (and note that, explicitly, "all paragraphs have equal authority" —that is, bold type is not more important in the IFRS than a normal font).

Regarding the presentation and disclosure of non-current assets or disposal groups classified as held for sale, the significant requirements are as follows (pars. 38– 42). An entity should present a non-current asset classified as held for sale and the assets of a disposal group classified as held for sale separately from other assets in the balance sheet. The liabilities of a disposal group classified as held for sale should be presented separately from other liabilities in the balance sheet. Those assets and liabilities are not to be offset and presented as a single amount. The major classes of assets and liabilities classified as held for sale are to be separately disclosed either on the face of the balance sheet or in the notes. An entity must present separately any cumulative income or expense (i.e., gains or losses) recognized directly in equity relating to a non-current asset (or disposal group) classified as held for sale. Such gains or losses would relate either to remeasurements, at fair value, or to currency translation difference on net investment under IAS 21, "The Effects of Changes in Foreign Exchange Rates." If, however, the disposal group is a newly acquired subsidiary that meets the criteria to be classified as held for sale on acquisition, disclosure of the major classes of assets and liabilities is not required. (Note that comparative figures are not restated, thus throwing the classification as held for sale into stark relief.)

An entity shall disclose the following information in the notes in the period in which a non-current asset (or disposal group) has been either classified as held for sale or sold:

1. A description of the non-current asset (or disposal group);

2. A description of the facts and circumstances of the sale, or leading to the expected disposal, and the expected manner and timing of that disposal;

3. The gain or loss recognized and, if not separately presented in the statement of comprehensive income, the caption in that statement that includes that gain or loss; and

4. If applicable, the segment in which the non-current asset (or disposal group) is presented in accordance with IFRS 8, "Operating Segments" (see Chapter 32).

The effects of changes in plans for sale must be explained and quantified.

OBSERVATION: There is a curious, and important, omission from the disclosure requirements of held-for-sale items. A non-current asset classified as held for sale is to be presented separately from other assets—but is it still a non-current asset? The rules of language and grammar indicate that it is: a non-current asset held for sale is logically a subclass of non-current assets. On the other hand, the item is likely, though not guaranteed, to meet criterion 3 of the definition of current asset given earlier in this chapter—that is, to be expected to be realized within 12 months. And, categorically, it is intended for sale, not for continuing use.

The definition and the disclosure sections of IFRS 5 are completely silent on this question. Nevertheless, it is clear that without bothering to specify so properly the IASB considers held-for-sale items as current. Recall the statement from the scope section of the IFRS (par. 3):

> Assets classified as non-current in accordance with IAS 1, "Presentation of Financial Statements," shall not be reclassified as current assets until they meet the criteria to be classified as held for sale in accordance with this IFRS. Assets of a class that an entity would normally regard as non-current and that are acquired exclusively with a view to resale shall not be classified as current unless they meet the criteria to be classified as held for sale in accordance with this IFRS.

This wording indicates an expectation of eventual reclassification as current assets. Further, the example of presentation given in the IFRS 5, "Implementation Guidance," indicates by its use of position and subtotals that a designation as current assets is assumed. Note, however, that the contents of an "Implementation Guidance" are *not* "requirements." The Guidance "accompanies, but is not part of, IFRS 5." IFRS 5 does not appear to *require* non-current resources held for sale to be presented as associated with current assets, but we have no doubt that their intention was to require precisely this.

PRESENTATION AND DISCLOSURE OF DISCONTINUED OPERATIONS

So far, we have not spent much time in this chapter on discontinued operations, though we considered the relevant definitions of a discontinued operation and component of an entity, and we discussed the rationale for distinguishing the results of discontinued and continuing operations in the context of user needs. The main reason for this omission is that there are no measurement issues involved. Both the classification and the measurement of held-for-sale resources required considerable specifications and discussion.

With discontinued operations as such, however, it is the disclosure requirements relating to the income statement that represent the only really significant issue. Notice from the definition that a component of an entity can only be discontinued if it has either already been disposed of, or has already been classified as held for sale (in addition to the other stated requirements). Thus, the criteria for being held for sale have to be considered, and satisfied, prior to the possibility of applying the discontinued operation requirements, under IFRS 5.

Once a discontinued operation is deemed to exist, the standard is reduced to a series of detailed disclosure requirements. These are essentially as follows (pars. 33 — 37). An entity shall disclose:

1. A single amount on the face of the income statement comprising the total of:

   (a) The post-tax profit or loss of discontinued operations, and

   (b) The post-tax gain or loss recognized on the measurement to fair value less costs to sell or on the disposal of the assets or disposal groups constituting the discontinued operation.

2. An analysis of the single amount in item 1(a) into:

   (a) The revenue, expenses, and pre-tax profit or loss of discontinued operations;

   (b) The related income tax expense as required by paragraph 81(h) of IAS 12 (see Chapter 21);

   (c) The gain or loss recognized on the measurement to fair value less costs to sell or on the disposal of the assets or disposal groups constituting the discontinued operation; and

   (d) The related income tax expense as required by paragraph 81(h) of IAS 12.

The analysis may be presented in the notes or in the statement of comprehensive income. If it is presented in the statement of comprehensive income, it should be presented in a section identified as relating to discontinued operations (i.e., separately from continuing operations). The analysis is not required for disposal groups that are newly acquired subsidiaries that meet the criteria to be classified as held for sale on acquisition.

3. The net cash flows attributable to the operating, investing, and financing activities of discontinued operations. These disclosures may be presented either in the notes or on the face of the financial statements. These disclosures are not required for disposal groups that are newly acquired subsidiaries that meet the criteria to be classified as held for sale on acquisition.

4. The amount of income from continuing operations and from discontinued operations attributable to owners of the parent. These disclosures may be presented either in the notes or in the statement of comprehensive income.

If an entity presents the components of profit or loss in a separate income statement, as described in paragraph 81 of IAS 1, a section identified as relating to discontinued operations is presented in that separate statement.

An entity shall re-present all the above disclosures for prior periods presented in the financial statements, so that the disclosures relate to all operations that have been discontinued by the balance sheet date for the latest period presented.

Adjustments in the current period to amounts previously presented in discontinued operations that are directly related to the disposal of a discontinued operation in a prior period must be classified separately in discontinued operations. The nature and amount of such adjustments must be disclosed.

If an entity ceases to classify a component of an entity as held for sale, the results of operations of the component previously presented in discontinued operations are to be reclassified and included in income from continuing operations for all periods presented. The amounts for prior periods shall be described as having been re-presented.

An entity that is committed to a sale plan involving loss of control of a subsidiary shall disclose the information required as above when the subsidiary is a disposal group that meets the definition of a discontinued operation.

Any gain or loss on the re-measurement of a non-current asset (or disposal group) classified as held for sale that does not meet the definition of a discontinued operation should be included in profit or loss from continuing operations (i.e., without separate disclosure).

CHAPTER 28
PROPERTY, PLANT, AND EQUIPMENT

CONTENTS

OVERVIEW

The accruals (matching) convention requires that fixed assets with a finite useful life should be gradually expensed over that life, in a manner such that annual expenses are pro rata with annual benefits. This process is known as *depreciation*.

IASB GAAP come from a variety of sources. The key relevant standards are:

- IAS 16, "Property, Plant, and Equipment"

- IFRS 3, "Business Combinations" (regarding goodwill)

- IAS 36, "Impairment of Assets"

- IAS 38, "Intangible Assets"

This chapter deals fully with IAS 16.

BACKGROUND

Assets have already been defined, as discussed in Chapter 2, as follows (Framework, par. 49a).

> An asset is a resource controlled by the enterprise as a result of past events and from which future economic benefits are expected to flow.

Assets are divided into fixed assets and current assets. The IAS terms are *non-current assets* and *current assets*, respectively. The distinction is formally defined in IAS 1 (par. 66).

An asset should be classified as a current asset when it:

1. Is expected to be realized in, or is intended for sale or consumption in, the entity's normal operating cycle; and

2. Is held primarily for the purpose of being traded;

3. Is expected to be realized within 12 months after the balance sheet date; and

4. Is cash or a cash equivalent (as defined by IAS 7, "Cash Flow Statements"), unless it is restricted from being exchanged or used to settle a liability for at least 12 months after the balance sheet date.

All other assets should be classified as non-current assets.

The definition of non-current assets is often misunderstood. A non-current asset is not an asset with a long life. The essential criterion is the *intention* of the owner, the intended *use* of the asset. A non-current asset is an asset that the firm intends to use within the business, over an extended period, in order to assist its daily operating activities. A current asset, on the other hand, is usually defined in terms of time. A current asset is an asset likely to change its form, that is, likely to undergo some transaction, within 12 months.

→ **PRACTICE POINTER:** Consider two firms, A and B. Firm A is a motor trader. It possesses some motor vehicles that it is attempting to sell, and it also possesses some desks used by the sales staff, management, and so on. Firm B is a furniture dealer. It possesses some desks that it is attempting to sell, and it also possesses some motor vehicles used by the sales staff and for delivery purposes. In the accounts of A, the motor vehicles are current assets and the desks are non-current assets. In the accounts of B, the motor vehicles are non-current assets and the desks are current assets. Note incidentally that a fixed asset that, after several years' use, is about to be sold for scrap, remains in the fixed asset part of the accounts even though it is about to change its form.

The crucial difference between IASB GAAP and U.S. GAAP is that IASB GAAP permit the upward revaluation of depreciable and non-depreciable non-current assets, whereas U.S. GAAP do not. U.S. GAAP also allow no distinction between investment properties and other properties.

PRINCIPLES OF ACCOUNTING FOR DEPRECIATION

The first major problem with depreciation, perhaps surprisingly, is to agree on what it is, and what it is for. The generally agreed view nowadays is that it is in essence a straightforward application of the matching, or accruals, convention. With a non-current asset, the benefit from the asset is spread over several years. The matching convention requires that the corresponding expense be matched with the benefit in each accounting period. This does not simply mean that the total expense for the asset's life is spread over the total beneficial life. It means, more specifically, that the total expense for the asset's life is spread over the total beneficial life *in proportion to the pattern of benefit*. Thus, to take a simple example, if a non-current asset gives half of its benefit, or usefulness, in year 1, one-third in year 2, and one-sixth in year 3, and the total expenses arising are $1,200, then the matching convention requires the charging of $600 in year 1, $400 in year 2, and $200 in year 3, in the annual profit calculation. This charge is known as the *depreciation charge*.

In order to calculate a figure for this charge it is necessary to answer four basic questions:

1. What is the cost of the asset?
2. What is the estimated useful life of the asset to the business? (This may be equal to, or may be considerably less than, its technical or physical useful life.)
3. What is the estimated residual selling value ("scrap value") of the asset at the end of the useful life as estimated?
4. What is the pattern of benefit or usefulness derived from the asset likely to be (not the *amount* of the benefit)?

It is perfectly obvious that the second, third, and fourth of these involve a good deal of uncertainty and subjectivity. The "appropriate" figures are all dependent on future plans and future actions. It is important to realize that even if the first figure, the cost of the fixed asset, is known precisely and objectively, the basis of the depreciation calculation as a whole is always uncertain, estimated, and subjective. The estimates should, as usual, be reasonable, fair, and prudent (whatever precisely this implies).

But the first figure is often not at all precise and objective, for several reasons.

→ **PRACTICE POINTER:** Problems in establishing a "cost" figure for a non-current asset include the following:

1. Incidental expenses associated with making the asset workable should be included, for example, installation costs carried out by the business's own staff, probably including some overhead costs.
2. The non-current asset may be constructed within the business by its own workforce, giving rise to all the usual costing problems of overhead definition and overhead allocation.

3. Interest on related borrowing during the construction process may, or may not, be capitalized (see Chapter 7, "Borrowing Costs").

4. Depending on the accounting policies used by the firm generally, the "basic" figure for the fixed asset may be revalued periodically. Additionally, if land is not depreciated but the building on the land is, then this requires a split of the total cost (or value) figure for the land and buildings together into two possibly somewhat arbitrary parts.

5. Major alterations/improvements may be made to the asset part way through its life. If these appear to increase the benefit from the asset over the remaining useful life, and perhaps also to increase the number of years of the remaining useful life, and are material, then the costs of these improvements should also be capitalized (i.e., treated as part of the non-current asset from then on). Maintenance costs, however, are "running" expenses and should be charged to the income statement as incurred. In practice, this distinction can be difficult to make.

The total figure to be depreciated, known as the *depreciable amount*, will consist of the cost of the asset less the scrap value. This depreciable amount needs to be spread over the useful life in proportion to the pattern of benefit. Once the depreciable amount has been found, with revision if necessary to take account of material improvements, several recognized methods exist for spreading, or allocating, this amount to the various years concerned. The more important possibilities are outlined below. It is essential to understand the implicit assumption that each method makes about the pattern of benefit arising and therefore about the appropriate pattern of expense allocation.

Methods of Calculating Depreciation

Straight-Line Method

The depreciable amount is allocated on a straight-line basis, that is, an equal amount is allocated to each year of the useful life. If an asset is revalued or materially improved, then the new depreciable amount will be allocated equally over the remaining, possibly extended, useful life.

Illustration of Straight-Line Method

Using the straight-line method, calculate the annual depreciation charge from the following data.

Cost ("basic" value figure)	$12,000
Useful life	4 years
Scrap value	$2,000
Annual charge	= ($12,000 – $2,000)/4
	= $2,500

This is by far the most common method. It is the easiest to apply, and also the preparation of periodic (e.g., monthly) accounts for internal purposes is facilitated. This method assumes, within the limits of materiality, that the asset is equally useful, or beneficial, each year. Whether this assumption is as frequently justified as the common usage of the method suggests is an open question.

Reducing-Balance Method

Under this method, depreciation each year is calculated by applying a constant percentage to the net book value (NBV) brought forward from the previous year. (Note that this percentage is based on the cost less depreciation to date.) Given the cost (or valuation) starting figure, and the useful life and "scrap" value figures, the appropriate percentage needed to make the net book value at the end of the useful life exactly equal to the scrap value can be found from a formula:

$$d = \sqrt[n]{S/C}$$

where d is the depreciation percentage, n is the life in years, S is the scrap value, and C is the cost (or basic value).

This formula is rarely used. In practice, when this method is used a standard "round" figure is usually taken, shown by experience to be vaguely satisfactory for the particular type of asset under consideration. Notice, incidentally, that the formula fails to work when the scrap value is zero, and produces an extreme and possibly distorted allocation of expense when the scrap value is very small.

Illustration of Reducing-Balance Method

Using the data of the previous illustration and assuming a depreciation percentage of 40%, calculate the depreciation charge for each of the 4 years using the reducing balance method.

Year 1	Cost	$12,000
	Depreciation 40%	4,800
Year 2	NBV	7,200
	Depreciation 40%	2,880
Year 3	NBV	4,320
	Depreciation 40%	1,728
Year 4	NBV	2,592
	Depreciation 40%	1,037
	NBV	$1,555

If the estimated scrap value turns out to be correct, then a "profit" on disposal of $445 would be recorded also in year 4. This is an example of a reducing-charge method, or of an accelerated depreciation method. The charge is highest in the first year and gradually reduces over the asset's life.

Several arguments can be advanced for preferring this approach to the straight-line method, at least in theory, as follows:

1. It better reflects the typical benefit pattern, at least of some assets.
2. It could be argued that, where the pattern of benefit is assumed to be effectively constant, the appropriate "expense," which needs to be correspondingly evenly matched, is not the pure depreciation element, but the sum of:

   (a) The pure depreciation element, and

   (b) The maintenance and repair costs.

Because (b) will tend to increase as the asset gets older, it is necessary for (a) to be reduced as the asset gets older, in the hope that the total of the two will remain more or less constant. This may be a valid argument in the most general of terms, but of course there is no reason why an arbitrary percentage applied in one direction should even approximately compensate for flexible and "chancy" repair costs in the other.

3. It better reflects the probable fact that the value (i.e., the market or resale value) of the asset falls more sharply in the earlier years. This argument, often advanced, is questionable in principle. Depreciation is concerned with appropriate allocation of expense, applying the matching convention. It is not concerned with an annual revaluation of the fixed assets, so whether or not a particular method is good or bad from this viewpoint is, or should be, irrelevant. As long as the original estimate of future benefit is still valid, the fact that current market value is small, at an intermediate time, is not of concern.

A particular variant found in practice in some countries is known as the double-declining balance method. This involves calculating the appropriate "straight line" depreciation percentage, then doubling it and applying the resulting percentage on the reducing balance basis.

Sum-of-the-Digits Method

The sum-of-the-digits method is another example of a reducing-charge method. It is based on a convenient "rule of thumb" and produces a pattern of depreciation charge somewhat similar to the reducing-balance method.

Using the same figures as before, we give the 4 years weights of 4, 3, 2, and 1, respectively, and sum the total weights. In general terms we give the n years weights of n, $n-1$, . . . , 1, respectively, and sum the total weights, the sum being $n(n + 1)/2$. The depreciable amount is then allocated over the years in the proportion that each year's weighting bears to the total.

Illustration of Sum-of-the-Digits Method

Using the data in the previous illustrations gives the following figures:

$$4 + 3 + 2 + 1 = 10 \text{ (the "sum" of the "digits")}$$

Depreciable amount = $12,000 − $2,000 = $10,000

Depreciation charges are:

Year		
	1	4/10 × 10,000 = $4,000
	2	3/10 × 10,000 = $3,000
	3	2/10 × 10,000 = $2,000
	4	1/10 × 10,000 = $1,000

This gives NBV figures in the balance sheet of $8,000, $5,000, $3,000, and $2,000 for year ends 1 — 4, respectively.

Output or Usage Method

The output or usage method is particularly suitable for assets where the rate of usage or rate of output can be easily measured. For example, a motor vehicle might be regarded as having a life of 100,000 miles, rather than a life of 4 years. The depreciable amount can then be allocated to each year in proportion to the recorded mileage, for example, if 30,000 miles are covered in year 1, then 3/10 of the depreciable amount will be charged in year 1. The life of a machine could be defined in terms of machine hours. The annual charge would then be:

$$\text{Depreciable amount} \quad \times \quad \frac{\text{Machine hours used in the year}}{\text{Total estimated life in machine hours}}$$

Revaluation or Arbitrary Valuation

The revaluation or arbitrary valuation approach is occasionally used with minor items such as loose tools. An estimated or perhaps purely arbitrary figure for the value of the items (in total) is chosen at the end of each year. Depreciation is then the difference between this figure and the figure from the previous year. Strictly, of course, this is not a method of depreciation at all, but a lazy alternative to it.

All of the above methods can be criticized on the grounds that they ignore the fact that the resources "tied up" in the fixed asset concerned have an actual cost to the business in terms of interest paid, or an implied (opportunity) cost in terms of interest foregone. This could well be regarded as an essential expense that should be matched appropriately against the benefit from the asset. The "actuarial" methods that attempt to take account of interest expense are complicated to apply and in financial accounting are hardly ever used.

OBSERVATION: The process of depreciation calculation is not designed to produce balance sheet numbers that are either particularly meaningful or particularly useful as measurements of value; in fact, they are measurements of unexpired costs.

It must be remembered that depreciation is a process of matching expenses in proportion to benefits. Given that the depreciable amount has been agreed, the annual charge is based on actual or implied assumptions as to the pattern of benefit being derived, and nothing else. In simple bookkeeping terms, all that is happening is that a transfer is being made from the non-current assets section in the balance sheet to the expenses section in the income statement. It is the expense that is being positively calculated, not the reduction in the asset figure. It follows from this that:

1. The asset figure for an intermediate year has no very obvious or useful meaning. It can only be defined in a roundabout way. For example, under historical cost accounting, it is the amount of the original cost not yet deemed to have been used or not yet allocated. This intermediate figure is often called "net book value," but it is *not* a value at all within the proper meaning of the word.

2. Depreciation has nothing to do with ensuring that the business can "afford" to buy another asset when the first one becomes useless. This is true even if we ignore the likelihood of rising price levels. Depreciation does not increase the amount of any particular asset, cash or otherwise.

3. However, depreciation, like any other expense figure, does have the effect of retaining *resources* (or total assets) in the business. By reducing profit, we reduce the maximum dividend payable (which would reduce resources) and, therefore, increase the "minimum resources remaining" figure. This is, in fact, a particular illustration of the idea of capital maintenance discussed in Chapter 10.

IASB GAAP

An early standard on depreciation, IAS 4, has long been withdrawn. IASB GAAP on depreciation are now contained in IAS 16, "Property, Plant, and Equipment," IFRS 3, "Business Combinations," and IAS 38, "Intangible Assets."

PROPERTY, PLANT, AND EQUIPMENT

IASB GAAP for the accounting treatment of property, plant, and equipment is provided by IAS 16. Originally issued in 1981, IAS 16 was revised in 1993, effective January 1, 1995, and revised again in 1998, effective accounting periods beginning on or after July 1, 1999. The 1998 changes were essentially concerned with consequential amendments arising from the issue of IAS 36, "Impairment of Assets" (see Chapter 20), and IAS 37, "Provisions, Contingent Liabilities, and Contingent Assets" (see Chapter 29). Further amendments were made in 2004, effective from January 1, 2005.

Further, minor amendments have been made by revisions to IAS 1, "Presentation of Financial Statements" (see Chapter 4), and IFRS 3, "Business Combinations" (see Chapter 8), mandatory from January 1, 2009, and July 1, 2009, respectively.

The standard notes that the general definition and recognition criteria for an asset given in the "The Conceptual Framework for Financial Reporting" (discussed in Chapter 2), must be satisfied before IAS 16 applies. Subject to that, IAS 16 applies to accounting for all property, plant, and equipment except when another IAS requires or permits a different accounting treatment (par. 2).

There are, in fact, a number of exclusions. It is explicitly stated (par. 3) that IAS 16 does not apply to biological assets related to agricultural activity (to which IAS 41 applies; see Chapter 34), nor to mineral rights and mineral reserves, such as oil, natural gas, and similar non-regenerative resources. However, it does apply to property, plant, and equipment used to develop or maintain these activities or assets but separable from those activities or assets. IAS 16 does not apply to property, plant, and equipment classified as held for sale in accordance with IFRS 5, "Non-Current Assets Held for Sale and Discontinued Operations" (see Chapter 27). IAS 16 also does not apply to the recognition and measurement of "exploration and evaluation assets" as defined in IFRS 6, "Exploration for and Evaluation of Mineral Resources" (see Chapter 36).

An enterprise applies IAS 40, "Investment Property," rather than IAS 16, to its investment property (see Chapter 25). With effect from January 1, 2009, IAS 40 applies to property being constructed or developed for future use as an investment property. IAS 40 also applies to existing investment property being redeveloped for future continued use as investment property.

In 2009, IFRIC 18, "Transfers of Assets from Customers," was issued, applying prospectively to transfer of assets received from customers after July 1, 2009. This addresses the requirements for agreements in which an entity receives an item of property, plant, or equipment from a customer and is required to use that item either to connect the customer to a network or to provide the customer with ongoing access to a supply of goods or services (such as a supply of electricity, gas, or water).

If the item meets the definition of an asset in the IASB's "Framework for the Preparation and Presentation of Financial Statements," the entity recognizes the asset as property, plant and equipment. The cost of the asset on initial recognition is its fair value. The fair value of the total consideration received or receivable (including the fair value of the asset) is allocated to each service or supply and the revenue for each service or supply is recognized in accordance with IAS 18, "Revenue."

If any other IAS permits a particular approach to the initial recognition of the carrying amount of property, plant, and equipment, then that standard will prevail regarding this initial carrying value, but IAS 16 would then apply to all other aspects, including depreciation. An example of this would be IFRS 3, "Business Combinations," which requires property, plant, and equipment acquired in a business combination to be measured initially at fair value (see Chapter 8).

The standard gives a number of key definitions as follows:

- *Property, plant, and equipment* are tangible assets that:
  - Are held for use in the production or supply of goods or services, for rental to others, or for administrative purposes; and
  - Are expected to be used during more than one period.
- *Depreciation* is the systematic allocation of the depreciable amount of an asset over its useful life.

- *Depreciable amount* is the cost of an asset, or other amount substituted for cost, less its residual value.
- *Useful life* is either:
  - The period of time over which an asset is expected to be used by an entity; or
  - The number of production or similar units expected to be obtained from the asset by an entity.
- *Cost* is (1) the amount of cash or cash equivalents paid, or the fair value of the other consideration given, to acquire an asset at the time of its acquisition or construction or (2) where applicable, the amount attributed to that asset when initially recognized in accordance with the specific requirements of other IFRSs (e.g., IFRS 2, "Share-Based Payment").
- The *residual value* of an asset is the estimated amount that an entity would currently obtain from disposal of the asset, after deducting the estimated costs of disposal, if the asset were already of the age and in the condition expected at the end of its useful life.
- *Entity-specific value* is the present value of the cash flows that an entity expects to arise from the continuing use of an asset and from its disposal at the end of its useful life, or that it expects to incur when settling liability.
- *Recoverable amount* is the higher of an asset's fair value less costs to sell and its value in use.
- *Fair value* is the amount for which an asset could be exchanged between knowledgeable, willing parties in an arm's-length transaction.
- An *impairment loss* is the amount by which the carrying amount of an asset exceeds its recoverable amount.
- *Carrying amount* is the amount at which an asset is recognized after deducting any accumulated depreciation and accumulated impairment losses.

IFRS 13, "Fair Value Measurement," mandatory from January 1, 2013, with earlier application "permitted," changes the definition of fair value, and introduces some consequential terminological amendments, as used in IAS 16. IFRS 13 is discussed in greater detail in Chapter 3.

Recognition of Property, Plant, and Equipment

An item of property, plant, and equipment should be recognized (par. 7) as an asset if, and only if:

1. It is probable that future economic benefits associated with the item will flow to the entity;
2. The cost of the item to the entity can be measured reliably.

In determining whether an item satisfies the first criterion for recognition, an entity needs to assess the degree of certainty attaching to the flow of future economic benefits on the basis of the available evidence at the time of initial recognition. Existence of sufficient certainty that the future economic benefits will flow to the entity necessitates an assurance that the entity will receive the rewards attaching to the asset and will undertake the associated risks. The second criterion for recognition is usually readily satisfied because the exchange transaction evidencing the purchase of the asset identifies its cost. In the case of a self-constructed asset, a reliable measurement of the cost can be made from the transactions with parties external to the enterprise for the acquisition of the materials, labor, and other inputs used during the construction process.

IAS 16 allows for the aggregation of items that may individually be insignificant (par. 9), giving "moulds, tools and dies" as an example. The aggregation is then treated as "*an* asset" if the above recognition criteria are met. When it is clear that, although an asset may initially be acquired as a whole, significant components of it will have significantly different useful lines, then the expenditure on the asset should be allocated to the component parts, and each part should be accounted for as a separate item. An aircraft and its engines are given as a likely example. This separate treatment allows depreciation figures to properly reflect the different consumption patterns of the various components.

→ **PRACTICE POINTER:** The standard goes out of its way to clarify that the criterion of probable future economic benefits from "the item" should be interpreted broadly. For example, resources acquired for safety or environmental reasons, whether legally required or only through custom or good public relations, will assist the entity to obtain future economic benefits from its other assets. Provided that the resultant carrying amount of the total assets does not exceed the recoverable amount from the total assets, the safety or environmental expenditures should be recognized as assets under IAS 16.

Subsequent Costs

The first and obvious point is that costs of day-to-day servicing of an item of property, plant, and equipment, often described as "repairs and maintenance," are expenses, not additions to costs. However, major parts of some items of property, plant, and equipment may require replacement at regular intervals. For example, a furnace may require relining after a specified number of hours of use; or parts of aircraft interiors, such as seats and galleys, may require replacement several times during the life of the airframe. Items of property, plant, and equipment may also be acquired to make a less frequently recurring replacement, such as replacing the interior walls of a building, or to make a non-recurring replacement. Under the recognition principle in paragraph 7, an entity recognizes in the carrying amount of an item of property, plant, and equipment the cost of replacing such a part of an item when that cost is incurred if the recognition criteria are met. The carrying amount of those parts that are replaced is derecognized in accordance with the derecognition provisions of the standard. Note that in order to facilitate this, the component parts of the original item need to have been accounted for separately in the first place.

A major inspection or refit, even if it does not "improve" the original item, may logically be treated the same way. Thus, paragraph 14 notes that a condition of continuing to operate an item of property, plant, and equipment (e.g., an aircraft) may be performing regular major inspections for faults regardless of whether parts of the item are replaced. When each major inspection is performed, its cost is recognized in the carrying amount of the item of property, plant, and equipment as a replacement if the recognition criteria are satisfied. Any remaining carrying amount of the cost of the previous inspection (as distinct from physical parts) is derecognized. This occurs regardless of whether the cost of the previous inspection was identified in the transaction in which the item was acquired or constructed. If necessary, the estimated cost of a future similar inspection may be used as an indication of what the cost of the existing inspection component was when the item was acquired or constructed.

Measurement of Property, Plant, and Equipment

IAS 16 divides its consideration of measurement issues into several different stages, that is, initial measurement, subsequent expenditure, and measurement subsequent to the initial recognition.

Initial Measurement

The essential requirement is straightforward and can be simply stated (par. 15). An item of property, plant, and equipment that qualifies for recognition as an asset should initially be measured at its cost. The cost of an item of property, plant, and equipment comprises its purchase price, including import duties and nonrefundable purchase taxes, and any directly attributable costs of bringing the asset to working condition for its intended use. Any trade discounts and rebates are deducted in arriving at the purchase price. Examples of directly attributable costs are:

1. The cost of site preparation;
2. Initial delivery and handling costs;
3. Installation costs;
4. Professional fees such as for architects and engineers; and
5. The estimated cost of dismantling and removing the asset and restoring the site, to the extent that it is recognized as a provision under IAS 37, "Provisions, Contingent Liabilities, and Contingent Assets" (see Chapter 29).

In practice, however, a number of complications are likely to arise. The standard goes into some detail about several aspects (pars. 18–28). It notes that in cases where payment is deferred beyond normal credit terms, defined or imputed interest must be removed from the total of the payments, thus reducing the cost to the cash purchase price equivalent. General and administration overheads are not likely to be "directly attributable costs" as the term is used above, but, for example, pension costs of direct labor could be.

The question of what is an essential cost of "bringing the asset to working condition" is likely to be difficult and subjective. The basic principle is that recognition of costs in the carrying amount of an item of property, plant, and equipment ceases when the item is in the location and condition necessary for it to be capable of operating in the manner intended by management. For example, the following costs are not included in the carrying amount of an item of property, plant, and equipment:

- Costs incurred while an item capable of operating in the manner intended by management has yet to be brought into use or is operated at less than full capacity;
- Initial operating losses, such as those incurred while demand for the item's output builds up;
- Costs of relocating or reorganizing part or all of an entity's operations;
- Costs of opening a new facility;
- Costs of introducing a new product or service (including costs of advertising and promotional activities);
- Costs of conducting business in a new location or with a new class of customer (including costs of staff training); and
- Administration and other general overhead costs.

The standard also feels the need to discuss the calculation of cost of self-constructed assets—to exclude any internal profits or abnormal wastage, for example—though all this is only normal practice. Assets held under finance leases are costed in accordance with IAS 17, "Leases" (see Chapter 26), and government grants are to be dealt with in accordance with IAS 20, "Accounting for Government Grants and Disclosure of Government Assistance" (see Chapter 19).

The standard makes dealing with barter exchanges involving property, plant, and machinery (pars. 24 — 26) very difficult. It notes that one or more items of property, plant, and equipment may be acquired in exchange for a non-monetary asset or assets or a combination of monetary and non-monetary assets. The cost of such an item of property, plant, and equipment is measured at fair value unless (a) the exchange transaction lacks commercial substance or (b) the fair value of neither the asset received nor the asset given up is reliably measurable. The acquired item is measured in this way even if an entity cannot immediately derecognize the asset given up. If the acquired item is not measured at fair value, its cost is measured at the carrying amount of the asset given up.

The standard gives complicated guidance on when commercial substance is likely to exist (par. 25) but forgets to tell us what to do if an exchange lacks commercial substance. The logical presumption would be that the "exchange" is not recognized at all.

Measurement Subsequent to Initial Recognition

The IASB has always operated on the basis that a strict adherence to historical cost is not required and, indeed, has recognized the possibility of rejecting historical cost accounting as the normal basis (see Chapter 10). Consistent with this approach, two alternative approaches to subsequent measurement are allowed under IAS 16 (pars. 30 and 31). The first is described as the cost model and is simply stated.

> After recognition as an asset, an item of property, plant, and equipment shall be carried at its cost less any accumulated depreciation and any accumulated impairment losses.

The second is the revaluation model:

> After recognition as an asset, an item of property, plant and equipment whose fair value can be measured reliably shall be carried at a revalued amount, being its fair value at the date of revaluation less any subsequent accumulated depreciation and subsequent accumulated impairment losses. Revaluations shall be made with sufficient regularity to ensure that the carrying amount does not differ materially from that which would be determined using fair value at the balance sheet date.

In the previous version of IAS 16, these models were presented as the benchmark treatment and the alternative treatment, respectively. They are now presented simply as two alternatives.

The fair value of land and buildings will usually be their market value as determined by professional qualified appraisers. It is interesting to note that the explicit statement in the 1993 version of IAS 16 that such valuation should presume continued "use of the asset in the same or a similar business" has been dropped from the current version. Now it is the fair value on the open market that should be used. When there is no evidence of market value because of the specialized nature of the plant and equipment and because these items are rarely sold, except as part of a continuing business, they are valued at their depreciated replacement cost. Appropriate specific price indexes may, if necessary, be used to determine replacement cost.

The frequency of revaluation required is not precisely defined. It is suggested in the standard (par. 34) that items that experience significant and volatile movements in fair value will require annual revaluation. For other items "every three or five years may be sufficient." All items within a class of property, plant, and equipment, however, are revalued simultaneously in order to avoid selective revaluation of assets and the reporting of amounts in the financial statements that are a mixture of costs and values at different dates. A class of assets may be revalued on a rolling basis, provided revaluation of the class of assets is completed within a short period of time and provided the revaluations are kept up to date. A class of property, plant, and equipment is a grouping of assets of a similar nature and use in an entity's operations.

IAS 16, paragraph 35, discusses the treatment of accumulated depreciation. The wording is obscure, and we quote the paragraph in full.

> When an item of property, plant, and equipment is revalued, any accumulated depreciation at the date of the revaluation is treated in one of the following ways:
>
> (a) Restated proportionately with the change in the gross carrying amount of the asset so that the carrying amount of the asset after revaluation equals its revalued amount. This method is often used when an asset is revalued by means of an index to its depreciated replacement cost; or
>
> (b) Eliminated against the gross carrying amount of the asset and the net amount restated to the revalued amount of the asset. This method is often used for buildings.

The amount of the adjustment arising on the restatement or elimination of accumulated depreciation forms part of the increase or decrease in carrying amount that is accounted for in accordance with paragraphs 39 and 40.

Item (a) appears to suggest the following. Suppose we have an asset to which IAS 16 applies, the cost is 10,000, the useful life is 5 years, the estimated residual value is nil, and it is now 3 years old. This will be recorded as:

Cost	Depreciation	Carrying Amount
10,000	6,000	4,000

The asset is now revalued, by index or otherwise, to a new gross figure of 15,000, that is, the new "cost" is 15,000. The depreciation is now "restated proportionately," that is, it is also increased by 50%. We thus end up with:

Gross Revaluation	Depreciation	Carrying Amount
15,000	9,000	6,000

This increase in carrying amount of 2,000 is then dealt with as discussed below.

Item (b) above suggests a different sequence. Suppose the asset is again recorded before revaluation:

Cost	Depreciation	Carrying Amount
10,000	6,000	4,000

It is now revalued to a current fair value *in its existing state* of 6,000. This means that the new carrying value is to be 6,000. Other balances will need to be altered or eliminated as shown.

Asset Revaluation Account			
Transfer of cost	10,000	6,000	Transfer of depreciation
Surplus (calculated)	2,000	6,000	New carrying value (given)
	12,000	12,000	

As indicated above, the treatment of increases and decreases arising on revaluation is dealt with in IAS 16, paragraphs 39 and 40. If an asset's carrying amount is increased as a result of a revaluation, the increase shall be recognized in other comprehensive income and accumulated in equity under the heading of revaluation surplus. However, the increase shall be recognized in profit or loss to the extent that it reverses a revaluation decrease of the same asset previously recognized in profit or loss.

If an asset's carrying amount is decreased as a result of a revaluation, the decrease shall be recognized in profit or loss. However, the decrease shall be recognized in other comprehensive income to the extent of any credit balance existing in the revaluation surplus in respect of that asset. The decrease recognized in other comprehensive income reduces the amount accumulated in equity under the heading of revaluation surplus.

Such a revaluation surplus reserve is not "realized," and is therefore not "earned," and not available for dividend. However, it is likely to become realized over time. Such revaluation surplus included in equity may be transferred directly to retained earnings when the surplus is realized. The whole surplus may be realized on the retirement or disposal of the asset. Some of the surplus, however, may be realized as the asset is used by the entity; in such a case, the amount of the surplus realized is the difference between depreciation based on the revalued carrying amount of the asset and depreciation based on the asset's original cost.

It is noteworthy that the word "may" is used three times in the last three sentences. The increase in carrying amount may be transferred to retained earnings eventually when the asset is disposed of, or gradually over the remaining useful life—thus in effect offsetting in the retained earnings balance the effect of "extra" depreciation. Note that in neither case is there any effect on the income statement for any year; this will be charged in full with the new depreciation expense. Alternatively, it appears that the increase could be left in revaluation surplus forever. Under a historical cost accounting philosophy, this last possibility seems illogical, although under a current cost philosophy it would be logically correct (see Chapter 10).

The Interpretations Committee issued IFRIC 1, "Changes in Existing Decommissioning, Restoration, and Similar Liabilities," in May 2004. It was effective for annual periods beginning on or after September 1, 2004. IFRIC 1 provides guidance on how to account for the effect of changes in the measurement of such existing liabilities. The details of IFRIC 1 are complicated, pedantic, and common sense.

Depreciation

The formal requirement of IAS 16 for the calculation of depreciation should by now have a familiar ring (par. 50).

The depreciable amount of an item of property, plant, and equipment should be allocated on a systematic basis over its useful life. The depreciation method used should reflect the pattern in which the asset's economic benefits are consumed by the entity. The depreciation charge for each period should be recognized as an expense, unless it is included in the carrying amount of another asset (e.g., as part of the manufacturing cost of inventories).

The residual value and the useful life of an asset is to be reviewed at least at each financial year-end and, if expectations differ from previous estimates, the change is accounted for as a change in an accounting estimate in accordance with IAS 8, "Accounting Policies, Changes in Accounting Estimates, and Errors."

Depreciation is recognized even if the fair value of the asset exceeds its carrying amount, as long as the asset's residual value does not exceed its carrying amount. Repair and maintenance of an asset do not negate the need to depreciate it. The depreciable amount of an asset is determined after deducting its residual value. In practice, the residual value of an asset is often insignificant and therefore immaterial in the calculation of the depreciable amount. The residual value of an asset may increase to an amount equal to or greater than the asset's carrying amount. If it does, the asset's depreciation charge is zero unless and until its residual value subsequently decreases to an amount below the asset's carrying amount.

OBSERVATION: This last point is rather significant. It recognizes and confirms that, although a depreciation charge is *required* for all items of property, plant, and machinery, the correctly calculated charge may well be zero.

The standard goes into detail about a number of aspects. Value of the asset above carrying amount does not obviate the requirement for annual depreciation. Useful life may be influenced by a number of factors (par. 56) including:

1. The expected usage of the asset by the entity;

2. The expected physical wear and tear, which depends on operational factors, such as the number of shifts for which the asset is to be used and the repair and maintenance program, and the care and maintenance of the asset while idle;

3. Technical or commercial obsolescence arising from changes or improvements in production, or from a change in the market demand for the product or service output of the asset; and

4. Legal or similar limits on the use of the asset, such as the expiration dates of related leases.

Land and buildings are separable assets with different accounting characteristics and should be considered separately, even if acquired as a single purchase.

The standard mentions three depreciation methods by name: straight-line, reducing (or diminishing) balance, and units of production (usage) method (par. 62). This list is neither exhaustive nor in order of preference. The method used for an asset is selected on the basis of the expected pattern of economic benefits and is consistently applied from period to period unless there is a change in the expected pattern of economic benefits from that asset. This implies that for any particular asset, with its own particular expected pattern of economic benefits, there is one particular appropriate method.

The depreciation method applied to an asset should be reviewed at least at each financial year-end and, if there has been a significant change in the expected pattern of consumption of the future economic benefits embodied in the asset, the method should be changed to reflect the changed pattern. Such a change is accounted for as a change in an accounting estimate in accordance with IAS 8, "Accounting Policies, Changes in Accounting Estimates, and Errors."

It is necessary to determine whether or not an item of property, plant, and equipment has become impaired. This area is covered by IAS 36, "Impairment of Assets" (see Chapter 20). Impairments or losses of items of property, plant, and equipment; related claims for, or payments of, compensation from third parties; and any subsequent purchase or construction of replacement assets are separate economic events and are accounted for separately as follows:

- Impairments of items of property, plant, and equipment are recognized in accordance with IAS 36, "Impairment of Assets";

- Derecognition of items of property, plant, and equipment retired or disposed of is determined in accordance with IAS 16;

- Compensation from third parties for items of property, plant, and equipment that were impaired, lost, or given up is included in determining profit or loss when it becomes receivable; and
- The cost of items of property, plant, and equipment restored, purchased, or constructed as replacements is determined in accordance with IAS 16.

Derecognition

The carrying amount of an item of property, plant, and equipment is derecognized:

- On disposal; or
- When no future economic benefits are expected from its use or disposal.

The gain or loss arising from the derecognition of an item of property, plant, and equipment shall be determined as the difference between the net disposal proceeds, if any, and the carrying amount of the item. The gain or loss is to be included in profit or loss when the item is derecognized (unless IAS 17, "Leases," requires otherwise on a sale and leaseback). Gains are not classified as revenue. This confirms that any element of revaluation reserve relating to the item will not pass through the income statement.

However, an entity that, in the course of its ordinary activities, routinely sells items of property, plant, and equipment that it has held for rental to others shall transfer such assets to inventories at their carrying amount when they cease to be rented and become held for sale. The proceeds from the sale of such assets shall be recognized as revenue in accordance with IAS 18, "Revenue." IFRS 5 does not apply when assets that are held for sale in the ordinary course of business are transferred to inventories (par. 68A, inserted in 2008).

The disposal of an item of property, plant, and equipment may occur in a variety of ways (e.g., by sale, by entering into a finance lease, or by donations). In determining the date of disposal of an item, an entity applies the criteria in IAS 18, "Revenue," for recognizing revenue from the sale of goods. IAS 17 applies to disposal by a sale and leaseback.

DISCLOSURE

The disclosure requirements are lengthy, and are essentially as follows (pars. 73 – 79). The financial statements should disclose, for each class of property, plant, and equipment:

1. The measurement bases used for determining the gross carrying amount;
2. The depreciation methods used;
3. The useful lives or the depreciation rates used;
4. The gross carrying amount and the accumulated depreciation (aggregated with accumulated impairment losses) at the beginning and end of the period; and
5. A reconciliation of the carrying amount at the beginning and end of the period showing:

(a) Additions.

(b) Assets classified as held for sale or included in a disposal group classified as held for sale in accordance with IFRS 5, "Non-Current Assets Held for Sale and Discontinued Operations," and other disposals.

(c) Acquisitions through business combinations.

(d) Increases or decreases resulting from revaluations and from impairment losses recognized or reversed in other comprehensive income in accordance with IAS 36, "Impairment of Assets."

(e) Impairment losses recognized in profit or loss in accordance with IAS 36.

(f) Impairment losses reversed in profit or loss in accordance with IAS 36.

(g) Depreciation.

(h) The net exchange differences arising on the translation of the financial statements from the functional currency into a different presentation currency, including the translation of a foreign operation into the presentation currency of the reporting entity.

(i) Other changes.

The financial statements must also disclose:

- The existence and amounts of restrictions on title and of property, plant, and equipment pledged as security for liabilities;

- The amount of expenditures recognized in the carrying amount of an item of property, plant, and equipment in the course of its construction;

- The amount of contractual commitments for the acquisition of property, plant, and equipment; and

- If it is not disclosed separately in the statement of comprehensive income, the amount of compensation—from third parties for items of property, plant, and equipment that were impaired, lost, or given up—that is included in profit or loss.

If items of property, plant, and equipment are stated at revalued amounts, the following must be disclosed:

- The effective date of the revaluation;

- Whether an independent valuer was involved;

- The methods and significant assumptions applied in estimating the items' fair values;

- The extent to which the items' fair values were (1) determined directly by reference to observable prices in an active market or recent market transactions on arm's-length terms or (2) were estimated using other valuation techniques;

- For each revalued class of property, plant, and equipment, the carrying amount that would have been recognized had the assets been carried under the cost model; and

- The revaluation surplus, indicating the change for the period and any restrictions on the distribution of the balance to shareholders.

In accordance with IAS 36 an entity discloses information on impaired property, plant, and equipment in addition to the above information. Users of financial statements may also find the following information relevant to their needs:

- The carrying amount of temporarily idle property, plant, and equipment;

- The gross carrying amount of any fully depreciated property, plant, and equipment that is still in use;

- The carrying amount of property, plant, and equipment retired from active use and not classified as held for sale in accordance with IFRS 5; and

- When the cost model is used, the fair value of property, plant, and equipment when this is materially different from the carrying amount.

Therefore, entities are encouraged to disclose these amounts.

CHAPTER 29
PROVISIONS, CONTINGENT LIABILITIES, AND CONTINGENT ASSETS

CONTENTS

OVERVIEW

The major purpose of IAS 37, "Provisions, Contingent Liabilities, and Contingent Assets," is to deal with two of the more difficult aspects of liabilities. In principle, one can envisage three types of obligation situation. The first is where the existence of the obligation and the amount of the obligation are definite. This gives rise to a liability proper. The second is where the existence of the obligation is definite but the amount of the obligation is uncertain. This gives rise to a provision, which must be recorded as an estimated liability in the balance sheet. The final situation is when the existence of the obligation is uncertain (the amount probably, but not necessarily, being uncertain, too), and some future event, not wholly within the control of the entity, will determine whether an obligation does or does not eventually arise.

This last situation gives rise to a contingent liability. A contingent liability is not recorded in the balance sheet, but it is disclosed in the notes to the accounts unless the possibility of an outflow of resources is "remote." The distinction between a provision and a contingent liability may in practice be a difficult and subjective one, although the definitions discussed below are clear enough.

The standard also deals with contingent assets, which are possible assets that arise from past events but whose existence will be confirmed or denied only by the occurrence or non-occurrence of one or more uncertain future events not wholly within the control of the enterprise. An example is a claim that an entity is pursuing through legal processes, where the outcome is uncertain. An enterprise should not recognize a contingent asset. A contingent asset should be disclosed where an inflow of economic benefits is "probable." When the realization of income is virtually certain, then the related asset is not a contingent asset and its recognition is appropriate.

By way of appendix, IAS 37 gives examples of the application of its principles.

Tables 29-1 and 29-2 give a summary and overview of the major requirements of the standard (with paragraph references to the standard itself).

BACKGROUND

As part of its original series of international standards, IASC issued IAS 10, "Contingencies and Events Occurring after the Balance Sheet Date," in 1974. Most of the original IAS 10, that is, all those parts dealing with contingencies, was replaced by IAS 37, "Provisions, Contingent Liabilities, and Contingent Assets," which is operative for annual financial statements beginning on or after July 1, 1999. The remaining parts of the old IAS 10 have since also been superseded, as discussed in Chapter 16.

IAS 37 deals with issues that must inevitably involve some difficult and subjective distinctions related to future expectations. It seeks to reduce the subjectivity by clear definitions and clearly stated requirements and by the inclusion of examples to illustrate the application of its principles. Nothing, however, can remove the need for intelligent and professional judgment on the part of accountants involved in the preparation and the auditing of the financial statements. The motto of the standard, though unstated, is perhaps that full necessary disclosure should always take place, whether or not the actual balance sheet itself is to be adjusted.

U.S. GAAP for provisions are broadly similar to IASB GAAP, though contained within several standards of which ASC 450, "Contingencies," is the most important.

Table 29-1: Provisions and Contingent Liabilities

Where, as a result of past events, there may be an outflow of resources embodying future economic benefits in settlement of (a) a present obligation or (b) a possible obligation whose existence will be confirmed only by the occurrence or non-occurrence of one or more uncertain future events not wholly within the control of the entity.

A contingent liability also arises in the "extremely rare" case where there is a liability that cannot be recognized because it cannot be measured reliably. Disclosures are required for the contingent liability.

If:	If:	If:
There is a present obligation that probably requires an outflow of resources.	There is a possible obligation or a present obligation that may, but probably will not, require an outflow of resources.	There is a possible obligation or a present obligation where the likelihood of an outflow of resources is remote.
Then:	**Then:**	**Then:**
A provision is recognized (par. 14).	No provision is recognized (par. 27).	No provision is recognized (par. 27).
Disclosures are required for the provision (pars. 84 and 85).	Disclosures are required for the contingent liability (par. 86).	No disclosure is required (par. 86).

Table 29-2: Contingent Assets

Where, as a result of past events, there is a possible asset whose existence will be confirmed only by the occurrence or non-occurrence of one or more uncertain future events not wholly within the control of the entity.

If:	If:	If:
The inflow of economic benefits is virtually certain.	The inflow of economic benefits is probable, but not virtually certain.	The inflow is not probable.
Then:	**Then:**	**Then:**
The asset is not contingent (par. 33).	No asset is recognized (par. 31).	No asset is recognized (par. 31).
	Disclosures are required (par. 89).	No disclosure is required (par. 89).

SCOPE OF APPLICATION

In general, IAS 37 applies to all entities. However, there are a number of rather complicated exceptions to this, which need to be considered. These are as follows:

1. IAS 37 does not apply to financial instruments (including guarantees) that are within the scope of IFRS 9, "Financial Instruments"(see Chapter 17).

2. IAS 37 does not apply to provisions, contingent liabilities, or contingent assets that result from executory contracts, unless the contract is onerous. Executory contracts are contracts under which neither party has performed any of its obligations or both parties have partially performed their obligations to an equal extent. An onerous contract is a contract in which the unavoidable costs of meeting the obligations under the contract exceed the economic benefits expected to be received under it.

3. The standard does not apply to items arising in insurance entities from contracts with their policyholders, but it does apply to provisions, contingent liabilities, and contingent assets of insurance entities, other than those arising from contracts covered by 4(e) below.

4. Where another international standard deals with a specific type of provision, contingent liability, or contingent asset, an entity applies that standard instead of IAS 37. For example, certain types of provisions are also addressed in standards on:

   (a) Construction contracts (see IAS 11, "Construction Contracts," discussed in Chapter 12);

   (b) Income taxes (see IAS 12, "Income Taxes," discussed in Chapter 21);

   (c) Leases (see IAS 17, "Leases," discussed in Chapter 26). However, as IAS 17 contains no specific requirements to deal with operating leases that have become onerous, IAS 37 applies to such cases;

   (d) Employee benefits (see IAS 19, "Employee Benefits," discussed in Chapter 14); and

   (e) Insurance contracts within the scope of IFRS 4, "Insurance Contracts" (see Chapter 35).

With the above exceptions, IAS 37 applies to all provisions, contingent liabilities, and contingent assets as defined in the standard.

→ **PRACTICE POINTER:** These terms, especially the word *provision*, may be used loosely in some jurisdictions with other meanings. For example, the terms *provision for depreciation* and *provision for doubtful debts*, are in common use. Such items are not provisions in the sense used by this standard, and the standard does not deal with them.

DEFINITIONS AND MEANINGS

Liabilities are defined as in IAS 1. A *liability* is a present obligation of the entity arising from past events, the settlement of which is expected to result in an outflow from the entity of resources embodying economic benefits. A *provision* is a liability of uncertain timing or amount (but not of uncertain existence).

Two types of obligation can be distinguished.

1. A *legal obligation* is an obligation that derives from:

   (a) A contract (through its explicit or implicit terms),

   (b) Legislation, or

   (c) Other operation of law.

2. A *constructive obligation* is an obligation that derives from an entity's actions where:

   (a) By an established pattern of past practice, published policies, or a sufficiently specific current statement, the entity has indicated to other parties that it will accept certain responsibilities, and

   (b) As a result, the entity has created a valid expectation on the part of those other parties that it will discharge those responsibilities.

A constructive obligation creates a liability just as much as a legal obligation does.

Again, contingent liabilities, as the term is used in the standard, can arise in two different ways.

A *contingent liability* is:

(a) A possible obligation that arises from past events and whose existence will be confirmed only by the occurrence or non-occurrence of one or more uncertain future events not wholly within the control of the entity, or

(b) A present obligation that arises from past events but is not recognized because:

    (i) It is not probable that an outflow of resources embodying economic benefits will be required to settle the obligation, or

    (ii) The amount of the obligation cannot be measured with sufficient reliability.

The meaning of the word *probable* in this definition is of some significance. This is discussed further below.

A *contingent asset* is a possible asset that arises from past events and whose existence will be confirmed only by the occurrence or non-occurrence of one or more uncertain future events not wholly within the control of the entity.

An *onerous contract* is one in which the unavoidable costs of meeting the obligations under the contract exceed the economic benefits expected to be received by it.

A *restructuring* is a program that is planned and controlled by management, and materially changes either:

(a) The scope of a business undertaken by an entity; or

(b) The manner in which that business is conducted.

The distinction between accruals and provisions is that accruals are liabilities to pay for goods or services that have been received or supplied but have not been paid, invoiced, or formally agreed with the supplier, including amounts due to employees (e.g., amounts relating to accrued vacation pay). Although it is sometimes necessary to estimate the amount or timing of accruals, the uncertainty is generally much less than for provisions. Accruals are often reported as part of trade and other payables, whereas provisions are reported separately.

In a theoretical sense, the distinction between provisions and contingent liabilities is perhaps less clear, as uncertainty exists in both cases. It may be suggested that:

1. Provisions are *present* obligations (of uncertain amount).

2. Contingent liabilities are either:

    (a) *Possible* obligations, because it has yet to be confirmed whether the enterprise has a present obligation that could lead to an outflow of resources embodying economic benefits; or

    (b) *Present* obligations that do not meet the recognition criteria in the standard (because either it is not probable that an outflow of resources embodying economic benefits will be required to settle the obligation or a sufficiently reliable estimate of the amount of the obligation cannot be made).

In practice they can be quite easily distinguished by the reader of financial statements, in that provisions *are* included in the balance sheet (with a corresponding charge in the income statement) and contingent liabilities are *not* included in the balance sheet.

RECOGNITION OF PROVISIONS

The standard states (par. 14) that a provision should be recognized when:

1. An entity has a present obligation (legal or constructive) as a result of a past event,

2. It is probable that an outflow of resources embodying economic benefits will be required to settle the obligation, and

3. A reliable estimate can be made of the amount of the obligation.

If these conditions are not met, no provision should be recognized.

Comparison of this statement with the definition of a liability given above shows that, in effect, all that paragraph 14 says is that a provision should be recognized when a liability exists and can be reliably estimated.

OBSERVATION: The terminology used by the standard is rather confusing. It states, for example, in paragraph 14 that if certain conditions are not met, then "no provision should be recognized." However, it has already been stated that provisions are recognized as liabilities and that "contingent liabilities" are not recognized as liabilities. It follows that an "unrecognized provision" is not an unrecognized provision. Rather, it is a contingent liability (which is not recognized, by definition). There is some circularity going on here!

Several terms used in paragraph 14 warrant some consideration. First of all, there may in certain circumstances (in "rare cases" according to the standard) be real uncertainty as to whether or not a present obligation exists. A lawsuit that is being disputed is a likely example. The standard says that after obtaining and assessing all possible evidence, where it is more likely than not that a present obligation exists at the balance sheet date, the entity recognizes a provision (if the recognition criteria are met). Where it is more likely that no present obligation exists at the balance sheet date, the entity discloses a contingent liability, unless the possibility of an outflow of resources embodying economic benefits is remote (as discussed below).

"More likely than not" clearly suggests that a 51% probability of the existence, arising from the past event, of a present obligation creates a provision. Equally clearly, 49% probability in such circumstances creates a contingent liability, which will not be recorded in the balance sheet itself.

OBSERVATION: It seems to us quite defensible in logic to argue that when something may or may not happen and there is no means of objective predetermination, the treatment should follow the simple balance of probabilities. It must be said, however, that this attitude is putting the demands of rationality and neutrality above the demands of prudence. On the other hand, since in either event full disclosure is ensured in one way or another, the reader of the financial statements should not be misled, which is arguably the crucial issue. The standard goes out of its way to state that the interpretation of "probable" as "more likely than not" in IAS 37 is unique to that standard, and it should not necessarily be assumed that the word "probable" as used in any other IASB standard or publication has the same meaning as in IAS 37.

The standard discusses past events at considerable length, although some of its points seem to be statements of the obvious and not all are worthy of comment here. An obligation will arise from a past event only where the settlement of the obligation can be enforced by law or, in the case of a constructive obligation, where the event (which may be an action of the entity) creates a valid expectation in other parties that the enterprise will discharge the obligation. The only liabilities recognized in an entity's balance sheet are those that exist at the balance sheet date. It is only those obligations arising from past events existing independently of an entity's future actions (i.e., the future conduct of its business) that are recognized as provisions.

It follows from the above that, for example, unavoidable decommissioning costs at the end of a plant's useful life do give rise to a provision during the life of the plant. However, if an entity intends to spend money on amending its factory processes but could avoid spending by changing its mode of operation, then it has no present obligation for that future expenditure, and no provision is required—indeed under the theoretical logic of the standard, no provision is permitted.

The standard points out that a "reliable estimate" is, of course, still an estimate. Estimates based on knowledge and experience, and statistical probability in the case of large numbers of possible obligations within the same class (as with product warranties for example), do provide adequate reliability. Except in extremely rare cases, an entity will be able to determine a range of possible outcomes and can therefore make an estimate of the obligation that is sufficiently reliable to use in recognizing a provision.

In the extremely rare case where no reliable estimate can be made, a liability exists that cannot be recognized. That liability is disclosed as a contingent liability.

CONTINGENT LIABILITIES, CONTINGENT ASSETS, AND RECOGNITION

As already indicated, the rule is quite simple: No contingent liability or contingent asset should be recognized—that is, no contingent liability or contingent asset should be recorded in the balance sheet. The requirements for disclosure in the notes to the financial statements are discussed below.

In respect of contingent items, it is necessary to reassess the situation regularly (the standard says "continually") to see whether the likelihood of inflows or outflows of resources has increased. If it becomes probable that an outflow of future economic benefits will be required for an item previously dealt with as a contingent liability, a provision is recognized in the financial statements of the period in which the change in probability occurs (except in the extremely rare circumstances where no reliable estimate can be made), that is, the item ceases to be a contingent liability. If it has become virtually certain that an inflow of economic benefits will arise, the asset and the related income are recognized in the financial statements of the period in which the change occurs; that is, the item ceases to be a contingent asset. If an inflow of economic benefits has become probable, an entity discloses the contingent asset (see the discussion on disclosure, below).

MEASUREMENT OF PROVISIONS

In essence, the amount recognized as a provision should be the best estimate of the expenditure required to settle the present obligation at the balance sheet date. It should be noted that, in principle, this is not necessarily the same as the best estimate of the expenditure likely to be required to settle the obligation at its likely date of settlement. Where the effect of the time value of money is material, however, the amount of a provision should be the present value of the expenditures expected to be required to settle the obligation. The discount rate should be a pretax rate that reflects current market assessments of the time value of money and the risks specific to the liability. The discount rate should not reflect risks for which future cash flow estimates have been adjusted. Note that where the effect of discounting would be material, discounting is a requirement, not an option.

Where the provision concerns a large population of items, then a statistical calculation of expected values is appropriate, with warranties on large volume sales, for example. If, say, experience suggests that 5% of sales will have minor faults at an average cost of $100 and 2% of sales will have major faults at an average cost of $1,000, and sales have been 20,000 units, then the provision would be calculated as follows:

$$(5\% \times 20,000 \times \$100) + (2\% \times 20,000 \times \$1,000) = \$100,000 + \$400,000 = \$500,000$$

Where a single obligation is under consideration, the situation is more complicated. It is worth quoting the comment of the standard, paragraph 40, in full.

> Where a single obligation is being measured, the individual most likely outcome may be the best estimate of the liability. However, even in such a case, the entity considers other possible outcomes. Where other possible outcomes are either mostly higher or mostly lower than the most likely outcome, the best estimate will be a higher or lower amount. For example, if an entity has to rectify a serious fault in a major plant that it has constructed for a customer, the individual most likely outcome may be for the repair to succeed at the first attempt at a cost of 1,000, but a provision for a larger amount is made if there is a significant chance that further attempts will be necessary.

OBSERVATION: At first sight there seems a danger of some confusion and inconsistency here. It will be recalled that in the context of the *recognition* of a provision, that is, the issue of whether or not a provision exists to be recorded, the "more likely than not" criterion is to be used. In paragraph 40, as quoted, the phrase used is "if there is a significant chance." This is not strictly an inconsistency, as paragraph 40 refers only to *measurement*, not to recognition. The meaning of "significant chance" is not discussed, but intuitively a chance could be regarded as significant with a probability considerably (significantly!) less than 50%.

The logical sequence must be carefully followed. First, is there a provision (more likely than not). If not, then measurement is not required. If yes, then measurement of a single obligation should follow paragraph 40, including the significant chance consideration.

The measurement of provisions needs to take full account of risk and uncertainty. Caution is needed in making judgments under conditions of uncertainty, so that income or assets are not overstated and expenses or liabilities are not understated. However, uncertainty does not justify the creation of excessive provisions or a deliberate overstatement of liabilities. Future events that may affect the amount required to settle an obligation should be reflected in the amount of a provision where there is sufficient objective evidence that they will occur.

The phrase "sufficient objective evidence" is an interesting one. IAS 37 gives the example of an expectation of future changes in technology reducing site clean-up costs on the future decommissioning of a plant. There would need to be independent (equals objective?) evidence of the expected existence and effectiveness of the technology involved.

Gains on the expected disposal of assets are not taken into account in measuring a provision, even if the expected disposal is closely linked to the event giving rise to the provision. Instead, an entity recognizes gains on expected disposals of assets at the time specified by the international standard dealing with the assets concerned.

In some situations significant or even total reimbursement of the cash outflow necessary to settle a provision may be expected, for example, because of insurance contracts or supplier warranties. In most cases, however, the entity will remain liable for the whole of the amount in question so that the entity would have to settle the full amount if the third party failed to pay for any reason. In this situation, a provision is recognized for the full amount of the liability, and a separate asset for the expected reimbursement is recognized only when it is virtually certain that reimbursement will be received if the entity settles the liability.

Whatever the original procedure for the measurement of a provision, provisions should be reviewed at each balance sheet date and adjusted to reflect the current best estimate. If it is no longer probable that an outflow of resources embodying economic benefits will be required to settle the obligation, the provision should be reversed. Note that such reversal is a requirement, not an option. Where discounting is used, the carrying amount of a provision increases in each period to reflect the passage of time. This increase is recognized as a borrowing cost.

APPLICATION OF RECOGNITION AND MEASUREMENT RULES

IAS 37 gives, in the body of the standard itself, not as appendices, discussions of the application of its principles to three particular areas. The standard is obviously concerned that adequate provisions should be made as soon as they are necessary. But it is at least equally concerned to prevent the creation of unnecessary or unnecessarily high provisions. This is to prevent creative accounting techniques such as income smoothing by the creation of extra provisions in profitable years, or "big bath" techniques, where management artificially accentuates a bad year by creating excessive provisions, thereby earning a steadily improving profit in upcoming years.

Future operating losses are simply dealt with. They do not meet the definition of a liability (being *future* events) and a provision cannot be provided for them. Relevant assets should, however, be tested for impairment under IAS 36, "Impairment of Assets" (see Chapter 20).

As discussed and defined in the "Scope of Application" section of this chapter, IAS 37 does not apply to executory contracts unless they are onerous. If an entity has a contract that is onerous, the present obligation under the contract should be recognized and measured as a provision. Before a separate provision for an onerous contract is established, an entity recognizes any impairment loss that has occurred on assets dedicated to that contract (see IAS 36, "Impairment of Assets," discussed in Chapter 20).

The third area of application discussed in IAS 37 is that of restructuring. The standard goes into considerable detail, to try to specify the circumstances in which provisions are or are not required as tightly as possible. In this case in particular, IASB is concerned to minimize the possibility of excessive or unjustified provisions. The definition of a restructuring given by IAS 37 is that it is a program that is planned and controlled by management, and materially changes *either:*

1. The scope of a business undertaken by an entity, *or*
2. The manner in which that business is conducted.

Examples of events that "may" fall within this definition are given as follows:

1. Sale or termination of a line of business;
2. The closure of business locations in a country or region or the relocation of business activities from one country or region to another;
3. Changes in management structure, for example, eliminating a layer of management; or
4. Fundamental reorganizations that have a material effect on the nature and focus of the entity's operations.

A provision for restructuring costs is recognized only when the general recognition criteria for provisions set out in paragraph 14 are met. IAS 37 spends no less than 12 paragraphs discussing the application of paragraph 14 to restructurings. IAS 37 states that a constructive obligation to restructure arises *only* when an entity:

1. Has a detailed formal plan for the restructuring, identifying at least:
    (a) The business or part of a business concerned;
    (b) The principal locations affected;
    (c) The location, function, and approximate number of employees who will be compensated for terminating their services;
    (d) The expenditures that will be undertaken; and
    (e) When the plan will be implemented.
2. Has raised a valid expectation in those affected that it will carry out the restructuring by starting to implement that plan or announcing its main features to those affected by it.

Whether or not these criteria are met is a question of fact to be determined in each case. The mere announcement, however formal, of a management intention is certainly not by itself sufficient. No obligation can arise related to the sale of an operation until the entity is committed to the sale by means of a binding sale agreement. Any restructuring provision should include only the direct expenditure arising from the restructuring, which are those that are both:

1. Necessarily entailed by the restructuring, and
2. Not associated with the ongoing activities of the entity.

Any expenditures relating to the *future* activities of the business, such as relocating or retraining staff, marketing, or investment in new processes, cannot be included as part of a restructuring provision. Identifiable future operating losses up to the date of a restructuring are not included in a provision, unless they relate to an onerous contract as defined in the standard.

DISCLOSURE

The disclosure requirements of IAS 37 are extensive and incapable of effective summarization. They are as follows.

For each class of *provision*, an entity should disclose:

1. The carrying amount at the beginning and end of the period;
2. Additional provisions made in the period, including increases to existing provisions;
3. Amounts used (i.e., incurred and charged against the provision) during the period;
4. Unused amounts reversed during the period; and
5. The increase during the period in the discounted amount arising from the passage of time and the effect of any change in the discount rate.

Comparative information is not required.

An entity should disclose the following for each class of provision:

1. A brief description of the nature of the obligation and the expected timing of any resulting outflows of economic benefits;
2. An indication of the uncertainties about the amount or timing of those outflows. Where necessary to provide adequate information, an entity

should disclose the major assumptions made concerning future events; and

3. The amount of any expected reimbursement, stating the amount of any asset that has been recognized for that expected reimbursement.

Unless the possibility of any outflow in settlement is "remote," an entity should disclose for each class of *contingent liability* at the balance sheet date a brief description of the nature of the contingent liability and, where practicable:

1. An estimate of its financial effect;

2. An indication of the uncertainties relating to the amount or timing of any outflow; and

3. The possibility of any reimbursement.

Where an inflow of economic benefits is probable, an entity should disclose a brief description of the nature of the *contingent assets* at the balance sheet date and, where practicable, an estimate of their financial effect.

The use of the phrase "where practicable" in relation to the disclosure of contingent liabilities and contingent assets should be noted. What is "impracticable" is not discussed. If any of the required information is omitted on the grounds of impracticability, then that fact must be stated. In "extremely rare" cases, disclosure of some or all of the information required can be expected to prejudice seriously the position of the entity in a dispute with other parties on the subject matter of the provision, contingent liability, or contingent asset. In such cases, an entity need not disclose the information but should disclose the general nature of the dispute, together with the fact that, and reason why, the information has not been disclosed.

OBSERVATION: As part of the FASB/IASB convergence project, the IASB issued an exposure draft of proposed amendments to IAS 37 in June 2005. The proposed changes appeared complicated and suggest a radically revised terminology, but they represent an attempted clarification of the essential requirements of the current IAS 37 rather than a radical change in direction. The proposals received some criticism and the project has been extensively delayed. In January 2010, the IASB published a limited Exposure Draft regarding the measurement of liabilities. Essentially this proposes to replace the "best estimate" original proposal with: "the amount that the entity would rationally pay at the measurement date to be relieved of the liability." This is in essence a fair value concept. The proposal has not been very well received. Watch this space!

APPENDICES TO THE STANDARD

As already indicated, IAS 37 gives a considerable number of examples of the application of the standard by way of appendix. These relate to the question of when a provision is to be *recognized,* and are not extended to the problems of the measurement of a recognized provision. Readers involved with difficult recognition decisions should read the appendix to IAS 37 carefully, and apply the examples directly or by analogy.

Also see the decision tree in Figure 29-1.

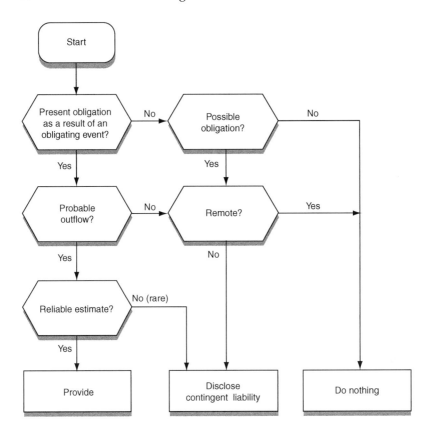

Figure 29-1: Decision Tree for Provisions and Contingent Liabilities

CHAPTER 30
RELATED PARTY DISCLOSURES

CONTENTS

OVERVIEW

The existence of related party relationships, that is, relationships where the independence necessary for arm's-length transactions does not exist, carries at least the possibility that transactions will take place that would not otherwise have done so or that the value of transactions may be different from what it would otherwise have been. The principle followed by IASB GAAP is that disclosure of the relationships and of the transactions is necessary, so that the reader of the financial statements is made aware of the lack of independence and its implications. There is no suggestion, however, that quantification of the monetary effect of the relationship is required. Disclosure is addressed, not measurement. The matter is dealt with by IAS 24, "Related Party Disclosures."

IAS 24 was originally effective from January 1, 1986, and survived unaltered until 2004, when a revised version was issued, effective for annual periods beginning on or after January 1, 2005, earlier adoption being encouraged. This revision was part of the improvements project and did not reconsider the fundamental approach. In particular, the limitation only to disclosure considerations was retained. However, the opportunity was taken to virtually rewrite the standard. The definition of related parties, and the application of the standard, were both tightened and widened, and in practice the relevance and applicability of IAS 24 was significantly increased.

The Standard was revised again in 2009, effective from January 1, 2011, with earlier application permitted. Again, no fundamental rethinking was done. The main changes were to the definition of a related party, and the granting of a partial exemption from the disclosure requirements for "government related entities." It is this new version that is discussed here.

SCOPE

The standard should be applied in:

- Identifying related party relationships and transactions;
- Identifying outstanding balances between an entity and its related parties;
- Identifying the circumstances in which disclosure of the two entries above is required; and

- Determining the disclosures to be made about those items.

IAS 24 requires disclosure of related party transactions and outstanding balances in the separate financial statements of a parent, venturer, or investor presented in accordance with IAS 27, "Consolidated and Separate Financial Statements." Entity financial statements of companies within a group should also follow the full disclosure requirements of the standard.

BACKGROUND

As indicated above, the principle of IAS 24 is that disclosure of related party implications is necessary (subject always to the fact that international standards are not intended to apply to immaterial items) to ensure an overall fair presentation in financial statements. U.S. GAAP (in ASC 820, "Fair Value Measurement") are consistent in principle with IASB GAAP, but more detailed. Under U.S. GAAP, the nature and extent of any transactions with all related parties should be disclosed, together with the amounts involved. All material related party transactions (other than compensation arrangements, expense allowances, and similar items) must be disclosed in the separate financial statements of wholly owned subsidiaries, unless these are presented in the same financial report that includes the parent's consolidated financial statements (including those subsidiaries).

DEFINITIONS

A number of important and precise definitions are given in paragraph 9.

A *related party* is a person or entity that is related to the entity that is preparing its financial statements (in this Standard referred to as the "reporting entity").

(a) A person or a close member of that person's family is related to a reporting entity if that person:

    (i) has control or joint control over the reporting entity;

    (ii) has significant influence over the reporting entity; or

    (iii) is a member of the key management personnel of the reporting entity or of a parent of the reporting entity.

(b) An entity is related to a reporting entity if any of the following conditions applies:

    (i) The entity and the reporting entity are members of the same group (i.e., that each parent, subsidiary and fellow subsidiary is related to the others);

    (ii) One entity is an associate or joint venture of the other entity (or an associate or joint venture of a member of a group of which the other entity is a member).

    (iii) Both entities are joint ventures of the same third party.

    (iv) One entity is a joint venture of a third entity and the other entity is an associate of the third entity.

(v) The entity is a post-employment benefit plan for the benefit of employees of either the reporting entity or an entity related to the reporting entity. If the reporting entity is itself such a plan, the sponsoring employers are also related to the reporting entity.

(vi) The entity is controlled or jointly controlled by a person identified in (a).

(vii) A person identified in (a)(i) has significant influence over the entity or is a member of the key management personnel of the entity (or of a parent of the entity).

A *related party transaction* is a transfer of resources, services or obligations between a reporting entity and a related party, regardless of whether a price is charged.

Close members of the family of a person are those family members who may be expected to influence, or be influenced by, that person in their dealings with the entity and include:

(a) that person's children and spouse or domestic partner;

(b) children of that person's spouse or domestic partner; and

(c) dependents of that person or that person's spouse or domestic partner.

Compensation includes all employee benefits (as defined in IAS 19, *Employee Benefits*), including employee benefits to which IFRS 2, *Share-Based Payments*, applies. Employee benefits are all forms of consideration paid, payable or provided by the entity, or on behalf of the entity, in exchange for services rendered to the entity. It also includes such consideration paid on behalf of a parent of the entity in respect of the entity. Compensation includes:

(a) short-term employee benefits, such as wages, salaries and social security contributions, paid annual leave and paid sick leave, profit-sharing and bonuses (if payable within 12 months of the end of the period) and non-monetary benefits (such as medical care, housing, cars and free or subsidized goods or services) for current employees;

(b) post-employment benefits such as pensions, other retirement benefits, post-employment life insurance and post-employment medical care;

(c) other long-term employee benefits, including long-service leave or sabbatical leave, jubilee or other long-service benefits, long-term disability benefits and, if they are not payable wholly within 12 months after the end of the period, profit-sharing, bonuses and deferred compensation;

(d) termination benefits; and

(e) share-based payment.

Control is the power to govern the financial and operating policies of an entity so as to obtain benefits from its activities.

Joint control is the contractually agreed sharing of control over an economic activity.

Key management personnel are those persons having authority and responsibility for planning, directing and controlling the activities of the entity, directly or indirectly, including any director (whether executive or otherwise) of that entity.

Significant influence is the power to participate in the financial and operating policy decisions of an entity, but is not control over those policies. Significant influence may be gained by share ownership, statute or agreement.

Government refers to government agencies and similar bodies, whether local, national or international.

A *government-related entity* is an entity that is controlled, jointly controlled or significantly influenced by a government.

These definitions are fully in line with other standards. They are also in many respects pervasive. Note for example that demonstrating actual influence is irrelevant to qualifying under the definition of a close relative, nor is demonstrating actual control or participation relevant to fitting within the definition of control or significant influence. Notwithstanding the greater degree of specification contained in this series of definitions, it is explicitly confirmed (par. 10) that the substance of a relationship, and not "merely" the legal form, determines whether or not the relationship involves related parties.

The standard notes that the following are "not necessarily" related parties:

1. Two entities simply because they have a director or other member of key management personnel in common, or because a member of key management personnel of one entity has significant influence over the other entity.

2. Two venturers simply because they share joint control over a joint venture.

3. Providers of finance, trade unions, public utilities, and government departments and agencies simply by virtue of their normal dealings with an entity (even though they may affect the freedom of action of an entity or participate in its decision-making process).

4. A customer, supplier, franchisor, distributor, or general agent with whom an entity transacts a significant volume of business, merely by virtue of the resulting economic dependence.

DISCLOSURE

Essentially there are two separate disclosure requirements to consider. The first exists when there is a related party relationship involving control. The requirement is that relationships between parents and subsidiaries must be disclosed irrespective of whether there have been transactions between those related parties. An entity must disclose the name of the entity's parent and, if different, the ultimate controlling party. If neither the entity's parent nor the ultimate controlling party produces financial statements available for public use, the name of the most senior parent that does so should also be disclosed. This is considered necessary so that readers of financial statements can form a view about the actual or potential effects of the related party relationships.

Further, an entity shall disclose key management personnel compensation in total and for each of the following categories:

- Short-term employee benefits
- Post-employment benefits
- Other long-term benefits
- Termination benefits
- Share-based payment

OBSERVATION: Note carefully the definition of "key management personnel" given earlier. It does not seem that the six disclosure requirements (total and the five categories above) are required individually for each such person. The word "personnel" presumably is used in its plural rather than singular form.

The second additional set of disclosure requirements relates to when there have been transactions between related parties. This applies to all related parties as defined, not only to control (parent and subsidiary) relationships as with the first requirement discussed above. Thus, if there have been transactions between related parties, an entity must disclose the nature of the related party relationship as well as information about the transactions and outstanding balances necessary for an understanding of the potential effect of the relationship on the financial statements. These disclosure requirements are in addition to the requirements above to disclose key management personnel compensation. At a minimum, disclosures are to include:

1. The amount of the transactions.
2. The amount of outstanding balances and:
   (a) Their terms and conditions, including whether they are secured, and the nature of the consideration to be provided in settlement; and
   (b) Details of any guarantees given or received.
3. Provisions for doubtful debts related to the amount of outstanding balances and
   (a) The expense recognized during the period in respect of bad or doubtful debts due from related parties.

These disclosures must be made separately for each of the following categories:

- The parent
- Entities with joint control or significant influence over the entity
- Subsidiaries
- Associates
- Joint ventures in which the entity is a venturer
- Key management personnel of the entity or its parent
- Other related parties

The following are examples of transactions that are disclosed if they are with a related party:

- Purchases or sales of goods (finished or unfinished)
- Purchases or sales of property and other assets
- Rendering or receiving of services
- Leases
- Transfers of research and development
- Transfers under license agreements
- Transfers under finance arrangements (including loans and equity contributions in cash or in kind)
- Provision of guarantees or collateral
- Commitments related to the future occurrence or non-occurrence of some particular event
- Settlement of liabilities on behalf of the entity or by the entity on behalf of another party

Disclosures that related party transactions were made on terms equivalent to those that prevail in arm's-length transactions can be made only if such terms can be substantiated. Items of a similar nature may be disclosed in aggregate except when separate disclosure is necessary for an understanding of the effects of related party transactions on the financial statements of the entity.

As discussed in the overview, exemptions in relation to government-related entities have been newly introduced. The key details are as follows (pars. 25 and 26):

25. A reporting entity is exempt from the disclosure requirements of paragraph 18 in relation to related party transactions and outstanding balances, including commitments, with:

(a) A government that has control, joint control or significant influence over the reporting entity; and

(b) Another entity that is a related party because the same government has control, joint control or significant influence over both the reporting entity and the other entity.

26. If a reporting entity applies the exemption in paragraph 25, it shall disclose the following about the transactions and related outstanding balances referred to in paragraph 25:

(a) The name of the government and the nature of its relationship with the reporting entity (i.e., control, joint control or significant influence);

(b) The following information in sufficient detail to enable users of the entity's financial statements to understand the effect of related party transactions on its financial statements:

(i) The nature and amount of each individually significant transaction; and

(ii) For other transactions that are collectively, but not individually, significant, a qualitative or quantitative indication of their extent. Types of transactions include those listed in paragraph 21.

OBSERVATION: The exemption discussed immediately above is said to have been introduced largely at the request of the Chinese government. More generally, this is a difficult area to regulate (and doubtless to audit). But it is important to expose implications of related party relationships which "may affect assessments of [entity] operations by users of financial statements, including assessments of the risks and opportunities facing the entity" (par. 8).

CHAPTER 31
REVENUE

CONTENTS

OVERVIEW

The primary issue in accounting for revenue is determining when to recognize revenue. Revenue is recognized when it is "probable" that future economic benefits will flow to the enterprise and these benefits can be measured reliably. IASB GAAP for this area are contained in IAS 18, "Revenue." This standard identifies the circumstances in which the criteria will be met and, therefore, revenue will be recognized. It also provides practical guidance on the application of these criteria. IFRIC 13, "Customer Loyalty Programmes," is also relevant.

BACKGROUND

The profit or earnings figure reported by an enterprise for an accounting period is in essence the result of a two-stage process. Stage 1 is to define and delineate the revenues to be recognized in the period. Stage 2 is to define and delineate the corresponding expenses, the net of the two figures being the profit. Many international standards are directly or indirectly about aspects of expense determination. But revenue is logically the first issue to consider, as the timing of revenue recognition significantly affects the timing of expense recognition—sales and cost of sales being an obvious and significant example.

The general principles outlined above are included in the IASB Framework (see Chapter 2). Key distinctions are discussed in detail below. IASB GAAP regarding revenues are contained in IAS 18, "Revenue," effective from January 1, 1995. This standard replaced an earlier standard called "Revenue Recognition," also numbered 18, which had been effective since 1982.

Perhaps rather surprisingly, neither U.S. nor U.K. GAAP contain a standard dealing with general principles, as opposed to specific applications, of revenue and its recognition. There are no significant differences of principle between these jurisdictions. It should not necessarily be assumed, however, that the typical interpretation of "probable" is the same across the various jurisdictions.

In the United States, revenue recognition guidance has been scattered throughout the various statements, directed to particular industries. In mid-2000, however, the staff of the SEC issued Staff Accounting Bulletin (SAB) 101, spelling out comprehensive, overall guidance on revenue recognition. The SAB had wide impact, particularly in the high-tech industry, and many companies were forced to restate their earnings as a result of that new guidance. In essence, SAB 101 (i.e., ASC 605) says that revenue is to be recorded when it is realized (or realizable) and earned, i.e., when the following criteria are met:

1. Persuasive evidence of an arrangement (with the customer) exists,
2. Delivery has occurred or services have been rendered,
3. The seller's price to the buyer is fixed or determinable, and
4. Collectability is reasonable assured.

The most interesting implementation questions posed by the new guidance arose where companies were offering a combination of services and had been recognizing up-front a large share of the total revenue. The new guidance says that revenue can only be recognized as the earning process is complete and as the seller discharges its obligations to the buyer.

In general principle, the guidance from the SEC Staff is consistent with the standards set forth in IAS 18, but case-by-case differences could be significant.

SCOPE AND DEFINITIONS

IAS 18 should be applied in accounting for revenue arising from the following transactions and events:

1. The sale of goods,
2. The rendering of services, or
3. The use by others of entity assets yielding interest, royalties, and dividends.

Revenue is formally defined in paragraph 7 as follows:

> *Revenue* is the gross inflow of economic benefits during the period arising in the course of the ordinary activities of an entity when those inflows result in increases in equity, other than increases relating to contributions from equity participants.

There are some subtleties in this definition, which require careful consideration. Under IAS definitions, revenue is a subset of income. Income is defined in "The Conceptual Framework for Financial Reporting" (see Chapter 2) as increases in economic benefits during the accounting period in the form of inflows or enhancements of assets or decreases of liabilities that result in increases in equity, other than those relating to contributions from equity participants. Income encompasses both revenue and gains. Revenue has been defined above.

Gains (Framework, par. 75) represent "other items that meet the definition of income and may, or may not, arise in the course of the ordinary activities of an enterprise."

This is not entirely clear either. The Framework says that revenue is "referred to by a variety of different names including sales, fees, interest, dividends, royalties and rent." Gains "include, for example, those arising on the disposal of non-current assets." Unrealized gains that are recognized in the income statement are part of income but are not revenue.

→ **PRACTICE POINTER:** The notion of "ordinary activities" is the central determinant of the distinction between revenue and gains. For example, sales of real estate would lead to revenue for a property development company, but to gains for an industrial or commercial enterprise.

The position of a disposal of a depreciating non-current asset leading to a surplus on disposal over the depreciated carrying value is not theoretically so clear. In our view this is logically seen as a correction to earlier depreciation estimates. Because these earlier depreciation charges are certainly operating expenses, then the surplus on disposal is logically an operating item too and therefore within the ordinary activities (but perhaps as negative expense not as revenue).

Revenue includes only the gross inflows of economic benefits received and receivable by the entity on its own account. Amounts collected on behalf of third parties such as sales taxes, goods and services taxes, and value-added taxes are not economic benefits that flow to the entity and do not result in increases in equity. Therefore, they are excluded from revenue. Under the same argument, the revenue of an agent is the commission earned, not the gross amount collected on behalf of the principal.

The standard comments on each of the three types of "transactions and events" are included within its scope. The sale of goods embraces goods produced by the entity for the purpose of sale and goods purchased for resale, such as merchandise purchased by a retailer or land and other property held for resale. The rendering of services typically involves the performance by the entity of a contractually agreed task over an agreed period of time. The services may be rendered within a single period or over more than one period. Some contracts for the rendering of services are directly related to construction contracts, for example, those for the services of project managers and architects. Revenue arising from these contracts is dealt with under IAS 11, "Construction Contracts" (see Chapter 12), not under IAS 18.

The use by others of entity assets gives rise to revenue in the form of (par. 5):

1. Interest—charges for the use of cash or cash equivalents or amounts due to the entity;

2. Royalties—charges for the use of long-term assets of the entity, for example, patents, trademarks, copyrights, and computer software; and

3. Dividends—distributions of profits to holders of equity investments in proportion to their holdings of a particular class of capital.

It should be noted that this set of three "forms" of revenue is exhaustive as far as the application of IAS 18 to the use by others of enterprises' assets is concerned.

Apart from the implications for the scope and coverage of IAS 18 arising from the above discussion, IAS 18 gives a number of explicit exclusions in paragraph 6. IAS 18 does not deal with revenue arising from:

1. Lease agreements (see IAS 17, "Leases," Chapter 26);

2. Dividends arising from investments that are accounted for under the equity method (see IAS 28, "Accounting for Investments in Associates," discussed in Chapter 15);

3. Insurance contracts of insurance entities (see IFRS 4, "Insurance Contracts," Chapter 35);

4. Changes in the fair value of financial assets and financial liabilities or their disposal (see IFRS 9 "Financial Instruments," Chapter 17);

5. Changes in the value of other current assets;

6. Initial recognition of, or from fair value changes in, biological assets related to agricultural activity (see IAS 41, "Agriculture," Chapter 34);

7. Initial recognition of agricultural produce (see IAS 41, "Agriculture," Chapter 34); and

8. The extraction of mineral ores (see IFRS 6, "Exploration for and Evaluation of Mineral Resources," Chapter 36).

The only other definition given by IAS 18 is the familiar concept of fair value. It is repeated here for completeness. See Chapter 3 regarding an eventual change in this definition.

Fair value is the amount for which an asset could be exchanged, or a liability settled, between knowledgeable, willing parties in an arm's-length transaction.

In addition to the above, IFRIC 15, "Agreements for the Construction of Real Estate," specifies that in certain circumstances IAS 18 may need to be applied to such agreements. See "Agreements for the Construction of Real Estate" in Chapter 12.

MEASUREMENT OF REVENUE

The above definition of fair value leads to what is ostensibly a simple rule, namely, that revenue should be measured at the fair value of the consideration received or receivable, taking into account the amount of any trade discounts and volume rebates allowed by the entity. When the inflow of cash or cash equivalents is deferred, the fair value of the consideration may be significantly less than the nominal amount of cash received or receivable. When the arrangement effectively constitutes a financing transaction, the fair value of the consideration is determined by discounting all future receipts using an imputed rate of interest. The imputed rate of interest is the more clearly determinable of either:

1. The prevailing rate for a similar instrument of an issuer with a similar credit rating, or

2. A rate of interest that discounts the nominal amount of the instrument to the current cash sales price of the goods or services.

Remember that, as always, the concept of materiality applies when considering whether discounting is necessary.

Sometimes goods or services are exchanged, or swapped, without a cash movement. Two possible situations can arise. If the exchange or swap is for goods or services that are "of a similar nature and value," then the exchange is not regarded as a transaction that generates revenue. This is often the case with commodities like oil or milk where suppliers exchange or swap inventories in various locations to fulfill demand on a timely basis in a particular location. However, when goods are sold or services are rendered in exchange for dissimilar goods or services, the exchange is regarded as a transaction that generates revenue. The revenue is measured at the fair value of the goods or services received, adjusted by the amount of any cash or cash equivalents transferred. Note carefully that it is the fair value of what is received that has to be considered, not the fair value of what was rendered. Note also that although fair value is by definition the result that would arise in an arm's-length transaction, the requirement to measure revenue at fair value applies to both arm's-length and non-arm's-length transactions. Again, it is the fair value of goods or services received that must be used.

IFRIC 18, "Transfers of Assets from Customers," now applies. This deals with the situation where an entity receives from its customers physical assets necessary to enable the entity to carry out its services to the customer. The provision of utility services, or outsourcing contracts, are situations likely to give rise to this.

Essentially, the entity concerned has firstly to decide whether the Framework definition of an asset is met, in particular as regards control. If it is, then the asset is recorded, typically as Property, Plant and Equipment (see Chapter 28). This would then satisfy the "dissimilar goods or services" requirement discussed above, and revenue would be recorded in accordance, as appropriate, with IAS 18.

SIC-31, "Revenue—Barter Transactions Involving Advertising Services," effective from December 31, 2001, provides detailed guidance to a very specific application of the general principles of IAS 18. It is apparently not uncommon in the advertising industry for two organizations to swap advertising services to and for each other, as a barter transaction, with or without some cash or other consideration also passing. The problem is that, in the general case, the fair value of the advertising *received* by an entity cannot be measured by that entity. SIC-31 requires that the revenue should be measured by the fair value of the advertising services *given* by the entity, provided specified conditions, which make that fair value reasonably objective, are met.

Note that SIC-31 only applies to an exchange of *dissimilar* advertising services. As already discussed, an exchange of similar services cannot generate revenue under IAS 18 anyway.

Care must be used in defining "a transaction" for the purpose of revenue measurement. The principle of substance over form is paramount. For example, when the selling price of a product includes an identifiable amount for subsequent servicing, or for updating, as is common with software packages, that amount is deferred and recognized as revenue over the period during which the service is performed. Conversely, the recognition criteria are applied to two or more transactions together when they are linked in such a way that the commercial effect cannot be understood without reference to the series of transactions as a whole. For example, an entity may sell goods and, at the same time, enter into a separate binding agreement to repurchase the goods at a later date. In this latter situation the substance of the two transactions is that there is, in effect, no sale at all and, therefore, no revenue.

SALE OF GOODS

IAS 18 requires that all of five conditions be satisfied before revenue from the sale of goods is recognized. These are (par. 14):

1. The entity has transferred to the buyer the significant risks and rewards of ownership of the goods.

2. The entity retains neither continuing managerial involvement to the degree usually associated with ownership, nor effective control over the goods sold.

3. The amount of revenue can be measured reliably.

4. It is probable that the economic benefits associated with the transaction will flow to the entity.

5. The costs incurred or to be incurred in respect of the transaction can be measured reliably.

Several of these criteria require further comment. For typical retail sales, the transfer of the significant risks and rewards occurs on the transfer of possession or of legal title to the buyer. However, an entity may retain a significant risk of ownership in a number of ways. Examples of situations in which the entity may retain the significant risks and rewards of ownership are:

- When the entity retains an obligation for unsatisfactory performance not covered by normal warranty provisions;

- When the receipt of the revenue from a particular sale is contingent on the derivation of revenue by the buyer from its sale of the goods;

- When the goods are shipped subject to installation and the installation is a significant part of the contract, which has not yet been completed by the enterprise; or

- When the buyer has the right to rescind the purchase for a reason specified in the sales contract and the entity is uncertain about the probability of return.

Again, the risks retained must be significant, that is, material, for the above to apply.

Requirement 2 deals with what is theoretically a question of fact in each particular situation. For example, if the seller transfers title to a buyer but retains control over that buyer's own marketing and pricing policies, then the reality of the transaction might be that the buyer is in substance acting as agent for the seller.

Requirements 3 and 5 are straightforward in principle, as profit cannot be adequately quantified without reliable measurement of revenue and expense. Reliable is, of course, a relative term, not an absolute. Requirement 4 may give problems in the case, for example, of exchange control restrictions. It may be uncertain that a foreign governmental authority will grant permission to remit the consideration from a sale in a foreign country. When the permission is granted, the uncertainty is removed and revenue is recognized. However, when an uncertainty arises about the collectability of an amount already included in revenue, the uncollectable amount or the amount in respect of which recovery has ceased to be probable is recognized as an expense rather than as a reduction of the amount of revenue originally recognized.

RENDERING OF SERVICES

There are two situations to be considered under rendering of services: when the outcome of the service transaction can be measured "reliably" and when it cannot. During the early stages of a transaction, it is often the case that the outcome of the transaction cannot be estimated reliably. Nevertheless, it may be probable that the entity will recover the transaction costs incurred. Therefore, revenue is recognized only to the extent of costs incurred that are expected to be recoverable. As the outcome of the transaction cannot be estimated reliably, no profit is recognized. This is a long-winded way of saying that the costs incurred to date are carried forward as assets. Naturally, if recovery of the transaction costs is not reasonably foreseeable, then the costs to date must be written off as expenses.

The second situation to be considered is where the outcome of the transaction can be measured "reliably." In such cases, the revenue associated with the transaction should be recognized by reference to the stage of completion of the transaction at the balance sheet date. The outcome of a transaction can be estimated reliably when all the following conditions are satisfied:

1. The amount of revenue can be measured reliably.
2. It is probable that the economic benefits associated with the transaction will flow to the entity.
3. The stage of completion of the transaction at the balance sheet date can be measured reliably.
4. The costs incurred for, and to complete, the transaction and can be measured reliably.

This is the percentage-of-completion method, which is required and discussed in detail in relation to construction contracts (see Chapter 12). IAS 18 explicitly states that the requirements of IAS 11, "Construction Contracts," are generally applicable to the recognition of revenue and the associated expenses for a transaction involving the rendering of services.

The above criteria are likely to be met provided that the entity has an effective internal budgeting and reporting system and that a clear agreement on terms has been reached with the customer. In practice, where a large number of regular acts of service are to be performed, revenue can be recognized on a simple time basis.

An interestingly problematic issue arises with customer loyalty programs, popular with, for example, airlines. A "sale" now involves immediate inflows, but also creates an expected future outflow (of uncertain amount, timing, and rate of take-up). Common practice is to recognize the full revenue immediately, and also to recognize an expense (and provision) for the expected costs of supplying the loyalty award.

The IASB has recently issued IFRIC 13, "Customer Loyalty Programmes," which is mandatory for annual periods beginning on or after July 1, 2008, earlier application being permitted. IFRIC 13 requires an entity that grants loyalty award credits (such as points or travel miles) to customers who buy other goods or services to allocate some of the proceeds of the initial sale to the award credits and recognize these proceeds as revenue only when they have fulfilled their obligations. The amount allocated to the award credits should be measured by reference to their fair value; that is, the amount for which the award credits could be sold separately (which will logically be less than the cost of actually supplying the loyalty award, to allow for expected non-take-up).

If the entity supplies the awards itself, it recognizes the amounts allocated to the award credits as revenue when the credits are redeemed and the entity fulfils its obligation to supply the awards. If a third party supplies the awards, the entity needs to assess first whether it is collecting the amount allocated to the award credits on its own behalf or as an agent for a third party. Note also that a correction to the unrecognized revenue may be needed from time to time to take account of expired unused loyalty rights.

OBSERVATION: The requirements of IFRIC 13 are entirely rational, but may seem like the proverbial sledgehammer attacking the nut. In theory, assuming perfect foresight, the change in reported earnings, and obligations, will be zero. There is also the conceptual problem that the expected cost of, for example, free flights is a liability, but deferred revenue is not.

INTEREST, ROYALTIES, AND DIVIDENDS

Two conditions are necessary for revenue arising from the use by others of entity assets leading to interest, royalties, or dividends. These are that (par. 29):

1. It is probable that the economic benefits associated with the transaction will flow to the entity, and

2. The amount of the revenue can be measured reliably.

Revenue should then be recognized on the following bases:

- Interest should be recognized on a time proportion basis using the effective interest method as set out in IAS 39, "Financial Instruments: Recognition and Measurement" (see Chapter 17).
- Royalties should be recognized on an accrual basis in accordance with the substance of the relevant agreement.
- Dividends should be recognized when the shareholder's right to receive payment is established.

It is important to distinguish, in all cases of revenue recognition, between uncertainty of recognition and uncertainty of collection of receivables after recognition. Revenue is recognized only when it is probable that the economic benefits associated with the transaction will flow to the enterprise. However, when an uncertainty arises about the collectability of an amount already included in revenue, the uncollectable amount, or the amount in respect of which recovery has ceased to be probable, is recognized as an expense, rather than as a reduction of the amount of revenue originally recognized.

DISCLOSURE

The disclosure requirements are straightforward and are given below (par. 35). An entity should disclose:

1. The accounting policies adopted for the recognition of revenue, including the methods adopted to determine the stage of completion of transactions involving the rendering of services;

2. The amount of each significant category of revenue recognized during the period including revenue arising from:

    (a) The sale of goods,

    (b) The rendering of services,

    (c) Interest,

    (d) Royalties,

    (e) Dividends; and

3. The amount of revenue arising from exchanges of goods or services included in each significant category of revenue.

ILLUSTRATIONS

IAS 18 contains an appendix, which gives no less than 20 illustrations of the application of the standard to particular types of situations. The appendix is illustrative only, and the examples do not modify or override the principles in the standard itself. Many of the illustrations are simple and/or repetitive of statements within the standard. Readers who study all these examples in the standard should note that the examples generally assume that the amount of revenue can be measured reliably, it is probable that the economic benefits will flow to the enterprise, and the costs incurred or to be incurred can be measured reliably.

We reproduce below two of the more interesting applications given. Both are debatable and the IAS attitude seems less prudent than U.S. GAAP would require.

Layaway Sales under Which the Goods Are Delivered Only When the Buyer Makes the Final Payment in a Series of Installments

Revenue from layaway sales is recognized when the goods are delivered. However, when experience indicates that most such sales are consummated, revenue "may" be recognized when a significant deposit is received, provided the goods are on hand, identified, and ready for delivery to the buyer.

Initiation, Entrance, and Membership Fees

In the case of initiation, entrance, and membership fees, revenue recognition depends on the nature of the services provided. If the fee permits only membership and all other services or products are paid for separately, or if there is a separate annual subscription, the fee is recognized as revenue when no significant uncertainty as to its collectability exists. If the fee entitles the member to services or publications to be provided during the membership period or to purchase goods or services at prices lower than those charged to nonmembers, it is recognized on a basis that reflects the timing, nature, and value of the benefits provided.

EXPECTED FUTURE DEVELOPMENTS

A convergence project is in hand, designed to produce a revised standard acceptable to both the IASB and FASB. An exposure draft was issued in the summer of 2010. This proposes some significant changes, including a requirement that entities may recognize revenue only as they satisfy distinct performance obligations by transferring control of goods or services to customers. This raises both theoretical and practical issues, in relation to the meaning and significance of control in this context. The principles are simple in that an entity recognizes revenue from contracts with customers only when it transfers goods or services to the customer. This revenue is measured at the amount of consideration the entity receives, or expects to receive.

Five steps follow from this.

- The identification of the contract with the customer.
- The identification of the contract's separate performance obligations.
- The determination of the transaction price.
- The allocation of the transaction price to the separate performance obligations.
- The recognition of revenue when the entity satisfies each performance obligation.

As briefly indicated above, changes in reported numbers may well occur if this Exposure Draft replaces the existing Standard. The exposure draft has received considerable criticism, and the IASB (and FASB) seem uncertain as to what the eventual new standard should require. An early final standard is not likely.

CHAPTER 32
SEGMENT REPORTING

CONTENTS

OVERVIEW

The key objective of segment reporting is to assist the user of financial statements in making judgments about the opportunities and risks facing an entity by the disclosure of finer information than that provided in the primary financial statements. The information is finer in that it provides an analysis of the entity's financial performance in the various market areas in which it operates. Market areas may be understood in the sense of product markets (business segments) and geographic markets (geographic segments), and one of the issues in segment reporting is whether these two types of segment should be given equal weight in the analysis. Disclosure of appropriate segment information enables the user of financial statements to observe the entity's performance by market area, for example, in terms of returns on assets employed and on sales and of cash flows. In addition, the entity's performance in the various segments can be examined in light of changes in sales and in assets employed in each segment.

For segment reporting to be truly useful, however, it must be comparable both over time for the same entity and cross-sectionally between entities. The latter is hard to achieve, especially regarding business segments, as this requires the segments themselves to be comparable, that is, similar in composition. Other potential pitfalls in achieving cross-sectional comparability in segment reporting are those relating to accounting methods and particularly the treatments of: (a) costs and assets common to more than one reportable segment; and (b) intersegment sales, with the attendant issue of transfer prices.

IFRS 8, "Operating Segments," issued in November 2006 to replace IAS 14, "Reporting Financial Reporting by Segment," reflects the view that the most relevant information about the components of an entity is that which management uses to make decisions about operating matters. Hence, the IFRS requires identification of operating segments on the same basis as that used for internal reports that are regularly reviewed by the entity's chief operating decision maker in order to assess performance and to allocate resources. While this approach may be expected to facilitate comparability over time, it does not address the issue of cross-sectional comparability. However, it may be that in spite of the efforts to address the latter issue in IAS 14 (see below), it is now regarded as a lost cause, since research appears to show that segment information based on this "management approach" is found more useful by analysts than segment information prepared in conformity with the accounting policies used for the consolidated financial statements. In part, this is because the management commentaries (such as the "Management Discussion and Analysis," or the "Operating and Financial Review") published in the Annual Report generally address the operating segments of the entity from the perspective of the management approach rather than that of the consolidated financial statements. Moreover, information based on this approach is likely to be useful in that it reflects the approach considered useful by management as a basis for assessing performance and allocating resources. Among other differences from IAS 14, IFRS 8 makes no distinction between primary and secondary segments.

IAS 14, "Reporting Financial Information by Segment," as revised in 1997, addressed the issue of cross-sectional comparability by providing sets of criteria to be used in arriving at the composition of a segment for financial reporting purposes. IAS 14 emphasized "similarity of risks and returns" as the overarching criterion in identifying the segments of an entity for financial reporting purposes. However, the structure of the entity's organization and internal financial reporting system were accepted as normally providing an acceptable basis for segment identification.

BACKGROUND

FAS-14, "Financial Reporting for Segments of a Business Enterprise," was issued in 1976 and was the first financial reporting standard (national or international) on this subject. Five years later, IAS 14, "Reporting Financial Information by Segment," was issued. During the 1990s, there was increasing recognition of the importance of segment information in analyzing entity performance. In 1997, the Financial Accounting Standards Board (FASB) responded to the criticism that FAS-14 did not require sufficient disclosure by replacing it with FAS-131 (ASC 280). In 1996, the IASB made a major revision to IAS 14 (and shortened its name to "Segment Reporting"). The revised IAS 14 was finally approved in July 1997. There was substantial cooperation between the IASB, the FASB, and the Canadian Institute of Chartered Accountants (CICA) in deciding the content of the new standards. Consequently, there is much similarity between ASC 280 and the revised IAS 14. However, there were also significant differences that are, in substance, the same as those between IAS 14 and IFRS 8 (issued in November 2006 as part of the program of convergence between IFRSs and U.S. GAAP) that are summarized below.

The main differences between IAS 14 and IFRS 8 are as follows:

1. *Identification of segments.* As the requirements of IFRS 8 are based on the information about the components of the entity that management uses to make operating decisions, the IFRS requires identification of operating segments on the basis of internal reports that are regularly reviewed by the entity's chief operating decision maker in order to assess performance and allocate resources to those segments. IAS 14 required the identification of two sets of segments: one set based on related products and services and the other set based on geographical areas, of which one set was regarded as the "primary" segment and the other as the "secondary" segment. In addition, where in a vertically integrated business structure a component of an entity sells exclusively or primarily to other operating segments of that entity, IFRS 8 considers that component as a (reportable) operating segment *if the management of the entity treats it as such.* Segments that are reportable as such under IAS 14, include only those that earn a majority of their revenue from sales to *external* customers.

2. *Measurement of segment information.* IFRS 8 requires the amount reported for an operating segment item to be the same as the measure reported to the chief operating decision maker for the purpose of assessing performance and allocating resources. IAS 14 required segment information to be prepared in conformity with the accounting policies applied in preparing the entity's (consolidated) financial statements. In addition, IAS 14 provided definitions of segment revenue, segment expense, segment result, segment assets, and segment liabilities. IFRS 8 does not provide such definitions but requires explanations of how segment profit or loss, segment assets, and segment liabilities are measured for each reportable segment.

The differences between IFRS 8 and U.S. GAAP (ASC 280) are intentionally minimal. There are differences in wording that reflect the need for IFRS 8 to be terminologically consistent with other IASB standards. In addition, IFRS 8 includes a requirement to disclose measures of segment liabilities if such amounts are regularly provided to the chief operating decision maker, although this is not a requirement of FAS-131. However, there were some disagreements among Board members regarding the fact that IFRS 8, in following FAS-131, neither provides definitions of segment profit or loss nor requires consistent attribution of assets and profit or loss to segments, and that it drops the definitions of segment revenue, expense, result, assets, and liabilities that are given in IAS 14. Some Board members believe that these definitions should have been retained in the new IFRS.

A minor amendment was made to IFRS 8 in April 2009, the effect of which is that the total assets of a reportable segment need be reported (together with the total liabilities) only if this information is "regularly reported to the chief operating decision maker."

CORE PRINCIPLE OF "OPERATING SEGMENTS"

IFRS 8, "Operating Segments," starts with a statement of the "core principle" of the standard, which is that an entity shall disclose information to enable users of its financial statements to evaluate the nature and financial effects of the business activities in which it engages and the economic environments in which it operates (IFRS 8, par. 1). IAS 14 contains no similar statement, but its core principle is the same.

SCOPE

IFRS 8 (like IAS 14) is applicable to the separate financial statements of an entity and the consolidated financial statements of a group with a parent that meets the following conditions:

- Its debt or equity instruments are traded in a public market, either on a stock exchange (domestic or foreign) or in an over-the-counter market, including local and regional markets; or
- It files, or is in the process of filing, its financial statements with a securities commission or other regulatory organization for the purpose of issuing any class of financial instruments in a public market.

If an entity that is not required to apply IFRS 8 (or IAS 14 prior to the effective date of IFRS 8) chooses to disclose information about the components of its business that are not in compliance with the IASB standard, then the information must *not* be described as segment information, as that would be misleading.

Segment information is also not required in parent financial statements when consolidated financial statements are published. However, subsidiaries with their own publicly traded securities should disclose their own segment information (IFRS 8, pars. 2–4, IAS 14, pars. 1–7).

OPERATING AND REPORTABLE SEGMENTS

According to IFRS 8, an *operating segment* is a component of an entity:

- That engages in business activities from which it may earn revenues and incur expenses, including revenues and expenses relating to transactions with other components of the same entity;
- Whose operating results are regularly reviewed by the entity's chief operating decision maker to make decisions about performance assessment and resource allocation; and
- For which discrete financial information is available.

An entity may produce reports in which its business activities are presented in more than one way. In such circumstances, operating segments may be identified by reference to criteria such as:

- The nature of the business activities of each component.

- The existence of managers responsible for them (generally, an operating segment has a segment manager who is directly accountable to the chief operating decision maker).
- Information presented to the board of directors.

Note: The terms "chief operating decision maker" and "segment manager" identify functions rather than individual managers with specific titles.

The characteristics described above may apply to more than one overlapping set of components for which managers are held responsible (as in a so-called *matrix form* of organization). According to IFRS 8, the core principle should be used to determine which set of components constitutes the operating segments.

A *reportable segment* is one that has been identified, and that, subject to the aggregation criteria stated below, meets the size criteria (quantitative thresholds) set out below (IFRS 8, pars. 5–11).

Aggregation Criteria and Quantitative Thresholds

Two or more operating segments may be aggregated into a single operating segment if:

1. Such aggregation is consistent with the core principle of IFRS 8.

2. The segments have similar economic characteristics (e.g., their long-term average gross margins are similar).

3. They are similar in terms of *all* of the following five aggregation criteria:

    (a) Nature of products and services

    (b) Nature of production process

    (c) Type or class of customer

    (d) Methods of distribution or of service provision

    (e) Nature of regulatory environment, where applicable (e.g., in banking, insurance, or public utilities) (IFRS 8, par. 12).

The *quantitative thresholds* for a reportable segment are that it must meet *one* of the following 10%-size criteria:

1. Its reported revenue, including intersegment sales and transfers, constitutes 10% or more of the combined revenue (intersegment and external) of all operating segments.

2. The absolute amount of its profit or loss is 10% or more of the greater (in absolute amount) of the combined reported profit (or, respectively, loss) of all the operating segments that did not report a loss (or, respectively, a profit).

3. Its assets are 10% or more of the combined assets of all operating segments.

Operating segments that do not meet any of the above criteria *may be classed as reportable* and hence separately disclosed *if management believes that such information would be useful* to financial statement users.

Operating segments that do not meet any of the quantitative thresholds listed above may be combined with others that also do not meet them *only if* they have similar economic characteristics and share at least three of the five *aggregation criteria* listed above.

If the total external revenue reported by the operating segments first identified as such constitutes less than 75% of its total revenue, an entity is required to identify additional operating segments (that do not meet any of the three size criteria above) as reportable until its operating segments include at least 75% of its revenue.

If management considers that an operating segment identified as reportable in the immediately preceding period, but that no longer meets the size criteria, is of continuing significance, information about that segment should continue to be reported separately. Similarly, if an operating segment is identified as reportable in the current period but failed to satisfy the size criteria in a prior period, segment data for the prior period is required to be restated to reflect that segment as being separately reportable, unless the information is no longer available and the cost of its reconstitution would be excessive.

Notwithstanding the above, if the total number of operating segments that are identified as reportable in a given period is greater than 10, the reporting entity must consider whether this number exceeds a practical limit in terms of reporting usefulness (bearing in mind the core principle).

Information about other business activities and operating segments not identified as reportable should be combined and disclosed in an "all other segments" category separately from other reconciling items in the reconciliations required, as described in the "Reconciliations" section below, together with the sources of the revenues included in that category (IFRS 8, pars. 13–19).

DIAGRAM FOR IDENTIFYING REPORTABLE SEGMENTS

The IASB's Guidance on Implementing IFRS 8, while not part of the standard, provides a useful diagram that summarizes the above as follows:

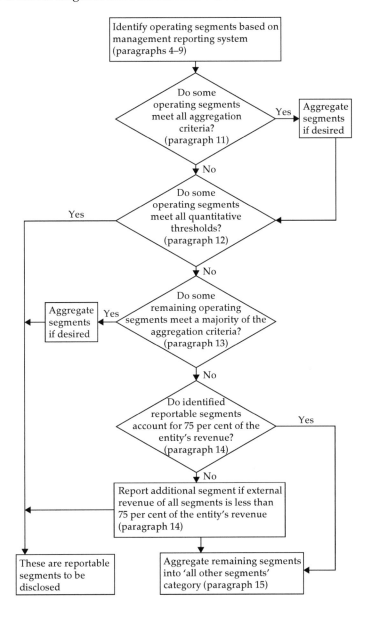

DISCLOSURES FOR REPORTABLE SEGMENTS

The section on segment disclosures in IFRS 8 begins with a repetition of the core principle cited above and continues by stating that, to give effect to this principle, an entity is required to disclose, for each period for which an income statement is presented, the following types of information:

- General information.
- Information about reported segment profit and loss, or assets and liabilities, and the basis of measurement used.
- Reconciliations of the totals of segment revenues, reported segment profit and loss, assets and liabilities, and other material segment amounts to corresponding entity-wide amounts in the entity's financial statements (IFRS 8, pars. 20–21).

General Information

General information includes the following:

1. Factors used to identify reportable segments, including:
   (a) The basis of organization, such as whether the entity is organized on the basis of
      (i) Products and services (i.e., business segments in IAS 14 parlance)
      (ii) Geographical areas (i.e., geographical segments in IAS 14 parlance)
      (iii) Regulatory environments
      (iv) A combination of such factors
   (b) Whether any operating segments have been aggregated.
2. Types of products and services from which each reportable segment derives its revenues (IFRS 8, par. 22).

Information about Profit/Loss and Assets/Liabilities

For each reportable segment, an entity is required to disclose a measure of each of the following:

- Segment profit and loss.
- If regularly provided to the chief operating decision maker, segment total assets and liabilities.

OBSERVATION: In considering the case of liabilities, it was noted that they are typically incurred centrally rather than at segment level. Moreover, there was a desire to avoid any arbitrary allocations of liabilities to segments.

The following specified amounts are also to be disclosed for each reportable segment, if they are included in the measure of segment profit or loss reviewed by the chief operating decision maker; or, even if they are not included in the measure of segment profit and loss, they are otherwise regularly reviewed by the chief operating decision maker:

- Revenues from external customers.
- Revenues from transactions with other operating segments of the entity.
- Interest revenue and/or expense.
- Depreciation and amortization.
- Material non-cash items other than depreciation and amortization.
- Material items of income and expense disclosed in accordance with IAS 1, "Presentation of Financial Statements," paragraph 86 (see Chapter 4).
- The entity's interest in the profit or loss of associates and joint ventures accounted for by the equity method.
- The amount of investment in associates and joint ventures accounted for by the equity method.
- The amounts of additions to non-current assets other than financial instruments, deferred tax assets, and post-employment benefit assets, as per IAS 19, "Employee Benefits," paragraphs 54–58 (see Chapter 14), and rights arising under insurance contracts.
- Income tax expense or income.

Interest revenue and expense are to be reported gross (i.e., not netted off) for each reportable segment, unless:

- A majority of the segment's revenues is from interest.
- The chief operating decision maker relies primarily on the *net* interest revenue in assessing the performance of the segment and making decisions about resources to be allocated to it.

When these conditions are satisfied, the net interest figure may be reported, accompanied by a statement that it is a net figure (IFRS 8, pars. 23–24).

Measurement

The amount of each segment item reported is to be *the measure reported to the chief operating decision maker* for the purpose of assessing the performance of the segment and making decisions about resources to be allocated to it. Hence, adjustments and eliminations made in preparing consolidated financial statements and allocations of revenues, expenses, gains, and losses are to be taken into account in arriving at the above amounts *only if they are taken into account in arriving at the measures of segment profit or loss that are used by the chief operating decision maker.* With regard to assets and liabilities, only those that are included in the measures of segment assets and liabilities used by the chief operating decision maker are to be reported. If amounts are allocated to reported segment profit or loss, or assets and liabilities, this must be done on a reasonable basis.

OBSERVATION: The notion of a "reasonable basis" for allocations is discussed in the IASB's Basis for Conclusions on IFRS 8, which is not part of the standard. The discussion, in fact, forms part of the FASB's Basis for Conclusions on FAS-131, which is included in the IASB's document. (The text of IFRS 8 has not been amended to reflect the fact that FAS-131 has now been superseded by ASC 280.) The thrust of the discussion is that items, such as expenses that are incurred at the consolidated level, may be allocated to segments in several different ways each of which could be considered reasonable while resulting in significantly different measures of segment profit or loss. In general, the Basis for Conclusions is wary of "arbitrary allocations" made for external reporting purposes. On the other hand, if allocations are made in arriving at measures used for management purposes, they presumably have some rationale. However, some allocations would clearly lack a reasonable basis, such as allocating part of pension expense to a segment that had no employees belonging to the pension plan.

If more than one measure of an operating segment's profit or loss, or assets or liabilities, is used by the chief operating decision maker, the measures to be reported, according to IFRS 8, are those that are believed by management to be determined in accordance with the measurement principles that are *most consistent with those used in measuring the corresponding amounts in the entity's financial statements.*

OBSERVATION: It is not clear why IFRS 8 uses the above criterion for making the choice. However, it has the pragmatic advantage of minimizing the amount of reconciliations needed (see below).

Explanations are required for the measurements of segment profit or loss, or segment assets and liabilities, including at least the following:

- The basis of accounting for any transactions between reportable segments.

- The nature of any differences between the measurements of the reportable segments' profits or losses and the entity's profit or loss *before income tax expense (or income) and discontinued operations,* and between the reportable segments' assets and liabilities and the entity's assets and liabilities, if these are not apparent from the reconciliations (see below), such as accounting policies and policies for the allocation of centrally incurred costs or jointly used assets or liabilities, and if such an explanation is necessary in order to understand the reported segment information.

- The nature of any changes from prior periods in the measurement methods used to determine reported segment profit or loss and the effect, if any, of these changes on the related measures.

- The nature and effect of any "asymmetrical" allocations to reportable segments, such as the allocation of depreciation expense without allocating the related depreciable assets (or vice versa) (IFRS 8, pars. 25–27).

Reconciliations

The accounting policies used in segment reporting may differ from those applied in the entity's financial statements. Reconciliations are required of the segment reporting information to the amounts in the entity's financial statements, as indicated below:

- The total amount of the reportable segments' revenues to the entity's revenue.

- The total of the reportable segments' measures of profit or loss to the entity's profit or loss *before tax expense (or tax income) and discontinued operations*; however, if tax expense (or tax income) is allocated to reportable segments, the entity *may* reconcile the total of its reportable segments' measures of profit or loss to its profit or loss after those items.

- The total of the reportable segments' assets to the entity's total assets.

- If segment liabilities are reported, the total of the reportable segments' liabilities to the entity's total liabilities.

- The total of the reportable segments' amounts for every other material item of information disclosed to the corresponding amount for the entity.

All material reconciling items (including items such as the amount of each material adjustment needed to reconcile the total of the reportable segments' measure of profit or loss to the entity's profit or loss that arises because of the use of different accounting policies) are required to be separately identified and described (IFRS 8, par. 28).

Restatements of Previously Reported Information

If an entity changes its internal organization structure in a way that alters the composition of its reportable segments:

- It should restate the corresponding information for earlier periods, including interim periods, unless the information is not available and would be too costly to develop.

- If this restatement is not made, the entity is required to disclose in the year in which the change occurs segment information for the current period on both the old and new bases of segmentation, unless the information on the old basis is not available and would be too costly to develop.

ENTITY-WIDE DISCLOSURES

The requirements set out below for information about products and services, geographical areas, and major customers apply to all entities within the scope of IFRS 8, *but only if this information is not otherwise provided as part of the reportable segment information described above.* Some entities may have only one reportable segment. Others may have business activities that are not organized on the basis of related products and services, or geographical areas of operations and their reportable segments may report revenues from a broad range of essentially different products and services, or more than one reportable segment may provide overlapping ranges of products and services. Likewise, reportable segments may hold assets, and report revenues from customers, in different geographical areas, or reportable segments may have overlapping geographical areas.

Information about Products, Services, and Geographical Areas

The following information is required, unless it is not available and would be too costly to produce, in which case this fact must be disclosed:

- Revenues from external customers for each product and service, or each group of similar products and services, the amounts reported being based on the financial information used to produce the entity's financial statements.

- Revenues from external customers attributed to

    — The entity's country of domicile

    — All foreign countries from which the entity derives revenues, in total and separately, for any individual country from which the amount is material, together with the basis for attributing revenues from external customers to individual countries.

- Non-current assets, excluding financial instruments, deferred tax assets, post-employment benefit assets, and rights arising under insurance contracts, that are located in

    — The entity's country of domicile, and

    — All foreign countries in which the entity holds assets, in total and separately, for any individual country in which the amount of such assets is material.

An entity may additionally provide subtotals of geographical information relative to groups of countries (IFRS 8, pars. 32–33).

Information about Major Customers

An entity is required to provide information about the extent of its reliance on major customers, namely customers for which revenues from transactions from that single customer amount to 10% or more of the entity's total revenues (a group of entities known to be under common control are considered to be a single customer). For each such customer, the total revenues from that customer and the identity of the segment or segments reporting those revenues are to be disclosed, but not the identity of the customer or the amount of revenues from the customer that each segment reports. A government (e.g., national, state, or provincial) and entities known to be under the control of that government are considered to be a single customer (IFRS 8, par. 34).

EFFECTIVE DATE

The effective date for IFRS 8, as amended in April 2009, is for annual periods beginning on or after January 1, 2010.

CHAPTER 33
SHARE-BASED PAYMENTS

CONTENTS

OVERVIEW

Although the most common way in which an entity pays for the goods and services that it receives is by the transfer of cash, this is by no means the only possibility. Barter (i.e., the direct exchange of goods and services), is a second one, and the granting of shares, or of rights or options to obtain shares on favorable terms, is a third. It is the treatment of this last possibility that is at issue here. It is argued that such grants represent, or will lead to, an outflow of resources, and therefore an expense may arise. IFRS 2, "Share-Based Payment," applies to virtually all share-based payments—that is, to transactions in which equity instruments of the entity represent part of the consideration; the main exclusion being business combinations. It requires an entity to recognize share-based payment transactions in its financial statements, including transactions with employees or other parties to be settled in cash, other assets, or equity instruments of the entity. For equity-settled share-based payment transactions, the IFRS requires an entity to measure the goods or services received and the corresponding increase in equity directly, at the fair value of the goods or services received, unless that fair value cannot be estimated reliably. If the entity cannot estimate reliably the fair value of the goods or services received, the entity is required to measure their value and the corresponding increase in equity indirectly, by reference to the fair value of the equity instruments granted.

It follows logically, then, that once the goods and services received have been recognized, they have to be dealt with in accordance with normal accounting principles. If they meet the definition of assets (see Chapter 2), they should be treated as assets, current or non-current, as appropriate. If not, they must be recognized as expenses, spread over future periods if the service is to be rendered over future periods, but otherwise immediately.

The wide scope of IFRS 2 should be noted. It includes share-based payments to employees, previously referred to in IAS 19, "Employee Benefits" (see Chapter 14) but is not limited to them. IFRS 2 is a requirement for annual periods beginning on or after January 1, 2005. IFRIC 8, "Scope of IFRS 2," and IFRIC 11, "Group and Treasury Share Transactions," are also relevant. Amendments relating to vesting conditions and cancellations were issued in January 2008, effective from January 1, 2009, and a minor amendment also was made by the recently revised IFRS 3, "Business Combinations" (see Chapter 8), effective from July 1, 2009. Earlier application is permitted in both cases.

BACKGROUND

The genesis of IFRS 2 has been lengthy and difficult. Its origins lie in a rapidly increasing use of the issue of share options to employees, especially but not uniquely to directors, in the United States and elsewhere. At the time of the creation of such options, there is typically no transfer of cash or other resource. If the option is eventually exercised gratis, it is easy to argue that no resources have ever flowed into or out of the entity and therefore that no expense needs to be recognized at any time. However, this argument is false in principle: the employee is accepting the options as part of a total remuneration package in return for which the employee grants labor resources to the entity. The total cost of these labor services is a proper expense of the entity over the period of those services.

Regulators have wrestled with this issue over a considerable period. The attempt to produce a GAAP requirement consistent with this logic in the United States, in FAS-123, "Accounting for Stock-Based Compensation" (i.e., ASC 718, "Compensation—Stock Compensation"), was met with a storm of political criticism, resulting, in effect, in an optional standard, although, at minimum, footnote disclosure of the expense effect is required. IAS 19 did not specify any recognition or measurement requirements for employee equity compensation benefits, nor did it require disclosure of the fair value of employee share options. This was said to be "in view of the lack of international consensus." The IASB has now summoned the courage, despite continuing threats of non-cooperation from some financial statement producers, to tackle the whole issue head-on. It is likely that other major regulators, including the FASB in the United States, will follow suit. In addition, the IASB has recognized that a consistent treatment of share-based payments is required, whether or not they relate to employees. IFRS 2 thus deals with the matter of share (i.e., stock) options to employees but has much more general application.

To argue that recognition and eventual expensing are required is easy. Measurement is a more difficult problem. If an option to acquire shares gratis in three years' time, possibly subject to certain conditions whose outcome is currently uncertain, is granted now, then two questions arise. First, should the evaluation of this agreement be focused on the grant date (now) or the vesting date (three years' time)? Second, on what basis should it be evaluated?

The IFRS is unequivocal in its answers to these questions. First, the transaction arises at grant date, so the grant date is the focus of both recognition and measurement. Second, the evaluation should be on a fair-value basis. When the fair value of the goods or services *received* can be measured reliably, it is this fair value that is used to measure both the goods and services, and the corresponding increase in equity. When this is not the case (and it will typically not be the case in relation to service agreements with employees), the fair value of the equity instruments *granted* is used. The principles of IFRS 2 are straightforward. Practical complications arise in relation to the quantification of fair value and the allocation of expense over future periods.

At the time of writing, U.S. GAAP has no comparable requirements. Developments are to be expected, but not quickly. ASC 718 applies in relation to employee equity options.

SCOPE

As already indicated, IFRS 2 is wide-ranging in its scope and application. The simple general rule is that it applies to all share-based payment transactions. This includes not only to those transactions in which the "payment" is actually *in* shares, but also to those in which the payment is by an amount of cash that is itself determined by the valuation of equity instruments or by a mixture or choice of both "payment" methods (par. 2). It is emphasized (pars. 3A and 4) that it is the substance of the transaction that matters. Thus, for example, the grant of share options to a whole class of shareholders, some of whom are also employees, does not involve IFRS 2.

There are two specific exceptions (pars. 5 and 6). First, an entity shall not apply IFRS 2 to transactions in which the entity acquires goods as part of the net assets acquired in a business combination to which IFRS 3, "Business Combinations," applies, or to the contribution of a business on the formation of a joint venture, or to common control transactions. Hence, equity instruments issued in a business combination in exchange for control of the acquiree are not within the scope of this IFRS. However, equity instruments granted to employees of the acquiree in their capacity as employees (e.g., in return for continued service) are within the scope of IFRS 2. Second, IFRS 2 does not apply to share-based payment transactions in which the entity receives or acquires goods or services under a contract within the scope of paragraphs 8–10 of IAS 32, "Financial Instruments: Presentation," or paragraphs 5–7 of IAS 39, "Financial Instruments: Recognition and Measurement," that is, relating to certain non-financial items.

IFRIC 8, "Scope of IFRS 2," was issued in January 2006. The issue addressed by IFRIC 8 concerns the situation where an entity cannot identify some or all of the goods or services received. The example given is where an entity gives shares to a particular disadvantaged section of the community to enhance its corporate image. Although the economic benefits to be derived cannot be identified, they can logically be presumed to exist. The fair value of these economic benefits cannot be measured (as they cannot be identified), but the fair value of the shares given can be. Under IFRIC 8, IFRS 2 applies, despite the fact that the goods or services received are unidentifiable. It follows from the standard measurement requirements of IFRS 2 (discussed under "Measurement" below) that the entity measures the goods or services presumed to be received as the difference between the fair value of the share-based payment and the fair value of any identifiable goods or services received or to be received. In the example given, this latter element will be zero. The measurement is made at the grant date, but for cash-settled transactions the liability is remeasured at each reporting date until it is settled. Effective January 1, 2010, IFRIC 8 is withdrawn, but these requirements are now inserted into the Standard itself (par. 13A).

DEFINITIONS

The standard gives a large number of definitions, all in Appendix A, which is described as "an integral part of the IFRS." Several of these definitions are presented and explained here, in a sequence intended to make them as logical as possible:

- *Share-based payment arrangement.* An agreement between the entity (or another group entity or any shareholder of any group entity) and another party (including an employee) that entitles the other party to receive:

    (a) cash or other assets of the entity for amounts that are based on the price (or value) of equity instruments (including shares or share options) of the entity or another group entity; or

    (b) equity instruments (including shares or share options) of the entity or another group entity,

    provided the specified vesting conditions, are met.

- *Share-based payment transaction.* A transaction in which the entity:

    (a) receives goods or services from the supplier of those goods or services (including an employee) in a share-based payment arrangement; or

    (b) incurs an obligation to settle the transaction with the supplier in a share-based payment arrangement when another group entity receives those goods or services.

- *Equity-settled share-based payment transaction.* A share-based payment transaction in which the entity:

    (a) receives goods or services as consideration for its own equity instruments (including shares or share options); or

    (b) receives goods or services but has no obligation to settle the transaction with the supplier.

- *Cash-settled share-based payment transactions.* A share-based payment transaction in which the entity acquires goods or services by incurring a liability to transfer cash or other assets to the supplier of those goods or services for amounts that are based on the price (or value) of equity instruments (including shares or share options) of the entity or another group entity.

OBSERVATION: These four definitions are fundamental for defining the scope and recording of transactions under IFRS 2. It is noteworthy that the key event that triggers consideration of whether IFRS 2 applies, at least theoretically, is the acquisition of goods and services. The question is not, Equity instruments have been issued: have goods and services been received as consideration, hence implying an asset or an expense? Rather, the question is, Goods and services have been acquired (or contracted for): have equity instruments been created as consideration, hence implying an increase in recorded equity, together with its double entry (as immediate asset or expense)? This second approach is consistent with the historical origins of the standard in the perceived necessity for expense recognition in relation to employee remuneration.

Several terms used in the above definitions are themselves defined and explained:

- *Equity instrument.* A contract that evidences a residual interest in the assets of an entity after deducting all of its liabilities.

- *Share option.* A contract that gives the holder the right, but not the obligation, to subscribe to the entity's shares at a fixed or determinable price for a specified period of time.

- *Vest.* To become an entitlement. Under a share-based payment arrangement, a counterparty's right to receive cash, other assets, or equity instruments of the entity vests when the counterparty's entitlement is no longer conditional on the satisfaction of any vesting conditions.

- *Vesting conditions.* The conditions that determine whether the entity receives the services that entitle the counterparty to receive cash, other assets or equity instruments of the entity, under a share-based payment arrangement. Vesting conditions are either service conditions or performance conditions. Service conditions require the counterparty to complete a specified period of service. Performance conditions require the counterparty to complete a specified period of service and specified performance targets to be met (such as a specified increase in the entity's profit over a specified period of time). A performance condition might include a market condition.

- *Vesting period.* The period during which all the specified vesting conditions of a share-based payment arrangement are to be satisfied.

Further significant definitions are as follows:

- *Grant date.* The date at which the entity and another party (including an employee) agree to a share-based payment arrangement, being when the entity and the counterparty have a shared understanding of the terms and conditions of the arrangement. At grant date the entity confers on the counterparty the right to cash, other assets, or equity instruments of the entity, provided the specified vesting conditions, if any, are met. If that agreement is subject to an approval process (for example, by shareholders), grant date is the date when that approval is obtained.

- *Intrinsic value.* The difference between the fair value of the shares to which the counterparty has the (conditional or unconditional) right to subscribe or that it has the right to receive, and the price (if any) the counterparty is (or will be) required to pay for those shares. For example, a share option with an exercise price of 15, on a share with a fair value of 20, has an intrinsic value of 5.

- *Market condition.* A condition upon which the exercise price, vesting, or exercisability of an equity instrument depends that is related to the market price of the entity's equity instruments, such as attaining a specified share price or a specified amount of intrinsic value of a share option, or achieving a specified target that is based on the market price of the entity's equity instruments relative to an index of market prices of equity instruments of other entities.

- *Measurement date.* The date at which the fair value of the equity instruments granted is measured for the purposes of the IFRS. For transactions with employees and others providing similar services, the measurement date is the grant date. For transactions with parties other than employees (and those providing similar services), the measurement date is the date the entity obtains the goods or the counterparty renders service.

- *Fair value.* The amount for which an asset could be exchanged, a liability settled, or an equity investment granted could be exchanged, between knowledgeable, willing parties in an arm's-length transaction.

Note that the new IFRS 13, "Fair Value Measurement" (see Chapter 3), does not apply to IFRS 2. An amendment to IFRS 2 (par. 6A), relevant from the date of application of IFRS 13, states that "when applying IFRS 2, an entity measures fair value in accordance with [IFRS 2], not IFRS 13." The above definition from IFRS 2 is not changed by IFRS 13, as par. D1 of that standard confirms by omission.

RECOGNITION

The requirement is straightforward and follows logically from the earlier discussion (pars. 7 and 8). An entity should recognize the goods or services received or acquired in a share-based payment transaction when it obtains the goods or as the services are received. The entity should recognize a corresponding increase in equity if the goods or services were received in an equity-settled share-based payment transaction or recognize a liability if the goods or services were acquired in a cash-settled share-based payment transaction. When the goods or services received or acquired in a share-based payment transaction do not qualify for recognition as assets, they are to be recognized as expenses.

OBSERVATION: It has been stated in recent paragraphs in relation to share-based payment transactions with employees that, first, the equity instruments granted must be valued at their fair value at the grant date, and second, that their recognition occurs gradually over the period of the service. This may all be very well in the simple case where the outcome of the whole transaction is reasonably certain. However, if vesting conditions are involved that may turn out not to be met, then the whole question of measurement, and of expense recognition over time, becomes much more difficult. Evidence as to the likely outcome, and of the eventual cash outflow in the case of cash-settled share-based payment transactions, will accumulate and likely point in different directions as time goes on. Much energy is expended in the standard on clarifying the exact procedures to be followed.

MEASUREMENT

The IFRS sets out measurement principles and specific requirements for three types of share-based payment transactions:

1. Equity-settled share-based payment transactions, in which the entity receives goods or services as consideration for equity instruments of the entity (including shares or share options);

2. Cash-settled share-based payment transactions, in which the entity acquires goods or services by incurring liabilities to the supplier of those goods or services for amounts that are based on the price (or value) of the entity's shares or other equity instruments of the entity; and

3. Transactions in which the entity receives or acquires goods or services and the terms of the arrangement provide either the entity or the supplier of those goods or services with a choice of whether the entity settles the transaction in cash or by issuing equity instruments.

These three types of share-based payment systems must be considered separately.

Equity-Settled Share-Based Payment Transactions

The basic rule is that the entity is required to measure the goods or services received and the corresponding increase in equity directly, at the fair value of the goods or services received, unless that fair value cannot be estimated reliably. If the entity cannot estimate reliably the fair value of the goods or services received, the entity must measure their value and the corresponding increase in equity, indirectly, by reference to the fair value of the equity instruments granted (par. 10).

If the transaction is with a party other than the employees, it can normally be assumed that the transaction is independent and at arm's-length, with a reasonably open market. Accordingly, there is a rebuttable presumption that the fair value of the goods or services received can be estimated reliably. That fair value is measured at the date the entity obtains the goods or the counterparty renders service. In rare cases, if the entity rebuts this presumption because it cannot estimate reliably the fair value of the goods or services received, the entity measures the goods or services received indirectly, by reference to the fair value of the equity instruments granted, measured at the date the entity obtains the goods or the counterparty renders service.

For transactions with the entity's own employees, though, it is likely in the general case to be impossible to obtain a meaningful figure for the fair value of the services rendered by the employees. The agreement between the entity and the employee, who by definition already have a contractual relationship, is neither independent nor open market. Therefore, to apply the IFRS 2 requirements to transactions with employees and others providing similar services, the entity must measure the fair value of the services received by reference to the fair value of the equity instruments granted. The fair value of those equity instruments should be measured at the grant date.

OBSERVATION: A common situation is that an employee receives an equity instrument that will vest at a later date or subject to uncertain future events. It might be suggested that value passes only when the equity instrument vests (i.e., becomes a definite entitlement of the employee). The IASB will have none of this; the grant date is the date of the agreement between the two parties (i.e., the acquisition of a *contingent right* by the employee), and hence the grant date is when the equity instrument should be evaluated and recorded.

However, in the case of such transactions with non-employees, where it is the fair value of the goods or services *obtained* that is evaluated and not the fair value of the equity instrument, the evaluation takes place in the case of services, when the service is rendered (i.e., when value passes). In general, this will be on a different date from (possibly later than) the grant date. There are thus two differences here between the treatment of transactions involving employees and those involving others, related to both the *method* of fair value evaluation and the *timing* of the date relating to which that fair value is evaluated.

In the case of the acquisition of goods, the recording treatment is simple (once the evaluation has taken place). The equity is increased, with a corresponding increase in the relevant asset accounts. These asset amounts are then treated as appropriate under other standards, and normally expensed at a later date.

In the case of the acquisition of services, the position is more complicated (pars. 14 and 15). If the equity instruments granted *vest* immediately, the counterparty is not required to complete a specified period of service before becoming unconditionally entitled to those equity instruments. In the absence of evidence to the contrary, the entity presumes that services rendered by the counterparty as consideration for the equity instruments have been received. In this case, on the grant date the entity recognizes the services received in full, with a corresponding increase in equity. It follows from these stated conditions that an immediate expense of the total amount is required. In many cases, however, the service will be rendered to the entity over a period of time, possibly extending well into the future. More possibly, if the equity instruments granted do not vest until the counterparty completes a specified period of service, the entity must presume that the services to be rendered by the counterparty as consideration of those equity instruments will be received in the future, during the vesting period.

It follows that the entity accounts for the services received, with corresponding increases in equity, at the appropriate points during this period, normally annually. In a genuine arm's-length transaction, where it is the fair value of the services obtained that is measured and recorded at the time of each rendering of service, no difficulties of principle or practice should arise.

However, in what is clearly expected by the IASB to be the more common scenario, often the fair value of the equity instrument granted needs to be *evaluated* as at the grant date but *recorded* as on the rendering of the service, as when services from employees are involved. Complexities do arise, and they are discussed below. Illustrations are given for the application of certain requirements; further illustrations are published by the IASB in its "Guidance on Implementing IFRS 2" (which is not formally part of IASB GAAP requirements). No set of illustrations can be exhaustive, and readers are urged to apply the principles when considering particular situations, not merely to seek analogy with non-definitive illustrations. Some detailed specifications, however, are included in Appendix B to IFRS 2 itself; these are part of the standard and are therefore definitive.

In a simple situation, the fair value of equity instruments granted is measured based on market prices, taking into account the terms and conditions upon which the equity instruments were granted. If market prices are not available, the entity shall estimate the fair value of the equity instruments granted by using a valuation technique to estimate what the price of those equity instruments would have been on the measurement date in an arm's-length transaction between knowledgeable, willing parties. The valuation technique should be consistent with generally accepted valuation methodologies for pricing financial instruments and should incorporate all factors and assumptions that knowledgeable, willing market participants would consider in setting the price (subject to the requirements of paragraphs 19–21 discussed below).

In practice, vesting conditions are likely to be involved, making the outcomes uncertain. The standard treats market conditions differently from other vesting conditions (par. 21). Market conditions have been defined formally earlier in the chapter. The point is that the outcome of the condition (i.e., its satisfaction or otherwise), is related to the market price of equity instruments of the entity at the specified date. Market conditions in this sense are taken into account when estimating the fair value of equity instruments granted, at the grant date. By implication, the greater the risk of non-achievement of a specified market condition, the greater the negative effect (other things being equal) on the estimation of fair value. Therefore, for grants of equity instruments with market conditions, the entity should recognize the goods or services received from a counterparty who satisfies all other vesting conditions (e.g., services received from an employee who remains in service for the specified period of service), regardless of whether that market condition is satisfied. This is because the possibility that the market conditions may not be satisfied is taken into account when estimating the fair value of the equity instrument.

Similarly, an entity shall take into account all non-vesting conditions when estimating the fair value of the equity instruments granted. Therefore, for grants of equity instruments with non-vesting conditions, the entity shall recognize the goods or services received from a counterparty that satisfies all vesting conditions that are not market conditions (e.g., services received from an employee who remains in service for the specified period of service), irrespective of whether those non-vesting conditions are satisfied.

Other (non-market) vesting conditions are treated differently (par. 19). These include completion by an employee of a specified length of service and the achievement of specified levels of profit or profitability by the entity. Vesting conditions other than market conditions should not be taken into account when estimating the fair value of the shares or share options at the measurement date. Instead, vesting conditions should be taken into account by adjusting the number of equity instruments included in the measurement of the transaction amount so that, ultimately, the amount recognized for goods or services received as consideration for the equity instruments granted is based on the number of equity instruments that eventually vest. Hence, on a cumulative basis, no amount is recognized for goods or services received if the equity instruments granted do not vest because of failure to satisfy a vesting condition (e.g., the counterparty fails to complete a specified service period) or a performance condition is not satisfied, subject to the requirements of paragraph 21.

To apply the requirements of paragraph 19, the entity recognizes an amount for the goods or services received during the vesting period based on the best available estimate of the number of equity instruments expected to vest and should revise that estimate, if necessary, when subsequent information indicates that the number of equity instruments expected to vest differs from previous estimates. On the vesting date, the entity revises the estimate to equal the number of equity instruments that ultimately vested, subject to the requirements of paragraph 21.

The Implementation Guidance issued by the IASB contains a number of worked illustrations of these requirements. They are not only instructive of the meaning and interpretation of the requirements in the standard itself, they also throw into high relief some of the implications of these detailed requirements. Reproduced, slightly adapted, are two of these examples (numbers 3 and 5), with the implications highlighted.

Illustration of a Grant with a Performance Condition in Which the Number of Equity Instruments Varies

At the beginning of year 1, entity A grants share options to each of its 100 employees working in the sales department. The share options will vest at the end of year 3, provided that the employees remain in the entity's employ, and provided that the volume of sales of a particular product increases by at least an average of 5% per year. If the volume of sales of the product increases by an average of between 5% and 10% per year, each employee will receive 100 share options. If the volume of sales increases by an average of between 10% and 15% each year, each employee will receive 200 share options. If the volume of sales increases by an average of 15% or more, each employee will receive 300 share options.

On the grant date, entity A estimates that the share options have a fair value of 20 per option. Entity A also estimates that the volume of sales of the product will increase by an average of between 10% and 15% per year and therefore expects that, for each employee who remains in service until the end of year, 3,

200 share options will vest. The entity also estimates, on the basis of a weighted-average probability, that 20% of employees will leave before the end of year 3.

By the end of year 1, seven employees have left and the entity still expects that a total of 20 employees will leave by the end of year 3. Hence, the entity expects that 80 employees will remain in service for the three-year period. Product sales have increased by 12% and the entity expects this rate of increase to continue over the next two years.

By the end of year 2, a further five employees have left, bringing the total to 12 to date. The entity now expects only three more employees will leave during year 3 and therefore expects a total of 15 employees will have left during the three-year period; and hence 85 employees are expected to remain. Product sales have increased by 18%, resulting in an average of 15% over the two years to date. The entity now expects that sales will average 15% or more over the three-year period, and therefore expects each sales employee to receive 300 share options at the end of year 3.

By the end of year 3, a further two employees have left. Hence, 14 employees have left during the three-year period, and 86 employees remain. The entity's sales have increased by an average of 16% over the three years. Therefore, each of the 86 employees receives 300 share options.

Application of Requirements

Year	Calculation	Remuneration Expense for Period	Cumulative Remuneration Expense
1	80 employees × 200 options × 20 × $1/3$	106,667	106,667
2	(85 employees × 300 options × 20 × $2/3$) − 106,667	233,333	340,000
3	(86 employees × 300 options × 20 × $3/3$) − 340,000	176,000	516,000

Illustration of a Grant with a Service Condition and a Market Condition

At the beginning of year 1, an entity grants to a senior executive 10,000 share options, conditional upon the executive remaining in the entity's employ until the end of year 3. However, the share options cannot be exercised unless the share price has increased from 50 at the beginning of year 1 to above 65 at the end of year 3. If the share price is above 65 at the end of year 3, the share options can be exercised at any time during the next seven years (i.e., by the end of year 10).

The entity applies a binomial option model, which takes into account the possibility that the share price will exceed 65 at the end of year 3 (at which point the share options become exercisable) and the possibility that the share price will not exceed 65 at the end of year 3 (at which point the options will be forfeited). It estimates the fair value of the share options with this market condition to be 24 per option.

Application of Requirements

Because paragraph 21 of the IFRS requires the entity to recognize the services received from a counterparty who satisfies all other vesting conditions (e.g., services received from an employee who remains in service for the specified service period), irrespective of whether that market condition is satisfied, it makes no difference whether the share price target is achieved. The possibility that the share price target might not be achieved has already been taken into account when estimating the fair value of the share options at grant date. Therefore, if the entity expects the executive to complete the three-year service period and the executive does so, the entity recognizes the following amounts in years 1, 2, and 3:

Year	Calculation	Remuneration Expense for Period	Cumulative Remuneration Expense
1	10,000 options $\times$ 24 $\times$ $1/3$	80,000	80,000
2	(10,000 options $\times$ 24 $\times$ $2/3$) — 8000	80,000	160,000
3	(10,000 options $\times$ 24) — 160,000	80,000	240,000

As noted above, these amounts are recognized irrespective of the outcome of the market condition. However, if the executive left during year 2 (or year 3), the amount recognized during year 1 (and year 2) would be reversed in year 2 (or year 3). This is because the service condition, in contrast to the market conditions, was not taken into account when estimating the fair value of the share options at grant date. Instead, the service condition is taken into account by adjusting the transaction amount to be based on the number of equity instruments that ultimately vest, in accordance with paragraphs 19 and 20 of the IFRS.

OBSERVATION: These two illustrations clearly reveal the differences in effect of the IFRS 2 requirements relating to the treatment of market and non-market vesting conditions. In the first illustration, at the grant date the entity grants share options to 100 employees. Each option has a fair value at grant date of 20 and the entity expects that 80 employees will meet the employment condition and that each will receive 200 options. This gives an immediate expected total expense of 80 $\times$ 200 $\times$ 20 = 320,000, of which one-third relates to year 1. The final outcome of the three years is the vesting of 300 options to each of 86 employees, giving a total expense over the three years of 86 $\times$ 300 $\times$ 20 = 516,000. Thus in the first illustration, the final outcome is the fair value at the *grant* date times the *actual* vesting quantities. The allocation of this total over the three years is determined by expectations at each year-end regarding the non-market vesting conditions.

In the second illustration, there is a market condition and a non-market condition. Given the fair value at the grant date (which will itself be influenced in amount by both conditions), the achievement or otherwise of the market condition has no effect. On the figures of the illustration, if the executive does in fact remain in employ until the end of year 3, a total expense of 240,000 is recorded, even if the market condition is not met and the employee never actually received the options. Conversely, if the employee in fact leaves before the end of year 3, a total expense of zero is recorded (even if, of course, the market condition itself is eventually met). Further, in the latter case, the zero total may consist of a large expense in one or some years and its eventual reversal in a later year.

It is readily apparent that reported earnings in any particular year, and therefore trends in reported earnings over time, may be significantly affected by the specifics of grant agreements.

In its "basis for conclusions on IFRS 2," the IASB discussed alternative arguments in many of these issues (pars. 1G170 –1G184). The approach eventually followed by the IASB is to support the principles chosen by the U.S. FASB in its ASC 718, but with a reduction in the element of choice allowed by the U.S. standard. Therefore, in effect, the IASB has supported IAS/US convergence to the degree it felt consistent with acceptable outcomes, but no further.

→ **PRACTICE POINTER:** The preceding illustration took the fair value at the grant date as given. The quantification of this fair value is often not easy. As indicated in the standard, the fair value will often need to be calculated based on estimates and an option pricing model. There are many such models. Their specification and application is not of itself a financial reporting issue, being a finance valuation problem. IFRS 2 contains Appendix B, which discusses the evaluation of fair value at some length; it is a full and integral part of IFRS 2 but disclaims any suggestion of being exhaustive. Practitioners should read it carefully. A minimum requirement, whatever detailed valuation model is used, is consistency within the entity, both over different options and over time.

Two further complexities or difficulties may arise, in relation to equity-settled share-based transactions, which are discussed in the standard. The first (pars. 24 and 25) concerns the "rare cases," in which the entity is unable to estimate the fair value of equity instruments granted at the measurement date (i.e., usually, at the grant date). In such a circumstance, the evaluation is based on the intrinsic value (as defined and illustrated in the definitions section of this chapter).

The second complexity occurs when modifications are made during the vesting period to the terms and conditions under which the equity instruments were granted (pars. 26 –29). An entity might, for example, reduce the exercise price of options granted to employees (i.e., reprice the options), which increases the fair value of those options. The requirements in the standard to account for the effects of modifications are expressed in the context of share-based payment transactions with employees. However, the requirements also apply to share-based payment transactions with parties other than employees that are measured by reference to the fair value of the equity instruments granted. In the latter case, any references to grant date instead refer to the date the entity obtains the goods or the counterparty renders service.

The basic principle is that the entity should recognize, as a minimum, the services received measured at the grant date fair value of the equity instruments granted, unless those equity instruments do not vest because of failure to satisfy a vesting condition (other than a market condition) that was specified at the grant date. This applies regardless of any modifications to the terms and conditions of which the equity instruments were granted or of a cancellation or settlement of that grant of equity instruments. In addition, the entity recognizes the effects of any modifications that increase the total fair value of the share-based payment arrangement or are otherwise beneficial to the employee. The rationale for this is that having adopted a grant date measurement method, the requirements for dealing with modifications and cancellations should ensure that the entity could not, through any modifications, avoid the recognition of remuneration expenses based on the original fair values at the grant date. Increases in benefits to the employee arising from the modifications, and fair value evaluation are, however, additionally recognized as expenses. With effect from January 1, 2009, the wording (pars. 28 and 28A) has been tightened up to ensure that the full recognition of remuneration expenses cannot be avoided.

Cash-Settled Share-Based Payment Transactions

This is the second type of share-based payment situation considered by IFRS 2. Although the amount of the consideration involved is determined in relation to an equity instrument, the consideration itself actually passes in cash or other assets, not in shares or any other equity instrument. In such a case, the basic requirement is that the entity should measure the goods or services acquired and the liability incurred at the fair value of the liability. Until the liability is settled, the entity remeasures the fair value of the liability at each reporting date and at the date of settlement, with any changes in fair value recognized in profit or loss for the period. As regards the last point, this treatment is different from that of equity-settled share-based payments discussed above. With cash-settled share-based payments, the liability is remeasured annually and the change recorded (and put through reported earnings). For both types of share-based payment, however, the payments should be recognized only to the extent that the corresponding goods or services have been acquired or received.

For example, an entity might grant share appreciation rights to employees as part of their remuneration package, whereby the employees will become entitled to a future cash payment (rather than an equity instrument), based on the increase in the entity's share price from a specified level over a specified period of time. The entity should recognize the services received, and a liability to pay for those services, as the employees render service. Some share appreciation rights vest immediately, and the employees are therefore not required to complete a specified period of service to become entitled to the cash payment. In the absence of evidence to the contrary, the entity presumes that the services rendered by the employees in exchange for the share appreciation rights have been received. Thus, the entity immediately recognizes the services received and a liability to pay for them. If the share appreciation rights do not vest until the employees have completed a specified period of service, the entity recognizes the services received, and a liability to pay for them, as the employees render service during that period. The liability is measured, initially and at each reporting date until settled, at the fair value of the share appreciation rights, by applying an option pricing model, taking into account the terms and conditions on which the share appreciation rights were granted, and the extent to which the employees have rendered service to date.

When the liability is actually settled, its fair value is, by definition, the amount of cash passing in settlement. There will be a final adjustment to the expenses charged at this point, in the case of services rendered.

→ **PRACTICE POINTER:** IFRS 2 applies to share-based payments for the acquisition of both services and goods; thus, the resources acquired through the liability may be recorded in the entity's balance sheet (e.g., as inventory), not as expense. The annual revaluation undertaken for cash-settled share-based payment transactions as described above is:

1. A remeasurement of the liability (at fair value).

2. To be taken, as regards the adjustments, to profit and loss account.

It follows that the carrying value of the asset is not adjusted even though the carrying value of the "corresponding" liability *is* adjusted.

Share-Based Payments with a Cash/Equity Settlement Alternative

Finally, there may be a mixture or choice of settlement methods between cash-settled and equity-settled transactions allowed under the original agreement. The basic rule here (par. 34) follows logically from earlier requirements. For share-based payment transactions in which the terms of the arrangement provide either the entity or the counterparty with the choice of whether the entity settles the transaction in cash (or other assets) or by issuing equity instruments, the entity accounts for that transaction, or the components of that transaction, (1) as a cash-settled share-based payment transaction if, and to the extent that, the entity has incurred a liability to settle in cash or other assets or (2) as an equity-based payment transaction, if, and to the extent that, no such liability has been incurred.

The element of choice might lie with either party. For a share-based payment transaction in which the terms of the arrangement provide the entity with the choice of whether to settle in cash or by issuing equity instruments, the entity determines whether it has a present obligation to settle in cash and accounts for the share-based payment transaction accordingly. It has a present obligation to settle in cash if the choice of settlement in equity instruments has no commercial substance (e.g., because the entity is legally prohibited from issuing shares); the entity has a past practice or a stated policy of settling in cash; or the entity generally settles in cash whenever the counterparty asks for cash settlement.

If the entity has a present obligation to settle in cash, it must account for the transaction in accordance with the requirements applying to cash-settled share-based payment transactions as above. If no such obligation exists, the entity accounts for the transaction in accordance with the requirements applying to equity-settled share-based payment transactions.

This is straightforward. The entity follows the reality of the situation. Correcting entries that adjust for any recorded equity interest settled in cash instead (treated as a repurchase) or that adjust for additional fair value owing at settlement (creating extra expense) are recorded as required.

If, on the other hand, an entity has granted the counterparty the right to choose whether a share-based payment transaction is settled in cash (or other assets) or by issuing equity instruments, the entity has granted a compound financial instrument, which includes both a debt component and an equity component (i.e., the counterparty's right to demand settlement in equity instruments rather than in cash). For transactions with parties other than employees, in which the fair value of the goods or services received is measured directly, the entity measures the equity component of the compound financial instrument as the difference between the fair value of the goods or services received and the fair value of the debt component, at the date when the goods or services are received. For other transactions, including transactions with employees, the entity shall measure the fair value of the compound financial instrument at the measurement date, taking into account the terms and conditions on which the rights to cash or equity instruments were granted (pars. 35 and 36).

The practical procedure is first to measure the fair value of the debt component, and second to measure the fair value of the equity component, taking into account that the right to receive cash is lost if the equity instrument is received. The standard notes that the latter element of the total fair value of the compound financial instrument may be zero.

The entity accounts separately for the goods or services received or acquired in respect of each component of the compound financial instrument. For the debt component, the entity recognizes the goods or services acquired and a liability to pay for those goods or services, as the counterparty supplies goods or renders service, in accordance with the requirements applying to cash-settled share-based payment transactions. For the equity component (if any), the entity should recognize the goods or services received, and an increase in equity as the counterparty supplies goods or renders service, in accordance with the requirements applying to equity-settled share-based payment transactions. At the date of settlement, the entity remeasures the liability to its fair value. If the entity issues equity instruments on settlement rather than paying cash, the liability is transferred direct to equity, as the consideration for the equity instruments issued. If the entity pays in cash on settlement rather than issuing equity instruments, that payment is applied to settle the liability in full. Any equity component previously recognized remains within equity. By electing to receive cash on settlement, the counterparty forfeited the right to receive equity instruments. However, this requirement does not preclude the entity from recognizing a transfer within equity (i.e., a transfer from one component of equity to another).

Thus, in summary, the entity's valuation of the compound financial instrument focuses first on the cash component and then on the equity component as the additional value of the alternative. The working out of these somewhat complex-sounding requirements is illustrated by a worked example in the IASB's Guidance on Implementations, reproduced below with some amendments.

Illustration of an Entity's Valuation of the Cash/Equity Financial Instrument

An entity grants to an employee the right to choose either 1,000 phantom shares, i.e., a right to a cash payment equal to the value of 1,000 shares, or 1,200 shares. The grant is conditional upon the completion of three years service. If the employee chooses the share alternative, the shares must be held for three years after vesting date.

At grant date, the entity's share price is 50 per share. At the end of years 1, 2 and 3, the share price is 52, 55 and 60, respectively. The entity does not expect to pay dividends in the next three years. After taking into account the effects of the post-vesting transfer restrictions, the entity estimates that the grant date fair value of the share alternative is 48 per share.

At the end of year 3, the employee chooses:

- Scenario 1: The cash alternative
- Scenario 2: The equity alternative

Application of Requirements

The fair value of the equity alternative is 57,600 (1,200 shares × 48). The fair value of the cash alternative is 50,000 (1,000 phantom shares × 50). Therefore, the fair value of the equity component of the compound instrument is 7,600 (57,600 – 50,000).

The entity recognizes the following amounts:

Year		Expense	Equity	Liability
1	Liability component:			
	(1,000 × 52 × $\frac{1}{3}$)	17,333		17,333
	Equity component:			
	(7,600 × $\frac{1}{3}$)	2,533	2,533	
2	Liability component:			
	(1,000 × 55 × $\frac{2}{3}$) – 17,333	19,333		19,333
	Equity component:			
	(7,600 × $\frac{1}{3}$)	2,533	2,533	
3	Liability component:			
	(1,000 × 60) – 36,666	23,334		23,334
	Equity component:			
	(7,600 × $\frac{1}{3}$)	2,534	2,534	
End Year 3	Scenario 1:			
	Cash of 60,000 paid			(60,000)
	Scenario 1 totals	67,600	7,600	0
	Scenario 2:			
	1,200 shares issued		60,000	(60,000)
	Scenario 2 totals	67,600	67,600	0

This illustration shows many of the characteristics of the application of IFRS 2 in a fairly complex situation. The fair value of the equity component of the compound instrument is calculated as a difference. Expenses are recognized on a time basis as the service is rendered. The cash-based element (the liability component) is re-evaluated each year at fair value, but the equity component is not (observe that the three years of expenses for this component are held constant based on the fair value calculated at grant date). On settlement, final adjustments are made as necessary.

2009 AMENDMENTS

IFRIC 11, "Group and Treasury Share Transactions," was issued in November 2006 to clarify two issues concerning accounting for share-based payment transactions. IFRIC 11 was applicable for annual periods beginning on or after March 1, 2007, with early application permitted. It has now been withdrawn, and its requirements incorporated into the Standard itself (pars. 43A–43D and B45–B61), with two further issues also considered.

The first issue is whether the following transactions should be accounted for as equity-settled or cash-settled under the requirements of IFRS 2:

1. An entity grants to its employees rights to equity instruments of the entity (e.g., share options) and either chooses or is required to buy equity instruments (i.e., treasury shares) from another party to satisfy its obligations to its employees.

2. An entity's employees are granted rights to equity instruments of the entity (e.g., share options), either by the entity itself or by its shareholders, and the shareholders of the entity provide the equity instruments needed.

The standard (par. B49) requires that share-based payment transactions in which an entity receives services as consideration for its own equity instruments are accounted for as equity-settled. This applies regardless of whether the entity chooses, or is required to buy, those equity instruments from another party to satisfy its obligations to its employees under the share-based payment arrangement. It also applies regardless of whether:

1. The employee's rights to the entity's equity instruments were granted by the entity itself or by its shareholders.

2. The share-based payment arrangement was settled by the entity itself or by its shareholders.

The second issue addresses the following share-based payment arrangements:

1. A parent grants rights to its equity instruments direct to the employees of its subsidiary: the parent (not the subsidiary) has the obligation to provide the employees of the subsidiary with the equity instruments needed.

2. A subsidiary grants rights to equity instruments of its parent to its employees: the subsidiary has the obligation to provide its employees with the equity instruments needed.

In arrangement (1), provided that the share-based arrangement is accounted for as equity-settled in the consolidated financial statements of the parent, the subsidiary shall measure the services received from its employees in accordance with the requirements applicable to equity-settled, share-based payment transactions, with a corresponding increase recognized in equity as a contribution from the parent.

In situation (2), the subsidiary shall account for the transaction with its employees as cash-settled. This requirement applies irrespective of how the subsidiary obtains the equity instruments to satisfy its obligations to its employees.

The third issue is how an entity that receives goods or services from its suppliers (including employees) should account for share-based arrangements that are cash-settled when the entity itself does not have any obligation to make the required payments to its suppliers. For example, consider the following arrangements in which the parent (not the entity itself) has an obligation to make the required cash payments to the employees of the entity:

1. The employees of the entity will receive cash payments that are linked to the price of its equity instruments.

2. The employees of the entity will receive cash payments that are linked to the price of its parent's equity instruments.

The subsidiary does not have an obligation to settle the transaction with its employees. Therefore, the subsidiary shall account for the transaction with its employees as equity-settled, and recognize a corresponding increase in equity as a contribution from its parent. The subsidiary shall remeasure the cost of the transaction subsequently for any changes resulting from non-market vesting conditions not being met in accordance with paragraphs 19–21. This differs from the measurement of the transaction as cash-settled in the consolidated financial statements of the group.

The fourth issue relates to group share-based payment arrangements that involve employees who have spent time over the vesting period in more than one group entity. If the subsidiaries concerned have no obligation to settle the share-based payment transactions with their own employees, they account for it on an equity-settled transaction. If a subsidiary does have an obligation to settle the transaction with its employees in its parent's equity instruments, it accounts for the transaction as cash-settled.

DISCLOSURES

These are detailed, and the requirements cannot be effectively summarized. They are reproduced below, complete with paragraph number:

44. An entity shall disclose information that enables users of the financial statements to understand the nature and extent of share-based payment arrangements that existed during the period.

45. To give effect to the principle in paragraph 44, the entity shall disclose at least the following:

   (a) A description of each type of share-based payment arrangement that existed at any time during the period, including the general terms and conditions of each arrangement, such as vesting requirements, the maximum term of options granted, and the method of settlement (e.g., whether in cash or equity). An entity with substantially similar types of share-based payment arrangements may aggregate this information, unless separate disclosures of each arrangement is necessary to satisfy the principle in paragraph 44.

(b) The number of weighted average exercise prices of share options for each of the following groups of options:

  (i) Outstanding at the beginning of the period;

  (ii) Granted during the period;

  (iii) Forfeited during the period;

  (iv) Exercised during the period;

  (v) Expired during the period;

  (vi) Outstanding at the end of the period; and

  (vii) Exercisable at the end of the period.

(c) For share options exercised during the period, the weighted average share price at the date of exercise. If options were exercised on a regular basis throughout the period, the entity may instead disclose the weighted average share price during the period.

(d) For share options outstanding at the end of the period, the range of exercise prices and weighted average remaining contractual life. If the range of exercise prices is wide, the outstanding options shall be divided into ranges that are meaningful for assessing the number and timing of additional shares that may be issued and the cash that may be received upon exercise of those options.

46. An entity shall disclose information that enables users of the financial statements to understand how the fair value of the goods or services received, or the fair value of the equity instruments granted, during the period was determined.

47. If the entity has measured the fair value of goods or services received as consideration for equity instruments of the entity indirectly, by reference to the fair value of the equity instruments granted, to give effect to the principle in paragraph 46, the entity shall disclose at least the following:

(a) For share options granted during the period, the weighted average fair value of those options at the measurement date and information on how that fair value was measured, including;

  (i) The option pricing model used and the inputs to that model, including the weighted average share price, exercise price, expected volatility, option life, expected dividends, the risk-free interest rate and any other inputs to the model, including the method used and the assumptions made to incorporate the effects of expected early exercise;

  (ii) How expected volatility was determined, including an explanation of the extent to which expected volatility was based on historical volatility; and

(iii) Whether and how any other features of the option grant were incorporated into the measurement of fair value, such as a market condition.

(b) For other equity instruments granted during the period (i.e., other than share options), the number and weighted average fair value of those equity instruments at the measurement date, and information on how that fair value was measured, including:

(i) If fair value was not measured on the basis of an observable market price, how it was determined;

(ii) Whether and how expected dividends were incorporated into the measurement of fair value; and

(iii) Whether and how any other features of the equity instruments granted were incorporated into the measurement of fair value.

(c) For share-based payment arrangements that were modified during the period:

(i) An explanation of those modifications;

(ii) The incremental fair value granted (as a result of those modifications); and

(iii) Information on how the incremental fair value granted was measured, consistently with the requirements set out in (a) and (b) above, where applicable.

48. If the entity has measured directly the fair value of goods or services received during the period, the entity shall disclose how that fair value was determined, e.g., whether fair value was measured at a market price for those goods or services.

49. If the entity has rebutted the presumption in paragraph 13, it shall disclose that fact, and give an explanation of why the presumption was rebutted.

50. An entity shall disclose information that enables users of the financial statements to understand the effect of share-based payment transactions on the entity's profit or loss for the period and on its financial position.

51. To give effect to the principle in paragraph 50, the entity shall disclose at least the following:

(a) The total expense recognized for the period arising from share-based payment transactions in which the goods or services received did not qualify for recognition as assets and hence were recognized immediately as an expense, including separate disclosure of that portion of the total expense that arises from transactions accounted for as equity-settled share-based payment transactions;

(b) For liabilities arising from share-based payment transactions:

(i) The total carrying amount at the end of the period; and

      (ii) The total intrinsic value at the end of the period of liabilities for which the counterparty's right to cash or other assets had vested by the end of the period (e.g., vested share appreciation rights).

52. If the information required to be disclosed by this IFRS does not satisfy the principles in paragraphs 44, 46, and 50, the entity shall disclose such additional information as is necessary to satisfy them.

The approach taken by the IASB in presenting these disclosure requirements is interesting. There are four key paragraphs, numbers 44, 46, 50, and 52, the first three of which are printed in bold in the published standard. Their importance is made clear by paragraph 52. All the rest of the requirements are operational detail as to how to apply the principles of paragraphs 44, 46, and 50. Paragraph 52 makes it explicit that the operational requirements specified (which are *requirements*, not illustrations) should not be assumed to be exhaustive. The *principles* are the key consideration.

OBSERVATION: IFRS 2 is somewhat controversial. Its basic ideas are very simple and very sensible, but its detailed applications can be, in certain situations, complicated and subjective. Those who wish to evade the logic of the standard and its benefits may attack this complexity and subjectivity. The IASB needs to stand firm on its principles, if not every detail.

PART III
INDUSTRY-SPECIFIC STANDARDS

CHAPTER 34
AGRICULTURE

CONTENTS

OVERVIEW

IAS 41, "Agriculture," is effective for annual financial statements beginning on or after January 1, 2003. It is a completely new standard dealing with the accounting treatment of agricultural activity. Agricultural activity is the management by an entity of the biological transformation of living animals or plants (biological assets) for sale, into agricultural produce or into additional biological assets. IAS 41 does not deal with the processing of agricultural produce after harvest.

IAS 41 requires that biological assets should be measured at their fair value less estimated point-of-sale costs, unless such market-based values are neither available nor capable of reliable estimation, when cost less depreciation and any impairment losses should be used. The standard requires that a change in fair value less estimated point-of-sale costs of a biological asset be included in the net profit or loss for the period in which it arises. This means, of course, that gains that are unrealized in transaction terms are to be included in operating profits.

IAS 41 was the last standard approved by the "old" IASC Board, at the end of 2000.

BACKGROUND

For a considerable time, the IASB had been issuing standards that explicitly excluded agricultural activity from their scope. For example:

- IAS 2, "Inventories," excluded "producers' inventories of livestock, agricultural and forest products . . . to the extent that they are measured at net realizable value in certain industries."

- IAS 16, "Property, Plant, and Equipment," did not apply to "forests and similar regenerative natural resources."

- IAS 18, "Revenue," did not deal with revenue arising from "natural increases in herds, and agricultural and forest products."

- IAS 40, "Investment Property," did not apply to "forests and similar regenerative natural resources."

Thus, there was no harmonizing force at work regarding financial reporting for agricultural activities. Taking a global view, agriculture is generally a small business activity, but this is tending to change. Thirdly, agriculture is a very significant industry in many countries, particularly in developing economies, where the resources available to develop local techniques and regulation are likely to be lacking. For all of these reasons, a standard on agriculture was felt to be desirable.

Much agricultural activity involves either the gradual physical expansion, and therefore increase in value, of a specific item, such as a tree or a cow, or the creation, without any market transaction, of a new item, such as a sapling grown from seed or the birth of a calf. In both these situations, the traditional accounting process based on recording the historical cost-of-purchase transactions, and then waiting until revenue is "earned" by means of a sale transaction, fails to fairly present the economic reality of the accumulation of agricultural resources. For this reason, IAS 41 focuses on the use of fair values in both the balance sheet and the calculation of revenues.

SCOPE

IAS 41 became formally operative for annual financial statements covering periods beginning on or after January 1, 2003. The standard should be used to account for the following when they relate to agricultural activity:

- Biological assets,

- Agricultural produce at the point of harvest, and

- Government grants related to biological assets measured on the fair value basis, and to government grants that require enterprises not to engage in specified agricultural activity.

IAS 41 does not apply to:

- Land related to agricultural activity (see IAS 16, "Property, Plant, and Equipment," Chapter 28, and IAS 40, "Investment Property," Chapter 25);

- Intangible assets related to agricultural activity (see IAS 38, "Intangible Assets," Chapter 22); and

- Government grants related to biological assets measured on the cost basis, to which IAS 20, "Accounting for Government Grants and Disclosure of Government Assistance" (see Chapter 19) is applied.

IAS 41 only applies to agricultural produce at the point of harvest. After that point, IAS 2, "Inventories" (see Chapter 24), or some other applicable IAS, is applied. It follows that IAS 41 does not apply to products associated with the processing of agricultural produce after the point of harvest. Consider, for example, a vintner who owns land on which vines are planted. These produce grapes, which he uses to produce wine. The land is not covered by IAS 41; the vines are, as biological assets; the grapes, as agricultural produce, are covered by

IAS 41 at the point of harvest, but not thereafter; the wine, whether in process or completed, is not covered by IAS 41.

TERMINOLOGY AND DEFINITIONS

The standard gives a series of definitions of specifically agriculture-related terms, as follows.

- *Agricultural activity* is the management by an entity of the biological transformation and harvest of biological assets for sale or for conversion, into agricultural produce, or into additional biological assets.
- *Agricultural produce* is the harvested product of the entity's biological assets.
- A *biological asset* is a living animal or plant.
- *Biological transformation* comprises the processes of growth, degeneration, production, and procreation that cause qualitative or quantitative changes in a biological asset.
- A *group of biological assets* is an aggregation of similar living animals or plants.
- *Harvest* is the detachment of produce from a biological asset or the cessation of a biological asset's life processes.
- Costs *to sell* are the incremental costs directly attributable to the disposal of an asset, excluding finance costs and income taxes.

Agricultural activity can cover a wide range of diverse operations. Three factors are said to be common to all agricultural activity.

1. Biological assets are capable of biological transformation.
2. Agricultural activity, to fall within IAS 41, must be managed. Thus, fish farming is an agricultural activity, whereas ocean fishing is not.
3. Changes in quantity or quality brought about by biological transformation are monitored and measured routinely as part of the management process.

In addition to these agriculture-related definitions, a number of general terms are defined for completeness, as follows.

- An *active market* is a market where all the following conditions exist:
  — The items traded within the market are homogeneous;
  — Willing buyers and sellers can normally be found at any time; and
  — Prices are available to the public.
- *Carrying amount* is the amount at which an asset is recognized in the balance sheet.
- *Fair value* is the amount for which an asset could be exchanged or a liability settled between knowledgeable, willing parties in an arm's-length transaction.
- *Government grants* are as defined in IAS 20, "Accounting for Government Grants and Disclosure of Government Assistance" (see Chapter 19).

The fair value concept is developed in the standard (in par. 9), which states that the fair value of an asset is based on its present location and condition. As a result, for example, the fair value of cattle at a farm is the price for the cattle in the relevant market less the transport and other costs of getting the cattle to that market. The implications of this are discussed below.

RECOGNITION AND MEASUREMENT

The recognition criteria are straightforward, and logically follow from the definition of an asset given in the IASB Framework (see Chapter 2). An entity should recognize a biological asset or agricultural produce when, and only when, all three of the following are satisfied.

1. The entity controls the asset as a result of past events.

2. It is probable that future economic benefits associated with the asset will flow to the entity.

3. The fair value or cost of the asset can be measured reliably.

Control, in this context, implies demonstrating ownership or responsibility, not necessarily inculcating obedience(!).

The essential measurement requirement of IAS 41, which is the core of the whole standard, can be simply stated. A biological asset should be measured on initial recognition and at each balance sheet date at its fair value less estimated costs to sell, except where the fair value cannot be measured reliably. Agricultural produce harvested from an entity's biological assets should be measured at its fair value less estimated costs to sell at the point of harvest. This amount is used as a substitute for "cost" at that date when applying IAS 2, "Inventories," or another applicable standard.

OBSERVATION: The precise implications of this measurement requirement are not so straightforward as the succinct statement given above might suggest. The definition of fair value has been quoted above. As regards assets, this is identical to the definition given in IAS 40, "Investment Properties" (see Chapter 24). IAS 40 explicitly states (in par. 37) that the fair value of investment property is "without any deduction for transaction costs."

This statement from IAS 40 should be contrasted with the statement from IAS 41, already quoted, that the fair value of cattle at a farm is the price for the cattle in the relevant market less the transport and other costs of getting the cattle to that market. Since the fair value under IAS 40 is explicitly identical for both buyer and seller, and the fair value "of cattle at a farm" under IAS 41 is explicitly *not* identical for both buyer and seller (being different by the transport, etc. costs), it would seem that these two statements are inconsistent. The only way they can be made consistent is to impute into the IAS 40 statement the two additional points that:

1. Costs of "getting" the property to the market must be deducted from fair value in the seller's books, and

2. It is in the nature of the property market that such costs are always zero.

It has to be said that IAS 40 gives no hint of this, and such an imputation seems somewhat far-fetched. Transport costs will indeed be zero, but "other" costs may not be.

The second point to underline is that, ignoring the above question of the definition of fair value, IAS 40 requires the relevant properties to be measured at fair value, period. IAS 41, in contrast, requires the relevant agricultural or biological assets to be measured at fair value less costs to sell as defined. This is not so much an inconsistency as an overt difference. It appears that fair value less costs to sell is effectively identical to the more traditional concept of net realizable value, which is defined in IAS 2, "Inventories" (see Chapter 24) (par. 6), as the estimated selling price in the ordinary course of business less the estimated costs of completion and the estimated costs necessary to make the sale. Net realizable value, and/or fair value less costs to sell, are more prudent concepts than fair value, period. It might be that this more prudent approach was necessary to get adequate support from the (pre-2001) IASC Board for the issue of the standard. This comment is speculation, but seems to be supported by a statement in an Appendix to IAS 41 (at par. B26) that "failure to deduct estimated point-of-sale costs (costs to sell) could result in a loss being deferred."

→ **PRACTICE POINTER:** The practical effect of all this is that biological assets under IAS 41 should be measured at the arm's-length exchange price, less transport and other such costs to market, and less point-of-sale costs such as commissions, levies, and taxes (i.e., less all "costs to sell").

IAS 41 makes a number of detailed comments about the determination of fair value. Biological assets or agricultural produce may conveniently be grouped according to key attributes. Contracts specifying prices at a future date are not necessarily relevant to the determination of fair values related to current market conditions. If several active markets are available with different prices, the market expected to be eventually used will give the relevant price to act as the basis of fair value estimation.

If an active market does not exist, an entity uses one or more of the following, when available, in determining fair value:

- The most recent market transaction price, provided that there has not been a significant change in economic circumstances between the date of that transaction and the balance sheet date;

- Market prices for similar assets with adjustment to reflect differences; and

- Sector benchmarks such as the value of an orchard expressed per export tray, bushel, or hectare, and the value of cattle expressed per kilogram of meat.

If no market-determined prices or values are available in relation to a biological asset in its present condition, then the discounted present value of expected net cash receipts may be used. In certain circumstances, essentially for biological transformation since initial cost incurrence is small, cost may be a reasonable approximation to fair value.

There is a presumption that fair value can be measured reliably for a biological asset. That presumption can be rebutted, but only on initial recognition for a biological asset for which market-determined prices or values are not available and for which alternative estimates of fair value are determined to be clearly unreliable. In such a case, the biological asset should be measured at its cost less any accumulated depreciation and any accumulated impairment losses. Once the fair value of such a biological asset becomes reliably measurable, an enterprise should measure it at its fair value less estimated point-of-sale costs.

In all cases, agricultural produce at the point of harvest must be measured at its fair value less the estimated point-of-sale costs.

So far, measurement has been discussed in the context of the balance sheet. It follows, both from the logic of the notion of economic gain and from the accounting relationship between the income statement and the balance sheet that, in essence, gain is represented by the increase in the recorded value of net assets. The required treatment of gains arising from the application of IAS 41 is that such gains are income; that is, they are part of the operating results for the period. More formally, a gain or loss arising on initial recognition of a biological asset at fair value less estimated point-of-sale costs and from a change in fair value less estimated point-of-sale costs of a biological asset should be included in profit or loss for the period in which it arises. A gain or loss arising on initial recognition of agricultural produce at fair value less estimated costs to sell should be included in profit or loss for the period in which it arises.

OBSERVATION: There are several arguments in favor of this approach. It follows logically from the decision to base measurement on fair value in the first place. More pragmatically, but just as importantly, it reports on progress regarding the very purpose of carrying out agricultural activity, namely the growth, in quality and quantity, of biological assets. Nevertheless, there are also arguments against this approach. Such gains are not realized within the traditional accounting meaning of the term and, although a high degree of reliability of fair value figures is often obtainable, it is still true to say that value figures *after* sale will generally be more reliable still.

In our view, if the fair value is accepted at all as the foundation for the valuation of biological assets and the initial valuation of agricultural produce, then taking the gains to income, as required by IAS 41, is the only logical and useful conclusion. The alternative would presumably have been the taking of these gains directly to equity. There are ideas emerging that consider reducing the distinction between these two alternatives through the creation of a single performance statement to replace both the income statement and the separate primary statement reflecting changes in equity as currently required by IAS 1 (see Chapter 4). These ideas are a long way from fruition at this time.

INTRODUCTION OF IFRS 13

In this chapter, the discussion of measurement is significantly changed in wording, though not in principle, by the introduction of IFRS 13, "Fair Value Measurement" (see Chapter 3). This standard is obligatory only from January 1, 2013, with earlier application being "permitted" (but not encouraged"). When an entity applies IFRS 13, the definition of an active market will be deleted, together with related discussion on how to determine fair value with and without the existence of an active market.

The deleted definition of an active market and the previous definition of fair provided in this chapter will both be replaced by the following:

> *Fair value* is the price that would be received to sell an asset or paid to transfer a liability in an orderly transaction between market participants at the measurement date. (See IFRS 13, "Fair Value Measurement").

As discussed in Chapter 3, the implications of IFRS 13 will be similar to the deleted parts of IAS 41. In particular, the price in the relevant market does not account for transaction costs, but does account for transport costs. However, par. 9 of IAS 41 remains unaltered. The situation will still remain, therefore, under IAS 41, as already stated: a biological asset should be measured on initial recognition, and at the end of each reporting period, at its fair value less costs to sell, except where the fair value cannot be measured reliably.

GOVERNMENT GRANTS

The fair-value-based valuation approach of IAS 41 gave the IASB a problem regarding the treatment of government grants. IAS 20, "Accounting for Government Grants and Disclosure of Government Assistance" (see Chapter 19), requires that government grants should not be recognized until there is reasonable assurance that:

- The entity will comply with the conditions attaching to them; and

- The grants will be received.

IAS 20 also requires that government grants should be recognized as income over the periods necessary to match them with the related costs that they are intended to compensate, on a systematic basis. As regards the presentation of government grants related to assets, IAS 20 permits two methods—setting up a government grant as deferred income or deducting the government grant from the carrying amount of the asset.

If the latter method is used in the context of a biological asset under IAS 41, then this will reduce the cost of the asset, and therefore increase the excess of a fair value over that "cost" on a dollar-for-dollar basis. Since this excess, under IAS 41, is taken directly to income, the effect is that the government grant itself is taken immediately to income, in direct conflict with the IAS 20 requirement to match the grant over the relevant periods.

IAS 41 resolves the conflict by requiring a delay in the recognition of such grants when the fair value basis is used. An unconditional government grant related to a biological asset measured at its fair value less estimated point-of-sale costs should be recognized as income when, and only when, the government grant becomes receivable. If a government grant related to a biological asset measured at its fair value less estimated point-of-sale costs is conditional, including where a government grant requires an entity not to engage in specified agricultural activity, an entity should recognize the government grant as income when, and only when, the conditions attaching to the government grant are met.

To illustrate, if a government grant is received in relation to a herd of cattle, which is repayable if the herd is not kept for three years, then none of the grant can be recognized as income until the three years have expired. However, if the amount repayable is reduced to 40% of the grant after the end of year two, then 60% of the grant could and should be taken to income at that point.

→ **PRACTICE POINTER:** The treatment of government grants denoted above applies under IAS 41 when the fair value less point-of-sale costs measurement basis applies (which will be the usual situation). However, if a government grant relates to a biological asset measured at its cost less any accumulated depreciation and any accumulated impairment losses, IAS 20, "Accounting for Government Grants and Disclosure of Government Assistance," is applied.

PRESENTATION AND DISCLOSURE

An entity should disclose the aggregate gain or loss arising during the current period on initial recognition of biological assets and agricultural produce and from the change in fair value less estimated costs to sell of biological assets. The entity should also provide a description of each group of biological assets.

The standard discusses how this last, vaguely worded requirement is to be interpreted. The objective that should underlie the interpretation of the word "group" in this context is to provide information that may be helpful in assessing the timing of future cash flows. The "description" may be narrative or quantified, but quantified descriptions of each group of biological assets, distinguishing between consumable and bearer biological assets or between mature and immature biological assets, are "encouraged." Consumer biological assets are those that are intended to be harvested as agricultural produce or sold as biological assets. Bearer biological assets are all others—that is, those likely to be self-regenerating. Thus, livestock intended for the production of meat are consumable biological assets. Livestock from which milk is produced are bearer biological assets. For example, an entity may disclose the carrying amounts of consumable biological assets and bearer biological assets by group. An entity may further divide those carrying amounts between mature and immature assets.

Further detailed disclosure requirements are given, as follows.

If not disclosed elsewhere in information published with the financial statements, an entity should describe:

- The nature of its activities involving each group of biological assets; and
- Non-financial measures or estimates of the physical quantities of:
  - Each group of the entity's biological assets at the end of the period, and
  - Output of agriculture produce during the period.

An entity should disclose the methods and significant assumptions applied in determining the fair value of each group of agricultural produce at the point of harvest and each group of biological assets.

An entity should disclose the fair value less estimated costs to sell of agricultural produce harvested during the period, determined at the point of harvest.

An entity should disclose:

- The existence and carrying amounts of biological assets whose title is restricted, and the carrying amounts of biological assets pledged as security for liabilities;
- The amount of commitments for the development or acquisition of biological assets; and
- Financial risk management strategies related to agricultural activity.

An entity should present a reconciliation of changes in the carrying amount of biological assets between the beginning and the end of the current period. Comparative information is not required. The reconciliation should include:

- The gain or loss arising from changes in fair value less estimated costs to sell;
- Increases due to purchases;
- Decreases due to sales or reclassification as held for sale under IFRS 5, "Non-Current Assets Held for Sale and Discontinued Operations" (see Chapter 27);
- Decreases due to harvest;
- Increases resulting from business combinations;
- Net exchange differences arising on the translation of financial statements of a foreign entity; and
- Other changes.

An entity should disclose the following related to agricultural activity covered by IAS 41:

- The nature and extent of government grants recognized in the financial statements;
- Unfulfilled conditions and other contingencies attached to government grants; and
- Significant decreases expected in the level of government grants.

When an entity has biological assets whose fair value cannot be measured reliably (i.e., the use of a cost-based measurement is necessary), then a number of additional disclosures are required, as follows.

If an entity measures biological assets at their cost less any accumulated depreciation and any accumulated impairment losses at the end of the period, the entity should disclose for such biological assets:

- A description of the biological assets;
- An explanation of why fair value cannot be measured reliably;

- If possible, the range of estimates within which fair value is highly likely to lie;
- The depreciation method used;
- The useful lives or the depreciation rates used; and
- The gross carrying amount and the accumulated depreciation (aggregated with accumulated impairment losses) at the beginning and end of the period.

If, during the current period, an entity measures biological assets at their cost less any accumulated depreciation and any accumulated impairment losses, the entity should disclose any gain or loss recognized on disposal of such biological assets, and the reconciliation of changes in the carrying amount of biological assets should disclose amounts related to such biological assets separately. In addition, the reconciliation should include the following amounts included in net profit or loss related to those biological assets:

- Impairment losses;
- Reversals of impairment losses; and
- Depreciation.

If the fair value of biological assets previously measured at their cost less any accumulated depreciation and any accumulated impairment losses becomes reliably measurable during the current period, an entity should disclose for those biological assets:

1. A description of the biological assets;
2. An explanation of why fair value has become reliably measurable; and
3. The effect of the change.

CHAPTER 35
INSURANCE CONTRACTS

CONTENTS

OVERVIEW

IASB GAAP on insurance, at their present stage of development as set out in IFRS 4, "Insurance Contracts," deal with insurance contracts in the accounts of the issuer of an insurance contract (i.e., the insurer). The "insurer" for this purpose is any entity that issues contracts meeting the definition of insurance contracts. An insurance contract is a contract under which one party (the insurer) accepts *significant insurance risk* from another party (the policyholder) by agreeing to compensate the policyholder if a specified uncertain event (the *insured event*) adversely affects the policyholder. As well as applying to all insurance contracts (including reinsurance contracts) that an entity issues, IFRS 4 applies to reinsurance contracts that an entity holds as a cedant, but not to a number of specified types of contract covered by other IFRSs. It does not apply to other assets and liabilities of an insurer, such as those that fall within the scope of IAS 39/IFRS 9, "Financial Instruments" (see Chapter 17), or to accounting by policyholders. As insurance contracts are a type of financial instrument, the definition of an insurance contract plays a key role in demarcating the scope of IFRS 4 from that of IAS 39/IFRS 9. Because IFRS 9 is gradually replacing IAS 39, but need not be adopted before annual reporting periods beginning on or after January 1, 2013 (or January 1, 2015, if the proposal in the August 2011 ED is accepted— see Chapter 17), though earlier adoption is permitted, a transitory situation exists, and so references in the text to IAS 39 also refer to IFRS 9, where appropriate.

IFRS 4, which constitutes phase 1 of the IASB's two-phase insurance project, requires limited improvements to accounting by insurers for insurance contracts and disclosures that (1) identify and explain the amounts in insurers' financial statements that arise from insurance contracts and (2) help users understand the amounts, timing, and uncertainty of cash flows from those contracts. It temporarily exempts an insurer from some requirements of other IFRSs, including the requirement to take account of the Framework in choosing accounting policies for insurance contracts. This is because the IASB wishes to avoid imposing in phase 1 requirements that could be modified in phase 2. However, IFRS 4 does impose the following prohibitions and requirements:

- It prohibits provisions for possible claims under contracts that are not in existence at the reporting date (e.g., catastrophe and equalization provisions)

- It requires a test for the adequacy of recognized insurance liabilities and an impairment test for reinsurance assets

- It requires an insurer to retain insurance liabilities in its balance sheet until they are discharged or canceled, or expire, and to present insurance liabilities without offsetting them against related reinsurance assets

IFRS 4 permits an insurer to change its accounting policies for insurance contracts only if this results in its financial statements presenting information that is either more relevant and no less reliable or more reliable and no less relevant (the criteria for relevance and reliability are those set out in IAS 8, "Accounting Policies, Changes in Accounting Estimates, and Errors"). In particular, the following practices cannot be introduced, although existing accounting policies that involve them may continue to be used:

- Measuring insurance liabilities on an undiscounted basis

- Measuring contractual rights to future investment management fees at an amount that exceeds their fair value, as implied by a comparison with current fees charged by others for similar services

- Using non-uniform accounting policies for subsidiaries' insurance liabilities

Under IFRS 4, an accounting policy may be introduced that involves remeasuring *designated insurance liabilities* consistently in each period to reflect current market interest rates (and other current estimates and assumptions), without such a change in accounting policy having to be applied consistently to *all* similar liabilities.

An insurer need not change its accounting policies for insurance contracts to eliminate excessive prudence, but if they are already measured with sufficient prudence the insurer should not introduce additional prudence.

There is a rebuttable presumption that if an insurer introduces an accounting policy that reflects future investment margins in the measurement of insurance contracts, its financial statements will become less relevant and reliable.

When an insurer changes its accounting policies for insurance liabilities, under IFRS 4 it may reclassify some or all of its financial assets applying the fair value option, as "at fair value with changes in fair value recognized in profit and loss"(abbreviated to *"at fair value through profit and loss"*). Such a change subsequent to initial recognition would not be permitted under IAS 39/IFRS 9 (see Chapter 17).

In addition, IFRS 4 clarifies the following:

- If an embedded derivative meets the definition of an insurance contract, it need not be accounted for separately at fair value

- An insurer should unbundle deposit components of some insurance contracts to avoid omitting assets and liabilities from its balance sheet

- It permits the practice known as "shadow accounting," whereby a recognized but *unrealized* gain or loss on an asset has the same direct effect on the measurement of insurance liabilities, related deferred acquisition costs, or related intangible assets, as a *realized* gain or loss

- It permits during phase 1, but does not require, the use of an expanded presentation of the fair value of insurance contracts acquired in a business or portfolio transfer so as to show an intangible asset representing the expected present value of contractual cash flows from the business acquired

IFRS 4 amends a number of other IFRSs, namely IAS 18, "Revenue"; IAS 37, "Provisions, Contingent Liabilities, and Contingent Assets"; and IAS 40, "Investment Property"; plus a very small amendment to IAS 19, "Employee Benefits."

In July 2010, the IASB published an exposure draft, ED/2010/8, "Insurance Contracts." See "Background" below.

BACKGROUND

In 1997, the then IASC set up a Steering Committee to carry out initial work on a project to develop a standard on accounting for insurance. This led to the publication of a Draft Statement of Principles (DSOP) that was submitted to the IASB, which started discussing it in November 2001. The Board did not approve the DSOP or invite formal comments on it but made it available on the IASB web site. However, the Board remained committed to the project, but because it was not considered feasible to complete in time for implementation in 2005, the project was split into two phases so that some aspects could be implemented in 2005. The proposals for phase 1 were published as ED 5, "Insurance Contracts," in July 2003. After reviewing the responses to ED 5, the Board issued IFRS 3 in March 2004.

U.S. GAAP for insurers are set out in the following FASB Accounting Standards Codification™ references (see *GAAP Guide Volume I*, Chapter 49):

- ASC 944, "Financial Services—Insurance."

- ASC 950, "Financial Services—Title Plant."

- ASC 450, "Contingencies."

- FIN-40, "Applicability of Generally Accepted Accounting Principles to Mutual Life Insurance and Other Enterprises."

The only definition of insurance contracts in U.S. GAAP appears in ASC 944, which provides an outline definition of an insurance contract and defines insurance risk. The definitions of insurance contracts and insurance risk in IFRS 4 were developed on the basis of the Board's review of those in FAS-113, now superseded by ASC 944.

In July 2010, the IASB published an exposure draft, ED/2010/8, "Insurance Contracts," intended to "provide a comprehensive framework [for accounting for insurance contracts], eliminate inconsistencies and weaknesses in existing practices, by replacing IFRS 4, 'Insurance Contracts' [which is] an interim standard . . . [and to propose] a comprehensive measurement approach for all types of insurance contracts issues by entities and reinsurance contracts held by entities) . . . " (ED/2010/8, pars. IN2–IN3). At the time of writing (June 2011), the IASB had not announced any final decision about the issuance of the new standard. In particular, the Board is pursuing convergence with the FASB and areas of disagreement remained. Nevertheless, the new standard, based on the exposure draft (but possibly with modifications), may be issued in the second half of 2011, as stated in the IASB's work plan. Accordingly, a substantial summary of the exposure draft is provided at the end of this chapter.

SCOPE

IFRS 4 is to be applied by an entity to:

- Insurance contracts (including reinsurance contracts) that the entity issues and reinsurance contracts that it holds; and

- Financial instruments that it issues with a discretionary participation feature.

The IFRS seeks to make limited improvements to accounting by insurers for insurance contracts as part of phase 1 of the insurance project and does not address other aspects of accounting by insurers, such as accounting for financial assets held or financial liabilities issued by insurers (see IAS 32, "Financial Instruments: Presentation," and IAS 39/IFRS 9, "Financial Instruments" (see Chapter 17)), except in transitional provisions for redesignation of financial assets when IFRS 4 is first applied. For ease of reference, IFRS 4 describes any entity that issues an insurance contract as an insurer, whether or not such an issuer is considered to be an insurer for legal or supervisory purposes.

A reinsurance contract is a type of insurance contract, and all references in the IFRS to insurance contracts therefore apply to reinsurance contracts.

IFRS 4 is not to be applied to a number of items that fall within the scope of other IFRSs (pars. 1–6):

- Product warranties issued directly by a manufacturer, dealer or retailer, which fall within the scope of IAS 18, "Revenue," and IAS 37, "Provisions, Contingent Liabilities, and Contingent Assets" (see Chapters 31 and 29, respectively).

- Employers' assets and liabilities under employee benefit plans (see IAS 19, "Employee Benefits," and IFRS 3, "Business Combinations," in Chapters 14 and 8, respectively), and retirement benefit obligations reported by defined benefit retirement plans (see IAS 26, "Accounting and Reporting by Retirement Benefit Plans," Chap. 14).

- Contractual rights or obligations contingent on the future use of, or right to use, a non-financial item (e.g., some license fees, royalties, contingent lease payments), as well as embedded guarantees of a lessee's residual value in a finance lease (see IAS 17, "Leases"; IAS 18, "Revenue"; and IAS 38, "Intangible Assets," in Chapters 26, 31, and 22, respectively).

- Financial guarantee contracts, *unless* the issuer has *previously* made an *explicit assertion that it regards such contracts as insurance contracts* and *has used accounting applicable to insurance contracts*, in which case it has the choice of applying to such contracts *either* IFRS 4 *or* the standards applicable to financial instruments (IAS 39/IFRS 9, IAS 32, and IFRS 7). This choice may be made by contract, although once it's made for a particular contract, it is irrevocable for that contract (see the Observation below).

- Contingent consideration payable or receivable in a business combination (see IFRS 3, Chapter 7).

- *Direct* insurance contracts that an entity *holds* (i.e., for which it is the policyholder). However, a cedant in a reinsurance contract applies the IFRS to reinsurance contracts that it holds.

OBSERVATION: The definition of *insurance contract* in IFRS 4, Appendix A, (a revision of the previous definition used to exclude insurance contracts from the scope of IAS 32 and IAS 39, which was less clear) begins by stating that an insurance contract is a contract under which one party (the insurer) accepts significant "insurance risk" from another party (the policyholder). The definition of *insurance risk* in the same Appendix states that it is risk, other than "financial risk," while the definition of *financial risk* states that it is "the risk of a possible future change in one or more of a specified interest rate, financial instrument price, commodity price, foreign exchange rate, index of prices or rates, *credit rating or credit index* or other variable, provided that in the case of a *non-financial* variable that variable is *not specific to a party to the contract.* . . ." The IASB clearly wished to exclude financial guarantee contracts from the scope of IFRS 4 and to include them in the scope of the (more demanding) standards dealing with financial instruments, both in light of the above definitions and because the various forms of credit insurance and associated derivatives, such as credit default swaps, fall into the category of financial instruments and are best treated under those standards. However, as IFRS 4 constitutes phase 1 of the IASB's two-phase insurance project, entities that have already treated certain financial guarantee contracts as insurance contracts are allowed to continue doing so (i.e., to apply IFRS 4) to avoid having to make system changes at this stage. The IASB expects to use the revised definition of an insurance contract given above in phase 2 of the insurance project.

Because the objective of IFRS 4 is to bring about *limited improvements* to accounting for insurance contracts by insurers, a considerable number of issues are left unresolved pending phase 2 of the IASB's Insurance project. The Board did not wish to introduce changes that might be subject to further modification in phase 2.

Embedded Derivatives

The requirement in IAS 39/IFRS 9 (see Chapter 17) to separate embedded derivatives from their host contract and measure them at "fair value through profit and loss" applies to derivatives embedded in an insurance contract unless the embedded derivative itself is an insurance contract.

IFRS 4 (pars. 7–9) introduces an exception to this. An insurer need not separate and measure at fair value a policyholder's option to surrender an insurance contract for a fixed amount (or an amount based on a fixed amount and an interest rate) even if the exercise price of the option differs from the carrying amount of the host insurance liability.

However, this exception does not apply to an embedded put or cash surrender option (1) if the surrender value varies in response to the change in a financial variable (such as an equity or commodity price or index) or a non-financial variable that is not specific to a party to the contract, or (2) if the holder's ability to exercise such an option is triggered by a change in such a variable (e.g., a put that can be exercised if a stock market index reaches a specified level.

Nor does this exception apply to options to surrender a financial instrument containing a discretionary participation feature.

Unbundling of Deposit Components

Some types of insurance contract contain an insurance component and a deposit component. Paragraphs 10–12 of IFRS 4 concern the unbundling of these two components. In unbundling, the insurer applies IFRS 4 to the insurance component and IAS 39/IFRS 9 to the deposit component. Unbundling is *required* if the insurer can measure the deposit component (including any embedded surrender options) separately (i.e., without considering the insurance component) and the insurer's accounting policies do not otherwise require it to recognize all obligations and rights arising from the deposit component. Unbundling is *permitted but not required* if the insurer can measure the deposit component separately as just mentioned but its accounting policies require it to recognize all obligations and rights arising from the deposit component, regardless of the measurement basis used to measure them. Unbundling is *not permitted* if an insurer is unable to measure the deposit component separately.

DEFINITIONS

Definitions of key terms in the IFRS are set out in Appendix A, which is an integral part of the standard. The definition of an insurance contract is the subject of further guidance in Appendix B, which is likewise an integral part of the standard.

The key IFRS 4 definitions of "financial risk," "insurance contract," "insurance risk," and "insured event" are given below:

- *Cedant.* The policyholder under a reinsurance contract.

- *Financial risk.* The risk of a possible future change in one or more of a specified interest rate, financial instrument price, commodity price, foreign exchange rate, index of prices or rates, credit rating or credit index or other variable, provided that in the case of a non-financial variable the variable is not specific to a party to the contract. Note that for insurance risk to exist (see below), even if the variable is specific to the holder, the holder must be exposed to adverse effects from the behaviour of the variable. (par. B14)

- *Insurance contract.* A contract under which one party (the insurer) accepts significant insurance risk from another party (the policyholder), by agreeing to compensate the policyholder if a specified uncertain future event (the insured event) adversely affects the policyholder. The adverse effect on the policyholder is a contractual precondition for payment.

- *Insurance liability.* An insurer's net contractual obligations under an insurance contract.

- *Insurance risk.* Risk, other than financial risk, transferred from the holder of a contract to the issuer. A contract that exposes the issuer to financial risk without significant insurance risk is not an insurance contract.

- *Insured event.* An uncertain future event that is covered by an insurance contract and creates insurance risk. At the inception of an insurance contract, at least one (but not necessarily more than one) of the following is uncertain: *whether* an insured event will occur; *when* it will occur; *how much* the insurer will need to pay if it occurs.

- *Liability adequacy test.* An assessment of whether the carrying amount of an insurance liability needs to be increased (or the carrying amount of related deferred acquisition costs or related intangible assets decreased), based on a review of future cash flows.

- *Reinsurance assets.* A cedant's net contractual rights under a reinsurance contract.

RECOGNITION AND MEASUREMENT

The main issues to be considered under recognition and measurement are:

- Some temporary exemptions given by IFRS 4 to insurers from applying IAS 8,
- Liability adequacy tests,
- Impairment of reinsurance assets,
- Changes in accounting policies by an insurer that already applies IFRSs or is adopting IFRSs for the first time,
- Insurance contracts acquired, and
- Discretionary participation features.

Temporary Exemption from Other IFRSs

IFRS 4 (pars. 13–14) exempts insurers from some of the implications of paragraphs 10–12 of IAS 8, "Accounting Policies, Changes in Accounting Estimates, and Errors" (see Chapter 6), with regard to the criteria to be used by an entity in developing an accounting policy if no IFRS applies specifically to an item, in the case of insurance contracts that it issues (including related acquisition costs and related intangible assets such as those acquired in a business combination) and reinsurance contracts that it holds.

However, the IFRS does not exempt an insurer from some of the implications of these criteria. Specifically:

- No provisions for possible future claims arising under insurance contracts that are not in existence at the reporting date (such as catastrophe provisions and equalization provisions) are to be recognized as liabilities.

- A liability adequacy test (see below) should be carried out.

- An insurance liability (or part of one) is to be removed from an insurer's statement of financial position when, and only when, under insurance contracts that are not in existence at the reporting date, the liability is extinguished—that is, the obligation specified in the contract is discharged or canceled, or expires.

- A cedant must not offset reinsurance assets against the related insurance liabilities, or income and expense from reinsurance contracts against the expense or income from the related insurance contracts.

- A cedant must consider whether its reinsurance assets are impaired.

OBSERVATION: In April 2009, the IASB issued ED/2009/3, "Derecognition," which would amend the wording of point 3 above to reflect the terminology of the ED and to introduce the term "derecognized" in place of "removed from [an insurer's] statement of financial position." The substance of the requirement is not changed.

Liability Adequacy Test

This test consists of an assessment, in the light of the estimated future cash flows, of whether the insurer's recognized insurance liabilities are adequate. Such assessments are to be carried out at each reporting date. If the assessment shows that the carrying amount of the insurance liabilities (less related deferred acquisition costs and related intangible assets—see below) is inadequate, the entire deficiency is recognized in profit or loss.

The test should consider current estimates of all contractual cash flows and of related cash flows, such as claims handling costs and cash flows resulting from embedded options and guarantees. If an insurer's accounting policies include a liability adequacy test that meets this requirement, with any deficiency being recognized in its entirety in profit or loss, IFRS 4 imposes no further requirements. The level of aggregation at which the test is applied is that specified by the insurer's accounting policies.

If an insurer's accounting policies do not meet this criterion, IFRS 4 requires that the insurer determine the carrying amount of relevant insurance liabilities less the carrying amount of any related deferred acquisition costs and any related intangible assets, such as those acquired in a business combination or portfolio transfer. However, related *reinsurance* assets are not considered, because an insurer accounts for them separately. The insurer is also required to determine whether the amount described above is less than the carrying amount that would be required if the relevant insurance liabilities were within the scope of IAS 37, "Provisions, Contingent Liabilities and Contingent Assets" (see Chapter 29). If it is less, the insurer must recognize the entire difference in profit or loss and decrease the carrying amount of the related deferred acquisition costs or related intangible assets or increase the carrying amount of the relevant insurance liabilities. This comparison is made at the level of a portfolio of contracts that are subject to broadly similar risks and are managed together as a single portfolio.

Impairment of Reinsurance Assets

A reinsurance asset is impaired if, and only if:

- There is objective evidence, as a result of an event that occurred after initial recognition of the reinsurance asset, that the cedant may not receive all amounts due to it under the terms of the contract; and

- The event in question has a reliably measurable impact on the amounts that the cedant will receive from the reinsurer.

If a cedant's reinsurance asset is impaired, the cedant is to reduce its carrying amount accordingly and recognize the impairment loss in profit or loss. (IFRS 4, par. 20).

Changes in Accounting Policies

The general rule (IFRS 4, par. 22) is that an insurer may change its accounting policies for insurance contracts only if the change makes the financial statements more relevant to the economic decision-making needs of users and no less reliable, or more reliable and no less relevant to those needs. The criteria of relevance and reliability to be applied are those in IAS 8 (see Chapter 6).

To justify a change in accounting policies for insurance contracts, an insurer needs to show that the change brings its financial statements closer to meeting those criteria, but it need not achieve full compliance with them. IFRS 4 (pars. 24–30) discusses changes in the following areas:

- Use of current market interest rates for remeasuring insurance liabilities,

- Continuation of certain existing practices,

- Prudence and excessive prudence,

- Present value of future investment margins and embedded value, and

Shadow accounting for the impact of recognized but unrealized gains and losses on assets on the measurement of insurance liabilities and on related deferred acquisition costs or related intangible assets.

Current Market Interest Rates

A change may be made to the accounting treatment of designated insurance liabilities and any related deferred acquisition costs and intangible assets so that they are remeasured at fair value to reflect current market interest rates, with the remeasurement gains and losses being recognized in profit or loss. At the same time, accounting policies may be introduced that require other current estimates and assumptions. Such a change in accounting policy is not a requirement, and if it is made it need not be applied to all other similar items (as IAS 8 would otherwise require). Once adopted, however, any such new accounting policy must be applied consistently to the designated items in all periods until they are extinguished.

Continuation of Existing Practices

The following practices may be continued but not introduced:

- Measuring insurance liabilities on an undiscounted basis (in current practice, general insurance claims liabilities are typically not discounted);

- Measuring contractual rights to future investment management fees at an amount that exceeds their fair value as implied by a comparison with current fees charged by other market participants for similar services (as per IAS 39, par. BC 104); and

- Using non-uniform accounting practices (e.g., local GAAP) for the insurance contracts (and any related deferred acquisition costs and intangible assets) of subsidiaries.

Prudence and Excessive Prudence

A change in accounting policies to eliminate excessive prudence (i.e., prudence in excess of what a neutral or objective approach would suggest) is not required in phase 1. However, if the existing practice is to measure with sufficient but not excessive prudence, the practice may not be changed to introduce additional prudence.

Present Value of Future Investment Margins and Embedded Value

IFRS 4 does not require an insurer to change its accounting policies to eliminate treatments of future investment margins that are at odds with the Board's views regarding appropriate measurement methodology. However, an insurer may not introduce such treatments. There is a rebuttable presumption that an insurer's financial statements will become less relevant and reliable if it introduces an accounting policy that reflects future investment margins in the measurement of insurance contracts unless those margins affect the contractual payments.

OBSERVATION: The cash flows from an asset are irrelevant for the measurement of a liability unless those cash flows affect either the cash flows arising from the liability or the liability's credit characteristics. The following practices are inconsistent with this principle: (a) using a discount rate to measure insurance liabilities that is based on the estimated return from the assets that are deemed to back the liabilities; and (b) the equivalent practice of projecting the returns on those assets at an estimated rate of return, discounting those projected returns at a different rate and including the result in the measurement of the liability.

Embedded values are often an important consideration in determining prices for acquisitions of insurers and insurance contracts, and in accounting for the insurance liabilities so assumed. Taking account of embedded values in measuring an insurance liability is an indirect method and as such involves discounting all cash flows arising from both the book of insurance contracts and the assets supporting the book, to arrive at a net measurement for the contracts and supporting assets, the measurement of the assets being deducted to arrive at the measurement of the book of contracts. Embedded value measurement methods currently in use, however, typically involve the practices described above that contravene what the IASB considers to be sound measurement methodology. Nevertheless, IFRS 4 permits the continued use of such embedded value measurements in phase 1. Moreover, a new accounting policy incorporating such measurements may be introduced subject to the following conditions (IFRS 4, pars. BC 143–144):

- The new accounting policy results in more relevant and reliable financial statements.

- This increase in relevance and reliability is sufficient to overcome the rebuttable presumption noted above, that an insurer's financial statements will become less relevant and reliable if it introduces an accounting policy that reflects future investment margins in the measurement of insurance contracts unless those margins affect the contractual payments. (It is highly unlikely that the rebuttable presumption could be overcome if, instead of the discount rate being used to determine the present value of a future profit margin (which is then allocated to future periods using a formula), the discount rate directly determines the measurement of the liability).

- The embedded values include contractual rights to future investment management fees at an amount that does not exceed their fair value as implied by a comparison with current fees charged by other market participants for similar services.

Shadow Accounting for the Impact of Recognized but Unrealized Gains and Losses

Some national requirements for some types of insurance contract involve the amortization of deferred acquisition costs (DAC) over the life of the contract as a constant proportion of the estimated gross profits (EGP). EGP include investment returns including realized, but not unrealized, gains and losses. Shadow accounting treats an unrealized gain in the same way as a realized gain, except that the unrealized gain and the resultant DAC amortization are (1) recognized in other comprehensive income rather than in profit or loss and (2) transferred to profit or loss when the gain is realized. Shadow accounting thus becomes relevant when, for example, an insurer changes its accounting policies so that financial assets are measured at fair value (as required by IFRSs) instead of on a cost basis. IFRS 4, paragraph 30 permits, but does not require, shadow accounting.

Illustration of Shadow Accounting

This example follows that in the Implementation Guide to IFRS 4, and ignores interest applied to DAC and EGP as well as re-estimation of EGP.

At the inception of a contract, an insurer has the following in relation to that contract:

- DAC of $20, and
- Present value at inception of EGP equal to $100

Hence, at inception DAC = 20% of EGP

Without shadow accounting, for each $1 of realized gross profits, the insurer amortizes DAC by $0.20. Thus, if the insurer sells assets and recognizes a gain of $10, the resultant DAC amortization is $2.

Under IFRSs, the insurer classifies its financial assets as available for sale and measures them at fair value with changes in fair value being recognized in other comprehensive income. In 2005, the insurer recognizes a remeasurement gain of $10 on the assets backing the contract. In 2006, the insurer sells the assets for an amount equal to their fair value at the end of 2005 and transfers the gain, now realized, to profit or loss.

If the insurer adopts shadow accounting, in 2005 it amortizes DAC by an additional $2, being 20% of the recognized remeasurement gain, and this additional amortization is recognized in other comprehensive income. When the assets are sold in 2006, no further adjustment to DAC is made, but the additional amortization of $2 is transferred from equity to profit or loss to reflect the realization of the gain to which it relates.

Insurance Contracts Acquired in a Business Combination or Portfolio Transfer

IFRS 3 (see Chapter 8) requires an insurer to measure at fair value, at the acquisition date, the insurance liabilities assumed and the insurance assets acquired in a business combination. IFRS 4 (pars. 31–33) permits, but does not require, the insurer to use an expanded presentation that splits the fair value of acquired insurance contract into two components:

1. A liability measured in accordance with the insurer's accounting policies; and

2. An intangible asset, representing the difference between (a) the fair value of the contractual rights acquired and the insurance obligations assumed and (b) the amount of the liability as measured above. (This intangible asset is generally amortized over the life of the related contract.).

The same type of presentation may also be used in respect of the acquisition of a portfolio of insurance contracts.

The intangible assets that are recognized as described above are excluded from the scope of IAS 36, "Impairment of Assets," and IAS 38, "Intangible Assets." However, there may be other intangible assets, such as customer lists and customer relationships, reflecting the expectation of future contracts that are not part of the contractual insurance rights and obligations acquired. IAS 36 and IAS 38 apply to such other intangibles.

Discretionary Participation Features

Discretionary participation features are found in some insurance contracts (such as bonuses payable to holders of "with profits" endowment life assurance policies) as well as in some financial instruments that are not insurance contracts. The treatments of these in IFRS 4 are as follows.

In Insurance Contracts

Some insurance contracts contain a discretionary participation feature as well as a guaranteed element. (An example is certain endowment life policies.) Under IFRS 4:

- The issuer of such a contract may, but need not, recognize the guaranteed element separately from the discretionary participation feature. In that case, the guaranteed element is classified as a liability, and the liability recognized cannot be less than the result of applying IAS 39/IFRS 9,

"Financial Instruments," to the guaranteed element. (If the total liability recognized is clearly higher than what would result from this, there is no need to determine the measurement.) If there is no separation, the whole contract is to be classified as a liability. In this case, there is no requirement to apply IAS 39/IFRS 9 to the guaranteed element, but a liability adequacy test must be required as set out in IFRS 4, paragraphs 15–19 (see above).

- If the discretionary participation feature is recognized separately, it is classified either as a liability or as a separate component of equity, or it may be split into liability and equity components using a consistent accounting policy for this split. IFRS 4 does not state criteria as to how the issuer determines in this case what is liability and what is equity. However, it does not permit the use of an intermediate classification that is neither liability nor equity.

- All premiums received may be recognized as revenue without separating out any portion that relates to the equity component. The resulting changes in the carrying value of the liability (i.e., the guaranteed element and the portion of the discretionary participation feature that is classified as a liability), is recognized as a corresponding expense in profit or loss. If part or all of the discretionary feature is classified as equity, a portion of profit and loss may be attributable to that feature and should be presented as an *allocation* of profit or loss (analogous to the treatment of a portion attributable to minority interests), not as expense or income.

In Financial Instruments

The above requirements apply to any financial instrument that contains a discretionary participation feature. In addition:

- If an issuer classifies the entire discretionary participation feature as a liability, the liability adequacy test set out in IFRS 4, paragraphs 15–19, should be applied to the whole contract, and the amount that would result from applying IAS 39/IFRS 9 to the guaranteed element need not be determined.

- If an issuer classifies part or all of that feature as a separate component of equity, the liability recognized for the whole contract should not be less than the amount that would result from applying IAS 39/IFRS 9 to the guaranteed element. That amount should include the intrinsic value of an option to surrender the contract but need not include its time value if the option is exempted from measurement at fair value by IFRS 4, paragraphs 7–9 (see the discussion on embedded derivatives under "Scope" above). The issuer need not (a) disclose the amount that would result from applying IAS 39/IFRS 9 to the guaranteed element, (b) present that amount separately, or (c) determine that amount if the total liability recognized is clearly higher.

- An issuer may continue to recognize the premiums for those contracts as revenue and recognize as an expense the resultant increase in the carrying amount of the liability.

DISCLOSURE

The disclosure requirements of IFRS 4 relate to:

- Explanations required for amounts recognized in financial statements that arise from insurance contracts.

- Information intended to help users to understand the amount, timing, and uncertainty of future cash flows from insurance contracts.

The disclosure requirements of IFRS 4 must be considered in conjunction with IFRS 7, "Financial Instruments: Disclosures" (see Chapter 17), for financial periods beginning on or after January 1, 2007, so as to be consistent with those of IFRS 7, with particular reference to information about risks and the amount, timing, and uncertainty of cash flows. According to IFRS 7, paragraphs 31–42, information about credit, market, and liquidity risk is required for insurance contracts that fall within the scope of IFRS 7. However, an insurer need not provide the maturity analysis required by IFRS 7 if it discloses instead information about the estimated timing of the net cash outflows resulting from recognized insurance liabilities. In addition, if an insurer employs an alternative method to manage sensitivity to market conditions, such as an embedded value analysis, this may be used to meet the IFRS 7, paragraph 41, requirement provided the explanations required by IFRS 7, paragraph 41 (see Chapter 17), are supplied (IFRS4, pars. 39–39A).

Explanation of Recognized Amounts

The basic requirement (IFRS 4, par. 36) is that an insurer must disclose information that identifies and explains the amounts in its financial statements arising from insurance contracts. Thus, the insurer should disclose:

1. Its accounting policies for insurance contracts and related assets, liabilities, income, and expense.

2. The recognized assets, liabilities, income, and expense (and in the case of cash flow statements prepared using the direct method cash flows) arising from insurance contracts. Also, a cedant shall disclose:

    (a) Gains and losses recognized in profit or loss on buying reinsurance.

    (b) If the cedant defers and amortizes gains and losses arising on buying reinsurance, the amortization for the period and the amounts remaining unamortized at the beginning and end of the period.

3. The process used to determine the assumptions that have the greatest effect on the measurement of the recognized amounts described above. When practicable, a quantified disclosure of those assumptions should also be given.

4. The effect of changes in assumptions used to measure insurance assets and liabilities, showing separately the effect of each change that has a material effect on the financial statements.

5. Reconciliations of changes in insurance liabilities, reinsurance assets, and, if any, related deferred acquisition costs.

Amount, Timing, and Uncertainty of Cash Flows

The basic requirement (IFRS 4, par. 38) is that an insurer disclose information that helps users of its financial statements to evaluate the nature and extent of risks arising from insurance contracts. Hence, an insurer must disclose:

1. Its objectives, policies, and processes for managing risks arising from insurance contracts and its policies for mitigating those risks.

2. Information about insurance risk (both before and after mitigation by reinsurance) including:

   (a) Sensitivity to insurance risk (see below).

   (b) Concentrations of insurance risk, including a description of how management determines concentrations and a description of the shared characteristic that identifies each concentration (e.g., type of insured event, geographical area, or currency).

   (c) Actual claims compared with previous estimates (i.e., *claims development*). This disclosure must go back to the period when the earliest material claim arose for which there is still uncertainty about the amount and timing of the claims payments, but need not go back more than 10 years. This information need not be disclosed for claims in respect of which uncertainty about the amount and timing of claims payments is typically resolved within one year.

3. Information about credit risk, liquidity risk, and market risk that IFRS 7, "Financial Instruments: Disclosure," requires (see Chapter 17) if the insurance contracts are within its scope. However, an insurer need not provide the maturity analyses required by IFRS 7, paragraph 39(a) and (b), if it discloses instead information about the estimated timing of the net cash outflows resulting from recognized insurance liabilities. In addition, if an insurer uses an alternative method to manage sensitivity to market conditions, such as an embedded value analysis, it may use that sensitivity analysis to meet the requirement in IFRS 7, paragraph 40(a), but in that case should also provide the disclosures required by IFRS 7, paragraph 41.

4. Information about exposures to market risk under embedded derivatives contained in a host insurance contract if the insurer is not required to, and does not, measure the embedded derivatives at fair value.

Sensitivity to Insurance Risk

To comply with the disclosure requirements regarding sensitivity to insurance risk, an insurer makes one or other of the following disclosures:

- A sensitivity analysis that shows how profit or loss and equity would have been affected if changes in the relevant risk variable that were reasonably possible at the end of the reporting period had occurred; the methods and assumptions used for this analysis; and any changes from the previous period in the methods and assumptions. However, if an insurer uses an alternative method to manage sensitivity to market conditions, such as an embedded value analysis, it may use that sensitivity analysis to meet the requirement in IFRS 7, paragraph 40(a), but in that case should also provide the disclosures required by IFRS 7, paragraph 41.

- Qualitative information about sensitivity and those terms and conditions of insurance contracts that have a material effect on the amount, timing, and uncertainty of the insurer's future cash flows.

EFFECTIVE DATE AND TRANSITION

IFRS 4 was applicable for annual periods beginning on or after January 1, 2005; earlier application was encouraged. If an entity applied IFRS 4 for an earlier period, it was required to disclose this fact.

SUMMARY OF ED 2010/8, "INSURANCE CONTRACTS"

Insurance contracts present some difficult issues of recognition and even more of measurement that the existing IFRS 4 does not address, or addresses only minimally. These issues concern both *insurance liabilities* (technical provisions) and *acquisition costs* (costs to sell, underwrite, and initiate) for new insurance contracts.

The exposure draft sets out a comprehensive measurement approach for all types of insurance contracts issued by entities and reinsurance contracts held by them, with a modified approach for the *pre-claims* liability of contracts with a duration of approximately one year or less (short-duration contracts) unless they contain embedded options or other derivatives that significantly affect cash flow variability.

Insurance Liabilities

The measurement model for liabilities involves the recognition of two separate components, as follows:

1. A direct measurement, which incorporates current, discounted estimates of future cash flows revised at each reporting date and adjusted for the effects of uncertainty about the amount and timing of those future cash flows (a *risk adjustment*); and

2. A margin that reports profitability of the contracts over their coverage period (a *residual margin*).

The risk adjustment represents the maximum amount that an insurer would rationally pay *to be relieved of the risk that the ultimate fulfillment cash flows exceed those expected* (i.e., the risk that the technical provision is inadequate). It is remeasured at the end of the reporting period and declines over time as the insurer is released from the risk. The risk adjustment is measured at a portfolio level of aggregation.

The residual margin is calibrated at inception to an amount such that the insurer *recognizes no gain on entering into an insurance contract*. This margin is released over the coverage period in a systematic manner, based on the passage of time unless the pattern of claims and benefits makes another pattern more appropriate.

OBSERVATION: The FASB prefers, pragmatically, to combine these two components into a single composite margin. The exposure draft asks respondents to express a preference for either the IASB's or the FASB's approach.

Acquisition Costs

For acquisition costs, the exposure draft requires that an insurer:

- Include *incremental acquisition costs* for contracts issued in the initial measurement in the present value of the contract *fulfillment cash flows*, adjusted for the effects of uncertainty. "Fulfillment cash flows" are the future cash outflows less future cash inflows that will arise as the insurer fulfills the insurance contract. Only those acquisition costs that are *incremental to an individual insurance contract* should be included. Those costs thus affect profit over the coverage period of the contract, rather than at inception.

- Recognize all other acquisition costs as an expense when incurred.

If the present value of the fulfillment cash flows is greater than zero (i.e., the expected present value of the future cash flows plus the risk adjustment exceeds the expected present value of the future cash inflows), the difference must be recognized immediately in profit and loss as an expense. In the opposite case, where the present value of the fulfillment cash flows is negative, the difference is included in the *residual margin* so that no gain is recognized upon entering into the contract.

Short-Duration Contracts

For *short-duration contracts* (unless they contain embedded options or other derivatives that significantly affect cash flow variability), the insurer uses an *unearned premium* approach to measure its *pre-claims liability*. The unearned premium is considered to be a reasonable approximation of the present value of the fulfillment cash flows and the residual margin. The insurer measures its pre-claims liability by allocating premiums over the coverage period. The pre-claims liability is the *pre-claims obligation* less the expected present value of future premiums (if any) that are within the boundary of the existing contract. The boundary is the point in time at which an insurer either is no longer required to provide coverage, or has the right or practical ability to reassess the risk of the policyholder and to set a price that fully reflects that risk. The pre-claims obligation for short-duration contracts is measured at initial recognition as the *premium received at initial recognition*, plus the expected present value of future premiums (if any) that are within the boundary of the existing contract, less the incremental acquisition costs (i.e., the unearned premium). Subsequently, measurement of the pre-claims obligation is reduced systematically over the coverage period of the contract.

Contracts with a Discretionary Participation Feature

The exposure draft retains the IFRS definition of an insurance contract, based on the transfer of significant insurance risk to the insurer. However, financial instruments that contain a discretionary participation feature do not meet this definition. Nevertheless, such instruments are within the scope of the exposure draft. The boundary of such a financial instrument is the point at which the contract holder no longer has a contractual right to receive benefits arising from the discretionary participating feature in that contract. The residual margin for such instruments is to be recognized in income over the life of the contract in a systematic way that best reflects the asset management services, that is, on the basis of (a) the passage of time, or (b) the fair value of the assets under management if that pattern differs significantly from the passage of time.

Other requirements of the exposure draft apply to contracts with a discretionary participation feature, even though they do not transfer significant insurance risk, but some requirements may be irrelevant or have no material effect.

Reinsurance

The proposals in the exposure draft would also apply to the reinsurance contracts held by an insurer. A cedant faces the risk that the reinsurer may default. The exposure draft proposed that the measurement of the reinsurance asset would incorporate, where appropriate, a reduction for the expected (i.e., probability weighted) present value of losses from default or dispute.

Disclosure

The exposure draft includes substantial disclosure requirements, including:

- Reconciliations from the opening to the closing aggregate contract balances;
- The methods and inputs used to develop the measurements; and
- The nature and extent of risks arising from insurance contracts.

CHAPTER 36
MINERAL RESOURCES

CONTENTS

OVERVIEW

IASB GAAP on accounting for exploration and evaluation in the extractive industries are set out in IFRS 6, "Exploration for and Evaluation of Mineral Resources," which joins IAS 41, "Agriculture," and IFRS 4, "Insurance Contracts," as an industry-specific standard. IFRS 6, like IFRS 4, is a stopgap standard with limited objectives, given the impossibility for the IASB of completing a comprehensive project on the relevant accounting and financial reporting issues in time for 2005, the year in which IFRSs became mandatory for listed corporations in the European Union (EU).

As such, IFRS 6 requires:

- Limited improvements to existing accounting practices for exploration and evaluation expenditures.

- When exploration and evaluation assets have been recognized, their assessment for impairment.

- The identification and explanation of amounts in an entity's financial statements that arise from the exploration for and evaluation of mineral resources, by means of disclosures that help users to appreciate the amounts, timing, and degree of certainty from any exploration and evaluation assets recognized.

Among the main features of the IFRS are that it permits an entity to develop an accounting policy for exploration and evaluation assets *without specifically considering the requirements of paragraphs 11 and 12 of IAS 8, "Accounting Policies"* (see Chapter 6). Thus, an entity adopting IFRS 6 may (as a *temporary measure*) continue to use its existing accounting policies applicable to exploration and evaluation assets, including those for recognition and measurement. (A majority of the Board took the view that, in the absence of further guidance in IFRS 6, which the Board was not in a position to provide, there might have been uncertainty about what would be acceptable in the light of IAS 8, including paragraphs 11 and 12.) In addition, this IFRS requires entities recognizing exploration and evaluation assets to perform an impairment test on those assets when facts and circumstances suggest that the carrying amount of the assets may exceed their recoverable amount. It also varies the *recognition* of impairment in IFRS 6 from that in IAS 36, "Impairment of Assets" (see Chapter 20), but *measures* the impairment in accordance with IAS 36 once the impairment is identified.

IFRS 6 involves slight amendments to a number of other IFRSs, namely IFRS 1, "First-Time Adoption of International Financial Reporting Standards"; IAS 16, "Property, Plant, and Equipment"; and IAS 38, "Intangible Assets."

BACKGROUND

The FASB has had a standard for financial accounting and reporting by oil- and gas-producing companies since 1979, when FAS-19, "Financial Accounting and Reporting by Oil- and Gas-Producing Companies," was amended by FAS-25, "Suspension of Certain Requirements for Oil- and Gas-Producing Companies— An Amendment of FASB Statement No. 19." At that time, there was a controversy in the U.S. over the FASB's attempt to exclude full-cost accounting, whereby the costs of unsuccessful property acquisition and exploration activities in a given geographical cost center (normally a country) are considered to be part of the cost (and hence, of the carrying value) of the reserves that are discovered.

In 1998, the then IASC established a Steering Committee to carry out initial work on accounting and financial reporting by entities engaged in extractive industries, and in 2000 the Steering Committee published an Issues Paper. However, in 2001, the IASB announced that it would restart the project only when agenda time permitted, and in September 2002 the Board decided that, in view of the 2005 deadline for adoption of IFRSs by listed corporations in the EU, it was not feasible to complete the necessary detailed analysis and due process in time. In January 2004, the Board published ED 6, the exposure draft of IFRS 6, and in April 2004 it approved a project to be undertaken by the national standard-setters in Australia, Canada, Norway, and South Africa to address accounting for extractive industries generally. In April 2010, the IASB published a Discussion Paper, "Extractive Industries," which was prepared by the six members of the project team constituted by the four national standard-setters.

As with a number of other standards (such as IFRSs 3 and 4), IFRS 6 represents the first stage in a two-stage process and is, in effect, a stopgap standard intended to produce a measure of convergence with U.S. GAAP in time for an effective date of January 1, 2006 as stated in the standard.

Four members of the IASB dissented from the issuance of IFRS 6, on the grounds that the temporary exemption from applying paragraphs 11 and 12 of IAS 8 is inappropriate, especially as there is at present no timetable for a second stage of the process of developing a definitive standard (i.e., completion of a comprehensive review of accounting for extractive activities). In June 2011, there are still no plans to prepare an ED in relation to the Discussion Paper mentioned above), so that the exemption may be in effect for a considerable time. Two of the dissenters also objected to the modification in IFRS 6 of the impairment recognition requirements of IAS 36.

On the other hand, the Board asserted that, with the above exceptions, all IFRSs (including IASs and interpretations) are applicable to entities engaged in the exploration for and evaluation of mineral resources that make an unreserved statement of compliance with IFRS in accordance with IAS 1, "Presentation of Financial Statements" (see Chapter 4).

U.S. GAAP applicable to the extractive industries are set out under ASC 932, "Extractive Activities—Oil and Gas" including ASU 2010-3, "Oil and Gas Reserves Estimation and Disclosures," which subsumes previously promulgated FASB Statements and Interpretations, namely FAS-19 as amended by FAS-25; FAS-69, "Disclosures about Oil- and Gas-Producing Activities"; FIN-33, "Applying FASB Statement No. 34 ['Capitalization of Interest Cost'] to Oil- and Gas-Producing Operations Accounted for by the Full-Cost Method"; and FIN-36, "Accounting for Exploratory Wells in Progress at the End of a Period". In addition, a number of Accounting Series Releases (ASRs) and Financial Reporting Releases (FRRs) have been issued by the SEC between 1976 and 1984. The SEC set out in ASRs 253, 257, and 258 and FRRs 14 and 17 its requirements if the full-cost method is used instead of the successful efforts method. U.S. GAAP are thus more developed than IASB GAAP but are specifically confined to oil and gas extraction. IFRS 6 can be applied in a manner that is compatible with U.S. GAAP, but it allows a measurement method (the revaluation model) that would not be consistent with FAS-19. In addition, the scope of IFRS 6 includes only exploration and evaluation assets, leaving development expenditures to be dealt with according to the IASB Framework and IAS 38, "Intangible Assets" (see Chapters 2 and 22). By contrast, FAS-19 includes in its scope development and production expenditures.

OBSERVATION: U.S. GAAP for oil- and gas-producing operations are in part the outcome of the political considerations that led to the amendment of FAS-19 by FAS-25, as a result of which assets are recognized that do not meet the criteria set out in the IASB Framework and in international standards generally. By not requiring entities to apply IAS 8, paragraphs 11 and 12, and allowing them to continue using existing accounting policies, IFRS 6 legitimized such accounting policies pending the comprehensive review.

SCOPE

In terms of entities, IFRS 6 is to be applied by all entities that are engaged in the exploration and evaluation of mineral resources. The standard is applicable only to exploration and evaluation expenditures incurred by such entities. It does not address other aspects of accounting by them, and in particular it is not applicable to expenditures incurred:

- *Before* the exploration for and evaluation of mineral resources, such as expenditures incurred before the entity has obtained legal rights to exploration in a given area (i.e., pre-exploration activities); or

- *After* the technical feasibility and commercial viability of extracting mineral resources are demonstrable (i.e., development activities).

The reasons for excluding these two areas were threefold. First, the Board did not wish to prejudge the comprehensive review of the accounting for these activities. Second, it concluded that an appropriate accounting policy for pre-exploration activities could be developed from an application of existing IFRSs and the IASB Framework, while the Framework and IAS 38, "Intangible Assets," provide guidance on the recognition of assets arising from development activities. Third, to expand the scope of IFRS 6 would require additional due process, including possibly another ED, which would result in further delay in meeting the deadline for entities that would be required to apply IFRSs, the initial date being January 1, 2005 (IFRS 6, pars. 3–5, 11, and BC 7–8).

DEFINITIONS

The following terms are used in the standard, with the meanings specified (Appendix A):

- *Exploration for and evaluation of mineral resources* are the *search* for mineral resources, including minerals, oil, natural gas, and similar non-regenerative resources *after the entity has obtained legal rights to explore in a specific area*, as well as the *determination* of the technical feasibility and commercial viability of extracting the mineral resources.

- *Exploration and evaluation expenditures* are expenditures incurred by an entity in connection with the exploration for and evaluation of mineral resources *before the technical feasibility and commercial viability* of extracting a mineral resource are demonstrable.

- *Exploration and evaluation assets* are exploration and evaluation expenditures recognized as assets in accordance with the entity's accounting policy.

RECOGNITION OF EXPLORATION AND EVALUATION ASSETS

An entity recognizing exploration and evaluation assets is required to apply paragraph 10 of IAS 8, "Net Profit or Loss for the Period, Fundamental Errors and Changes in Accounting Policies," when developing its accounting policies for such assets. It is also required to follow IFRS 6, paragraphs 9 and 10 (see below), in determining which exploration and evaluation expenditures are recognized as assets. However, as a temporary measure it is exempted from the requirement to follow paragraphs 11 and 12 of IAS 8, which specify sources of authoritative guidance that must be considered in developing an accounting policy for an item if no IFRS applies specifically to that item (IFRS 6, pars. 6 and 7).

Elements of Cost of Exploration and Evaluation Assets

IFRS 6 requires an entity to determine a policy specifying which expenditures are recognized as exploration and evaluation assets and to apply the policy consistently. In doing so, it should consider the degree to which the expenditure can be associated with finding specific mineral resources. The following examples are given of types of expenditure that might be included in the initial measurement; the list is intended neither to be exhaustive nor to indicate that such expenditures should be so included:

- Acquisition of rights to explore
- Topographical, geological, geochemical, and geophysical studies
- Exploratory drilling
- Trenching
- Sampling
- Activities in relation to evaluating the technical feasibility and commercial viability of extracting a mineral resource

Expenditures related to the development of mineral resources are not to be recognized as exploration and evaluation assets but should be considered for recognition as assets arising from development in the light of guidance from the Framework and IAS 38 (IFRS 6, pars. 9 and 10).

OBSERVATION: IAS 8, paragraph 10, requires management, in the absence of a standard or interpretation that specifically applies to a transaction, other event, or condition, to use its judgment in developing and applying an accounting policy that results in information that is both relevant and reliable. IAS 8, paragraphs 11 and 12, requires management, in making such a judgment, to consider the applicability of the following sources, in hierarchical order:

1. Standards and interpretations dealing with similar issues;
2. The definitions, recognition criteria and measurement concepts in the Framework; and
3. The most recent pronouncements of other standard-setting bodies using a similar conceptual framework, the accounting literature, and industry practices.

The sources to which IAS 8, paragraphs 11 and 12, would point in this case notably include IAS 16 for tangible assets and IAS 38 for intangibles. The Board's problem concerned particularly the latter. The Board considered that the recognition criteria of IAS 38 were more restrictive than those that are commonly used for exploration and evaluation assets, and that application of IAS 38 might result in an overly conservative treatment of exploration and evaluation expenditures (i.e., an overstatement of expenses). Given the absence of internationally accepted standards for such expenditures, the diversity of existing practices, and in particular the unresolved issue of the acceptability of the full-cost method, the Board took the view that until a comprehensive review of accounting for extractive industries had been completed, an entity should be permitted to continue following the accounting policies it was using when it first applied IFRS 6, provided they satisfy the requirements of paragraph 10 of IAS 8 with regard to recognition as well as paragraphs 9 and 10 of IFRS 6 (the latter being hardly restrictive, except as regards the exclusion of development expenditure). Thus, the Board did not feel ready to take the bull by the horns as regards the inappropriate recognition of assets under the full-cost method.

MEASUREMENT OF EXPLORATION AND EVALUATION ASSETS

A distinction is made between measurement at recognition and after recognition.

Measurement at Recognition

At recognition, exploration and evaluation assets are to be measured at cost (IFRS 6, par. 8).

Any obligations for removal and restoration incurred during a period, as a consequence of mineral resource exploration or evaluation activities, must be recognized in accordance with IAS 37, "Provisions, Contingent Liabilities, and Contingent Assets" (IFRS 6, par. 11).

Measurement after Recognition

Entities are given a choice between the *cost model* and the *revaluation model* as set out in IAS 16 for property, plant, and equipment and in IAS 38 for intangible assets. If the revaluation model is used, this must be done consistently with the classification of the assets as tangible or intangible (IFRS 6, par. 12).

OBSERVATION: The revaluation model for tangible assets, and that for intangibles, have somewhat different requirements for the determination of fair value. For intangibles, reference to an *active market* is required, whereas for property, plant, and equipment, the requirement is only for *market-based evidence*. The requirement in paragraph 12 is intended to prevent "accounting arbitrage" between the two. Any revaluation of exploration and evaluation assets as a result of their being acquired in a business combination should be carried out in accordance with IFRS 3 (IFRS 6, BC31). IFRS 13, "Fair Value Measurement," will be applicable to fair value measurements under IFRS 6 for annual periods beginning on or after January 1, 2013.

Changes in Accounting Policies

A change in accounting policies for exploration and evaluation expenditures is permitted only if it demonstrably makes the financial statements either (1) *more relevant* and *no less reliable* or (2) *more reliable* and *no less relevant* to the economic decision-making needs of users, using the IAS 8 criteria for relevance and reliability. However, the change need not achieve full compliance with those criteria (IFRS 6, pars. 13 and 14).

PRESENTATION OF EXPLORATION AND EVALUATION ASSETS

The issue in presentation is one of classification, namely whether the assets are presented as tangible or as intangible. Some are treated as intangible (e.g., drilling rights), whereas others are clearly tangible (e.g., drilling rigs and vehicles).

Classification of Exploration and Evaluation Assets

Exploration and evaluation assets are to be classified as tangible or intangible *according to the nature of the assets acquired*, and the classification shall be applied consistently. Insofar as a tangible asset is consumed in developing an intangible asset, the amount reflecting that consumption (e.g., depreciation) is part of the cost of the intangible; however, this does not turn the tangible asset into an intangible asset (IFRS 6, pars. 15 and 16)

OBSERVATION: Pending completion of the comprehensive review of accounting practices for the extractive industries, the Board did not wish to lay down criteria in IFRS 6 as to which exploration and evaluation assets should be classified as tangible or intangible. It preferred to state that the elements of exploration and evaluation assets should be *classified according to their nature* (this classification being applied consistently).

IMPAIRMENT OF EXPLORATION AND EVALUATION ASSETS

The main issues that arise in connection with impairment of exploration and evaluation assets concern the facts and circumstances that should trigger an impairment test and the level of aggregation at which the assets are assessed for impairment.

Facts and Circumstances That Should Trigger an Impairment Test

An exploration and evaluation asset should be assessed for impairment when facts and circumstances suggest that its carrying amount may exceed its recoverable amount. In such a case, any resulting impairment loss shall be measured, presented, and disclosed in accordance with IAS 36, except that IAS 36 will not be applied in respect of the following:

- The criteria for identifying the need for an impairment test are those stated in IFRS 6, paragraph 20.

- The level at which the impairment test is to be carried out is specified in IFRS 6 paragraph 21.

The term "assets" used in paragraph 20 applies equally to separate exploration and evaluation assets or to a cash-generating unit (IFRS 6, pars. 18 and 19).

One or more of the following indicate the need for an impairment test of exploration and evaluation assets, to be carried out in accordance with IAS 36 subject to paragraph 21 below, any impairment loss being recognized as an expense as required by IAS 36 (the list is not exhaustive):

- The period for which the entity has the right to explore in a specific area has expired during the reporting period or will expire in the near future and is not expected to be renewed.

- Substantive expenditure on further exploration for and evaluation of mineral resources in a specific area is neither budgeted nor planned.

- Exploration for and evaluation of mineral resources in a specific area have not led to the discovery of commercially viable quantities of mineral resources and the entity has decided to discontinue such activities in the area.

- Sufficient data exist to indicate that, although a development in the area is likely to proceed, it is unlikely that the carrying amount of the exploration and evaluation asset will be fully recovered from successful development or by sale (IFRS 6, par. 20).

The Level at Which an Impairment Test Is to Be Carried Out

An entity is required to determine an accounting policy for allocating exploration and evaluation assets to cash-generating units or groups of cash-generating units for the purpose of assessing such assets for impairment. No such unit or group of units shall be larger than a segment based on either the entity's primary reporting format or its secondary reporting format determined in accordance with IFRS 8, "Reportable Segments" (see Chapter 31). The level at which impairment testing of exploration and evaluation assets is to be carried may thus comprise one or more cash-generating units (IFRS 6, pars. 20 and 21).

OBSERVATION: Exploration and evaluation assets may not generate identifiable cash flows, especially in the case of entities that perform only exploration. In such cases, there is insufficient information about the mineral resources in a specific area for the entity to make reasonable estimates of the assets' recoverable amount, because the activities have not reached a stage at which information to estimate future cash flows is available. Thus, it is not possible to estimate either fair value less costs to sell, or value in use, as required by IAS 36. Application of IAS 36 in such cases would typically lead to an immediate write-off of exploration assets, unlike existing methods of accounting for such assets, which the Board did not wish to ban at this time. Hence, the Board decided that IFRS 6 would permit exploration and evaluation assets not to be tested for impairment until the entity had sufficient data to determine technical feasibility and commercial viability. When such information becomes available, or other facts and circumstances (as indicated above) suggest that an exploration and evaluation asset might be impaired, the assets must be assessed for impairment.

DISCLOSURE

In respect of the amounts recognized in its financial statements arising from the exploration for and evaluation of mineral resources, an entity is required to disclose information that identifies and explains them, namely:

- Its accounting policies for exploration and evaluation expenditures, including the recognition of exploration and evaluation assets, which shall be recognized as a separate class of assets.

- The amounts of assets, liabilities, income and expense and operating and investing cash flows rising from the exploration for and evaluation of mineral resources.

- The disclosures required by IAS 16 and IAS 38, as applicable, consistently with how the assets are classified as tangible or intangible.

(IFRS 6, pars. 23– 25)

EFFECTIVE DATE AND TRANSITIONAL PROVISIONS

The IFRS was applicable for annual periods beginning on or after January 1, 2006, earlier application being encouraged, but such earlier application was to be disclosed.

Cross-Reference

ORIGINAL PRONOUNCEMENTS
TO 2012 IAS/IFRS GUIDE CHAPTERS

This locator provides instant cross-reference between an original pronouncement and the chapter(s) in this publication in which a pronouncement is covered. Original pronouncements are listed on the left and the chapter(s) in which they appear in the 2012 IAS/IFRS Guide on the right. Minor amendments and insertions are becoming increasingly common and are not regarded as "revisions" in the sense used below.

INTERNATIONAL ACCOUNTING STANDARDS

ORIGINAL PRONOUNCEMENT	2012 *IAS/IFRS GUIDE REFERENCE*
Framework for the Preparation and Presentation of Financial Statements	Issued 1989. The Conceptual Framework for Financial Reporting, ch. **2**
IAS 1 Presentation of Financial Statements	Revised 2004, 2005, 2007, 2009, 2011. Supersedes IAS 1 (1975, 1997), IAS 5 (1976), IAS 13 (1979). Presentation of Financial Statements, ch. **4**
IAS 2 Inventories	Revised 2004. Supersedes IAS 2 (1977, 1993). Inventories, ch. **24**
IAS 3 Consolidated Financial Statements	Superseded and withdrawn.
IAS 4 Depreciation Accounting	Superseded and withdrawn.
IAS 5 Information to Be Disclosed in Financial Statements	Superseded and withdrawn.
IAS 6 Accounting Responses to Changing Prices	Superseded and withdrawn.
IAS 7 Statement of Cash Flows	Revised 1992. Supersedes IAS 7 (1977). Cash Flow Statements, ch. **9**
IAS 8 Accounting Policies, Changes in Accounting Estimates, and Errors	Revised 2004. Supersedes IAS 8 (1978, 1993). Part superseded by IAS 35 (1998). Accounting Policies, Changes in Accounting Estimates, and Errors, ch. **6**
IAS 9 Research and Development Costs	Superseded and withdrawn.
IAS 10 Events after the Balance Sheet Date	Revised 2004. Supersedes IAS 10 (1978, 1999) with respect to events occurring after the balance sheet date. Events after the Reporting Period, ch. **16**
IAS 11 Construction Contracts	Revised 1993. Supersedes IAS 11 (1979). Construction Contracts, ch. **12**

IAS 12
Income Taxes

Revised 1996, with later insertions.
Supersedes
IAS 12 (1979). See also SIC-21, SIC-25.
Income Taxes, ch. **21**

IAS 13
Presentation of Current Assets and Current
Liabilities

Superseded and withdrawn.

IAS 14
Segment Reporting

Superseded by IFRS 8, Operating Segments,
and withdrawn.
Segment Reporting, ch. **32**

IAS 15
Information Reflecting the Effects of Changing
Prices

Issued 1981. Withdrawn 2005.
Changing Prices and Hyperinflationary
Economies, ch. **10**

IAS 16
Property, Plant, and Equipment

Revised 2004. Supersedes IAS 16 (1982, 1998).
Property, Plant, and Equipment, ch. **28**

IAS 17
Leases

Revised 2004. Supersedes IAS 17 (1982, 1997).
See also SIC-17.
Leases, ch. **26**

IAS 18
Revenue

Revised 1998. Supersedes IAS 18 (1982).
Revenue, ch. **31**

IAS 19
Employee Benefits

Revised 2005. Supersedes IAS 19 (1993, 1998).
Employee Benefits, ch. **14**

IAS 20
Accounting for Government Grants and
Disclosure of Government Assistance

Issued 1983. See also SIC-10.
Government Grants and Government
Assistance, ch. **19**

IAS 21
The Effects of Changes in Foreign Exchange
Rates

Revised 2004. Supersedes IAS 21 (1983, 1993).
Foreign Currency Translation, ch. **18**

IAS 22
Business Combinations

Superseded and withdrawn.

IAS 23
Borrowing Costs

Revised 2007. Supersedes IAS 23 (1984, 1993).
Borrowing Costs, ch. **7**

IAS 24
Related Party Disclosures

Revised 2009. Supersedes IAS 24 (1984, 2004).
Related Party Disclosures, ch. **30**

IAS 25
Accounting for Investments

Superseded and withdrawn.

IAS 26
Accounting and Reporting by Retirement
Benefit Plans

Issued 1987.
Employee Benefits, ch. **14**

IAS 27
Consolidated and Separate Financial
Statements

Revised 2004, 2007, and further revised and
renamed Separate Financial Statements in 2011
with effect for annual periods from January 1,
2013. Supersedes IAS 27 (1989).
See also SIC-12.
Consolidated Financial Statements and
Disclosures of Interests in Other Entities, ch. **11**

IAS 28
Investments in Associates

Revised 2004 and further revised and renamed The Equity Method and Joint Ventures in 2011. Supersedes IAS 28 (1998). The Equity Method, ch. **15**

IAS 29
Financial Reporting in Hyperinflationary Economies

Issued 1989. Changing Prices and Hyperinflationary Economies, ch. **10**

IAS 30
Disclosures in the Financial Statements of Banks and Similar Financial Institutions

Superseded and withdrawn.

IAS 31
Interests in Joint Ventures Consolidated Financial Statements, ch. **10**

Revised 2004. Supersedes IAS 31 (1990). To be superseded by IFRS 11, Joint Arrangements, and IFRS 12, Disclosure of Interests in Other Entities, for annual periods from January 1, 2013.

IAS 32
Financial Instruments: Presentation

Revised 2004. Supersedes IAS 32 (1995, 1999). Amended by IAS 39 (1999). Disclosure elements replaced by IFRS 7 from January 1, 2007. Financial Instruments, ch. **17**

IAS 33
Earnings per Share

Revised 2004. Supersedes IAS 33 (1997). Earnings per Share, ch. **13**

IAS 34
Interim Financial Reporting

Issued 1998. Interim Financial Reporting, ch. **23**

IAS 35
Discontinuing Operations

Superseded and withdrawn.

IAS 36
Impairment of Assets

Revised 2004. Supersedes IAS 36 (1998). Impairment of Assets, ch. **20**

IAS 37
Provisions, Contingent Liabilities and Contingent Assets

Issued 1998. Supersedes part of IAS 10 (1978). Provisions, Contingent Liabilities, and Contingent Assets, ch. **29**

IAS 38
Intangible Assets

Revised 2005. Supersedes IAS 38 (1998, 2004). IAS 9 (1993). Intangible Assets, ch. **22**

IAS 39
Financial Instruments: Recognition and Measurement

Revised 2004. Supersedes IAS 39 (1999). Financial Instruments, ch. **17**

IAS 40
Investment Property

Revised 2004. Supersedes IAS 40 (2000). Investment Property, ch. **25**

IAS 41
Agriculture

Issued 2001. Agriculture, ch. **34**

INTERNATIONAL FINANCIAL REPORTING STANDARDS

IFRS 1
First-Time Adoption of International Financial Reporting Standards

Issued 2003. First-Time Adoption of International Financial Reporting Standards, ch. **5**

Index

References are to page numbers.

GOO